THE
ALFRED HITCHCOCK
ENCYCLOPEDIA

THE ALFRED HITCHCOCK ENCYCLOPEDIA

Stephen Whitty

ROWMAN & LITTLEFIELD
Lanham • Boulder • New York • London

Published by Rowman & Littlefield
A wholly owned subsidiary of The Rowman & Littlefield Publishing Group, Inc.
4501 Forbes Boulevard, Suite 200, Lanham, Maryland 20706
www.rowman.com

Unit A, Whitacre Mews, 26-34 Stannary Street, London SE11 4AB

British Library Cataloguing in Publication Information Available

Library of Congress Cataloging-in-Publication Data
Names: Whitty, Stephen, 1959– author.
Title: The Alfred Hitchcock encyclopedia / Stephen Whitty.
Description: Lanham, Maryland ; London : Rowman & Littlefield, 2016. | Includes bibliographical references and index.
Identifiers: LCCN 2015051217 (print) | LCCN 2016004225 (ebook) | ISBN 9781442251595 (cloth : alk. paper) | ISBN 9781442251601 (electronic)
Subjects: LCSH: Hitchcock, Alfred, 1899–1980–Encyclopedias.
Classification: LCC PN1998.3.H58 W55 2016 (print) | LCC PN1998.3.H58 (ebook) | DDC 791.4302/33092–dc23 LC record available at http://lccn.loc.gov/2015051217

♾ ™ The paper used in this publication meets the minimum requirements of American National Standard for Information Sciences—Permanence of Paper for Printed Library Materials, ANSI/NISO Z39.48-1992.

Printed in the United States of America

To my wife, Jacqueline—
my partner in life and art and
first, last, and best reader.

CONTENTS

ACKNOWLEDGMENTS

Even a one-man encyclopedia is not a one-man job. I owe a great deal to Leslie Halliwell, whose groundbreaking *Filmgoer's Companion* showed me more than 40 years ago that it was indeed possible for a single person to undertake a mad task like this, and to David Thompson, whose later *A Biographical Dictionary of Film* proved that a fact-crammed reference book could still be idiosyncratic and opinionated. I never would have begun this project without their early, formidable examples.

I need to also acknowledge the books and sites that formed the backbone of my own research. Donald Spoto's several works, of course (but particularly his passionate *The Dark Side of Genius*); Patrick McGilligan's more measured but also important *Alfred Hitchcock: A Life in Darkness and Light*; Robin Wood's seminal work of criticism, *Hitchcock's Films*; and, of course, the go-to reference book for the director's own memories, *Hitchcock/Truffaut*. A particularly helpful website is www.the.hitchcock.zone.com, which has myriad links to period reviews, news articles, interviews, and documentary transcripts. (Other sources can be found in the reference lists to individual entries and in the bibliography.)

I would also very much like to thank all the people I interviewed over the last 20 years, sometimes multiple times, about Alfred Hitchcock, the man and the filmmaker—particularly (although not only) Jay Presson Allen, Karen Black, Peter Bogdanovich, Brian De Palma, Bruce Dern, Farley Granger, Norman Lloyd, Shirley MacLaine, Kim Novak, Patricia Hitchcock O'Connell, and Eva Marie Saint. They were all generous to a fault, and any faults in this book are my own.

"Why should we take Hitchcock seriously?" More than half a century ago, that was how Robin Wood began his slim book, *Hitchcock's Films*. At the time, it was not an absurd question to ask.

Today, of course, Alfred Hitchcock is probably the most famous director in history—and, perhaps, the most analyzed artist since William Shakespeare. His life and work continue to be discussed in academia and revisited in popular culture. Two autobiographical movies (*Hitchcock, The Girl*) have been recently released; a famous book-length interview with him (*Hitchcock/Truffaut*) is the subject of its own new documentary. His films—including some once thought lost—are currently available in a multitude of formats and continue to inspire new works (a television prequel to *Psycho*, a comedy stage version of *The 39 Steps*, in-development remakes of *The Birds* and *Strangers on a Train*).

But in 1965, when Wood asked that question, Alfred Hitchcock was, at best, only damned with faint praise as the "Master of Suspense." Although Peter Bogdanovich had interviewed the director for a good, concise monograph in 1963, Wood's pioneering work was the first lengthy English-language work to strip away the usual condescension and, indeed, take Hitchcock seriously—not just as an assembler of entertaining thrillers or even a slick craftsman but as someone whose works spoke to guilt, doubt, alienation, and all the anxieties of the modern world, an artist to be given the same consideration we give any great author. Yet at the time, Wood's strong, simple answer to his own rhetorical question—we should take him seriously because he's a serious artist—was still met with raised eyebrows.

Shortly after Wood's book, however, the exhaustive *Hitchcock/Truffaut* came out. There was another wave of appreciations following Hitchcock's Irving G. Thalberg Memorial Award from the Academy of Motion Picture Arts and Science in 1968, a more harshly critical summing-up after the bleak disaster of *Topaz* the next year—and then a further, more positive reappreciation after the surprise success of *Frenzy* in 1972.

And Hitchcock, never publicity shy, took full advantage of the new interest, making time for interviews and public appearances, including sitting for a PBS documentary, agreeing to a *New York Times Magazine* piece, and retelling his favorite anecdotes on a multi-episode run of TV's *The Dick Cavett Show*. His films were re-released to theaters and revived for television. Meanwhile burgeoning cinema studies departments turned out new scholars yearly and new pieces regularly. His reputation increased. Since the filmmaker's death in 1980, that interest has only grown. And grown more controversial.

In 1983, Donald Spoto's groundbreaking critical biography *The Dark Side of Genius: The Life of Alfred Hitchcock* took a lengthy look at the man's art and his life, portraying him as an increasingly obsessed loner whose fetishes finally led him to both dark masterpieces and gross acts of sexual harassment. Twenty years later, Patrick McGilligan's gentler *Alfred Hitchcock: A Life in Darkness and Light* offered, right from its title, a more evenhanded approach, praising the films while dismissing some of the worst accusations in Spoto's book (although, ironically, also offering a few new ones). And in between those two biographies—and continuing to this day—has been an ever-increasing pile of purely aesthetic analyses, taking so many different approaches that as a whole they raise a new and perhaps even more controversial question.

Which Hitchcock should we take seriously? Is it the misogynist director—who liked to quote the writing advice of the French dramatist Victorien Sardou ("Torture the women!"); took exquisite care filming scenes of his heroines being strangled, stabbed, raped, and shot; and was himself accused of verbally abusing and sexually harassing some of the actresses on his sets? Whose films are built around the objectifying and diminishing effects of the male gaze, which reduces women to mere legs and lips and hair and ultimately turns violence against them into popular entertainment? Should we look to him?

Or is it to the feminist filmmaker—who identified so strongly with his heroines that he often told his stories from their points of view; who took such enormous care with his leading ladies that many returned happily to work with him again and again; who collaborated closely and confidently with female colleagues like Joan Harrison, Edith Head, and his own wife,

Alma Reville? Whose films often centered on the oppression of women and dramatically detailed how a patriarchal culture and male-dominated power structure kept them in bondage, forced them into prostitution, denied them any real independence?

Which Hitchcock should we study? Is it the popular entertainer—who ultimately judged the failure or success of any production based on how warmly it had been received by audiences, who stuck to the most commercial genre available to him, who liked to work with only the biggest Hollywood stars? Who coldly crafted images, storyboarding every moment in the film, insisting his actors do nothing that interfered with the movements and angles of his camera, creating movies in which emotion, plot, plausibility are all sacrificed to the perfection of every shot? Whose films are among the world's best known and whose profits made him enormously wealthy?

Or is it the experimental artist—who immediately embraced German expressionism and Soviet montage, who delighted in taking on new technical challenges or disrupting narrative rules, who cast stars against type and character actors in starring roles? The anguished creature of emotion who consciously worked out his own worries about sin and temptation, his own conflicts between freedom and duty, in every film he made? Who shone those massive studio lights into the darkest, shabbiest corners of his own mind—and thereby illuminated something secret and painful and powerful in all of us? Whose films are continually analyzed by serious scholars and working filmmakers alike?

Which Hitchcock should we take seriously? All of them. Because in the end they are all equal and essential Hitchcocks and integral to the creation of those films. And if those works do not, on first glance, seem to always accurately reflect our world, then they brilliantly, dreamily create their own—a complicated, indeed constantly contradictory, one in which women are simultaneously villain and victim, heroes are always guilty and somewhat innocent, figures of respect and authority rarely deserve the first and routinely abuse the latter, and we as an audience are both encouraged to watch and made to feel ashamed for not looking away.

And my hope is that this book, while adding one more volume to the already heavy shelves of works on the director, will go some way toward putting all those Hitchcocks together, between two covers— the sentimentalist who dreamed of making *Mary Rose* and the nihilist who lingered over *The Birds*, the showman who turned himself into a household name and the genius who used that power to make deeply personal, stubbornly noncommercial films like *Vertigo* and *The Wrong Man*.

So, here you will find discussions of his films from their preproduction struggles through their postproduction reception, biographies of his most frequent collaborators, essays on his most commonly recurring methods and motifs, fresh new critiques of the work itself. You will also find stories, in the words of people who witnessed it, of his often cruel humor and high-handed treatment of colleagues—and you will find other stories, sometimes from the same colleagues, of his professionalism, his generosity, and his care.

As this is first and foremost a reference book for students, entries are arranged alphabetically; words appear in all capital letters on first reference point to separate, related entries. Story synopses are supplied, sources are given, and when a biographical fact is seriously in dispute, both versions are discussed.

Yet it's also my hope, though, that as well as being consulted by scholars, this book will simply be read by admirers— either in several sessions, front to back, or piecemeal, with the Hitchcock buff dipping in and out at any point. For what do we remember first of a Hitchcock film but those Hitchcock moments? A key clutched in a hand. The sudden rattle of a shower curtain being pulled aside. A crop-dusting plane suddenly turning and heading for us. This book is filled with nothing but moments like those—quick, crisp fragments of emotion, sudden close-ups of love and horror. They're all here, separate images, waiting to be assembled.

Make your own montage.

REFERENCES

Peter Bogdanovich, *The Cinema of Alfred Hitchcock* (New York: Museum of Modern Art Film Library/Doubleday, 1963), 1–2; Patrick McGilligan, *Alfred Hitchcock: A Life in Darkness and Light* (New York: HarperCollins, 2003), 62–64, 163–64; Donald Spoto, *The Dark Side of Genius: The Life of Alfred Hitchcock* (New York: Da Capo Press, 1999), 458, 474–76; Robin Wood, *Hitchcock's Films* (New York: Paperback Library, 1969), 7.

A NOTE ON THE TEXT

Consistency is the hobgoblin of little minds but the heart and soul of a reference book. So for entries on individual films or television shows, the titles are their original ones (Hitchcock's early English films were often retitled for America); the running times are the longest ones officially recorded (as silents were projected at various speeds and some films lost footage along the way). Dates refer to the year the film was first released. The studio listed in credits is the distributor (which, during Hitchcock's time in Great Britain, was usually separate from the producing studio; if different, then this is noted in the text).

I've tried to limit producer credits to those active principals listed onscreen, making an exception for people known to regularly work anonymously (such as Hitchcock) and have confined official screenwriting credits to those actually acknowledged in the film's titles (although writers known to have contributed ideas or uncredited rewrites to a particular film are mentioned in the text). I've included Alma Reville's early "continuity" credits as part of the writers' credits, as that's how that position was grouped onscreen at the time, although it no longer has such prominence. Also, note that in some cases, particularly on television episodes, the person credited onscreen for editing or music may have been the head of the department rather than the uncredited staff members who may have done the bulk of the actual work; be aware, too, that some artists used slightly different credits on different films (e.g., cinematographer Jack Cox was occasionally billed as Jack E. Cox).

For biographical entries, I've used the most commonly reported birthdates, noting any controversy; for birthplaces, I've given the town (unless, in the case of foreign countries, the village is so obscure that a state or county is more readily recognizable). Honorary titles are included only if the performer regularly used them professionally (so "Sir Cedric Hardwicke" but plain "Julie Andrews"). All films reviewed were recently rescreened, usually on film or on DVD; for the very few that were unavailable in those formats, VHS tapes or online versions had to suffice.

Although I obviously hope the facts as presented are correct (typos and errors do creep in and will be corrected in any later edition), all the opinions here as to the talents and motives of the individuals discussed and the intentions and effects of the films analyzed are my own. You may find some of those judgments of value; you may find many of them arguable; you may find a few of them grossly mistaken. But if they end up doing nothing more than encouraging you to go out and see a Hitchcock film tonight—either to rediscover an old favorite or to discover one you somehow missed—I will be very happy indeed.

ACADEMY AWARDS

Although Hitchcock is often mentioned as one of the greatest talents never honored by the Academy of Motion Picture Arts and Sciences, it wasn't as if he were ignored—he was nominated five times for best director for *REBECCA*, *LIFEBOAT*, *SPELLBOUND*, *REAR WINDOW*, and *PSYCHO*, and many of his films garnered nominations (and even wins) for other people. Indeed, his first year in Hollywood, two of his films, *Rebecca* and *FOREIGN CORRESPONDENT*, were nominated for best picture, with *Rebecca* taking home the prize. (The next year, Joan Fontaine won the best actress award for his *SUSPICION*.)

It was an impressive start. But Hitchcock himself never took home the Oscar in competition, which is why many thought the honorary Irving G. Thalberg Award he received in 1968 for his body of work was not so much overdue as a bit of a half-hearted consolation prize. Feeling miffed, too, perhaps was Hitchcock; walking to the podium to accept the bust from Robert Wise, he merely said, "Thank you very much indeed," and walked off again.

Reference

Mason Wiley and Damien Bona, *Inside Oscar, 10th Anniversary Edition* (New York: Ballantine Books, 1996), 103–4, 120, 412.

ADAPTATIONS

Although Hitchcock was constantly on the lookout for movie ideas and picked up options on many novels before they were published (usually bidding anonymously to keep down the price), generally he viewed books and plays as raw material meant to be shaped according to his needs.

They formed an important base for what was to come; without the spine of a well-turned plot, his original stories (*SABOTEUR*, say, or *NORTH BY NORTHWEST*) tended to turn into a collection of colorful incidents set against a variety of interesting backdrops. But the novels and plays he bought were rarely more than blueprints, and the lesser known the works were, the more content he seemed.

That's not to say the director didn't appreciate good writing; early in his career he adapted plays by Noel Coward, John Galsworthy, and Sean O'Casey. Many of the scenarists he worked with (THORNTON WILDER; JOHN STEINBECK; DOROTHY PARKER; and, less successfully, RAYMOND CHANDLER) were well-known authors in their own right, and a few internationally famous novelists (Vladimir Nabokov, GRAHAM GREENE) were briefly pursued for collaborations as well. For Hitchcock, however, films were about motion and emotion, not reason and prose; the demands of the screen had to be met, and he didn't shrink from rewriting

Alfred Hitchcock poses for a typically droll publicity photo on the set of *Alfred Hitchcock Presents*, circa mid-1950s. *Photofest*

famous writers, whether they were Joseph Conrad (turning *The Secret Agent* into *SABOTAGE*) or W. Somerset Maugham (transforming *Ashenden* into *SECRET AGENT*), or contriving entirely new endings or characters if that would help.

Still, there are some missed opportunities there, particularly among authors who shared his obsessions with guilt and sin. One has to wonder, after *STRANGERS ON A TRAIN*, what other movies he could have made from PATRICIA HIGHSMITH's work or what a Hitchcock version of one of Greene's "entertainments," such as *Stamboul Train*, might have looked like. There is, in the end, only room for one auteur in a film, but a second author might have given some of Hitchcock's work an even extra bit of depth—or at least a stimulating second point of view.

Reference

Donald Spoto, *The Dark Side of Genius: The Life of Alfred Hitchcock* (New York: Da Capo Press, 1999), 114–15, 508.

AGEE, JAMES (1909–1955)

A powerful, poetic, and self-destructive writer born in Knoxville, TN. When he was six, his father died in an automobile accident, which would roughly scar his life (and lead to one of his most famous works, published posthumously, the Pulitzer Prize–winning *A Death in the Family*, which won a second Pulitzer when Tad Mosel adapted it into the play *All the Way Home*).

Agee would be celebrated for his work on the rural poor *Let Us Now Praise Famous Men* in 1941 and end his brief life working on a variety of screenplays, including *The African Queen* and *Night of the Hunter* (although some of his work was rewritten and the second screenplay was drastically cut).

In between, he worked as a film critic for *Time* and *The Nation* and championed films from *Henry V* to *Monsieur Verdoux*. But he enjoyed slapstick and thrillers, too, and while he brushed off *SPELLBOUND* ("Just so much of the id as could be safely displayed in a Bergdorf Goodman window"), he singled out Hitchcock's *NOTORIOUS* for special praise, noting the director's use of the SUBJECTIVE CAMERA, his skill with actresses, and his ability to manufacture "expressive little air pockets of dead silence."

He remains an influence on critics today, both in his effortless style and his refusal to give in to snobbery or consensus. He died of a massive heart attack in a Manhattan taxi at age 45 on his way to a doctor's appointment.

References

James Agee, *Agee on Film*, vol. 1 (New York: Grossett Universal Library, 1969) 179–80, 213–14; "James Agee (1909–1955): Chronology of His Life and Work," *Agee Films*, http://www.ageefilms.org/ageebio.html; "James Agee," *Encyclopaedia Britannica*, http://www.britannica.com/biography/James-Agee.

AHERNE, BRIAN (1902–1986)

Worcestershire-born performer, the son of an architect who made his stage debut in 1911. Some 20 years later, he would finally make his way to Hollywood, where, after a supporting-actor nomination for *Juarez*, he settled into a profitable career as a second-string leading man.

Marrying JOAN FONTAINE just before she began *REBECCA* ("Couldn't you do better than that?" costar LAURENCE OLIVIER waspishly asked her), he would later take the CARY GRANT role and play opposite her on a radio version of *SUSPICION*; in 1953, Hitchcock cast him in a small part as the crown prosecutor in *I CONFESS*.

Aherne would go on to play King Arthur twice, including 1954's *Prince Valiant*, then switch largely to television work; he retired from the screen at 65. He died in Venice, FL, at 83.

References

"Brian Aherne," *IMDb*, http://www.imdb.com/name/nm0000731/bio?ref_=nm_ov_bio_sm; "Brian Aherne, An Actor for 75 Years," *Sun-Sentinel*, February 11, 1986;

Donald Spoto, *Laurence Olivier: A Biography* (New York: Harper Paperbacks, 1993), 170–71.

ALBERTSON, FRANK (1909–1964)

Born in Fergus Falls, MN, he entered the movie business as a prop boy in 1922, eventually stepping in front of the camera for character parts. He's best remembered today for the role of wealthy Sam Wainwright in *It's a Wonderful Life*, but he worked regularly for Hitchcock; he had a bit in the 1956 *THE MAN WHO KNEW TOO MUCH*, appeared on several episodes of *ALFRED HITCHCOCK PRESENTS*, and was Tom Cassidy, the source of Marion Crane's stolen money, in *PSYCHO*. He died in Santa Monica at 55 in 1964.

References

"Frank Albertson," *IMDb*, http://www.imdb.com/name/nm0007214/bio?ref_=nm_ov_bio_sm; Alfred E. Twomey and Arthur F. McClure, *The Versatiles: Supporting Character Players in the Cinema, 1930–1955* (New York: Castle Books, 1969) 28.

ALCOHOL

A gourmet as well as a gourmand, Hitchcock enjoyed fine wines and spirits—sometimes a little too much. (The famous disorienting effect in *VERTIGO* of the background both dropping away and rushing forward was his attempt to replicate a feeling he'd once had while drunk.) As early as *FOREIGN CORRESPONDENT*, he was in the habit of having several glasses of champagne with his lunch; STAR JOEL MCCREA remembers him frequently seeming to doze off during takes.

When drinking appears in Hitchcock's films, though—in *STRANGERS ON A TRAIN*; *FRENZY*; and, forcibly, *NORTH BY NORTHWEST*—it's generally treated as a character flaw and a source of friction. (His original idea for *CHAMPAGNE*—

rejected by the studio—was to follow a worker in a bottling plant to Paris, where she would see just how unromantic the product could be.) Liquor leads to a loss of control and explosions of emotion, and in Hitchcock's precisely ordered and carefully repressed world, that's to be shunned. (In private life, one of Hitchcock's cruelest practical JOKES would be to deliberately trick people into getting wildly, humiliatingly drunk.)

A central plot point in *NOTORIOUS*—the movie, after all, depends on those vintage bottles of wine down in the cellar—alcohol also leads to one of its bitterest scenes as CARY GRANT mistakes the effects of poisoning for drunkenness and disgustedly assumes INGRID BERGMAN has gone back to drinking. He may be a spy who lives by deceit, yet he can't stop taking measure of her supposed personal failings and judging her harshly for them, and drinking is just one more of her sins.

References

Patrick McGilligan, *Alfred Hitchcock: A Life in Darkness and Light* (New York: HarperCollins, 2003), 261; François Truffaut, *Hitchcock/Truffaut*, rev. ed. (New York: Touchstone, 1985), 57–58, 246.

ALFRED HITCHCOCK: A LIFE IN DARKNESS AND LIGHT

If JOHN RUSSELL TAYLOR's *Hitch*, published in 1978, stands as very much the authorized biography of the director and DONALD SPOTO's *THE DARK SIDE OF GENIUS: THE LIFE OF ALFRED HITCHCOCK*, first published in 1983, remains the primary portrait of the filmmaker as a sad SEXUAL harasser, then this 2003 book, written by PATRICK MCGILLIGAN, navigates a more forgiving, sympathetic middle ground. Unlike Taylor, McGilligan covers some ugly events in Hitchcock's life, including a suddenly clumsy pass at actress

BRIGITTE AUBER; unlike Spoto, McGilligan is far more likely to take Hitchcock's side in any he-said/she-said complaints or at least present alternate explanations.

Sometimes this makes *A Life in Darkness and Light* particularly valuable. (McGilligan, for example, convincingly rebuts a story about a cruel bit of schoolboy sadism Spoto presents as fact.) Sometimes, it seems the author protests too much—McGilligan not only entertains the idea that INGRID BERGMAN did try to seduce the director, as Hitchcock privately maintained, but also seems unwilling to accept the possibility that the filmmaker harassed TIPPI HEDREN; he also suggests that ALMA REVILLE may not have exactly been sitting chastely at home either, an assertion later picked up by the film *HITCHCOCK*.

A thorough researcher, McGilligan adds quite a bit to our understanding of Hitchcock's early life and his wartime propaganda work; the author of books on screenwriting and the blacklist, he casts an important new light on those subjects, too. But he doesn't write as searchingly about the art of Hitchcock's films as Spoto does, is less likely—rightly or wrongly—to tie it to the director's life, and (given continuing, corroborating statements from other coworkers) seems obtusely wrong about Hedren. An invaluable biography and a strong case for the defense, however one best read not instead of Spoto's book but alongside.

References
"Discover Author Patrick McGilligan," *HarperCollins Publishers*, http://www.harpercollins.com/authors/6508; Patrick McGilligan, *Alfred Hitchcock: A Life in Darkness and Light* (New York: HarperCollins, 2003), 20, 381, 550–51, 647.

THE ALFRED HITCHCOCK HOUR
As the 1960s went on, television series seemed to divide themselves into half-hour comedies and hour-long dramas; half-hour dramas became rare, and anthologies were quickly disappearing, giving way to the predictability of STARS and storylines that returned week after week.

The Twilight Zone, another popular half-hour portmanteau show, would struggle on until 1964, but the 30-minute *ALFRED HITCHCOCK PRESENTS* tried to get ahead of the curve by going to an hour's length in 1962, first on CBS and then on NBC. Hitchcock directed one of them, "I SAW THE WHOLE THING," which starred JOHN FORSYTHE as a man defending himself on a hit-and-run charge, but the director was less involved than he had been on the original series; the new format eked out another few seasons for the show, but by then an embattled Hitchcock—recovering from several health problems and his recent blowup with discovery TIPPI HEDREN—decided to let it lapse.

References
Tim Brooks and Earle Marsh, *The Complete Directory to Prime Time Network TV Shows*, 8th ed. (New York: Ballantine Books, 2003), 29; Jack Edmond Nolan, "Hitchcock's TV Films," *Film Fan Monthly* (June 1968), 3–6; Donald Spoto, *The Dark Side of Genius: The Life of Alfred Hitchcock* (New York: Da Capo Press, 1999), 370.

ALFRED HITCHCOCK PRESENTS
After the success of *REAR WINDOW*, Hitchcock's agent, LEW WASSERMAN—already one of Hollywood's biggest power brokers and eventually a studio head—urged the director to expand into television. Hitchcock would be happy he agreed when he saw the deal Wasserman was able to strike, generous even by today's standards—a fee of $125,000 an episode for a brief filmed introduction and epilogue and all rights to revert to Hitchcock after the first broadcast.

Hitchcock's involvement in the short mystery series was supposed to be minimal; he brought in trusted old collaborators JOAN HARRISON (who had begun her career in England as his secretary) as the executive producer and eventually NORMAN LLOYD (who had memorably hung from the Statue of Liberty in *SABOTEUR*) as her associate. Directors, screenwriters, and cast would change from episode to episode, as was typical of the anthology programs then in vogue.

Hitchcock's chief assignment was to set the tone with his blackly comic introductions—and then at the end ensure viewers that, no matter what seemed to have happened on that week's episode, the guilty parties had been eventually brought to justice. Audiences, no doubt, took that with a grain of salt, as they did Hitchcock's lampooning of the show's commercial breaks (insults that maddened the sponsors until they realized that the "bad" publicity actually increased sales).

The director, though, took too much pride in his own name—he was already one of the first "brand" directors—to leave everything else up to others. If it was a season premiere, the material particularly interested him (episodes about GUILT and doubt), or he was fond of the actors (VERA MILES, whom he had just signed to a five-year contract), then he would often take a hand.

He ended up directing 17 of the series' half-hour episodes. They are, in order of production, "BREAKDOWN," "REVENGE," "THE CASE OF MR. PELHAM," "BACK FOR CHRISTMAS," "WET SATURDAY," "MR. BLANCHARD'S SECRET," "ONE MORE MILE TO GO," "THE PERFECT CRIME," "LAMB TO THE SLAUGHTER," "A DIP IN THE POOL," "POISON," "BANQUO'S CHAIR," "ARTHUR," "THE CRYSTAL TRENCH," "MRS. BIXBY AND THE COLONEL'S COAT," "THE HORSE PLAYER," and "BANG! YOU'RE DEAD."

Originally, the show was seen as an outgrowth of some of Hitchcock's lighter films and macabre sense of humor; his tongue-in-cheek introductions, in particular, were modeled after the sardonic mood of *THE TROUBLE WITH HARRY*. Yet a show that was supposed to be influenced by the director's features influenced them, as well; the stark BLACK-AND-WHITE photography, real-life locations, and shabby realism of *THE WRONG MAN* and even much of *PSYCHO* owe something to the TV show (which, in the case of *Psycho*, also contributed some crew members, including cinematographer JOHN L. RUSSELL, used to working quickly and economically).

The show ran in half-hour episodes, alternating between the CBS and NBC networks from 1955 through 1961; in 1962 it moved to a 60-minute format under the title *THE ALFRED HITCHCOCK HOUR* and, after going off the air in 1965, eventually went into syndication. Other tie-ins included a digest magazine (still publishing), a comic book, and a line of hardcover and paperback collections; the show was revived as a new, syndicated series in 1985, which included remakes of some of its most famous original episodes.

References

Tim Brooks and Earle Marsh, *The Complete Directory to Prime Time Network TV Shows*, 8th ed. (New York: Ballantine Books, 2003), 29; Jack Edmond Nolan, "Hitchcock's TV Films," *Film Fan Monthly* (June 1968), 3–6; Donald Spoto, *The Dark Side of Genius: The Life of Alfred Hitchcock* (New York: Da Capo Press, 1999), 360, 369–75.

ALLEN, JAY PRESSON (1922–2006)

San Angelo–born Texan debutante and would-be actress who turned to writing—

strictly for the money, she insisted. "My first novel (*Spring Riot*, 1948) I wrote to finance my divorce," she said. "It was pure ignorance. I thought you just wrote books and publishers bought them. And in fact that's exactly what did happen."

When live television began, she jumped in, later moving on to movies. "I had no ambitions to be a screenwriter," she said. "I would never have taken a screenwriting job if it hadn't been Hitchcock." But he had run into problems with *MARNIE* when his first choice of screenwriter EVAN HUNTER argued with him over a scene of marital rape that Hitchcock was set on including. So he asked Allen to take over, and she eagerly signed on. For the rest of her life, she insisted that the scene was not about an actual rape and that Hitchcock was the perfect collaborator. "He was wonderful to me, a great friend and an extraordinary teacher," she said. "I didn't have a clue at first—I didn't even know how to cut between scenes."

Although it has its fierce partisans today, the film was a critical and commercial failure at the time. Some blamed STAR TIPPI HEDREN's stiff performance; others the brutal scene between SEAN CONNERY and Hedren's heroine on her wedding night. (Years later, Hedren would say that Hitchcock himself had harassed and abused her throughout filming.) Allen's take on the film's problems off and on the set? At times over the years, she would go into detail, blaming some of them on Hitchcock's infatuation with Hedren, which she somewhat sympathetically described as "an old man's cri de coeur." At other times, she would shut the topic down with a simple "I don't want to discuss it."

After *Marnie*, Allen went back to the theater, wrote the screenplays for *Cabaret* and *Prince of the City*, and did anonymous rewrite jobs. By her 70s, she was a frequent interview subject and honoree at film festivals and just as tartly plainspoken as she'd ever been. "You get to a certain age and

these sort of things roll in," she said once of the accolades that were piling up. "I suppose it means I should get myself to an estate planner."

She died at home in Manhattan at 84.

References

Jay Presson Allen, interview with the author, June 1999; "Jay Presson Allen," *IMDb*, http://www.imdb.com/name/nm0696319/bio?ref_=nm_ov_bio_sm; Patrick McGilligan, ed., *Backstory: Interviews with Screenwriters of the 60s* (Berkeley: University of California Press, 1997), 15–41; *The Trouble with Marnie*, directed by Laurent Bouzereau (2000), documentary, http://the.hitchcock.zone/wiki/The_Trouble_with_Marnie_%282000%29_-_transcript.

ALLGOOD, SARA (1879–1950)

Formidable Irish actress who rose from tragedy. She was put in an orphanage after the death of her father and lost both her husband and child to the flu epidemic of 1917. A leading figure of the Irish stage, she made her movie debut in 1919; she appears in Hitchcock's *BLACKMAIL* and stars in his 1930 version of *JUNO AND THE PAYCOCK*, a faithful if uncharacteristically stage-bound adaptation of the Sean O'Casey play (and the role she had immortalized at the Abbey Theatre).

By the time of the Second World War, Allgood was in Hollywood, where she would appear in *How Green Was My Valley, Jane Eyre*, and the Hitchcockian *The Spiral Staircase*, among others; although she never worked with Hitchcock again, she did appear in the 1944 version of *The Lodger*, a new adaptation of the thriller that had made his career in 1927. She died in California of a heart attack at 70.

References

"Sara Allgood," *IMDb*, http://www.imdb.com/name/nm0021329/bio?ref_=nm_ov_bio_sm; Alfred E. Twomey and Arthur

F. McClure, *The Versatiles: Supporting Character Players in the Cinema, 1930–1955* (New York: Castle Books, 1969), 28.

ALWAYS TELL YOUR WIFE
(GB 1923)

DIRECTOR: Hugh Croise.
SCREENPLAY: Hugh Croise, from the play by Seymour Hicks.
PRODUCER: Seymour Hicks.
CINEMATOGRAPHY: Uncredited.
EDITOR: Uncredited.
CAST: Seymour Hicks (James Chesson), Stanley Logan (Jerry Hawkes), Ellaline Terriss (Mrs. Chesson), Gertrude McCoy (Mrs. Hawkes).
RUNNING TIME: 20 minutes. Black and white.
RELEASED THROUGH: Seymour Hicks Productions.

Happily married Jim receives a telegram from an ex-lover, who demands he meet her for dinner and give her some money if he doesn't want her to reveal their romantic past to his wife; his wife finds the telegram and is even more furious when Jim lies about it. She gets her revenge when Jim feigns illness and she concocts a series of noxious home remedies to "cure" him.

A two-reel comedy based on a play already filmed once before in 1914. At some point, original director Hugh Croise either took ill or was fired by producer, writer, and STAR SEYMOUR HICKS; Hicks took over some of the direction, enlisting Hitchcock—whose studio jobs then had ranged from title designer to art director—as well. (Hitchcock's own recent directorial debut, *NUMBER 13*, had been abandoned once funding ran out.) Neither man nor several other crew members took credit; Hitchcock's specific contributions are difficult to judge, as only about the first half of the film survives.

Reference
Henry K. Miller, "Always Tell Your Wife," *BFI Screenonline*, http://www.screenonline.org.uk/film/id/1422787/index.html.

ANDERSON, DAME JUDITH
(1897–1992)

Adelaide-born performer and a great and groundbreaking actress, she made her stage debut in Australia in 1915—but it would be two decades before she established herself as a respected and formidable STAR on Broadway and in London, playing Gertrude to JOHN GIELGUD's *HAMLET* in 1936, and Lady Macbeth to LAURENCE OLIVIER's Scottish thane in 1937.

Hitchcock's *REBECCA* in 1940 was her first sizable film role; she played Mrs. Danvers, the housekeeper of Max de Winter's glorious estate, Manderley, and the elegantly evil tormentor of his second wife, oh so carefully sowing seeds of self-doubt, self-loathing, and eventually suicide. Hitchcock emphasized the character's almost supernatural quality by rarely showing her in motion; poor JOAN FONTAINE suddenly turns around, and there she is, waiting.

Anderson was nominated for an Oscar for the role; although she did not win, the attention led to several more juicy Hollywood parts, including the icy Ann Treadwell of *Laura* in 1944, the older woman who lovingly subsidizes the decidedly disloyal Vincent Price. She also played Emily Brent in the first and best version of the Agatha Christie mystery *And Then There Were None* in 1945. "I may play demons," she proudly said late in life, "but I never played a wimp!"

For the rest of her eclectic career, Anderson moved happily among Broadway, television, and Hollywood; she once played Hamlet, was in several productions of *Medea* (the title role in 1947, the nurse in 1982), did three years on the TV soap *Santa Barbara*, and even appeared as the Vulcan high priestess T'Lar in *Star Trek III: The Search for Spock.*

Anderson died in Santa Barbara, CA, in 1992.

References

"Judith Anderson," *IBDb*, http://ibdb.com/person.php?id=29864; "Judith Anderson," IMDb, http://www.imdb.com/name/nm0000752/bio?ref_=nm_ov_bio_sm; Eric Pace, "Dame Judith Anderson Dies, An Actress of Powerful Portrayals," *New York Times*, January 4, 1992, http://www.nytimes.com/1992/01/04/arts/dame-judith-anderson-dies-at-93-an-actress-of-powerful-portrayals.html.

ANDERSON, LINDSAY (1923–1994)

British writer and filmmaker best known for *This Sporting Life* and *If . . . .* he founded the early and influential British film magazine *Sequence* in 1947 with Gavin Lambert and Karel Reisz. Writing about Hitchcock in the late '40s, Anderson criticized the filmmaker as having gone into serious decline since he went to Hollywood (an interesting position compared to ROBIN WOOD's, who initially only found Hitchcock's American work worthy of lengthy attention).

Anderson dismissed most of Hitchcock's films as dreadfully contrived (*NOTORIOUS* is a "succession of vulgar, superficial effects") and woefully apolitical ("His films are interesting neither for their ideas nor their characters. None of the early films can be said to carry any sort of 'message'"). But this point of view, particularly at this dull stage of Hitchcock's career—with *THE PARADINE CASE* and *ROPE* behind him and only *UNDER CAPRICORN* and *I CONFESS* just ahead—was a common one. It would take the 1950s, *STRANGERS ON A TRAIN*, and the French critics to rescue the director's reputation.

References

"About Lindsay," *Lindsay Anderson Memorial Foundation*, http://www.lindsayanderson.com/about; Lindsay Anderson, "Alfred Hitchcock," in *Focus on Hitchcock*, edited by Albert LaValley (Englewood Cliffs, NJ: Prentice Hall, 1972), 48–59.

ANDREWS, JULIE (1935–)

With her bell-clear four-octave range and wholesome English looks, the Surrey-born performer was a STAR almost from the time she was a child—and certainly became one as a young adult, when at 19 she made her Broadway debut in *The Boyfriend*. Two years later, she followed that onstage with *My Fair Lady*—and by the mid-'60s, she had conquered Hollywood as well, with the back-to-back hits of *Mary Poppins* and *The Sound of Music*.

After the audience's less-than-thrilled response to Hitchcock's exciting new discovery TIPPI HEDREN, a big bankable female star was exactly what the studio thought his next movie needed. So although the director preferred EVA MARIE SAINT for *TORN CURTAIN*, UNIVERSAL persuaded him to star Andrews (with another box-office behemoth, PAUL NEWMAN, as an added bit of insurance). Hitchcock, who resented what he saw as their exorbitant salaries—$750,000 apiece—remained unconvinced; almost passive-aggressively, he seemed to spend more time and effort on the picture's character actors than the two stars.

"She was not right for *Torn Curtain*," he said years later. "She was a musical-comedy star, and it was not fair to her to call her a scientist. But she was what they call 'hot,' and the commercial aspect seemed more important than anything else at the time. In those days, we thought we needed stars, but today we know better."

Although his lack of interest in his lead actors surprised Andrews at the time, she simply, typically, pushed ahead. "I accepted for the chance to work with Hitchcock, and he taught me more about film and lenses than anyone," Andrews said later. "It was a wonderful education but he was obviously more interested in manipulating people, and in getting a reaction from the audience, than he was in directing us."

Neither Andrews nor Newman make much impression in the movie, and—significantly—whenever a list is drawn up of the "Hitchcock BLONDES," Andrews is never remembered, although her costar, who had his own problems with the film, praised her unreservedly. ("The last of the really great dames," Newman said.)

Although Andrews's career faltered in the early '70s, she went on to make a number of fine movies with her husband Blake Edwards, including the underrated spy thriller *The Tamarind Seed* in 1974 as well as the comedies *10*, *Victor Victoria*, and *S.O.B.* She still acts and is a prolific author of children's books.

References

Guy Flatley, "I Tried to Be Discreet with That Nude Corpse," *New York Times*, June 18, 1972, http://the.hitchcock.zone/wiki/New_York_Times_%2818/Jun/1972%29_-_I_Tried_to_Be_Discreet_With_That_Nude_Corpse; "Julie Andrews," *IMDb*, http://www.imdb.com/name/nm0000267/bio?ref_=nm_ov_bio_sm; "Julie-Pedia," *Julie Andrews Online*, http://www.juliean drewsonline.com/2015/juliepedia.html; Patrick McGilligan, *Alfred Hitchcock: A Life in Darkness and Light* (New York: Harper-Collins, 2003) 664; David Shipman, ed., *Movie Talk: Who Said What about Whom in the Movies* (New York: St. Martin's Press, 1988), 4; Donald Spoto, *The Dark Side of Genius: The Life of Alfred Hitchcock* (New York: Da Capo Press, 1999), 490–91.

ANECDOTES

Always keenly aware of the value of good press—he worked with a personal publi-

cist after the release of *THE LODGER*, not a common ploy among '20s British filmmakers—Hitchcock was not just a careful guardian of his own image but also the canny creator of it. By the time of his arrival in Hollywood, he had begun to construct a specific, nearly trademarked idea of what a "Hitchcock film" meant and who its prime force was.

Part of that strategy was to cultivate reporters. It's doubtful that any great director ever gave quite as much time to the press as Hitchcock did, particularly when a new project was about to be released; the filmmaker would sit for literally hours of tape-recorded questioning, even on the set during the shoot, or give long television INTERVIEWS—provided that the interviewer was properly awed by his precious time with the "Master of Suspense."

Typically, though, for a man who preplanned his films in excruciating detail, those interactions were as free from accident—or, frankly, spontaneity—as he could manage. Many celebrities tend to retell and slightly revise the same stories over time, but Hitchcock's were done by rote until a constant reader could almost recite them with him. ("His answers tend more to mask than reveal," wrote interviewer ANDRE BAZIN, who even in the early '50s noted the director's change-the-subject tendency to respond to even the most probing questions with "straight-faced jesting.")

And there were a number of prepared responses HITCH was always ready to trot out on command. There is, for example, the story of how, when he was a child, his father conspired with police to lock him in a cell to reprimand him after some transgression; the director's "mistakes" of angering the audience by actually having the bomb go off in *SABOTAGE* or letting the flashbacks turn out to be lies in *STAGE FRIGHT*; his detailed descriptions of various VISUAL EFFECTS; his statement that "actors should be treated like cattle" (all of which make up a large part of *HITCH-COCK/TRUFFAUT*).

Hitchcock was a droll raconteur with a supply of slightly dirty stories and true-crime trivia that could enliven any interview (particularly if it was the first one with him you had ever conducted or read). But—as most JOKES and factoids do—they often served only as a deliberate distraction from more probing questions and perhaps more uncomfortable truths.

What was his relationship with his father (and his MOTHER, considering how strongly domineering women figure in his films)? Why did he never mention his siblings? What part did his CATHOLIC upbringing play in his films' treatment of temptation and GUILT? Is any narrative choice that dismays or disappoints an audience by nature a mistake? When does an artist know to go for an intricate shot or elaborate MONTAGE over a simple angle or long take? How can an actor's improvisations enliven or enrich a scripted work?

Rarely did any interviewer ask these or indeed any follow-up question; almost consistently did Hitchcock merely barrel on to the next anecdote—the origination of MACGUFFIN, the definition of *SUSPENSE*, his favorite practical jokes, the peculiar details of how the police finally caught Dr. H. H. CRIPPEN. They are interesting anecdotes the first three or four times, but eventually they pall. And the more of them he piled up, the harder they became to get past.

Alfred Hitchcock loved mysteries, but his deepest secrets were the feelings he hid in plain sight behind a camouflage of wit.

References

Andre Bazin, "Hitchcock vs. Hitchcock," in *Focus on Hitchcock*, edited by Albert LaValley (Englewood Cliffs, NJ: Prentice Hall, 1972), 60–69; François Truffaut, *Hitchcock/Truffaut*, rev. ed. (New York: Touchstone, 1985), 110, 189–90.

ANGEL, HEATHER (1900–1986)

Her romantic name seemed made for marquees, but the bulk of Heather Angel's film work was in supporting parts and done over barely a dozen years, with her steadiest jobs coming in the B-movie *Bulldog Drummond* series. The British farmer's daughter from Oxford started out well, with roles in the 1932 *The Hound of the Baskervilles* and, after going to Hollywood, the 1935 *The Informer*, but her career cooled; she is the maid in *SUSPICION* and, in *LIFEBOAT*, the mourning mother. Angel married director Robert Sinclair that year and soon retired from acting, except for the very occasional part or voiceover; in a gruesome real-life mystery, Sinclair died protecting her from an unknown assailant, presumably a burglar, in their home in 1970. The killer was never caught. She died in Los Angeles from cancer in 1986.

References

"Heather Angel," *IMDb*, http://www.imdb.com/name/nm0029456/bio?ref_=nm_ov_bio_sm; "Heather Angel, 77, Is Dead; Acted in More Than 60 Films," *New York Times*, December 16, 1986, http://www.nytimes.com/1986/12/16/obituaries/heather-angel-77-is-dead-acted-in-more-than-60-films.html.

ARCHIBALD, WILLIAM (1917–1970)

Anglo–West Indian choreographer, dancer, and writer who first gained prominence in the 1940s through his stage collaborations with Katherine Dunham. Later, he helped adapt the early Paul Anthelme play *Nos Deux Consciences* into *I CONFESS*, turned

Henry James's *The Turn of the Screw* into his own stage play (and then the screenplay for) *The Innocents*, and directed several early plays by Lanford Wilson. He died in New York at 53 of infectious hepatitis.

References

"Odds and Ends—3: William Archibald," *Caffe Cino Pictures*, https://caffecino.word press.com/2008/01/01/odds-and-ends-3/oaearchibald-2; "William Archibald," *IMDb*, http://www.imdb.com/name/nm0033780/bio?ref_=nm_ov_bio_sm.

ARMSTRONG, CHARLOTTE (1905–1969)

American mystery writer and author of the novels *A Dram of Poison* and *The Unsuspected*, among many others. Three of her stories appear in the Alfred Hitchcock fiction anthologies, and she wrote three teleplays for *ALFRED HITCHCOCK PRESENTS*, including the very good "The Five-Forty-Eight," based on a John Cheever tale. The early Marilyn Monroe film *Don't Bother to Knock* comes from her book *Mischief*; director CLAUDE CHABROL, an early Hitchcock devotee, later adapted two more of her novels, *The Balloon Man* (as *La Rupture*) and *The Chocolate Cobweb* (as *Merci Pour le Chocolat*). She died in California at 64.

References

"Charlotte Armstrong," *IMDb*, http://www.imdb.com/name/nm0035655; "Charlotte Armstrong," *Internet Speculative Fiction Database*, http://www.isfdb.org/cgi-bin/ea.cgi?13507.

"ARTHUR" (US; ORIGINALLY AIRED SEPTEMBER 27, 1959)

DIRECTOR: Alfred Hitchcock.
SCREENPLAY: James P. Cavanaugh, based on Arthur Williams's story.
PRODUCERS: Joan Harrison, Norman Lloyd.

CINEMATOGRAPHY: John L. Russell.
EDITOR: Edward W. Williams.
ORIGINAL MUSIC: Frederick Herbert.
CAST: Laurence Harvey (Arthur Williams), Hazel Court (Helen Brathwaite).
RUNNING TIME: 30 minutes with commercials. Black and white.
ORIGINALLY BROADCAST BY: CBS.

One of the more gruesome episodes of *ALFRED HITCHCOCK PRESENTS*, with poultry farmer Laurence Harvey fatally dispatching nagging girlfriend Hazel Court, then disposing of her body by grinding it up into chicken feed and distributing it to his livestock. While the material seems more suited for an old EC Comic than the sophisticated director, it actually continues the exploration of long-held phobias (BIRDS and eggs) and a favorite theme (domineering women); the bad-taste JOKE of the twist only prefigures the darkness that was to come with *PSYCHO*.

References

Tim Brooks and Earle Marsh, *The Complete Directory to Prime Time Network TV Shows*, 8th ed. (New York: Ballantine Books, 2003), 29; Jack Edmond Nolan, "Hitchcock's TV Films," *Film Fan Monthly* (June 1968), 3–6.

ASHCROFT, PEGGY (1907–1991)

Formidable Croydon-born performer who played Desdemona to Paul Robeson's Othello in 1931 onstage (and real-life lover to him off) and quickly added to that a slew of legendary Shakespearean performances, including Juliet in a production of *Romeo and Juliet*, in which JOHN GIELGUD and LAURENCE OLIVIER regularly traded the roles of Romeo and Mercutio.

In the Hitchcock canon, she has the brief, bittersweet part of the "crofter's wife" in *THE 39 STEPS* who takes pity on the fugitive ROBERT DONAT and sees that her uncaring husband provides the man with shelter. A good woman trapped in a loveless union, she's just one of the first in a long line of Hitchcock's unhappily marrieds.

She died in London at 83.

References
Brian McFarlane, "Dame Peggy Ashcroft," *BFI Screenonline*, http://www.screenon line.org.uk/people/id/457078; "Peggy Ash-croft," *IMDb*, http://www.imdb.com/name/nm0001919/bio?ref_=nm_ov_bio_sm.

ATTERBURY, MALCOLM (1907–1992)
A child of wealth and privilege—his father was the president of the Pennsylvania Railroad—the Philadelphia-born Atter-bury went into acting early, beginning his career in vaudeville and spending much of the rest of his life as a supporting actor in films and TV, often playing plainspoken country folk. He is a blackmailer in the *ALFRED HITCHCOCK PRESENTS* episode "Help Wanted" and a rural lawman in *THE BIRDS*; his most famous (albeit uncredited) role may be as the man waiting for a bus in *NORTH BY NORTHWEST* who makes the observation to CARY GRANT, "That plane's dusting crops where there ain't no crops." He died at age 85 in Beverly Hills.

References
"Malcolm Atterbury," *IMDb*, http://www.imdb.com/name/nm0041021/bio?ref_=nm_ov_bio_sm; "Malcolm Atterbury: Overview," *TCM*, http://www.tcm.com/tcmdb/person/6746|104140/Malcolm-Atterbury.

AUBER, BRIGITTE (1928–)
Parisian-born performer whose earliest films were for Marcel Carne and Julien Divivier. Hitchcock cast her as the gamine Danielle in *TO CATCH A THIEF*. He was patient with her on the set, and she looked to him as a mentor; she was then deeply shocked several years later, when, parked in her car after a casual dinner in Paris, he

suddenly leaned over and kissed her "full on the mouth." She quickly fended him off, diplomatically explaining that she had a boyfriend, but she told PATRICK MCGIL-LIGAN that Hitchcock's behavior was an "enormous disappointment." Despite the director's apologies, their friendship faded. She continued to act until recently, mostly in French and on television.

References
"Brigitte Auber," *IMDb*, http://www.imdb .com/name/nm0041270/bio?ref_=nm _ov_bio_sm; "Brigitte Auber," *Wikipe-dia*, https://en.wikipedia.org/wiki/Brigitte _Auber; Patrick McGilligan, *Alfred Hitch-cock: A Life in Darkness and Light* (New York: HarperCollins, 2003), 550; Thilo Wydra, *Grace: A Biography* (New York: Skyhorse, 2014), 172–74, 176–79.

AUTEUR THEORY
The critical concept that the director is the sole "author" of any film and that every cre-ative choice made holds his or her signature.

The auteur theory is almost as old as the movies and existed long before the French gave it a name; even in the '10s and '20s, no one would ever have doubted that D. W. Griffith, Cecil B. DeMille, or Erich von Stroheim were the primary forces behind their motion pictures.

Directors had a slightly lower status in silent comedies, however, where STARS—Charlie Chaplin, Stan Laurel—truly "directed" their films, whether they were credited or not. And when sound films (and their dialogue) appeared, talk of the direc-tor's preeminence could draw an eye roll or worse from screenwriters; weary of Frank Capra's constant credit-grabbing, longtime collaborator Robert Riskin once reportedly turned in a blank script and snapped, "Here, just give it that Capra touch."

The popular cult of the director, with his iconic riding boots and megaphone, also tended to ignore the powerful influence that studio moguls had, particularly during the '30s and '40s, when giants like Irving Thalberg and DAVID O. SELZNICK supervised every aspect of a production, from first-draft script to final cut. You may not immediately remember the names of the different directors of *Cat People* and *The Body Snatcher*; you recognize each, though, by the consistent mark of its meticulous producer, Val Lewton.

But all the exceptions aside, auteurs were busy in movies from the start, and even at the height of the studio-made, factory-assembled era, there were directors, from Douglas Sirk to Vincente Minnelli, who gave their movies a particular look and, even more important, a personal sensibility and a way of looking at the world because an auteur doesn't merely stage, photograph, and edit things in a similar, signature fashion. At best that's mere style; at worst, a stunning lack of imagination. No, in addition to a consistent aesthetic approach, a true auteur usually addresses specific, consistent themes or concerns. For John Huston, it might be an individual's determination to hold on to a personal code despite the odds; for Howard Hawks, the quiet grace under pressure of men trying to do a difficult job. But what these directors said was as important as how they said it, and they often said the same thing in a dozen different ways.

Some auteurs—Huston, Billy Wilder, Preston Sturges—were screenwriters themselves, and this helped them articulate their philosophies onscreen. Others—Ford, James Whale, Capra—tended to work within the same genre and often with the same small group of writers, which allowed them to seek out and fully explore particular themes.

The case for Hitchcock as auteur may be the easiest of all to make. Although he could change the style to suit the content (long, "stage-y" takes for his adaptation of *JUNO AND THE PAYCOCK*) or amuse himself with self-imposed restrictions (the no-cuts edict for *ROPE*), his films have a similar look, usually incorporating a smoothly moving camera, occasional subjective shots, extreme close-ups for emphasis, and a strong reliance on MONTAGE. Standard Hollywood "coverage"—a long master shot of two people in conversation, say, with contrasting over-the-shoulder close-ups of each, all to be cut together later in editing—was something he avoided. Instead, each shot in every scene had a specific function and was planned out long in advance in elaborate storyboards. (By the time he got to the set, Hitchcock often said, his real work was done: All he had to do was shoot the film and then splice it together.)

Yet for a director whose first job in films had been designing the title cards for silent movies, Hitchcock kept a youthful and even experimental approach well into his 60s. Whether it was making a ceiling out of plate glass (so he could film from below, *THE LODGER* anxiously pacing) to that nearly subliminal flash of dead Mrs. Bates at the end of *PSYCHO* more than 30 years later, he continually delighted in finding new things the medium could do.

Beyond the signature style, though, there were his themes—or, perhaps, obsessions. Most will get their own deserved entries later on in this book, but some must be at least mentioned here because they are the strongest intellectual proof of his auteur status. The constraints of unwilling BONDAGE (*THE 39 STEPS, SABOTEUR*), the pains of domineering MOTHERS or maternal figures (*REBECCA, THE BIRDS*), the sweaty pleasures of secret FETISHES (*VERTIGO, MARNIE*), the pull of VOYEURISM (*REAR WINDOW, Psycho*), the TRANSFERENCE of GUILT (*STRANGERS ON A TRAIN, THE WRONG MAN*)—these are the things that any true Hitchcock film is made of.

Of course, Hitchcock worked in genre films, which made underestimating him easy; worse, unlike Ford and Hawks, who tended toward westerns and war films, Hitchcock's films often included strong leading roles for women and romantic conflicts, which made them even more tempting for male critics to dismiss. They were not serious, as LINDSAY ANDERSON would assert in a typical critique of Hitchcock's Hollywood films in 1949; they did not contain progressive political messages.

It took the French to take another look at Hitchcock as, after the war, American films began to be better distributed again and noir began to take hold. A new generation of critics—many of whom, like ERIC ROHMER, CLAUDE CHABROL, and FRANÇOIS TRUFFAUT, would go on to their own great filmmaking careers—began to write respectful reappreciations, conduct awed INTERVIEWS, and publish admiring books. Cinemas revived his films; cinephile journals, such as CAHIERS DU CINEMA, lionized him. (Truffaut would eventually produce an essential, later updated, book-length interview.)

Meanwhile, in America, ANDREW SARRIS—who had met Truffaut in Paris—began writing for The Village Voice in the late '50s. Although he (much to his later embarrassment) failed to praise Vertigo in 1958, he wrote a rave for Psycho in 1960; two years later, his "Notes on the Auteur Theory" popularized the concept of the director as author. In 1968, his The American Cinema: Directors and Directions separated filmmakers into tiers; he placed Hitchcock, along with 13 colleagues, in the unassailable "Pantheon."

Although Sarris's ranking of directors was (and remains) controversial—and that other great critic of the times, PAULINE KAEL, seemed locked in eternal argument with him about nearly everything—his influence was enormous. And while that influence has sometimes been pernicious—Do we really need to discuss the signature craft of that auteur Michael Bay?—it has also been valuable. For if nothing else, it gave us a portrait of the "Master of Suspense" as he really was—artist, author, and prime mover of some of the richest American movies ever made. He is an auteur, and we are the better for it.

References

Michael Powell, "A Survivor of Film Criticism's Golden Age," *New York Times*, July 9, 2009, http://www.nytimes .com/2009/07/12/movies/12powe.html ?_r=2&pagewanted=all; Andrew Sarris, *The American Cinema: Directors and Directions, 1929–1968* (New York: Dutton, 1968), 19–37, 56–61; Andrew Sarris, "Notes on the Auteur Theory in 1962," *Film Culture* 27 (Winter 1962–1963), 1–8.

AVENTURE MALGACHE (GB 1944)

DIRECTOR: Alfred Hitchcock.
SCREENPLAY: Jules Francois Clermont.
PRODUCERS: Uncredited.
CINEMATOGRAPHY: Gunther Krampf.
EDITOR: Uncredited.
ORIGINAL MUSIC: Benjamin Frankel.
CAST: The Moliere Players.
RUNNING TIME: 32 minutes. Black and white.
RELEASED THROUGH: Unreleased.

A short propaganda film made in England for Britain's Ministry of Information featuring a number of French actors who had escaped the Occupation and (for safety's sake) appeared here without taking individual onscreen credit. Hitchcock, who had been fiercely criticized for not returning to England during the war (and also for *LIFE-BOAT*, which some critics found—unfairly—insufficiently anti-Nazi), bravely flew back to direct this film and the similar *BON VOY-AGE*, although once he arrived, his own circumstances were relatively posh. (He took a suite at Clairidge's, where he polished the script with old friend ANGUS MACPHAIL.) The final result, though, which detailed disagreements among factions of the Free French forces, was controversial and, its producers worried, potentially libelous; as a result, it was shelved for decades, although it is available today on DVD.

Reference
Patrick McGilligan, *Alfred Hitchcock: A Life in Darkness and Light* (New York: Harper-Collins, 2003), 346–48.

B

"BACK FOR CHRISTMAS" (US; ORIGINALLY AIRED MARCH 4, 1956)

DIRECTOR: Alfred Hitchcock.
SCREENPLAY: Francis Cockrell, based on the story by John Collier.
PRODUCER: Joan Harrison.
CINEMATOGRAPHY: John L. Russell.
EDITOR: Edward W. Williams.
ORIGINAL MUSIC: Stanley Wilson.
CAST: John Williams (Herbert Carpenter), Isabel Elsom (Hermione Carpenter).
RUNNING TIME: 30 minutes with commercials. Black and white.
ORIGINALLY BROADCAST BY: CBS.

JOHN WILLIAMS's character murders his wife and buries her in the cellar; he doesn't realize she had some home-improvement plans of her own. Another example of Hitchcock's late-period interest in unhappy marriages, given a nicely cold *The Gift of the Magi* twist.

References

Tim Brooks and Earle Marsh, *The Complete Directory to Prime Time Network TV Shows*, 8th ed. (New York: Ballantine Books, 2003), 29; Jack Edmond Nolan, "Hitchcock's TV Films," *Film Fan Monthly* (June 1968), 3–6.

BAGDASARIAN, ROSS (1919–1972)

Fresno-born entertainer who made his Broadway debut in cousin William Saroyan's *The Time of Your Life* in 1940; the two later cowrote the novelty song "Come On-a My House," a big hit in 1951 for singer Rosemary Clooney. In 1954, he appeared in *REAR WINDOW* as the composer living across the courtyard from JAMES STEWART; he appears in Hitchcock's cameo in that film and eventually ends the film on a date with "Miss Lonelyhearts." (Two years later, he also recorded a song called "The Trouble with Harry," although it has nothing to do with the Hitchcock film of the same name.)

Bagdasarian's biggest and most improbable success came in the late '50s, when he began experimenting with different tape speeds during recording sessions of comedy pop songs; "Witch Doctor" was the first hit in 1958, followed later that year by the Chipmunk Song ("Christmas Don't Be Late"). Other records and a TV cartoon series followed, with Bagdasarian continuing to do all the voices (including that of the Chipmunk's long-suffering human guardian, "David Seville").

Bagdasarian died of a heart attack in California at age 52. His son, Ross Jr., now vocalizes for the singing rodents.

Ingrid Bergman truly established herself as one of the essential "Hitchcock blondes" in *Notorious*.
RKO Radio Pictures/Photofest © RKO Radio Pictures

References

John Bush, "Ross Bagdasarian: Biography," *Billboard*, http://www.billboard.com/artist/1532935/ross-bagdasarian/biography; Tom Simon, "David Seville and the Chipmunks," *Tom Simon*, http://www.tsimon.com/chipmunk.htm.

BAKER, DIANE (1938–)

Coolly patrician performer who was born into a sometime-show-business family in Los Angeles (her mother had appeared in several early Marx Brothers comedies) and later studied drama and dance in Manhattan. She made her movie debut in *The Diary of Anne Frank* in 1959.

Hitchcock chose her to play Lili Mainwaring, SEAN CONNERY's suspicious sister-in-law in 1964's *MARNIE*, where she witnessed some of the director's on-set behavior toward TIPPI HEDREN, as he worked to keep other cast members away from her or dictated her daily routine. It disturbed Baker, who avoided talking about it for years but has come forward recently to corroborate some of Hedren's account: "What happened with Tippi, that was unique and certainly inappropriate and I feel for her—she lost a couple of years out of her career because of it. It's her story, and a lot of it she's only spoken about recently, but during the shoot I was fully aware there was some sort of huge dispute going on between them; I mean, they weren't speaking, at all."

Baker also said Hitchcock (who had previously sounded out the brunette actress about signing her to a contract) had been "inappropriate a couple of times" with her as well, including a clumsy pass when he came into her dressing room and suddenly kissed her; shocked, she wordlessly showed him the door. She said she later spoke about it to a casting agent at the studio. "Everything got back to him, and when he learned that I was unhappy and complaining, his attitude toward me changed completely," Baker said. "I was glad not to be under contract to him, the way Tippi was—I could finish the job and get away." When Baker finally saw the edited film, she realized some of her scenes had been trimmed.

Baker appeared the same year in *Strait-Jacket* from Hitchcock imitator William Castle, the next year in the HITCHCOCKIAN *Mirage*, and had a long career on television. She remains active today; the youngest generation may remember her best as the distraught senator in *The Silence of the Lambs* who, while pleading for her daughter's rescue, garners an unwelcome compliment from Dr. Hannibal Lecter ("Love your suit").

References

Diane Baker, interview with the author, September 2015; "Biography," *Diane Baker*, http://www.ebakerstreet.com; Donald Spoto, *Spellbound by Beauty: Alfred Hitchcock and His Leading Ladies* (New York: Harmony Books, 2008), 263–69.

BALCON, SIR MICHAEL (1896–1977)

A middle-class boy from Birmingham who had to give up his education to help support his family, Balcon had worked in the jewelry trade and as an executive assistant at a rubber plant before, in 1921, starting a film distribution company. Within a few years he and his partner, Victor Saville, had taken over the Famous Players–Lasky Studios and began producing their own product under the name GAINSBOROUGH PICTURES.

The studios they had bought came with trained staff, including a young Alfred Hitchcock, who had not yet directed; Gainsborough would give him his chance and serve as his home for his earliest films.

Balcon later encouraged the young director to shoot several coproductions in Germany, where the company had business interests; the travel not only broadened the far-from-worldly filmmaker but also exposed him to essential EXPRESSIONIST influences. And when it seemed Hitchcock's *THE LODGER* was going to be left on the shelf, Balcon championed the film, lined up important allies, and was instrumental in securing its release—and saving the filmmaker's career.

Balcon left Gainsborough shortly after its release of Hitchcock's 1935 masterpiece *THE 39 STEPS*; five years later, the mogul would also break bitterly with his former protégé when Hitchcock seemed happy to stay in his new American home even as Britain went to war. An appalled Balcon—who was the child of Jewish immigrants and had helped artists flee Nazi Germany—publicly called out these expatriates in 1940 as "deserters"; adding insult to injury, he identified Hitchcock only as a former "plump junior technician."

By then, the producer had already moved on to Ealing, soon to become a byword for such beautifully crafted, obdurately British films as *Dead of Night, The Lavender Hill Mob, Kind Hearts and Coronets,* and *The Man in the White Suit.* "We made films at Ealing that were good, bad and indifferent, but they were indisputably British," Balcon said later. "They were rooted in the soil of the country." Although Ealing's fortunes faded, Balcon lived long enough to see the resurgence of British cinema in the 1960s; the last film he worked on was 1963's *Tom Jones.* Long enough, too, to finally roughly mend fences with Hitchcock, although it wasn't until the mid-'60s, when they met again at an industry dinner.

Balcon died in East Sussex at age 81; one of his grandchildren is Daniel Day-Lewis.

References

Brian McFarlane, "Sir Michael Balcon," *BFI Screenonline,* http://www.screenonline.org .uk/people/id/447085/index.html; "Michael Balcon," *IMDb,* http://www.imdb.com/ name/nm0049608/bio?ref_=nm_ov_bio _sm; Donald Spoto, *The Dark Side of Genius: The Life of Alfred Hitchcock* (New York: Da Capo Press, 1999), 235–36.

BALSAM, MARTIN (1919–1996)

Bronx-born, Actors Studio–trained performer who was busy in postwar theater and live TV. He had a good part in the film version of *12 Angry Men* in 1957 and a role in an *ALFRED HITCHCOCK PRESENTS* episode the year later; that and his no-nonsense professionalism made him an easy choice to play private detective Milton Arbogast in *PSYCHO* in 1960. "I think the

average guy has always identified with me," he said once.

Balsam would do another *Alfred Hitchcock Presents* in 1961, later help Hitchcock discovery TIPPI HEDREN through her expensive screen tests, and continue to play stolid, salt-of-the-earth characters, particularly in genre films like *Cape Fear* and *The Anderson Tapes;* he won a supporting actor Oscar in 1965 for *A Thousand Clowns.*

Balsam died in 1996 while on vacation in Rome.

References

"Martin Balsam," *IMDb,* http://www.imdb .com/name/nm0000842/bio?ref_=nm_ov _bio_sm; Lawrence Van Gelder, "Martin Balsam Is Dead at 76: Ubiquitous Character Actor," *New York Times,* February 14, 1996, http://www.nytimes.com/1996/02/14/nyre gion/martin-balsam-is-dead-at-76-ubiqui tous-character-actor.html.

"BANG! YOU'RE DEAD" (US; ORIGINALLY AIRED OCTOBER 17, 1961)

DIRECTOR: Alfred Hitchcock.
SCREENPLAY: Harold Swanton, based on the story by Margaret Vosper.
PRODUCERS: Joan Harrison, Norman Lloyd.
CINEMATOGRAPHY: John L. Russell.
EDITOR: Edward W. Williams.
ORIGINAL MUSIC: Joseph E. Romero.
CAST: Billy Mumy (Jackie Chester).
RUNNING TIME: 30 minutes with commercials. Black and white.
ORIGINALLY BROADCAST BY: NBC.

Young Jackie's busy running around with a toy gun, annoying everyone he meets with his plans to shoot. What none of them knows is that the gun is real. One of the rare but effective "message" stories on *ALFRED HITCHCOCK PRESENTS.*

References
Tim Brooks and Earle Marsh, *The Complete Directory to Prime Time Network TV Shows*, 8th ed. (New York: Ballantine Books, 2003), 29; Jack Edmond Nolan, "Hitchcock's TV Films," *Film Fan Monthly* (June 1968), 3–6.

BANKHEAD, TALLULAH (1902–1968)
Born into an old and politically prominent Alabama family, she seemed cheerfully determined to disgrace, Tallulah Bankhead won a movie magazine contest in 1915 and somehow persuaded her father to let her move alone to New York; there she showed even fewer inhibitions, having a number of affairs, developing a taste for drugs ("Cocaine isn't habit forming and I know, because I've been taking it for years"), and by 1918 starting to appear regularly onstage.

Her movie career took off in the 1930s, but Bankhead's greatest successes continued to be on Broadway; when her stage hits *Dark Victory* and *The Little Foxes* were adapted for the movies, however, Bette Davis grabbed both parts. Bankhead, though, got one of her rare Hollywood leads in Hitchcock's *LIFEBOAT*, in which she played the glamorous Constance Porter, now marooned at sea after a U-boat attack. Elegant and shamelessly shallow at first, bit by bit Connie's pretensions are stripped away, along with her possessions; in the end, even her diamond bracelet is sacrificed, turned into bait in hopes of catching a fish. She slowly radicalizes too, finding herself strongly attracted to a muscular Marxist played by JOHN HODIAK.

Apart from a cameo in *Stage Door Canteen*, the 1944 film had been Bankhead's first movie appearance in a dozen years; according to Hitchcock, she was just as wild on set as she'd ever been, scandalizing everyone by climbing in and out of the prop lifeboat without benefit of underwear. (The director later jokingly claimed he was unable to do anything about it, as he couldn't decide whether it was the "make-up man's department or the hairdresser's.")

The role won Bankhead the best actress prize from the NEW YORK FILM CRITICS CIRCLE ("Dahlings, I was wonderful," she informed the crowd as she accepted) but failed to revive her film career; she soon returned to the stage and mostly stayed there, apart from some attempts at television. Her last screen appearance was in the horror-hag film *Fanatic* in 1965; she died in Manhattan in 1968. Her last request was for a bourbon.

References
David Shipman, ed., *Movie Talk: Who Said What about Whom in the Movies* (New York: St. Martin's Press, 1988), 10; Donald Spoto, *The Dark Side of Genius: The Life of Alfred Hitchcock* (New York: Da Capo Press, 1999), 268–69; "Tallulah Bankhead," *IBDb*, http://ibdb.com/person.php?id=66814; "Tallulah Bankhead," *IMDb*, http://www.imdb.com/name/nm0000845/bio?ref_=nm_ov_bio_sm.

BANKS, LESLIE (1890–1952)
Born in Liverpool, Banks was a bright young Oxford student headed for a career in the church when he heard the call of the theater instead; he had begun a serious career on the stage before the First World War took him to the battlefield. Banks returned with half his face disfigured; instead of retiring, he boasted, he would use his scarred profile for serious roles, his unblemished side for comedic ones. The former definitely served to his advantage in his Hollywood debut, playing the mad,

man-hunting Count Zaroff in 1932's *The Most Dangerous Game*.

Returning to England, Banks had leading roles in two essential Hitchcock pictures—the original 1934 *THE MAN WHO KNEW TOO MUCH*, in which he's the father of the kidnapped child, and one of the cutthroat smugglers in *JAMAICA INN* in 1939, Hitchcock's last film before the director departed to America and Hollywood. Banks went on to appear in *Went the Day Well?*, LAURENCE OLIVIER's *Henry V*, and the thriller *The Door with Seven Locks*; he died of a stroke at age 61.

References
"Leslie Banks," *IMDb*, http://www.imdb .com/name/nm0052203/bio?ref_=nm_ov _bio_sm; Brian McFarlane, "Leslie Banks," *BFI Screenonline*, http://www.screenon line.org.uk/people/id/454219/index.html; David Thomson, *The New Biographical Dictionary of Film* (New York: Knopf, 2002), 51.

"BANQUO'S CHAIR" (US; ORIGINALLY AIRED MAY 3, 1959)

DIRECTOR: Alfred Hitchcock.
SCREENPLAY: Frances Cockrell, based on the story by Rupert Croft-Crooke.
PRODUCERS: Joan Harrison, Norman Lloyd.
CINEMATOGRAPHY: John L. Russell.
EDITOR: Edward W. Williams.
ORIGINAL MUSIC: Frederick Herbert.
CAST: John Williams (Inspector Brent), Kenneth Haigh (John Bedford).
RUNNING TIME: 30 minutes with commercials. Black and white.
ORIGINALLY BROADCAST BY: CBS.

One of the better supernatural stories on *ALFRED HITCHCOCK PRESENTS* (and perhaps a nod to Hitchcock's history of practical JOKES). A retired police inspector gives a dinner party and hires an actress to play the ghost of a murdered woman in hopes of revealing the killer. Unbeknownst to him, however, a real ghost has already accepted the role.

References
Tim Brooks and Earle Marsh, *The Complete Directory to Prime Time Network TV Shows*, 8th ed. (New York: Ballantine Books, 2003), 29; Jack Edmond Nolan, "Hitchcock's TV Films," *Film Fan Monthly* (June 1968), 3–6.

BARING, NORAH (1905–1985)
Petite London-born performer, chiefly on stage. Her brief film career began in the early '20s; she is best remembered today for her lead in *MURDER!* as the young actress—coincidentally if confusingly named "Diana Baring"—on trial for her life. Baring retired from the screen after becoming a mother in 1934, although she published an INTERVIEW with Hitchcock the next year in *Film Pictorial*; she died in Surrey at age 79 of pneumonia.

References
"Norah Baring," *The Hitchcock Zone*, http://the.hitchcock.zone/wiki/Norah _Baring; "Norah Baring," *IMDb*, http:// www.imdb.com/name/nm0054689/ bio?ref_=nm_ov_bio_sm.

BARNES, GEORGE (1892–1953)
With a cinematography career that went back to the days of Thomas H. Ince, Barnes was known for his evocative lighting and pioneering the use of deep-focus compositions. (Gregg Toland was a protégé.) His first credit was for *Vive la France!* in 1918, one of his last for the special-effects-heavy *The War of the Worlds* in 1953, and in between he turned his hand at such dissimilar yet distinctive classics as *Jesse James*,

Meet John Doe, Jane Eyre, and *Force of Evil,* adapting his style to Gothic dark shadows or gritty film noir.

At DAVID O. SELZNICK's insistence, he would be Hitchcock's first American cinematographer, on *REBECCA,* giving Manderley's fluttering curtains a ghostly look and Hitchcock's ever-moving EYE a smoothly mobile camera that glided along with it without complaint; it won him an Oscar. He returned to work with Hitchcock on *SPELLBOUND,* where—avoiding the usual hazy clichés—he shot GREGORY PECK's dreams and flashbacks with a crisp, high-contrast focus that was sharp as a straight razor. His last credit was the Bing Crosby drama *Little Boy Lost.*

References

"George Barnes," *IMDb,* http://www.imdb .com/name/nm0055604/bio?ref_=nm _ov_bio_sm; Thomas Staedeli, "Portrait of the Cinematographer George Barnes," *Cyranos,* http://www.cyranos.ch/spbarg-e htm.

BARRY, JOAN (1903–1989)

London-born performer onstage since her early teens. (She is not to be confused with the American actress of the same name who brought a controversial paternity suit against Charlie Chaplin.) Barry's most unusual screen credit was actually uncredited; when ANNY ONDRA's Czech accent was judged too impenetrable for Hitchcock's *BLACKMAIL,* Barry was called upon to dub her lines. (The process was just as crude as *Singin' in the Rain* would later satirize; during filming, Barry simply stood off camera and recited the dialogue while Ondra moved her lips.) Barry got her own Hitchcock film in 1931 with *RICH AND STRANGE,* but her career turned out to be brief; after marrying in 1934, she retired. She died at age 85 in Marbella, Spain.

References

"Joan Barry," *IMDb,* http://www.imdb .com/name/nm0054689/bio?ref_=nm_ov _bio_sm; Donald Spoto, *The Dark Side of Genius: The Life of Alfred Hitchcock* (New York: Da Capo Press, 1999), 119.

BARRYMORE, ETHEL (1879–1959)

Member of one of America's oldest (and still ongoing) acting dynasties, she made her Broadway debut in 1895 and her first film in 1914; she had an early success in *A Doll's House,* won a wedding proposal from a young Winston Churchill (she turned him down), and became a strong and courageous voice for Actors' Equity. She never, though, quite embraced the movies, an industry she likened to a "Sixth Avenue peepshow." ("Half the people in Hollywood are dying to be discovered and the other half are afraid they will be," she quipped.) Although she won an Oscar for her part as CARY GRANT's Cockney mother in *None but the Lonely Heart,* her roles in Hollywood tended toward the dowager type; she was, in fact, nominated again for playing the much-abused Lady Sophie Horfield in Hitchcock's *THE PARADINE CASE* (although ironically the scenes that probably won her the nomination were cut before the film's official release by producer DAVID O. SELZNICK). In any case, Barrymore lost to Celeste Holm for *Gentleman's Agreement.* She died in Los Angeles at age 79.

References

"Ethel Barrymore," *IMDb,* http:// www.imdb.com/name/nm0000856/ bio?ref_=nm_ov_bio_sm; "Ethel Barrymore Is Dead at 79," *New York Times,* June 19, 1959, http://www.nytimes.com/ learning/general/onthisday/bday/0815 .html; "Ethel Barrymore Biography," *TCM,* http://www.tcm.com/tcmdb/ person/10733|49240/Ethel-Barrymore.

BASS, SAUL (1920–1996)

Bronx-born artist who began his career in postwar Hollywood working on movie posters; his signature style revolved around bold uses of type, stark cut-out silhouettes, and slashing geometric forms. After seeing his work on the advertising for *Carmen Jones*, its director, Otto Preminger, encouraged Bass to branch out into title sequences; his credits for Preminger's *The Man with the Golden Arm* and *Anatomy of a Murder* are among his best and most copied.

Bass's opening titles typically translated the film's themes and mood into design elements, setting the stage for the drama to come. His first work for Hitchcock was the credit sequence for *VERTIGO*, with its swirling, hypnotic spirals. He followed that with the propulsive opening credits for *NORTH BY NORTHWEST* in 1959, then the deliberately jarring titles for *PSYCHO*, their antic energy and broken lines hinting at the violent madness just ahead.

As part of his work on *Psycho*, though, Bass—as he had recently on *Spartacus*—served as a visual or, as he was billed, "pictorial" consultant, a job that included drawing up the storyboards for complicated sequences—basically blueprints for the filming. The ones Bass did for the Arbogast murder were thrown out—Hitchcock thought they made the detective look like the killer—but the ones for the shower scene were followed quite closely.

This led to a dispute years later, when Bass claimed that not only had he designed the famous sequence but also he had helped direct it, an assertion STAR JANET LEIGH and others heatedly denied. (The issue was at least arguable; while Bass had never instructed the performers or worked with the cameraman, he had suggested many of the shots and reportedly shot test footage.) For his part, Hitchcock never worked with

Bass again and in INTERVIEWS credited him only with his storyboards for the Arbogast scene—which, he emphasized, he'd had to discard as unsuitable.

Bass continued to design innovative title sequences (*It's a Mad, Mad, Mad, Mad World*), posters (*The Shining*), and countless corporate logos; the one film he directed, the sci-fi *Phase 4*, has slowly achieved a cult status for its striking visuals. His last credit was for the titles in Martin Scorsese's *Casino*. Bass died in Los Angeles in 1996.

References

Pat Kirkham, "Reassessing the Saul Bass and Alfred Hitchcock Collaboration," *West 86th*, Spring 2011, http://www.west86th.bgc.bard.edu/articles/kirkham-bass-hitchcock.html; Janet Leigh with Christopher Nickens, *Psycho: The Classic Thriller* (New York: Harmony Books, 1995), 65–76; Stephen Rebello, *Alfred Hitchcock and the Making of Psycho* (New York: HarperPerennial, 1991), 100–118, 122–23; "Saul Bass," *IMDb*, http://www.imdb.com/name/nm0000866/bio?ref_=nm_ov_bio_sm; François Truffaut, *Hitchcock/Truffaut*, rev. ed. (New York: Touchstone, 1985), 273.

BASSERMANN, ALBERT (1867–1952)

A prominent classical actor in Germany, the Mannheim-born performer worked with both the legendary Max Reinhardt onstage and newcomer Ernst Lubitsch on film; when Hitler came to power, though, Bassermann began planning his escape. (Reportedly the dictator so admired the actor that he ensured him he could continue working safely in the Reich—if he merely divorced his Jewish wife.) The couple fled to Switzerland, eventually settling in the United States, where Bassermann painstakingly set about learning English; one of his first parts, as the diplomat in

FOREIGN CORRESPONDENT, had to be memorized phonetically. (Impressively, he won an ACADEMY AWARD nomination anyway.) Bassermann continued to act regularly, both onstage and in films, where Hollywood tended to cast him as wise old doctors. He returned to Europe after Hitler's defeat; his last movie role was in the British classic *The Red Shoes*. He died of a heart attack at age 84 on a plane to Zurich.

References

"Albert Bassermann," *Encyclopaedia Britannica*, http://www.britannica.com/bio graphy/Albert-Bassermann; "Albert Bassermann," *IMDb*, http://www.imdb.com/name/nm0060168/bio?ref_=nm_ov_bio_sm.

BATES, FLORENCE (1888–1954)

Far more interesting than most of the roles she played, the formidable San Antonio matron was, successively, a piano prodigy, a math whiz (and graduate of the University of Texas), one of the first female lawyers in the state of Texas, an antiques dealer, a Spanish-English radio pundit, and the owner of a Los Angeles bakery. It was only as she neared 50, however, that she took up acting after almost accidentally landing a part at the Pasadena Playhouse; enjoying her experience onstage, she began her last, and most famous, career as a character actress.

Bates had had only one bit part in the movies when she screen-tested for Hitchcock in 1939; impressed nonetheless, he cast her as JOAN FONTAINE's imperious employer Mrs. Van Hopper in *REBECCA*, just the first of the domineering women who will try to rule that shy heroine's life. Bates never rose to stardom but soon became a familiar and comforting face in films, appearing first in movies like *The Mask of Dimitrios*, *I Remember Mama*, and *Portrait of Jennie* and later on such early TV sitcoms as *The George Burns and Gracie Allen Show* and *I Love Lucy*. Bates was only 65 when she died in Burbank of a heart attack.

References

"Florence Bates," *IMDb*, http://www.imdb.com/name/nm0060904/bio?ref_=nm_ov_bio_sm; Christy Putnam, "Florence Bates: It's a Grand Feeling!" https://sue sueapplegate.wordpress.com/2013/11/10/florence-bates-its-a-grand-feeling; Alfred E. Twomey and Arthur F. McClure, *The Versatiles: Supporting Character Players in the Cinema, 1930–1955* (New York: Castle Books, 1969), 39.

BAXTER, ANNE (1922–1985)

A granddaughter of Frank Lloyd Wright and the child of a Seagram's executive who was raised in Manhattan and privately schooled, Baxter should have had her life mapped out for her at birth—a map that, likely, would not have included detours to Broadway; Hollywood; and, for a while, a remote cattle ranch in Australia. But a thirst for acting and adventure hit her hard in childhood, and by 16, she was in California, screen-testing for the lead role in *REBECCA*.

She didn't get the part (she was, too clearly, still a teenager), but she got a contract at Fox out of it (where she would win a supporting actress Oscar for her role as the doomed Sophie in *The Razor's Edge* in 1946—"my only great performance," she called it). She starred in Orson Welles's butchered *The Magnificent Ambersons*, but her role as the duplicitous title character in *All about Eve* is probably her most remembered; she eventually worked for Hitchcock in *I CONFESS* after the studio abruptly vetoed his first choice, Anita Bjork, once they discovered she was an unwed and unashamed mother.

"He was very particular about wardrobe and hair," Baxter remembered of her first meetings with Hitchcock. "I felt I wasn't as pretty as he wanted a woman to be in his films, and as he wanted me to be. There was a lot of Pygmalion in him, and he was proud of how he transformed actresses." She remained slightly uncomfortable on the set, particularly as costar MONTGOMERY CLIFT was drinking heavily and often seemed to go blank during scenes.

Baxter would later appear in an episode of THE ALFRED HITCHCOCK HOUR (and as a rather campy Nefretiri in Cecil B. De Mille's The Ten Commandments), but her career slowed after she married a rancher in 1960 and moved away from Los Angeles; she wrote about her Australian experiences and others in her memoir Intermission. She died of a brain aneurysm in New York at 62.

References

"Anne Baxter," IMDb, http://www.imdb .com/name/nm0000879/bio?ref_=nm_ov _bio_sm; Anne Baxter, Intermission: A True Story (New York: G. P. Putnam's Sons, 1976), 63; Donald Spoto, The Dark Side of Genius: The Life of Alfred Hitchcock (New York: Da Capo Press, 1999), 338–40.

BAZIN, ANDRE (1918–1958)

Seminal critic and theorist born in Angers, France, who cofounded CAHIERS DU CINEMA in 1951; his aesthetic convictions (including a firm preference for LONG TAKES and deep focus) are still debated today. Yet despite his antipathy toward directors whose style called too much attention to themselves, he was an advocate of the filmmaker as visionary, and his writing—and his magazine—became the rock upon which the AUTEUR THEORY was built.

This did not mean that Bazin agreed with the devotion shown some filmmak-

ers by many of his contributors, particularly those "partisans" whom he thought overpraised Hitchcock wildly; Bazin, who preferred the "invisible" style of a William Wyler or Howard Hawks, found Hitchcock's fondness for MONTAGE distracting at best and, when INTERVIEWING him on the set of TO CATCH A THIEF, definitely began the interview with a certain bias. (His opening question: "Traditional criticism often reproaches you for brilliant but gratuitous formalism . . .")

Despite the stiffness of their give and take, worsened by the need for a translator, it is an interesting piece primarily because the men's tastes are so different. (Bazin admires ROPE, which the director finds dull; Hitchcock wants to talk about REAR WINDOW, but the critic is uninterested.) But the article also has some unexpected revelations—Hitchcock, for example, dismissing the now-revered NOTORIOUS as simply a well-made but shallow entertainment. And it gets at an unexpected truth— sometimes the greatest judge of an artist's work is neither the artist nor the critic but the audience. And time.

Bazin died in Nogent-sur-Marne, France, at 40 of leukemia.

References

Andre Bazin, "Hitchcock vs. Hitchcock," in Focus on Hitchcock, edited by Albert LaValley (Englewood Cliffs, NJ: Prentice Hall, 1972), 60–69; Katherine Blakeney, "An Analysis of Film Critic Andre Bazin's Views on Expressionism and Realism on Film," Student Pulse 1, no. 12, http://www .studentpulse.com/articles/86/an-analysis -of-film-critic-andre-bazins-views-on -expressionism-and-realism-in-film; Dave Kehr, "Cahiers Back in the Day," Film Comment (September/October 2001), http://www.filmcomment.com/article/ cahiers-back-in-the-day.

BEL GEDDES, BARBARA
(1922–2005)

Born in New York, Barbara Bel Geddes showed a wide range early on, winning an Oscar nomination for the warmly nostalgic *I Remember Mama* in 1948, then originating the role of the hungry, sexy Maggie in the first Broadway production of *Cat on a Hot Tin Roof* in 1955. Yet her liberal political leanings caused some trouble for a while in Hollywood during the McCarthy era; when she did manage to get cast later, it was mostly in quietly empathetic, maternal roles.

She played to both sides for Hitchcock, though, first as the motherly, long-patient Midge in *VERTIGO*, then the mutton-wielding murderess in his TV production of "LAMB TO THE SLAUGHTER." She actually appeared on Hitchcock's TV show four times, although it's not sure whether that was the doing of Hitchcock, who remained sympathetic to colleagues who had been blacklisted, or associate producer NORMAN LLOYD (who had once run afoul of Hollywood's political witch hunters himself).

After a successful, late-in-life run on TV's *Dallas* as the matriarch Miss Ellie, Bel Geddes retired to Maine, where she busied herself with painting—just like Midge. She died there in 2005.

References

"Actress Barbara Bel Geddes Has Died," *Today*, August 10, 2005, http://www.today .com/popculture/actress-barbara-bel-ged des-has-died-2D80556262; *Barbara Bel Geddes*, http://www.barbarabelgeddes.com; "Barbara Bel Geddes," *IMDb*, http://www .imdb.com/name/nm0000895.

BELLOC LOWNDES,
MARIE ADELAIDE (1868–1947)

Extraordinarily prolific Franco-English writer who, despite her upbringing—her mother was the feminist Bessie Parkes, a forceful proponent for women's property rights—published under her married name and was and is almost invariably referred to simply as "Mrs. Belloc Lowndes." Born into a particularly literate family (her brother was Hillaire Belloc), her first book, a study of the Prince of Wales, appeared anonymously at age 30; her greatest success, in 1914, would be *The Lodger*, a novel about Jack the Ripper.

Hitchcock would adapt it as *THE LODGER: A STORY OF THE LONDON FOG* (and, for years, nurse the idea of his own remake); another of her novels, *What Really Happened*, would become an episode of *THE ALFRED HITCHCOCK HOUR*. Although *The Lodger* remained her most famous work (and would be adapted at least four other times for the screen), she wrote dozens of other books, both fiction and nonfiction; her novel *Letty Lynton* was made into a Joan Crawford movie in 1932. "Rather, sort of, (a) cottage loaf," said Hitchcock, likening her to a round, double-tiered bread. "A very devout Catholic, rather a bit of a social snob, but she wrote the most horrifying murder stories."

She died at age 79 in Hampshire, England.

References

Alfred Hitchcock, interview by Keith Berwick, *Speculation*, Channel 28, 1969, http://the.hitchcock.zone/wiki/Speculat ion_%28Channel_28,_1969%29); "Marie Adelaide Lowndes," *Encyclopaedia Britannica*, http://www.britannica.com/ biography/Marie-Adelaide-Lowndes; Elyssa Warkentin, "Marie Belloc Lowndes Rewrites the Ripper," *Nineteenth Century Gender Studies* (Spring 2011), http:// www.ncgsjournal.com/issue71/warkentin .htm.

BENCHLEY, ROBERT
(1889–1945)

A deliciously droll, Worcester, MA–born humorist—as a student at Harvard, he wrote an assigned paper on a US-Canadian fishing treaty from the cod's perspective—Benchley had already been a popular critic and essayist when he followed the great migration of Manhattan talents out to Hollywood. An early Jazz Age trip didn't take, but he returned again in the '30s, where he soon became busy working on scripts, writing and starring in his own comic shorts (*How to Sleep* won an Oscar in 1935), and taking on supporting roles, usually as an incompetent lecturer or sodden businessman wandering through scenes like a vaguely worried walrus. In *FOREIGN CORRESPONDENT*, he is the hack reporter Stebbins; he also rewrote some of the film's dialogue. He died, reportedly from cirrhosis, in New York at age 56.

References

"Robert Benchley," *IMDb*, http://www.imdb.com/name/nm0070361/bio?ref_=nm_ov_bio_sm; "Robert Benchley: His Writings and Sayings and His Life and Times," *Robert Benchley Society*, http://www.robertbenchley.org/sob.

BENDIX, WILLIAM (1906–1964)

A former batboy for the New York Yankees (he was reportedly fired for obediently bringing Babe Ruth a mammoth order of hot dogs, which left the Babe too gaseous to play his best), Bendix was a failed New Jersey grocer until he started finding stage work in the '30s as part of a federal work program. Moving to Hollywood in the early '40s, he played a steady succession of working-class characters (including the title role in *The Babe Ruth Story*) and ended his career on television in the blue-collar sitcom *The Life of Riley*. He is Gus Smith, the wounded and eventually delirious German American sailor on Hitchcock's *LIFEBOAT*; the operation he's forced to undergo there, with only liquor for an anesthetic and a rudely sterilized pocketknife for a scalpel, is one of the film's most horrifying scenes.

Bendix died from complications of pneumonia at age 58 in Los Angeles; ironically, he had just settled out of court with a TV network for wrongful dismissal when they had canceled a contract because they insisted he was too ill to work.

References

"Obituary: Mr. William Bendix," *Times*, December 16, 1964, http://the.hitchcock.zone/wiki/The_Times_%2816/Dec/1964%29_-_Obituary:_Mr_William_Bendix; "William Bendix," *IMDb*, http://www.imdb.com/name/nm0000904/bio?ref_=nm_ov_bio_sm.

BENNETT, CHARLES
(1899–1995)

A West Sussex–born actor-turned-playwright, Bennett gave a notable stage success to TALLULAH BANKHEAD with *BLACKMAIL*, which Hitchcock later decided to turn into a film. The two men's meeting was apparently congenial; Bennett would go on to adapt or write most of the director's best British films, including *THE MAN WHO KNEW TOO MUCH*, *THE 39 STEPS*, *SECRET AGENT*, *SABOTAGE*, and *YOUNG AND INNOCENT*.

The string of successes led to offers for both men; Bennett ended up preceding Hitchcock to Hollywood in 1938, when he got a contract from UNIVERSAL. The two men would work again at that studio on *FOREIGN CORRESPONDENT* and *SABOTEUR*; Bennett's later projects would range from an early, live TV adaptation of *Casino Royale* to the classic horror tale *Curse of the Demon*, although little of it would approach the quality of his work with Hitchcock.

Although it's a perverse if familiar failing of the AUTEUR THEORY to completely overlook the writer—the actual, technical "auteur"—Bennett's contribution to Hitchcock's films can't be overestimated. He is the scenarist on nearly every notable Hitchcock talkie, save *THE LADY VANISHES*; his screenplays are uniformly sophisticated, particularly about relationships, and often feature a teasing SEXUAL tension. Yes, their frequent man-on-the-run plots are one of the elements most often identified as HITCHCOCKIAN. But isn't that element perhaps "Bennett-esque" as well?

Hitchcock worked so closely with his scenarists (often aided, sometimes anonymously, by ALMA REVILLE) that it's difficult to parse who did what, but it's certainly true that the director's work with Bennett is some of the most consistent of his career; perhaps because, unlike some other collaborators, Bennett never pushed to claim credit; even as Hitchcock sometimes seized more than his share, the two men remained fond friends (although later, after the director's death, Bennett would grumble a bit about the way his contributions had been overlooked).

Bennett died in Los Angeles at age 95; at the time, he was busy writing a new screenplay of *Blackmail* in hopes of mounting a remake.

References

"Charles Bennett," *IMDb*, http://www.imdb.com/name/nm0071657/bio?ref_=nm_ov_bio_sm; David Shipman, "Obituary: Charles Bennett," *Independent*, June 22, 1995, http://the.hitchcock.zone/wiki/The_Independent_%2822/Jun/1995%29_-_Obituary:_Charles_Bennett.

BERGMAN, INGRID (1915–1982)

Born in Stockholm, Bergman realized she wanted to be an actress from the start, and although her artistic father disagreed slightly—he saw her as an opera singer—when in 1932 she won the same dramatic scholarship that Greta Garbo had, the future seemed clear.

In 1939, DAVID O. SELZNICK put her under contract and brought her to America; her first Hollywood film, *Intermezzo: A Love Story*, was a remake of one of her Swedish hits. From the start her natural appearance and unaffected demeanor—she refused to relentlessly pluck her eyebrows or wear much makeup and spoke in a softly natural if slightly accented voice—made her stand apart.

Her greatest role was, of course, in *Casablanca*—just the way she looked at Humphrey Bogart was enough to immediately clinch his status as a leading man—but it was the Selznick connection that soon brought her into contact with another of his contracted talents, Alfred Hitchcock. Following in MADELEINE CARROLL's dainty footsteps, she became one of the first "Hitchcock BLONDES"—elegantly reserved in public, bubbling with passion in private.

Like those who came later in the director's work—GRACE KELLY in the 1950s, TIPPI HEDREN in the 1960s—Bergman defined her decade. She also set the tone for Hitchcock's conflation of onscreen and offscreen obsession, the first of the blonde icons who would become increasingly, disturbingly central to the director's fantasies.

Shortly after they began their first picture together, Hitchcock began telling friends that Bergman had cornered him in his bedroom at a dinner party and refused to leave until he made love to her. PATRICK MCGILLIGAN defends the story as possible; DONALD SPOTO decries it as the director's own wishful fantasy. That seemed to be how the forgiving Bergman portrayed it. "People will believe what they want to believe," she said years later of their relationship. "I loved him, but not his way. Well, I wanted to keep his friendship, and I did."

Interestingly, although Bergman was technically the closest to the Hitchcock ideal—the Nordic blonde—unlike the icily perfect Kelly, onscreen she projected vulnerability and a messy, conflicted personal life. Her characters are often struggling with uncontrollable feelings, emotional weaknesses, even mounting self-loathing; their challenge is, with the help of a man, to find a kind of equilibrium again.

She made only three movies for Hitchcock. In the first, the contrived but entertaining *SPELLBOUND*, she is the sensible if repressed therapist who ministers to GREGORY PECK's complicated complexes while trying to keep her own surprising love at bay; in the last, the fiercely felt but rather muddled *UNDER CAPRICORN* (a period story—one of the director's least favorite genres), she is a troubled alcoholic, possibly being gaslit (a familiar thing for Bergman) by someone in her husband's house. It is a flawed film, although it gives her at least one great scene, shot in a single, punishingly long take.

But the second film for Hitchcock, *NOTORIOUS*, is unimpeachable—an adult thriller of complicated emotions in which Bergman plays the daughter of a convicted Nazi. Loyal to America, loving her father, her feelings are tumultuous from the start—and become even more so when a man she grows to care for, an American agent, asks her if, for patriotism's sake, she would agree to take another man, a suspected Nazi sympathizer, to bed. Should she do what the American asks her to do, even as it earns his moral disapproval? Or should she refuse to do what he wants and garner his professional disappointment? It's an impossibly frustrating situation, made even worse by the man's refusal to give her any real guidance, and Bergman's

performance (which also includes one of the great kisses in screen history, with the easy-to-kiss CARY GRANT) is indelibly heart-wrenching.

Shortly after *Under Capricorn*, however, Bergman began a new collaboration with the Italian director Roberto Rossellini; she ended up having his child out of wedlock and leaving her husband and daughter in America. She was denounced on the floor of the Senate and remained persona non grata in Hollywood for half a decade. But she and Hitchcock—who, whenever she was agonizing over a scene, would gently remind her "Ingrid, it's only a movie"— remained friends forever.

They didn't work together again, however. "You see, she only wanted to appear in masterpieces," the director later complained to FRANÇOIS TRUFFAUT. "When she was pleased with a picture she'd just finished, she would think, 'What can I do after this one?' Except for *Joan of Arc*, she could never conceive of anything that was grand enough; that's very foolish!"

Nonetheless, an Academy Award for best actress in *Anastasia* in 1956 signaled that hypocritical Hollywood had finally "forgiven" Ingrid Bergman; her career continued, eventually including the lively *Indiscreet* and *Murder on the Orient Express*, for which she won a best supporting actress Oscar. In 1978, she collaborated with another famous Swede, Ingmar Bergman, on *Autumn Sonata*. It would be her last performance in a theatrical picture. In 1980, knowing he was gravely ill, she made a special point of seeing Hitchcock a final time. He wept.

She died in 1982 in London. Isabella Rossellini, the actress and filmmaker, is one of her children.

References

Ingrid Bergman and Alan Burgess, *My Story* (New York: Delacorte Press, 1980), 55, 149–52, 177–78; "Ingrid Bergman,"

IMDb, http://www.imdb.com/name/ nm0000006/bio?ref_=nm_ov_bio_sm; Patrick McGilligan, *Alfred Hitchcock: A Life in Darkness and Light* (New York: HarperCollins, 2003), 381; *The Official Ingrid Bergman Web Site*, http://www.ingridberg man.com/about/bio.htm; Donald Spoto, *Spellbound by Beauty: Alfred Hitchcock and His Leading Ladies* (New York: Harmony Books, 2008), 138–39; François Truffaut, *Hitchcock/Truffaut*, rev. ed. (New York: Touchstone, 1985), 189.

BERNSTEIN, SIDNEY (1899–1993)

Essex-born son of a real estate investor who slowly amassed a diverse portfolio of holdings. It was the chain of cinemas that interested him most, though, and by the mid-'20s, he had cofounded the London Film Society, become friendly with Hitchcock and IVOR MONTAGU, and begun importing foreign films, particularly the stirring Soviet works of Sergei Eisenstein.

A staunch antifascist, it was Bernstein who, in the '40s, encouraged Hitchcock to make the propaganda films *AVENTURE MALGACHE* and *BON VOYAGE* to aid the war effort and asked him to take over the supervision of what would become *MEMORY OF THE CAMPS*; later they would join in forming TRANSATLANTIC PICTURES. The duo managed to make *ROPE* and *UNDER CAPRICORN*, but both films underperformed with audiences; Transatlantic's third production, *STAGE FRIGHT*, was eventually taken over by WARNER BROS. as the Bernstein-Hitchcock partnership dissolved.

It ended, however, without rancor and with profitable futures for both; serving as his own uncredited producer, Hitchcock went on to the most productive decade of his career, while Bernstein pioneered British independent television in 1956 with his company Granada. In 1969, the media baron became a real one, Lord Bernstein; a decade later, he retired. He died in London at 94; his last wish was that the Holocaust documentary he and Hitchcock had worked on be restored and finally shown on television, a project his daughter Jane Wells, a documentarian in her own right, successfully took on.

References
Anthony Howard, "Obituary: Lord Bernstein," *Independent*, February 6, 1993, http://www.independent.co.uk/news/peo ple/obituary-lord-bernstein-1471201.html; Tise Vahimagi, "Sidney Bernstein," *BFI Screenonline*, http://www.screenonline.org uk/people/id/531117.

BEST, EDNA (1900–1974)

A champion swimmer from Sussex, the fair-haired, pale-eyed athlete was well cast as Jill Lawrence, the skier and sharpshooter who has to call on her marksmanship skills to save her child in the 1934 version of *THE MAN WHO KNEW TOO MUCH*, her best-known movie role. Although Best had great success on the English stage in plays from *Charley's Aunt* and *Peter Pan* to *The Constant Nymph*, the movies remained a more difficult arena, even after her Hitchcock hit; a relocation to Hollywood in the late '30s brought mostly supporting parts, although they included the films *Intermezzo: A Love Story*, *The Late George Apley*, and *The Ghost and Mrs. Muir* (she played Martha, the maid). She died in Switzerland at age 74.

References
Edna Best, http://www.ednabest.co.uk; "Edna Best," *IMDb*, http://www.imdb .com/name/nm0078923/bio?ref_=nm_ov _bio_sm.

BIRDS

Birds (and their eggs) appear in many of Hitchcock's films, even apart from the most famous, titular one. In *SABOTAGE*, the code for the bombing is "The birds will sing at 1:45." (Later, after watching the cartoon *WHO KILLED COCK ROBIN?* Mrs. Verloc stabs her murderous husband.) The predatory Jack Favell gnaws on a filched drumstick in *REBECCA*, the lovers' chicken dinner grows cold and goes untouched in *NOTORIOUS*, and an angry ex-comrade throws a raw egg at Robie in *TO CATCH A THIEF*.

In *SUSPICION*, the coroner carves into his game hen as if it were a corpse; in *TOPAZ*, gulls fatally give away a surveillance job, and a spy camera is concealed inside a chicken. In *FRENZY*, the overworked inspector returns home to a revolting meal of tiny quail; in the Hitchcock-directed episode "ARTHUR" on *ALFRED HITCHCOCK PRESENTS*, the murderer turns a corpse into poultry feed.

These examples might seem like coincidences—and not unusual ones, given the international popularity of chicken dinners—but the avian metaphor becomes far more explicit in *PSYCHO*. Our heroine, Marion Crane, comes from Phoenix; she takes refuge in a motel whose proprietor, Norman Bates, decorates the walls of the cabins—or at least one special cabin—with pictures of songbirds and spends his spare time at taxidermy, stuffing his feathered friends with cotton-wool and stitching on glass eyes. He prefers working on birds rather than other animals, he says, because they're such "passive creatures."

At first, the symbolism seems a reference to how Norman sees himself—quiet, helpless, a caged bird DOMINATED by his MOTHER. ("We're all in our own private traps," he insists. "We scratch and claw but only at the air, only at each other.") Later, it becomes clearer though, that the stuffed animals aren't a metaphor for Norman but

for his mother—sightless, soundless, lifeless. These silent winged creatures aren't just passive but death itself, and while this visiting Crane may hail from Phoenix, she will not be reborn, and in the end, her dead gaze will be as flatly unblinking as theirs.

The metaphor becomes the movie entire in *THE BIRDS*, of course, in which the creatures—without warning, although not perhaps without motive—turn on the human race, which has spent countless years selling them as pets, treating them as pests, or frying them up as blue-plate specials. Whether this is true vengeance or merely rabid madness remains unanswered—there is no thought to be read behind their black gaze—but a single shot, from high up in the clouds, suggests something huge and implacable at work. Far below, a gas station burns, tiny humans run in terror—but who is it that is watching so impassively? Is this a bird's-eye view? Or God's?

It is tempting to draw a simple and Freudian line from these images of birds and eggs directly to Hitchcock's childhood; his father was, among other things, a poultry dealer, and the stink of chicken coops (and the probable permanence of cheap eggs on the family table) was undoubtedly a large part of young Alfred's memories. But how much more poetic not to look for a single rational explanation for it, rooted in long-ago memories or childhood aversions. How much more moving to see birds, as Hitchcock's films do, as something inhuman and unknowable and strangely swiftly violent.

Which makes them, in the end, perhaps not so inhuman after all.

Reference
Donald Spoto, *The Dark Side of Genius: The Life of Alfred Hitchcock* (New York: Da Capo Press, 1999), 14–16.

THE BIRDS (US 1963)

DIRECTOR: Alfred Hitchcock.
SCREENPLAY: Evan Hunter, based on the short story by Daphne du Maurier.
PRODUCER: Uncredited (Alfred Hitchcock).
CINEMATOGRAPHY: Robert Burks.
EDITOR: George Thomasini.
SOUND CONSULTANT: Bernard Herrmann.
CAST: Tippi Hedren (Melanie Daniels), Rod Taylor (Mitch Brenner), Suzanne Pleshette (Annie Hayworth), Jessica Tandy (Lydia Brenner), Veronica Cartwright (Cathy Brenner).
RUNNING TIME: 119 minutes. Color.
RELEASED THROUGH: Universal.

Melanie Daniels, a spoiled and troubled heiress, has caught the eye of San Francisco lawyer Mitch Brenner and vice versa—but their relationship veers between ambiguous and antagonistic. Looking for a resolution, perhaps, Melanie travels to his weekend home in the small town of Bodega Bay, bringing a gift of lovebirds for his baby sister. Shortly after her arrival, though, she's attacked by a seagull—and soon surprised to find out that Mitch has his own flock of women around him, including an overprotective mother and Annie, a rueful ex-lover.

They don't complicate things as much as the local birds do, however, who soon begin to launch, en masse, unprovoked attacks against the villagers. An elderly man is found dead in his farmhouse, his eyes pecked out, and flocks of vicious birds attack schoolchildren. Annie dies trying to protect them, and the small downtown becomes a fiery disaster area, with no one sure of the animals' motive.

Finally, Melanie and Mitch's family take refuge inside their home; after a long and violent night and the birds' massive onslaught on Melanie, the extended family sneaks out in the morning as the momentarily pacified animals simply roost and watch. There is no explanation, however, for what caused these vicious attacks. And there is no guarantee that they will not begin again.

The Birds is the bleakest of all Alfred Hitchcock films. There are arguments to be made, certainly, for *VERTIGO, PSYCHO*, and *FRENZY*. But *Psycho* is tinged with humor, however black; *Frenzy* ends with the murderer caught and society put back in order. Even *Vertigo* admits the power of love. *The Birds* is pitch-dark, almost nihilist.

Why did that seagull attack? Why are songbirds pecking out people's EYES, chasing children, swarming down chimney flues? There is no answer. There is simply the fact that something you thought you understood, something you may have taken for granted or might even have enjoyed, now wants nothing but your bloody destruction. And all you can do is run or die.

Nature is not the only thing that seems to be breaking down. There is not one intact family or healthy relationship in the entire film; Mitch's father is dead, Melanie's mother deserted her, and Annie lives alone, drinking brandy and thinking about Mitch (a record album of the doomed-love epic *Tristan und Isolde*, a Hitchcock favorite, within reach). Mitch's mother is described as unloving, and Melanie feels herself unloved; significantly, only after the horrors of the birds' assaults traumatize them both—and the mother is able to embrace this substitute child and the child able to accept that embrace—is the film finally allowed to end.

That may be the birds' real dramatic purpose, in terms of the characters' development, but what do the animals themselves want? At times, almost everyone in the film tries to come up with some sort of explanation. ("It's the end of the world," proclaims an Irish drunk in the local diner, and he may be the closest to the truth.) Looking carefully, you might notice that the attacks often seem to occur right after arguments or moments of conflict—our feathered friends making the emotional disputes between people real and red in tooth and claw. But really, there is no explanation here. Only horror.

The film had its beginnings in the early '60s in newspaper stories Hitchcock had been noticing about unprovoked bird attacks; the detail appealed to both the frightened boy in him (who disliked birds to begin with) and the canny businessman (who realized he still held the movie option on a DAPHNE DU MAURIER short story about an avian attack). As Hitchcock disliked breaking in new writers, he first called JOSEPH STE-FANO, who had just provided him with *Psycho*, but Stefano had no interest; eventually Hitchcock turned to mystery novelist EVAN HUNTER, and the two worked together amicably. (Although later, much to Hunter's disgust, Hitchcock inserted several scenes of his own at the last minute, including the one on the hilltop when Mitch and Melanie talk of a "mother's care.")

The movie would also mark the debut of TIPPI HEDREN, a Hitchcock discovery (she had been a model and done some TV commercials) who was to be the new Hitchcock BLONDE. He had previously signed VERA MILES to a personal contract, but she was more interested in being a mother than a movie STAR, and he eventually, disgustedly, let her contract lapse, a relief, Miles later said, as she had already seen how controlling he could be, trying to not only determine every step in her career but also the very clothes she wore off the set.

He also, Hedren later claimed, tried to do far more than that with her, and when she rebuffed his advances, he turned first cold, then cruel. While some of the off-the-set specifics remain unverifiable, it is true that he seemed particularly posses-sive of her and, during the final onscreen avian assault on the actress, insisted on having live birds physically thrown at her; he demanded take after take, and after five days of increasingly intense shooting, a doctor finally demanded a week's rest for the anguished, sobbing actress.

That cruelty and coldness marks the movie. Significantly, it is the only Hitchcock sound film that contains no music. (BER-NARD HERRMANN, who designed the aural mix of mechanized bird cries, drew a credit as "sound consultant.") Nor, beyond the shell-shocked Melanie's finally accep-tance of a maternal embrace, does it have any sense of closure or even a proper ending; the attacks pause, however briefly, and the movie stops. There is no "End" title.

Whatever control he exerted over his leading lady, Hitchcock is—apart from some unconvincing process shots and some overly romantic close-ups of Hedren—inarguably in complete charge of the film-making and in top form throughout. There is a skillful use of deep focus when Melanie is on the phone with Mitch and Annie lis-tens in the foreground; an attack on Mela-nie, trapped within a glass phone booth, recalls a scene from D. W. Griffith's *Broken Blossoms*, in which Lillian Gish hides from her abusive father in a cramped closet.

It also continues a visual motif begun right at the start of the film in the pet store, in which humans are confined—in small places or by their damaged pasts—while the animals roam wild and free. "The human beings are in cages and the birds are on the outside," Hitchcock later observed, adding, perhaps sadly, "When I shoot something like that, I hardly think the public is likely to notice it."

But the starkest and most significant shot in the film comes during the attack on the gas station, where the camera—high, high up in the clouds—looks down dispassionately at a landscape where something is burning, some people are running, and nothing is of any consequence. It is sometimes described, naturally enough, as being from a bird's-eye view. But it is really a view from the heavens.

And it is from the vantage point of a God who—in the utterly despairing viewpoint of this film and its AUTEUR—can no longer bring Himself to care.

References

Kyle B. Counts and Steve Rubin, "The Making of 'The Birds,'" *Cinemafantastique* 10, no. 2 (Fall 1980), http://the.hitchcock.zone/wiki/Cinemafantastique_%281980%29 _-_The_Making_of_Alfred_ Hitchcock%27s_The_Birds; Richard Freedman, "'Psycho' Actress Defends Hitchcock," *Spokesman Review*, June 25, 1983, http://the.hitchcock .zone/wiki/The%20Spokesman-Review%20 %2825%2FJun%2F1983%29%20-%20 %27Psycho%27%20actress%20defends%20 Hitchcock; Greg Garrett, "Hitchcock's Women on Hitchcock," *Literature Film Quarterly* 27, no. 2 (1999), http://the .hitchcock.zone/wiki/Literature_Film_Quar terly_%281999%29_-_Hitchcock's_women _on_Hitchcock; Patrick McGilligan, *Alfred Hitchcock: A Life in Darkness and Light* (New York: HarperCollins, 2003), 611–29; Donald Spoto, *The Dark Side of Genius: The Life of Alfred Hitchcock* (New York: Da Capo Press, 1999), 448–66; Donald Spoto, *Spellbound by Beauty: Alfred Hitchcock and His Leading Ladies* (New York: Harmony Books, 2008), 243–57; François Truffaut, *Hitchcock/Truffaut*, rev. ed. (New York: Touchstone, 1985), 285–97.

BLACK, KAREN (1939–2013)

Born in Park Ridge, IL, this precociously intelligent performer studied theater at Northwestern University and eventually gravitated to the burgeoning world of underground filmmaking; her first substantial credits were in Francis Ford Coppola's *You're a Big Boy Now*, Dennis Hopper's *Easy Rider*, Bob Rafelson's *Five Easy Pieces*, and Jack Nicholson's *Drive He Said*.

Her cross-eyed looks and unconventional line readings made her a hard sell for some productions, though; a juicy role as a femme fatale in Hitchcock's *FAMILY PLOT* seemed like it might bring more mainstream work. It had been UNIVERSAL's idea; Black was a "name" at the time, and reportedly the studio demanded Hitchcock cast her although he was intent on casting the lesser-known BARBARA HARRIS as the female lead. (Annoyed by their growing salaries and demands, Hitchcock had not worked with marquee names since *TORN CURTAIN*.) He agreed to the tradeoff (although, Harris later said, he was less than thrilled with Black).

Black said she enjoyed working on the film, however, even after Hitchcock gave her an unexpected kiss and put his tongue in her mouth. ("He was an exuberant spirit," was her explanation.) "We'd do limericks together," she said of her time on set with Hitchcock. "One day he pulled up his shirt to show me his belly-button—which he didn't have. He'd had an operation and when they sewed him up they took it away. His belly-button was gone!"

But *Family Plot* came and went, too, and despite some occasionally interesting projects (a few loyal supporters, such as Robert Altman, continued to give her good parts), Black was soon reduced to titles like *Killer Fish* and *It's Alive III*. She never stopped working, although the films got more obscure and the roles less prominent; she remained both a cult favorite and den mother to new talent. She died at 74 of pancreatic cancer in Los Angeles.

References

Greg Garrett, "Hitchcock's Women on Hitchcock," *The Hitchcock Zone*,

http://the.hitchcock.zone/wiki/Litera
ture_Film_Quarterly_%281999%29
_-_Hitchcock%27s_women_on_Hitchcock;
"Karen Black," *IMDb*, http://www.imdb
.com/name/nm0000947/bio?ref_=nm_ov
_bio_sm; Patrick McGilligan, *Alfred Hitchcock: A Life in Darkness and Light* (New
York: HarperCollins, 2003), 726; Robrt L.
Pela, "Barbara Harris Knew Bill Clinton
Was White Trash," *Phoenix New Times*,
October 24, 2002, http://www.phoenixnew
times.com/arts/barbara-harris-knew-bill
-clinton-was-white-trash-6410220.

BLACK-AND-WHITE CINEMATOGRAPHY

Although Hitchcock could use COLOR brilliantly—think of the autumnal explosions that dominate ROBERT BURKS's images in *THE TROUBLE WITH HARRY*, the violent Communist reds of *TORN CURTAIN*, or the otherworldly green light that bathes KIM NOVAK in *VERTIGO*—it's often used merely, judiciously, as an accent. When we think of his films, we tend to think in monochrome. Some of that, of course, was merely due to the era he shot most of them in, when color was an extravagance at best; some of it was due to other considerations. (To shoot *PSYCHO* in color would not only have driven up the budget but also made the shower scene almost unwatchable.)

But it suits the content, too. Hitchcock's moral world is one of black and white and all the grays in between—of evil and good and varying degrees of guilt and innocence—and the palette is made for it. The light of the moon, the darkness of the shadow, the silvery gleam of a knife raised high—these are the real hues of Hitchcock. "Color will give me the chance to portray what I want to portray most—lack of color," he predicted in the late '30s, when he was still stuck with monochrome. "I know that it sounds paradoxical, but think

it over. How can I show the drabness of a slum street compared with the glory of a lovely landscape when I must photograph them both in tones of grey?"

Reference

"Some Thoughts on Colour by Alfred Hitchcock," *Adelaide Advertiser*, September 4, 1937, http://the.hitchcock.zone/wiki/Adelaide_Advertiser_%2804/Sep/1937%29_-_Some_Thoughts_on_Color_by_Alfred_Hitchcock.

THE BLACKGUARD (GB 1925)

DIRECTOR: Graham Cutts.
SCREENPLAY: Alfred Hitchcock, based on the novel by Raymond Patton.
PRODUCERS: Sir Michael Balcon, Erich Pommer.
CINEMATOGRAPHY: Theodor Sparkuhl.
EDITOR: Uncredited.
CAST: Jane Novak (Princess Irene), Walter Rilla (Michael Caviol), Bernard Goetzke (Levinsky).
RUNNING TIME: 70 minutes. Black and white.
RELEASED THROUGH: Wardour Films.

Michael Caviol, an ambitious violinist, has pledged since childhood to love nothing but his art—a promise that becomes difficult to keep once he meets a beautiful princess. Come the Russian Revolution, Caviol decides he must do everything he can to protect her—even if it means opposing his former mentor Levinsky, now a Communist leader.

The first in a planned series of Anglo-German coproductions, with GRAHAM CUTTS directing and Hitchcock, as had become customary, doing nearly everything else—not only writing the screenplay but also serving as assistant director and art director. Typical of producer SIR MICHAEL BALCON, the cast included an

American import, Jane Novak, in hopes of juicing the box office; typical of Hitchcock's scripts at this time, the plot involved a melodramatic love story and some unconvincing elements of fantasy.

Reference

Patrick McGilligan, *Alfred Hitchcock: A Life in Darkness and Light* (New York: Harper-Collins, 2003), 62.

BLACKMAIL (GB 1929)

DIRECTOR: Alfred Hitchcock.
SCREENPLAY: Alfred Hitchcock, Benn W. Levy, from the play by Charles Bennett.
PRODUCERS: Uncredited (John Maxwell).
CINEMATOGRAPHY: Jack Cox.
EDITOR: Emile de Ruelle.
ORIGINAL MUSIC: Jimmy Campbell, Reginald Connolly.
CAST: Anny Ondra (Alice White), John Longden (Detective Frank Webber), Sara Allgood (Mrs. White), Cyril Ritchard (The Artist).
RUNNING TIME: 84 minutes. Black and white.
RELEASED THROUGH: Wardour Films.

After an argument with Frank, her police-detective boyfriend, Alice goes off with a rakish artist who invites her up to his studio. Not surprisingly, perhaps, he intends to show her more than his etchings; when he assaults her, she finally grabs a knife and stabs him, then flees. But she's left behind her glove, and Frank, after being assigned the case, soon begins to realize she's the prime suspect.

So, however, does an artist's model, who saw Alice go up to the studio; he begins, quietly at first, to blackmail the couple into paying for his silence, until Frank decides it would be easier to simply frame the blackmailer for the crime. The blackmailer flees, Frank gives chase, and it ends at the British museum, where the man falls to his death, Frank is congratulated on closing the case, and Alice goes free, with only two living souls aware of her guilt.

"The first full-length all-talkie movie made in Great Britain!" the posters breathlessly announced, although that wasn't strictly true. (The sound-on-disc mystery *The Clue of the New Pin* with JOHN GIELGUD had come out earlier that year.)

Actually, it wasn't supposed to be an all-talkie anyway; at first, the skittish production company, BRITISH INTERNATIONAL PICTURES, was only willing to pay for one or two scenes with sync recording. Hitchcock blithely ignored them, however, shooting most of the film with sound; the only problem was Czech actress ANNY ONDRA, whose accent was nearly impenetrable. Hitchcock's solution was to have her merely mouth her dialogue, while actress JOAN BARRY stood off camera and spoke the lines into a microphone.

Despite the early technical limitations, a confident Hitchcock takes full advantage of the new medium of sound; particularly impressive is an almost EXPRESSIONISTIC sequence in which, after the stabbing, an innocent family meal is haunted by the repetition of the word *knife*. And his visual sense is as ensured as always, particularly in his use of special effects. (A tricky matte technique done with mirrors, the Schüfftan process, was used to seemingly place actors in the British Museum.) The film even ends with a grand chase set against the backdrop of a famous landmark—a script suggestion from the very young Michael Powell, a protégé of Hitchcock back then and a hint of what was to come in *SABOTEUR* and *NORTH BY NORTHWEST*.

But more striking is the film's continued refining of Hitchcock's great themes—of GUILT; of duty; of ever-changing, flexible morality. (Like the later *SABOTAGE*, it's a movie where the killer actually goes unpunished, her crime concealed by her lawman lover.) It was not only a sizable hit for the filmmaker; it was also a turning point where Hitchcock the director began to become HITCH the brand.

References

"Blackmail," *BFI*, http://explore.bfi.org .uk/4ce2b6a55273b; "On Set with Alfred Hitchcock," *BFI*, http://www.bfi.org.uk/ news/set-alfred-hitchcock; Tom Ryall, *Alfred Hitchcock and the British Cinema* (London: Continuum International, 1996), 96; François Truffaut, *Hitchcock/Truffaut*, rev. ed. (New York: Touchstone, 1985), 63–69.

THE BLIND MAN

A slightly fantastic thriller based on the idea that the retinas of a murder victim might retain the image of his killer; when the recipient of an EYE transplant finds this out to be true, a dangerous chase is on. Begun after *PSYCHO*, this project proceeded far enough that ERNEST LEHMAN had worked up a script and JAMES STEWART agreed to star, but Disneyland refused to allow Hitchcock to shoot some pivotal scenes at the park, and the project eventually fell apart—as would several more over the next few years, until he finally began production on *THE BIRDS*.

Reference

Patrick McGilligan, *Alfred Hitchcock: A Life in Darkness and Light* (New York: Harper-Collins, 2003), 608–9.

BLOCH, ROBERT (1917–1994)

Born in Chicago and raised in Milwaukee, WI, Bloch began writing as a teenager; a fan letter to horror icon H. P. Lovecraft gained him not only a mentor but also an entrée to "the pulps," particularly *Weird Tales*, where he quickly became a regular contributor.

Although Bloch, like many, began by copying Lovecraft's stories of the monster-haunted Cthulhu Mythos, his own instincts were for psychological horror, bad puns, and twist endings; some of his fiction was told in the first person by unreliable narrators who turned out to be the villains. Despite the gruesome violence and sick humor, Bloch protested it was all in good fun. "I have the heart of a small boy," he liked to say. "I keep it in a jar on my desk." In 1959, he published *Psycho*, a slim novel—based loosely on the real-life crimes of ED GEIN—about an amateur taxidermist who lived with the preserved corpse of his mother while sometimes "becoming" his parent and slaughtering women. The movie rights were bought by an unknown source for $9,000.

The source turned out to be Alfred Hitchcock, who—with screenwriter JOSEPH STEFANO—immediately set about revising and revamping Bloch's story. The first major change they made was staying with the heroine—Mary in the novel, Marion in the screenplay—for much more of the beginning to trick you into thinking she was going to be around for a while. The second was to make Norman—a pudgy, balding drunk in Bloch's story—into a likable, handsome young man. They kept the smart gimmick of the novel (a split-personality twist that, frankly, Bloch had already used before). But they deepened and broadened everything else, adding an almost existential sense of hopelessness and filling the film with verbal and visual clues to its themes of divided selves and secret compulsions.

Bloch never saw more than that first small check from the movie sale, but the film's enormous success established him as a brand-name author; he went on to write many episodes of *ALFRED HITCHCOCK PRESENTS* and *THE ALFRED HITCHCOCK HOUR* as well as short stories, screenplays, and novels. Although he wrote and published several more *Psycho* sequels, Hollywood was uninterested; the eventual film follow-ups came from other hands.

Bloch died in Los Angeles in 1994.

References

Robert Bloch, *Psycho* (New York: Award Books, 1975); Patrick McGilligan, *Alfred Hitchcock: A Life in Darkness and Light* (New York: HarperCollins, 2003), 608–9; "Obituary: Robert Bloch," *Independent*, September 26, 1994, http://the.hitchcock .zone/wiki/The_Independent_%2826/ Sep/1994%29_-_Obituary:_Robert_Bloch; Stephen Rebello, *Alfred Hitchcock and the Making of Psycho* (New York: HarperPerennial, 1991), 7–14, 31–50.

BLONDES

Perhaps it was the usual fetish. ("The perfect woman of mystery," he said once, "is one who is blonde, subtle and Nordic.") Or, perhaps, it was just, as he sometimes JOKED, that their paleness showed off the blood better, "like the virgin snow." But right from the very first truly "Hitchcock film," *THE LODGER*, women with golden hair would be the director's favorite victims or heroines or both—EDNA BEST in the first *THE MAN WHO KNEW TOO MUCH* (and DORIS DAY in the second), EVA MARIE SAINT in *NORTH BY NORTH-WEST* (her character a perfect emblem of the type, from her icy duplicity to her forward sensuality). And those were just the women who dropped in for a film; beyond them you had the real "Hitchcock blondes," great STARS like MADELEINE CARROLL, INGRID BERGMAN, and GRACE KELLY who became favorite and frequent collaborators, young and insecure actresses whose careers were molded for better (JOAN FONTAINE) or worse (TIPPI HEDREN).

Being Hitchcock, even as he embraced the common fetish, he abhorred the obvious. He didn't use blondes as a symbol of purity or innocence. (When we first see JANET LEIGH in *PSYCHO*, she's in her underwear, locked in an illicit embrace; give her a few more scenes, and she'll be a thief on the run.) Nor was he a fan of the pneumatic blondes of the '50s, full of as many superfluous curves as a Studebaker; mystery is what Hitchcock preferred in his stars as well as his plots. No, his blondes are knowing yet still unknowable, promising but just out of reach. For Hitchcock, the real eroticism came from Kelly, prim as a convent schoolgirl, leaning toward CARY GRANT in *TO CATCH A THIEF* with a basket of chicken and asking mischievously "Leg? Or breast?" Someone like KIM NOVAK in *VERTIGO*, with her voluptuous figure (and obvious dislike for support garments), he found vaguely distasteful. Pulchritude, in his fantasy, always came on a pedestal.

And yet, he couldn't resist dirtying these golden statues, trying to knock off some of their shine. Carroll's wrists were rubbed raw and bloody by the handcuffs he had her wear for *THE 39 STEPS*, and Fontaine turned into a mass of nerves in *REBECCA* after he made sure she knew how much the rest of the cast disliked her. The literal tortures he put Hedren through on the set of *THE BIRDS* are well documented. They may have all seemed like some subtle, Nordic symbol of sex, but to the deeply, complicatedly CATHO-LIC Hitchcock, their carnal beauty was both something to be guiltily admired and deserving of punishment onscreen (and sometimes, reportedly, shamefully, off).

References

"Alfred Hitchcock Quotes," *Wikiquote*, https://en.wikiquote.org/wiki/Alfred _Hitchcock; Sidney Gottlieb, ed., *Alfred Hitchcock: Interviews* (Jackson: University Press of Mississippi, 2003), 195; Donald

Spoto, *The Dark Side of Genius: The Life of Alfred Hitchcock* (New York: Da Capo Press, 1999), 431; Donald Spoto, *Spellbound by Beauty: Alfred Hitchcock and His Leading Ladies* (New York: Harmony Books, 2008), 51–57, 92–96, 246–57.

BOGDANOVICH, PETER (1939–)

A New Yorker who was both a youthful devotee of Orson Welles and later, in some ways, a B-movie version of him; despite heady early success with a string of fine films, his last few decades have been marked by one failed, or at least flawed, project after another, while he continues to regale younger fans with stories of the way things used to be.

Bogdanovich began his movie career as a film programmer and interviewer; when a retrospective of Hitchcock's work was mounted at New York's Museum of Modern Art in 1963, Bogdanovich INTERVIEWED the filmmaker and wrote the accompanying 48-page booklet, the first extended work in English to approach Hitchcock as more than a mere entertainer. He later went on to do a number of profiles, mostly for *Esquire* (including a terrific one with JAMES STEWART), collected in the book *Pieces of Time*. Those jobs led to a meeting with Roger Corman; a fast turnaround on an excellent original thriller, *Targets*; and then a string of critical and popular hits: *The Last Picture Show*; *What's Up, Doc*; *Paper Moon*. Then the winning streak left him, and the brutal murder of his lover, Dorothy Stratten, pretty much sidelined him for years.

Bogdanovich continues to work and has mostly turned to acting, although he released an ensemble comedy, *She's Funny That Way*, in 2015; his books, *Who the Devil Made It* and *Who the Hell's in It?*, are good collections of his many interviews, including ones with Hitchcock and many of his STARS.

References
Peter Bogdanovich, *Who the Hell's in It* (New York: Knopf, 2004), 3–37; "Peter Bogdanovich," *IMDb*, http://www.imdb.com/name/nm0000953; Peter Tonguette, "Peter Bogdanovich," *Senses of Cinema*, http://sensesofcinema.com/2004/great-directors/bogdanovich.

BOILEAU, PIERRE (1906–1989)

French crime novelist who, with partner THOMAS NARCEJAC, wrote dozens of thrillers, young-adult mysteries, and authorized sequels to Maurice Leblanc's novels about the jewel thief Arsene Lupin. Hitchcock, who was scouting constantly for new stories to adapt, had originally tried to buy the rights to their *Celle Qui N'Etait Plus*; they went instead to HENRI-GEORGES CLOUZOT who made it into *LES DIABOLIQUES* in 1955. (Prefiguring *PSYCHO*, the film had a nasty scene inside a bathroom—and an ad campaign that warned audiences not to give away the twist.) Hitchcock then bought one of their subsequent books, *D'Entres les Morts*, and began transforming it into *VERTIGO*.

He and his screenwriters made a significant change, however; whereas in the novel, you only learn about Judy's masquerade at the end, Hitchcock had a scene put in toward the last third, when she sits down and writes a letter confessing everything. It was a bold move, and Hitchcock even doubted the wisdom of it himself; until the film's final release, he tried cuts both with and without the scene. But ultimately he left it in, as the clearest proof of his strongest storytelling belief: Surprise is a simple shock; suspense is the anticipation of one.

Boileau continued to work with Narcejac, most notably on the screenplay to *Les Yeux san Visage* (*Eyes without a Face*) in 1959 and to publish for decades. Boileau died in 1989, Narcejac in 1998.

References

"Boileau-Narcejac," *Wikipedia*, https://en.wikipedia.org/wiki/Boileau-Narcejac; Patrick McGilligan, *Alfred Hitchcock: A Life in Darkness and Light* (New York: Harper-Collins, 2003), 563–64.

BONDAGE

"Being tied to something," Hitchcock said disingenuously to FRANÇOIS TRUFFAUT as their INTERVIEW turned to the hand-cuffed hero in *THE LODGER*. "It's somewhere in the area of FETISHISM, isn't it?"

Hitchcock, of course, knew that it was, but given the constraints of CENSORSHIP, he was only able to hint at SEXUALITY and its sideshows onscreen for much of his movie career. An arguably helpful thing, too; the arrival of new cinematic freedoms happened to coincide with his own darkening moods, and rape became a more explicit part of his later films, particularly in the gruesome *FRENZY*.

For much of his work, though, metaphor has to do the job, and there are hints of bondage throughout. In two of his supposedly light entertainments, *THE 39 STEPS* and *SABOTEUR*, the hero and heroine are literally handcuffed together; the very title of *ROPE* refers to the murder weapon (but also the ties that bind together the two, presumably gay, murderers). In "FOUR O'CLOCK," a Hitchcock-directed episode of the TV show *SUSPICION*, a would-be murderer is tied up by burglars and left next to his own ticking bomb; in *THE LADY VAN-ISHES*, the missing Miss Froy is wrapped up in bandages like a mummy.

But more than a cheeky reference to sex or a simple plot device (or both, as in *THE LODGER*), Hitchcock films often use bondage as an emotional idea, as a vision of people unwillingly and unhappily tied to others. It can be the ties of marriage (Alicia in *NOTORIOUS*) or divorce (Sam in *PSY-CHO*); it may be the bonds of familial loyalty (Charlie in *SHADOW OF A DOUBT*), ideology (*SABOTAGE*), or religious duty (*I CON-FESS*). Frequently it is as simple and crass as money—those golden handcuffs that keep Johnnie close in *Suspicion* and Bruno plotting in *STRANGERS ON A TRAIN*.

But in Hitchcock's world, many of us are bound—in bad and unequal relationships with lovers, parents, society. And the fastest way to cut those bonds is usually the most violent.

Reference

François Truffaut, *Hitchcock/Truffaut*, rev. ed. (New York: Touchstone, 1985), 47.

BON VOYAGE (GB 1944)

DIRECTOR: Alfred Hitchcock.
SCREENPLAY: Angus MacPhail, J. O. C. Orton, Arthur Calder-Marshall.
PRODUCERS: Uncredited.
CINEMATOGRAPHY: Gunther Krampf.
EDITOR: Uncredited.
ORIGINAL MUSIC: Benjamin Frankel.
CAST: John Blythe (Sgt. John Dougall).
RUNNING TIME: 26 minutes. Black and white.
RELEASED THROUGH: British Ministry of Information.

One of two propaganda films made by Hitchcock for Britain's Ministry of Information on behalf of the war effort (and perhaps to blunt some of the criticism he'd received from SIR MICHAEL BALCON and others for staying safely in America while Britain was being bombed). A small experiment in conflicting narratives, it has an RAF pilot recounting his voyage through enemy territory; one of his debriefers then offers a different, more sinister interpretation of what the man did (or did not) see along the way. Hitchcock would later explore the idea of untrustworthy flashbacks in *STAGE FRIGHT*. The film received a brief release in France and is available on DVD.

Reference

François Truffaut, *Hitchcock/Truffaut*, rev. ed. (New York: Touchstone, 1985), 159–61.

BOYLE, ROBERT F. (1909–2010)

Los Angeles–born architect who lost his job during the Depression; the only work he could find was at the city's movie studios as a draftsman. He eventually worked his way up to art director and showed a particular skill for large-scale fakery; it was he who constructed the replica of the Statue of Liberty used at the end of *SABOTEUR* and, more than 15 years later, the Mount Rushmore heads used for the climax of *NORTH BY NORTHWEST*.

He had some skill with smaller things, though, too, working on *SHADOW OF A DOUBT* and *MARNIE* and wrangling dozens of live animals on the set of *THE BIRDS*. "We needed to find out which birds we could use best, and finally settled on two types," he explained later. "Sea gulls, which were very greedy beasts that would always fly toward the camera if there was a piece of meat, and crows, which had a strange sort of intelligence."

A loyal Hitchcock collaborator ("It was a meeting of equals"), Boyle was having preproduction meetings with him for *THE SHORT NIGHT* when the project was finally dropped due to the director's ill health. Boyle retired shortly thereafter; he is the subject of a documentary, *The Man on Lincoln's Nose*, coproduced by the director's daughter, PATRICIA HITCHCOCK.

He died in Los Angeles of natural causes at age 100.

References

Kyle B. Counts and Steve Rubin, "The Making of 'The Birds,'" *The Hitchcock Zone*, http://the.hitchcock.zone/wiki/Cine mafantastique_%281980%29_-_The _Making_of_Alfred_Hitchcock%27s_The _Birds; "Robert Boyle," *Economist*, August 19, 2010, http://www.economist.com/ node/16843186; "Robert Boyle," *IMDb*, http://www.imdb.com/name/nm0102327.

THE BRAMBLE BUSH

Proposed Hitchcock movie about a former Communist who sneaks back into America under a false identity—unluckily for him, that of a murder suspect. Hitchcock commissioned several scripts during the early '50s, but none seemed to offer anything beyond standard thrills, and the location shooting he'd hoped for threatened to be expensive. Eventually he abandoned the project and turned to the already-written, easily staged *DIAL M FOR MURDER*. The proposed Hitchcock film has no relation to the later Richard Burton film of the same title.

Reference

Patrick McGilligan, *Alfred Hitchcock: A Life in Darkness and Light* (New York: HarperCollins, 2003), 466–68.

"BREAKDOWN" (US; ORIGINALLY AIRED NOVEMBER 13, 1955)

DIRECTOR: Alfred Hitchcock.
SCREENPLAY: Francis Cockrell, Louis Pollock.
PRODUCER: Joan Harrison.
CINEMATOGRAPHY: John L. Russell.
EDITOR: Edward W. Williams.
ORIGINAL MUSIC: Stanley Wilson.
CAST: Joseph Cotten (William Callew).
RUNNING TIME: 30 minutes with commercials. Black and white.
ORIGINALLY BROADCAST BY: CBS.

Grim story of a man paralyzed in an auto accident and thought to be dead; we listen to his increasingly anguished thoughts as his body is retrieved and brought to the mortuary. An interesting example of internal monologue—a rare narrative choice for Hitchcock—and the first episode shot for ALFRED HITCHCOCK PRESENTS, although "REVENGE" would eventually be chosen for the debut.

References

Tim Brooks and Earle Marsh, *The Complete Directory to Prime Time Network TV Shows*, 8th ed. (New York: Ballantine Books, 2003), 29; Jack Edmond Nolan, "Hitchcock's TV Films," *Film Fan Monthly* (June 1968), 3–6.

BRISSON, CARL (1893–1958)

Danish-born boxer-turned-performer, whose pugilistic skills made him a natural lead for *THE RING* in 1927, both his first film and Hitchcock's first movie from an original story. He returned, less successfully, for the director's *THE MANXMAN* in 1929 (and actually introduced the standard "Cocktails for Two" in *Murder at the Vanities* in 1934) but retired from the screen soon thereafter when his accent made roles in English-language films difficult to get. He died at age 64 in Copenhagen of jaundice; his son, Frederick, produced several hit musical films and married Rosalind Russell.

References

"Carl Brisson," *IMDb*, http://www.imdb.com/name/nm0109895/bio?ref_=nm_ov_bio_sm; Hans J. Wollstein, *Strangers in Paradise: The History of Scandinavian Actors in American Films from 1910 to World War II* (Lanham, MD: Scarecrow Press, 1994), 47–52.

BRITISH INTERNATIONAL PICTURES

Film studio founded by Scottish lawyer John Maxwell in 1927. It later went through a variety of names and permutations, buying British Pathe in the '30s, renaming itself the Associated British Picture Corporation, and eventually entering into partnership with WARNER BROS., before turning to television production. It was at BIP, however, that Hitchcock found a home, making 10 films over five years—*THE RING, THE FARMER'S WIFE, CHAMPAGNE, THE MANXMAN, BLACKMAIL, JUNO AND THE PAYCOCK, MURDER!, THE SKIN GAME, RICH AND STRANGE*, and *NUMBER 17*. It was the most work he would do for any single studio and the most diverse; only 3 of the 10 films were thrillers. Yet by the early '30s, his streak seemed to be cooling; after briefly trying to turn him into a producer with *LORD CAMBER'S LADIES*, the studio let his contract lapse.

References

Patrick McGilligan, *Alfred Hitchcock: A Life in Darkness and Light* (New York: HarperCollins, 2003), 148–49; Donald Spoto, *The Dark Side of Genius: The Life of Alfred Hitchcock* (New York: Da Capo Press, 1999), 100–103, 117–23.

BROOK, CLIVE (1887–1974)

Perfectly mannered, well-groomed leading man whose patent-leather hair and dashing way with evening clothes was emblematic of the Noel Coward era and enlivened many British films. He made his stage debut shortly after the First World War and would go on to play Sherlock Holmes three times and costar with MARLENE DIETRICH in the outré *Shanghai Express*, where, writes David Thomson, "his restraint was oddly sexy, his disdain alluring." Brook finished his career in the John Huston thriller *The List of Adrian Messenger* in 1963. Forty years before, he appeared in three films on which Hitchcock had contributed the screenplays: *THE PASSIONATE ADVENTURE, WOMAN TO WOMAN*, and *THE*

WHITE SHADOW; although the last film was long thought to be completely lost, it was recently revealed that half of it had been discovered in New Zealand. Brook died at age 87 in London.

References

"Clive Brook," *IMDb*, http://www.imdb.com/name/nm0111612; "Rare Alfred Hitchcock Film Footage Discovered," *BBC News*, August 3, 2011, http://www.bbc.com/news/entertainment-arts-14384626; David Thompson, *The New Biographical Dictionary of Film* (New York: Knopf, 2002), 109–10.

BROWNE, ROSCOE LEE (1925–2007)

The son of a Baptist minister from New Jersey, Browne served with distinction in World War II and returned to attend college, excel in various track-and-field events, and go on to teach French and literature. The lecture hall, however, was merely a poor substitute for the stage; by his early 30s, Browne abandoned the campus for cattle-call auditions and was soon landing parts in Joe Papp's early Shakespearean productions in New York. Blessed with a deeply cultured voice and an elegantly cynical attitude, Browne was a singular presence onstage and in film during the Black Power era; today he is perhaps best remembered from an episode of *All in the Family*, where he witheringly puts Archie Bunker in his place, and the movie *The Cowboys*, in which he helps John Wayne lead a cattle drive made up of gangly boys. (Although politically Browne and Wayne were polar opposites, during the film they reportedly bonded over their love of poetry.) He plays the French agent Phillipe Dubois in *TOPAZ*; his last film job was serving as narrator for the farce *Epic Movie* in 2007. The firmly private "lifelong bachelor" died at age 81 of stomach cancer.

References

Robert Fikes, "Roscoe Lee Browne," *BlackPast*, http://www.blackpast.org/aah/browne-roscoe-lee-1925-2007; "Roscoe Lee Browne," *IMDb*, http://www.imdb.com/name/nm0001975.

BRUCE, NIGEL (1895–1953)

"Eh, what? Jolly good. Well, cheerio, then." To even read the name *Nigel Bruce* is to immediately hear his voice in your ear and remember scores of his performances—chiefly the devoted if dim Dr. Watson he played to Basil Rathbone's brilliant and acerbic Sherlock Holmes. It wasn't quite true to the character—in the Doyle canon, Watson is more of a help than a hindrance—but it gave the series good humor, humanized the otherwise insufferable Holmes, and immortalized Bruce.

Born into the aristocracy—he was a descendent of the legendary king of Scots, Robert the Bruce—Bruce lost his father at 17, his mother a few years later. His older brother inherited the title of baronet; Bruce went into the army, where he was badly wounded in France, and ended the First World War in a wheelchair. After his recovery, though, he went on the stage, appearing first in comedies and then transitioning to film. In 1934, after several successful Broadway appearances, he went to Hollywood.

But if he left England, he also took some of it with him; Bruce kept his British citizenship, captained the Hollywood Cricket Club, and became a leading member of Hollywood's fabled expat ENGLISH COLONY, which would furnish Hitchcock with much of the cast of *REBECCA*, including Bruce as Major Lacy (who's memorably cut off by his wife with a simple "You're very much in the way here, go someplace else"). He would work again with Hitchcock on *SUSPICION* as Beaky, Johnnie's preposterously silly school chum;

the film was based on a novel published years before, yet the part seemed to have been written specifically for Bruce, and he caught every nuance of the character's sweet cluelessness.

Bruce's screen work was diverse, ranging from *The Charge of the Light Brigade* to Chaplin's *Limelight*, but it was as Watson in 14 Sherlock Holmes films that he gained his greatest fame. Apart from the first two, shot at Fox and true to the period, the movies were B-features at best; producers at UNIVERSAL tended to pitch them somewhere between war-time propaganda and horror thrillers, with low comedy relief an ever-present annoyance. Yet Bruce is, in every one, as comfortable and comforting as a ratty old cardigan and, for many, inextricably linked to fond memories of childhood matinees and "The game's afoot!" "I am in no way a distinguished man," he said after the Holmes films ended, "but if I died tomorrow, I can honestly claim to have been what few men can call themselves—a really happy one."

He died in Santa Monica of a heart attack at age 58.

References
Nigel Bruce, "Games, Gossip and Greasepaint," *Picasa Web Albums*, https://picasaweb.google.com/118245811686959745462/NigelBruceMemoirsGamesGossipAndGreasepaintInformationExtracts; "Nigel Bruce," *IMDb*, http://www.imdb.com/name/nm0115558/bio?ref_=nm_ov_bio_sm; Alfred E. Twomey and Arthur F. McClure, *The Versatiles: Supporting Character Players in the Cinema, 1930–1955* (New York: Castle Books, 1969), 54.

BUCHAN, JOHN (1875–1940)
A lawyer, journalist, novelist, and politician—with long stints serving in Africa and five years as the governor general of Canada—Buchan wrote *The Thirty-Nine Steps* in 1915 while in bed recovering from an ulcer. The book was a best seller and led to many other thrillers, some featuring the same calm protagonist Richard Hannay; adapting the novel in 1935 into *THE 39 STEPS*, Hitchcock and the scenarist played up the comic elements; made its first mysterious victim a woman; and added a heroine, a romance, and a pursuit in handcuffs. (Hitchcock often thought of filming another Hannay adventure, *GREENMANTLE*, but could never quite figure out how to adapt it.)

Other directors have adapted *The Thirty-Nine Steps*, though none as well, and it was even turned into a knockabout farce for the stage; a few of the author's other novels, particularly *THE THREE HOSTAGES*, have been adapted for television or the screen, too, while Hannay got his own British TV series in the late '80s. Buchan's books are somewhat pulpy (and prone to ethnic stereotyping) but still fast-paced and inventive; GRAHAM GREENE and Ian Fleming were both schoolboy fans, and the Hannay books were clearly an influence on their own spy fiction.

Buchan died of a stroke in Montreal while in office at age 64.

References
"John Buchan: Biography," *Cleave Books*, http://www.cleavebooks.co.uk/grol/buchan/zbuchan.htm; Donald Spoto, *The Dark Side of Genius: The Life of Alfred Hitchcock* (New York: Da Capo Press, 1999), 144–45, 256.

BUMSTEAD, HENRY (1915–2006)
Art director and production designer in films since 1948. He first worked with Hitchcock on the 1956 *THE MAN WHO KNEW TOO MUCH* and would eventually help devise the look of *VERTIGO, TOPAZ,* and *FAMILY PLOT*. (The various interiors on *Vertigo*—particularly Scottie's apartment and Judy's hotel room—show his

signature approach, an attention to detail rooted both in the realism of the setting and the emotional background of the character.) Starting with *High Plains Drifter*, Bumstead formed a particularly strong partnership with Clint Eastwood; he would work on 14 of the director's films, concluding with *Flags of Our Fathers* and *Letters from Iwo Jima*; he died before either film was released. He was 91.

References

"Henry Bumstead," *IMDb*, http://www.imdb.com/name/nm0120317/bio?ref_=nm_ov_bio_sm; Dennis McLellan, "Henry Bumstead, 91: Veteran Production Designer," *Los Angeles Times*, May 27, 2006, http://articles.latimes.com/2006/may/27/local/me-bumstead27.

BURKS, ROBERT (1909–1968)

Born in Chino, CA, Burks began his career as a special-effects technician at WARNER BROS. in the '30s, eventually branching out into cinematography; he got his first director of photography credit in 1949 on *The Fountainhead* and in 1951 drew the assignment of shooting Hitchcock's STRANGERS ON A TRAIN.

Their partnership would continue through *MARNIE*, with Burks shooting every Hitchcock picture except *PSYCHO* (on which, trying for a faster, cheaper, and perhaps grittier look, Hitchcock turned to JOHN L. RUSSELL of his *ALFRED HITCHCOCK PRESENTS* TV crew). A gifted and adaptable technician, Burks could work in BLACK AND WHITE, COLOR, even 3-D. (In addition to Hitchcock's *DIAL M FOR MURDER*, one of the last examples of the '50s fad, he also did perhaps its most famous example, *House of Wax*.) Rarely did his work draw attention to itself.

And yet Burks's ever-adaptable style (he was equally comfortable on set or on location) marks so much of the director's work. The lush, change-of-seasons colors of *THE TROUBLE WITH HARRY* and the gorgeous Monegasque sunshine of *TO CATCH A THIEF*; the newsreel bleakness of *THE WRONG MAN* and moody monochrome of *I CONFESS*—Burks could capture whatever needed to be caught. And he could bring things to the screen that other, equally flexible cinematographers might miss—the crazy carnival world of *Strangers on a Train* (including the heart-in-your-throat shots of the madly spinning carousel), the frame-within-a-frame VOYEURISM of *REAR WINDOW*, the nauseating focal-length dislocations of *VERTIGO*.

Although Burks had won an Oscar for *To Catch a Thief* (and nominations for *Rear Window* and *Strangers on a Train*), the partnership with Hitchcock ended after *Marnie*; while the movie was no more marred by its zooms and oddly obvious back-projection than by TIPPI HEDREN's forced performance, Hitchcock was already wracked by self-doubt and would go on to summarily curtail associations with many talents he had previously collaborated with and depended on, including Burks and composer BERNARD HERRMANN.

Burks died in a fire in his California house in 1968.

References

James Morrison, "Robert Burks," *Internet Encyclopedia of Cinematographers*, http://www.cinematographers.nl/GreatDoPh/burks.htm; "Robert Burks," *IMDb*, http://www.imdb.com/name/nm0122079/bio?ref_=nm_ov_bio_sm.

BURR, RAYMOND (1917–1993)

Born in British Columbia, Raymond Burr grew up in California and by 20 was already appearing at the Pasadena Playhouse. But his greatest performance may have been the public one he gave of a made-up "private life"—over the years he successively claimed to have been in the navy, have been wounded at Okinawa, attended various colleges, and (most offensively) had a beloved son who tragically died of leukemia.

None of it seemed to have any basis in fact. Most, perhaps, were meant as distractions from the truth—that Burr, despite a studio-publicized "romance" with young Natalie Wood and a brief arranged marriage, was gay. And this was not an era when any actor—even one generally called upon to play the villain—could be anything but a red-blooded heterosexual.

So when Burr appeared in *REAR WINDOW* as the pathetic murderer Lars Thorwald—a shy, desperately unhappy man who only wants to be left alone—listen again as he begs JAMES STEWART "What do you want from me?" Watch again as you see him, blinking in the cruel light of the flashbulbs, trying to keep his secret. And think about what he must have been thinking about to prepare for this role.

After *Rear Window*, Burr changed directions to play TV's calmly successful lawyer *Perry Mason*, the paralyzed chief of police on *Ironside*—and then return again for a string of successful Perry Mason TV movies. He worked constantly, with breaks only for regular charity work and trips to Hawaii, where he raised orchids.

He died in California in 1993. He left his entire estate to his lover of 33 years.

References

Andrew Mersmann, "Robert Benevides of the Raymond Burr Winery," *Passport*, http://www.passportmagazine.com/robert-benevides-raymond-burr-winery; "Raymond Burr," *IMDb*, http://www.imdb.com/name/nm0000994; Michael Seth Starr, *Hiding in Plain Sight: The Secret Life of Raymond Burr* (Milwaukee: Applause, 2008), 59–64.

CADY, FRANK (1915–2012)

Born in small-town Susanville, CA, weedy Frank Cady was a journalist, Stanford graduate, and educator who fell in love with acting during a 1930s stint in England (where he apprenticed at a London theater and even made an appearance on the then-very-rudimentary TV service of the BBC). The Second World War put an abrupt end to that career, but afterward Cady returned to the stage and managed to rack up a long string of small parts in very good noirs—*He Walked by Night, D.O.A., The Asphalt Jungle, Ace in the Hole*—where his thin voice and meek appearance made him a natural for frightened witnesses, seedy suspects, and expendable bystanders. He was often uncredited; typically, his character in *REAR WINDOW*—the man with the apartment above the Thorwalds'—wasn't even given a name. His most famous character was, however, as the grocer Sam Drucker, the lone voice of sanity on CBS's trio of corn-pone comedies of the '60s, simultaneously appearing on *Green Acres, Petticoat Junction*, and *The Beverly Hillbillies*. He died at his home in Wilsonville, OR, at 96.

References

"Frank Cady," *IMDb*, http://www.iMdb com/name/nm0128326/bio?ref_=nm_ov _bio_sm; Daniel E. Slotnik, "Frank Cady, Kept Store on 'Green Acres,' Dies at 96," *New York Times*, June 11, 2012, http:// www.nytimes.com/2012/06/12/arts/televi sion/frank-cady-actor-on-green-acres-dies -at-96.html?_r=0.

CAHIERS DU CINEMA

A venerable French film journal, it rose in 1951 from the interests (and membership groups) of two serious Parisian film societies and boasts a long line of critics who went on to become acclaimed directors in their own right—from such early contributors as ERIC ROHMER, FRANÇOIS TRUFFAUT, CLAUDE CHABROL, Jacques Rivette, and Jean-Luc Goddard to such later lights as Leos Carax and Olivier Assayas.

Although it is still extant, the magazine's most influential era was in the mid-'50s, as the young Truffaut launched both a sneering attack on the safe, literary, good-taste films of earlier French cinema ("the tradition of quality") and a ringing defense of Hollywood films often seen as mere entertainments, such as the westerns of Howard Hawks and melodramas of Nicholas Ray. Hitchcock came in for special, approving attention—even in 1954 receiving his own issue—with the young *Cahiers* critics responding enthusiastically both to his PURE CINEMA explosions of thrilling MONTAGE and his consistent CATHOLIC concerns with sin and GUILT.

Of course, not everyone agreed. In his own piece, "Hitchcock vs. Hitchcock," the

Norman Lloyd, left, holds on, barely, to Robert Cummings at the climax of *Saboteur*. *Universal Pictures/Photofest © Universal Pictures*

magazine's cofounder ANDRE BAZIN— whose preference was for neorealism and "invisible" style—would declare of his young colleagues, "I cannot say that the combined efforts of Scherer, Astruc, Rivette, and Truffaut have entirely con- vinced me of Alfred Hitchcock's flawless genius." Still, the young cultists made many converts. Truffaut, Chabrol, and Rohmer would all eventually INTERVIEW and write book-length studies of the director, and Truffaut's writings on the AUTEUR

THEORY would form the basis for not only the coming reappreciation of Hitchcock and other often underestimated filmmakers but also for much of modern film criticism.

The aesthetics and politics of the magazine have, naturally enough, changed with the decades and with the editors. As Truffaut and others left to make their own films (and lead the FRENCH NEW WAVE), the magazine went through love affairs with modernism, postmodernism, and Marxism. At one point, the entire enterprise was put together by a Maoist collective (which, bizarrely, banned the use of photographs in the magazine); during another era, reviews of reality TV shows began to appear. Never has *Cahiers* regained the stature—the absolutely essential quality—it had in the 1950s, when whether you agreed with it or not, any serious cinephile had to read it. But whatever its fortunes (and in a literal sense, they're scant—the publication has almost always lost money), the magazine remains an essential part of film history, one that not only rescued the art's past from the rubbish heap but also encouraged its future for decades to come. This book, and many hundreds more, would not be here without it.

References

Andre Bazin, "Hitchcock vs. Hitchcock," in *Focus on Hitchcock*, edited by Albert LaValley (Englewood Cliffs, NJ: Prentice Hall, 1972), 60–69; Philip French, "A Short History of Cahiers du Cinema," *The Observer*, March 13, 2010, http://www.theguardian.com/books/2010/mar/14/cahiers-du-cinema-emilie-bickerton; Dave Kehr, "Cahiers Back in the Day," *Film Comment* (September/October 2001), http://www.filmcomment.com/article/cahiers-back-in-the-day.

CALHERN, LOUIS (1895–1956)

Brooklyn born, Missouri-raised high school athlete-turned-vaudeville-performer. His large head and hawklike profile made him a leading man in early silents and then, as he moved into middle age, a supporting actor often cast in positions of authority, whether as the diplomat in the anarchic *Duck Soup* or as CARY GRANT's highly pragmatic boss in *NOTORIOUS*.

With his worldly mien and beautiful speaking voice, Calhern won an Oscar nomination for playing Oliver Wendell Holmes in 1950's *The Magnificent Yankee* (a part he'd already played onstage). He is best known today, though, for two other roles he played that year: a singing Buffalo Bill in *Annie Get Your Gun* and the duplicitous lawyer in *The Asphalt Jungle* who funds the heist.

Married four times (including to actresses Ilka Chase and Natalie Schaefer), Calhern was a fine interpreter of Shakespeare, too, playing the title role in Joseph L. Mankiewicz's 1953 film of *Julius Caesar* and the lead in a 1950 Broadway production of *King Lear*. He died of a heart attack at age 61 while on location in Japan to shoot *The Teahouse of the August Moon*.

Paul Ford replaced him in the film, and any typically wry Calhern character would have chuckled mirthlessly at the irony; Calhern had only gotten his own part in *Annie Get Your Gun* when the original star, Frank Morgan, suffered a sudden fatal heart attack at age 59.

References

"Louis Calhern," *IMDb*, http://www.iMdb.com/name/nm0129894/bio?ref_=nm_ov_bio_sm; Alfred E. Twomey and Arthur F. McClure, *The Versatiles: Supporting Character Players in the Cinema, 1930–1955* (New York: Castle Books, 1969), 56.

CALTHROP, DONALD (1888–1940)

Skilled British performer onstage since 1906 and in films since 1916. Calthrop appeared in five Hitchcock movies: *BLACKMAIL* (as the blackmailer), *MURDER!, NUMBER 17, JUNO AND THE PAYCOCK*, and the revue *ELSTREE CALLING*, although this busy schedule seems to be due more to his own industry and the insular world of British filmmaking than any particularly strong connection with the filmmaker. Among Calthrop's other credits are the English version of *F.P.I. Doesn't Answer* (based on an early sci-fi novel by Curt Siodmak and simultaneously shot in German and French), the 1935 *Scrooge* (he played Bob Cratchit), and *Fire over England*, the movie on which LAURENCE OLIVIER and Vivien Leigh fell in love. The actor—who tragically lost two sons at the Battle of Dunkirk in 1940—died that same year in Eton of a heart attack at 52. He had nearly finished filming *Major Barbara*; his part was completed with a stand-in and some dubbing.

References

"Donald Calthrop," *IMDb*, http://www.iMdb.com/name/nm0130740/bio?ref_=nm_ov_bio_sm; Anthony Slide, "Donald Calthrop," *BFI Screenonline*, http://www.screenonline.org.uk/people/id/454022.

CAMEOS

When FRANÇOIS TRUFFAUT asked Hitchcock about his tradition for onscreen cameos starting with *THE LODGER*, the director was typically dismissive. "It was strictly utilitarian," Hitchcock insisted. "We had to fill the screen. Later on it became a superstition and eventually a gag."

In truth, it was something more than that. Hitchcock may have appeared in *The Lodger* when they needed an extra player; after the film was finished, however, he began working with a publicist (a rare thing for a director in 1920s England) and started constructing both a product brand and a personal image. The cameo became part of that and particularly part of his iconography as the "Master of Suspense." Never during his days in Britain would he contribute a cameo to a comedy or straight drama. But he almost invariably shows up in his thrillers, a portly Englishman in a dark suit with an even darker sense of sly humor, often struggling with mass transit, a package, or some other quietly exasperating fact of daily life.

The branding took work. At the time, the few directors who moviegoers recognized tended to be either famous industry figures (such as D. W. Griffith, one of the four founders of United Artists) or actors themselves (such as Erich von Stroheim). Hitchcock was neither. But by appearing in his own films and eventually making a bit of a game of it (can you spot him?), he became both a familiar figure and a celebrity. Later on, his appearances on his TV series and in his own trailers, the merchandising of his name and silhouette on everything from magazines to comic books, and his tireless appearances on talk shows would make him the most recognizable director in the world.

The only downside—apart from encouraging some critics to view him as more of a showman than an artist—was that it could keep audiences focusing on playing "Where's Hitch?" rather than actually following the plot. "By now it's a rather troublesome gag," he told Truffaut in 1962, "and I'm very careful to show up in the first five minutes or so, as to let the people look at the rest of the movie with no further distraction."

Here is a list of Hitchcock's popularly confirmed cameos in his own films, as compiled by the excellent online resource, *The Hitchcock Zone* (http://the.hitchcock.zone/welcome). Although there has been effort by some scholars to read meaning and metaphor into these appearances, it's a bit of a reach; most symbolize nothing beyond the director's efforts to promote his image while perhaps having a chuckle or two doing it. (Note that some of these cameos are difficult to see in today's full-screen—that is, panned-and-scanned—home-video versions. Times given are approximate.)

THE LODGER (1927). About five minutes into the film, sitting in a newsroom with his back to the camera, talking on the phone. (Although identified by Truffaut as a second cameo, the extra in a later scene watching IVOR NOVELLO's arrest seems to be another actor.)

BLACKMAIL (1929). About 10 minutes into the film on the London Underground, trying to read while a small boy pesters him.

MURDER! (1930). About an hour into the film, strolling past the crime scene.

THE MAN WHO KNEW TOO MUCH (1934). About 30 minutes in on the sidewalk as a bus passes by.

THE 39 STEPS (1935). About five minutes in, tossing away some trash, as ROBERT DONAT brings "Miss Smith" back to his apartment.

YOUNG AND INNOCENT (1937). About 15 minutes in, waiting outside the courthouse, wearing a cap, and carrying a tiny camera.

THE LADY VANISHES (1938). Near the very end of the film in Victoria Station, smoking.

REBECCA (1940). About two hours into the film, walking past GEORGE SANDERS in the street. (A slightly longer cameo, with him waiting outside a phone booth while Sanders makes a call, was cut.)

FOREIGN CORRESPONDENT (1940). About 10 minutes in, passing JOEL MCCREA in the street while reading the paper.

MR. AND MRS. SMITH (1941). About 40 minutes in, walking past the hotel.

SUSPICION (1941). About 45 minutes in, mailing a letter.

SABOTEUR (1942). About an hour in, standing with a woman outside the drugstore. (A more elaborate cameo with Hitchcock and screenwriter DOROTHY PARKER was vetoed and played with other actors; a second one, with Hitchcock making a pass at a woman in sign language, didn't make it past the CENSORS.)

SHADOW OF A DOUBT (1943). About 15 minutes in, his back to the camera, on the TRAIN playing cards. His hand contains 13 spades—a good hand for bridge but perhaps a hint of the film's deadly theme.

LIFEBOAT (1944). His most ingenious appearance. About 25 minutes in, WILLIAM BENDIX picks up a newspaper; Hitchcock's picture appears in an advertisement for "Reduco: The Sensational New Obesity Slayer."

SPELLBOUND (1945). About 45 minutes in, getting out of a hotel elevator.

NOTORIOUS (1946). About an hour in, getting a glass of champagne at the party (and doing his own unknowing part to engineer CLAUDE RAINS's crucial trip to the wine cellar).

THE PARADINE CASE (1947). About 35 minutes in, carrying a cello.

ROPE (1948). Another brilliant gag. About 50 minutes in, his famous self-drawn caricature turned into a red neon sign is glimpsed through one of the apartment's windows.

Another Reduco ad, the director explained. (Some sources insist he's visible during the credits sequence as well, walking past the apartment building with a woman, but this seems to be an extra player.)

UNDER CAPRICORN (1949). About 15 minutes in, his only appearance in period costume, standing on the steps of Government House. (Some sources say he can also be glimpsed about 10 minutes earlier in the crowd watching a parade.)

STAGE FRIGHT (1950). About 35 minutes in, passing by JANE WYMAN while giving her a questioning look (perhaps because she's in disguise; perhaps because she seems made up to resemble his daughter PATRICIA HITCH-COCK).

STRANGERS ON A TRAIN (1951). About 10 minutes in, carrying a double bass and trying to board the train.

I CONFESS (1953). Little more than two minutes in, glimpsed at the top of a flight of steps.

DIAL M FOR MURDER (1954). About 10 minutes in, seen in the class photo displayed by RAY MILLAND. (As in *Rope* and *Lifeboat*, the film's constrained setting and limited number of characters required some imagination to fit in an appearance.)

REAR WINDOW (1954). About 25 minutes in, across the courtyard, winding a clock in ROSS BAGDA-SARIAN's apartment.

TO CATCH A THIEF (1955). About 10 minutes in, sitting obliviously next to CARY GRANT on the bus.

THE TROUBLE WITH HARRY (1955). About 20 minutes in, wearing a raincoat and walking past JOHN FORSYTHE's paintings.

THE MAN WHO KNEW TOO MUCH (1956). About 25 minutes in, his back to the camera, watching the acrobats in Morocco along with DORIS DAY and JAMES STEW-ART.

THE WRONG MAN (1956). Both his earliest-in-the-story and deliberately most serious appearance, Hitchcock shows up within the first minute in silhouette to introduce the movie.

VERTIGO (1958). About 10 minutes in, walking in front of the shipyard.

NORTH BY NORTHWEST (1959). About two minutes in, during the opening credits, he misses the bus. (About 45 minutes later, on the train, there is also an overweight woman in a blue dress who some watchers have speculated is Hitchcock in drag, although this seems highly unlikely.)

PSYCHO (1960). About five minutes in, he can be seen through the window of JANET LEIGH's office, standing outside with his back to the camera and wearing a Stetson.

THE BIRDS (1963). About two minutes in, leaving a pet shop with two terriers (his own).

MARNIE (1964). About five minutes in, walking out of a hotel room—and seeming to catch us looking at him.

TORN CURTAIN (1966). About five minutes in, at the International Congress of Physicists. His back to the camera, he sits in the hotel lobby, awkwardly holding a toddler on his knee.

TOPAZ (1969). About a half-hour in at the airport, briefly sitting in—and then getting up from—a wheelchair.

FRENZY (1972). About three minutes in, he stands in a crowd, wearing a bowler hat and listening to a politician talk about cleaning up the Thames. He is not impressed.

FAMILY PLOT (1976). About 40 minutes in, his shadow casting the familiar jowly silhouette on the frosted-glass door of the city registrar's office.

References

"The Hitchcock Cameos," *The Hitchcock Zone*, http://the.hitchcock.zone/wiki/The_Hitchcock_Cameos; François Truffaut, *Hitchcock/Truffaut*, rev. ed. (New York: Touchstone, 1985), 49.

CARDIFF, JACK (1914–2009)

Born in Norfolk, the son of two music hall performers, Cardiff acted as a child both onstage and in the silents; at 15, he moved on to working behind the scenes at Britain's small studios. He was still a lowly gofer and "clapper boy" on Hitchcock's THE SKIN GAME in 1931 but eventually began getting jobs as a cinematographer and in 1937 was the first to shoot on three-strip Technicolor in Britain for the Henry Fonda film *Wings of the Morning*.

After the war and a stint shooting British propaganda films in India, Cardiff returned to the English movie industry, where he became known as a specialist in capturing deeply saturated, nearly unreal COLORS. He would shoot several films, including the almost painfully vibrant *Black Narcissus* and *The Red Shoes* for Michael Powell and Emeric Pressburger; when for *The African Queen* John Huston needed someone comfortable with unforgiving climates and rich hues, he called Cardiff.

In between working for Powell and Pressburger and Huston, Cardiff would shoot UNDER CAPRICORN for Hitchcock, only the director's second film in Technicolor and his first film back in Britain in 10 years. Echoing ROPE, his previous film, *Under Capricorn* used a moving camera and very long takes, a challenge for both Cardiff and the actors; unfortunately the film was not a hit with audiences and was the final nail in the coffin of TRANSATLANTIC PICTURES, Hitchcock's short-lived production company. "I think a film of *Capricorn* being made would have been far more successful than *Capricorn* itself," Cardiff wryly observed.

After *The African Queen*, Cardiff was frequently called upon for epics, action films, or difficult shoots; his credits quickly grew to include *War and Peace*, *The Vikings*, and even *Rambo: First Blood Part II*. (Despite an early success with *Sons and Lovers* in 1962, his career as a director was not as smooth.) More than 75 years after his first job on a movie set, Cardiff was still shooting; he died at age 94 in Ely, England.

References

Cameraman: The Life and Work of Jack Cardiff, http://www.jackcardiff.com; "Jack Cardiff," *IMDb*, http://www.imdb.com/name/nm0002153/bio?ref_=nm_ov_bio_sm; Patrick McGilligan, *Alfred Hitchcock: A Life in Darkness and Light* (New York: HarperCollins, 2003), 422–24.

CAREY, MACDONALD (1913–1994)

Bland midwesterner who began on Chicago radio programs during the Depression and later transitioned to Broadway and then a Hollywood studio contract. A dependable but unremarkable actor, he was typical of the leading men (ROBERT CUMMINGS, JOHN HODIAK) Hitchcock felt himself saddled with in the early '40s, when DAVID O. SELZNICK would loan him out to other studios whose list of contract players was somewhat lacking.

Carey was a prime example. In *SHADOW OF A DOUBT*, for example, he plays Jack Graham, JOSEPH COTTEN's pursuer and, eventually, TERESA WRIGHT's love interest. He is a sober, dedicated professional hunting down a dangerous serial killer, but does he interest any viewer? Or leave them doubting for a moment that Wright's life with him will be one of stultifying safety? Still, Hitchcock would use the actor later for his TV shows on episodes of *ALFRED HITCHCOCK PRESENTS* and *THE ALFRED HITCHCOCK HOUR*. Like Carey, both installments were competent and unmemorable. The actor finally found a more congenial home on daytime TV, where for nearly 30 years he played Tom Horton on *Days of Our Lives*.

He died of lung cancer at age 81 in Beverly Hills; one of his daughters, Lynn Carey, was a *Penthouse* centerfold, rock singer, and star of Russ Meyer films, including *Beyond the Valley of the Dolls*.

References
"Macdonald Carey," *IMDb*, http://www .imdb.com/name/nm0136994; Richard Severo, "Macdonald Carey, 81, Film Actor with a Soap Opera Career, Dies," *New York Times*, March 22, 1994, http://www .nytimes.com/1994/03/22/obituaries/mac donald-carey-81-film-actor-with-a-soap -opera-career-dies.html.

CARROLL, LEO G. (1886–1972)
Tweedy, avuncular actor whose quiet professionalism made him one of Hitchcock's favorites; the director used him six times over nearly 20 years, starting with *REBECCA* and continuing with *SUSPICION, SPELLBOUND, THE PARADINE CASE, STRANGERS ON A TRAIN*, and *NORTH BY NORTHWEST*. (Only CLARE GREET, whose credits include the unfinished silent *NUMBER 13*, appeared in more, with seven—eight if you count *LORD CAMBER'S LADIES*, which Hitchcock merely produced.)

Born in Buckinghamshire, England, to a devoutly Catholic family (he was named after Pope Leo XIII), Carroll made his stage debut in 1912; by the early '30s he was in America, first in summer stock and then on Broadway and in Hollywood. He made his first film, *Sadie McKee*, in 1934 with Joan Crawford; played Marley's Ghost in the 1938 *A Christmas Carol*; and was Joseph in the 1939 *Wuthering Heights*.

As the doctor in *Rebecca*, he was merely one of the many members of the ENGLISH COLONY to lend some British verisimilitude to Hitchcock's California-shot thriller; in *Suspicion*, he is Captain Melbeck, one of the feckless Johnnie's easy marks. Both parts—trustworthy, sympathetic—made him an excellent choice for *Spellbound*, in which he finally got to play the villain (and had to handle the complicated acting job of going from confident murderer to despairing suicide within a brief, single scene). He was excellent, too, in *North by Northwest*, as the professor, a spymaster who plays the game of espionage like a particularly diverting match of chess. It was that role that led to his last, and perhaps most signature, success, as Mr. Waverly, the sometimes slightly distracted secret agent handler on TV's *The Man from U.N.C.L.E.* (and its brief spinoff, *The Girl from U.N.C.L.E.*) from 1964 through 1968.

He died in Hollywood of pneumonia at age 85.

References
"Leo G. Carroll," IMDb, http://www.imdb .com/name/nm0001991/bio?ref_=nm_ov _bio_sm; Alfred E. Twomey and Arthur F. McClure, *The Versatiles: Supporting Character Players in the Cinema, 1930–1955* (New York: Castle Books, 1969), 60.

CARROLL, MADELEINE (1906–1987)
Elegant, erudite British performer from Staffordshire and the child of an Irish professor and his French-born wife. Carroll later grad-

uated from the University of Birmingham with a B.A. in French. But her pale blonde hair and porcelain looks were obvious even in the classroom, and after appearing in a play her senior year, she knew she was meant to become an actress. "I understood then how people get 'a call,'" she said later.

Her father, who had planned for her to continue her studies at the Sorbonne as he had and then take up an academic career, was opposed; in fact, she was turned out of the house and had to take a job teaching in a girl's school to support herself. But by 1927, she was appearing on the stage and by the following year had made her movie debut. She would rapidly go on to make *The American Prisoner* with CARL BRISSON, *French Leave* with CHARLES LAUGHTON, and *Escape* with EDNA BEST.

In 1931, she married an English officer and soon announced her retirement from acting. That was surprising but not unprecedented—at the time, many actresses retired upon marriage—but Carroll returned to the screen in 1933 with a new studio contract and offers coming in from Hollywood. In 1935, she made perhaps her best-remembered film, *THE 39 STEPS*, for Hitchcock and became, some say, the "first Hitchcock BLONDE."

The honor is not an inarguable one; the director had used fair-haired women before as both heroines and victims. But Carroll was the true archetype in a long line of cinematic flaxen-haired symbols, all of whom followed the rigid rules first set down for those characters here and broadened and darkened by Hitchcock over the ensuing decades. In a drama, they would question, challenge, or confront the hero right from the start (*SPELLBOUND*, *NOTORIOUS*); in a chase film, they would arrive later in the narrative as an outright obstacle or nemesis (*SABOTEUR, NORTH BY NORTHWEST*). They could not really be trusted (*VERTIGO, MARNIE*). Their

SEXUALITY was often hidden or teasingly withheld (*PSYCHO, TO CATCH A THIEF*). And for all this, they would eventually be punished onscreen—dragged around in handcuffs, strangled, even stabbed.

As the sexy, suspicious, and ultimately supportive heroine to ROBERT DONAT's man on the run, Carroll set the standard in *The 39 Steps*, and although privately she would complain of Hitchcock's occasional treatment of her—putting her through chase scenes that left her wet and uncomfortable or snapping on handcuffs that left her delicate skin red and raw—the film was an enormous hit for both of them, with Carroll's removal of her sodden stockings a particularly erotic moment for 1935 cinema.

She returned to star for Hitchcock again in *SECRET AGENT*, but the results weren't to be quite as acclaimed—JOHN GIELGUD was no substitute for a then-ailing Robert Donat, and the plot was trickier and more downbeat. Still, it led to further offers from Hollywood, resulting in *Lloyds of London*, *The General Died at Dawn*, and in 1937 the charming *The Prisoner of Zenda*. She was billed on one poster as the "most beautiful woman in the world," and it's a sign of her genuine appeal that the audience greeted this rather bold proclamation with nothing but assent.

Then in 1940, her baby sister Marguerite was killed during the London blitz, and Carroll was changed utterly. Although she continued to take on a few assignments—including *My Favorite Blonde* with Bob Hope—she got out of her Hollywood contract. By now divorced from her first husband and married to Sterling Hayden (although that would only last a few more years), she gave up acting. She moved to Europe and devoted herself to the war effort. She had already turned her French chateau into an orphanage; she then became a nurse for the Red Cross under the name Madeline

Hamilton and took a job at a busy military hospital in Italy.

After the war, Carroll remained in Europe, where she remarried, this time to a French producer, and worked on radio programs and documentaries meant to foster better international relations, provide aid to Holocaust survivors, and care for the displaced and often disabled children of the conflict. Charity became her focus; although she would occasionally appear in films, on the stage, and eventually on TV, her work on behalf of children, especially through UNICEF, became the driving force in her life. Eventually she retired to Spain, where she lived with her two yapping Yorkies, Tricky and Dicky.

She died at 81 in Marbella, Spain.

References
"Biography," *Madeleine Carroll*, http://www.madeleinecarroll.com/biography; "Madeleine Carroll," *IMDb*, http://www.imdb.com/name/nm0140914/bio?ref_=nm_ov_bio_sm; Richard Pendlebury, "From Hollywood Starlet to Wartime Angel," *Daily Mail*, February 22, 2007, http://www.dailymail.co.uk/femail/article-437780/From-Hollywood-starlet-wartime-angel.html; Donald Spoto, *Spellbound by Beauty: Alfred Hitchcock and His Leading Ladies* (New York: Harmony Books, 2008), 52–66.

CARTWRIGHT, VERONICA (1949–)
Bristol-born child STAR in films since 1958. Busy on early American TV, she would play Violet in *Leave It to Beaver*, appear in the Ray Bradbury adaptation "I Sing the Body Electric" on *The Twilight Zone*, and costar in two episodes of *ALFRED HITCHCOCK PRESENTS*. In 1963, she played ROD TAYLOR's sister (and the object of many BIRDs' enmity) in *THE BIRDS*, bringing the film some of its sharpest notes of helpless hysteria and its only plaintive one of hope as, at the end, she begs to take her pet lovebirds with her and her fleeing family.

Like many child stars, Cartwright grew faster than her career; her most famous roles as an adult remain the 1978 *Invasion of the Body Snatchers* and the original *Alien*. (She is not to be confused with her three-years-younger sister, Angela, who starred in *The Sound of Music* and TV's *Lost in Space* and who also appeared on *Alfred Hitchcock Presents*.)

References
Veronica Cartwright, http://www.veronica-cartwright.com; "Veronica Cartwright," *IMDb*, http://www.imdb.com/name/nm0001021/bio?ref_=nm_ov_bio_sm.

"THE CASE OF MR. PELHAM" (US; ORIGINALLY AIRED DECEMBER 4, 1955)

DIRECTOR: Alfred Hitchcock.
SCREENPLAY: Frances Cockrell, based on the novel by Anthony Armstrong.
PRODUCERS: Joan Harrison.
CINEMATOGRAPHY: John L. Russell.
EDITOR: Edward W. Williams.
ORIGINAL MUSIC: Stanley Wilson.
CAST: Tom Ewell (Albert Pelham), Raymond Bailey (Dr. Harley).
RUNNING TIME: 30 minutes with commercials. Black and white.
ORIGINALLY BROADCAST BY: CBS.

A doppelgänger slowly, effectively, begins to take over a man's life, finding easy acceptance among the original's acquaintances. An odd and unresolved episode of *ALFRED HITCHCOCK PRESENTS* that digs a little deeper into Hitchcock's favored theme of DOUBLES.

References
Tim Brooks and Earle Marsh, *The Complete Directory to Prime Time Network*

TV Shows, 8th ed. (New York: Ballantine Books, 2003), 29; Jack Edmond Nolan, "Hitchcock's TV Films," *Film Fan Monthly* (June 1968), 3–6.

CATHOLICISM

"I don't think I can be labeled a Catholic artist," Alfred Hitchcock mildly protested to FRANÇOIS TRUFFAUT. Many critics disagree.

Certainly the roots were there (and, as even Hitchcock immediately went on to admit, "It may be that one's early upbringing influences a man's life and guides his instinct"). His father's side of the family had drifted in and out of the faith, but Hitchcock's mother, Emma, was Irish and more devout; as the director later JOKED, the day he was born was "one of the only Sundays in my mother's life when she missed church."

Although his own relationship with the sacraments was less stringent—he remained a generous donor, though by old age he had fallen away from regular services and, writes DONALD SPOTO, even grown suspicious of priests—Hitchcock was a fairly conventional Catholic through middle age. His wife, ALMA REVILLE, had to convert before their marriage; he went to mass regularly and was delighted when his daughter, PATRICIA HITCHCOCK, married into the family of a prominent American archbishop.

As a child, Hitchcock had been educated by the Jesuits, a traditionally rigorous, intellectual order. The experience schooled him in logic and discipline but also left him with a sense of fear—in a sneaky form of torture, corporal punishment for any offense was scheduled, so that the student was forced into dreadful anticipation—and of human duality, "a consciousness of good and evil, that both are always with me."

Hitchcock left his all-boys school around the age of 14, and the ways in which the Jesuits had prepared him for the real world were limited. On one hand, he had taken classes in religion, drawing, elocution, choir, and all the usual academic subjects (including Latin, German, and French); on the other, teachings on SEXUALITY were limited to occasional paeans to chastity, the "angelic virtue." Not only were the details of reproduction avoided but also discussion of gender itself; in fact, Hitchcock remained so ignorant of female biology that, while shooting *THE PLEASURE GARDEN*, he was confused when an assistant told him one of the actresses couldn't do a swimming scene because she was menstruating. "What's that?" the filmmaker asked. He was 25.

And so, born during the last gasp of the Victorian era and raised in England by Irish Catholics (who, perhaps because they were surrounded by Protestants, clung even more stubbornly to their traditions), Hitchcock was very much an old-school, old-fashioned believer. Almost any worldly pleasure offered an occasion of sin; women were either on pedestals or in bordellos, Mary the Holy Mother of God or Mary Magdalene, a sinning (if eventually saved) woman of the streets. But how did this affect his art?

Certainly, it is there in his treatment of GUILT and innocence. He was raised, as he admitted, to believe that good and evil are both within us, that the struggle for one's soul was constant. Beyond that, though, his beliefs took a darker turn. In Catholic teaching, the end is not predestined; one has free will and the power to resist. After all, Christ himself was tempted; the only difference between a saint and a sinner is that the sinner not only knowingly gives into the temptation but also refuses to repent.

Yet Hitchcock was not so forgiving. In his cinematic world, the momentary desire is almost as bad as the act itself. Guy doesn't actually kill his wife in *STRANG-ERS ON A TRAIN*—but he wants her dead, and he profits by her murder, and so he must suffer. In *ROPE*, Professor Cadell may not believe his lectures on Nietzsche are truly meant to justify eliminating "the inferior"—but shouldn't he have realized that at least one obviously disturbed student might disagree? No one is innocent. And as for the truly guilty—well, the Jesuits might have preached salvation, but in the church of Alfred Hitchcock, repentance is not enough.

In *I CONFESS*, any sexual indiscretion Logan might have engaged in with a married woman happened before he became a priest—and yet it will still lead to blackmail and death. In *PSYCHO*, Marion Crane has already decided to return the stolen money (even begun to figure how much more she owes, after impulsively buying that car)—and still the knife comes for her. Regrets always come too late; "sorry" doesn't matter.

Yet if guilt and desire and sin and punishment are ever present in almost all of Hitchcock's films, what is far rarer is the essential Christian teaching of meek acceptance and dramatic self-sacrifice. Even Father Logan, who seems willing to go to jail in *I Confess* rather than break the seal of the confessional, is not so much sacrificing himself for the murderer's sake as safeguarding his own salvation; to break his vows would be a grievous sin. In the end, he's really only thinking about himself.

No, in Hitchcock's world of murder, only a few true martyrs exist. Not surprisingly, all of them are women, and they divide, with the usual clear lines, into Madonnas and whores. On the saintly side, there is Midge, the wry maternal virgin of *VERTIGO*, who loves Johnnie and is willing to sacrifice almost anything for him—yet realizes in the end that he has to save himself. There is Mama Balestrero in *THE WRONG MAN*, the dedicated, widowed

mother who prays (and begs her son to pray) for a miracle—and actually seems to get one, as religious icons look down from the shabby walls.

And, across the divide, there is Alicia in *NOTORIOUS*, who begins the film lost in drink and despair and will soon go to bed with a poisonous villain for the good of her country and, ironically, the love of a man—potentially sacrificing herself, and her soul, for others. And Annie in *THE BIRDS*—a frank, worldly, slightly cynical woman—who will give her life for her ex-lover's little sister, dying on the steps of her own childless home.

These women are out there, Hitchcock says, and if we are lucky, they will step forward to try to help us find our way. But it may not be enough. Our feet are turned toward Hell from our birth, and with every stray and uncontrolled thought, we take another step.

References
Richard Alleva, "The Catholic Hitchcock: A Director's Sense of Good and Evil," *Commonweal*, July 12, 2010, https://www.commonwealmagazine.org/catholic-hitchcock; "Catechism of the Catholic Church," *The Holy See*, http://www.vatican.va/archive/ccc_css/archive/catechism/p3s1c1a8 htm; Bess Twiston Davies, "Hitchcock: Monster or Moralist?" *Times*, September 5, 2008, http://the.hitchcock.zone/wiki/The_Times_%2805/Sep/2008%29_-_Hitchcock:_monster_or_moralist; Patrick McGilligan, *Alfred Hitchcock: A Life in Darkness and Light* (New York: HarperCollins, 2003), 17–18, 20–21; Donald Spoto, *The Dark Side of Genius: The Life of Alfred Hitchcock* (New York: Da Capo Press, 1999), 15, 19–20, 22–23, 551–52.

CENSORSHIP
In 1972, the British censors demanded trims in the brutal rape scene in *FRENZY*.

This caused some outcry among the director's fans—far more brutal films, such as Sam Peckinpah's *Straw Dogs* and Stanley Kubrick's *A Clockwork Orange*, had recently passed without changes, while no Hitchcock film had been cut in Britain since *PSYCHO*. Hitchcock, however, remained unruffled, saying it was only a few frames. "I am not given to goriness, you know," he told the London *Times*, adding "These things are always a matter of degree, and it always depends on whether you do it with taste or not. . . . I do not get seriously censored, because I have enough experience in this business to know what is sensible." That he had good sense, though, and usually good taste did not mean that he avoided the censors entirely.

Although the director's SEXUAL experience can only have been scant before his marriage—when, at the age of 25, he was told one of his actresses in *THE PLEASURE GARDEN* was indisposed because she was having her period, he needed to have someone explain what it meant—he had a schoolboy's love of naughty limericks, crude practical JOKES, and dirty puns, many of them revolving around his own last name. As he grew older and more powerful, he would try to shock his leading ladies with obscene stories. ("I heard worse things when I was in convent school," an unblushing GRACE KELLY told him and won his adoration.) Later, he would try to shock audiences by pushing things even further with images the screen had rarely seen.

During his early days in Britain, Hitchcock's relation to studio and government censors was calm but oppositional. Although some of the disagreements were political—he claimed later that stories of a "sociological importance" he had wanted to do (a film on the general strike of 1926, for example) were vetoed by producers before they ever got to the script stage—most of the arguments were over sexual material.

Particularly infuriating was that the government authorities applied double standards—"The censor bans scenes in British films which he permits to pass in American films of a similar type," he told the *Daily News* of Perth in 1930. English films, Hitchcock concluded, were sadly lacking in "sex appeal."

Still, he managed to work around the bluenoses. Sometimes this was mere cleverness, as in setting necessary expository scenes in dressing rooms or shared accommodations, where women bustled about getting in and out of scanty lingerie (as in the opening moments of *THE LADY VANISHES*), yet the dialogue rendered the sequence essential to the film—always a strong argument against cutting. Sometimes the workaround took a more ingenious approach. At one point, directors personally showed their films to the censor; Hitchcock, discovering the man was nearly blind in one eye, would pick problematic moments to ask a question, forcing the gentleman to turn his head and miss what was about to happen onscreen.

When Hitchcock reached America, though, he found that a sly wink and a clever subterfuge were not enough to get past the industry's Production Code or to get "objectionable" material passed by the independent, all-powerful Hays Office.

His first project, *REBECCA*, turned out to be a problem almost immediately. Producer DAVID O. SELZNICK did not believe in altering one word of a best seller once he bought it for the movies; the movie censors, reading ROBERT E. SHERWOOD's first draft, found it in violation of their standards due to an "illicit" love relationship, a murderer going unpunished, and "quite inescapable inferences of sex perversion."

Further drafts would retool *Rebecca* to—rather tortuously—absolve Maxim of Rebecca's death. Even more work would be required by BEN HECHT on *NOTORI-OUS*, too, which censor Joe Breen found particularly distasteful in not only its details of Alicia's sexual past but also the film's original ending, which had her succumbing to the poisoning and emerging as a sort of martyr. It was essential, Breen wrote, that the word *tramp* be used less frequently; also, it would be better if Alicia lived and were rescued by Devlin (after which they could head, presumably, to the nearest all-night chapel).

These were small-minded complaints and frustrating situations, but as they were occurring at the script stage, at least there was time to find a solution before shooting began; sometimes the solutions truly improved the film (such as the long, constantly interrupted, endlessly erotic kiss filmed for *Notorious*, staged so as to get around the censorious stopwatch usually applied to such embraces). Far worse were those times when the movies were finished and then ran afoul of the censors and had to be cut.

In *REAR WINDOW*, for example, the board objected that "Miss Torso" appeared to be topless in one shot; Hitchcock, who had deliberately inserted the scene as a bargaining chip, happily took it out on the condition that other material now be allowed in. In *NORTH BY NORTHWEST*, they demanded that in the line "I never make love on an empty stomach," *make* be changed to *discuss*; Hitchcock acquiesced, smiling to himself that they hadn't noticed the final, impudently phallic shot of the TRAIN hurtling into a tunnel.

More often problems would happen when the film went into its widest release and ran into additional censors in other parts of America (some states still maintained their own, even stricter, boards for years) or other countries. Maryland drastically cut the scenes in *STRANGERS ON A TRAIN* when Bruno kills Miriam (and then

nearly relives it, choking Mrs. Cunningham); India scissored out the scene in *Rear Window* when Grace Kelly sat on JAMES STEWART's lap; Ireland banned *Notorious* and *I CONFESS* in their entirety; and France and Italy did the same for *ROPE*.

No film brought more trouble from the beginning than *Psycho*. The movie starts with a woman and a divorced man half-naked in a hotel room; it ends with an almost subliminal shot of a stuffed corpse. In between there are two bloody murders, one of a nude woman. Almost none of this, the censors said, was remotely acceptable.

But their power was waning, standards were shifting, and Hitchcock knew this. He scheduled a reshoot of the sexy hotel room tryst, inviting the censors onto the set; when they didn't show, he left the scene as it was. Similarly, when the censors couldn't agree just what they could see in the shower scene (except for a few frames of the corpse's buttocks, which Hitchcock immediately cut), he told them he would re-edit the film further; instead, he simply resubmitted the same version a few days later. Although the censors still found problems—the shot of a flushing toilet was thought to be in particular bad taste—the film ultimately emerged unscathed.

Other stories of censorship battles, however, are less well documented and feel a bit like Hitchcock inventing excuses after the fact or apologies for compromises he himself willingly made. For example, although the director always said the contrived happy ending of *SUSPICION* was forced on him when RKO refused to let him have CARY GRANT turn out to be a killer, DONALD SPOTO has pointed to studio correspondence proving that the film's theme—a woman's paranoia—had been Hitchcock's preferred one all along.

In fact, as much as Hitchcock railed against the censors and fought their intrusions—as had Billy Wilder, Ernst

Lubitsch, Preston Sturges, and every other sophisticate in Hollywood—in some ways, he benefitted from them. He had always trusted his wife, ALMA REVILLE, to give scripts a final read, films one last look, before he considered them finished. The industry's censors served as a second, similar check and balance, and while their objections were often absurd, that they forced Hitchcock to at least justify some of his choices was not always a bad thing, as the years to come would show. For the power of the censors began to wane just as Hitchcock's taste for shocking material began to increase—and, Spoto argues, allow him to express, and live out onscreen, some of his darkest personal obsessions.

Certainly, after the victories of *Psycho*, the director's films grew ever more gruesome. The close-up of the dead, disfigured farmer in *THE BIRDS*; the marital rape of the nearly comatose *MARNIE*, the long drawn-out murder in *TORN CURTAIN*—these are not shots or situations the director would have even considered a decade before. But now, there was no one to stop him from dwelling on them or from putting them onscreen. In 1959, Audrey Hepburn's own good taste would derail *NO BAIL FOR THE JUDGE*, a movie that was to feature her being dragged off to Hyde Park and assaulted; by the '70s, Hitchcock could film a rape in close-up for *Frenzy* and even end it with the dead victim's staring face, her tongue hanging uselessly from her mouth. His final, unrealized project, *THE SHORT NIGHT*, was built around another brutal, sexual assault, a scene he discussed in careful detail during the long and ultimately abandoned development of the script.

It is absolutely true that censorship constrained Hitchcock for most of his career and sometimes forced ridiculous compromises; it would be utterly idiotic to wish that there had been more of it. But it's also true that once those constraints were dropped and he was free to go where he wished, he was also free to trade subtle metaphor for explicit imagery, as he explored ever darker and more dangerous territory. And his attitude toward that new freedom (honest artistry or crass provocation?) and motivation for dramatizing that new material (a revulsion against the violence visited on women or a vicarious participation in it?) has been debated ever since. And will continue to be.

References

Rudy Behlmer, ed., *Memo from David O. Selznick* (New York: Viking Press, 1972), 261, 284–85; "Censor Trims Hitchcock Film," *Times*, January 3, 1972, http://the .hitchcock.zone/wiki/The_Times_%2803/ Jan/1972%29_-_Censor_trims_Hitch cock_film; Gerald Gardner, *The Censorship Papers: Movie Censorship Letters from the Hays Office, 1934–1968* (New York: Dodd, Mead, 1987), 84–96; Stephen Rebello, *Alfred Hitchcock and the Making of Psycho* (New York: HarperPerennial, 1991), 76–78, 145–46; "Retort to Film Censors," *Daily News* (Perth), April 16, 1930, http://the.hitchcock.zone/wiki/ The_Daily_News_%28Perth%29_%2816/ Apr/1930%29_-_Retort_to_Film_Censors; Donald Spoto, *The Dark Side of Genius: The Life of Alfred Hitchcock* (New York: Da Capo Press, 1999), 213–15, 243–44, 537–38; François Truffaut, *Hitchcock/ Truffaut*, rev. ed. (New York: Touchstone, 1985), 34.

CHABROL, CLAUDE (1930–2010)

A child of the bland, petit bourgeois (both his father and grandfather had been druggists), Chabrol was fascinated by detective stories and movies since childhood; although he ostensibly matriculated at the Sorbonne to study pharmacology, he graduated with a degree in literature. Friendships with fellow cinephiles FRAN-ÇOIS TRUFFAUT, Jacques Rivette, ERIC ROHMER, and Jean-Luc Goddard soon followed; they would form the critics' core of the magazine *CAHIERS DU CINEMA* and, later, the originators of the FRENCH NEW WAVE.

Chabrol collaborated with Truffaut on a Hitchcock INTERVIEW for the journal, and then cowrote a book-length study of the director's work up through *THE WRONG MAN*; by the time the book was published in France in 1957 (it would appear much later in America as *Hitchcock: The First Forty-Four Films*), Chabrol was already directing his first film, *Le Beau Serge*, inspired very loosely by *SHADOW OF A DOUBT*.

He would continue directing with marked regularity until his death; many of his films—*Les Biches, La Femme Infidele, Merci Pour la Chocolat, La Ceremonie*—while functioning as social critiques, would often feature a violent crime and, while standing stylistically apart from Hitchcock's films in terms of pace and MONTAGE, examine the same thematic concerns of GUILT and TRANSFERENCE. If BRIAN DE PALMA came the closest to copying the appearance of Hitchcock's films, Chabrol may have been best at invoking their soul.

He died in Paris at 80.

References

"Claude Chabrol," *IMDb*, http://www.imdb.com/name/nm0001031/bio?ref_=nm_ov_bio_sm; "Claude Chabrol: Biography," *NewWaveFilm.com*, http://www.newwavefilm.com/french-new-wave-encyclopedia/claude-chabrol.shtml.

CHAMPAGNE (GB 1928)

DIRECTOR: Alfred Hitchcock.
SCREENPLAY: Eliot Stannard, Alfred Hitchcock, based on a story by Walter C. Mycroft.
PRODUCER: Uncredited (John Maxwell).
CINEMATOGRAPHY: Jack E. Cox.
EDITOR: Uncredited.
CAST: Betty Balfour (The Girl), Gordon Harker (The Father), Jean Bradin (The Boy), Theo Von Alten (The Man).
RUNNING TIME: 93 minutes. Black and white.
RELEASED THROUGH: Wardour Films.

Betty, a spoiled and willful heiress, runs away with her boyfriend—of whom her father heartily disapproves, warning her that the man's only after her money. But before their ship to Paris has even docked, the couple has fought and separated—a separation made somewhat wider by Betty's interest in a mysterious stranger.

Her father catches up with her in France with a bit of devastating news—the family champagne business has been wiped out and, along with it, her entire inheritance. When a robber also deprives her of her jewelry, Betty is forced to take a job in a restaurant. Her boyfriend disapproves—and the mysterious stranger reappears to court her.

Eventually her father arrives to tell her the truth—their fortunes are intact and his story was merely a ruse to ascertain her boyfriend's true intentions. More outraged than relieved, Betty decides to run away with the stranger but reconsiders—too late, once their ship has sailed for America.

Luckily her boyfriend is already onboard—as is her father, who confesses that the stranger was someone he'd asked to keep an eye on her. Parent and child reconcile, and Betty and her boyfriend make up—although, as the film ends, it seems another quarrel is around the corner.

This is not the movie Hitchcock had intended to make.

His first idea, he claimed years later, was a sort of rake's progress, following the life of a French girl who worked in a factory bottling the bubbly stuff. She imagines the drink leads to all sorts of glamorous scenarios but, after finally making it to the big city, sees only drunkenness and violence. She returns to her factory job, now viewing the sparkling wine as poison. This was not the sort of movie BRITISH INTERNATIONAL PICTURES wanted to produce, however, particularly once they had hired the popular comic actress Betty Balfour.

So, quickly working with another screenwriter—often finishing a scene only minutes before it had to be shot—Hitchcock came up with a sort of protoscrewball comedy, full of silly millionaires, MISTAKEN IDENTITIES, and a constant battle of the sexes. (That his wife, ALMA REVILLE, was then pregnant might have encouraged the film's rather unromantic view of marriage, but any truly serious ideas were left unexplored.)

Typical of Hitchcock's often international productions during the silent era—the boyfriend was played by a French actor, the mysterious stranger by a German/Russian one—it was not in any way a happy experience. Hitchcock despised beginning with an unfinished script and, according to famed director Michael Powell (then only a stills photographer on the set), referred to the leading lady foisted upon him as a "piece of suburban obscenity." (The one bright spot of the whole affair was a trick shot Hitchcock devised, shooting a close-up through the bottom of a champagne glass.)

Although the studio promoted the film as "light, frivolous, frothy" and coming from the "premier British director and one of the finest in the world," its international reception was mixed (the *Variety* review called the whole thing "dire"), and Hitchcock later disavowed the entire production, calling it the "lowest ebb in my output." It's difficult, however, to truly fairly judge the movie today; apparently all surviving prints were struck from the "back-up" negative, comprising alternative takes. The original release version—starring, as the studio had trumpeted, "Britain's Queen of Happiness"—seems lost.

References

"Champagne," *Variety*, September 5, 1928, 28; Patrick McGilligan, *Alfred Hitchcock: A Life in Darkness and Light* (New York: HarperCollins, 2003), 103–5; François Truffaut, *Hitchcock/Truffaut*, rev. ed. (New York: Touchstone, 1985), 57–61; Kieron Webb and Bryony Dixon, "London— Restoring Hitchcock," *Journal of Film Preservation* (October 2012), http://the. hitchcock.zone/wiki/Journal_of_Film _Preservation_%282012%29_-_London _-_Restoring_Hitchcock.

CHANDLER, RAYMOND (1888–1959)

American-born, English-raised writer whose first attempts at poetry led to little and whose fallback career in the California oil industry disappeared with the arrival of the Depression (and the flowering of his lifelong troubles with alcohol). Teaching himself to write pulp fiction the same way he had taught himself bookkeeping, the middle-aged Chandler began selling stories to the detective magazines; his first novel, *The Big Sleep*, arrived in 1939 and helped rewrite the mystery story, popularizing the idea of the private detective as a wounded idealist with a tendency for poetic narration, vivid turns of speech, and a chivalrous ideal of womanhood.

Although most of Chandler's novels were adapted for the films, he had a hand in none of them; Hollywood chiefly hired him to write screenplays based on other people's mysteries, including James M. Cain's *Dou-*

ble Indemnity for Billy Wilder (where his style gave the film much of its rich dialogue and his drinking helped convince Wilder to make *The Lost Weekend*) and PATRICIA HIGHSMITH's *STRANGERS ON A TRAIN* for Hitchcock.

"If my books had been any worse, I should not have been invited to Hollywood," Chandler said later. "If they had been any better, I should not have come."

The collaboration with Hitchcock was not a happy one. Chandler (who by the end was referring to the director as "that fat bastard") complained that Hitchcock's idea of character was "primitive," that his plots too often "lose their grip on logic," and that he cared less about the dialogue in a scene than "shooting it upside down through a glass of champagne"; Hitchcock, deeming Chandler's efforts unusable, supposedly made a great show of holding his nose and throwing his last draft into the trash. (Chandler kept screen credit, although the script was largely rewritten by CZENZI ORMONDE.)

"If you wanted something written in skim milk, why on earth did you bother to come to me in the first place?" Chandler wrote Hitchcock after the frustrating collaboration came to an end. "What a waste of money! What a waste of time! It's no answer to say that I was well paid. Nobody can be adequately paid for wasting his time."

Chandler never mailed the letter. Neither did he ever really work in Hollywood again (although he later turned one of his rejected scripts into the novel *Playback*). He had one more good book in him, his greatest, *The Long Goodbye*, but after his beloved wife died, the alcoholism and depression won. He died at age 70 in La Jolla, CA.

References

Dorothy Gardiner and Kathrine Sorley, ed., *Raymond Chandler Speaking* (Boston: Houghton Mifflin, 1962), 132–35; Paul Jensen, "Raymond Chandler: The World You Live In," *Film Comment* (November 1974), 18–26; Patrick McGilligan, *Alfred Hitchcock: A Life in Darkness and Light* (New York: HarperCollins, 2003), 444–50; David Shipman, ed., *Movie Talk: Who Said What about Whom in the Movies* (New York: St. Martin's Press, 1988), 31; Donald Spoto, *The Dark Side of Genius: The Life of Alfred Hitchcock* (New York: Da Capo Press, 1999), 322–24; Tom Williams, *A Mysterious Something in the Light: The Life of Raymond Chandler* (Chicago: University of Chicago Press, 2013), 270–78.

CHEKHOV, MICHAEL (1891–1955)

A nephew of Anton Chekhov, Michael studied at the Moscow Art Theatre under Konstantin Stanislavski, who hailed him as a sensitive new talent (too sensitive, perhaps; Michael had a nervous breakdown after the school's probing, psychological exorcisms). Later, Michael would move away from Stanislavski's very personal approach, developing his own theories based more on imagination and a kind of internalized physicality.

Chekhov, who had been teaching first in Eastern Europe, then Germany, then England, finally moved to America in 1939, where he established an acting school; he also returned to film acting after more than a decade with a role in *Song of Russia*. In *SPELLBOUND*, he is Dr. Brulov, where he plays Constance's gruff old mentor ("The mind of a woman in love is operating on the lowest level of the intellect!"); it was a scene-stealing part and won him an Academy Award nomination.

Chekhov continued to act as well as draw new hopefuls to his classes; in the 1950s, some of his students included Yul Brynner, Jack Palance, and a very young Clint Eastwood. Chekhov died in Beverly

Hills of a heart attack at 64; his books are still a strong influence on many young performers, and the Michael Chekhov Acting Studio in New York still guides new generations.

References

"About Michael Chekhov," *MICHA: Michael Chekhov Association*, http://www .michaelchekhov.org/michael-chekhov/ about-michael-chekhov; "Michael Chekhov," *IMDb*, http://www.imdb.com/name/ nm0155011/bio?ref_=nm_ov_bio_sm; *Michael Chekhov Acting Studio*, http:// www.michaelchekhovactingstudio.com/ workshops.htm.

CIANNELLI, EDUARDO (1888–1969)

The gifted and erudite son of a Neapolitan physician, Ciannelli was himself a surgeon until falling in unconditional love with music; he would go on to sing baritone in operas at La Scala and later appear on Broadway in the '20s in *Rose-Marie*. Typically, once he reached Hollywood, he was chiefly cast as gangsters or other swarthy types (he is the maniacal Indian rebel in *Gunga Din*), although most of his villains were marked by their quietly intense focus.

Despite being stereotyped, Ciannelli appeared in a number of excellent movies, including *Marked Woman*, *For Whom the Bell Tolls*, *The Mask of Dimitrios*, and *Gilda*; he is the villainous Mr. Krug in *FOREIGN CORRESPONDENT* and, more than 20 years later, appeared on two episodes of *ALFRED HITCHCOCK PRESENTS*.

He died of cancer in Rome at 81.

References

"Eduardo Ciannelli," *IMDb*, http:// www.imdb.com/name/nm0161862/ bio?ref_=nm_ov_bio_sm; Alfred E. Twomey and Arthur F. McClure, *The Versatiles: Supporting Character Players in the Cinema, 1930–1955* (New York: Castle Books, 1969), 65.

CLIFT, MONTGOMERY (1920–1966)

Gifted, beautiful, damned.

Born in Nebraska, the son of an erratically successful stockbroker and a mother who aspired to high society, Clift was educated by private tutors and lived a pampered, sheltered life until he showed an interest in amateur theatricals at 13; his mother encouraged him to turn professional, eventually moving with him to New York. At 17, Clift got his first Broadway lead; parts in the hits *The Skin of Our Teeth* and *Our Town* would follow.

Despite his misgivings about Hollywood and its businessmen—he walked out of an early meeting at MGM—Clift eventually signed for the film *Red River* in 1946. Although Howard Hawks's western, released two years later, is ostensibly about a generational conflict between two cowboys, it also seemed to presage one between kinds of film actors—John Wayne's iconic, personality-driven style forced to face Clift's more unpredictable, METHOD approach.

Clift was not the first of the "new" New York actors to bring their casual, sometimes mumbled naturalism to Hollywood—in some ways, John Garfield, trained in the Group Theatre, preceded him by a decade—but Clift planted a flag that later arrivals, like Marlon Brando and James Dean, would pick up and proudly wave, and Clift's good looks made him an immediate STAR. Intrigued, Hitchcock first approached Clift for a leading role in *ROPE*, but the actor reportedly turned it down because the gay subtext struck too close to home; he would finally sign with the director to make *I CONFESS*.

Yet their two approaches—with the young actor constantly questioning everything and the veteran director expecting him to simply perform on cue—couldn't be more at odds; whether it ever actually happened or not, the director's favorite tart JOKE about what he once told an actor who dared to ask about his motivation ("Your paycheck" was the reply) probably has its roots in this experience. Hitchcock much preferred the older generation of stars.

"He was a Method actor, and neurotic as well," Hitchcock later said. "'I want you to look in a certain direction,' I'd say, and he'd say 'Well, I don't know whether I'd look that way.' Now immediately you're fouled up because you're shooting a precut picture. He's got to look that way because you're going to cut to something over there. So I have to say to him, 'Please, you'll have to look that way, or else.'"

Of course the fact that Clift arrived on set with not only his own approach (and acting coach) but a serious drinking problem alienated the two men even further. Eventually Hitchcock would barely speak to him at all, relaying instructions through an assistant or costar KARL MALDEN (who also grew annoyed as shooting went on, and Clift seemed to be working to upstage him). Clift's drinking intensified, and—according to DONALD SPOTO—during at least one party, Hitchcock egged him on, daring the drunken actor to finish a snifter of brandy in a gulp. (Clift did and passed out.)

The film was not a success. Still, while audiences objected to the character of a flawed priest and most reviews singled out the frustrations inherent in the plot—Clift plays a man whose signature action is that he can't act—few blamed the star. In fact, the next year, Clift would enjoy one of his greatest successes in *From Here to Eternity*.

In 1956, however, while filming *Raintree County*, he smashed his car into a tree after leaving a party at Elizabeth Taylor's house. Taylor ran to the accident and saved Clift from choking on his own shattered teeth; he was rushed to a hospital, where doctors and plastic surgeons worked on his badly broken nose, fractured jaw, and severely scarred right profile.

It would have been a disaster for any performer; for someone heralded as one of the most beautiful men in the movies (with an already deeply insecure and addictive personality), it was the end. It just took a long time coming. Although there were flashes of fragile brilliance in *The Misfits*, it was clear the actor's concentration was gone; when frustrated directors turned on him, Clift turned only deeper into himself. (He's the "only person I know who is in even worse shape than I am," Marilyn Monroe mused.)

Joseph L. Mankiewicz tried to have Clift fired from *Suddenly, Last Summer* when it turned out he could only remember a line or two at a time; although he was brilliant in *Judgment at Nuremberg*, UNIVERSAL sued him for putting John Huston's lugubrious *Freud* behind schedule. And yet still Clift's friends—mostly women—rallied fiercely around him. (At the end of the *Suddenly, Last Summer* shoot, after making sure they had truly gotten their last shot and concluded their business, Katharine Hepburn spat in Mankiewicz's face.)

Nearly unemployable after 1962's *Freud* lawsuit, Clift returned to Manhattan and his own self-made fog. (PETER BOGDANOVICH, then a young man working at a revival house, remembers Clift coming in one day to see *I Confess* and standing unsteadily at the back of the theater, just smoking and weeping.)

He died alone in his New York bedroom of a heart attack at age 45.

References

Peter Bogdanovich, *Who the Hell's in It* (New York: Knopf, 2004), 92–96; Philip

French, "Screen Legends: Montgomery Clift," *Guardian*, January 16, 2010, http://www.theguardian.com/film/2010/jan/17/screen-legend-montgomery-clift; "Montgomery Clift," *IMDb*, http://www.imdb.com/name/nm0001050/bio?ref_=nm_ov_bio_sm; David Shipman, ed., *Movie Talk: Who Said What about Whom in the Movies* (New York: St. Martin's Press, 1988), 36; Donald Spoto, *The Dark Side of Genius: The Life of Alfred Hitchcock* (New York: Da Capo Press, 1999), 338–41; David Thomson, *The New Biographical Dictionary of Film* (New York: Knopf, 2002), 164.

CLOUZOT, HENRI-GEORGES (1907–1977)

One of the filmmakers often called the "French Hitchcock," although Hitchcock would perhaps more accurately be described as a contemporary (and a rival) than an influence. Clouzot began working in the movies in the early '30s, a decade later than Hitchcock, but the two men were always intrigued by similar themes, even occasionally pursuing the same projects; the French director's most productive period—the wartime era through the '50s—corresponds roughly with Hitchcock's own.

Born in Niort to a bookseller (whose business later failed), Clouzot was interested in drama and music from an early age; by the 1930s, he was working in Germany's film industry, primarily translating scripts, but lost his job as the racial discrimination laws began to take effect and his continuing friendship with Jewish producers made him suspect. After a long bout with tuberculosis, Clouzot returned to France just in time for the Occupation; he resumed his work in the movies, this time taking a job with the German-supervised Continental Films. Clouzot began by directing mysteries, although *Le Corbeau*, released in 1943, was rather more a bitter story of a small and small-minded town torn apart by anonymous hate mail.

The film was unpopular with everyone but the people; although audiences rushed to it, Vichy propagandists criticized it as being an insult to the national character, and the studio fired the director. Yet the Liberation only brought worse troubles; Clouzot was branded a Nazi collaborator and given a lifetime ban from the cinema. With many French artists and intellectuals protesting his sentence, Clouzot was eventually allowed to return to work, directing a new adaptation of *Manon* and several more thrillers. Unlike Hitchcock, however, the style was more subdued, and the theme tended to hew closer to betrayal and deception than temptation and GUILT.

The Wages of Fear, released in 1953, was a more straightforward adventure thriller, with four men given the job of driving a truck full of nitroglycerine, and was both an international hit and a prize-winner at Cannes. Moving quickly, Clouzot snapped up the rights to the PIERRE BOILEAU and THOMAS NARCEJAC novel *Celle Qui N'Etait Plus*. (By some accounts, even as Hitchcock was preparing to put in a bid.) It became his next film, *LES DIABOLIQUES*, the story of a sickly wife and abused mistress who join forces to murder their tormentor.

The film has often, too easily, been cited as a major influence on *PSYCHO*, with its murder in a bathtub and twist ending; in fact, the Hitchcock film takes its shower scene from the ROBERT BLOCH novel, and its view of SEXUAL relationships is far more obsessive and corrupting than the mere sleaziness on view in Clouzot's film. But its marketing (with audiences warned about giving away the surprise) and its popularity definitely first alerted Hitchcock to how profitable grimy BLACK-AND-WHITE horror could be. (A few years later, William Castle's *Macabre* would clinch the deal.)

Hitchcock, however, had definitely learned one lesson: When the rights to the Boileau and Narcejac novel *D'entre les Morts* came available, he bought them immediately and started turning it into *VERTIGO*.

Although Clouzot had another hit with the Brigitte Bardot courtroom drama *La Verite*, his success grew spotty; one major film, *Les Espions*, never even got an American release, and another, *L'Enfer*, was left unfinished. His wife and frequent leading lady Vera Clouzot died of a heart attack; his own health problems reoccurred. Nor did the continuing comparisons to Hitchcock help. "I admire him very much and am flattered when anyone compares a film of mine to his," Clouzot said graciously, but it was a one-way road; the young French critics who adored the American "Master of Suspense" found their native-born one distressingly shallow, and any comparisons they drew usually found Clouzot lacking.

Increasingly depressed, the director filmed some concerts for French TV and pursued other projects, completing only one more movie, the sadomasochistic drama *La Prisonniere* in 1968.

Clouzot died in his Paris apartment at age 69.

References

Ivan Butler, *Horror in the Cinema* (New York: A. S., 1970), 103–12; "Henri-Georges Clouzot," *The Criterion Collection*, https://www.criterion.com/explore/7-henri-georges-clouzot; "Henri-Georges Clouzot," IMDb, http://www.imdb.com/name/nm0167241/bio?ref_=nm_ov_bio_sm.

COBURN, CHARLES (1877–1961)

Irascible, liver-lipped authority figure who seemed to be born old, perhaps because he was 61 when he finally made his movie debut after a stage career that had begun at the turn of the century. The Georgia-born performer was frequently cast in comedic roles, most memorably as Barbara Stanwyck's con-man confederate in *The Lady Eve* and as the matchmaking boarder in *The More the Merrier*, which won him an Oscar, but he was a sternly unsympathetic impediment to romance in *Made for Each Other* and an outright villain in *Kings Row*. His one role for Hitchcock was in *THE PARADINE CASE* as Mrs. Paradine's solicitor, adding his usual bluster and shaking jowls to a movie already, thanks to CHARLES LAUGHTON, blessed with a surfeit of them. A stalwart right-winger—he served on the board of the Motion Picture Alliance for the Preservation of American Ideals—he died at 84 of a heart attack in New York.

References

"Charles Coburn," IMDb, http://www.imdb.com/name/nm0002013/bio?ref_=nm_ov_bio_sm; Alfred E. Twomey and Arthur F. McClure, *The Versatiles: Supporting Character Players in the Cinema, 1930–1955* (New York: Castle Books, 1969), 68.

COLLIER, CONSTANCE (1878–1955)

Born in Berkshire, this statuesque and extravagantly theatrical creature was onstage from the time she was 3 and had her earliest and greatest successes at the turn of the century in the stage productions of Sir Herbert Beerbohm Tree. Later, she would branch out into films (she's in *Intolerance*) and, eventually, coaching other younger actors.

She lost her husband to the Spanish influenza epidemic and later had a long friendship with the gay composer and actor IVOR NOVELLO, who would go on to star in *THE LODGER*; a play Collier and Novello wrote, *Down Hill*, would also form the basis for Hitchcock's similarly titled film in 1928. But by then, Collier was already in Hollywood, patiently coaching terrified silent screen stars on how to speak for the talkies.

Collier had a good part in *Stage Door* as an aged actress (a much more pathetic version of her real self) and another one in *ROPE* as the aunt of the murdered boy. She was also in the noirs *Whirlpool* and *The Dark Corner* and coached many young performers; even Katharine Hepburn made sure to book some classes before daring to return to the stage with *As You Like It* in 1950.

She died at age 77 in Manhattan.

References

"Constance Collier," *IMDb*, http://www.imdb.com/name/nm0171887/bio?ref_=nm_ov_bio_sm; Alfred E. Twomey and Arthur F. McClure, *The Versatiles: Supporting Character Players in the Cinema, 1930–1955* (New York: Castle Books, 1969), 69.

COLLINGE, PATRICIA (1892–1974)

Dublin-born performer onstage since the early 1900s, she began playing romantic ingénues and aged into playing flighty, slightly damaged older women—she took over from Josephine Hull in *Arsenic and Old Lace* on Broadway and played Birdie in both the stage production and movie of *The Little Foxes*.

In Hitchcock's *SHADOW OF A DOUBT*, she is the tender, tremulous Emma, the quickly beating heart of the picture who so loves her brother Charles that her daughter Charlie can't bear to reveal him as the murderer he is. (That Collinge's character shares a first name with Hitch-

cock's own late mother is perhaps not coincidental.) She is not one of the "useless women" that Charles likes to woo and strangle; in her own small domain, she is more than competent—observe how she dismisses the detective (posing as a photographer) when he tries to interfere with her baking. But she is fragile, and it is her life that Charlie will sacrifice anything to protect.

In real life, Collinge was far more level-headed than the women she often played; when, despite the efforts of veteran authors THORNTON WILDER and Sally Benson, TERESA WRIGHT and MACDONALD CAREY were having trouble playing one scene in *Shadow of a Doubt*, she quickly and calmly rewrote it herself. (Collinge, who also had plays and short stories to her credit, reportedly helped Hitchcock punch up the script of his next picture, *LIFEBOAT*, as well.)

By the next decade, Collinge was working almost exclusively on television; a Hitchcock favorite, she appeared on no fewer than a half-dozen episodes of his television series, including "The Landlady" (adapted by ROBERT BLOCH from a chilly story by ROALD DAHL), "The Cheney Vase," and "The Rose Garden" with JOHN WILLIAMS.

She died at 81 in New York City.

References

Beyond Doubt: The Making of Alfred Hitchcock's Favorite Film, directed by Laurent Bouzereau (2000), documentary, http://www.imdb.com/name/nm0172048/bio?ref_=nm_ov_bio_sm; "Patricia Collinge," *IMDb*, http://www.imdb.com/name/nm0172048/bio?ref_=nm_ov_bio_sm.

COLOR

Alfred Hitchcock was a commercial director in the best sense of the word; to him, motion pictures were a mass medium, and if your pictures weren't reaching the masses, then you must have done something wrong.

With that in mind, he embraced new technologies and new ways of storytelling as they emerged. When sound came in, he found way to incorporate it into his own style; he agreed to try 3-D and, when the old CENSORS disappeared, pushed the boundaries with startlingly frank new images.

Color was not a commonplace option for filmmakers, even in Hollywood, until the '40s, and Hitchcock approached it with curiosity and respect, imaginatively exploring its uses while always avoiding what he saw as a garish, "postcard effect." "Color for reason, not just color to knock people's eyes out," he explained. "Make color an actor, a defined part of the whole. Make it work as an actor, instead of scenery."

And Hitchcock's very first films in color are full of that considered restraint. The skyline we see through the apartment windows in *ROPE* has a subtly shifting palette; the sunny Australian streets and brooding bedrooms of *UNDER CAPRICORN* stand in stark contrast to each other, an effect that owed much to cinematographer JACK CARDIFF (and has lost much, given the current, sorry state of that film's prints).

Even when color became more popular in the '50s, Hitchcock—like Vincente Minnelli, like John Huston, two other directors with artistic backgrounds—drew a distinct line between which films were suitable for its hues and which demanded monochrome. A downbeat film like *I CONFESS*, a brooding realistic one like *THE WRONG MAN*—these were made for BLACK-AND-WHITE. The travelogue scenery of the 1956 *THE MAN WHO KNEW TOO MUCH* or *TO CATCH A THIEF*—these begged for color. Yet despite general mood or practical considerations (shooting the self-financed *PSYCHO* in black and white was not only cheaper but also easier on the censor), Hitchcock would also use color in very specific ways.

In its most famous instance, he would use it for a splash of violence in the otherwise black-and-white *SPELLBOUND*, as the villain turns the revolver on himself—and, as staged, us—and his suicide explodes the screen in a burst of crimson. (Long missing from TV prints, the red has finally been restored on home-entertainment versions.) Color also fills a largely narrative purpose in *MARNIE*, whose heroine—like that of the hero in *Spellbound*—suffers from a deeply repressed childhood trauma. In her case, it's not white that brings on her fits but deep red, the color of blood. It's a color that reappears in *THE TROUBLE WITH HARRY*, too, but in keeping with that comedy, it's only the color of pretty autumn leaves; there may be a corpse in the film, but he's nearly bloodless and purely decorative.

Sometimes, though, the associations are more ambiguous, like the bilious hues that start off the fake medium's séance in *FAMILY PLOT*, the emerald dress that Miss Lonelyhearts puts on in *REAR WINDOW*, the pale-mint suit Melanie wears in *THE BIRDS*, or the almost underwater green that bathes the transformed Judy in *VERTIGO*. Was there something erotic to that shade in Hitchcock's eyes or something dangerous? Perhaps both. Decades later, he would recall his early childhood, going to see stage melodramas: "I remember the green light," he said. "Green for the appearances of ghosts and villains."

References

"Some Thoughts on Colour by Alfred Hitchcock," *Adelaide Advertiser*, September 4, 1937, http://the.hitchcock .zone/wiki/Adelaide_Advertiser_%2804/ Sep/1937%29_-_Some_Thoughts_on

_Color_by_Alfred_Hitchcock; Donald Spoto, *The Dark Side of Genius: The Life of Alfred Hitchcock* (New York: Da Capo Press, 1999), 22; François Truffaut, *Hitchcock/Truffaut*, rev. ed. (New York: Touchstone, 1985), 245.

COMPSON, BETTY (1897–1974)

Beaver, UT–born actress who went into show business as a teenager to help support her widowed mother. By 1915, she was appearing in silent slapstick comedies, sometimes appearing in more than three dozen two-reelers a year. Promoted as the "Prettiest Girl in Pictures," within five years she was producing her own movies. In 1924, a STAR-starved British film industry imported her to play the difficult double role in *WOMAN TO WOMAN*; Hitchcock, the young screenwriter and assistant director on that film, was particularly taken by her pale blonde looks, and the two became close friends.

Although Compson was an Academy Award nominee for 1928's *The Barker*, a marriage to the alcoholic (and tax-avoiding) director James Cruze left her bankrupt at the start of the '30s; a long string of forgettable pictures badly hampered her career. By the 1940s, any Hollywood work was hard to come by; the recently arrived Hitchcock made a point of giving her a small part in *MR. AND MRS. SMITH*, so she could keep her Screen Actors Guild benefits.

She died in Glendale at 77 from a heart attack.

References

"Betty Compson," *IMDb*, http://www.imdb.com/name/nm0173993/bio?ref_=nm_ov_bio_sm; "Hollywood Star Walk: Betty Compson," *Los Angeles Times*, http://projects.latimes.com/hollywood/star-walk/betty-compson; Patrick McGilligan, *Alfred Hitchcock: A Life in Darkness and Light* (New York: HarperCollins, 2003), 58–59.

CONNERY, SEAN (1930–)

Edinburgh-born sailor, bodybuilder, lifeguard, artist's model, and coffin polisher who, looking for extra cash, tried out for the chorus in a touring company of *South Pacific*; his perfect pecs won him a part as one of the frequently shirtless Seabees. When the production went on to England, Connery, a featured player by now, went with it and began studying drama out of borrowed books.

By the late '50s, Connery was working regularly, building a career in everything from the British TV production of *Requiem for a Heavyweight* to the Disney film *Darby O'Gill and the Little People* (and building a reputation as an authentically dangerous man when, approached by gun-wielding gangster Johnny Stompanato on the set of a Lana Turner film, Connery reportedly knocked him down with one punch). "I have always moved around and kept my eyes open and been prepared to raise my middle finger at the world," he told *Playboy* in 1965. "I always will."

It was that attitude that had won him the role of James Bond in 1962. Names from David Niven to Patrick McGoohan had been floated, but producers Cubby Broccoli and Harry Saltzman realized that it was far easier to fake class than courage; any man looked like a gentleman in a tuxedo, but to look like a hard fellow, you had to be one. (Ironically, one of the rejected Bonds, Niven, had actually been a commando in World War II; Connery had been invalided out of the navy due to ulcers.)

Connery sailed through the Bond films with a wry quip and an occasional furrowed brow, but he knew that he needed to start laying foundations for a real career beyond that; smartly, he made sure that, in between spy pictures, he took on more challenging assignments, so he did the oddball comedy *A Fine Madness* and the stark war drama *The Hill*. For Hitchcock, he did *MARNIE*, a challenge on several levels—not only was he supposed to convincingly pass as an old-money, East Coast American, but also he had to make a sympathetic character out of a man who rapes his obviously disturbed wife on her wedding night. The first task was difficult enough, but the second proved to be—as it should have proven—insurmountable.

Of course there had always been something chauvinistic in the Connery persona; even then, in the preliberated '60s, Bond's habit of slapping fannies and slinging double entendres raised a few hackles (as would Connery's much-repeated comment that some women simply needed a "smack.") But in *Marnie*, Mark Rutland is crude from the start, and the marital rape is the breaking point. Until then, Rutland just seems to have an odd fetish: He wants to go to bed with a thief. But by forcibly taking his comatose wife, he lurches into villainous status; her subsequent suicide attempt moves the act out of cheap romance novel (or *Gone with the Wind* fantasy) into the abhorrent.

Yet although the first screenwriter hired, EVAN HUNTER, argued against the rape, Hitchcock (who'd been dwelling on this sort of assault since at least the script for *NO BAIL FOR THE JUDGE* a half-dozen years before and may have harbored vengeful feelings against his current leading lady, TIPPI HEDREN) insisted. And not perhaps to his credit but probably to Hitchcock's appreciation, Connery went along.

Handsome, confident, and unburdened by the METHOD, Connery was exactly the sort of old-fashioned leading man Hitchcock liked and felt he no longer had, as CARY GRANT and JAMES STEWART headed into their 60s; enthused, he tried to sign Connery to a personal contract. But Connery, who went his own way (and could not help but see what a personal contract had done to Hedren), declined; the two men never worked together again.

Once Connery mostly shed himself of Bond and his toupees, he became a slightly more vulnerable and definitely more likable character onscreen; though no less masculine, his exploration of his own flaws and acknowledgment of an ever-encroaching age made him even more appealing. He is marvelously romantic in *Robin and Marian* and sturdily commanding in *The Untouchables* (which finally won him an Oscar); he brought some necessary good humor to *Indiana Jones and the Last Crusade* and, even in his dotage, was a credible action hero and leading man in trifles like *The Rock* and *Entrapment*.

But, like Grant, when it seemed only supporting roles lay ahead, he stepped back; better to go out as a star, he thought, then hang on as a character actor. He lives quietly and very well, continuing to turn down roles—he was an early choice for Gandalf in *The Lord of the Rings* saga—and occasionally raising his voice on behalf of Scotland to urge complete independence.

After all, it always worked so well for him.

References

"Playboy Interview: Sean Connery," *Playboy*, November 1965, http://seanconnery online.com/art_playboy1165.htm; "Sean Connery," *Biography*, http://www.biography.com/people/sean-connery-9255144; "Sean Connery," *IMDb*, http://www.imdb.com/name/nm0000125/bio?ref_=nm_ov_bio_sm; David Thomson, *The New Biographical Dictionary of Film* (New York: Knopf, 2002), 173.

COOK, WHITFIELD (1909–2003)

Montclair, NJ–born son of an engineer who was interested in writing from an early age. He went to the Yale School of Drama and published short stories in a variety of the mass-market "slicks," including *Cosmopolitan* and *Redbook*. He later collected several of these stories and in 1944 turned them into a play, *Violet*; it lasted exactly 23 performances on Broadway.

It also, however, fatefully starred the budding actress PATRICIA HITCH-COCK, then 16; as her father was busy in London at that time working with SID-NEY BERNSTEIN, her mother accompanied her to New York for the show's (abbreviated) run.

Cook and ALMA REVILLE became friends and, later, collaborators of a sort, as he contributed early drafts of *STAGE FRIGHT* and *STRANGERS ON A TRAIN*. But did they become more than that? PATRICK MCGILLIGAN thinks so; based on INTERVIEWS with Cook and a reading of his diaries, McGilligan's *ALFRED HITCHCOCK: A LIFE IN DARKNESS AND LIGHT* describes an "intermittent romance" that included possible weekends alone at the Hitchcock retreat near Santa Cruz. (This charge later made its way into the film *HITCHCOCK*, although the actress playing Reville, Helen Mirren, said she frankly found the assertion the two had an affair "not remotely proved.")

There is no record of Alfred Hitchcock's reaction to Cook's relationship with his wife, whatever it was; typically hagiographic, their daughter's biography, *Alma Hitchcock: The Woman behind the Man*, remembers Cook only as a family friend. (Complicating everything is that Cook was reportedly bisexual—and that both Hitchcocks remained friends with him throughout their lives and happily served as witnesses at his wedding.) Whatever the extent of the bonds, Cook's collaborations with the Hitchcocks ended in the early '50s; after that, he chiefly wrote for television (although never either of Hitchcock's TV series) and published a number of novels.

He died at 94 in New London, CT.

References
John Anderson, "Alfred Hitchcock's Secret Weapon Becomes a Star," *New York Times*, November 18, 2012, http://www.nytimes.com/2012/11/18/movies/hitchcock-and-the-girl-remember-alma-reville.html?_r=0; Pat Hitchcock O'Connell and Laurent Bouzereau, *Alma Hitchcock: The Woman behind the Man* (New York: Berkeley Trade, 2004), 123–26; Patrick McGilligan, *Alfred Hitchcock: A Life in Darkness and Light* (New York: HarperCollins, 2003), 364–65, 428, 432; "Whitfield Cook," *IMDb*, http://www.imdb.com/name/nm0177336.

COOPER, GLADYS (1888–1971)

Beautiful child actress onstage from the age of seven who grew up and old and into Mrs. Windle Vale, one of the most terrifying mothers in Hollywood movies, in *Now, Voyager*.

As a young woman, Cooper was a favorite of W. SOMERSET MAUGHAM's, appearing in the original London stagings of several of his plays, including *The Letter*; by 1940, she was in Hollywood, where she made her American movie debut in *REBECCA* playing Maxim's elegantly arch sister, the largely sympathetic but still stinging Beatrice Lacy. ("Oh, don't care about me—I can see by the way you dress you don't give a hoot how you look.") Her other movie characters were generally even more disapproving, as Cooper went on to play a series of formidable dowagers, including Henry Higgins's mother in *My Fair Lady*. On TV, she appeared on *ALFRED HITCHCOCK PRESENTS* and two episodes of *THE ALFRED HITCH-COCK HOUR*; on *The Twilight Zone*, she is the old woman resisting the entreaties of Robert Redford's handsome Grim Reaper.

Busy right until the end—her last stage success was in a revival of *The Chalk Garden*—she died in Henley-on-Thames at age 82 of pneumonia.

References

"Gladys Cooper," *IMDb*, http://www.imdb.com/name/nm0178066/bio?ref_=nm_ov_bio_sm; Alfred E. Twomey and Arthur F. McClure, *The Versatiles: Supporting Character Players in the Cinema, 1930–1955* (New York: Castle Books, 1969), 73.

COPPEL, ALEC (1907–1972)

Australian playwright and novelist who had a hit with his story for *The Captain's Paradise*, the Alec Guinness comedy from 1953 on which he shared screenplay credit; he did some anonymous work on Hitchcock's *TO CATCH A THIEF* two years later.

After several story credits for *ALFRED HITCHCOCH PRESENTS*, the director brought Coppel back for *VERTIGO*, where he was one of at least three writers to take a crack at the tricky PIERRE BOILEAU and THOMAS NARCEJAC novel; whatever his approach, his script was discarded, and a new writer, SAMUEL A. TAYLOR, was brought in to start from scratch.

Although Coppel would sell another script to *THE ALFRED HITCHCOCK HOUR*, his succeeding efforts tended toward black comedy (*The Gazebo*) and supposedly riotous sex farces (*The Bliss of Mrs. Blossom*); he died in London of liver cancer at age 64.

References

"Alec Coppel," *IMDb*, http://www.imdb.com/name/nm0178785; Steven Vagg, "Alec Coppel: Australian Playwright and Survivor," *Australasian Drama Studies*, https://www.questia.com/library/journal/1P3-2055166241/alec-coppel-australian-playwright-and-survivor.

COREY, WENDELL (1914–1968)

Bland, pale-eyed leading man from small-town Massachusetts who tended to play cops, doctors, and the heroine's dependable but unexciting fallback boyfriend. Starting onstage in summer stock, he soon joined the Federal Theater Project and had his first big success on Broadway in 1945 with *Dream Girl*, which led to a contract with Paramount.

He's in the essential noirs *Sorry, Wrong Number* and *The File on Thelma Jordan* and appears in *REAR WINDOW* as Jeff's doubting policeman friend; he would later star in the *ALFRED HITCHCOCK PRESENTS* episode "POISON" based on the story by ROALD DAHL.

Corey was reportedly a congenial and amusing cast member, with a strong interest in politics. (He later served in various positions with the Screen Actors Guild and the Academy of Motion Picture Arts and Sciences and was elected to the Santa Monica City Council.) But his career slipped badly in the '60s, and drinking became a serious problem; he died in Woodland Hills, CA, of cirrhosis of the liver at 54.

References

"Obituary: Wendell Corey," *Times*, November 11, 1968, http://the.hitchcock.zone/wiki/The_Times_%2811/Nov/1968%29_-_Obituary:_Wendell_Corey; "Wendell Corey, *IMDb*, http://www.imdb.com/name/nm0179819/bio?ref_=nm_ov_bio_sm.

COTTEN, JOSEPH (1905–1994)

Charming, gently drawling Virginian who worked in advertising and journalism before turning to the theater; he made his Broadway debut in 1930. Four years later, he met Orson Welles, then 19 and already a busy radio actor; the two became lifelong friends and collaborators, and Cotten would be there for Welles's first New York stage production (*Horse Eats Hat*, 1936) and his first short film (*Too Much Johnson*, 1938). "I'm afraid you'll never make it as an actor," Welles told him early on. "But as a STAR, I think you might well hit the jackpot."

The two friends would make their extraordinary Hollywood debut together in 1941 in *Citizen Kane* and go on to collaborate on many other projects, including Welles's *The Magnificent Ambersons* and *Touch of Evil*, as well as Carol Reed's *The Third Man*; in 1943, Cotten was signed by DAVID O. SELZNICK, who kept him busy at home and on loan-out; his films for the mogul include the deliriously romantic fantasy *Portrait of Jennie*, the sturdy homefront melodrama *Since You Went Away*, and the overripe western *Duel in the Sun*.

"I was a so-called star because of my limitations," Cotten once modestly observed. "I couldn't do any accents. So I had to pretend. Luckily I was tall, had curly hair and a good voice. I only had to stamp my foot and I'd play the lead—because I couldn't play character parts."

It was while under contract to Selznick that Cotten was cast in fellow Selznick employee Alfred Hitchcock's *SHADOW OF A DOUBT* as Uncle Charlie, the sophisticated city relative of a small-town family (and secretly a serial strangler of women). He is one of Hitchcock's many charming villains (as the director was fond of pointing out, disagreeable villains found it harder to attract victims), and Cotten, cast against type, is superb in the role—tight, contained, steely, and full of good-mannered menace. Particularly fine is the scene where he's talking with cavalier viciousness about the "swine" who fill the world and the "silly wives" who, once widowed, squander their husbands' money; when his horrified niece Charlotte exclaims, "But they're human beings!" Hitchcock breaks the fourth wall and has Charlie look directly at the camera, and us. "Are they?" he asks coldly.

Shadow of a Doubt was Hitchcock's first great American film, and he would often mention it as his favorite; at the end of the decade, he would bring Cotten

back to play another man with a secret in *UNDER CAPRICORN*, but the film was slow and somewhat uninvolving and as much a disappointment for both men as *Shadow of a Doubt* had been a triumph.

The two would reteam later on three episodes of *ALFRED HITCHCOCK PRESENTS*, including the Hitchcock-directed "BREAKDOWN" (in which Cotten is left paralyzed by a car crash and presumed dead) and "Together," directed by a young Robert Altman (in which Cotten finds himself trapped with the corpse of his murdered mistress). A longtime friend, Cotten was a regular at Hitchcock family parties—daughter PATRICIA HITCHCOCK had a mild crush on him as a teenager—and served as a witness when the director became an American citizen.

As the actor moved into his 60s, however, his career inevitably slowed, and by the 1970s, the jobs tended toward disaster movies and Euro-horrors (although he also shows up in the stylish *The Abominable Dr. Phibes* and the memorable *Soylent Green*). He died in Los Angeles at 88 of pneumonia; cancer had robbed him of his voice four years before. Yet we can hear it still—soft and warm and gentle.

References
"Joseph Cotten," *IMDb*, http://www.imdb.com/name/nm0001072/bio?ref_=nm_ov_bio_sm; David Shipman, ed., *Movie Talk: Who Said What about Whom in the Movies* (New York: St. Martin's Press, 1988), 42; David Thomson, *The New Biographical Dictionary of Film* (New York: Knopf, 2002), 183.

COX, JACK E. (1896–1960)
London-born cameraman in films since 1913. Although later Alfred Hitchcock would portray him as a raw novice who benefited from his own early tutelage, when they worked together in the late '20s,

Cox (who sometimes dropped the middle initial in credits) was actually more experienced than the young director and already known as a specialist in "trick" or difficult shots.

Nor was the quality of his work dependent on Hitchcock. After their association, Cox would continue to do good films, particularly in the '30s, shooting *Mimi* (a well-reviewed version of *La Boheme*), the Boris Karloff chiller *The Man Who Changed His Mind*, and the original *Doctor Syn* with George Arliss. When the British film industry faltered, Cox did, too, but, busy and adaptable, continued to shoot right through the '50s, working on both broad comedies (*Just My Luck*, *The Square Peg*) and inexpensive genre pictures (*Alias John Preston*, *Devil Girl from Mars*).

His longest association, however, was with Hitchcock, for whom he photographed 11 films (including *MARY*, the German-language version of *MURDER!*), and he was instrumental in capturing some of the young director's earliest, most ambitious visual ideas—the shot through the wine glass in *CHAMPAGNE*, the tricky special effects sequence in the British Museum in *BLACKMAIL*. Cox's silent work is particularly evocative—with its happy freaks and grimacing patrons, the carnival he captured in *THE RING* would not be out of place in the films of F. W. MURNAU or even Federico Fellini.

He died at age 64 in Surrey.

References

"Jack E. Cox," *IMDb*, http://www.imdb.com/name/nm0185055; Patrick McGilligan, *Alfred Hitchcock: A Life in Darkness and Light* (New York: HarperCollins, 2003), 95–96.

CRIPPEN, H. H. (1862–1910)

Michigan-born homeopath and self-styled doctor who, with his second wife—his first had died of a stroke—moved to London in 1897. Unable to obtain a medical license, he sold patent medicines and oversaw the second Mrs. Crippen's attempts at a music hall career. The marriage, marred by her adultery almost from the start, was soon a shambles; eventually, Crippen began seeing a young typist from his office.

In 1910, Cora Crippen disappeared; Crippen told friends that she had left for America (with a lover, he later added), and his mistress, Ethel Neave, subsequently moved into the house. When she was seen wearing Cora's jewelry, one of the woman's friends became suspicious; Scotland Yard came to question Crippen and searched the home.

They found nothing, but Crippen panicked, and he and Neave fled, eventually boarding a ship for Canada with Neave disguised as a boy. Alerted to the couple's disappearance, Scotland Yard sent teams to search the house again; only on their fourth try did they dig up a newly laid basement floor and find a torso. Authorities were notified and boarded the ship before it docked; "Thank God it's over," Crippen said.

A true-crime aficionado since childhood, Hitchcock was particularly fascinated by the Crippen case and would often bring it up in INTERVIEWS, recounting the details with relish; a fact he particularly enjoyed was that Crippen had chatted amiably with the ship's wireless officer only moments after the radioman had sent word to Scotland Yard that the suspect was onboard. In fact, Crippen was the first criminal to be apprehended thanks to a telegram.

But the story also reoccurs in many Hitchcock works. The general shape of the narrative—the mousy and put-upon husband who finally snaps and murders his domineering wife, only to be caught through a small mistake—was one the director would often return to, particularly during the years of his television shows. And the other details—the clue of the left-behind jewelry (*VERTIGO*, *SHADOW OF A DOUBT*, *REAR WINDOW*) and the disposal of an inconvenient body (*FRENZY*, *THE TROUBLE WITH HARRY*, *PSYCHO*, *Rear Window* again) would show up in many of his films. (The idea of cross-dressing—with its undercurrent of shameful FETISH and secret gratification—runs from *MURDER!* through *Psycho*.)

In real life, the couple was eventually returned to England for trial, with Cora's body identified by a scar on the torso (although Crippen's defense pointed out correctly that, as that skin sample from the body had hair, it couldn't be scar tissue). Neave was acquitted and moved to America; Crippen was convicted and hung.

They never did find Cora's head.

References

"Hawley Harven Crippen: Killing, Murder, 11th October 1910," *Proceedings of the Old Bailey*, http://www.oldbaileyonline.org/browse.jsp?id=t19101011-74-offence-1&div=t19101011-74; "A London Murder Mystery: Dr. H. H. Crippen and Ethel Le Neve," *Tower Project Blog*, https://towerproject.blog.lib.cam.ac.uk/?p=3571; Donald Spoto, *The Dark Side of Genius: The Life of Alfred Hitchcock* (New York: Da Capo Press, 1999), 32–34; François Truffaut, *Hitchcock/Truffaut*, rev. ed. (New York: Touchstone, 1985), 222–23.

CRONYN, HUME (1911–2003)

Born into one of Canada's leading families (his father was a member of Parliament, his mother one of the beer-brewing Labatts), Cronyn studied drama at McGill University, later continuing his work at the American Academy of Dramatic Arts in New York; he made his Broadway debut in 1934.

Cronyn married actress JESSICA TANDY in 1942 and the next year made his movie debut in Hitchcock's *SHADOW OF A DOUBT*; he would reteam with Hitchcock the next year for *LIFEBOAT*, work on the screenplays of *ROPE* and *UNDER CAPRICORN*, and go on to appear on several episodes of *ALFRED HITCHCOCK PRESENTS*.

A small and wiry man—he had been a formidable featherweight boxer back in Canada—Cronyn had a coldly methodical mien, which often led to him being cast as unsympathetic, even villainous, characters. (He is Cora's maneuvering lawyer in *The Postman Always Ring Twice*, the sadistic captain in *Brute Force*.) Late in life, he was to transfer to crusty curmudgeons in *Cocoon* and, a Broadway hit with Tandy, *The Gin Game*.

Hitchcock, though, cast him as quiet, detail-oriented men—Herbie, the mild bachelor and crime fan in *Shadow of a Doubt*; Sparks, the radio operator in *Lifeboat*. And although the director later expressed some dissatisfaction with his friend's literary skills, Cronyn would go on to be instrumental in bringing Tennessee Williams's early work to New York and have an unexpected hit play of his own with *Foxfire*.

He died of prostate cancer in Fairfield, CT, at 91.

References

"Hume Cronyn," *IMDb*, http://www.imdb.com/name/nm0002025/bio?ref_=nm_ov_bio_sm; Kenneth Jones, "Actor Hume Cronyn Dead at 91; Starred with Wife Jessica Tandy in Plays and Films," *Playbill*, June 16, 2003, http://www.playbill.com/news/article/actor-hume-cronyn-dead-at-91-starred-with-wife-jessica-tandy-in-plays-and-f-113803; François Truffaut, *Hitchcock/Truffaut*, rev. ed. (New York: Touchstone, 1985), 186.

"THE CRYSTAL TRENCH" (US; ORIGINALLY AIRED OCTOBER 4, 1959)

DIRECTOR: Alfred Hitchcock.
SCREENPLAY: Stirling Silliphant, from the story by A. E. W. Mason.
PRODUCERS: Joan Harrison, Norman Lloyd.
CINEMATOGRAPHY: John F. Warren.
EDITOR: Edward W. Williams.
ORIGINAL MUSIC: Frederick Herbert.
CAST: Patricia Owens (Stella Ballister), James Donald (Mark Cavendish).
RUNNING TIME: 30 minutes with commercials. Black and white.
ORIGINALLY BROADCAST BY: CBS.

A not particularly dramatic story of a woman waiting for a thaw to free her long-dead husband's corpse from a glacier; like much of Hitchcock's movie work from the 1950s on, this episode of *ALFRED HITCH-COCK PRESENTS* has a rather jaundiced view of relationships.

References

Tim Brooks and Earle Marsh, *The Complete Directory to Prime Time Network TV Shows*, 8th ed. (New York: Ballantine Books, 2003), 29; Jack Edmond Nolan, "Hitchcock's TV Films," *Film Fan Monthly* (June 1968), 3–6.

CUMMINGS, ROBERT (1910–1990)

Missouri-born performer in love from an early age with aviation. His cousin and godfather, Orville Wright, gave him lessons early, and Cummings became the first licensed flight instructor in the country while he was still a teenager. Family finances forced him to drop out of Carnegie Tech; eventually he ended up in New York, where, hearing that an overabundance of females had the American Academy of Dramatic Arts paying male students a stipend, he signed up.

Cummings began acting in real life, too. To capitalize on the current demand for English performers, he presented himself as "Blade Conway" at New York auditions; in Hollywood, where westerns were in vogue, he introduced himself as starstruck cowboy "Bruce Hitchens." He gathered credits under both aliases (and, somewhere along the way, shaved two years off his age). Once he began getting steady work, though, it was under his real name, often cast as a decent, hardworking American; this was the character he played in 1942 in one of his biggest hits, *King's Row*, and his first picture for Hitchcock, *SABOTEUR*, where he was a young munitions worker caught up in a Nazi plot.

Later, Hitchcock—who'd really wanted Gary Cooper for the lead—blamed Cummings for the film's relative lack of heft, complaining that an "actor of stature" would have gained more of the audience's empathy. "He's a competent performer but he belongs to the light-comedy class of actors," the director said. "Aside from that he has an amusing face, so that even when he's in desperate straits, his features don't convey any anguish."

Yet whatever Hitchcock's disappointment with Cummings's lack of STAR power (the director was displeased with having to use PRISCILLA LANE, too, who "simply wasn't the right type for a Hitchcock picture"), any criticism of him being miscast is unfounded; it's precisely Cummings's every-day, working-class quality that gives *Saboteur* much of its power. We may expect ROBERT DONAT to win over MADELEINE CARROLL in *THE 39 STEPS* or CARY GRANT to talk his way out of an auction house in *NORTH BY NORTH-WEST* because Donat is smoothly charming and Grant is always intelligently alert; when Cummings woos Lane or manages his escape from a charity ball, the scenes have that much more drama because it seems like that much more of a victory for such an ordinary man.

It's possible, of course, that Hitchcock was only disappointed in Cummings's performance in retrospect; in any case, he used the actor again in *DIAL M FOR MURDER* as GRACE KELLY's old love (and most loyal advocate). Shortly afterward, Cummings found a congenial home on TV, where he starred in several series, often playing a popular bachelor (including *My Living Doll*, in which Julie Newmar costarred as a sexy robot).

In private life, however, Cummings, was far more complicated than any of his characters. He went through five marriages and, despite his very vocal touting of health food and "clean living"—he wrote *How to Stay Young and Vital* and briefly ran a questionable nutritional supplement company—was an amphetamine addict who received regular treatments from "Dr. Feelgood," a prescriber to stars and presidents.

He died at 80 of renal failure and pneumonia at the Motion Picture and Television Country House and Hospital in Woodland Hills, CA.

References

Peter B. Flint, "Robert Cummings Is Dead at 82; Debonair Actor in TV and Films," *New York Times*, December 4, 1990, http://www.nytimes.com/1990/12/04/obituaries/robert-cummings-is-dead-at-82-debonair-actor-in-tv-and-films.html; "Robert Cummings," *IMDb*, http://www.imdb.com/name/nm0191950/bio?ref_=nm_ov_bio_sm; François Truffaut, *Hitchcock/Truffaut*, rev. ed. (New York: Touchstone, 1985), 145–46.

CURTIS, BILLY (1909–1988)

Born Luigi Curto, the Massachusetts native had dwarfism, a condition he used to even-

tually leave his shoe store job and go into show business as "Little Billy" and as a member of the Singer Midgets. It was as part of that troupe that he appeared in *The Terror of Tiny Town*, an "all-midget" western; he was also one of the Munchkins in *The Wizard of Oz* (and, according to Judy Garland, the most persistent in trying to seduce her).

In Hitchcock's *SABOTEUR*, Curtis is with the circus where Barry seeks asylum; the least sympathetic member of the troupe, he's "the general," the one who wants to turn him over to the authorities (and as such is derided as a fascist by the "human skeleton" Bones). Curtis went on to appear in many genre pictures (*The Incredible Shrinking Man*, *The Angry Red Planet*, the robot in *Gog*); his best, late-career credit was as Mordecai in *High Plains Drifter*.

He died of a heart attack at age 79 and to the end of his days never understood why people snickered at *The Terror of Tiny Town*. "I played the good guy who put the bad guy behind bars at the end—just like John Wayne," he said later. "And I kissed the pretty girl—just like he did. So what the hell's so funny?"

References

"Billy Curtis," *IMDb*, http://www.imdb.com/name/nm0193260/bio?ref_=nm_ov_bio_sm; "Billy Curtis," *Wikipedia*, https://en.wikipedia.org/wiki/Billy_Curtis; Burt A. Folkart, "Actor, Double: Billy Curtis; Midget Had Film Career," November 12, 1988, *Los Angeles Times*, http://articles.latimes.com/1988-11-12/news/mn-388_1_billy-curtis.

CUTTS, GRAHAM (1884–1958)

Brighton-born cinema pioneer who left an engineering career to get into film distribution in 1909; by the early '20s, he was directing, specializing in melodramas and controversial issues, such as *Cocaine* (drug addiction) and *Flames of Passion* (illegitimate children).

Joining SIR MICHAEL BALCON at GAINSBOROUGH PICTURES, he used Hitchcock on five of his silent films as an assistant director (a position that often ended up including work on the scripts as well as art direction, editing, and sometimes uncredited directing). Cutts was suspicious of the young man's eagerness, however, a feeling that grew darker as Hitchcock began to get his own directing assignments; even before *THE LODGER* was finished, Cutts told mogul C. M. WOOLF the film was an absolute disaster. (As a result, the film came very close to not being released; only Balcon's intervention, and some clever re-editing by IVOR MONTAGU, saved the movie and probably Hitchcock's career.)

In truth, it was Cutts who was soon to be in trouble. His personal life had always been complicated, and already obdurately middle-aged by the time the talkies arrived, he had trouble adapting to the new format; although he made one of the earliest Sherlock Holmes sound films, *The Sign of Four*, in 1932, he was eventually reduced to making "quota quickies"—disposable movies made purely to fulfill the requirement that British theaters show a certain percentage of British films. (Hitchcock gave him a small job, shooting some insert shots for *THE 39 STEPS*, in 1935.) Cutts directed his last feature in 1940 and died, 18 long years later, at age 74; his daughter has a cameo in *NORTH BY NORTHWEST* as the hospital patient who wishes CARY GRANT would stay just a little longer.

References

Donald Spoto, *The Dark Side of Genius: The Life of Alfred Hitchcock* (New York: Da Capo Press, 1999), 67; François Truffaut, *Hitchcock/Truffaut*, rev. ed. (New York: Touchstone, 1985), 49–51.

D

DAHL, ROALD (1916–1990)

Acerbic, darkly humorous British author who was able to write both youthful adventures for adults (the screenplay for *You Only Live Twice*) and adult entertainments for children (*Matilda, Charlie and the Chocolate Factory*), many of them gilded with the shining, well-polished resentments of class and privilege. He particularly excelled at short stories of exquisite malice and coldly served revenge, six of which were adapted (one by Dahl himself) for *ALFRED HITCHCOCK PRESENTS*; all are memorable, particularly "LAMB TO THE SLAUGHTER," directed by Hitchcock, and "Man from the South," helmed by NORMAN LLOYD. Popular and feted, controversial and combative to the end, Dahl died of cancer at age 74 in Oxford.

References

Tim Brooks and Earle Marsh, *The Complete Directory to Prime Time Network TV Shows*, 8th ed. (New York: Ballantine Books, 2003), 29; Martin Gram Jr. and Patrik Wikstrom, *The Alfred Hitchcock Presents Companion* (Whiteford, MD: OTR, 2001); Jack Edmond Nolan, "Hitchcock's TV Films," *Film Fan Monthly* (June 1968), 3–6; *Roald Dahl*, https://www.roald dahl.com/home/grown-ups; "Roald Dahl," *IMDb*, http://www.imdb.com/name/nm0001094/bio?ref_=nm_ov_bio_sm.

DALI, SALVADOR (1904–1989)

Brilliant, maddening, eccentric, calculating artist who collaborated on projects with filmmakers from Luis Bunuel to Walt Disney, while both confusing and attracting millions of admirers. Dali was born in Figueres, Spain, and would remain deeply linked to Catalonia throughout his life. At 18, however, he moved to Madrid to study art; expelled four years later, he went to Paris, where he met Picasso, cultivated an outrageous moustache, and eventually began collaborating on films with art school friend Luis Bunuel, beginning with 1929's *Un Chien Andalou*.

The nature of the collaboration is hazy—Dali, who later quarreled with Bunuel, would claim he did some of the filming, while others suggest he had only worked on the script—but the short movie, beginning with its deliberately repulsive image of a woman's EYE (actually a dead cow's) being slit by a razor, was a sensation. That it was not an outrage as well disappointed Dali, who had hoped for controversy, even riots in the theater; that came with their next film, *L'Age d'Or*, condemned by the right-wing as being a tool of "Judaism, Masonry, and rabid, revolutionary sectarianism," but by then the Dali-Bunuel partnership was ending.

During the '30s, Dali's fame increased exponentially, with gallery shows throughout Europe and in New York; bitterly criti-

Doris Day provides a typically strong emotional moment in the 1956 *The Man Who Knew Too Much*. *Paramount Pictures/Photofest © Paramount Pictures*

cized by the artistic elite for his self-promotion but embraced by (or at least now familiar to) much of the mainstream, Dali relocated to America in 1940. Although his refusal to condemn Fascism and his ultimate praise of Spanish dictator Francisco Franco earned him more enmity (George Orwell called him a "good draughtsman and a disgusting human being"), Dali—who cited Harpo Marx, Walt Disney, and Cecil B. DeMille as three of his favorite surrealists—soon found a congenial home and commissions in Hollywood. He wrote a script for Disney, *Destino* (finally filmed in 2003); he worked on the dream sequences for the movies *Moontide*; *SPELLBOUND*; and even, uncredited, *Father of the Bride*.

Hitchcock had initially approached Dali for *Spellbound* because he loathed the blurry, foggy effect often given movie dreams; what he appreciated in the Spanish surrealist's work, he later said, were the same sort of noon-day sharpness and clean angles he saw in Chirico—"the long shadows, the infinity of distance, and the converging lines of perspective." But the studio was opposed to Hitchcock's chief inspiration (to shoot the dream sequence outside, in natural light, for even more clarity) and many of Dali's suggestions were unworkable. He "had some strange ideas," the director told Truffaut decades later. "He wanted a statue to crack like a shell falling apart, with ants crawling all over it, and underneath, there would be Ingrid Bergman, covered by the ants! It just wasn't possible."

Neither was having the sequence last 20 minutes, which Bergman said had been the original plan. (Other sources put the original length of the sequence at closer to five minutes.) DAVID O. SELZNICK ordered WILLIAM CAMERON MENZIES to reshoot some of it and a chunk of it to be cut. Still, what the sequence did contain—eyes sliced with scissors, faceless men, a distorted wheel—did feel like Dali and made the nightmare one of Hollywood's most distinctive. But Dali would always be too outré for studio productions, too distinctive for collaborative efforts, and shortly after the war, the artist returned to his Spain, his paintings, his public spectacles, and his provocations.

His only other cinematic efforts are a documentary on a search for hallucinogenic mushrooms (he narrated) and a planned role in Alejandro Jodorowsky's version of *Dune* (which was years in pre-production but never made). He died of heart failure at 84 at home in the town where he was born.

References

Rudy Behlmer, ed., *Memo from David O. Selznick* (New York: Viking Press, 1972) 355; James Bigwood, "Solving a Spellbound Puzzle," *American Cinematographer* 72, no. 6 (June 1991), 34; Leonard Leff, "Selznick International's Spellbound," *The Criterion Collection*, https://www.criterion.com/current/posts/223-selznick-international s-spellbound; Patrick McGilligan, *Alfred Hitchcock: A Life in Darkness and Light* (New York: HarperCollins, 2003), 360–64; George Orwell, "Benefit of Clergy: Some Notes on Salvador Dali," *The Orwell Prize*, http://theorwellprize.co.uk/george-orwell/by-orwell/essays-and-other-works/benefit-of-clergy-some-notes-on-salvador-dali; "Salvador Dali," *Biography*, http://www.biography.com/people/salvador-dal-40389; "Salvador Dali," *IMDb*, http://www.imdb.com/name/nm0198557/?ref_=fn_al_nm_1; Donald Spoto, *The Dark Side of Genius: The Life of Alfred Hitchcock* (New York: Da Capo Press, 1999), 277–78; Bob Thomas, *Selznick* (New York: Pocket Books, 1972), 225; François Truffaut, *Hitchcock/Truffaut*, rev. ed. (New York: Touchstone, 1985), 163–65.

DALL, JOHN (1920–1970)

New York–born stage actor who made his first Broadway appearance in 1944 in *Dear Ruth*; his movie debut followed the next year in *The Corn Is Green*. Tall and well-spoken, he projected a mocking and slightly effete personality that served him well in Hitchcock's *ROPE*, where he played one of the two presumably gay murderers; it was less helpful in finding other parts. He is the obsessed shooter in *Gun Crazy*; an ancient Roman in *Spartacus*; and, in his last movie role, a mythical usurper in 1961's *Atlantis, the Lost Continent*. Most of his other work was limited to guest roles on TV series, and later he began to drink heavily. Deeply closeted, he was briefly married in the 1940s; he died in Los Angeles at age 50 of a heart attack, leaving his body to medical science.

References
"John Dall," *Gay for Today*, http://gayforto day.blogspot.com/2007/05/john-dall.html; "John Dall," *IMDb*, http://www.imdb.com/ name/nm0197982/bio?ref_=nm_ov_bio_sm.

DANO, ROYAL (1922–1994)
Born in New York into a working-class Irish family, Dano left home at 12 in the midst of the Depression to travel the country; he eventually returned home to attend classes at NYU and then served in the army, where he helped put on shows during World War II. He appeared on Broadway in *Finian's Rainbow* and gave what was reportedly a striking performance as "The Tattered Man" in an early version of John Huston's *The Red Badge of Courage*, but Huston said the scene was so grim that, during a preview screening, "damn near a third of the audience got up and walked out"; it was quickly cut, as was much of the rest of the picture.

Whether that sidelined Dano's chance for stardom or not, he never lacked for work, his deep voice and mournful looks winning him many years of supporting parts, mostly in period pieces. He played Abraham Lincoln in a five-part run on TV's *Omnibus* (and later supplied the presidential voice for Disneyland's robotic rail splitter); he is Elijah in Huston's *Moby Dick*, Peter in *King of Kings*, and on almost too many TV westerns to count. For Hitchcock, he appeared as the humorless deputy sheriff in *THE TROUBLE WITH HARRY* and on three episodes of *ALFRED HITCH-COCK PRESENTS* and *THE ALFRED*

HITCHCOCK HOUR. His last role was in the Stephen King horror film *The Dark Half*.

He died in Los Angeles of a heart attack following a car crash at age 71.

References
"Royal Dano," *IMDb*, http://www.imdb .com/name/nm0200455/bio?ref_=nm _ov_bio_sm; Richard Harland Smith, "The Enigma of Royal Dano," *TCM Movie Morlocks*, http://moviemorlocks .com/2014/02/21/the-enigma-of-royal -dano.

THE DARK SIDE OF GENIUS: THE LIFE OF ALFRED HITCHCOCK
Exhaustive look at the director by DONALD SPOTO, combining extensive biographical research with a close analysis of the work; it is especially valuable for its details on Hitchcock's childhood, the films' productions, and the insight—as both a gay man and a CATHOLIC—that Spoto brings to the movies' symbols and subtexts. (Originally an academic by training, Spoto has a doctorate in theology from Fordham.) Coming after the approving, authorized JOHN RUSSELL TAYLOR 1978 bio, *Hitch: The Life and Times of Alfred Hitchcock*, Spoto's posthumous study struck some at the time as gossipy, even scandalous; particularly criticized were Spoto's reports that the director had emotionally abused TIPPI HEDREN, harassed other actresses, and in later years slipped into heavy drinking and an obsession with violent fantasies.

Loyally denied at the time by partisans, including Taylor, HUME CRONYN, and NORMAN LLOYD—and by PATRICIA HITCHCOCK, the auteur's daughter—over the years, many of Spoto's biographical claims have become more firmly established as facts. Even PATRICK MCGILLIGAN's *ALFRED HITCHCOCK: A LIFE IN DARKNESS AND LIGHT*, while providing alternate interpretations and refuting a few of Spoto's assertions, produced more charges (such as the director's heretofore unremarked-upon pass at BRIGITTE AUBER). Although Spoto's book can't be taken as the final word on the man's life, it still stands as an essential introduction.

"It is not a heroic portrait of Alfred Hitchcock that Donald Spoto has presented here," Christopher Lehmann-Haupt wrote at the time in the *New York Times*'s admiring review. "It is instead the picture of a severely repressed, even twisted, Victorian gentleman. Some readers may therefore wish to challenge Mr. Spoto's conclusion that Hitchcock was a great artist. . . . But this much is certain. Mr. Spoto makes us see that Hitchcock was much more than a Hollywood entertainer."

References

Christopher Lehman-Haupt, "The Dark Side of Genius," *New York Times*, March 15, 1983, http://www.nytimes .com/1983/03/15/books/books-of-the -times-032380.html; John Russell Taylor, "Hitch Hatchet Job," *Times*, March 19, 1983, http://the.hitchcock.zone/ wiki/The_Times_%2819/May/1983%29 _-_Hitch_hatchet_job; "Interview with: Donald Spoto—Biographer/Historian," *Writers Store*, https://www.writersstore. com/interview-with-donald-spoto-biogra pher-historian.

DAWSON, ANTHONY
(1916–1992)

Born in Edinburgh, Dawson's long, lean, lined face added a touch of menace even to unthreatening characters; he had several small parts in British films in the early '40s and then returned to acting full time after the war. A small but good role came in 1948's prestigious *The Queen of Spades*, with Edith Evans and Anton Walbrook. By the early '50s, he was working in America, where he was busy in New York with TV roles and in the original Broadway production of *DIAL M FOR MURDER*, in which he played the blackmailer; it was around that time that Alfred Hitchcock, already planning the movie adaptation, invited him to a dinner party with GRACE KELLY.

Later at home, the phone rang; Dawson picked it up to hear "that wonderful fat man's Cockney voice" offering him the chance to reprise his role in the movie. "I mumbled my thanks and put the phone down, feeling rather dazed, electrified, stunned; all of these," Dawson wrote later in *Rambling Recollections*, his unpublished memoirs. "The full impact of this call from Hitch was very soon to come home to me."

Shabby and uncertain, Dawson's blackmailer stands as the seedy opposite to RAY MILLAND's elegant husband yet also helps to emphasize Milland's cold-blooded criminality; desperate and dishonest as his criminal is, Dawson's greedy villainy pales next to Milland's icy evil. Dawson makes a strong impression, and his ultimate death at Kelly's hands remains a standout moment in this talky film (and even more so in 3-D, although the film is usually exhibited in its "flat" format).

Dawson remained busy after that, even if it was mostly playing cads and cowards; he worked for Hitchcock again in a three-part *ALFRED HITCHCOCK PRESENTS* "I Killed the Count" and was the traitorous Professor Dent in *Dr. No* and the evil Marques in *Curse of the Werewolf*. (He would also provide the uncredited hands and lap of the cat-loving Blofeld in *From Russia with Love* and *Thunderball*; another actor dubbed the voice.) Although the roles grew smaller, Dawson continued to lurk about ominously in films until the end; he died in Sussex of cancer at age 75.

References

"Antony Dawson," *IMDb*, http://www
.imdb.com/name/nm0206060/bio?ref
_=nm_ov_bio_sm; Anthony Eric Gillon
Dawson, "A Tribute to Anthony Dawson,"
Anthony E. G. Dawson, http://anthonydaw
son.thelasis.com/pop1.html.

DAY, DORIS (1922–)

Multitalented performer born Doris Mary
Ann Kappelhoff in Cincinnati. Her father,
Frederick, was a local music teacher and—
although the family split when she was
young—may have been her earliest musical
encouragement. She performed locally as
half of a dance act in her very early teens;
when a car accident stopped that burgeoning career, she began to sing.

By 17 (or possibly even 15; some
sources list her birthdate as 1924), Kappelhoff had changed her name to Day and
begun touring, eventually signing with the
Les Brown band; her honeyed voice and
cautiously hopeful material—"Till the End
of Time," "My Dreams Are Getting Better
All The Time," and especially "Sentimental Journey"—formed a beloved homefront
soundtrack.

By 1948, Day was in movies, frequently
put in pinafores and cast in gaslit romantic comedies, with pictures like *On Moon-
light Bay* and *By the Light of the Silvery
Moon* evoking a postwar nostalgia for the
supposedly simpler, safer times of turn-of-
the-century America. ("She was the home
fire," David Thomson writes, "that refused
to admit the cold war.") But when her contract with WARNER BROS. expired, Day
decided not to renew it and to look for
meatier, more serious parts.

A very early standout brought a
return to the studio for 1955's *Love Me or
Leave Me*, with Day playing the Depres-
sion-era torch singer Ruth Etting; it was
another period piece, true, but the mood
was dark, with James Cagney in a late-
career triumph as Etting's domineering
husband, Martin "the Gimp" Snyder. Cagney, who'd worked with her on *The West
Point Story*, pushed the studio to give Day
the role; she repaid his confidence by giving a surprisingly strong performance as
a woman in thrall to her untrustworthy
spouse (a relationship, sadly, reportedly
paralleled by Day's own union with third
husband Terry Melcher).

The next year, Day teamed with
JAMES STEWART for Hitchcock's new
version of *THE MAN WHO KNEW TOO
MUCH*. This was a change of pace for the
director on several levels; although he had
referenced his own earlier films before,
he had never outright remade one. Nor
was there a love story here, outside of the
mother's devotion to her kidnapped little
boy; the couple is married but perhaps not
completely happily, and their relationship
is about to come under severe strain.

Day was nervous about her performance, a concern that grew into a real
worry when she felt Hitchcock was ignor-
ing her on the set. Expecting to be fired, she
finally pulled him aside and told him if he
didn't like what she was doing, she'd quit.
"If you weren't doing what I liked," he told
her, "you'd know." And so, back to work.

Indeed, Day conveyed a real feeling of anguish and loss as the parent of a
kidnapped child; a true feeling of betrayal,
too, at an emotionally distant husband who
has stopped her career and at one point
even doses her with sedatives without her
knowledge.

Although Day hardly projected Hitchcock's favored sophisticated appeal (and
never seems to be included in periodic
stories on the "Hitchcock BLONDES"),
the director was in fact very pleased with
his leading lady (whom he'd chosen after
seeing her in the noirish *Storm Warning*);
that one of the songs she sang in the film,
"Que Sera Sera," became a number-2 hit

(and an Oscar winner) was a lovely bonus that helped push the film's popularity even further.

Hitchcock and Day did not work together again, though, and despite some flirtations with the thriller genre (*Julie, Midnight Lace*), Day soon settled into a series of musicals and very popular romantic comedies. Many costarred Rock Hudson and featured Day in constant, outraged flight from his advances; that a 40-ish actress who'd spent her teenage years on the road with an all-male band could play quite so prim seemed absurd ("I knew Doris Day before she was a virgin," Oscar Levant cracked), but the films were popular.

Until they weren't. As the '60s sexual revolution took hold, Day began to seem out of touch with the times, an alienation she was actually happy to embrace; although she had a charming, huskily intimate speaking voice and a lovely figure, Hollywood had never really asked her to explore her sensuality, and she was quite happy with that. She turned down the Mrs. Robinson part in *The Graduate* ("vulgar and offensive"), gave up on the movies, and opted instead for TV sitcoms and talk shows.

She has been essentially retired since the mid-'90s, devoting most of her time to animal rights. Although she remains, by some measures, Hollywood's biggest female STAR (10 years in the top 10 at the box office, an unmatched 4 times at number 1), her accomplishments seem (unfairly) half-forgotten today; her only Oscar nomination was for *Pillow Talk* in 1959, and a recent push to present her with an honorary award came to naught. To which you can only imagine her saying—*Que sera, sera.*

References

Doris Day, http://www.dorisday.com; "Doris Day," *IMDb*, http://www.iMdb .com/name/nm0000013/bio?ref_=nm_ov _bio_sm; A. E. Hotchner, *Doris Day: Her Own Story* (New York: William Morrow, 1975), 164–66; Patrick McGilligan, *Alfred Hitchcock: A Life in Darkness and Light* (New York: HarperCollins, 2003), 517–21; Donald Spoto, *The Dark Side of Genius: The Life of Alfred Hitchcock* (New York: Da Capo Press, 1999), 363–65; David Thomson, *The New Biographical Dictionary of Film* (New York: Knopf, 2002), 211.

DEATH

It was TRUFFAUT who said that Hitchcock filmed his murders like love scenes and his love scenes like murders. Look again when Roger and Eve first kiss in *NORTH BY NORTHWEST* and his large hands encircle her—it's not clear at first whether Roger means to embrace the woman or strangle her. There's a similar streak of antagonism, if not outright threat, in *SABOTEUR, THE 39 STEPS, SUSPICION, LIFEBOAT*, and many others.

But conversely there is little tenderness in Hitchcock's movie murders, which are always up close and brutal. And while love is not a part of them, sex often is—at least the quick, violent, unwanted sex of a SEXUAL assault, with the director often cutting between close-ups of the women's legs, wildly writhing, and the very intent glint in the man's narrowed EYES.

STABBING, usually with a phallic knife, is one of the most common methods in Hitchcock's films—*The 39 Steps, THE MAN WHO KNEW TOO MUCH, North By Northwest, PSYCHO*—the blade usually thrust into some unsuspecting victim from behind, the brutally sudden penetration meant to leave them gasping and helpless in some dark and terrified metaphor for forcible sodomy. STRANGULATION, perhaps the most intimate form of murder, appears regularly, too (*STRANGERS ON A TRAIN, DIAL M FOR MURDER, ROPE, FRENZY*), while the old blunt instrument is an occasional standby, although often wielded by a woman against a man (*MARNIE*, "LAMB TO THE SLAUGHTER"). And, of course, there are the usual dull, impersonal deaths by revolver and rifle and some fatal falls.

Murder is rarely quick in Hitchcock films, too, which may suggest a certain sadism on the director's part; actually, there is a moral component to it, as well. A life is not, should not, be easy to take; to suggest that it's a simple thing is not only amoral but also, at the very least, unrealistic. In *TORN CURTAIN*, for example, the centerpiece of the film is the killing of Gromek, and the most startling thing is how difficult it is. He is stabbed, he is beaten, and finally he is pushed into a gas oven and asphyxiated. Bond may kill someone with a high-powered rifle and a quip; in Hitchcock's spy films, you look into the man's EYES and use your bare hands.

"My first thought again was to avoid the cliché," Hitchcock said later. "In every picture somebody gets killed and it goes very quickly. They are stabbed or shot and the killer never even stops to look and see whether the person is dead or not. And I thought it was time to show that it was very difficult, very painful and it takes a very long time to kill a man."

Women, though, can be easier to dispatch in his movies, particularly if they're willing to meet you halfway. The way the second Mrs. De Winter stands at those high windows while Mrs. Danvers whispers to her; the way Lina sticks so patiently by Johnnie in *Suspicion* even though she's convinced herself he's a murderer; even the way Miriam turns so expectantly, happily, to the silently stalking Bruno in *Strangers on a Train*—in Hitchcock's films, yes, some men are born killers. But some women are born victims, too.

Reference

François Truffaut, *Hitchcock/Truffaut*, rev. ed. (New York: Touchstone, 1985), 311.

DE BANZIE, BRENDA (1909–1981)

Manchester-born performer who made her British stage debut at 16 in the chorus of *DuBarry Was a Lady*. She had a strong career in the theater throughout the '50s (including the hit thriller *Murder Mistaken*) and eventually branched into films.

Generally cast as lonely and dissatisfied women, she made her first screen appearance in the mystery *The Long Dark Hall* in 1951 and was a standout in both *Hobson's Choice* and *The Entertainer*; in 1956 in *THE MAN WHO KNEW TOO MUCH*, she was Lucy Drayton, the unhappy wife and conflicted accessory of the kidnapper. She later costarred in an ill-considered Hitchcock remake, *The Thirty-Nine Steps*, and appeared in *The Pink Panther*; other parts were less prominent. She died at age 71 of complications following brain surgery.

References

"Brenda De Banzie," *IMDb*, http://www.imdb.com/name/nm0207219/bio?ref_=nm_ov_bio_sm; "Underrated Performer of the Week: Brenda De Banzie," *Classic Film and TV Café*, http://www.classicfilmtvcafe.com/2010/03/underrated-performer-of-week-brenda-de.html.

DENNY, REGINALD (1891–1967)

Richmond-born son of a British family long involved with opera and the theater; he made his stage debut at 7 and nearly 70 years later was still going, playing King Boris on TV's *Batman*. In between, Denny tended to play light comedies or supporting roles in dramas; in *REBECCA*, he is Frank Crawley, the quietly efficient estate manager for Manderley (and one of Rebecca's many besotted admirers). He later appeared in *The Locket*, *My Favorite Brunette*, and *Abbott and Costello Meet Dr. Jekyll and Mr. Hyde*.

More personally satisfying, perhaps, was his career in aviation; a gunner in the Royal Flying Corps during World War I, Denny occasionally worked as a stunt pilot and in 1934 opened the first in a chain of model-airplane hobby shops. By World War II, he was a pioneer in drone technology, turning out radio-controlled aircraft for the US Army. He sold the company to Northrop in 1952.

Denny died at 75 after suffering a stroke in England.

References

"Reginald Denny," *IMDb*, http://www.imdb.com/name/nm0219666/bio?ref_=nm_ov_bio_sm; "Reginald Denny: The Dennyplane," *Hargrave: The Pioneers*, http://www.ctie.monash.edu.au/hargrave/dennyplane.html; Alfred E. Twomey and Arthur F. McClure, *The Versatiles: Supporting Character Players in the Cinema, 1930–1955* (New York: Castle Books, 1969), 82.

DE PALMA, BRIAN (1940–)

Is he one of our greatest filmmakers, a master artist who uses Brechtian distancing and metafictional devices to comment on the very art he's making, as critics like PAULINE KAEL have claimed? Or just one of our most self-satisfied popcorn salesmen who simply, shamelessly, copies twists and tricks from Alfred Hitchcock? ("Once a year, Brian De Palma picks the bones of a dead director," a satirical *Saturday Night Live* trailer once claimed, "and gives his wife a job.") The consensus on Brian De Palma has gone back and forth.

Born to a Newark, NJ, surgeon, De Palma was an early computer enthusiast and science fair standout who went to Columbia University to major in physics; attending screenings of films by Orson Welles and Hitchcock changed that idea, and he ended up getting his master's in theater at Sarah Lawrence before embarking on a movie career.

"I still remember sitting in the balcony at Radio City Music Hall in 1958 and watching *VERTIGO*," he said of his freshman year in college, "and when KIM NOVAK went over the side the second time I thought, I don't believe this. But that touched me, all of it, particularly the JAMES STEWART character. . . . I think if you look at them, there's a great sense of helplessness in my movies, a lot of impotent characters."

At first, based in New York, De Palma moved between experimental films and documentary work (combining the two in *Dionysus in '69*, chronicling a production of Euripides's *The Bacchae* by the Performance Group). Much of De Palma's work was political and deliberately provocative, breaking the fourth wall, experimenting with different film stocks, or using split-screen effects to project multiple images. Several—*Greetings*; *Hi, Mom!*—featured the young actor Robert De Niro.

After having his first Hollywood film, the farcical *Get to Know Your Rabbit*, taken away from him, De Palma turned to independent filmmaking and genre subjects with *Sisters*. Starring Margot Kidder and Jennifer Salt (and William Finley, a friend from his avant-garde days), the movie told a grotesque story of Siamese twins, fractured personalities, and brutal murders. Sold to audiences as the "most genuinely frightening film since Hitchcock's *PSYCHO!*"—and with a leading character dispatched early on by knife, elements of VOYEURISM, and a score by BERNARD HERRMANN—it was easy to see the parallels. Yet the film's BLACK-AND-WHITE cinema verité flashbacks are pure De Palma; its split-screen techniques are contrary to everything Hitchcock preached about MONTAGE. It had its own style.

Later films would have more obvious connections to the older director, although whether those took the form of homage, debt, or outright theft depended on the critic. Kael was an early, and ardent supporter; screenwriter I. A. L. Diamond accused the young director of simply making a "career out of ripping off Hitchcock." Others took a more balanced view. "*Sisters, Raising Cain, Body Double, Obsession*, which is a virtual remake of *Vertigo*—it's incredible all the variations he spun on Hitchcock," observed Kent Jones, a festival programmer and the director of the 2015 documentary *HITCHCOCK/TRUFFAUT*. "But saying that De Palma's movies were superior—I don't know, when was the last time any of these people took a look at *Vertigo*? Or *MARNIE*, or *REAR WINDOW*?"

Certainly the Hitchcock influences are there, although they go beyond storytelling tricks, like transgender disguises or carefully orchestrated murder plots, too; themes like the compulsive FETISHISM of *Rear Window* and the DOUBLES of *THE WRONG MAN* and *Vertigo* show up as well (most obviously in *Body Double*, which makes SEXUALLY explicit what *Rear Window* only hinted at). Yet to see De Palma only as a mere imitator is unfair. Although his films are smartly if self-consciously edited (like *The Untouchables*, which cheekily copies the Odessa steps sequence from *Battleship Potemkin*), he is even fonder of long tracking shots than Hitchcock was, sometimes incorporating dizzyingly over-the-top 360-degree pans; his humor is more bitter, too, and his films often end on notes of utter despair or absurdist resignation.

And many of his sequences stand on their own as bravura bits of filmmaking. In *Dressed to Kill*, Angie Dickinson and a mysterious stranger play a game of hide and seek in a museum; in *Body Double*, Craig Wasson follows a mysterious woman through a mall. Both scenes end very differently, but they share an assured use of a constantly moving camera, a clever sense of pacing, and a serious take on the thin line between a romantic attraction and a dangerous obsession and how easily it can be crossed.

Since the commercial failure of *Raising Cain*, De Palma has shown less interest in the themes and tricks of Hitchcock. *Carlito's Way*, released in 1993, was a superior gangster drama; the spy adventure *Mission Impossible*, released in 1996, a competent job for hire. Unfortunately, few of his recent films have connected with audiences or any but the most rabid admirers—although 2007's *Redacted* intriguingly revisited his old interests in politics and voyeurism, *Passion*, from 2012, was barely released.

So is Brian De Palma an original thinker who uses the medium to comment on the medium? Or a clever imitator who borrows some of his greatest effects from an even greater filmmaker? The answer, inarguably, is—both.

References

Brian De Palma, interview with the author, February 2007; "Brian De Palma," *Biography*, http://www.biography.com/people/brian-de-palma-9272033; "Brian De Palma," *IMDb*, http://www.imdb.com/name/nm0000361/bio?ref_=nm_ov_bio_sm; Kent Jones, interview with the author, February 2007; Noel Murray and Scott Tobias, "Primer: Brian De Palma," *AV Club*, http://www.avclub.com/article/brian-de-palma-52964; David Thomson, *The New Biographical Dictionary of Film* (New York: Knopf, 2002), 227–28.

DERN, BRUCE (1936–)

Chicago-born son of a renowned and well-connected family (the poet Archibald MacLeish was his granduncle, Adlai Stevenson his godfather) whose decision to pursue an acting career was an "act of rebellion" and caused a small scandal within the family. "My family was very disappointed in me," he said of the day he announced his choice. "They were all great men, and they made it very clear they did not think I was going to be a great man."

It took Dern a while to find his footing. He is a murder victim in 1964's *Hush, Hush, Sweet Charlotte* and starred the same year in an equally fatal flashback in *MARNIE* as a drunken and very unlucky sailor. He also appeared on two episodes of *THE ALFRED HITCHCOCK HOUR*, playing a suspicious drifter and a suspected pervert. Despite his roots in the midwestern aristocracy, Dern's reedy voice and hard stare helped typecast him as sneering villains or ignorant trash in the movies; onscreen, he rode with outlaw bikers, sewed heads onto bodies, and in *The Cowboys* gained movie infamy by shooting John Wayne in the back. (When Wayne warned him that audiences were going to "hate his guts" for that scene, Dern answered, "Yeah, but they'll sure love me in Berkeley!")

There were some attempts to broaden his image. Dern had a good part in *Silent Running*; in *FAMILY PLOT*, Hitchcock cast him as George, the good-natured but not particularly bright boyfriend of Blanche, a fake psychic. Dern (who with his well-bred, midwestern manners still refers to the late director as "Mr. Hitchcock") later claimed to have helped him direct some of the scenes, when the filmmaker's health problems interfered; for his part, Hitchcock assured Dern that this was the movie that would finally make him a STAR.

Whether the first assertion was true or not, the second was definitely not. The film was not a huge success, and Dern went back to being an underrated (if definitely busy) character actor, mostly in smaller-budgeted films. *Nebraska* in 2013 offered a rare sympathetic lead and even won him an Oscar nomination. He did not win.

References

Bruce Dern, interview with the author, November 2013; "Bruce Dern," *IMDb*, http://www.imdb.com/name/nm0001136/bio?ref_=nm_ov_bio_sm.

DEVANE, WILLIAM (1937–)

Albany, NY–born performer whose square jaw and thick hair made him a favorite of casting directors looking for someone to play a politician; he was Robert F. Kennedy off-Broadway, John F. Kennedy in the TV movie *The Missiles of October*, and a variety of straight and crooked politicians in television shows from *The West Wing* to *Stargate*. Interestingly, his father had once been a chauffeur to Franklin Delano Roosevelt when he was New York's governor. "I was around politicians my whole life," Devane said. "My Uncle Frannie was a captain on the police force. My Uncle Bill was the water commissioner. When I said I wanted to be an actor it was received as kind of good news. It was a step better than wanting to be a cop."

His ability to smile widely when saying even the most menacing things made him perfect for not just elected officials but also more streetwise villains; in *FAMILY PLOT*, he was Edward Shoebridge, a self-created orphan who changed his name and worked as a kidnapper and San Francisco jeweler. As it turned out, Devane was both Hitchcock's first and third choice for the role. When the actor's schedule didn't allow him to join the production, Hitchcock began shooting his scenes with Roy Thinnes, instead; when Devane became available, Hitchcock abruptly fired Thinnes and brought Devane on for reshoots (although Thinnes can supposedly be glimpsed in some longshots).

Devane continues to work and play characters with slightly slippery morals and great toothy smiles.

References

Patrick McGilligan, *Alfred Hitchcock: A Life in Darkness and Light* (New York: Harper-Collins, 2003), 725–26; Bernard Weinraub, "They Told Devane He'd Be Typecast as a Kennedy," *New York Times*, October 15, 1995, http://www.nytimes.com/1995/10/15/tv/cover-story-they-told-devane-he-d-be-typecast-as-a-kennedy-but-which-one.html; "William Devane," *IMDb*, http://www.imdb.com/name/nm0001137/bio?ref_=nm_ov_bio_sm.

LES DIABOLIQUES (FRANCE 1955)

DIRECTOR: Henri-Georges Clouzot.
SCREENPLAY: Henri-Georges Clouzot, Jerome Geronimi, Rene Masson, Frederic Grendel, based on the novel *Celle Qui N'Etait Plus* by Pierre Boileau and Thomas Narcejac.
PRODUCERS: Henri-Georges Clouzot (Georges Lourau, uncredited).
CINEMATOGRAPHY: Armand Thirard.
EDITOR: Madeleine Gug.
ORIGINAL MUSIC: Georges Van Parys.
CAST: Simone Signoret (Nicole Horner), Vera Clouzot (Christina Delassalle), Paul Meurisse (Michel Delassalle). In French.
RUNNING TIME: 116 minutes. Black and white.
RELEASED BY: Cinedis.

At a cheap French boarding school, the food is always on the edge of spoiling, the swimming pool is full of muck—and the headmaster is both running through his wife's money and knocking about his girlfriend, one of the teachers. The two women, though, find they have more in common than not, and the tough teacher talks the frail wife—who actually owns the school but has a weak heart—into joining her in a plan to drown the headmaster in a bathtub and dump his body in the pool.

The women carry out the murder and get rid of the corpse—but later, when the pool is drained, there's no body to be found. Wife and girlfriend grow more and more concerned until the body reappears—rising from a bathtub in the school. The wife has a heart attack and dies. As she was supposed to—all was a plan between husband and mistress to kill her and get her money. Except the two are quickly arrested—and now a new ghost walks the halls of the old school.

Often cited as influenced by Hitchcock, *Les Diaboliques* was an influence on him as well, both in subject matter (stymied in purchasing the rights to the same novel, he soon bought another one by the authors, PIERRE BOILEAU and THOMAS NARCEJAC, turning it into *VERTIGO*) and marketing (the warnings against late admissions and giving away the twist, which would be reused for *PSYCHO*). Yet Clouzot, who definitely shared much with the English director (including a rather jaundiced view of actors and a delight in constructing thrillers like "a game") brought his own tastes and talent to the tale.

Simone Signoret's mistress, for example, has an aggressive, almost masculine SEXUALITY you wouldn't see in Hitchcock's films, while instead of that director's stark contrasts and straight lines, Clouzot creates a gray, murky underwater feeling and an almost palpable sense of damp decay. If *SHADOW OF A DOUBT* and *Psycho* show murder blooming in the sunshine, *Diaboliques* is slowly sprouting like a mushroom from a rotten log.

The film was an enormous hit and has been remade, with credit and without, several times since. Cinephiles would be wise to avoid the many poor-quality versions available and opt for the Criterion edition; music fans are advised to look carefully and see if they can spy a junior version of French rock-and-roller Johnny Hallyday as one of the students.

References

Ivan Butler, *Horror in the Cinema* (New York: A. S. Barnes, 1970), 103–12; "Diabolique," *The Criterion Collection*, https://www.criterion.com/films/575-dia bolique.

DIAL M FOR MURDER (US 1954)

DIRECTOR: Alfred Hitchcock.
SCREENPLAY: Frederick Knott, based on his play.
PRODUCER: Uncredited (Alfred Hitchcock).
CINEMATOGRAPHY: Robert Burks.
EDITOR: Rudi Fehr.
ORIGINAL MUSIC: Dimitri Tiomkin.
CAST: Grace Kelly (Margot Wendice), Ray Milland (Tony Wendice), Robert Cummings (Mark Halliday), Anthony Dawson (Captain Lesgate/Swann), John Williams (Chief Inspector Hubbard).
RUNNING TIME: 105 minutes. Color. 3-D.
RELEASED THROUGH: Warner Bros.

A retired tennis player, Tony likes living well but is getting tired of doing it with his wife Margot's money—so he blackmails Swann, a disgraced old schoolmate, into agreeing to slip into the apartment that night and murdering Margot so it looks like a burglary gone wrong.

But while Tony is away with Margot's old lover, Mark, establishing his alibi, it's the murder that goes wrong—Swann is killed, stabbed by Margot with a pair of scissors. Quickly, Tony shifts plans—planting one of Margot's love letters to Mark in Swann's pocket to make it look as if Margot merely killed her blackmailer.

Mark is suspicious, but Margot is quickly arrested, convicted, and sentenced to death. Only on the morning of her hanging is Mark, working with the police, able to prove that Tony was behind all of it, finding the key he left for Swann to let himself into the apartment. Tony goes off to prison like a good sport, and Margot is freed.

Dial M for Murder was a bit of treading water for Hitchcock—*I CONFESS* had been a disappointment, and several other projects he'd planned, including *THE BRAMBLE BUSH*, had fallen apart. Filming a hit play (which had already been done once for British television) seemed like a safe choice.

A bit too safe, perhaps. Playwright FREDERICK KNOTT was good at setting up tricky situations and shifting alliances among thieves (the early scenes between Tony and Captain Lesgate, a.k.a. "Swann," are similar to the ones between Roat and Sam in his later play *Wait until Dark*), but the plotting is a trifle clever for its own good, and the crucial importance of the hidden key is both overdone and underwhelming. "I could have phoned that one in," Hitchcock said later—as usual, unable to resist either a pun or self-criticism.

He had been encumbered from the start, however, by the studio's decision to shoot in 3-D. Although the director was as open to new technology as he'd been when the talkies first arrived, like those early sound cameras, the 3-D ones were enormous, limited in function, and difficult to maneuver; it was hard to get the extreme close-ups he sometimes wanted or to move the camera as much as he liked. All of this made what already seemed like a rather stagey film even more static and stiff. (Actually, the movie that might have benefitted from 3-D, with its deep perspectives, was *REAR WINDOW*—but by the time it was in production, the fad had faded.)

Still, some of the old Hitchcock occasionally shines through in *Dial M for Mur-*

der. Like so many of his '50s films, it's about an unhappy marriage—certainly the unhappiest among his works, as the wife is an adulteress and the husband a would-be murderer. It shows both his modern mastery of COLOR (with Margot's clothes going from gay to gray as her situation worsens) and his old skill with EXPRESSIONISTIC suggestion (Margot's trial conveyed with a close-up or two staged against nearly blank backgrounds). And his ever-sharp eye for detail, like the glint he was so careful to catch on the fatal scissors ("A murder without gleaming scissors is like asparagus without hollandaise sauce," he observed. "Tasteless"). And, in a filmography full of erotic death, the attack on Margot is one of the most graphic, with her dressed only in a filmy white nightgown, her legs moving beneath the silky fabric while her assailant grabs her from behind, the scissoring of her legs mimicking the tool she's about to grab and shockingly thrust into his back.

Despite a terrific performance from GRACE KELLY and a droll one from RAY MILLAND (Hitchcock had wanted CARY GRANT, but once again, the STAR refused to play a villain), the movie was only a modest success; although ANTHONY DAWSON and JOHN WILLIAMS both ably repeated their stage performances, ROBERT CUMMINGS was bland as ever as Mark, and by the time the film was released, the 3-D fad was finished (most theaters got standard 2-D prints). Hitchcock would have better luck with his next film, *Rear Window.*

References

B. Kite, "Staged Fright," *Village Voice*, December 30, 2003, http://www.village voice.com/film/staged-fright-6397459; Patrick McGilligan, *Alfred Hitchcock: A Life in Darkness and Light* (New York: HarperCollins, 2003), 469–72; Donald Spoto,

The Dark Side of Genius: The Life of Alfred Hitchcock (New York: Da Capo Press, 1999), 341–45; François Truffaut, *Hitchcock/Truffaut*, rev. ed. (New York: Touchstone, 1985), 209–11.

DIETRICH, MARLENE (1901–1992)

Schöneberg-born performer who dreamed of becoming a classical violinist but eventually found work as a chorus girl in the touring Girl-Kabarett and then moved on to movies. She became a STAR in 1929 playing Lola-Lola in Josef von Sternberg's *The Blue Angel,* the sexy young singer who becomes an old professor's self-destructive obsession. Quickly moving onto Hollywood, she and von Sternberg created a series of extraordinary melodramas, as known for their silvery rays of light and rich textures as for Dietrich's slashing cheekbones and gender-bending attitudes; burning hot but quickly, she was a top star by the early '30s, "box-office poison" just a few years later.

It was then that the Nazis approached her, hoping to woo her back to Germany; Dietrich's response was to take out American citizenship and, when the war began, do everything she could to aid the Allied war effort. After the war, Dietrich's career—which had been revived in '39 with the self-mocking *Destry Rides Again*—picked up again, as she played a variety of knowing, unknowable older women.

She played that part for Hitchcock in *STAGE FRIGHT,* in which she was Charlotte Inwood, a stage diva, the lover of a younger man—and, just possibly, the brutal killer of her own husband. It was a good part for Dietrich but not a good film, and although she had a big star's perquisites—a wardrobe by Dior, a song to sing by Cole Porter, and reportedly a loud dressing-room affair with the leading man, MICHAEL WILDING—she apparently disliked the film and her costar JANE WYMAN.

Dietrich had a few movie successes after that—she is very good in the Billy Wilder courtroom thriller *Witness for the Prosecution* and iconic under that improbable black wig in Orson Welles's *Touch of Evil*—and then spent much of the next decade as a concert performer. Well into her 60s by then, she would prepare by painfully taping her skin taut and squirming into corseted, painfully slimming gowns, almost literally willing herself back into the shape of the irresistible Lola-Lola.

Declining health and several bad falls forced her retirement; Dietrich ended up a recluse, retreating to her Paris apartment and talking to her many friends and admirers over the phone but letting only a few ever see her face. It was important that her image—and our memories of her own, self-made SEXUAL iconography—remained perfect and untouched by time.

She died at age 90 in Paris. According to her will, only after the reunification of Germany was her body returned home and buried in her beloved Berlin.

References

"Biography," *Marlene Dietrich*, http://www .marlene.com/bio.html; "Marlene Dietrich," *IMDb*, http://www.imdb.com/name/ nm0000017/bio?ref_=nm_ov_bio_sm; Patrick McGilligan, *Alfred Hitchcock: A Life in Darkness and Light* (New York: HarperCollins, 2003), 431–37; Donald Spoto, *The Dark Side of Genius: The Life of Alfred Hitchcock* (New York: Da Capo Press, 1999), 316; Donald Spoto, *Spellbound by Beauty: Alfred Hitchcock and His Leading Ladies* (New York: Harmony Books, 2008), 190–92; David Thomson, *The New Biographical Dictionary of Film* (New York: Knopf, 2002), 236–38.

"A DIP IN THE POOL" (US; ORIGINALLY AIRED JUNE 1, 1958)

DIRECTOR: Alfred Hitchcock.
SCREENPLAY: Robert C. Dennis, based on the story by Roald Dahl.
PRODUCERS: Joan Harrison, Norman Lloyd.
CINEMATOGRAPHY: John F. Warren.
EDITOR: Edward W. Williams.
ORIGINAL MUSIC: Uncredited.
CAST: Keenan Wynn (William Botibol), Fay Wray (Mrs. Renshaw).
RUNNING TIME: 30 minutes. Black and white.
ORIGINALLY BROADCAST BY: CBS.

A vulgar, braying American makes a bet on how far the cruise ship he's on will travel; when he tries to ensure the outcome, he ends up only fatally cheating himself. A typically cold story about dishonesty from ROALD DAHL, a favorite of *ALFRED HITCHCOCK PRESENTS*; Dahl's "Man from the South," however, directed by NORMAN LLOYD, made for a far better episode.

References

Tim Brooks and Earle Marsh, *The Complete Directory to Prime Time Network TV Shows*, 8th ed. (New York: Ballantine Books, 2003), 29; Jack Edmond Nolan, "Hitchcock's TV Films," *Film Fan Monthly* (June 1968), 3–6.

DOLLY SHOTS

In cinematography, a shot in which the camera is on a wheeled platform pushed along to either move in or out on a person or object or to follow them as they move in or out of frame. Dating back a hundred years, dolly shots often serve very utilitarian functions and provide a sometimes-useful alternative to cutting to a close-up. One can dolly in on a clue a murderer leaves behind as he exits a room to emphasize its importance and dolly out from the end of a dialogue scene to underline its firm finality.

Like many directors who began their careers in the silents, where image is all, Hitchcock understood dolly shots in all their complexity and used them in complicated ways. In the incredibly difficult-to-shoot *ROPE* and *UNDER CAPRICORN*—which required breakaway sets and special props—they are part of the essential grammar, almost never-ending, following people from room to room and adding to the tension. In *VERTIGO*, they are coupled with a zoom to strand us in the middle of Scottie's awful disabling disorientation, as things seem to move forward and fall away at the same time (a shot now known as the "Hitchcock zoom" or the "*Vertigo* effect"). In *PSYCHO*, they are part of the rhythm as much as the music, slowly moving ahead of Arbogast as he climbs up those fateful STAIRS or bringing us into Lila's mind as she approaches the house; in *FRENZY*, they take the pitiless approach of a disinterested God, following the murderer and his victim up the stairs to his room—and then silently retreating to leave them to their fates.

Dolly shots are definitely part of Hitchcock's style, although only one part—his signature "look," while much celebrated, is not easily defined. As much as Hitchcock believed in moving the camera in long unbroken takes, he also believed in MONTAGE; some of his shots could last six minutes or more, and others flash by almost subliminally. He did whatever worked for that particular emotional moment in that particular scene. Everything was put in service of PURE CINEMA.

So he could do an extraordinary crane shot, like the one that pulls back in *Psycho* as Norman carries his mother out of her room (and cleverly also obscures just what "Mother" is) or the one that swoops down in *NOTORIOUS* to show the tiny

key clutched in Alicia's hand or in *YOUNG AND INNOCENT* to reveal the murderer. Or he could jump to quick cuts for the attacks in *THE BIRDS* or *TORN CURTAIN*. Or provide sit-back-and-watch close-ups as JOSEPH COTTEN calmly outlines his own madness in *SHADOW OF A DOUBT* or Henry Jones so coldly sums up the inquest's findings in *Vertigo*, both breaking the fourth wall to stare directly at us.

But whatever the scene, Hitchcock's movies never stood still. And rarely did his camera.

Reference

"Dolly Shot," *Media College*, http://www.mediacollege.com/video/shots/dolly.html.

DOMINATION

The Hitchcock filmography is full of images of BONDAGE and submission—starting with *THE LODGER*, the first truly "Hitchcock film," which begins with a mocking equation of handcuffs and a wedding ring and climaxes with a trussed-up suspect hauled up before a mob like a crucified Christ.

But the ropes don't work without someone to tie them, and there's no submission without someone to kneel before. Hitchcock's own relationship to these power struggles is complex—like many who were intimidated in childhood (his father, determined to punish him for some long-forgotten infraction, brought him down to the police station and had the constables lock him up), he could be intimidating in adult life (establishing his own on-set dominance by playing practical JOKES on crew members or deliberately discomfiting his STARS). And those complications are explored in the films in which—even when they seem to be victims—women almost inevitably prevail.

Yes, the fiancé who taunts his girl with handcuffs in *The Lodger* literally holds the key—but he will be put in his place before the film ends. Richard Hannay may tease Pamela as they spend their days bound together in *THE 39 STEPS*—but he is unable to take any advantage of her, and she's the one who eventually slips the bond and steals away. And while Scottie is absurdly controlling of Judy in *VERTIGO*, in the end, she's the one who holds the cards, and when the hand turns out to go against them both, there's nothing Scottie can do but stand there, impotently. Norman can peep and pant all he wants in *PSYCHO*—but when he really needs to do something physical, he has to pull on a wig and put on a dress.

That's because, although men seem to be the sole protagonists in Hitchcock films, it's almost always the women who—in handcuffs or not, dead or not, impersonated or not—still hold the actual power.

Maxim de Winter is rich, haughty, and (when he wants to be) irresistibly charming—but there is no doubt that *REBECCA* ruled and ruined his life (and that Mrs. Danvers presumes to take her place, at least as a controlling feminine force). Devlin is a master American spy and Alexander Sebastian a silky Nazi in *NOTORIOUS*—but they are both in thrall to Alicia Huberman and Sebastian especially to his mother.

Domineering wives are a constant in Hitchcock, of course. Guy Haines is figuratively chained to his shrewish spouse, Miriam, in *STRANGERS ON A TRAIN* (a chain that only the flirtatious, feminine Bruno can break). In *REAR WINDOW*, Jeff is wary of marriage, seeing unhappiness every time he spies on his neighbors—including Mr. Thorvald, who eventually murders his complaining wife. (The number of Hitchcock TV shows centering on nagging wives done in by put-upon husbands is dizzying.)

The smothering ministrations of devoted mothers leave their painful mark, too. Mitch is still a bachelor in *THE BIRDS*

because he's devoted to his kid sister and their hypercritical mother—and Melanie, who has her own ugly memories of being denied a "mother's care," can't find a way to break into that closed circle until she's reduced to nearly infantile helplessness. The murderous Bob Rusk in *FRENZY*, like Norman Bates, has clearly been formed by his smothering mother. And then there is poor *MARNIE* (one of the truest, saddest female victims in Hitchcock), who as a confused and sleepy child thought she was rescuing her mother—and has paid for that act of mistaken bravery with decades of guilt and remorseless disapproval of everything that wasn't "respectable."

No, it's almost always a female who is in charge (and, in a situation with several women, always the oldest). And even when men, driven mad by their powerlessness, seek revenge against all females, it's always a woman who's their undoing. Charles in *SHADOW OF A DOUBT*, Thorwald in *Rear Window*, even Norman in *Psycho*—they're not caught by the gruff male detectives on their trails. They're undone by the fearless persistence of the young women softly smiling in their faces, slowly untangling their lies, steadily pushing their ways into these Bluebeards' secret rooms.

Hitchcock's movies may see women as Madonnas. They may see them as whores. They may see them, most frequently, as exciting performers who pretend to be the first and are secretly the other. But the one thing his movies—for all their perceived misogyny—rarely see them as is powerless.

Reference

Donald Spoto, *The Dark Side of Genius: The Life of Alfred Hitchcock* (New York: Da Capo Press, 1999), 16, 109–12, 219.

DONAT, ROBERT (1905–1958)

Manchester-born, ineffably charming British performer who first took elocution lessons to help with a childhood stammer. He found precocious success with Shakespeare onstage but took a while to find his place in films. In fact, fearful of the camera and terribly awkward, he failed one screen test after another; only after the final disaster, when he burst into laughter at himself, did he win over mogul Alexander Korda, who signed him to a contract.

Donat made an impression in *The Private Life of Henry VIII* and then went to Hollywood in 1934 for *The Count of Monte Cristo* but turned down *Captain Blood* (thereby handing Errol Flynn a career) and returned to England for *THE 39 STEPS*; a contemporary English critic hailed Donat's "easy confident humour" and exulted, "for the first time on our screen we have the British equivalent of a Clark Gable."

Donat's gentle, almost careless performance as the film's hero took some work on everyone's part; on the first day of shooting, Hitchcock deliberately "lost" the key to the handcuffs to force some bonding between his leading man and the slightly frosty MADELEINE CARROLL. It must have been successful. In the end, Donat's easy, offhanded grace not only sets the film's tone but also creates the template for later, seemingly effortless (albeit truly difficult) Hitchcock performances from MICHAEL REDGRAVE and CARY GRANT.

Hitchcock wanted the actor for his next film, *SECRET AGENT* (and, indeed, for several of his films to come), but Donat was always unavailable, often due to ill health; later, Donat went on to star in *The Citadel*, for which he got an Oscar nomination as best actor, and *Goodbye, Mr. Chips*, for which he won (beating out, among others, Clark Gable for *Gone with the Wind* and JAMES STEWART for *Mr. Smith Goes to Washington*).

There was at the time some gossip that Donat's had been a sympathy vote because he was ill; indeed, he had quietly suffered a breakdown in 1937 and, thanks to increasingly debilitating asthma attacks, would work only sporadically, sometimes having to withdraw from productions. According to some, his illness was mostly psychosomatic, springing from his own internalized fears and self-doubt; he was, they said, simply too gentle for this life.

He died in London at 53 of a brain tumor.

References

"Mr. Donat Captures Hollywood," *Milwaukee Journal*, July 9, 1939, https://news .google.com/newspapers?nid=1499&dat= 19390709&id=JYdSAAAAIBAJ&sjid=GC IEAAAAIBAJ&pg=5946,5134780&hl=en; "Robert Donat," *IMDb*, http://www.imdb .com/name/nm0232196/bio?ref_=nm _ov_bio_sm; "Robert Donat Tells His Life Story," *Courier-Mail*, June 23, 1938, http:// trove.nla.gov.au/ndp/del/article/40995382; Donald Spoto, *Spellbound by Beauty: Alfred Hitchcock and His Leading Ladies* (New York: Harmony Books, 2008), 54–55; David Thomson, *The New Biographical Dictionary of Film* (New York: Knopf, 2002), 241.

DOR, KARIN (1938–)

Wiesbaden-born performer who made her German-movie debut as a teenager and soon became a regular in Edgar Wallace thrillers and international productions like *The Face of Fu Manchu*. Her appearance as the duplicitous Helga in the Bond blockbuster *You Only Live Twice* brought a brief flurry of guest shots on American TV shows and a role in *TOPAZ*, where she played the passionate Juanita de Cordoba.

"Of all the directors I have worked with, Hitchcock was my favorite," she said in 2012. "I adored and loved him as a director. At the end of every filming day on *Topaz* he would come to my trailer with his secretary and they would bring me German recipes because he knew I liked to cook. We had a marvelous, immediate, simpatico relationship."

It ended after the film, however, and her career after *Topaz* was intermittent, once again swinging back and forth between international thrillers and German television, where she continues to be busy today.

References

"Karin Dor," *IMDb*, http://www.imdb.com/name/nm0233312/bio?ref_=nm_ov_bio_sm; "Karin Dor," *Listal*, http://www.listal.com/karin-dor.

DOUBLES

Hitchcock's CATHOLIC education gave him a "consciousness of good and evil, that both are always with me," he once said. But if the director felt they were always inside him, then in his movies they are often externalized, as characters are split in two or doubled by their reversed reflections. (In one of the episodes he directed for *ALFRED HITCHCOCK PRESENTS*, "THE CASE OF MR. PELHAM," the twinning actually becomes real.) These doppelgänger stories are not quite the same as his MISTAKEN IDENTITY plots, which usually set a light-hearted chase in motion (until the grimly sober *THE WRONG MAN*, which tries to atone for them). Those stories are about the fluidity of IDENTITY; his "double" movies are about its complexity and the way that one person can contain two characters—or two characters can each contain half of one person.

You can see this in *THE LODGER*, when the young mysterious gentleman steps out of the fog to rent a room. At first, we—and eventually his landlady—come to suspect he is the Avenger, the serial killer prowling London and murdering BLONDES. Eventually it's revealed that

he is, in fact, a vigilante in pursuit of the Avenger, hoping to make him pay for murdering his sister. But doesn't that make him an avenger as well? A remorseless killer who has put himself above the law?

Or in *SHADOW OF A DOUBT*, where young Charlotte so eagerly wishes for her Uncle Charlie to come visit to shake up her staid family the way only he can. She adores him, feels a kinship with him—and he encourages that and the slightly superior sense they share that—compared to the sleepwalkers around them—they alone are alive and alert.

And in *STRANGERS ON A TRAIN*, where Bruno and Guy—over an ordered "pair of doubles" in the bar car—talk about their similar situations. Guy is trapped in a marriage to a shrewish woman; Bruno feels under the thumb of his insensitive father. They have so much in common. If only they could—"criss-cross!"—solve each other's problems. The difference, of course, is that Charlotte and Guy are perfectly normal, charming people who sometimes see others as annoying or troublesome; Charlie and Bruno are sociopaths who often see others as inhuman and expendable.

But in Hitchcock's unforgiving world there is only a small difference between the intention and the act; once someone has had an evil thought, the evil is already half-committed. There is really less difference between Charlotte and Charlie, Guy and Bruno, than we might like to think. And so the connection between those two characters is constantly underlined, both through clear camera grammar (*Shadow of a Doubt* introducing Charlie and Charlotte in separate but parallel series of shots, as they gloomily get up from bed; *Strangers on a Train* intercutting between the two men's striding legs) and more subtle visual cues (Charlie and Charlotte going to the "Til Two" bar, Miriam's dropped glasses showing two images of Guy looming above her).

In other Hitchcock films, though, the doubling occurs less as a copy than as a reflection—the same yet subtly reversed (a metaphor the director often makes concrete by making sure the scenes include mirrors, a visual motif continued in *VERTIGO* and *PSYCHO*).

Doubling is, in fact, the entire theme of *Vertigo*, in which Scottie tries to combine two women who are, or seem to be, polar opposites. Madeleine is sleek, chic, and contained, her hair as perfectly done and endlessly circling as one of San Francisco's streets; Judy is brassy, uneducated, and alive, her body moving restlessly under her clothes as if trying to break free. The two are completely unalike—until, we realize ahead of Scottie, that they are the same person. The Madeleine he thought he knew, in fact, doesn't exist; she's a construct, and he's merely telling the performer who played her that he prefers the fictional character she created to the real person she is (a painful preference that many real-life actresses know well and KIM NOVAK makes particularly, personally heartbreaking here).

The division of identity begins right at the start of *Psycho*, as Marion, the quiet responsible secretary, stands before a mirror with an envelope of money in her hands and deliberately reinvents herself as a runaway embezzler. (She even soon changes from nice-girl white lingerie to bad-girl black.) But her personality crisis is nothing compared to the man she'll soon meet, Norman Bates, who literally dresses up and takes on the personality of his mother "whenever danger or desire" suddenly appears.

Yet complex as he is, Norman may be even more complicated than he or we know. (He's certainly beyond the grasp of the psychiatrist who tries to sum him up in a diagnosis.) Norman murders Marion because he thinks his mother would,

because he thinks of his mother as puritanical and jealous. Yet, we find out later, his mother had a lover—and it was Norman who found them together in bed and murdered them both. So who really is the violent puritan? Isn't Norman's disguise as his murderous mother just a way of disguising his own ugly, homicidal urges?

The movie continues the theme of doubling as Marion's lover, Sam, returns to the story and sister Lila makes an appearance. That Lila looks like Marion is easily explained, but Sam's resemblance to Norman Bates—brought home as they face each other over the motel check-in desk, a mirror on the wall—is more striking. Both tall, good-looking, dark-haired men, yes—but also both men with debts and small family businesses, Sam struggling to pay off his father's bills and his own alimony, Norman trying to keep going a motel where few people check in and even fewer check out. Couldn't Sam have been Norman with more kinks in his childhood? Couldn't Norman have been Sam if his own father had never died? (That Hitchcock cast the dull square JOHN GAVIN as Sam and the boyishly charming ANTHONY PERKINS as Norman only makes the contrast, and our conflicting feelings, more dramatic.)

Of course, Hitchcock was not only a Catholic schoolboy but also a child who memorized TRAIN timetables for fun and a teenager who excelled at draftsmanship; he loved patterns and order, and much of the doubling in his films speaks to that. There are husband-and-wife heroes and villains in *THE MAN WHO KNEW TOO MUCH* and two very different couples circling each other in *FAMILY PLOT*. Those doublings spring chiefly from his insistence on balance, in storyline as well as composition.

These, though—the competing avengers of *The Lodger*, the murderer/victims of *Shadow of a Doubt* and *Strangers on a Train*, the many, sometimes fractured mirror images of *Psycho*—remind us that there is good and evil in all of us. As the Jesuits' teachings, Hitchcock insisted, reminded him every day of his life.

References
Richard Alleva, "The Catholic Hitchcock: A Director's Sense of Good and Evil," *Commonweal*, July 12, 2010, https://www.com monwealmagazine.org/catholic-hitchcock; Donald Spoto, *The Dark Side of Genius: The Life of Alfred Hitchcock* (New York: Da Capo Press, 1999), 20.

excuse to begin interspersing clips of US presidents and Soviet premiers. That turns what began as an intriguing essay into a muddled polemic and leaves a film about identity without one.

Reference
Stephen Whitty, "'Double Take' Movie Review: Alfred Hitchcock Times Two," *NJ.com*, http://www.nj.com/entertainment/ movies/index.ssf/2010/06/double_take _movie_review_alfred_hitchcock_times _two.html.

DOUBLE TAKE (BELGIUM 2009)

DIRECTOR: Johan Grimonprez.
SCREENPLAY: Johan Grimonprez, from a story by Tom McCarthy.
PRODUCERS: Emmy Oost, Nichole Gerhards, Hanneke Van der Tas.
CINEMATOGRAPHY: Martin Testar.
EDITORS: Dieter Diependaele, Tyler Hubby.
ORIGINAL MUSIC: Christian Halten.
CAST: Alfred Hitchcock, Janet Leigh, Farley Granger (file footage).
RUNNING TIME: 80 minutes. Color and black and white.
RELEASED BY: Kino International.

DOWNHILL (GB 1928)

DIRECTOR: Alfred Hitchcock.
SCREENPLAY: Eliot Standard, based on the play *Down Hill* by Constance Collier and Ivor Novello.
PRODUCERS: Uncredited (Sir Michael Balcon, C. M. Woolf).
CINEMATOGRAPHY: Claude L. McDonnell.
EDITOR: Lionel Rich (Ivor Montagu, uncredited).
CAST: Ivor Novello (Roddy Berwick), Robin Irvine (Tim Wakely).
RUNNING TIME: 80 minutes. Black and white.
RELEASED THROUGH: Wardour Films.

An experimental "documentary" that conflates a Jorge Luis Borges essay on IDENTITY with a fictional ANECDOTE about the day that, called away from the set of *THE BIRDS*, Alfred Hitchcock met a future version of himself gone back in time.

The idea is certainly a unique one, as is its execution; most of the film is made up of cleverly repurposed, re-edited, and otherwise revised footage, drawn from Hitchcock home movies, various newsreels, and clips from many of his films (including his own cameos). It might have made a brilliant short, particularly if it stuck to Hitchcock's own theme of DOUBLES and opposites—alas, the early '60s period isn't happenstance but an

Roddy and Tim are best friends at a posh English boarding school, despite the fact that Roddy is born to wealth and Tim is there on a scholarship, and they share everything—including a flirtation with a waitress in the town. But then Tim gets her pregnant, and she nastily blames Roddy—and Roddy accepts the blame, feeling he can weather the trouble easier.

The trouble, though, is worse than he expects—he is not only expelled from school but also shunned by his father. Leaving home, handsome but unsuited for any real occupation, he becomes an actor—eventually losing even that position and sinking to the status of second-rate gigolo, separating older women from small sums of money.

Eventually penniless and dreadfully ill, he's shipped home by some sailors who take pity on him—and the prodigal son is welcomed back by his father, who's since learned about the terrible lie and his son's sacrifice.

Thematically, this is another of the early British Hitchcocks that don't seem to fit easily into his career. The story is crudely melodramatic, and there are few of the concerns that we see in his later films. Still, if the story—with its noblesse oblige, old school ties, and family scandal—feels Victorian, then so was Hitchcock. And if its concept—right down to a stripped-to-the-waist shot of matinee idol IVOR NOVELLO—seems calculatedly commercial, then so, too, could be Hitchcock.

It is interesting, though, to see flashes of his favorite theme, GUILT, coupled with the rarer one of self-sacrifice. (It happens very rarely in Hitchcock films, and it's almost always a woman's choice.) It's a film full of dangerous and domineering women, as well. And visually, it shows both his skill with pure imagery (like *THE RING*, there are very few title cards; like *VERTIGO*, the COLOR green signals danger; like *SPELLBOUND*, there is an interesting hallucinatory sequence) and his urge for concrete metaphor. (As Novello's status is slipping, we cut a little obviously to a subway escalator—headed down, of course.)

While not quite the follow-up to *THE LODGER* that both Novello and Hitchcock might have hoped—and GAINSBOROUGH PICTURES was counting on—it still pointed to greater triumphs to come, at least for the filmmaker. Novello's star, sadly, was already slipping.

References

Mark Duguid, "Downhill," *BFI Screenonline*, http://www.screenonline.org.uk/film/id/437747/index.html; Geoffrey Macnab, "Homme Fatal," *Guardian*, January 10, 2004, http://the.hitchcock.zone/wiki/The_Guardian_%2810/Jan/2004%29_-_Homme_fatal:_Ivor_Novello; François Truffaut, *Hitchcock/Truffaut*, rev. ed. (New York: Touchstone, 1985), 51.

DU MAURIER, DAPHNE (1907–1989)

London-born daughter of actor Sir Gerald du Maurier and granddaughter of author George du Maurier. A skilled and popular novelist whose stories often combined Gothic menace and doomed romance, she was a loyal favorite of filmmakers.

Hitchcock adapted her works three times, for *JAMAICA INN*, *REBECCA*, and *THE BIRDS*, although each experience was quite different. His version of *Jamaica Inn* changed the story (and neither she nor the director was pleased with the finished film); his version of *Rebecca* was as faithful as the Hollywood CENSORS would allow (and was an enormous hit). *The Birds*, meanwhile, was a more distant connection; although she had written a short story of the same name about unexplained avian attacks, neither the setting of the movie's story nor its characters are hers.

Her many other novels include *Frenchman's Creek*, *My Cousin Rachel*, and *The Scapegoat*, all made into films; in addition, she adapted *Rebecca* into a stage play, and her short story "Don't Look Now" served as a springboard for the Nicolas Roeg movie.

Hitchcock knew the du Mauriers, mostly through his admiration of Sir Gerald, who appeared in *LORD CAMBER'S LADIES* and served as the butt of several of the director's typically rude practical JOKES. (He once invited the man to a costume party; when the actor arrived, decked out in face paint and kilt like some ancient Scot, he found that the dress code was black tie.) Hitchcock's relationship with Daphne was more professional and less satisfying; producer DAVID O. SELZNICK's insistence that not a word of *Rebecca* be changed (a demand pushed hard by the author, who had loathed *Jamaica Inn*) was a particular thorn, and it's hard not to think that her reappearance in the credits of *The Birds* was simply a canny move by Hitchcock to associate a very unusual property with a best-selling name.

Interestingly, du Maurier may not have restricted her mysteries to her fiction; after the film *Rebecca* was released, a Brazilian author came forward to say that du Maurier had lifted material from her own novel about a drab second wife, *The Successor*; after du Maurier's death, a history of her family also claimed that she was bisexual, a fact she had guiltily hid from her homophobic father. Of course it is true that, on the face of it, both *The Successor* and *Rebecca* owe their own large debt to *Jane Eyre* and that, conveniently, the dead are unable to bring lawsuits. It seems fitting that, decades after her death at 81, Daphne du Maurier would still have a bit of mystery swirling around her, like the fog of Manderley.

References

Rudy Behlmer, ed., *Memo from David O. Selznick* (New York: Viking Press, 1972), 266–72; Peter J. Conradi, "The Fantastical World of the du Mauriers," *Financial Times*, March 1, 2013, http://www.ft.com/cms/s/2/4d0dc798-7f6e-11e2-97f6-00144feabdc0.html; "Jamaica Inn," *Irish Film Institute*, http://issuu.com/irishfilminstitute/docs/irish_film_institute_march_2013; Harrison Smith, "Was 'Rebecca' Plagiarized?" *Saturday Review of Literature*, November 29, 1941, http://www.unz.org/Pub/SaturdayRev-1941nov29-00003.

DURGNAT, RAYMOND (1932–2002)

Film writer and educator who moved between universities and film journals, England and America. His many books on filmmakers and films include ones on Greta Garbo, Samuel Fuller, and *W. R.: Mysteries of the Organism*. In 1974, he published *The Strange Case of Alfred Hitchcock*, at the time a rare and therefore important bit of naysaying; the more laudatory *A Long Hard Look at 'Psycho'* came out almost 30 years later.

Unafraid to be a lone voice in a profession often prey to consensus, Durgnat was a politically engaged man who still referred to Marxist theory as a "trap," a devotee of great directors who nonetheless called the AUTEUR THEORY "moth-eaten dogma." His writing could be full of insight and color (he was also a poet) but also meander and sometimes seem willfully obscure.

His first Hitchcock book made the common critics' mistake of reviewing other reviewers, attacking many of the films for not being what their most fervent supporters claimed them to be; his book on *Psycho* was more on point and quite exhaustive but sadly arrived posthumously. Durgnat died at age 69 in London.

Reference

Kevin Gough-Yates, "Raymond Durgnat," *Guardian*, May 20, 2002, http://www.theguardian.com/news/2002/may/24/guardianobituaries.

EASY VIRTUE (GB 1928)

DIRECTOR: Alfred Hitchcock.
SCREENPLAY: Eliot Stannard, based on the play by Noel Coward.
PRODUCER: Sir Michael Balcon.
CINEMATOGRAPHY: Claude L. McDonnell.
EDITOR: Uncredited (Ivor Montagu).
CAST: Isabel Jeans (Larita Filton), Franklin Dyall (Aubrey Filton), Robin Irvine (John Whittaker), Eric Bransby Williams (Claude), Violet Farebrother (John's mother).
RUNNING TIME: 94 minutes. Black and white.
RELEASED THROUGH: Woolf and Freedman Film Service.

Blamed for an artist's suicide, unjustly accused of adultery, and divorced by her wealthy but disreputable husband, beautiful but misunderstood Larita leaves England for the French Riviera to hopefully begin a new life far away from the headlines. There, she swiftly meets, falls in love with, and marries John, a wealthy young man. But he seems far less worldly than she, and so Larita keeps her past a secret.

The couple returns to England, where John introduces her to his family. His immediately disapproving mother finds Larita's face vaguely familiar, though, and she grows even more suspicious. Eventually, at a formal party, the truth is revealed, and the hypocritical gentry draw back in horror from this woman of "easy virtue"; Larita agrees to a divorce so that John can marry a far more suitable young woman.

To make a silent movie out of a Noel Coward play seems a stubborn exercise in futility—like making a statue out of a symphony—but the 1924 comedy-drama had been a stage hit in both America and London, and Hitchcock's bosses at GAINSBOROUGH were eager to adapt it for the screen. Still, the screenplay heavily rewrites its source, beginning with a courtroom scene, proceeding to a flashback, and then cutting to the Riviera; only when the couple arrives back home in England does Coward's original play begin in earnest. And even then, only a brief exchange or two of dialogue makes its way into the title cards, most of which were written by Hitchcock.

"It contained the worst title I've ever written," Hitchcock told FRANÇOIS TRUFFAUT years later, referring to the trial scene. "The photographers gather outside. Eventually she appears at the courthouse STAIRS, her arms out, and says 'Shoot, there's nothing left to kill!'"

Although there are some more inventive moments in the film—such as a scene in which we follow the dramatic progress of a conversation solely by watching the face of the switchboard operator listening

Rhonda Fleming, surrounded by eyes—a constant Hitchcockian symbol—on the dream-sequence set of *Spellbound. United Artists/Photofest © United Artists*

in—and touches of those favorite themes of GUILT and domineering MOTHERS, it felt, as *DOWNHILL* did, very much like a work for hire. A financial failure, it was the director's last film for Gainsborough; he would now move on to BRITISH INTERNATIONAL PICTURES. The play was filmed again in 2008 as a rather more obvious comedy with Jessica Biel.

References

David Robinson, "When Hitchcock Adapted Noel Coward," *Times*, April 28, 1977, http://the.hitchcock.zone/wiki/The_Times_%2828/Apr/1977%29_-_When_Hitchcock_adapted_Noel_Coward; Donald Spoto, *The Dark Side of Genius: The Life of Alfred Hitchcock* (New York: Da Capo Press, 1999), 98–101; François Truffaut,

Hitchcock/Truffaut: Revised Edition (New York: Touchstone, 1985), 51–52.

EDOUART, FARCIOT
(1894–1980)
California-born cinematographer whose colorful Gallic name enlivened decades of movie credits. The son of a portrait photographer, he began working as a studio cameraman while still in his teens.

After serving in World War I (where he briefly was attached to the camouflage division), he returned to Hollywood, where he appropriately specialized in disguising fantasy as reality. Edouart's specialty was in rear projection, a process he helped pioneer and refine, in which live action and a projected background are combined. Although the results can seem crude today, particularly if done on the cheap, Edouart had a light touch and a constant desire to push things further; his refinements won him 10 technical and scientific awards from the Academy of Motion Picture Arts and Sciences over his long career.

Occasionally called upon for science fiction films (the bold-for-their-time *Dr. Cyclops* and *When Worlds Collide*), Edouart was even more prized for his ability to lend a verisimilitude to epics like *Lives of a Bengal Lancer* and *It's a Mad, Mad, Mad, Mad World*. Still, perhaps his best work combined reality and fantasy, daily life and dreams—as in his work on Billy Wilder's *The Lost Weekend* and Hitchcock's *VERTIGO*. He retired in 1974 after 52 years as head of Paramount's special effects department and died at 85 in Kenwood, CA.

References
"Farciot Edouart," *Film Reference*, http://www.filmreference.com/Writers-and-Production-Artists-De-Edo/Edouart-Farciot.html; "Farciot Edouart," *IMDb*, http://www.imdb.com/name/nm0249643/bio?ref_=nm_ov_bio_sm.

ELSTREE CALLING (GB 1930)

DIRECTORS: Andre Charlot, Alfred Hitchcock, Jack Hulbert, Paul Murray.
SCREENPLAY: Adrien Brunel, Walter C. Mycroft, Val Valentine.
PRODUCER: John Maxwell.
CINEMATOGRAPHY: Claude Friese-Greene.
EDITOR: Emile de Ruelle, A. C. Hammond.
ORIGINAL MUSIC: Sydney Baynes, Teddy Brown, John Reynders, Idris Lewis.
CAST: Donald Calthrop, Gordon Harker, Tommy Handley, Anna May Wong, as themselves.
RUNNING TIME: 86 minutes. Black and white.
RELEASED THROUGH: Wardour Films.

Britain's first movie musical was actually a revue meant to compete with current Hollywood portmanteaus, such as *Paramount on Parade*, stitching together an assortment of comic sketches and songs within a loose framework (in this case, a family frustratingly trying to tune into the broadcast on their still-experimental television set).

The directors were all currently under contract to BRITISH INTERNATIONAL PICTURES; the performers are mostly music hall STARS of the period (apart from Anna May Wong, a refugee from Hollywood racism trying to capitalize on her recent British success in *Piccadilly*); the sketches, as suggested by the presence of *CHAMPAGNE* screenwriter Walter C. Mycroft, were mediocre at best.

Hitchcock's own contribution is unclear. One source confidently credits him with directing the GORDON HARKER scenes (likely, as the two had already worked on three other pictures together, including *THE RING*), others suggest he did the murder sketch as well and reshot some other scenes with DONALD CALTHROP, who'd just appeared in *BLACKMAIL*. Yet another source suggests he spent no more than a day on the set.

Hitchcock's take on the entire effort? "Of no interest whatever," he told FRANÇOIS TRUFFAUT.

References

"First British Talkie Revue," *Yorkshire Post*, February 11, 1930, http://the.hitch cock.zone/wiki/Yorkshire_Post_%2811/ Feb/1930%29_-_First_British_Talkie _Review; Patrick McGilligan, *Alfred Hitchcock: A Life in Darkness and Light* (New York: HarperCollins, 2003), 132–33; Donald Spoto, *The Dark Side of Genius: The Life of Alfred Hitchcock* (New York: Da Capo Press, 1999), 122–23; François Truffaut, *Hitchcock/Truffaut*, rev. ed. (New York: Touchstone, 1985), 69.

EMERY, JOHN (1905–1964)

The son of two theater actors, Emery excelled at playing charming, romantic, but almost inevitably undependable gentlemen. A skilled Shakespearean on the Broadway stage, in Hollywood he became a sort of second-string John Barrymore (who had befriended him early in his career) and made his film debut in James Whale's *The Road Back* in 1937.

For Alfred Hitchcock, Emery would be the suspicious Dr. Fleurot in *SPELLBOUND* and, years later, a worm who turned in "Servant Problem," an episode of *ALFRED HITCHCOCK PRESENTS*; in between his other jobs included various parts on TV's *I Love Lucy*, playing Vincent Price's theatrical nemesis in *The Mad Magician*, and spearheading the scientific mission of *Rocketship X-M*. His most dramatic role, however, was undoubtedly surviving four years as TALLULAH BANKHEAD's husband. "It was like the rise, decline and fall of the Roman Empire," he observed later with typical cool humor. He died in New York at 59 of cancer.

References

"John Emery," *IMDb*, http://www.imdb .com/name/nm0256305/bio?ref_=nm_ov _bio_sm; Alfred E. Twomey and Arthur F. McClure, *The Versatiles: Supporting Character Players in the Cinema, 1930–1955* (New York: Castle Books, 1969), 90.

ENGLISH COLONY

Although British actors had been part of the Hollywood community since its inception, with music hall comics from Charlie Chaplin to Stan Laurel finding a happy home in silent comedies, the talkies brought an insatiable need for people who could handle dialogue—which meant, for gangster pictures and snappy comedies, an influx of New Yorkers and, for period pictures and romances, a veritable British invasion of Los Angeles.

"Of recent years the English set in Hollywood has become an established thing," an Australian newspaper reported back to its readers in 1937. "They have formed their own cricket club, polo teams, tennis club and golf club. They hunt together, play together, swim together—all united by the common bond—loyalty to the Union Jack."

It was a clubby group and could be an exceedingly insular and judgmental one, and when the Hitchcocks arrived in America in 1939, they did not feel compelled to join. (DONALD SPOTO goes further, suggesting they felt snubbed by the expats; PATRICK MCGILLIGAN, however, disagrees and insists they mixed easily when they cared to.) Hitchcock did draw on its members, though, for *REBECCA*—C. AUBREY SMITH, Col. Julyan in that film, was pretty much the colony's grand old man—and many of the supporting actors in that film and in Hitchcock films to come (LEO G. CARROLL, NIGEL BRUCE) came from its ranks as well.

After the war, the colony began to dissipate, dispersed by a new wave of international productions and ignored by a new generation of angry young men and women. It is lampooned (along with the American funeral industry) quite brilliantly by Evelyn Waugh in his novel *The Loved One*; he was obviously taking notes during his 1947 trip to Hollywood to discuss the adaptation of *Brideshead Revisited*. (Wisely, Waugh accepted MGM's lavish hospitality but denied them the book rights.)

References

"The English Colony in Hollywood," *Sydney Morning Herald*, March 2, 1937, http://trove.nla.gov.au/ndp/del/article/17348532; Patrick McGilligan, *Alfred Hitchcock: A Life in Darkness and Light* (New York: HarperCollins, 2003), 243–44; Donald Spoto, *The Dark Side of Genius: The Life of Alfred Hitchcock* (New York: Da Capo Press, 1999), 210, 216.

EROICA

Beethoven's Symphony no. 3, at first dedicated to Napoleon, whom the composer saw as heroically spreading the ideals of liberty; he was, when the French leader declared himself emperor, to violently change his opinion. An old 78 record of the work figures in *PSYCHO*, discovered by Lila Crane in Norman Bates's cluttered bedroom, where it both suggests the disordered state of Norman's mind (classical records jockeying for space with stuffed animals) and suggests—like the mysterious privately bound hardcover she finds—"erotica" as well. It is one of the few classical compositions to be directly referenced in Hitchcock's films; the other, Richard Wagner's *Tristan und Isolde*, shows up as a record album in Annie's home in *THE BIRDS* and is clearly a musical inspiration for BERNARD HERRMANN's score for *VERTIGO*.

Reference

"Historical Overview," *Beethoven's Eroica*, http://www.beethovenseroica.com/Pg2_hist/history.html.

ESMOND, JILL (1908–1990)

London-born child of two actors who would end up following them onstage after some training at the Royal Academy of Dramatic Arts. By the late '20s, she was an established actress, with successes both on the West End and on Broadway, and a cultured and elegant persona. In 1930, she married LAURENCE OLIVIER, who was then still trying to find fame as an actor but was a very persistent suitor; the next year she made her film debut in Hitchcock's *THE SKIN GAME*, another of the director's early-career stage adaptations, playing the member of a respectable upper-class family (which is, nonetheless, willing to consider blackmail when necessary).

Esmond dialed back her own career as Olivier's grew, a decision she would regret when he began an affair with Vivien Leigh; although Esmond named Leigh in the 1940 divorce, she rarely spoke about the split afterward and resumed working, although her moment had passed. Her last film was *A Man Called Peter* in 1955; she died at 82 in London, having survived Olivier by one year. She never remarried.

References

Burt A. Folkart, "Jill Esmond: Actress and Former Wife of Olivier," *Los Angeles Times*, August 1, 1990, http://articles.latimes.com/1990-08-01/news/mn-1554_1_jill-esmond; "Jill Esmond," *IMDb*, http://www.imdb.com/name/nm0260728; Donald Spoto, *Laurence Olivier: A Biography* (New York: Harper Paperbacks, 1993), 83–84, 173.

EVELYN, JUDITH (1909–1967)

Born in Seneca, SD, she made her Broadway debut two days before Pearl Harbor in the thriller *Angel Street*. She would go on to work regularly on the stage and quite busily in television, although her parts in movies were generally small.

Interestingly, her two most famous movie roles were silent. In *REAR WINDOW*, she was Miss Lonelyhearts, the depressed single woman across the courtyard from JAMES STEWART; in *The Tingler*, she was Mrs. Higgins, the deaf-mute wife of the theater owner who is given a memorable (and, to fans of *LES DIABOLIQUES*, familiar) bathroom scare.

Evelyn appeared in two episodes of *ALFRED HITCHCOCK PRESENTS*, as well as many other TV anthologies, but her oddest brush with history came in 1939, when she and her father were sailing from Europe to Canada aboard the *Athena*; it was torpedoed in the Irish Sea by a German U-boat. It was the first submarine attack of the war, and all but six passengers drowned, her father among them.

Evelyn died in New York of cancer at 58.

References

"Biography: Judith Evelyn," *TCM*, http://www.tcm.com/tcmdb/person/58803|90572/Judith-Evelyn/biography.html; "Judith Evelyn," *IMDb*, http://www.imdb.com/name/nm0263393/bio?ref_=nm_ov_bio_sm.

EXPRESSIONISM

Twentieth-century artistic movement that rejected many of the realist tendencies in art, literature, and dance, often using exaggeration, symbolism, and deliberately fantastic effects to evoke a mood of mental anguish and emotional despair. Although international in nature, it was especially strong in Germany between the wars, where anxious artists were particularly attuned to a coming age of dehumanization.

Expressionism soon found fertile ground in the new art of cinema; *The Cabinet of Dr. Caligari*, made in 1920, is generally considered the best early example, with its cockeyed sets, painted shadows, and mentally unstable narrator.

The movement was a strong, early influence on Hitchcock, who by the mid-'20s had been sent by SIR MICHAEL BALCON to helm several joint productions in Germany. Always an alert and eager student, Hitchcock would observe firsthand what filmmakers like F. W. MURNAU were doing—he even watched him on the set of *The Last Laugh*—and incorporate it into his own work. Like them, he would develop a determination to dramatize how people's lives could be caught up in large and faceless forces and an urge to express those emotional states in purely visual yet not necessarily realistic ways.

"*THE LODGER* is the first picture possibly influenced by my period in Germany," he reflected later, perhaps referring to its shots through transparent floors or recurring close-ups of flashing neon signs. But it was only the first picture. The shadows of German expressionism—the empty cavernous sets of *REBECCA*, the distorted image of the murder in *STRANGERS ON A TRAIN*, the dark romantic fatalism of *VERTIGO*—would fall over Hitchcock's work for decades to come.

References

Siegfried Kracauer, *From Caligari to Hitler: A Psychological History of the German Film* (Princeton, NJ: Princeton University Press, 2004), 68–75; Patrick McGilligan, *Alfred Hitchcock: A Life in Darkness and Light* (New York: HarperCollins, 2003), 63–64; Donald Spoto, *The Dark Side of Genius: The Life of Alfred Hitchcock* (New York: Da Capo Press, 1999), 67–71.

EYE

People watching people watching other people—this is the hall of mirrors that a Hitchcock film can become, as cinema audiences (who are, by definition, paying VOYEURS) are lured into stories about spies, peeping toms, and stalking serial killers.

The plot device of sweaty-palmed voyeurism and the artist's choice of the pitilessly appraising MALE GAZE occur again and again in these films, but both find their symbol in the human eye.

In *STRANGERS ON A TRAIN*, it's symbolized in the glasses that Miriam whips off, flirtatiously, before her murder—not only showing her own blindness to the coming danger but also then giving us a distorted view of Bruno's own twisted world. In *REAR WINDOW*, it's cartoonishly emphasized, absurdly exaggerated into the giant lens of a camera—like some monstrous phallus balanced carefully on Jeff's knee as he stares out of his own window and into other rooms, other lives.

And in *PSYCHO*, another film about looking, the eyes are everywhere—in the sudden suspicious glance Marion gets as she drives out of town with the stolen money, in the large-lashed gaze Norman turns on her as she undresses, and in Marion's own final unblinking stare, as sightless as those of the stuffed birds on Norman's walls or the hollows in Mrs. Bates's skull.

Yes, in Hitchcock's world, the eye is the window to the soul—but that soul is often a very dark and sunless place, indeed.

FAMILY PLOT (US 1976)

DIRECTOR: Alfred Hitchcock.
SCREENPLAY: Ernest Lehman, based on *The Rainbird Pattern* by Victor Canning.
PRODUCER: Uncredited (Alfred Hitchcock).
CINEMATOGRAPHY: Leonard J. South.
EDITOR: J. Terry Williams.
ORIGINAL MUSIC: John Williams.
CAST: Karen Black (Fran), Bruce Dern (George Lumley), William Devane (Arthur Adamson), Barbara Harris (Blanche Tyler), Cathleen Nesbitt (Julia Rainbird).
RUNNING TIME: 121 minutes. Color.
RELEASED THROUGH: Universal.

Blanche makes a modest living running séances and giving psychic readings for gullible clients, her insights helped along occasionally by information from cab-driver boyfriend (and would-be actor) George, who sometimes plays private detective. One day, instead of her usual "sardines," however, Blanche hooks a whale—Mrs. Rainbird, an elderly millionaire who wants to find a long-missing, given-up-for-adoption heir.

George and Blanche go on the case, but what they don't realize is that the heir doesn't want to be found—he long ago murdered his adoptive parents, changed his name to Arthur Adamson, and is now a high-stakes kidnapper who, with his glamorous lover Fran, is collecting a small fortune in ransoms, which he demands be paid in jewels.

Realizing he's being investigated and assuming the worst, Adamson has a confederate try to kill Blanche and George by sabotaging their car's brakes. It doesn't work, though, and eventually Blanche goes to Arthur's home to tell him about the inheritance—except she spies his latest kidnapping victim. Arthur decides to kill Blanche, but George arrives and helps lock the criminals up and calls the police—while Blanche finds the glittering ransom.

Family Plot ends with Blanche winking at the audience—which, in a way, is very much how Hitchcock ended his career. Although he hoped otherwise at the time, this was the director's last film—and, like the final works of many great artists, from Shakespeare on, it is one of light fantasy and forgiveness. Although there is murder in its backstory, it is one of the least violent of Hitchcock's films (and a stark contrast to his previous one, *FRENZY*); it ends with its desperate criminals locked in their own cozy cell, the police on the way, and a nice fat reward due to be paid. No wonder Blanche is so happy.

The story—adapted by ERNEST LEHMAN, who knew Hitchcock's tastes well, having written *NORTH BY NORTH-*

Cary Grant and Joan Fontaine in *Suspicion*. The actress's second film with the director, it won her the Oscar. *RKO Radio Pictures/Photofest © RKO Radio Pictures*

WEST and worked with him on *NO BAIL FOR THE JUDGE*—touches lightly on favorite Hitchcock themes and devices. There are, for example, the mismatched/ mirrored couples—the clumsy investigators George and Blanche versus the cool criminals Arthur and Fran. There is also

a nicely arbitrary bit of narrative misdirection—as when, having lulled us into thinking this is a story about a daffy *Blithe Spirit* medium, Hitchcock has George and Blanche drive past Fran, a mysterious femme fatale in dark glasses, and abruptly has the camera leave them and follow her story instead. (It's like the bait-and-switch plotting of *PSYCHO*—although done, as so much of this film is, in good fun.) And there's a lovely example of MONTAGE, in which—cutting almost exclusively between a two-shot of George and Blanche in their car and point-of-view shots of what they see through the windshield—Hitchcock constructs a both minimally designed yet deliberately comical over-the-top scene of their car speeding out of control on a steep mountain road.

Yet for a director so obsessed with GUILT—and a story about murder, kidnapping, and fraud—*Family Plot* is, ultimately, a film about forgiveness. Mrs. Rainbird wants to forgive herself and bring her heir back into the family; Blanche and George need to accept each other for the flawed people they are. Only by forgetting their past can they move on with their futures.

Hitchcock always intended the film to be a bit of a romp and pushed for that from preproduction (when he urged Lehman to play things for comedy) through post- (when he encouraged composer JOHN WILLIAMS, with whom he had not worked before, to have fun with the score). That mood is sometimes overstressed. The image of George as a pseudo–Sherlock Holmes (complete with pipe) is awfully obvious; the harpsichord in Williams's music says "whimsical" a little too loudly. Sadly, the film—much of it shot on the UNIVERSAL backlot—also has a cheap, sort of second-string look, with some poor process shots (using a new optical process the studio pushed Hitchcock to use).

And, admittedly, the casting has a bit of a budget look to it, too, especially measured against the director's usual STAR-conscious demands. Initial thoughts, for George, had included Jack Nicholson and,

for Arthur, Roy Scheider; instead Hitchcock got BRUCE DERN and WILLIAM DEVANE. (KAREN BLACK was a different sort of compromise; only by casting a "name" as Fran would the studio allow Hitchcock to cast the lesser-known BARBARA HARRIS, whom he really wanted, as Blanche.)

Yet the casting works. The mischievous, elfin Harris steals the movie as the delightful Blanche, and Devane (who replaced the unsatisfactory Roy Thinnes after filming had already begun) is very good as the slickly villainous Arthur. Black is an interesting figure in her wig and glasses, and Dern is certainly more believably helpless than Nicholson would have been. In a way, the absence of stars actually helps the film—it feels more casual, more improvisational, more friendly.

More, well, forgiving.

References

Karen Black, interview with the author, July 1995; Bruce Dern, interview with the author, November 2014; Greg Garrett, "Hitchcock's Women on Hitchcock," *Literature Film Quarterly* (Spring 1999), http://the.hitchcock.zone/wiki/Literature_Film_Quarterly_%281999%29_-_Hitchcock%27s_women_on_Hitchcock; Patrick McGilligan, *Alfred Hitchcock: A Life in Darkness and Light* (New York: HarperCollins, 2003), 725–29; Robrt L. Pela, "Barbara Harris Knew Bill Clinton Was White Trash," *Phoenix New Times*, October 24, 2002, http://www.phoenixnewtimes.com/arts/barbara-harris-knew-bill-clinton-was-white-trash-6410220; Donald Spoto, *The Dark Side of Genius: The Life of Alfred Hitchcock* (New York: Da Capo Press, 1999), 527–38; François Truffaut, *Hitchcock/Truffaut*, rev. ed. (New York: Touchstone, 1985), 339–42.

THE FARMER'S WIFE (GB 1928)

DIRECTOR: Alfred Hitchcock.
SCREENPLAY: Eliot Stannard, based on the play by Eden Phillpotts.
PRODUCER: John Maxwell.
CINEMATOGRAPHY: Jack E. Cox.
EDITOR: Uncredited (Alfred Booth).
CAST: Jameson Thomas (Samuel Sweetland), Lillian Hall-Davis (Araminta Dench), Gordon Harker (Churdles Ash).
RUNNING TIME: 129 minutes. Black and white.
RELEASED THROUGH: Wardour Films.

Recently widowed and with his grown daughter now married and moved away, prosperous farmer Samuel Sweetland decides to remarry and, with the help of his servants Ash and Minta, comes up with a list of local "eligibles." Unfortunately, his courting skills are rusty, and he meets with one disaster after another—with one woman too neurotic, another uninterested, and a third rejecting him as too old. Returning home, though, Sweetland suddenly sees Minta not just as his faithful housekeeper but also as a warm and sympathetic soul. He proposes, and she accepts—much to the anger of one of the women who rejected him who's now decided perhaps he's not too old after all.

Hitchcock did several play adaptations during the early part of his career and several comedies, but *The Farmer's Wife* is perhaps the most successful. Although some of its interior scenes are staged a little flatly and ELIOT STANNARD's adaptation depends too heavily on titles, the film moves quickly, and there is some lovely location shooting in the English countryside.

And while the shoot itself wasn't particularly smooth—at one point the cameraman took ill and Hitchcock had to take over—at least it was all done with familiar and congenial colleagues largely from BRITISH INTERNATIONAL PICTURES. (Stannard is credited with eight Hitchcock screenplays; LILLIAN HALL-DAVIS and GORDON HARKER had been in *THE RING* and would soon appear in *CHAMPAGNE*, and both Harker and JAMESON THOMAS would return for the revue *ELSTREE CALLING*.) Afterward, Hitchcock celebrated the end of the shoot by hosting a lavish dinner for the cast (at which, in one of his practical JOKES, the waiters had been instructed to be as rude and clumsy as possible).

The film opened to good reviews, although only a few years later, Hitchcock would look back on it a little sadly, noting that Thomas had to leave his career to take care of his dying wife and that costar Hall-Davis, who had an "acute inferiority complex," had recently passed under "tragic circumstances." (She had, in fact, cut her throat and stuck her head in the gas oven.) For one of his most lighthearted films touched with physical comedy, it would always carry some grim memories.

References

Charles Barr, *English Hitchcock* (Petaluma, CA: Cameron Books, 2002), 52–53; Alfred Hitchcock, "My Screen Memories," *Film Weekly* (March 1936), http://the.hitchcock .zone/wiki/Film_Weekly_%281936%29 _-_My_Screen_Memories.

FETISHES

"Being tied to something," Hitchcock said to FRANÇOIS TRUFFAUT, as their epic INTERVIEW turned to the handcuffed hero in *THE LODGER*. "It's somewhere in the area of fetishism, isn't it?"

"I don't know, but I have noticed that handcuffs have a way of recurring in your movies," Truffaut replied a little cluelessly.

They got off the subject then, talking about photographs of arrested suspects, but Hitchcock tried to bring it back later. "There's also a SEXUAL connotation, I think," he says. "When I visited the Vice Museum in Paris I noticed there was considerable evidence of sexual aberrations through restraint. You should go there sometime."

But instead of exploring this, Truffaut—often more prize student than probing interviewer—brings up the title of an obscure F. W. MURNAU project before dropping the topic completely. Too bad.

Of course, as Truffaut also rightly—obviously—observed earlier, handcuffs are the "most concrete—the most immediate—symbol of the loss of freedom." And in many Hitchcock films, that symbol is sometimes visual (the various heroes and heroines linked together by a pair of police bracelets) and sometimes invisible (the heroes and heroines chained to domineering females, debts, duty, or dead parents). But yes, there's another connotation too, to handcuffs—to willing BONDAGE—and Hitchcock was clearly aware of it.

The "area of fetishism" is one that many Hitchcock films travel in, beginning with his own, not uncommon, fetish for BLONDES. Fair-haired women appear in many of his movies, sometimes as victims, sometimes as femmes fatales, and often as some shifting combination of the two, although it seems the women who deceive with hair dye or wigs (*VERTIGO, MARNIE, FAMILY PLOT*) are always the least worthy of the hero's trust and the most likely to find unhappiness.

The typical male's fetish for breasts and buttocks is not one Hitchcock movies indulge in, however; in fact, his heroines tend to have pleasant but relatively unremarkable figures, with voluptuousness (*Vertigo, PSYCHO*) somehow equated with sin and deceit. His camera, though, will linger on bare, vulnerable legs—the vacationers dawdling in their hotel room in *THE LADY VANISHES*, the terrified honeymooner in *Marnie*, Margot's writhing limbs in *DIAL M FOR MURDER*. Taken together, it indicates perhaps an obsession not so much with women's bodies or even women themselves as with innocence—rare, precious, and easily lost.

Moving beyond the fetishization of objects to actual practices, Hitchcock films examine several distinct sexual perversions. The first, of course, is VOYEURISM, which deserves its own entry, and occurs in many Hitchcock films, most famously *REAR WINDOW*. But then voyeurism is part and parcel of the art itself, the essential act from which cinema springs: A filmmaker takes pictures of people in intimate situations; then we sit in a theater and watch them. Born in the "peepshows" where the earliest, crudest movies lived, the passive fetish of watching actively binds audience and director together—yet another reason it is, perhaps, the most common fetish of all.

Alternatively, one of the least common fetishes in real life (but, given Hitchcock's preferred genre, one of the most frequent in his films) is hybristophilia, in which the fetishist is sexually attracted to criminals. In many of his films, this is treated lightly—for example, in the chase films (*THE 39 STEPS, SABOTEUR*), in which the woman has a love-hate attraction for the suspicious man on the run, or the caper films (*Family Plot, TO CATCH A THIEF*), in which the bad-boy criminal exerts a certain sexual fascination.

In the pitch-dark *Marnie*, though, the core of the film is, as Hitchcock frankly told Truffaut in '62, the "fetish idea. A man wants to go to bed with a thief because she is a thief, just like other men have a yen for a Chinese or a colored woman. Unfortunately this concept doesn't come across on screen. . . . To put it bluntly, we'd have to have SEAN CONNERY catching the girl robbing the safe and show that he felt like jumping at her and raping her on the spot."

That specific scene was discarded but only because Hitchcock feared the audience wouldn't believe it. But it was only the criticism of THE PLAUSIBLES he feared, not the risk of depicting (even justifying) a sexual assault; he was quite insistent that *Marnie* include Mark raping his bride on their honeymoon in an attempt to "cure" her of her frigidity. He was so insistent on this fact—carefully going over the scene, close-up by close-up in preproduction—that, when screenwriter EVAN HUNTER objected to it, Hitchcock had him replaced with JAY PRESSON ALLEN, a novice screenwriter and perhaps one more easily led.

Rape is, of course, not just a vicious crime but a fetish as well, and it is one that Hitchcock began trying to include explicitly in his films in the '50s. His *NO BAIL FOR THE JUDGE*, slated for 1958, was to contain a rape scene, but Audrey Hepburn turned it down, and the picture was shelved; the shower murder in *Psycho* and the final avian attack in *THE BIRDS* are at the very least symbolic sexual assaults. And even the real marital rape in *Marnie* did not exorcise this obsession; it occurs several times, once with grisly detail in *FRENZY*, while another sexual assault figures in his last, long-developed, and finally abandoned project *THE SHORT NIGHT*.

Whether the newly literal emphasis on sexual violence was a function of just a lessening of cinematic CENSORSHIP or a deeply personal response from the filmmaker—and it is noteworthy that the scenes began roughly after the ending of his working relationship with GRACE KELLY and gained feverish heat during his tempestuous partnership with TIPPI HEDREN—is something for the psychiatrists and biographers to argue over. But it is the darkest part of Hitchcock's work and, of all the erotic obsessions he put onscreen, the one that grows only more disturbing over time.

References
Patrick McGilligan, *Alfred Hitchcock: A Life in Darkness and Light* (New York: HarperCollins, 2003), 636–37; Donald Spoto, *The Dark Side of Genius: The Life of Alfred Hitchcock* (New York: Da Capo Press, 1999), 411–12; François Truffaut, *Hitchcock/Truffaut*, rev. ed. (New York: Touchstone, 1985), 47, 301.

THE FIGHTING GENERATION (US 1944)

DIRECTOR: Uncredited.
SCREENPLAY: Stephen Longstreet.
PRODUCER: David O. Selznick.
CINEMATOGRAPHY: Uncredited.
EDITOR: Uncredited.
ORIGINAL MUSIC: Uncredited.
CAST: Jennifer Jones (Nurse).
RUNNING TIME: 2 minutes. Black and white.
RELEASED THROUGH: RKO.

Very brief short, set in a hospital, made to encourage the purchase of war bonds. It was shot in one day at RKO. No director is credited, but some sources suggest Hitchcock supervised the filming; the fact that it stars Jennifer Jones, still married to ROBERT WALKER but already the pampered obsession of Hitchcock's boss, DAVID O. SELZNICK, bolsters the case.

Reference
"The Fighting Generation," *IMDb*, http://www.imdb.com/title/tt1375299/companycredits?ref_=ttfc_ql_5.

FILM NOIR
An attitude more than a genre or even a style, film noir refers to a group of movies—chiefly American but also British and French and

filling the years between 1940 and 1960—in which the plot generally revolves around a crime and the overwhelming mood is one of weary fatalism.

Yet even given its rather broad boundaries, noir has certain visual totems, archetypes, and traditional settings. The dramas usually unfold in a big city (whether the film is shot on an expressionistically altered backlot or realistically caught location). There is a woman who can't be trusted to do the right thing and a man who generally, albeit reluctantly, will. There are trench coats and cigarettes and rain that never washes anything away.

Mostly, though, there's a feeling of tough truths—of a hero who's suddenly jolted awake. "He felt like somebody had taken the lid off life and let him see the works," Dashiell Hammett wrote of a traumatized character in *The Maltese Falcon* in 1930, and it's that thought that all of movie noir would spring from a decade later—that there's an unseen and ugly world around us, controlling us, and all it takes is one happenstance act, one missed TRAIN, one turn down the wrong alley, to bring it out.

There is classic western noir (Raoul Walsh's *Pursued*, Robert Wise's *Blood on the Moon*) and modern sci-fi noir (Ridley Scott's *Blade Runner*, the Wachowskis' *The Matrix*), but the crime dramas of the '40s and early '50s account for most of the best of the genre while mirroring a real and continually growing feeling in America that life had become unstable and unpredictable (but only perhaps because unseen powers were at work).

It is not a style that Hitchcock is automatically associated with, perhaps because it lived most fully among the studios' B-movie productions; Hitchcock long had a naturally commercial preference for big STARS, plush sets, and neatly resolved endings over gritty actors, bleak cityscapes,

and unhappy climaxes. Still, his themes of an ordinary man accidentally caught up in strange conspiracies—*FOREIGN CORRESPONDENT*, *SABOTEUR*—are definitely ones that fit into noir. So is the character of the smiling and socially respected villain who may be a Nazi or—in *SHADOW OF A DOUBT* or *STRANGERS ON A TRAIN*—a murderous psychopath.

But if Hitchcock is not immediately tagged—as FRITZ LANG is—as a noir director, then it may be because he only began to truly embrace its despairing attitude in the late '50s; as other filmmakers were moving on, his movies were growing darker. The idea of getting a sudden, unwelcome look at "the works"—isn't that at the heart of *THE WRONG MAN*, in which, through nothing more than happenstance and coincidence, an innocent is plunged into the hell of the justice system? And what is more noir than the inside-out reversals of *VERTIGO*, in which the private detective is revealed to have been a dupe, his dream woman turns out to be just that—and all he can do at the end is stand impotently, literally at the edge of nothing?

For—settings, style, and stereotypes aside—if noir is a feeling that the bottom can drop out beneath your feet at any moment, then that is a road that most of Hitchcock's heroes walk.

References

Dashiell Hammett, *The Novels of Dashiell Hammett: The Maltese Falcon* (New York: Knopf, 1965), 335; Alain Silver, Elizabeth M. Ward, James Ursini, Robert Porfirio, eds., *The Film Noir Encyclopedia* (New York: Overlook Press, 2010), 1–6.

FINCH, JON (1942–2012)

The son of an investment banker, Finch was born into privilege in Surrey and won a place at the London School of Economics but had already discovered amateur theatricals and folk singing and decided to try performing instead. After military service—including some time in the reserves of Britain's hardened special forces—he turned to acting full time, with TV spots on the popular shows *Crossroads* and *Z-Cars*. By 1970, the handsome leading man had made his movie debut thanks to Hammer, with parts in two of their period horrors, *The Vampire Lovers* and the somewhat campy *The Horror of Frankenstein*; the next year brought *Sunday Bloody Sunday* and Roman Polanski's controversial *Macbeth*, with Finch in the title role.

After briefly considering David Hemmings, Hitchcock cast Finch in *FRENZY* in 1972 as Richard Blaney, an ex-military man with a taste for brandy and violent confrontation; he is suspected of murdering his wife (and soon a string of London women), and the curious and complicated thing about the film is that, even though he plays the hero, you feel under certain circumstances he might have done it; like *In a Lonely Place*, it's a film where, even exonerated, the protagonist remains far from innocent.

Finch's performance is intense but thanks to the script a little one-note; he begins the film in an angry, argumentative mood, and things only get quickly worse (particularly on the set, where Hitchcock took an immediate dislike to him once he dared question some dialogue). In any case, it was not the sort of movie made to earn Finch many accolades; his decision to turn down *Live and Let Die* and become the next Bond closed off another avenue.

Not that Finch seemed to care. "I never wanted to be a big STAR," he insisted once. "I usually do one film a year, so I always have enough money to enjoy myself and keep myself out of the public eye. It's a very pleasant life, not one of great ambition."

In his 30s, Finch was diagnosed with diabetes; his health was spotty for the rest of his life, causing him to drop out of Ridley Scott's *Alien* as the unlucky astronaut who becomes the creature's first host; John Hurt replaced him in the role. Much of Finch's subsequent work was in cheap foreign thrillers, although decades after *Alien* Scott would give him a small part in 2005's *Kingdom of Heaven*. It would be Finch's last screen appearance.

His body was found in his flat in Hastings after friends and family had not heard from him in some time. He was 70.

References
Ronald Bergan, "Jon Finch Obituary," *Guardian*, January 13, 2013, http://www.theguardian.com/film/2013/jan/13/jon-finch; "Jon Finch," *IMDb*, http://www.imdb.com/name/nm0277424/bio?ref_=nm_ov_bio_sm; *The Story of Frenzy*, directed by Laurent Bouzereau (2001), documentary, http://the.hitchcock.zone/wiki/The_Story_of_Frenzy_%282001%29_-_transcript.

FLAMINGO FEATHER
A proposed adaptation of a Cold War adventure novel by controversial South African writer Laurens van der Post, this got far along enough in preproduction in the mid-'50s for Hitchcock to approach JAMES STEWART about playing the lead and even to travel to Africa to scout locations. But the logistics—and politics—were discouraging, and the project was dropped.

Reference
Patrick McGilligan, *Alfred Hitchcock: A Life in Darkness and Light* (New York: HarperCollins, 2003), 539–40.

FLEMING, RHONDA (1923–)
Flame-haired, porcelain-skinned performer and that rare creature, a Hollywood native. She was discovered by an agent while still in Beverly Hills High School and was doing

small parts in films (the sort billed as "Girl at Dance," "Girl on Train") almost immediately.

SPELLBOUND finally gave her a character with a name, the violent and SEXUALLY aggressive Mary Carmichael—who, in raking her fingernails across an orderly's hand, will give the film its first instance of the parallel lines that so terrify John Ballantyne. (She shows up later in the film in Ballantyne's dream as the "kissing bug.") The small but indelible part led to others, particularly in the HITCHCOCKIAN *The Spiral Staircase* and the classic FILM NOIR *Out of the Past*.

The growing popularity of Technicolor brought new opportunities for the vibrant redhead; she was a particularly popular choice for westerns, period pieces, and 3-D extravaganzas. By the 1960s, she was doing mostly TV work; her last "major" film was *The Nude Bomb* in 1980. Over the years, Fleming also pursued a singing career, charity work, and—despite being married six times at last count—"Project Prayer," a morality crusade to return God to public schools.

References

"Biography," *Rhonda Fleming*, http://www.rhondafleming.com; Drew Pearson, *Washington Merry-Go-Round*, May 14, 1964, http://dspace.wrlc.org/doc/bit stream/2041/50658/b18f14-0514zdisplay .pdf; "Rhonda Fleming," *IMDb*, http://www.imdb.com/name/nm0281766/ bio?ref_=nm_ov_bio_sm.

FONDA, HENRY (1905–1982)

Nebraska-born performer who, like many actors, contained interesting contradictions. While exuding the unsophisticated American Midwest, he was from a Genovese clan that, by way of the Netherlands, had been in America since colonial days. Often playing sympathetic paternal figures, he was, according to children Peter and Jane, a painfully distant father whose emotional remoteness was broken only by bursts of anger.

At first interested in journalism, Fonda turned to acting at the encouragement of Marlon Brando's mother, Dodie, a drama coach. Dropping out of college, he did summer stock in New England, where he met lifelong friend JAMES STEWART; the two men made their first forays on the Broadway stage together and then Hollywood (where for a while they were roommates). Tall, lean, and handsome, Fonda found success early on film. He is haunted (and hunted) as the fugitive in *You Only Live Once*, memorable as a slowly falling-out-of-love suitor in *Jezebel*, but it was as Tom Joad—the rootless Okie-turned-Christ-figure at the heart of *The Grapes of Wrath*—that he became an indelible and richly silent American icon, a wealth of bit-back righteous anger in every "hmm" and "well."

"I am not a very interesting person," he insisted later in life. "I haven't ever done anything except be other people. I ain't really Henry Fonda! Nobody could be. Nobody could have that much integrity." Still, it was a persona that fit Fonda well—the mostly stoic, intensely stubborn, highly decent man who did the difficult thing without much fuss or furor; even his small-minded martinet in *Fort Apache* is an upright man convinced of the correctness of his cause. Yet although Fonda could occasionally use that stiffness well in comedy (as in *The Lady Eve*), he did not project much sex appeal; there was something too unbending in him, too uncompromising. He could play the perfect, naïve butt of a worldly heroine's JOKES (Barbara Stanwyck and Lucille Ball would delightedly dance rings around him), but he was ill-suited for the give and take of glossy movie romances.

This made him a poor choice for the usual Hitchcock hero but the perfect embodiment of Manny Balestero in *THE WRONG MAN*, Manhattan's dullest jazz musician, a man with the face of a starved saint and an early martyr's capacity for suffering. It was a character made for Fonda. Manny doesn't need to display passion or even anger; what Manny has to do is endure, from the frustrating, increasingly Kafkaesque turns of the justice system to, eventually, the madness and violence rained down on him by his own wife. It is a bleak but perfectly calibrated performance, marked more by quiet sadness than shocked surprise—even when his wife strikes him with a hairbrush—and the movie serves as a grim preparation for the masculine despair his old friend Stewart would provide in *VERTIGO*.

Fonda, who had enlisted in World War II and taken a long break from Hollywood after, had a second surge on film in the '50s and '60s. He repeated his Broadway success in *Mr. Roberts* and was the voice of sanity in *12 Angry Men*; he embodied an idealist's view of American politicians in *Advise and Consent*, *The Best Man*, and *Fail Safe*, adding to his image of staunch morality and quiet self-sacrifice. Much against his instincts, he agreed to put all that aside to play Frank in Sergio Leone's *Once upon a Time in the West*; as a child murderer with eyes as cold as a wintry lake, Fonda creates not only one of the great western villains but also one of the movie's most memorable monsters.

It was perhaps his last great performance, but typically, he won his only Oscar for playing his most human and sentimental one in *On Golden Pond*, in which he had several achingly personal scenes with his daughter, Jane, acting out the rapprochement on screen they had never managed in life.

He died in Los Angeles at 77 of heart disease.

References

"Henry Fonda," *Biography*, http://www.biography.com/people/henry-fonda-9297981; "Henry Fonda," *IMDb*, http://www.imdb.com/name/nm0000020/bio?ref_=nm_ov_bio_sm; David Thomson, *The New Biographical Dictionary of Film* (New York: Knopf, 2002), 298–99.

FONTAINE, JOAN (1917–2013)

British performer born in Tokyo and mostly raised in northern California, whose mother had been on the stage and whose elder sister, Olivia de Havilland, became an immediate movie STAR at 19 with *Captain Blood*. Fontaine was already on the stage at that point but discouraged by her mother, who thought she would only distract people from her sister's success. (In fact, she was told not to act under the de Havilland name.)

Dropped from her RKO contract after several undistinguished years, Fontaine later found herself in (or, some say, engineered) a dinner-party seat next to DAVID O. SELZNICK, then trying to cast *REBECCA* (and engender some of the same publicity his talent search for *Gone with the Wind* had brought). Fontaine pushed for the part and underwent a half-year's worth of auditions and screen tests before finally securing it.

Hitchcock had not been an early ally—he thought the then-22-year-old too girlish and much preferred Margaret Sullavan—but eventually agreed with Selznick that her real-life uncertainty as an overshadowed younger sister might be perfectly suited for the film's heroine, a shy bride who feels she can't live up to everyone's memories of her husband's first wife.

Yet it was Hitchcock's genius—or perhaps his cruelty—that, once he realized this connection, he played upon it. "He was a Svengali," Fontaine remembered later. "He wanted control over me and he seemed to relish the cast not liking one another. . . . It kept him in command and it was part of the upheaval he wanted. He kept me off balance, much to his own delight. He would constantly tell me that nobody thought I was any good except himself and that nobody really liked me."

It was sadistic, but it was also useful; as Fontaine would also admit, "Of course this helped my performance, as I was supposed to be terrified of everyone, and it gave a lot of tension to my scenes." Fearing perhaps that the young actress did not know how to play the character, Hitchcock deliberately turned her into the character—uncertain, awkward, full of self-doubt. It won her an Oscar nomination.

She was nominated again for her lead in her next picture for Hitchcock, *SUSPI-CION*. It was a curious honor—on the set, Fontaine (who had been so bullied by the director on their last film) now complained that he paid no attention to her at all; her costar CARY GRANT, perhaps realizing Fontaine had the dominant part, muttered that she was upstaging him. (That the script was being constantly rewritten—and, after a bad sneak preview, an entirely new ending shot—did not help matters.) And still, Fontaine won the Oscar for it—the only one any performer ever took home for a Hitchcock film.

The victory established her as a Hollywood star—and, because she'd defeated her sister, nominated that same year for *Hold Back the Dawn*, added insult to a sibling relationship that had never been warm and would grow only colder as they competed for parts. "I married first, won the Oscar before (she) did and if I die first, she'll undoubtedly be livid because I beat her to it!" Fontaine cracked later.

Fontaine is very good opposite Orson Welles in the 1943 *Jane Eyre*—that Gothic heroine practically the archetype for the

modern one in *Rebecca*—and lovely in 1948's classic *Letter from an Unknown Woman*, a project that she put together through her own company. On- and offscreen, she projected an air of intelligence, breeding, and quietly strong feminism.

Her film career was less vibrant in the 1950s, although she appeared in a number of costume epics, including *Ivanhoe* (and, as a winking favor to Welles, as a page in his *Othello*); she did considerable television (including an episode of *ALFRED HITCH-COCK PRESENTS*) and was working as late as the mid-'90s.

She died at 96 in Carmel Highlands, CA—beating her sister to that life event, too, as she predicted.

References

Rudy Behlmer, ed., *Memo from David O. Selznick* (New York: Viking Press, 1972), 281–84; Joan Fontaine, *No Bed of Roses* (New York: William Morrow, 1978), 90, 106–8; "Joan Fontaine," *Biography*, http://www.biography.com/people/joan-fontaine-20987191; "Joan Fontaine," *IMDb*, http://www.imdb.com/name/nm0000021/bio?ref_=nm_ov_bio_sm; Donald Spoto, *Spellbound by Beauty: Alfred Hitchcock and His Leading Ladies* (New York: Harmony Books, 2008), 90–99, 114.

FOOD

Eating certainly occupied a large part in Alfred Hitchcock's life—as it would almost have to in anyone whose weight would occasionally push past 300 pounds. Yet although his wife, ALMA REVILLE, taught herself fine French cooking (PATRICIA HITCHCOCK's biography of her mother includes recipes), he was often more gourmand than gourmet; those who dined with him often remarked about the broiled steak at lunch, the Dover sole at dinner, the meals that were as simple and unchanging as the rows of dark suits in his closet.

In "normal" life, food offers a respite from our cares. In Hitchcock films, they only remind us of them, where family meals become battlegrounds. In *BLACK-MAIL*, a conversation around the kitchen table turns into a symphony of GUILT and paranoia; in *SHADOW OF A DOUBT*, it leads Uncle Charlie to talk of the "swine" he moves among (and both exterminates and profits from, like any farmer).

The more elegant the food, the more drastic the disappointment. In *FRENZY*, Chief Inspector Oxford tries to escape the gruesomeness of the murder case by going home to a family dinner; he longs for sausage and mash, but instead, his ambitious wife serves pretentious French swill full of animal gristle and gelatinous sauces. In fact, as *FRENZY* suggests, the more loving a meal is meant to be in Hitchcock, the more easily it can all go bad. The chicken dinners that grow cold in *NOTORIOUS* as the lovers quarrel, Lisa's catered meal in *REAR WINDOW* that only strikes Jeff as too posh and perfect, like her—these are meant to be intimate, romantic suppers, and yet they only symbolize (or even spur on) the couple's disharmony.

Gluttony is indeed one of the seven deadly sins—but in Hitchcock's films, no sensual pleasure goes unpunished, and even the small delight one would take in looking forward to a simple meal is bound to end in punishment. After all, the gentleman in "LAMB TO THE SLAUGHTER" was probably looking forward to his dinner, too—until his wife clubbed him over the head with it.

References
Pat Hitchcock O'Connell and Laurent Bouzereau, *Alma Hitchcock: The Woman behind the Man* (New York: Berkeley Trade, 2004), 226–54; Donald Spoto, *The Dark Side of Genius: The Life of Alfred Hitchcock* (New York: Da Capo Press, 1999), 170, 267, 320.

FORD, WALLACE (1898–1966)
Bolton-born performer who was somehow separated from his parents as a child and sent to an orphanage; he would pass through 17 foster homes before being adopted by a Canadian farmer, whom he later claimed treated him as nothing more than free labor. Running away from that Winnipeg home at 11, he toured with a kiddie vaudeville troupe, worked odd jobs, and hitched rides on freight trains. (Born Samuel Grundy, he later renamed himself after a friend who was killed in a railway accident.) By his middle 20s, Ford was a successful stage actor; when the talkies arrived in Hollywood, so did he.

His earliest screen appearances are in *Freaks* (where he's one of the few sympathetic "normal" characters) and in John Ford's *The Informer*. He would make a dozen more for Ford, as well as working steadily in everything from westerns to old-dark-house horrors; for Hitchcock he plays MACDONALD CAREY's camera-toting partner in *SHADOW OF A DOUBT* and, in *SPELLBOUND*, the hotel-lobby lothario who tries to pick up Dr. Peterson. When his movie career began to slow down, like many supporting actors, he made a profitable transition to TV.

He died at 68 of a heart attack in Woodland Hills, CA.

References
"Wallace Ford," *Hollywood.com*, http://www.hollywood.com/celebrities/wallace-ford-57304596; "Wallace Ford," *IMDb*, http://www.imdb.com/name/nm0285922/bio?ref_=nm_ov_bio_sm.

FOREIGN CORRESPONDENT
(US 1940)

DIRECTOR: Alfred Hitchcock.
SCREENPLAY: Charles Bennett and Joan Harrison, with additional dialogue by Robert Benchley and James Hilton, based on the memoir *Personal History* by Vincent Sheean.
PRODUCER: Walter Wanger.
CINEMATOGRAPHY: Rudolph Mate.
EDITOR: Dorothy Spencer.
ORIGINAL MUSIC: Alfred Newman.
CAST: Joel McCrea (Johnny Jones), Laraine Day (Carol Fisher), Herbert Marshall (Stephen Fisher), George Sanders (ffolliott), Albert Bassermann (Van Meer), Edmund Gwenn (Rowley), Eduardo Ciannelli (Krug).
RUNNING TIME: 120 minutes. Black and white.
RELEASED THROUGH: United Artists.

Frustrated with the recycled government press releases he's getting from his foreign correspondents, the *New York Globe*'s editor decides to send a young police reporter overseas instead to bring a fresh eye to foreign coverage and, perhaps, uncover the "crime" of world war that now seems to be threatening Europe.

Unsophisticated and unprepared, Johnny Jones—who's told to file under the more impressive name of Huntley Haverstock—works quickly, soon meeting Stephen Fisher and his daughter Carol, who head a major peace group, and the veteran Dutch diplomat Van Meer.

When Van Meer is seemingly assassinated in front of his eyes, Jones chases after the killer—only to discover that the murder was that of a double and that Van Meer is being held (and tortured) by foreign agents who are trying to get him to give up essential government secrets.

Going to see the Fishers, Jones is shocked to find one of the enemy agents

there. He privately tells Stephen Fisher, who tells him he will handle it. In fact, Fisher is working with the assassins—and they decide to hire a "bodyguard" for Jones who will, instead, eliminate him. Jones, however, escapes the attempt (accidentally killing the assassin) and now realizes that Fisher is a traitor. Working quickly, he finds Van Meer and confronts Fisher—who was working without his daughter's knowledge. All three are on a plane back to America when it is shot down by the Germans; Fisher gives up his life to save them.

Rescued by an American ship, Jones telephones his scoop to his editor and then, back in London, gives a radio broadcast warning Americans about the coming war.

Hitchcock's second movie in Hollywood, *Foreign Correspondent*, feels more like one of his mid-'30s British ones.

Loaned out by DAVID O. SELZNICK (who pocketed a hefty differential each time he sent the director out to work for someone else), Hitchcock was given the assignment of making a film out of journalist Vincent Sheean's memoirs, which producer Walter Wanger had purchased five years before. But it soon became clear that there was not enough in the foreign correspondent's book to make a movie.

Screenwriter CHARLES BENNETT (who had written six of Hitchcock's English films, and was already in Hollywood) and Hitchcock's longtime assistant JOAN HARRISON (who had already cowritten *REBECCA* and *JAMAICA INN*) then set about to concoct a completely new adventure, albeit one that drew on favorite Hitchcock touches.

So, as in *THE 39 STEPS*, there is an eminently respectable gentleman who turns out to be a traitor; as in *THE LADY VANISHES*, there is a senior citizen entrusted with a potentially dangerous bit of information about the secret clause in a peace treaty. And as in *THE MAN WHO KNEW TOO MUCH*, there is some travelogue—in this case, the studio-created Holland of picturesque windmills (one of which is signaling to enemy aircraft by turning *against* the wind). For Hitchcock—and fans of his earlier work—it all must have felt a little cozy. There was even a bit of added familiarity in the supporting cast, which included HERBERT MARSHALL (*MURDER!*) and, cast against type as the nefarious "bodyguard," EDMUND GWENN (*THE SKIN GAME*).

The film is very much a light entertainment but—as was often the case for Hitchcock when on loan-out to cheaper studios—not quite the STAR-driven A-production he had envisioned. (The director wanted Gary Cooper and Barbara Stanwyck for his leads; he had to settle for JOEL MCCREA and Laraine Day.) The script, meanwhile, manages to be both overcomplicated (the ending is protracted, and the reporter character played by GEORGE SANDERS largely superfluous) and simplistic, and the tacked-on scene—by an uncredited BEN HECHT—of Jones's final radio broadcast feels like the hastily added propaganda it is (although Joseph Goebbels, knowing good agitprop when he saw it, praised the antifascist film as a "masterpiece").

Yet beyond the film's flaws and compromises—many of them caused by it being reworked and rewritten during production to try to keep up with current events—it's full of strong HITCHCOCKIAN touches.

There is, for example, the nice visual moment when, fleeing across the roof of the Hotel Europe, Jones accidentally breaks the building's neon sign (turning its announcement into "Hot Europe," suggesting the flames to come). There's also the fake assassination, with the killer escaping into a sea of bobbing umbrellas, and the moment when Jones notices the wrong-way windmill (a moment of dawning comprehension echoed decades later in

NORTH BY NORTHWEST when the man notices the crop duster is dusting crops where there "ain't no crops").

A few other scenes resonate, too. The "enhanced interrogation techniques" used against Van Meer—drugs, bright lights, constant music, sleep deprivation—were grim then and seem particularly relevant today. The character of the avuncular working-class assassin, particularly as played by Gwenn, is also striking, adding a particularly GRAHAM GREENE-ish touch to the narrative.

And then there is Hitchcock's favorite moment in the film, when—in a single shot from inside the cockpit—we see Jones's plane go crashing into the Atlantic and a torrent of water come flooding in. It was done with back projection, a rice-paper screen, and two tanks of water, and it was the sort of purely technical puzzle (and solution) that often delighted the director—and occasionally helped distract him from a story that had little to offer in either character or theme.

References

Donald Spoto, *The Dark Side of Genius: The Life of Alfred Hitchcock* (New York: Da Capo Press, 1999), 225–37; Jeff Stafford and John M. Miller, "Foreign Correspondent," *TCM*, http://www.tcm.com/tcMdb/title/75400/Foreign-Correspondent/articles.html.

FOREVER AND A DAY (US 1943)

DIRECTORS: Edmund Goulding, Sir Cedric Hardwicke, Frank Lloyd, Victor Saville, Robert Stevenson, Herbert Wilcox, Rene Clair.
SCREENPLAY: Charles Bennett, Alan Campbell, Norman Corwin, C. S. Forester, Peter Godfrey, Jack Hartfield, Lawrence Hazard, Sig Herzig, James Hilton, Michael Hogan, Christopher Isherwood, Emmet Lavery, W. P. Lipscomb, Gene Lockhart, Frederick Lonsdale, Alice Duer Miller, R. C. Sherriff, Donald

Ogden Stewart, John Van Druten, Claudine West, Keith Winter.
PRODUCERS: Edmund Goulding, Sir Cedric Hardwicke, Frank Lloyd, Victor Saville, Robert Stevenson, Herbert Wilcox, Rene Clair.
CINEMATOGRAPHY: Uncredited.
EDITOR: Uncredited.
ORIGINAL MUSIC: Uncredited.
CAST: Kent Smith (Gates Trimble Pomfret), Ruth Warrick (Lesley Trimble), Herbert Marshall (Curate), C. Aubrey Smith (Adm. Eustance Trimble), Edmund Gwenn (Stubbs), Ray Milland (Lt. Bill Trimble), Dame May Whitty (Lucy Trimble), Claude Rains (Ambrose Pomfret), Charles Laughton (Bellamy), Brian Aherne (Jim Trimble), Nigel Bruce (Maj. Garrow), Gladys Cooper (Mrs. Barringer), Robert Cummings (Ned Trimble), Sir Cedric Hardwicke (Mr. Dabb).
RUNNING TIME: 104 minutes. Black and white.
RELEASED THROUGH: RKO.

During World War II, American reporter Gates Trimble Pomfret, assigned to war-torn London, decides to sell off the old family house; Lesley Trimble, a distant British relative, urges him not to and shares some of the stories of the home and their ancestors.

A film made for the Allied war effort and for British morale with an almost absurd number of directors, writers, and STARS volunteering, the film unfolds as a long series of short flashbacks, and most of the behind-the-camera talents (all working separately on various segments) went uncredited. Alfred Hitchcock was reportedly one of many contributors to the screenplay; although he was originally supposed to be one of the directors as well, he withdrew due to a schedule conflict with SHADOW OF A DOUBT and was replaced by Rene Clair.

Reference
"Forever and a Day," *AFI Catalog of Feature Films,* http://www.afi.com/members/catalog/DetailView.aspx?s=&Movie=436.

FORSYTHE, JOHN (1918–2010)
New Jersey–born, Brooklyn-raised performer who exuded calm urbanity. The son of a stockbroker, he handled the public announcements at Ebbets Field for the Brooklyn Dodgers, was a bit player at WARNER BROS., and then after the war returned to New York and the theater. The preppy Forsythe took classes at the Actors Studio (where, he said later, "They called me the Brooks Brothers bohemian") and appeared on Broadway in *All My Sons* and *Mister Roberts.* Stage work and live TV kept him based in New York, where he'd begun to raise a family.

He joined the cast of Hitchcock's *THE TROUBLE WITH HARRY* in Vermont, where he played the free-spirited artist who wants to paint SHIRLEY MACLAINE in the nude; he was pleasant but no more convincing as an iconoclast onscreen than he'd been in the Actors Studio rehearsal spaces.

But Forsythe's lovely speaking voice and distinguished looks kept him going on television, where he found a comfortable home, appearing on *ALFRED HITCHCOCK PRESENTS* and *THE ALFRED HITCHCOCK HOUR.* He would also return to work for the director on *TOPAZ,* playing the supporting part of an American intelligence agent.

His most profitable place remained the small screen, however, where he eventually appeared in a string of series spanning a half-century—*Bachelor Father, The John Forsythe Show, To Rome with Love, Charlie's Angels, Dynasty, The Colbys,* and *The Powers That Be.*

He died of pneumonia at 92 in Santa Ynez, CA.

References

"John Forsythe," *IMDb*, http://www.imdb.com/name/nm0001234/bio?ref_=nm_ov_bio_sm; Claudia Luther, "John Forsythe Dies at 92," *Los Angeles Times*, April 3, 2010, http://www.latimes.com/news/la-me-john-forsythe3-2010apr03-story.html#page=1.

FOSTER, BARRY (1927–2002)

Nottinghamshire-born performer who, after a failed attempt at an advertising career, won a drama scholarship to the Central School of Speech and Drama (where he became friends with a young Harold Pinter, then acting under the name David Baron; Foster would later act in several of Pinter's plays, while Pinter's wife, VIVIEN MERCHANT, would appear with Foster but share no scenes in *FRENZY*). After graduation, Foster joined a traveling repertory company, chiefly doing classics; he made his London stage debut in 1955. Later, he would appear in the films *The Family Way*, *Robbery*, and *Twisted Nerve* and have a TV hit in the British series *Van der Valk*.

"I'm neither very tall nor very short," he said once, explaining his busy career. "You can't look at my face and say 'he's the killer' or 'the guy next door,' or 'the mad scientist.' All I've got is my curly hair—which everyone thinks is a wig anyway."

Hitchcock cast Foster in *Frenzy* after seeing him in *Twisted Nerve*, a sick psycho thriller (with, nonetheless, a standout score by BERNARD HERRMANN). It undoubtedly helped that the fair-haired actor resembled Michael Caine, who had already turned down the Hitchcock film—but Foster gave his own fine performance, keeping the character seesawing between icy villainy and warm Cockney charm.

After, Foster returned to the stage; notched good parts in a number of strong TV and movie productions, including *Smiley's People*, *A Woman Called Golda*, and *Maurice*; and starred in several revivals of the *Van der Valk* series.

He died in Guildford at 74 of a heart attack.

References

"Barry Foster," *IMDb*, http://www.imdb.com/name/nm0287687/bio?ref_=nm_ov_bio_sm; "Barry Foster," *Telegraph*, February 12, 2002, http://www.telegraph.co.uk/news/obituaries/1384538/Barry-Foster.html; *The Story of Frenzy*, directed by Laurent Bouzereau (2001), documentary, http://the.hitchcock.zone/wiki/The_Story_of_Frenzy_%282001%29_-_transcript.

"FOUR O'CLOCK" (US; ORIGINALLY AIRED SEPTEMBER 30, 1957)

DIRECTOR: Alfred Hitchcock.
SCREENPLAY: Frances Cockrell, from the story by Cornell Woolrich.
PRODUCERS: Alfred Hitchcock, Joan Harrison.
CINEMATOGRAPHY: John L. Russell.
EDITOR: Edward W. Williams.
ORIGINAL MUSIC: Stanley Wilson.
CAST: E. G. Marshall (Paul Steppe), Nancy Kelly (Fran Steppe), Richard Long (Dave).
RUNNING TIME: 60 minutes, with commercials. Black and white.
ORIGINALLY BROADCAST BY: NBC.

A suspicious husband decides to plant a time bomb to explode during one of the afternoon trysts he assumes his wife is having with her lover; surprised in the house by burglars, he's left tied up, now forced to sit and watch the clock tick away. Perhaps the purest illustration of Hitchcock's old definition of SUSPENSE VS. SURPRISE, this was made as the debut episode of a new TV anthology program, *SUSPICION*, on which longtime colleague JOAN HARRISON served as de facto producer.

References
Tim Brooks and Earle Marsh, *The Complete Directory to Prime Time Network TV Shows*, 6th ed. (New York: Ballantine Books, 1995), 1002; Jack Edmond Nolan, "Hitchcock's TV Films," *Film Fan Monthly* (June 1968), 3–6.

FRENCH NEW WAVE
A self-proclaimed tsunami of artistic innovation, the rebellious nouvelle vague generation drew its most famous early directors—Jean-Luc Godard, FRANÇOIS TRUFFAUT, ERIC ROHMER, and CLAUDE CHABROL—from the ranks of *CAHIERS DU CINEMA*'s most frequent contributors. Truffaut, Rohmer, and Chabrol had all INTERVIEWED—and championed the work of—Alfred Hitchcock. Some would later explore his themes (e.g., the DOUBLE, with Julie Christie playing two different mysterious BLONDES in Truffaut's *Fahrenheit 451*, Jean-Claude Brialy and Gerard Blain playing contrasting characters in Chabrol's *Les Cousins*) and genre (Truffaut's *The Bride Wore Black* and *Mississippi Mermaid*; Chabrol's many crime stories, including *Landru*, *Les Biches*, and *La Femme Infidele*).

Stylistically, though, the new wave directors forged their own path, at first drawing from the work of the Italian neorealists and early American independent filmmakers, such as Morris Engel (*The Little Fugitive*). Driven by a desire to both explore and expose the artificiality of cinema—and work within their limited means—many of their early films featured handheld camera work, on-location shooting, and abrupt edits. Deep down, though, they shared little but a determination not to tell stories that had been told before and do things as they had always been done.

But if many of them had initially been inspired by Hitchcock, did they eventually inspire him, as well? The distressingly flat, featureless world of Marion Crane's Phoenix wouldn't be out of place in a Godard film, while her abrupt departure from the narrative is its own kind of deliberately jarring jump cut. *PSYCHO* is not, in style or subject, a new wave film. Yet it's interesting to wonder if Hitchcock would have attempted it had he not seen what the French critics who'd once knelt before him were now doing behind their own cameras.

References
Dave Kehr, "Cahiers Back in the Day," *Film Comment* (September/October 2001), http://www.filmcomment.com/article/cahiers-back-in-the-day; *NewWaveFilm.com*, http://www.newwavefilm.com/new-wave-cinema-guide/nouvelle-vague-where-to-start.shtml.

FRENZY (US 1972)

DIRECTOR: Alfred Hitchcock.
SCREENPLAY: Anthony Shaffer, based on the novel *Goodbye Piccadilly, Farewell Leicester Square* by Arthur LaBern.
PRODUCER: Alfred Hitchcock.
CINEMATOGRAPHY: Gilbert Taylor.
EDITOR: John Jympson.
ORIGINAL MUSIC: Ron Goodwin.
CAST: Jon Finch (Richard Blaney), Barry Foster (Robert Rusk), Barbara Leigh-Hunt (Brenda Blaney), Anna Massey ("Babs" Milligan), Alec McCowen (Chief Inspector Oxford), Vivien Merchant (Mrs. Oxford).
RUNNING TIME: 116 minutes. Color.
RELEASED THROUGH: Universal.

Recently fired from his job as a bartender and bitter at the bad luck and failed businesses that have left him nearly penniless, Richard Blaney shows up at his ex-wife Brenda's matchmaking service, hoping for a handout and perhaps a bit of sympathy. Instead, the short-tempered Blaney quarrels with his ex loudly—and publicly (although she still slips some money into his pocket when he isn't looking).

The next day, Blaney's friend Robert Rusk turns up at the lonely-hearts office, too, hoping to be set up with another date; when Brenda tells him she refuses to deal with him any longer due to clients' reports of his sexual sadism, he rapes and strangles her—the latest in a series of unsolved "necktie murders" that have left London in a panic.

With reports coming in of Blaney's drunken rages and circumstantial evidence tying him to Brenda's murder, Chief Inspector Oxford sees him as the likeliest suspect. He becomes the only suspect after Rusk murders Blaney's latest girlfriend, Babs, too—and, while pretending to help Blaney hide from the police, frames him for that death as well.

Knowing now that Rusk is the killer but unable to convince the police, Blaney eventually escapes from prison, determined to murder him. Instead he and Oxford get to Rusk's apartment only to discover the corpse of his latest victim, a necktie knotted around her neck. The tieless Rusk, arriving with a steamer trunk to haul away the body, is arrested.

The last great Hitchcock film, *Frenzy* marks a late but lively return to form and a startling new frankness.

Pressured by UNIVERSAL to stay away from large, STAR-driven budgets—and perhaps realizing that his last two movies, both espionage thrillers, had flopped—Hitchcock began looking in the early '70s for both something different and familiar. The choice eventually narrowed to *Goodbye Piccadilly, Farewell Leicester Square*, a novel about a serial killer; its theme contained not only a nod to his original hit, *THE LODGER*, but also its setting suggested a return to London (where, ALMA REVILLE pointed out, there was a vast number of terrific, stage-trained actors whom he can sign very cheaply). Hitchcock sent the novel out to ANTHONY SHAFFER—who had just scored a big stage success with *Sleuth*—and made early trips to scout locations (largely in the neighborhood where his father's food shop had been) and to put together a cast.

Although several crew members remarked on the director's health—arthritis was making it increasingly difficult for him to get about, and he was wracked with concern over his wife, who had a small stroke during the production—Hitchcock seemed energized by the return home and delighted in the veteran actors who knew their parts backward and forward yet could improvise a bit of business when necessary. Only JON FINCH, his moody star, caused him any annoyance; as he had on *I CONFESS* with MONTGOMERY CLIFT, Hitchcock took his small revenge by shooting around him and limiting his close-ups whenever possible. (The only other trouble came after shooting, when Hitchcock decided he loathed Henry Mancini's score; a new one was promptly commissioned from another composer.)

Hitchcock's first movie in England since the less-than-satisfactory *UNDER CAPRICORN* and *STAGE FRIGHT*—and his most recent effort after the dull *TORN CURTAIN* and disastrous *TOPAZ*—*Frenzy* is surprisingly confident, even self-congratulatory from the start. The film begins with a slow approach up the Thames, with stirring music and the seal of the city of London in the upper-right corner of the frame—the entire sequence looks like the triumphal march of a conquering hero come back to claim his crown.

And then the naked body of a woman floats by. The stark nudity is a first for a Hitchcock film, but even more shocking is the disregard, even contempt, the film seems to show for women's bodies and lives. This, the first corpse in the movie, arrives only seconds after a politician has remarked on the "waste" clogging the river; later, noting the fact that the strangler's victims have all been raped first, a smiling stranger JOKES, "Every cloud has a silver lining."

Indeed, once they've provided sex—usually against their will—women's bodies have little purpose in *Frenzy*. The murderer throws them in the Thames like rubbish, packs them in a trunk like old clothes, or simply leaves them lying about; Babs, the film's most sympathetic character, is literally stuffed into a sack of potatoes (and then provides a gruesome bit of slapstick humor as, when cut out of the bag, she keeps stubbornly sticking her cold dead foot in the killer's face).

This sort of scene risks going beyond black comedy into cold heartlessness, and coupled with Hitchcock's increasing fascination with violence against women as a plot device—bookended by the aborted projects *NO BAIL FOR THE JUDGE* and *THE SHORT NIGHT* and marked by *PSYCHO*, *THE BIRDS*, and especially *MARNIE*—it's difficult to watch *Frenzy* for the first time without a feeling of distaste. Is it merely ironic that the villain—handsome, well-dressed, and quick with a joke—is far more sympathetic than our moody, hard-drinking hero? Can the graphic rape scene be anything but misogynistic?

And yet.

And yet Hitchcock, rather than hiring flagrantly erotic actresses for the victims—as Sam Peckinpah did in *Straw Dogs* with Susan George—casts the rather maternal BARBARA LEIGH-HUNT as Brenda and the quietly plain ANNA MASSEY as Babs, resisting any urge to vicariously SEXUALIZE the violence. And although, yes, Brenda's murder is dwelled on at gruesome length, that also allows Hitchcock to merely suggest the film's other deaths; Babs's strangulation is seen in brief, almost subliminal flashbacks, while the other two victims appear only after the fact.

Of course, it's Brenda's murder that marks—and for many mars—this film. She is pushed against a wall, knocked down, and grabbed; her clothes are literally ripped from her body. (In the scene's saddest moment, she's glimpsed, midassault, trying with pathetic modesty to tuck her breast back into her brassiere.) When we last see her, she looks almost like a comic-book parody of a murder victim, her EYES blank, her tongue lolling.

Played in a desperate, sweaty silence punctuated only by the rapist's groaning, exultant "Lovely! Lovely! Lovely!" the rape and murder is a grotesque scene—and, most likely, the one that led Michael Caine, first choice for the part of the villain, to turn down the entire project as "disgusting," later saying he had a sort of "moral thing" against playing sadists who murdered women (a qualm he apparently conquered before signing on for BRIAN DE PALMA's Hitchcock homage *Dressed to Kill*).

Yet even as it dwells on the pain and humiliation visited on Brenda, the movie also observes and mourns her helplessness—in some ways, all our helplessness. Polite, even prim, Brenda wears a tiny gold cross around her throat; as the rapist looms over her, grunting, she half-dazedly recites the Twenty-third Psalm. And when he stops and curses her and begins to take off his tie—when she finally realizes who and what he is and that she has only seconds to call for aid—she screams, "Jesus, help me, help me!" It goes unheard.

And later, when the murderer takes an unsuspecting Babs upstairs to his apartment, the camera—the audience—follows quickly, nosily, expectantly. Until he takes her inside and the door shuts, and we know precisely what horror is about to follow. At which point the camera retreats—backing down the

STAIRS, unwilling to look, unable to help, dedicated to nothing except simply moving cravenly away. We are on our own in this world, and nobody—no heavenly deity, no godlike director—is going to save us.

Frenzy marked many things for Hitchcock. On the brightest side, it showed a 73-year-old director who (despite his own health problems and worry about his wife's) was still full of vigor and imagination. It showcased London's bustling Covent Garden—Hitchcock's own childhood neighborhood, where his father had been a merchant—and preserved it on film, just as developers were readying to tear it down. And it spotlighted a strong array of fine British actors, from leads Finch and BARRY FOSTER to, in smaller parts, the marvelous Billie Whitelaw and Jean Marsh. On its darkest side? It seemed to relish the abuse of women, turning rape into vicious entertainment.

Except a second or third viewing of *Frenzy* turns that reading on its head. Yes, the businessmen joke about the "silver lining" of being raped before you're murdered—but even the crudest misogynist would find nothing amusing about the assault visited on the sweet, nurturing Brenda. Because, ultimately, *Frenzy* isn't about the titillating aspects of rape; it doesn't present sadism and sexual DOMINATION as spicy fantasies. It simply shows us a pleasant, middle-aged lady—and the word *lady* is very deliberate—being abused and murdered, even as she cries out to God for help. And it dares us to look away, asking, In what kind of world can such things be?

And the answer is, only in the kind of world that Hitchcock saw in *VERTIGO*, in *Psycho*, in *Marnie* and *The Birds*—a world without sense, without help, without hope.

References

Ronald Bergan, "Jon Finch Obituary," *Guardian*, January 13, 2013, http://www .theguardian.com/film/2013/jan/13/jon-finch; Patrick McGilligan, *Alfred Hitchcock: A Life in Darkness and Light* (New York: HarperCollins, 2003), 704; Donald Spoto, *The Dark Side of Genius: The Life of Alfred Hitchcock* (New York: Da Capo Press, 1999), 505–17; *The Story of Frenzy*, directed by Laurent Bouzereau (2001), documentary, http://the.hitchcock.zone/wiki/The_Story_of_Frenzy_%282001%29_-_transcript; Peter Waymark, "Murder with Comedy at Covent Garden Market," *Times*, August 3, 1971, http://the.hitchcock.zone/wiki/The_Times_%2803/Aug/1971%29_-_Murder_with_comedy_at_Covent_Garden_Market.

FREUD, SIGMUND (1856–1939)

Austrian-born doctor hailed as the father of modern psychiatry. His influence remains immense, and his theories form a quiet but constant background to Hitchcock's stories, which often feature FETISHES, perversions, and neurotics with MOTHER fixations. Although Hitchcock showed no interest in a "serious" movie treatment of mental illness, such as *The Snake Pit*, he clearly knew the material and took the subject itself seriously; the most sensible character in *SPELLBOUND* is the rather Freudian analyst Dr. Brulov, and the only explanation we get of Norman Bates's behavior in *PSYCHO* comes courtesy of the state psychiatrist, Dr. Fred Richman.

The director, though, seems to have drawn the line at being analyzed himself, saving the detailing of his fears and obsessions for the movies; whether he profited from that or not, generations of audiences continue to.

Reference

Patrick McGilligan, *Alfred Hitchcock: A Life in Darkness and Light* (New York: HarperCollins, 2003), 173, 355.

FULTON, JOHN P. (1902–1966)

Nebraska-born son of an artist and theatrical designer who, in accordance with his father's wishes, trained as an engineer and surveyor. Still, by the early '20s, he'd abandoned that to work in Hollywood as a camera assistant. He was soon particularly known for his special-effects work with multiple exposures and traveling mattes; his successes ranged from the still-wondrous *The Invisible Man* in 1933 to the 1956 *The Ten Commandments*.

Although he never realized his dream of being a director, Fulton explored and expanded the world of optical effects far beyond what other cameramen had tried; even on such low-budget films as *I Married a Monster from Outer Space*, his shots were rooted in reality yet strangely dreamlike.

He first worked for Hitchcock on *SAB-OTEUR*, uncredited, on the Statue of Liberty sequence; their other collaborations would include *SHADOW OF A DOUBT, REAR WINDOW, TO CATCH A THIEF, THE TROUBLE WITH HARRY,* and *VERTIGO.*

He caught an infection while shooting a film in Spain and died in a London hospital at 63.

References

Bruce Eder, "John P. Fulton," *New York Times*, http://www.nytimes.com/movies/person/90755/John-P-Fulton/biography; "John P. Fulton," *IMDb*, http://www.imdb.com/name/nm0298483/bio?ref_=nm_ov_bio_sm; "The Wild and Wonderful World of John P. Fulton," *Matte Shot*, http://nzpetesmatteshot.blogspot.com/2010/08/wild-and-wonderful-world-of-john.html.

GABEL, MARTIN (1912–1986)

Philadelphia-born performer, particularly busy in the New York theater as an actor and on television as a narrator and personality. A charter member of Orson Welles's Mercury Theatre players, he seemed to specialize in playing not heroes but their dogged antagonists—he was Javert in Welles's radio version of *Les Miserables*, Cassius in the company's production of *Julius Caesar*—NORMAN LLOYD played Cinna—and went on to re-create Professor Moriarty and Stephen A. Douglas onstage.

Hollywood was less open to his talents, almost invariably casting him in gangsters, in pictures both worth watching (*Deadline U.S.A.*) and not (*Lady in Cement*). His one film as a director, *The Lost Moment*—an atmospheric adaptation of Henry James's *The Aspern Papers*, with Mercury Theatre alum Agnes Moorehead—was a prestigious flop. In Hitchcock's *MARNIE*, he was the businessman Sidney Strutt, from whom Marnie steals at the beginning of the film—and then runs into again at a party at her husband's home.

Offstage, Gabel was a good businessman, too, quietly investing in a number of hit plays, including the long-running *Life with Father*. His marriage to actress Arlene Francis lasted 40 years, and the two often appeared on the popular TV quiz show *What's My Line?*

He died of a heart attack at 73 at their home in Manhattan.

References

Glenn Fowler, "Martin Gabel, Actor, Director and Producer, Is Dead at 72," *New York Times*, May 23, 1986, http://www.nytimes.com/1986/05/23/obituaries/martin-gabel-actor-director-and-producer-is-dead-at-73.html; "Martin Gabel," *IMDb*, http://www.imdb.com/name/nm0300010/bio?ref_=nm_ov_bio_sm.

GAINSBOROUGH PICTURES

Founded in 1924, when SIR MICHAEL BALCON bought its Islington studios from PARAMOUNT, the London-based Gainsborough released Hitchcock's first five pictures as director—*THE PLEASURE GARDEN, THE MOUNTAIN EAGLE, THE LODGER, DOWNHILL*, and *EASY VIRTUE*—and, through its close relationships and coproductions with Germany's UFA studios, introduced its young director to the EXPRESSIONIST style and dark themes then prominent in German cinema.

Hitchcock would move on to BRITISH INTERNATIONAL PICTURES, which offered him more money, but he returned in the mid-'30s to make several movies for Balcon at Gainsborough's sister studio GAUMONT-BRITISH. The entire company was eventually taken over by the Rank Organization, and during the war, Gainsborough began to specialize in florid costume dramas. Rank closed the actual studio space in 1949 and eliminated the fading

Alfred Hitchcock, Cary Grant, and Ingrid Bergman in between shots of *Notorious*, a career high point for all three. *RKO Radio Pictures/Photofest © RKO Radio Pictures*

brand in 1951. Its one-time home is now a block of apartments.

References

"Gainsborough Pictures," *BFI Screenonline*, http://www.screenonline.org.uk/film/id/448996; Patrick McGilligan, *Alfred Hitchcock: A Life in Darkness and Light* (New York: HarperCollins, 2003), 93, 190.

GARMES, LEE (1898–1978)

Peoria-born filmmaker who began in 1916 as a painter's assistant at Thomas H. Ince's studios but soon graduated to cameraman. His work in silents ranged from Dorothy Gish comedies to Rin Tin Tin adventures. Early on, Garmes—who pioneered the use of incandescent lights in filming—showed a remarkable grasp of texture and shadow;

his career took off in the early '30s at the always-stylish PARAMOUNT, where his work with Josef von Sternberg created a chiaroscuro world full of exotic fantasy and MARLENE DIETRICH melodrama.

Although his work on *Gone with the Wind* was too obviously artistic for DAVID O. SELZNICK, who famously fired him from the production, he would work on other Selznick productions, including the warm *Since You Went Away* and the overheated *Duel in the Sun*; for Hitchcock's *THE PARADINE CASE*, he gave Alida Valli an almost glowing beauty (although NORMAN LLOYD always thought that naming his own mad character "Garmes" in the Selznick-supervised *SPELLBOUND* a few years before had been Hitchcock's, or Selznick's, inside dig at the cinematographer).

Yet despite his painstaking approach and widespread renown for "Rembrandtesque" lighting, Garmes was adaptable, able to capture the misty fantasy of *Portrait of Jennie*, the deep noir of *Nightmare Alley*, or the ugly violence of the grimy *Lady in a Cage*; an innovator until the end, he was one of the earliest (if oldest) voices promoting the use of videotape.

He died at 80 in Los Angeles.

References

"Lee Garmes," *IMDb*, http://www.imdb.com/name/nm0005716/bio?ref_=nm_ov_bio_sm; "Lee Garmes," *Mec Films*, http://www.mecfilms.com/leebio.htm; Norman Lloyd, interview with the author, July 2015.

GAUMONT-BRITISH

Sister studio to GAINSBOROUGH PICTURES. Hitchcock did some of his best mid-'30s work there for SIR MICHAEL BALCON and IVOR MONTAGU, where his pictures included *SABOTAGE* (where he had quarrels with Montagu over the budget), *YOUNG AND INNOCENT*, and *THE LADY VANISHES*. The entire company was eventually taken over by the Rank Organization, and during the war, Gainsborough began to specialize in florid costume dramas. Rank closed the actual studio space in 1949 and eliminated the fading brand in 1951. Its one-time home is now a block of apartments.

References

Gaumont British Picture Corporation Limited, http://www.gaumontbritish.com; Patrick McGilligan, *Alfred Hitchcock: A Life in Darkness and Light* (New York: Harper Collins, 2003), 190.

GAVIN, JOHN (1931–)

Tall, dull, and handsome leading man who grew up in California, went through prep school and Stanford (majoring in economics and Latin-American affairs), and was a naval intelligence officer during the Korean War. A career in business or politics seemed likely, but while serving as a technical adviser on a movie about the navy, he was encouraged to take a screen test; much to his shock, UNIVERSAL drew up a contract on the spot and at "so much money I couldn't resist."

It was a smart fallback decision for the studio; they already had Rock Hudson on the roster and thought it good business to have another ready-made, six-foot-plus STAR to put in his place (or at least threaten him with). But Gavin had no acting experience and little natural ability; pushed into Ross Hunter's string of remade melodramas (*Back Street, Imitation of Life*), he was rarely more than a pair of broad shoulders, a deep voice, and a good haircut.

If he was handsome, dependable, and utterly unexciting, though, that made him a good choice for Sam Loomis in *PSYCHO*; Gavin looks like the sort of quietly decent sort who'd be paying off his father's debts and alimony and completely unable to figure out what to do with a lively lover like JANET LEIGH's teasing Marion Crane. His casting also helped the film's sneaky theme of doubles; there are times when, watching him face down ANTHONY PERKINS in tight two-shots, you think the two could be brothers.

Years later, Gavin would claim that he found *Psycho* to be an uncongenial experience and the sex and violence terribly disturbing; indeed, Hitchcock was icy to him on the set, finding him insufficiently ardent in the opening bedroom scene with Leigh, and a little flat throughout. If anything, though, the resulting insecurity only helps Gavin's performance, which is built around obvious discomfort and painful confusion. (He can barely get out the words "Why was he . . . dressed like that?" as he sits in the police station after Norman Bates's arrest.)

Still, the dissatisfied Hitchcock—who sometimes referred to Gavin as "The Stiff"—would use him in two episodes of *THE ALFRED HITCHCOCK HOUR*, and the actor would later have a very good, lightly self-parodying role as the straight-arrow boyfriend in George Roy Hill's *Thoroughly Modern Millie*. He would also come frustratingly close to playing James Bond. (He was actually signed for *Diamonds Are Forever* but was paid off and dismissed once SEAN CONNERY finally agreed to star.)

Alternately embarrassed by his own work ("When I started out in front of the cameras I was green—raw, scared and just plain awful") and defensive ("Some of those early roles were unactable—even LAURENCE OLIVIER couldn't have done anything with them"), Gavin increasingly began pursuing other interests, including business and politics. In 1981, Ronald Reagan appointed him ambassador to Mexico, a post he held for five years. Since, he has mostly pursued business opportunities; his last acting credit was on an episode of TV's *Fantasy Island* in 1981.

"For a long time I wondered if I shouldn't have gone into something worthwhile, such as being a doctor," Gavin mused in the '70s, after the film parts had stopped coming. "I've only recently realized there's the actor in every human being—and to let it out, let it happen is a very wonderful, very giving thing. But I would have been so much happier in the past if I realized that sooner. You see, I would have relaxed."

References

Doris Klein Bacon, "John Gavin Is Our Man in Mexico," *People*, August 29, 1983, http://www.people.com/people/archive/article/0,,20085787,00.html; Marian Christy, "Handsome John Gavin, Under-dressed, Puts Down Label of Clotheshorse," *Reading Eagle*, August 29, 1973, https://news.google.com/newspapers?nid=1955&dat=19730829&id=jQsrAAAAIBAJ&sjid=cZoFAAAAIBAJ&pg=6276,4744274&hl=en; "John Gavin," *IMDb*, http://www.imdb.com/name/nm0001260/bio?ref_=nm_ov_bio_sm; Stephen Rebello, *Alfred Hitchcock and the Making of Psycho* (New York: HarperPerennial, 1991), 65, 86–88.

GEIN, ED (1906–1984)

Wisconsin-born farmer and handyman raised in isolation by an alcoholic father and abusive, fundamentalist MOTHER. His father died of a heart attack in 1940, and Ed Gein's older brother Henry died under mysterious circumstances while fighting a fire on their farm in 1944; one year later, after several strokes, his mother died, too, leaving Ed alone.

Gein boarded up most of the house and spent his days reading pulp-magazine stories of head-hunters, cannibals, and Nazi death-camp atrocities; he spent his nights robbing graves and bringing the bodies home, where he tanned them like leather and used them to decorate furniture, stitched into clothes, and fashioned into masks. He may have eaten some parts as well. He did not rob his mother's grave, but he robbed those around hers, in a rough circle, and used the masks, corset, and leggings he made out of their skin to then dress up as a woman and "become" her.

In 1957, Bernice Wordern disappeared from her nearby hardware store; left behind was a receipt that police connected to Gein. Going out to his farm, they discovered Wordern's body, headless, strung up in a shed "dressed out like a deer"; entering the house, they found rooms full of body parts, including a "mask" they later identified as being the preserved face of Mary Hogan, a bar owner who had disappeared three years before.

Gein pled not guilty by reason of INSANITY, was found unfit to stand trial, and confined to a maximum-security asylum. In 1968, he was finally deemed sane enough for court; he was tried and convicted of Wordern's murder and then sent back to a mental hospital. In the meantime, his house was burned down, presumably by outraged townspeople; the Ford he had used to haul the bodies home was sold to a carnival owner, who for a few profitable months charged people a quarter to look inside "the Ed Gein ghoul car."

Gein's case was, of course, Robert Bloch's inspiration for PSYCHO, although the novelist made several changes (the real Gein didn't run a motel, disinter his mother, or kill a woman in a shower), and JOSEPH STEFANO's script made even more revisions, changing him from a grizzled, drunken middle-aged loner into a pleasant young man with a neat sports jacket and ready smile.

Since then, the more gruesome details of Gein's case, particularly the cannibalism and human taxidermy—Gein had learned how to preserve hides from his father—have inspired several other famous horror films, including *The Silence of the Lambs* and *The Texas Chainsaw Massacre*. He has also been the subject of several more lightly fictionalized movies (*Deranged*) and was an early obsession of Errol Morris, then beginning his career as a documentarian, who actually interviewed him in the mental hospital; the movie was never made.

Gein died in 1984 and is buried in the same cemetery he once plundered. His own grave is unmarked.

References

"Obsessive Love for His Mother Drove Gein to Slay, Rob Graves," *Milwaukee Journal*, November 21, 1957, https://news.google.com/newspapers?nid=jvrRlaHg2sAC&dat=19571121&printsec=frontpage&hl=en; Harold Schechter, *Deviant: The Shocking True Story of Ed Gein, the Original Psycho* (New York: Gallery Books, 1998), xi, xii, 14; Troy Taylor, "Dead Men Do Tell Tales: Ed Gein," *American Hauntings*, http://www.prairieghosts.com/ed_gein.html.

GELIN, DANIEL (1921–2002)

Angers-born performer who left home at 16 to become an actor and made his film debut in 1940, soon finding a home in dramas as a sensitive leading man. Over the first half of a long career, he would work with HENRI-GEORGES CLOUZOT, Max Ophuls, Sacha Guitry, Jean Cocteau, and Louis Malle; Hitchcock cast him as Louis Bernard, the titular (and early) victim in the 1956 version of *THE MAN WHO KNEW TOO MUCH*. Later, substance abuse and a melodramatic romantic life took their toll, and the assignments grew less impressive. He was married three times and had four children—although he always refused to acknowledge actress Maria Schneider, whom he'd had by a French model.

He died in Paris at 81.

References

"Daniel Gelin," *IMDb*, http://www.imdb.com/name/nm0004625/bio?ref_=nm_ov_bio_sm; "Daniel Gelin, 81: Versatile French

Actor Had 60-Year Career," *Los Angeles Times*, November 30, 2002, http://articles.latimes.com/2002/nov/30/local/me-passings30.6.

GERAGHTY, CARMELITA (1901–1966)

Insouciant, Indiana-born performer who was mostly raised in New York, then Hollywood, where her father was a favored scriptwriter of Douglas Fairbanks. Because her parents disapproved of her going into show business, she used a pseudonym at first; eventually she got parts in Mack Sennett two-reelers and in 1924 was named a WAMPAS Baby Star.

The next year she went on to costar with VIRGINIA VALLI in Hitchcock's *THE PLEASURE GARDEN* (SIR MICHAEL BALCON was then pioneering the idea of importing Hollywood names to enliven British productions); the women's extravagances while on location bled the budget of an already-troubled project. Returning to Hollywood in 1926, Geraghty played Jordan Baker in the first version of *The Great Gatsby*, an adaptation that F. Scott Fitzgerald loathed. ("It's rotten and awful and terrible and we left," Zelda wrote after a screening.) No prints of the film survive.

Geraghty's career was equally short-lived; a creature of the carefree Jazz Age, by the crash, her name was at the bottom of cast lists, and by the early '30s, most of the work she found was in cheap westerns. She married an MGM producer in 1934 and retired two years later; she took up painting and later in life began to exhibit with some success.

She died of a heart attack at 65 in Manhattan.

References

"Carmelita Geraghty," *IMDb*, http://www.imdb.com/name/nm0313867/bio?ref_=nm_ov_bio_sm; Alfred Hitch-cock, "My Screen Memories," *Film Weekly* (May 1936), http://the.hitchcock.zone/wiki/Film_Weekly_%281936%29_-_My_Screen_Memories; François Truffaut, *Hitchcock/Truffaut*, rev. ed. (New York: Touchstone, 1985), 31–39.

GIELGUD, JOHN (1904–2000)

London-born performer whose father's family were long-exiled Eastern European aristocrats (they had lost their castle in a premature revolt against Czar Nicholas I). His mother's family included many famed British actors, including the great Shakespearean interpreter Dame Ellen Terry. In Gielgud's case, breeding did tell; over an extraordinarily long career, he rarely gave a performance that did not draw on both family inheritances, combining his hawk-like profile and chilly hauteur with a speaking voice that sounded like silver bells. His parents, though, were not in favor of his dreams of an acting career, and the teenage Gielgud had to promise that, if he were not successful by 25, he would get a job in an office.

Still, he began his career in the family business—literally—by working for his cousin Phyllis Nelson-Terry as an understudy; later he would enroll at the Royal Academy of Dramatic Art under the tutoring of the equally mellifluous CLAUDE RAINS. By the late '20s, Gielgud was a regular fixture on the West End, at the Old Vic, and on Broadway, where he had particular success in the works of Chekhov, Shakespeare, and Noel Coward. There was no need for an office job; he had made his family's deadline.

Gielgud made his movie debut in 1924 and appeared in the very early talkie *The Clue of the New Pin* in 1929 but disliked the modern craft of movie acting at first; his experience on Hitchcock's *SECRET AGENT* in 1936 was an unpleasant one for both, as Hitchcock had decided, too late, the character was passive and unsympathetic, and Gielgud craved the sort of dramatic guidance the filmmaker was uninterested in providing.

Of course it did not help that Hitchcock had really hoped to get ROBERT DONAT for the lead so he could reteam the STARS of his smash THE 39 STEPS or that while filming the exhausted Gielgud was also appearing on the West End in Romeo and Juliet with Peggy Ashcroft. "I had to get up very early in the morning and was always fidgeting to get away by five or six for the evening performance, so I grew to dislike working for the cinema," Gielgud wrote later of the shoot. "Of course I was paid more money than in the theatre, but I had a feeling that no one thought I was sufficiently good-looking."

Gielgud would appear on film only once more until Julius Caesar in 1953. (He worked chiefly on the stage, where he did rapturously received productions of Crime and Punishment, Hamlet, and Richard II.) But he found James Mason's work onscreen in Julius Caesar intriguing, as well as the Hollywood fees being earned by younger protégées like LAURENCE OLIVIER; Gielgud would do more and more film work over the decades to come, while always returning regularly to the stage.

Although his brilliantly conceived, musically delivered performances were soon out of step with the working-class dramas beginning to take over the theater, Gielgud—who had already survived the scandal of a 1953 arrest in a men's room for soliciting sex—would remain an accomplished star. He would give many great live performances, including his own one-man show The Ages of Man, a collection of Shakespeare's speeches and sonnets, and Home, in which he appeared with lifelong friend Sir Ralph Richardson; his many movies ranged from Becket and Gandhi to Arthur and Caligula. He never retired.

Gielgud died at home a year after the death of his long-time companion, Martin Hensler. He was 96.

References

John Gielgud, *Early Stages: An Autobiography* (San Francisco: Mercury House, 1989), 159–60, 164; "John Gielgud," *IMDb*, http://www.imdb.com/name/nm0000024/bio?ref_=nm_ov_bio_sm; Patrick McGilligan, *Alfred Hitchcock: A Life in Darkness and Light* (New York: HarperCollins, 2003), 183–84; "Sir John Gielgud," *Encyclopaedia Britannica*, http://www.britannica.com/biography/John-Gielgud; Donald Spoto, *The Dark Side of Genius: The Life of Alfred Hitchcock* (New York: Da Capo Press, 1999), 152–54; François Truffaut, *Hitchcock/Truffaut*, rev. ed. (New York: Touchstone, 1985), 105.

GILLIAT, SIDNEY (1908–1994)

Born in Cheshire, the son of a newspaper editor, Gilliat started in films doing a bit of everything, including small parts; he reportedly wrote some of the titles for Hitchcock's CHAMPAGNE in 1928 and the next year did some preproduction research for the Isle of Man set of THE MANXMAN.

Neither job won him a screen credit, but he soon partnered with FRANK LAUNDER to turn out screenplays; their fifth effort, THE LADY VANISHES, became (after briefly gaining the interest of another director and then being rewritten) Alfred Hitchcock's 1938 hit and the first to feature the director's name on theater marquees.

Gilliat would do some work on Hitchcock's JAMAICA INN (and he and Launder would do a sort of spin-off of The Lady Vanishes, Night Train to Munich, for Carol Reed), but as Hitchcock observed, the screenwriters were not happy seeing directors get most of the credit on films; Gilliat and Launder soon turned to producing and directing their own scripts, including *Captain Boycott*, *Green for Danger*, and the *St. Trinian's* comedies.

He died in Wiltshire at age 86.

References

Gilbert Adair, "Obituary: Sidney Gilliat," *Independent*, June 2, 1994, http://the.hitch cock.zone/wiki/The_Independent_%2802/ Jun/1994%29_-_Obituary:_Sidney_Gilliat; David Cairns, "Individual Features: The Cinema of Launder and Gilliat," *BritMovie*, http://www.britmovie.co.uk/2008/08/26/ individual-pictures-the-cinema-of -launder-and-gilliat; Patrick McGilligan, *Alfred Hitchcock: A Life in Darkness and Light* (New York: HarperCollins, 2003), 206–8, 222–23; "Sidney Gilliat," *IMDb*, http://www.imdb.com/name/nm0319148/ bio?ref_=nm_ov_bio_sm; Donald Spoto, *The Dark Side of Genius: The Life of Alfred Hitchcock* (New York: Da Capo Press, 1999), 172–74.

THE GIRL (GB 2012)

DIRECTOR: Julian Jarnold.
SCREENPLAY: Gwyneth Hughes, based on the book *Spellbound by Beauty*, by Donald Spoto.
PRODUCERS: Amanda Jenks, Marvin Saven, Genevieve Hofmeyr.
CINEMATOGRAPHY: John Pardue.
EDITOR: Andrew Hulme.
ORIGINAL MUSIC: Phillip Miller.
CAST: Sienna Miller (Tippi Hedren), Toby Jones (Alfred Hitchcock), Imelda Staunton (Alma Hitchcock).
RUNNING TIME: 91 minutes. Color.
ORIGINALLY BROADCAST BY: BBC/Showtime.

A docudrama based chiefly on the chapters in DONALD SPOTO's book *Spellbound by Beauty: Alfred Hitchcock and His Leading Ladies*, detailing the director's relationship with TIPPI HEDREN, beginning with him signing her to a contract and ending with their professional and personal split after *MARNIE*. Sienna Miller does a fair job of playing Hedren without ever quite capturing her glacial beauty; as Hitchcock, Toby Jones is less successful, looking like a man trapped in bad makeup and a padded suit.

The film hews pretty closely to Spoto's book, statements made by the late EVAN HUNTER, and interviews given by Hedren, and the actress—who was consulted by the producers and by Miller—gave the film approving marks. Still, she said it was a little relentless, portraying none of the playfulness that Hitchcock showed, too, at least before his obsessiveness grew intolerable. "It wasn't a constant barrage of harassment," she admitted in interviews to promote the broadcast. "If it had been constantly the way we have had to do it in this film, I would have been long gone."

Of course, the film was also strongly criticized, albeit sometimes by people who hadn't been present for the events it covered. Director Sacha Gervasi and actor Anthony Hopkins—who had their own picture about the making of *PSYCHO* coming up, *HITCHCOCK*—found it lacking, with Gervasi calling it "one-note" and Hopkins politely wondering if it were really "necessary to put all that into a movie." Longtime Hitchcock defenders Tony Lee Moral (author of several books on Hitchcock's films) and JOHN RUSSELL TAYLOR (the director's authorized biographer) were among those who also questioned the movie's facts or called its conclusions "absurd." An entire site, *Save Hitchcock* (www.savehitchcock.com), sought to rebut the allegations.

For her part, Hedren said she thought the film was largely accurate and hoped it would be helpful. "I hope that young women who do see this film know that they do not have to acquiesce to anything that they do not feel is morally right. . . . There was absolutely nothing I could do legally, whatsoever. There were no laws about this kind of a situation. If this had happened today, I would be a very rich woman. But I can look at myself in the mirror, and I can be proud. I feel strong. I lived through it beautifully."

References
Nick Clark, "Who Was the Real Sir Alfred?" *Independent*, August 15, 2015, http://www .independent.co.uk/arts-entertainment/ films/news/who-was-the-real-sir-alfred -hitchcock-director-sacha-gervasi-backs -auteur-against-sadistic-monster-por trayed-in-the-girl-8462209.html; "Hop- kins' Hitch with Hedren," *Evening Stan- dard*, January 8, 2013, http://www.standard .co.uk/news/londoners-diary/hopkinss -hitch-with-hedren-8442836.html; Mayer Nissim, "'Hitchcock' Anthony Hopkins: 'The Girl' Wasn't Necessary," *Digital Spy*, January 9, 2013, http://www.digitalspy .com/movies/news/a449727/hitchcock -anthony-hopkins-the-girl-wasnt-necessary .html#~p598JM9MbifAbW; Rob Salem, "Hitchcock and Hedren Now a TV Movie," *Star*, October 19, 2012, http://www.thestar .com/entertainment/television/2012/10/19/ hitchcock_and_hedren_now_an_hbo _movie.html; *Save Hitchcock*, http://save hitchcock.com.

GRAHAM, WINSTON (1908–2003)
Prolific Manchester-born author who pub- lished his first novel in 1934 and his last in 2002. His most successful were installments in the Poldark series, set on the Cornish coast during the late-18th and early-19th centuries and creating a broad historical saga set among the great families of the area. They were adapted several times for British television.

Graham also wrote thrillers, a num- ber of which became modestly budgeted British films—*Take My Life*, *Night with- out Stars*, *Fortune Is a Woman*. The noir- ish *MARNIE*, however, published in 1961, was quietly bought by Alfred Hitchcock, who initially saw it as a way to lure GRACE KELLY away from Monaco and back to the screen. It did not work, nor did Graham's story reach the screen quite unchanged— Hitchcock immediately changed the setting to America, softened the ending (which was even bleaker in the book), and tried to make Marnie's predatory SEXUAL black- mailer somewhat more sympathetic (start- ing with casting SEAN CONNERY).

If any of it annoyed Graham, then he, quite typically, kept his mouth shut, depos- ited his check, and went back to writing a new book.

He died at 95 in London.

References
Dennis Barker, "Obituary: Winston Gra- ham," *Guardian*, July 14, 2003, http:// www.theguardian.com/news/2003/jul/14/ guardianobituaries.booksobituaries; *Win- ston Graham and Poldark*, http://www.win stongraham.org.

GRANGER, FARLEY (1925–2011)
San Jose, CA–born performer from a rich family fallen on hard times. It was while they were living in straitened circumstances in Los Angeles that their teenage son took up amateur theatricals and was discovered by a studio scout. He managed to film small parts in two movies—and then shipped out to Hawaii with the navy, where, he later boasted, he lost his virginity twice in one night (first to a young woman in a bor- dello and then to one of the sailors waiting downstairs in the parlor).

Returning to Hollywood after the war, Granger resumed his career, starting with the gritty classic *They Live by Night* in 1948; Hitchcock signed him that same year for *ROPE*, playing the more GUILT-ridden of the two murderers. Despite the technical difficulties of the shoot, Granger enjoyed working with the director. "Hitchcock was very open about everything," Granger says. "He often invited me to the house for dinner. He had a great wine cellar and we'd all get drunk together. That was sort of the family pastime, I think."

After a few more movies, including the noir dramas *Side Street* and *Edge of Doom*, Granger would return to appear in Hitchcock's *STRANGERS ON A TRAIN*. "We just had a jolly old time on that one," he said later. "The crew loved (Hitchcock), because he knew what he was doing. . . . Every day you went to work you knew you were working on something wonderful."

But if Granger was good in it, then he was a little too soft, a little too petulant, for most Hollywood movies. His characters tended to be passive, even submissive young men—in both *Rope* and *Strangers on a Train* his protagonists are clearly DOMINATED by the movie's aggressive, boastful murderers. Other pretty, introverted young actors could occasionally twist their mouths in a snarl; in his performances, Granger mostly pouted. That was not an advantage in getting leading-man parts.

Nor was the actor's sexuality; unlike others at that time, he was relatively open about his fondness for both men and women and didn't shy away from characters who seemed to share that orientation. (For a long time he was in a relationship with ARTHUR LAURENTS, who wrote the *Rope* screenplay.)

This hardly bothered Hitchcock, who had been friendly with gay actors since IVOR NOVELLO back in the silents. (Of course, it was also true that Hitchcock found gay men and lesbians exotic, even a little scary—many of his villains, from the "half-caste" in *MURDER!* to Leonard in *NORTH BY NORTHWEST*, either hint at or declare their HOMOSEXUALITY.)

Other people, however, were less broadminded, particularly mogul Samuel Goldwyn, who had Granger under contract and had been disturbed early on to hear of the young actor's friendships with certain "theatrical" talents.

"I got called into Goldwyn's office, and told I was not to be seen with Aaron Copland anymore. That he was a 'known homosexual.' And first I laughed and then I got very mad and said, 'Look, I'll be seen with whoever I want.' And I stormed out," Granger said. "I mean, who were these little pissants? . . . You had (gossip columnists) Hedda Hopper and Louella Parsons hanging over the whole town like a couple of storm clouds. But I just didn't pay any attention to it. I just lived my own life."

Tired of the studio typecasting and Hollywood homophobia, eventually Granger bought himself out of his contract and went off to Europe in search of better parts. A fine one almost immediately arrived in Luchino Visconti's *Senso* with ALIDA VALLI. But other roles of that caliber proved hard to come by. Granger came back to America to find that other STARS were now at the top (and suspected that Goldwyn had blackballed him with other producers). He did some television work and then returned to Europe, but the days of lavish international productions were ending; what he was mostly offered now (and almost invariably accepted) were cheap crime pictures with sadistic plots and titles like *Kill Me, My Love!* and *The Red-Headed Corpse*.

Eventually Granger came back to America, this time for good, where he shared a modest Manhattan apartment with his longtime partner, Robert Calhoun; did some stage work and a soap opera; and finally retired to write his memoirs—dishing the dirt with the same cool attitude he'd once fired across a wide wooden desk at Sam Goldwyn.

He died at 85 in New York.

References

"Farley Granger," *IMDb*, http://www.imdb
.com/name/nm0335048/bio?ref_=nm_ov
_bio_sm; Neil Genzlinger, "Farley Granger,
Screen Star of the 1950s, Dies at 85," *New
York Times*, March 29, 2011, http://www
.nytimes.com/2011/03/30/arts/actor-farley
-granger-dies-at-85.html; Farley Granger,
interview with the author, April 2007; Farley Granger with Robert Calhoun, *Include
Me Out: My Life from Goldwyn to Broadway* (New York: St. Martin's Press, 2007),
67–71, 107–110.

GRANT, CARY (1904–1986)

"Everyone wants to be Cary Grant," he
liked to tell reporters. And then pause—his
timing was always perfect—before adding
"Even I want to be Cary Grant." It was hard
work, but he made it look easy.

He was born Archibald Leach in Bristol, the son of a coldly pragmatic father
and an emotionally unstable mother who
had never gotten over the death of an older
child. When Archie was nine, his father
secretly had her committed; when Archie
asked where she was, he simply told her she
had gone "on holiday" without saying goodbye. The next year, Elias Leach divorced his
wife and remarried, now telling Archie that
his mother had died. (Her son wouldn't find
out the truth for another two decades, years
after he had become a STAR.)

Little Archie was soon unwelcome in
the new household and failing grammar
school; his solution was to run off and join
the circus or at least a troupe of acrobats.
By 16, he had followed the group to America, where they played everywhere from
Coney Island to ornate vaudeville houses;
Archie's specialty was stilt-walking. When
after two years the rest of the company
packed up for England, Leach stayed on.
There was nothing to go back to, anyway.

Eventually he landed in Hollywood,
where PARAMOUNT gave him a contract
and a name change—and Mae West, looking for a leading man for *She Done Him
Wrong*, spotted him on the lot and told her
director, "If he can talk, I'll take him." Still,
his early pictures with West and MAR-
LENE DIETRICH only presented him as
simple eye candy, a fantasy figure for the
studio's leading ladies to make eyes at.

He showed some of what he could
do as a rascally Cockney in *Sylvia Scarlett*
opposite Katharine Hepburn, but the film
flopped; the real turning point came with
The Awful Truth in 1937, one of the truly
perfect screwball comedies, and a success
that led to *Holiday*, *Bringing Up Baby*, *His
Girl Friday*, and *The Philadelphia Story* (as
well as the change-of-pace dramas *Only
Angels Have Wings*, *In Name Only*, and the
roaring boys' adventure *Gunga Din*).

At which point, Hitchcock showed up.
Grant would make four films for the director—SUSPICION and NOTORIOUS, and
then (after being lured out of a premature,
mid-'50s retirement) *TO CATCH A THIEF*
and *NORTH BY NORTHWEST*. The movies were spread out over two decades and
skipped from genre to genre—thriller, spy
film, romantic caper, and then a spy film
again. But in some ways, they were the
same film because in many ways Grant
played the same character, the perfect
character: The man whose love cannot be
trusted.

Like everyone in Hollywood, Hitchcock knew that "Cary Grant" was a construct, a creature of invention, a dream;
unlike most studio-made stars, Grant lived
the lie with a grin, treated IDENTITY like
a game. He joked about "Archie Leach,"
named a pet terrier after him, even sneaked
a reference to the fellow into *His Girl Friday*. He made no secret of his real origins.
In fact, he invited you to help, drew you
into his deception (and would do so even
in the movies in which—every so often—
he would shoot a quick helpless look at the

camera, breaking the fourth wall, making you share in the game).

And something in Grant's public double life—beyond whatever private secret life he may have had—appealed to Hitchcock. It had always been part of his genius to see something more than celebrity in his stars and cast them accordingly; if Hitchcock hated directing actors, then it was only because he felt he shouldn't have to. (And if he had to, then it was because he had failed earlier on; if you matched the right actor to the right role, then there was little else you had to do.)

And so the parts Hitchcock cast Grant in were very specific. In *Suspicion*, he is a man his wife suspects of thievery (and worse); in *Notorious*, he is a spy who tricks and pushes a woman he loves into sleeping with the enemy; in *To Catch a Thief*, he is a suitor who is using a beauty and her diamonds for his own purposes; in *North by Northwest*, he is a shamelessly shallow bachelor who believes in nothing but self-preservation.

He is the man that every woman falls in love with and then spends the rest of the relationship worrying about, checking up on, trying to decode, attempting to make excuses for. He is the man whom you can depend on to be undependable. He is the man whom you know will always do the right thing—for him—and whom you can only pray will also do the right thing for you when it finally counts.

These are Hollywood movies, of course, and so of course Grant does do the right thing at last. But there is a certain kind of slippery selfishness even in Grant's heroes that you would never see in JAMES STEWART's work for Hitchcock, let alone GREGORY PECK's. It never crosses into outright villainy, perhaps. (Despite what Hitchcock and Grant later occasionally said in INTERVIEWS, DONALD SPOTO suggests that the two never seriously planned

for his character in *Suspicion* to be a murderer.) But it didn't have to. In Hitchcock's movies, Grant is every lover's worst nightmare, the beloved who has his own agenda, his own past, his own plans, and keeps all of them from you—until you catch him in a lie, at which point he only tells a bigger one, smiling. And you believe him because you want to.

It is a very specific character, and kudos to the director (and to the star) for seeing that in him, but it would not work for every film. Grant could have played the secretive Max in *REBECCA* or the coldly deceptive Tony in *DIAL M FOR MURDER*; he probably couldn't have played the damaged John Ballantyne in *SPELLBOUND* or rueful Rupert in *ROPE*. It was not that Cary Grant could not have played a villain. It's that Cary Grant could never have played anyone who doubted himself. No, for Hitchcock, Grant was always the cocky confidence man, the grinning liar, the poisoned bonbon—and even as the films end happily, it's difficult to imagine an easy marriage ahead for any of the women he takes into his arms just before the final credits.

Of course, no one was more attuned to his image than the actor himself, and a large part of that image was being able to credibly play a leading man; still, in typical Hollywood fashion, as he got older, his costars got younger, the portrayal of passion more and more subdued.

Grant (smartly) insisted that the script of the very HITCHCOCKIAN *Charade* (in which he's once again a charming liar) be rewritten so Audrey Hepburn was the romantic aggressor; to have a 59-year-old silver fox chasing after a 33-year-old gamine might be distasteful. The next year *Father Goose* required similar careful treatment with Leslie Caron, but by 1966 and *Walk, Don't Run*, a remake of *The More the Merrier*, it was no longer necessary;

the once-ageless Grant was now cast in the avuncular, supporting role.

He promptly retired afterward, and although there was still much in life to enjoy—serving on corporate boards, doing occasional public appearances, doting on his only child, the daughter of his fourth, penultimate marriage to Dyan Cannon—he never appeared in another movie. And in some ways it was his last and gentlest lie, leaving us with the Cary Grant we grew up with, the lover who never aged, the man Archie Leach invented. "I pretended to be somebody I wanted to be and I finally became that person," he said once. "Or he became me. Or we met at some point."

He died at 82 of a cerebral hemorrhage in Davenport, IA.

References

Peter Bogdanovich, *Who the Hell's in It* (New York: Knopf, 2004), 97–124; "Cary Grant," *Biography*, http://www.biography.com/people/cary-grant-9318103; "Cary Grant," *IMDb*, http://www.imdb.com/name/nm0000026/bio?ref_=nm_ov_bio_sm; Patrick McGilligan, *Alfred Hitchcock: A Life in Darkness and Light* (New York: HarperCollins, 2003), 493–94; Donald Spoto, *The Dark Side of Genius: The Life of Alfred Hitchcock* (New York: Da Capo Press, 1999), 243–44; David Thomson, *The New Biographical Dictionary of Film* (New York: Knopf, 2002), 351–52.

GREEN, HILTON A. (1929–2013)

Movie brat born to B-movie director Alfred E. Green and former silent STAR Vivian Reed. After college, he entered the movie business as an assistant director, serving in that capacity mostly on TV shows, including an episode of *SUSPICION* (the tense, ticking-bomb story "FOUR O'CLOCK," directed by Alfred Hitchcock) and more than 40 installments of *ALFRED HITCHCOCK PRESENTS*.

He was part of the TV crew that Hitchcock took with him to make *PSYCHO*, knowing that they were all used to working quickly and efficiently; Green went on to direct one episode of *Alfred Hitchcock Presents*, assistant-direct another show on *THE ALFRED HITCHCOCK HOUR*, and then returned as assistant director for *MARNIE* and (years later, uncredited) as a production manager on *FAMILY PLOT*.

The association stood him in good stead when, after Hitchcock's death, UNIVERSAL decided to produce a *Psycho* sequel. After a director and screenwriter were hired (and an initially reluctant ANTHONY PERKINS signed on, too), Green was brought on as a producer, primarily to reinforce the message that the project was being made with respect. After calling PATRICIA HITCHCOCK and getting her blessing, Green agreed.

The success of the film would allow Green to go on to produce other films, including *Sixteen Candles*, although Hitchcock remained a particularly profitable specialty; Green also produced *Psycho III* and *Psycho IV*, appeared in a half-dozen documentaries on Hitchcock and his films, and consulted on Gus Van Sant's shot-for-shot *Psycho* remake in 1998.

He died at 84 in Pasadena.

References

"Film Legend and 1960's Psycho Hilton Green Dies in Pasadena Home, 84," *Pasadena Now*, October 4, 2013, http://www.pasadenanow.com/main/film-legend-and-1960-psychos-hilton-green-dies-in-pasadena-home-84/#.VeiLtZdUV5s; "Hilton A. Green," *IMDb*, http://www.imdb.com/name/nm0337906/bio?ref_=nm_ov_bio_sm.

GREENE, GRAHAM (1904–1981)

A product of the Victorian age, a CATHOLIC, a perceptive critic and screenwriter, and a prolific author of thrillers whose characters were often wracked by GUILT and caught up in far-flung conspiracies—you would think that Graham Greene would have been a constant and natural collaborator with Hitchcock. You would be wrong.

Already a young, published novelist, Greene reviewed films from 1935 to 1940 (with a break when a particularly harsh remark about Shirley Temple's appeal brought a libel suit and a well-timed trip out of the country); he was there for the best of Hitchcock's English period. And, it seems, he didn't like any of it. A fan of espionage stories, he said that Hitchcock's *THE 39 STEPS* had "inexcusably" spoiled JOHN BUCHAN's original novel, and what Hitchcock did to W. SOMERSET MAUGHAM's Ashenden stories in *THE SECRET AGENT* was "deplorable."

No fan of the director, he would broaden the criticism many years later to include *CAHIERS DU CINEMA*, too, and give his final word on the subject, maintaining that, "whatever Monsieur Truffaut may say," Hitchcock's films merely "consist of a series of small, 'amusing,' melodramatic situations. . . . [T]hey mean nothing: they lead to nothing."

Not surprisingly, Greene made a single contemporary exception for Hitchcock's bleakest, grubbiest thriller of the '30s, *SABOTAGE*, admitting that while "I have sometimes doubted Mr. Hitchcock's talent," many of the sequences—Greene singles out the bomb on the bus, the screening of *WHO KILLED COCK ROBIN?*, the knifing at the kitchen table—were first rate. "As a director, he has always known exactly his right place to put the camera," the critic smartly observed, "and there is only one right place in any scene."

Some of Greene's criticisms have weight, of course—most of Hitchcock's films, particularly in that early period, were more plot-driven than character-oriented, and plausibility was never something the filmmaker valued very highly. Some of his

other objections were clearly colored by Greene's having admired both Buchan and Maugham's thrillers since childhood (and already writing his own spy stories, with their own very different sensibilities).

Later, Greene who had first sold a novel to the movies in 1934, would get regular checks from Hollywood, sometimes for original screenplays; three of his thrillers were turned into films by American studios during the '40s, when Hitchcock was regularly assigned similar properties, and the director's friendly old nemesis, DAVID O. SELZNICK, eventually lent a producer's hand to Greene's *The Third Man*, made in 1949 by Carol Reed. At one point, the novelist was even approached to do the script for *I CONFESS*, an intriguing notion. Still, Greene and Hitchcock never worked together.

Yet perhaps their work is not so far apart. The specter of temptation that waits behind our every step, the idea that guilt might haunt a man guilty of nothing but a briefly sinful wish—those ideas concern both those men. As do the small touches of the everyday that give life to even their most fantastic entertainments—the slightly shabby, insistently chatty assassin of Hitchcock's *FOREIGN CORRESPONDENT* is as much a character out of a Greene novel as the completely fictitious, utterly endangered spy in Greene's *Our Man in Havana* seems like one out of a Hitchcock film.

So no, the two men never collaborated. Yet in some ways, they never needed to.

References

Graham Greene, *The Pleasure Dome: The Collected Film Criticism of Graham Greene* (London: Oxford University Press, 1980), 1–2, 74–75, 122–23; "Graham Greene," *Encyclopaedia Britannica*, http://www.britannica.com/biography/Graham-Greene; Patrick McGilligan, *Alfred Hitchcock: A Life in Darkness and Light* (New York: HarperCollins, 2003), 441.

GREENMANTLE
Another JOHN BUCHAN thriller, the author's own sequel to his *The Thirty-Nine Steps*, and one that Hitchcock always wanted to do; in this one, set during World War I, hero Richard Hannay has to foil Germany's plans to ignite a worldwide Islamic revolt. But although Hitchcock pursued this for several years after arriving in America—CARY GRANT, he thought, would have been a suitable lead—the rights were too expensive.

Reference
Patrick McGilligan, *Alfred Hitchcock: A Life in Darkness and Light* (New York: Harper-Collins, 2003), 247–48, 264–65, 306–7.

GREET, CLARE (1871–1939)
Leicestershire-born stage veteran who made her movie debut at age 50 in *The Rotters* and would go on to play mostly small parts as older women, almost invariably servants; a list of her credits includes a number of characters described only as "Landlady," "Cook," and "Registry Office Cleaner" (although at least she got to play Mrs. Hudson, the landlady, in the early Sherlock Holmes film, *The Sign of Four*).

She was the most frequent (if occasionally uncredited) cast member in Hitchcock films, appearing in seven, starting with the unfinished *NUMBER 13* in 1922 (which she helped finance when money ran low) and concluding with *JAMAICA INN*, her last picture, in 1939. She also appeared in *LORD CAMBER'S LADIES*, which Hitchcock only produced—her steady work perhaps a sign of his gratitude for her early help.

She died at 67 in London.

References
"Alfred Hitchcock's Most Wanted Actresses," *Alfred Hitchcock Geek*, http://www.alfredhitchcockgeek.com/2010/08/alfred-hitchcocks-most-wanted-actresses.html; "Clare Greet," *Cyranos*, http://www.cyranos.ch/spgree-e.html; "Clare Greet,"

IMDb, http://www.imdb.com/name/nm0339504.

GRIFFITH, MELANIE (1957–)
Manhattan-born performer and daughter of TIPPI HEDREN and advertising executive Peter Griffith. The couple divorced when she was four. Then a 30-ish model and now a single mother, Hedren quickly accepted Alfred Hitchcock's offer of a movie contract.

Hitchcock's possessiveness of his new STAR led him to not only isolate her from her fellow actors but also her child; later, Griffith would remember that suddenly "I wasn't allowed even to visit my mom at the studio." After production finally wrapped, Hitchcock presented Griffith with a doll fashioned after her mother and dressed in a replica costume from the film; it would have been a thoughtful gift if the wooden box it came in hadn't resembled a coffin.

A little more than 20 years later, Griffith would rekindle the Hitchcock connection by starring in BRIAN DE PALMA's fevered *VERTIGO/REAR WINDOW* mash-up *Body Double*, playing the pornographic actress Holly Body; she would also appear on the revived *ALFRED HITCHCOCK PRESENTS* show in a remake of the original episode "Man from the South." After a career high point in *Working Girl*, however, Griffith's career began to slip, interrupted by personal problems and substance-abuse issues; although she continues to act, it's mostly as a guest star on television shows.

References
Jay Carr, "Melanie Griffith: Poised for Stardom," *Boston Globe*, December 22, 1988, http://the.hitchcock.zone/wiki/Boston_Globe_%2822/Dec/1988%29_-_Melanie_Griffith_poised_for_stardom; "Melanie Griffith," *IMDb*, http://www.imdb.com/name/nm0000429/bio?ref_=nm_ov_bio_sm.

GUILT

In a standard Hollywood mystery or mass-market thriller, the question of guilt is both central—Who committed the crime?—and simple. The criminal may be known to us at the start (or never discovered at all); he may be kept offscreen until the end or turn out to be the (anti)hero. But guilt is present chiefly as a legal concept: Who did this? The concept of guilt is far murkier in Hitchcock.

Legally speaking, many of Hitchcock's villains—Uncle Charlie in *SHADOW OF A DOUBT*, Bruno in *STRANGERS ON A TRAIN*, Norman in *PSYCHO*, Bob Rusk in *FRENZY*—could probably plead not guilty by reason of INSANITY; arguably, they can't tell right from wrong. They are not innocent in any broad sense, yet they can't really be fully blamed for their acts. They are walking aberrations, accidents, misfiring circuits in the human machine.

It's Hitchcock's other, supposedly saner murderers who are his real concern. Because they aren't so much innocent as guiltless—they do know right from wrong and simply do not care. They are killers who act out of not psychosis but greed and calm expediency. Vandamm dispatches assassins to kill the troublesome Roger Thornhill in *NORTH BY NORTHWEST*, Tony hires a man to strangle his wife in *DIAL M FOR MURDER*, Fry burns a coworker alive in *SABOTEUR*—these men don't lose sleep over their deeds. They don't even miss meals. And it's that they can sin without guilt is what, in Hitchcock's world, truly makes them villains, while feeling not only regretful but morally responsible—even though you may not have even personally done anything wrong—is what marks you as a Hitchcock hero. In Hitchcock, only the good feel guilty.

Legal culpability rarely enters into it. The childhood death of John Ballantyne's brother in *SPELLBOUND* was an accident; Guy assumed that Bruno's murderous promise in *Strangers on a Train* was a drunken JOKE. The death of *REBECCA* was an accident, too (and one she carefully helped incite); the murder of the drunken sailor in *MARNIE*, the act of a terrified toddler. These are not crimes any jury would convict you of, probably not even sins in the eyes of any loving God. In some cases, they are acts completely beyond our control, stemming solely from illness or happenstance. Should Scottie really feel guilty for having *VERTIGO*? Should Manny really blame himself for being mistakenly arrested in *THE WRONG MAN*? Yet all these characters carry that guilt with them, sometimes for decades, letting it twist their lives, sour their love affairs.

In fact, in Hitchcock's world—built so solidly on the rigid Catechism of his youth—it does not matter whether you actually commit an illegal act. In his unforgiving eyes, just temptation is bad enough; it's not necessary that you go through with the crime, merely that you considered it, like Guy in *Strangers on a Train*, or even accidentally profited by it, like Father Logan in *I CONFESS*. Even somehow just witnessing it—like Jeff peeping into a killer's apartment in *REAR WINDOW*—is enough to condemn you as a kind of accomplice. Taken to its logical extreme in some of the films, this becomes Hitchcock's trickiest, nastiest bit of audience manipulation, in which he first encourages us to identify with the criminal and then upbraids us for it.

It's no accident that the actors playing his villains—ROBERT WALKER in *Strangers on a Train*, ANTHONY PERKINS in *Psycho*, JOSEPH COTTEN in *Shadow of a Doubt*—are almost always far more charming and attractive than the people trying to stop them. It's not merely a bit of style that, during their crimes, the photography will often switch to a subjective camera, encouraging our identification with them even further—those are our hands reaching for Miriam in *Strangers on a Train*, our hands mopping up the blood in *Psycho*.

In Hitchcock's world, there is always more than enough guilt to go around. And simply by sitting passively in the audience, unblinkingly watching the violence, even vicariously enjoying it, we're sinners, too—as guilty as the killers and the man who created them.

References
Richard Alleva, "The Catholic Hitchcock: A Director's Sense of Good and Evil," *Commonweal*, July 12, 2010, https://www.commonwealmagazine.org/catholic-hitchcock; "Catechism of the Catholic Church," *The Holy See*, http://www.vatican.va/archive/ccc_css/archive/catechism/p3s1c1a8.htm.

GWENN, EDMUND (1877–1959)
London-born performer whose announcement that he intended not to go into the civil service after university but onto the stage instead earned his father's red-faced wrath and a demand he leave the family home permanently. It was, the actor recalled later, a "scene without parallel in Victorian melodrama." Eventually, Gwenn would become part of a family of actors. (He was distantly related, through a very brief marriage, to JOHN GIELGUD; his cousin, Cecil Kellaway, was the ill-fated restaurateur in the 1946 *The Postman Always Rings Twice*.) However, the first few years were lean.

As his career went on, Gwenn proved himself skilled at both popular farce (*What the Butler Saw*) and drama (*THE SKIN GAME*); he became a particular favorite of George Bernard Shaw, who invited him to join his company, where he had a fine run in *Man and Superman*. Gwenn added cinema to his repertoire in 1916 and re-created his success in *The Skin Game* for a 1921 silent; 10 years later, he would reprise it a final time for Hitchcock's version. Hitchcock would also cast him as Johann Strauss the Elder in his disastrous *WALTZES FROM VIENNA*, one of the lowest ebbs in the director's British career.

The two men had a more happy reunion in America in 1940, where Hitch-cock brought Gwenn on to play Rowley, the cheerful "bodyguard" in *FOREIGN CORRESPONDENT* who has a nasty habit of throwing his charges from great heights; chattily keeping up a stream of conversation while coldly judging trajectories and keeping an eye out for witnesses, he's one of Hitchcock's most memorable early villains.

Although Gwenn had the range for a variety of parts—he costarred with DAME JUDITH ANDERSON, Katharine Cornell, and Ruth Gordon in a legendary 1942 Broadway production of *Three Sisters*—once he settled in Hollywood, he tended to be cast as chatty parsons, wise professors, and otherwise harmless codgers. In *Mister 880*, he is a little old counterfeiter; in *Miracle on 34th Street*, he is Kris Kringle himself. When Hitchcock revisited his first hit, *THE LODGER*, as a radio play in 1940, he cast Gwenn as the landlord; his brother, Arthur Chesney, had played the same part in the original film.

Hitchcock brought Gwenn back in 1955 for *THE TROUBLE WITH HARRY* as Captain Albert Wiles, the first to discover Harry's inconvenient corpse in the woods; it's a marvelously deadpan performance and one of the few—along with MILDRED NATWICK's—that seemed to catch the very dry, very British humor that Hitchcock was trying to translate to the screen. Gwenn also appeared in *Them!* (as one of the experts fighting the giant ants) and the infamous *Bonzo Goes to College*; his last role was for Hitchcock again, on *ALFRED HITCHCOCK PRESENTS*.

He died in Woodland Hills, CA, at 81 of pneumonia.

References
"Edmund Gwenn," *IMDb*, http://www.imdb.com/name/nm0350324/bio?ref_=nm_ov_bio_sm; Alfred E. Twomey and Arthur F. McClure, *The Versatiles: Supporting Character Players in the Cinema, 1930–1955* (New York: Castle Books, 1969), 106.

H

HALL-DAVIS, LILLIAN (1898–1933)

London-born performer who hid her working-class origins (and insecurity) by pretending to come from a better neighborhood, eventually adding a posh hyphen to her name. She had an early success with *The Admirable Crichton* in 1918 and the controversial silent *Maisie's Marriage* in 1923 and was the busy STAR of many European epics, including the 1924 Italian spectacle *Quo Vadis*. For Hitchcock, who once called her his "favorite actress," she seemed to serve as a symbol of fragile feminine virtue; in *THE RING*, she was the simple country girl led astray by her boyfriend's new riches, while in *THE FARMER'S WIFE*, she was the true love the hero nearly overlooks.

The transition to sound movies proved to be difficult, however; her career slowed, then stopped, and she fell into a deep depression. In 1933, her 14-year-old son returned home from school to find a suicide note in the hall and the apartment door locked; when neighbors broke in, she was found dead, her throat cut with a razor and her head in the oven. She was 35.

References

"Film Actress' Death: Inquest on Miss Lilian Hall-Davis," *Times*, October 28, 1933, http://the.hitchcock.zone/wiki/The_Times_%2828/Oct/1933%29_-_Film _actress's_death:_inquest_on_Miss_Lilian _Hall-Davis; Alfred Hitchcock, "My Screen Memories," *Film Weekly* (May 1936), http://the.hitchcock.zone/wiki/Film _Weekly_%281936%29_-_My_Screen _Memories; "Lillian Hall-Davis," *IMDb*, http://www.imdb.com/name/nm0356233/ bio?ref_=nm_ov_bio_sm.

HAMILTON, PATRICK (1904–1962)

Sussex-born writer whose novels may be more respected by writers than read by the public. His famous admirers ranged from GRAHAM GREENE to Doris Lessing, and only recently Nick Hornby called Hamilton's *Twenty Thousand Streets under the Sky* the "stretch of motorway" that connected Charles Dickens and Martin Amis.

However literary his novels were, however, Hamilton's plays were true popular successes—*ROPE*, first performed in 1929, and *Gas Light*—two words in Hamilton's original—first performed in 1938. Both played in London and New York and were eventually bought for the movies. (Also purchased was Hamilton's novel *Hangover Square*, although Hollywood, hoping to continue Laird Cregar's recent success in *THE LODGER* remake, made it into a Victorian melodrama.) Often set in England's shabbier resorts and grimier backstreets and fueled by cynicism, Marxism, and cheap drink, Hamilton's books are sometimes surreal, often pitch dark, literally as well as metaphorically;

Hitchcock and composer Bernard Herrmann pose playfully during recording sessions for the 1956 *The Man Who Knew Too Much. Paramount Pictures/Photofest © Paramount Pictures*

his characters live by night, and George Bone, the protagonist of *Hangover Square*, is given to murderous blackouts.

A melancholic, even somewhat misanthropic man who divided his adult life between the bottle and the typewriter, Hamilton published his last novel,

Unknown Assailant, in 1955 and returned full time to drinking; he died of cirrhosis of the liver in Norfolk at age 58.

References

"Season's Readings," *Guardian*, December 3, 2004; A. Stevens, "Welcome Back,

Patrick Hamilton," *Guardian*, April 16, 2007, http://www.theguardian.com/books/booksblog/2007/apr/16/welcomebackpatrickhamilton.

HAMLET

One of the more intriguing unproduced Hitchcock projects, this idea originated with the director himself in the summer of 1945—a modern-dress, modern-language version of the story, with the hero caught in a sort of murder-mystery and the "To be or not to be" soliloquy done as a monologue from a psychoanalyst's couch. CARY GRANT was approached and enthusiastic, and at one point, it was planned as the first release from TRANSATLANTIC PICTURES, with Grant possibly joining Hitchcock and SIDNEY BERNSTEIN as a third partner in the venture.

Then two things intervened. First, Hitchcock and Bernstein decided that *UNDER CAPRICORN*, with the in-demand INGRID BERGMAN, would be a more auspicious debut. Then in 1947, a writer named Irving Fiske sued Hitchcock and Grant, claiming that he had written something called *Hamlet in Modern English* and that their work infringed on his copyright. He asked for $1.25 million in damages—the legal challenge pushing *Hamlet* further back on the company's list of productions.

Eventually, Transatlantic, finding Bergman to be temporarily unavailable, went ahead with a still different film, *ROPE*; the *Hamlet* case dragged on through a series of delays (with the penny-conscious Grant, undoubtedly to his relief, finally being dropped from the lawsuit). The whole thing finally reached the courts in 1954; after hearing slightly over two weeks of testimony, the judge stopped the trial, threw out the lawsuit, and told Fiske to pay Hitchcock $5,000 in legal costs. The rest was silence.

References

"Filming Hamlet," *Aberdeen Journal*, September 5, 1945, http://the.hitchcock.zone/wiki/Aberdeen_Journal_%2805/Sep/1945%29_-_Filming_Hamlet; Caroline Moorehead, *Sidney Bernstein: A Biography* (London: Jonathan Cape, 1984), 173–74.

HARDWICKE, SIR CEDRIC (1893–1964)

Worcestershire-born performer whose life and career followed the path of many British actors of his generation—early work in stock companies, service in World War I, then prominent success in the West End followed by the inevitable, remunerative (but hardly challenging) trip to Hollywood to be cast as mad scientists, clergymen, or ancient Romans.

Born into a medical family, Hardwicke was expected to follow in his father's footsteps but didn't have the grades for medical school; the Royal Academy of Dramatic Art was less interested in his scholarly skills, however, and admitted him as a student. He was on the London stage by 1912 and later toured South Africa and Rhodesia. After fighting in France during the war, he returned to great success, particularly in some of the best works of George Bernard Shaw; he also appeared in the original London production of *Showboat*, was nominated for a Tony on Broadway, and at the early age of 41 won a knighthood.

By the late '30s, however, he moved to Hollywood to continue the film work he'd begun in 1926; although he was in several prestige productions early on, he was too often mired in second-string horror pictures, such as *The Invisible Man Returns* and *The Ghost of Frankenstein*, where his reserved underplaying often allowed flashier STARS to steal the show.

"I believe that God felt sorry for actors, so he created Hollywood to give them a place in the sun and a swimming pool," Hardwicke said once. "The price they had to pay was to surrender their talent."

His natural reserve suited him well, though, as General McLaidlaw, Lina's disapproving father, in *SUSPICION*; years later, Hitchcock would bring him back for *ROPE* as Mr. Kentley, the father of the murdered boy. Hardwicke's gentle shyness and growing concern about his son's unexpected absence gives the film its true heart; every time we're tempted to laugh at one of Brandon's morbid JOKES, Kentley's face stops it in our throats.

Hardwicke would go on to do several other fine films, including *The Winslow Boy* and LAURENCE OLIVIER's *Richard III*; making full use of his beautifully precise speaking voice, he provided the narration for several movies, too, including *The War of the Worlds*. He would have a late-in-life success playing the old pharaoh Sethi in Cecil B. De Mille's *The Ten Commandments*, and TV drama anthologies kept him busy; *ALFRED HITCHCOCK PRESENTS* used him twice. His last film was *The Pumpkin Eater* in 1964.

He died in New York after a long bout with cancer at age 71. His estate had been so drained by medical bills that a collection had to be taken up to pay for his funeral.

References

"Cedric Hardwicke," *IMDb*, http://www.imdb.com/name/nm0362567/bio?ref_=nm_ov_bio_sm; Daniel Blum, *Daniel Blum's Screen World* (Cheshire, CT: Biblo-Moser, 1966), 220; Brian McFarlane, "Sir Cedric Hardwicke," *BFI Screenonline*, http://www.screenonline.org.uk/people/id/483436.

HARKER, GORDON (1885–1967)

London-born actor most reliably cast as cocky (and morally flexible) working-class blokes. Born into a theatrical fam-ily and onstage since the early 1900s, he made his movie debut in 1921 and made three films for Hitchcock (*THE RING, THE FARMER'S WIFE*, and *CHAMPAGNE*), four if you count his appearances in the multidirector revue *ELSTREE CALLING*.

Unlike some silent-film actors, Harker benefitted from the arrival of sound, which allowed him to give full reign to his East End attitude; he was particularly popular with directors of mysteries, who found he could convincingly play either a cop or a crook as circumstances required. Along the way, he would also appear in *The Phantom Light* in 1935, an early fantasy from Michael Powell, and have his own brief movie series appearing as Inspector Hornleigh, a London detective. He also—fine casting—played Alfred Doolittle in an early TV broadcast of *Pygmalion* in 1948.

Harker died at age 81 in London.

References

"Gordon Harker," *IMDb*, http://www.imdb.com/name/nm0363104/bio?ref_=nm_ov_bio_sm; Brian McFarlane, "Gordon Harker," *BFI Screenonline*, http://www.screenonline.org.uk/people/id/463253.

HARMONY HEAVEN (GB 1930)

DIRECTOR: Thomas Bentley.
SCREENPLAY: Randall Faye, Frank Launder, Arthur Wimperis.
PRODUCER: Uncredited.
CINEMATOGRAPHY: Theodor Sparkuhl.
EDITOR: Sam Simmonds.
ORIGINAL MUSIC: John Reynders.
CAST: Polly Ward (Billie Breeze), Stuart Hall (Bob Farrell), Trilby Clark (Lady Mistley), Jack Raine (Stuart).
RUNNING TIME: 61 minutes. Black and white.
RELEASED THROUGH: Wardour Films.

Early backstage musical from BRITISH INTERNATIONAL PICTURES about a struggling composer and his plucky girl-friend, it was shot in primitive COLOR and cowritten by FRANK LAUNDER, who would go on to cowrite THE LADY VAN-ISHES. Some sources, including FRAN-ÇOIS TRUFFAUT, credit Hitchcock as codirector (PATRICK MCGILLIGAN sup-posed he spent, at most, a "few days" on the set), which has allowed at least one site to sell overpriced DVDs of this "rare Hitch-cock film." Other sources, however, dis-agree, asserting that, although Hitchcock's involvement was once announced, he never worked on the project. For his own part, Hitchcock never mentioned the picture.

References

"Harmony Heaven," *Hitchcock Zone*, http://the.hitchcock.zone/wiki/Harmony _Heaven_%281929%29; Patrick McGil-ligan, *Alfred Hitchcock: A Life in Dark-ness and Light* (New York: HarperCollins, 2003), 127; François Truffaut, *Hitchcock/ Truffaut*, rev. ed. (New York: Touchstone, 1985), 353.

HARRIS, BARBARA (1939–)

Evanston, IL–born performer, daughter of a pianist and a businessman, who was already doing serious Chicago theater in her teens and went on to become a found-ing member of the Compass Players, the first improv group in America, and serve as a central part of its more famous successor, Second City. Harris later said she adored improv, but "I was a small-town, middle-class girl who wore a cashmere sweater very nicely and ended up on Broadway because that's the way the wind was blowing." She would go on to star in the original produc-tions of *The Apple Tree* and *On a Clear Day You Can See Forever* (both of which were written for her) as well as *Mother Courage*.

On film, Harris's delicately winsome features and quick reactions won her a limited but select number of strong comic roles, from *A Thousand Clowns* to the orig-inal *Freaky Friday*. (She also had a memo-rable part in *Nashville*.) Hitchcock particu-larly wanted her for *FAMILY PLOT*, but the studio wanted a bigger STAR (Goldie Hawn was one suggestion); when Hitch-cock persisted, UNIVERSAL pushed him to at least cast KAREN BLACK—then more of a name—in the other female role. Hitch-cock agreed, but—as Harris said later—the director, who "always wanted emotionless people in his movies," was unimpressed by the bigger star's need to indicate every feel-ing in every close-up.

"There was a scene in our film, where Karen Black was acting, acting, acting—all that Lee Strasberg human-struggle stuff," Harris remembered. "And it took her so long to get those tears going, and Mr. Hitchcock turned to the cameraman and said, 'We will just photograph the actors' feet in this scene.' He wanted a beautiful woman who wasn't showing her life's his-tory."

Hitchcock was apparently quite happy with Harris, however, who gave Blanche a slightly daffy, *Blithe Spirit* feel mixed in with physical comedy and turn-on-a-dime emotions; in a rare bit of generous approval for a director so keen on absolute control, he not only accepted the improvised wink to the camera in her final close-up but also kept it in the film.

Harris continued to act but less and less and largely by her own choice; she had come to realize, she said, that she liked the process more than the performance, the rehearsal more than the show. She had a small part in *Peggy Sue Got Married* and another in *Grosse Point Blank*. Since 2002, she has lived in Arizona where, she says, she blissfully goes unrecognized.

References

"Barbara Harris," *IMDb*, http://www.imdb.com/name/nm0364455/bio?ref_=nm_ov_bio_sm; Patrick McGilligan, *Alfred Hitchcock: A Life in Darkness and Light* (New York: HarperCollins, 2003), 722–23; Robrt L. Pela, "Barbara Harris Knew Bill Clinton Was White Trash," *Phoenix New Times*, October 24, 2002, http://www.phoenixnewtimes.com/arts/barbara-harris-knew-bill-clinton-was-white-trash-6410220; Donald Spoto, *The Dark Side of Genius: The Life of Alfred Hitchcock* (New York: Da Capo Press, 1999), 531.

HARRISON, JOAN (1907–1994)

Surrey-born writer and producer who began her life in films in 1933 as Alfred Hitchcock's secretary. She would remain a trusted collaborator and loyal confidante throughout his career, even after establishing her own in the 1940s as a respected screenwriter and one of Hollywood's few female producers.

The daughter of a newspaper publisher, Harrison showed an early interest in writing at St. Hugh's College, Oxford, where she reviewed films for the student paper in between studying philosophy, economics, and politics; she considered a career in serious journalism and after graduation would continue her studies at the Sorbonne. She was in her mid-20s when she saw a newspaper ad—"Young lady, highest educational qualifications, must be able to speak, read and write French and German fluently." The job turned out to be working for Hitchcock, who was then preparing the first *THE MAN WHO KNEW TOO MUCH* and needed a secretary. He hired her after an interview, although she later wondered if what clinched it for her was when he asked her to remove her hat and saw that she was blonde.

The over-qualified Harrison was, by her own admission, terrible as a regular secretary but very good as a selfless assistant and creative associate who could tackle any number of jobs, including, in *The Man Who Knew Too Much*, playing a small part (as a secretary—one of the director's beloved in-JOKES). Soon she was sitting in and contributing to script conferences, as well. Her jobs soon grew to include spotting—and then improving—potential screen properties. She received her first screen credit for helping to adapt *JAMAICA INN* and—after following Hitchcock to America as part of his deal with DAVID O. SELZNICK—shared writing credits on his next four films: *REBECCA*, *FOREIGN CORRESPONDENT*, *SUSPICION*, and *SABOTEUR*.

Harrison became not only an important professional aide but also a close friend who occasionally vacationed with the family; although it may indeed have been the yellow hair that initially attracted him, Hitchcock respectfully listened to her opinions, encouraged her further efforts, and made sure she was credited for all of them. The lecherous boss grabbing his pretty assistant? As much as he may have been attracted to her, that was one cliché Hitchcock went to particular lengths to avoid.

But eventually Harrison—with the director's reluctant approval—struck out on her own. She would continue to do uncredited rewrite work on other people's screenplays but in 1944 would begin her own career as a producer with the noir thriller *Phantom Lady*, based on a CORNELL WOOLRICH story. Other offbeat thrillers—*Uncle Harry, They Won't Believe Me*, and *Ride the Pink Horse*—would follow, and most of them were HITCHCOCKIAN in the best ways, featuring strong heroines; untrustworthy heroes; tricky plots; and stylish, shadowy compositions.

Although—given the script work, sometimes uncredited, she had done for him over a decade—perhaps it could be said they were in the "Harrison tradition," as well.

Harrison moved to television work in the 1950s and soon resumed her association with Hitchcock, serving as an associate, executive, or full producer of more than 300 episodes of his two shows. (She also produced 40 episodes of the similar TV anthology SUSPICION, including the one Hitchcock directed, "FOUR O'CLOCK.") A later, more horror-oriented series she did on her own, *Journey to the Unknown*, was less successful, lasting only 15 episodes. She retired after producing the TV movie *Love Hate Love* in 1971 (written by her husband since 1958, novelist Eric Ambler).

She died in London at 87.

References

"Joan Harrison," *IMDb*, http://www.imdb.com/name/nm0365661/bio?ref_=nm_ov_bio_sm; "Joan Helps Hitchcock Find Those TV Chillers," *Chicago Tribune*, May 5, 1963, http://archives.chicagotribune.com/1963/05/05/page/274/article/joan-helps-hitchcock-find-those-tv-chillers; Patrick McGilligan, *Alfred Hitchcock: A Life in Darkness and Light* (New York: HarperCollins, 2003) 514–15, 522–24; Donald Spoto, *The Dark Side of Genius: The Life of Alfred Hitchcock* (New York: Da Capo Press, 1999), 147–49, 188–89, 220–21.

HARTLEY, MARIETTE (1940–)

Weston, CT, performer born into an upper-class, politically connected family that—she later wrote—was so alcoholic and dysfunctional it was like the "back end of an O'Neill drama." (Her maternal grandfather was John B. Watson, the controversial psychologist and founder of "behaviorism.") During Hartley's teens, however, she found an outlet in acting and soon began winning TV roles. In 1962, she made her movie debut in Sam Peckinpah's lovely *Ride the High Country*; two years later, she played Susan in *MARNIE*.

"Hitchcock had seen me in *Gunsmoke* and hired me," she said later in an authorized documentary about the film. "He and I had a wonderful time, with great repartee, he was very funny and giving, showing me the storyboarding which were exquisitely beautiful, I was so thrilled. Hitch had his own look; I feel so blessed that I was able to work with him."

And yet, she said another time, he could be mercurial, mysterious, emotionally withholding. Toward the end of production, when relations between them had reached the point where he would no longer speak to Hartley directly—according to fellow cast members TIPPI HEDREN and DIANE BAKER, he was already quarreling with them, too, and had made passes at both—"I went up to him and asked if in some way I had offended him," Hartley later said. "His reply was, 'Miss Hartley, I think you have problems with men.'"

Although there were a few more movies—*Marooned*, *The Return of Count Yorga*—Hartley, who had always had a busy TV career, has mostly been seen on the small screen since the mid-'70s. Her most famous role may have been in a wry series of Polaroid commercials with James Garner, which left many viewers convinced they were married. (Eventually, she had T-shirts printed up, reading "I am not James Garner's wife!") She continues to act, mostly on television, and remains a strong advocate for mental health initiatives.

References

Alvin Klein, "A Bittersweet Homecoming for Mariette Hartley," *New York Times*, February 6, 1994, http://www.nytimes.com/1994/02/06/nyregion/theater-a-bittersweet-homecoming-for-mariette-hartley.html?pagewanted=2&src=pm; "Mari-

ette Hartley," *IMDb*, http://www.imdb
.com/name/nm0366866/bio?ref_=nm
_ov_bio_sm; Patrick McGilligan, *Alfred
Hitchcock: A Life in Darkness and Light*
(New York: HarperCollins, 2003), 646; *The
Trouble with Marnie*, directed by Laurent
Bouzereau (2000), documentary, http://the
hitchcock.zone/wiki/The_Trouble_with
Marnie%282000%29_-_transcript.

HAY, IAN (1876–1952)

Educator and soldier born in Manchester
as John Hay Beith, who emerged as a popular playwright and memoirist after the First
World War. His account of his battalion
during the early days of battle, *The First
Hundred Thousand*, was a best seller in 1915,
and in 1919, his play *Getting Together* was
turned into the movie *The Common Cause*.
Known for his light and conversational
style, he is credited with dialogue on three
of Hitchcock's '30s films—*THE 39 STEPS*,
SECRET AGENT, and *SABOTAGE*—and his
plays *The Middle Watch* and *Tilly of Blooms-
bury* have been adapted many times.

He served in the public relations
department of the British War Office until
retirement, just before turning 65; he died
at age 76 in Hampshire.

References

"Ian Hay," *IMDb*, http://www.imdb.com/
name/nm0067308/bio?ref_=nm_ov_bio
_sm#trivia; "Ian Hay," *Only Two Rs*, https://
only2rs.wordpress.com/2006/05/04/14.

HAYES, JOHN MICHAEL
(1919–2008)

Worcester, MA–born author who moved
early on from journalism to radio scripts.
Settling in California after the war, he
wrote for a number of hit series, including
the mystery programs *The Adventures of
Sam Spade* and *Inner Sanctum*, and eventually transitioned to a job at UNIVERSAL
(then Universal-International) in 1952.

Over his career, Hayes would have
some success with soapy melodramas
(he did the movie adaptations of *BUt-
terfield 8* and *Peyton Place* and the supposed Hollywood exposé *Harlow*), but
his most prominent association was with
Alfred Hitchcock, for whom he wrote four
pictures—*REAR WINDOW, TO CATCH
A THIEF, THE TROUBLE WITH HARRY*,
and *THE MAN WHO KNEW TOO
MUCH*—before the relationship acrimoniously dissolved.

The first, *Rear Window*, is still the
strongest. The original CORNELL WOOL-
RICH story had the VOYEURISTIC gimmick but no real romance; reportedly, an
early treatment by Josh Logan had added
a heroine, and now Hitchcock gave Hayes
the job of fleshing her out. Also very specific instructions. "We have to have a girl,"
Hayes recalled the director telling him,
"and I want to use GRACE KELLY." Hayes
spent a couple of weeks with the actress
to get to know her better and decided to
make her character (like his wife) a fashion
model. He also worked hard at giving the
script humor, providing THELMA RIT-
TER with a number of tart wisecracks as
JAMES STEWART's cynical visiting nurse.

"I brought dialogue, character and
humor to Hitch," Hayes said later (as if
those elements had been absent in the
director's previous three decades of work).
"He had the suspense, and we melded very
well. He liked my sometimes flippant dialogue, and so did the audience."

What the director didn't care for was
Hayes's obvious confidence and happiness to take credit even when credit was
due; when the screenwriter won an Oscar
nomination for the screenplay and even an
Edgar Award from the Mystery Writers of
America, the director was visibly annoyed.
"He resented my receiving an award when
he didn't," Hayes said. Still, the collaboration continued on the slight but elegant

To Catch a Thief, also with Kelly, and the disappointing *The Trouble with Harry* (both of which, nonetheless, showed off Hayes's gift for humor and slightly more-risqué-than-usual lines). A better, deeper effort was the remake of *The Man Who Knew Too Much.* Hitchcock explained the basic story but told Hayes not to watch the original film before he wrote the script; Hayes's new screenplay gave the main characters a complicated, somewhat troubled marriage and grounded the thriller in a human reality the first movie had lacked.

During preproduction, however, Hitchcock called in ANGUS MACPHAIL, whom he had known since the British silents and had last worked with on *SPELLBOUND,* telling Hayes that the old writer was now his new collaborator. According to Hitchcock, MacPhail contributed technical advice and a good deal of the spy plot and would receive a cowriting credit; according to Hayes, MacPhail was a "dying alcoholic" who contributed nothing. When Hitchcock insisted on the shared credit, Hayes submitted the screenplay to the Writers Guild for arbitration; ultimately, the guild decided that only Hayes should be named.

MacPhail, who seemed to be further from death than Hayes remembered—he lived another six years—went on to work on the screenplay for *THE WRONG MAN* and did some early work on *VERTIGO,* before begging off. Hayes, however, never worked for Hitchcock again. They had already been quarreling over low fees, a never-paid bonus, and Hayes's attempts to enlist the actors of *To Catch a Thief* in his rewrite battles; this final, public squabble put a period to it. When Hayes's name came up in the FRANÇOIS TRUFFAUT INTERVIEWS, Hitchcock vaguely and ungenerously dismissed the author of four of his strongest '50s pictures as a "radio writer" who did the dialogue and a gimmick or two.

"I enjoyed working with Hitchcock professionally," Hayes said later. "But he was egotistical to the point of madness."

Hayes continued to write—the adventure story *Iron Will* from 1994 is his—and to teach writing at Dartmouth. He died at 89 in Hanover, NH.

References

"John Michael Hayes," *IMDb,* http://www .imdb.com/name/nm0371088/bio?ref_=nm _ov_bio_sm; Patrick McGilligan, *Alfred Hitchcock: A Life in Darkness and Light* (New York: HarperCollins, 2003), 500, 529–32; Patrick McGilligan, ed., *Backstory: Interviews with Screenwriters of the 60s* (Berkeley: University of California Press, 1997), 174–92; "Obituary: John Michael Hayes," *Guardian,* December 5, 2008, http://the .hitchcock.zone/wiki/The_Guardian_%2805/ Dec/2008%29_-_Obituary:_John_Michael _Hayes; "Obituary: John Michael Hayes," *Los Angeles Times,* November 27, 2008, http://the.hitchcock.zone/wiki/Los_Ange les_Times_%2827/Nov/2008%29_-_Obitu ary:_John_Michael_Hayes; Donald Spoto, *The Dark Side of Genius: The Life of Alfred Hitchcock* (New York: Da Capo Press, 1999), 345–46, 360–61, 366–67; François Truffaut, *Hitchcock/Truffaut,* rev. ed. (New York: Touchstone, 1985), 222, 227.

HEAD, EDITH (1897–1981)

San Bernardino fashion maven, whose first career was in academia—after graduating with honors from the University of California, Berkeley, she earned a master's from Stanford in romance languages. By the early '20s, she was teaching French at the Hollywood School for Girls. Interested in the extra money a second specialty would bring, Head took night classes in drawing so she could teach art to her pupils, as well; in fact, rather than bringing her more students, it earned her an interview at PARAMOUNT, where—after blithely displaying a portfolio plumped up with other people's work—she won a job as a "sketch artist" in 1924.

She first worked with Alfred Hitchcock on NOTORIOUS, where she designed INGRID BERGMAN's elegant party gown; she and the director would work together 10 more times, on REAR WINDOW, TO CATCH A THIEF, THE TROUBLE WITH HARRY, THE MAN WHO KNEW TOO MUCH, VERTIGO, THE BIRDS, MARNIE, TORN CURTAIN, TOPAZ, and FAMILY PLOT. (She was in preproduction on his THE SHORT NIGHT until that film was finally abandoned.) Throughout her career, with him and other directors, she was known for working closely with actresses and became a favorite designer of many, including Barbara Stanwyck, Dorothy Lamour, SHIRLEY MACLAINE, and Natalie Wood.

As she had in her first studio interview—and as had her male bosses before her—Head sometimes grandly signed her name to other people's work; it was well known that at least two of her Oscars, for Roman Holiday and Sabrina, were for clothes emanating from other designers, including Hubert de Givenchy. Still, there is a link connecting much of her work, with her designs deliciously feminine, even flirty. ("A dress," Head opined, "should be tight enough to show you're a woman, and loose enough to show you're a lady.")

Probably because she worked so closely with the STARS themselves, they are also, invariably, flattering and unfussy, with clean lines. And they immediately tell you something about the character—the clothes that INGRID BERGMAN wears at the beginning of Notorious when she's careless and drunken and single are quite different from the ones she wears when she is meeting CARY GRANT and different still from the ones she wears when at home with CLAUDE RAINS. Fashion follows form.

This was a decision, of course, firmly embraced by Hitchcock, who would come to pay more and more meticulous attention to his actresses' clothes and hair. It was a symbol of control, of course, but also of characterization—the cheap, revealing dresses worn by KIM NOVAK's Judy in Vertigo, the stiff but sexy gown sported by GRACE KELLY in To Catch a Thief. And it was something that Head appreciated.

"Alfred Hitchcock is the only person who works on a script with such detail that a designer could go ahead and make the clothes without discussing them with him," she said in a long 1979 interview with American Film. "Unless there is a story reason for a COLOR, we keep the colors muted, because Hitchcock believes they can detract from an important action scene. He uses color, actually, almost like an artist, preferring soft greens and cool colors for certain moods."

Although the power—and resources—of the costume designer had shrunken vastly since the end of the studio system, Head continued to work regularly, sometimes on TV and often for period pictures such as The Sting (for which she won her eighth and final Oscar). Her last credit was on Dead Men Don't Wear Plaid in 1982, nearly 60 years after she had begun her career. She died at 83 in Los Angeles of bone marrow disease.

References

Allison P. Davis, "The Cut: 30 Fantastic Movie Costumes by the Legendary Edith Head," New York Magazine, October 28, 2013, http://nymag.com/thecut/2013/10/30-fantastic-movie-costumes-by-edith-head.html#; "Dialogue on Film: Edith Head," American Film (May 1978), http://the.hitchcock.zone/wiki/American_Film_%281978%29_-_Dialogue_on_Film:_Edith_Head; "Edith Head," Biography, http://www.biography.com/people/edith-head-9332755; "Edith Head," IMDb, http://www.imdb.com/name/nm0372128/bio?ref_=nm_ov_bio_sm.

HECHT, BEN (1894–1964)

A hugely talented and prolific writer born in New York, raised in Wisconsin, who fled to Chicago at 16 to become a newspaperman. Both location and occupation formed him as, he remembered decades later, he "ran everywhere in the city like a fly buzzing in the works of a clock, tasted more than any fit belly could hold, learned not to sleep and buried myself in a tick-tock of whirling hours that still echo in me." Hecht covered crime for the *Chicago Daily News*, went to Europe as a war correspondent, and then returned to shine as a columnist; it was an era of scoops, scandals, and knock-down battles between rival reporters. Hecht loved all of it (and recaptured it later in his hit play with Charles MacArthur, *The Front Page*, and his memoirs, *A Child of the Century*).

In 1926, he got a telegram from Herman Mankiewicz, a fellow reporter who had left for work in Hollywood as a screenwriter; it was going even better than "Mank" had dared hope. "Millions are to be grabbed out here and your only competition is idiots," he wired his friend. "Don't let this get around." Hecht may or may not have kept the secret, but he soon took the train, establishing himself early on with *Underworld* in 1927, which won best screenplay at the first Academy Awards ceremony. Hecht quickly became known as the fastest—and most expensive—writer in the industry; at one point, DAVID O. SELZNICK was paying him $3,500 a day.

Hecht's high price was due largely to his skill as a script doctor, coming in at the start of—or even the end of—production to fix a sick screenplay; his first work with Hitchcock was hastily concocting the final speech-to-America scene for *FOREIGN CORRESPONDENT*. Like most of his work for the director—rewrites and touch-ups on *LIFEBOAT*, *THE PARADINE CASE*, and *ROPE*—it would go uncredited but not unnoticed on the screen. For his two best scripts for Hitchcock, however, *SPELLBOUND* and *NOTORIOUS*—not accidentally, also two of Hitchcock's best '40s films—he took full credit.

Both are notable enough just on the surface; *Spellbound* was one of the first Hollywood films to treat psychiatry with any seriousness, while *Notorious* helped pioneer the modern spy-thriller genre. But more than that, Hecht's scripts for Hitchcock were remarkable for the depth of their characters' relationships and the complexity of the heroines. *Notorious* was particularly striking, as Alicia goes from betrayed daughter to self-loathing drunkard to vulnerable and hopeful lover—a lover who is then, essentially, patriotically pimped out to crack a Nazi conspiracy.

Alicia is a complicated character, a sinning saint (and nearly a martyr) who has few parallels in Hitchcock's work. But strong women are a constant in Hecht's screenplays, whether it's the comical fraud of *Nothing Sacred* or the fiery heroine of *Wuthering Heights* (or, probably, the heroines in all the other screenplays he reportedly worked on but was never credited for, such as *Gilda* and *Duel in the Sun*); as a strong man, Hecht celebrated confident women and prized adult relationships.

He liked Hitchcock but found few adults in Hollywood or in other movies. The people he worked with, he wrote, were generally "nitwits on a par with the lowest run of politicians I had known"; the art the industry produced, he feared, was an "eruption of trash that has lamed the American mind and retarded Americans from becoming a cultured people." The only reason he stayed, he insisted, was that screenwriting provided "tremendous sums of money for work that required no more effort than a game of pinochle."

So he also wrote plays. He wrote novels. And during the Second World War, he worked hard to spread the truth about the Holocaust at a time when it was still minimized or even denied; after the war, he became a loud and loyal supporter of a new Jewish state to the point of paying for a ship to transport settlers and even unhesitantly supporting terrorist attacks on British occupiers by the Irgun gang. (As a result, for a while his films were banned in Britain; even in their obituary, a still-outraged *Times* referred to his views as "virulent.")

The publication of *A Child of the Century* brought Hecht new respect in 1954—although he always considered his novels to be his most serious work—but Hecht continued to churn out new pages and rewritten ones for films from *Monkey Business* to (uncredited) *7 Faces of Dr. Lao*. He died at 70 in New York of thrombosis.

References

"Ben Hecht," *Encyclopaedia Britannica*, http://www.britannica.com/biography/Ben -Hecht; "Ben Hecht," *IMDb*, http://www .imdb.com/name/nm0372942/bio?ref_=nm _ov_bio_sm; Florice Whyte Kovan, *Ben Hecht Biography and Works*, http://benhecht books.net; "Obituary: Mr. Ben Hecht," *Times*, April 20, 1964, http://the.hitch cock.zone/wiki/The_Times_%2820/ Apr/1964%29_-_Obituary:_Mr_Ben_Hecht.

HEDREN, TIPPI (1930–)

Last and most controversial of the "Hitchcock BLONDES."

The small-town, Minnesota-born daughter of a storekeeper, Tippi—a family nickname, her real name is Nathalie—began modeling as a teenager, mostly for local department stores. After high school, she moved to New York to pursue her career; she appeared twice on the cover of *Life* magazine and landed a soft-drink commercial.

By the early '60s, though, she was entering her 30s, living in Los Angeles, divorced, and the mother of a four-year-old child, Melanie; the offer of a seven-year personal contract with Alfred Hitchcock (who had spotted her in that soda advertisement) seemed like an enormous breakthrough, although Hedren's movie experience had been limited to a bit part more than 10 years before in the ROBERT CUMMINGS musical *The Petty Girl*. "It was never my ambition to be an actress, much less a movie STAR," she said later. "I had never thought of myself that way. I was a model, and I had come to Los Angeles not only to try for better work than was available in New York, but also because I wanted my daughter to grow up in a home with a yard and trees and a neighborhood to roam and play in."

Hitchcock had his own ambitions. After years of dealing with stars who were under contract to studios (or to other producers, such as DAVID O. SELZNICK) he wanted an actress he could literally call his own, available at any time for any project; a previous contract with VERA MILES (who, inconveniently, kept getting married and having children) had yielded little. Now he would try again.

Although he had no one but himself to convince of Hedren's suitability, Hitchcock put as much care and cash into the actress's screen test as he would into an actual film. EDITH HEAD was told to design not only clothes for the auditions but a personal wardrobe for Hedren as well; MARTIN BALSAM, fresh from *PSYCHO*, was brought on to do the test shoots with her. The scenes were taken from Hitchcock's previous hits with JOAN FONTAINE, GRACE KELLY, and INGRID BERGMAN.

But with all the molding, the careful control, it really seemed like only one movie was being reprised. "It was really very clear, wasn't it?" screenwriter SAMUEL A.

TAYLOR asked later. "He was doing *VER-TIGO*." Taylor had, of course, one of the screenwriting credits on *Vertigo*, so perhaps it was clear to him; other observers were less sure of what Hitchcock's real attitude was or convinced that it was any different than it had ever been. The director had always had very specific views of how his leading ladies should appear on the screen; he would give very specific instructions to the costume designer (usually Head) or choose the clothes off the rack himself. Hairstyles, shoes—all were taken into consideration.

But before, Hitchcock had mostly worked with women who were under contract to others, who were already stars and often were already married. Hedren was single, uncertain, and signed exclusively to him. And that led him to fashion a very tight leash for his new discovery. Although, as filming began, some observers still saw nothing beyond his usual meticulous control of image—albeit, in this case, a living person's image—others thought his relationship to Hedren was turning somewhat darker.

ROD TAYLOR, her costar in *THE BIRDS*, remembers Hitchcock—who on the set referred to Hedren simply as "the girl"—keeping her segregated from the rest of the cast and crew, even forbidding them from sharing rides. "He was very firm about that—oh, I must not ride with her, as if that would taint his goddess," Taylor said. "He was putting a wall around her, trying to isolate her from everyone so that all her time would be spent only with him."

"He started telling me what I should wear on my own time, what I should be eating and what friends I should be seeing," Hedren remembered later. "He suggested that such and such a person was not good enough for my company, or that someone I might have a social engagement was not right. And he became angry and hurt if I didn't ask his permission to visit friends in the evening or on a weekend."

Then, Hedren said, things grew worse. Riding in a car to the location one day, the director grabbed her in an embrace. She pushed him away but gave him the "benefit of the doubt"—that he was just trying to keep her off balance before an emotional scene, the way he would whisper dirty words in her ear before a take, trying to shake her up (the same way he had purposefully undermined Fontaine's confidence on the set of *REBECCA*).

But later, as she began to worry this was more than just a director's trick, Hedren felt trapped. "I couldn't just resign or quit my contract—there would have been a major lawsuit and I was a single mom with a little girl to support," Hedren said later, pointing out this was years before anyone thought of suing over sexual harassment. "I would have been blacklisted all over town—would have been unable to find work anywhere. So I tried to cope."

But then the final bit of shooting came on *The Birds*, built around the climactic scene in which the heroine goes upstairs alone to be attacked by a flock of pecking animals. In the script, it is the final assault on the character of Melanie Daniels, the attack that breaks down her last bit of cocky independence to make her into the docile child that Mitch and his mother seem to want. But on the set it seemed to be an assault on the actress Tippi Hedren, an attack to demolish her final bit of resolve.

She had been told it would be an easy scene, that they would use mechanical birds. Instead it took nearly a week and employed live animals—some of which were literally thrown at her, others of which were tied to her clothes so they couldn't get away. On the fifth day of shooting, Hedren finally collapsed on the set in hysterics. She went home and, on medical advice, stayed away from the production for a week. Eventually the filming was completed, and the movie moved into postproduction.

Hedren's performance in *The Birds* isn't confident or particularly natural—unsurprising, given that this was her first real job as an actress and that Hitchcock seemed to be working hard to bully and control her. She has one or two real moments onscreen with JESSICA TANDY and SUZANNE PLESHETTE, but her scenes with Taylor feel forced. And, with his love of MONTAGE and PURE CINEMA, at times Hitchcock directs her as if she were a marionette, particularly in the sequence of the birds' assault on downtown, in which Hedren's artificially posed close-ups are intercut with different scenes of destruction.

Hitchcock may have begun to realize that his much vaunted discovery was not going to be the new Grace Kelly he had imagined and whom he still desperately missed; in fact, he had already tried to lure the old Kelly back for his next picture, *MARNIE*. But she had turned him down—it's hard to imagine how he thought a reigning royal could ever have played a SEXUALLY repressed kleptomaniac—and so now he pushed ahead with Hedren.

This was an even more difficult role than *The Birds*, calling for a wide range of complicated emotions, many of which even the character herself wasn't supposed to understand; there wouldn't be any horrific shocks or special effects to act as a distraction, either (nor would critics give her the benefit of the doubt of only being in her first movie). The stresses were going to be high. And, according to Hedren, Hitchcock soon added to them. He continued his old methods (referring to her as "the girl," isolating her from other crew members, sternly ordering her leading man not to touch her). He invented new ones, too; DIANE BAKER, a costar, recalled him standing outside Hedren's dressing room and talking disparagingly of his discov-ery in a voice pitched deliberately loud so Hedren couldn't help but overhear.

Eventually, according to Hedren, his behavior progressed to include more obvious, blatantly personal demands. The entire set had been fraught with sexual tension for some time; Baker said Hitchcock was "inappropriate a couple of times [with me] and I made it very clear I was not interested," while MARIETTE HARTLEY remembers him first turning icy to her and then announcing "Miss Hartley, I think you have problems with men." Finally, Hedren said, the director flatly told her that she was going to become his mistress—or he would ruin her career.

These are stories of something that happened 50 years ago; not surprisingly, there are many who dispute them. For years, Hedren said little about it (and even smilingly attended some salutes to the director); although she went on the record to a degree for DONALD SPOTO's *THE DARK SIDE OF GENIUS*, her story has seemed contradictory at times; as late as 2005, she was denying the director had ever made an actual pass. But her tale is told at more length and with ugly detail in Spoto's 2008 *Spellbound by Beauty* (and was the impetus behind the movie *THE GIRL*). *Marnie* screenwriter JAY PRESSON ALLEN, Baker, and various costars and coworkers have also come forward to corroborate Hedren's story, too, at least in part.

Also supplying evidence, no matter how legally inadmissible, are the films themselves. In *The Birds*, Hedren plays a chilly, ironic beauty who is methodically attacked and broken down until she's reduced to helplessness; in *Marnie*, Hedren is a cold and amoral thief and liar who is raped by her husband and then traumatized by being forced to relive an assault from her childhood. Both movies are about icy princesses being brutalized—ultimately for their own good, the stories insist—and reduced through cruel victimization to their properly submissive status.

"He was always trying to put his own personal feelings up on the screen and I think that was one of the things he was doing with *Marnie*," observed Hitchcock colleague and longtime production designer ROBERT F. BOYLE, who worked on both Hedren films. "He was doing it through Tippi, and through his filmmaking, and exploring some of his own feelings and his compulsive behavior."

Still, others continue to deny it. When the stories first received mainstream attention with the publication of *The Dark Side of Genius*, many reacted to them with shock or disbelief, with a few noting that these charges weren't made until the man wasn't alive to defend himself. PATRICK MCGILLIGAN's 2003 *ALFRED HITCHCOCK: A LIFE IN DARKNESS AND LIGHT* offered the strongest defense of the director, and there is an entire website, *Save Hitchcock* (www.savehitchcock.com), that rallies support for the dead filmmaker. It's been forthcoming, too. "I feel bad about all the stuff people are saying about him now, that he was a weird character," KIM NOVAK has said. "I did not find him to be weird at all. I never saw him make a pass at anybody or act strange to anybody."

But this much isn't in dispute: Tippi Hedren never became Alfred Hitchcock's mistress. And Alfred Hitchcock did help ruin her career. He kept her under contract for two years yet, she says, stubbornly refused to loan her out for other directors' projects. Finally, he sold her contract to UNIVERSAL (where, as its third largest stockholder, he essentially still remained her boss). Hedren had a small part in Charles Chaplin's disastrous *A Countess from Hong Kong* in 1967; she did some television work and made the film *The Harrad Experiment*. She was dropped by the studio

after a disagreement over a TV western; by the mid-'70s, her movie career was pretty much over.

Hedren continued to work though, if at other things. She became very active in charities, particularly in regard to animal welfare (a drive, interestingly, she shared with former Hitchcock blondes Novak and DORIS DAY); she did work with Vietnamese refugees, helping involve them in the new nail salon industry. She raised her daughter, MELANIE GRIFFITH. She occasionally took a part on oddly familiar projects—she was in a poor TV sequel to *The Birds*, *The Birds II: Land's End*; appeared in a television remake of *SHADOW OF A DOUBT*; and contributed a cameo to Griffith's appearance on the rebooted *The New Alfred Hitchcock Presents*.

And eventually she began talking about what her years with Hitchcock were really like—detailing both his brilliance and his darkness—without fear, without rancor, but also without hesitation. "He ruined my career," she has said. "But he didn't ruin my life."

References

Peter Ackroyd, "Alfred Hitchcock Was an Overgrown Schoolboy," *Daily Mail*, March 21, 2015, http://www.dailymail .co.uk/home/event/article-3002550/Alfred -Hitchcock-overgrown-schoolboy-school boy-s-obsession-sex.html; Diane Baker, interview with the author, September 2015; Andrew Billen, "The Birds Attacked Me but Hitch Was Scarier," *Times*, April 4, 2005, http://www.thetimes.co.uk/tto/arts/ film/article2426913.ece; Kyle B. Counts and Steve Rubin, "The Making of 'The Birds,'" *Cinemafantastique* 10, no. 2 (Fall 1980), http://the.hitchcock.zone/wiki/Cine mafantastique_%281980%29_-_The_Mak ing_of_Alfred_Hitchcock%27s_The_Birds; Patrick McGilligan, *Alfred Hitchcock: A Life in Darkness and Light* (New York: HarperCollins, 2003), 626–28, 645–49; Rosie Millard, "Hitchcock's Girl," *FT Magazine*, July 27, 2012, http://www.ft.com/intl/cms/s/2/14e3358c-d5f1-11e1-a5f3-00144feabdc0.html#axzz2HbGxCPMO; Rob Salem, "Hitchcock and Hedren Now a TV Movie," *Star*, October 19, 2012, http://www.thestar.com/entertainment/television/2012/10/19/hitchcock_and_hedren_now_an_hbo_movie.html; Donald Spoto, *The Dark Side of Genius: The Life of Alfred Hitchcock* (New York: Da Capo Press, 1999), 449–52, 457–60, 467–68, 475–76; Donald Spoto, *Spellbound by Beauty: Alfred Hitchcock and His Leading Ladies* (New York: Harmony Books, 2008), 245–77; David Thomson, *The New Biographical Dictionary of Film* (New York: Knopf, 2002), 386–87; "Tippi Hedren," *IMDb*, http://www.imdb.com/name/nm0001335/bio?ref_=nm_ov_bio_sm; *The Trouble with Marnie*, directed by Laurent Bouzereau (2000), documentary, http://the.hitchcock.zone/wiki/The_Trouble_with_Marnie_%282000%29_-_transcript; François Truffaut, *Hitchcock/Truffaut*, rev. ed. (New York: Touchstone, 1985), 327.

HELMORE, TOM (1904–1995)

London-born performer of well-tailored elegance who dutifully followed his father into the family's accounting firm while looking for movie parts in his spare time; he made his screen debut in 1927 with his first feature appearance—extra work—in Hitchcock's *THE RING*. It would be another year or two before he was a familiar face; by the '30s, he was a busy supporting player in British films, often in mysteries and light comedies. (Hitchcock gave him another small part in *SECRET AGENT* in 1936.)

By the 1950s, Helmore was in America and a regular on a variety of television shows; Hitchcock used him on two episodes of *ALFRED HITCHCOCK PRESENTS* and gave him at last a real film role in *VERTIGO* as Gavin Elster, the husband who hired Scottie to keep an eye on his wife. By the '60s, Helmore's career was winding down; he was one of ROD TAYLOR's friends in *The Time Machine* and had a small role in *Advise and Consent*; his last appearance was in a 1972 episode of *Night Gallery*.

He died at 91 in Longboat Key, FL.

References
"Tom Helmore," *IMDb*, http://www.imdb.com/name/nm0375738/bio?ref_=nm_ov_bio_sm; "Tom Helmore, 91, Actor Best Known for Comedy," *New York Times*, September 15, 1995, http://www.nytimes.com/1995/09/15/obituaries/tom-helmore-91-actor-known-best-for-comedy.html.

HERO

In myth and classical literature, a protagonist—usually of royal if sometimes concealed origins—who embarks on a quest or journey, suffers many trials, and either triumphs through his own noble virtues or is undone by his own tragic flaws. The figure—perhaps more simply and accurately called the protagonist—has a different role in Hitchcock's films.

Hitchcock's heroes are frequently the least heroic characters in his films, riddled by self-doubt and self-loathing. While their opponents are confident, Hitchcock's heroes hesitate; while his villains invariably exude charm and trustworthiness, his heroes often alienate others and attract suspicion. Most of them carry GUILT—yet for things they didn't do or couldn't avoid. The heroes of *THE 39 STEPS, NORTH BY NORTHWEST*, and *THE MAN WHO KNEW TOO MUCH* all have stabbing victims literally fall at their feet and expire; the hero of *SABOTEUR* accidentally kills a man by using a fire extinguisher that's been secretly filled with gasoline.

Often this guilt festers into genuine psychological trauma. In *VERTIGO*, haunted by letting one man fall to his death, Scottie is then driven into a clinical depression when his illness stops him from preventing another death; in *SPELLBOUND*, the amnesiac Ballantyne has a guilt complex over a childhood accident; the icy kleptomaniac *MARNIE* has effectively but disastrously repressed memories of childhood violence.

Hitchcock's heroes are flawed in ways his villains never are; in fact, often in an act of TRANSFERENCE, the villains push their guilt and their weaknesses onto the men opposed to them. In *ROPE*, Rupert fears it was his influence that drove Brandon to plan a "thrill killing"; in *STRANGERS ON A TRAIN*, it's Guy who worries it's his own blithe conversation that drove Bruno to kill. And who is the likelier murderer in *FRENZY*—Bob Rusk, the charming Cockney merchant, or Richard Blaney, the hard-drinking, habitually angry ex-serviceman? (Typically, even their identical-but-reversed initials— BR versus RB—suggest the mirrored images and DOUBLES that reoccur throughout Hitchcock's films, in which heroes and villains sometimes seem interchangeable.)

Brandon and Bruno, though, have no guilt—nor do presumably the real traitors in *The 39 Steps* and *Saboteur*, the plotting husband in *Vertigo*, or the psychopath in *Frenzy*. That is something that only a Hitchcock hero has—along with a dislike of emotional commitment and an occasional desire to see some independent women taken down a peg, which may come awfully, uncomfortably close to abuse.

None of which makes them classically heroic, and all of which can make them fascinating.

Reference

"Hero," *Encyclopaedia Britannica*, http://www.britannica.com/art/hero-literary-and-cultural-figure.

HERRMANN, BERNARD (1911–1975)

New York musician who took violin lessons at the urging of his opera-loving father and later studied composition at New York University and Juilliard. An obvious if somewhat prickly prodigy, he had his own small chamber orchestra by 20 and by 23 was a staff conductor at CBS radio. There, Herrmann's duties grew to include not only programming and conducting live broadcasts of modern and classical works but also scoring dramas; it was through those that he met Orson Welles and began collaborating with him on his own work for the network. When Welles went to Hollywood and RKO with the Mercury Theatre, Herrmann went with him.

Herrmann's score for *Citizen Kane* is, in its own way, as careful a collection of styles as the movie itself—commercial fanfare for the documentary; period pop; opera; and then the slow, dark dirge that surrounds so much at Xanadu. *The Magnificent Ambersons* seemed slated to be another fine score, too, but when the studio cut it along with the movie, Herrmann angrily insisted his credit be removed from the titles.

Between the two collaborations with the director, Herrmann had already scored (and won his only Oscar for) *The Devil and Daniel Webster* in 1941; he would go on to compose a moving score for *Jane Eyre* (in which Welles acted), a thunderously melodramatic one with bits of classical music; for *Hangover Square*; an achingly romantic score for *The Ghost and Mrs. Muir*, one of Herrmann's favorites; and the modern THEREMIN-based electronic music for *The Day the Earth Stood Still*.

Typically, Herrmann's scores were marked by short repetitive phrases, an avoidance of leitmotif, and a creative approach to orchestration; his work life was similarly marked by an insistence on absolute control over his own art and a rarely disguised contempt for musically illiterate directors or studio heads who only wanted something "commercial" they could use to sell the movie.

Although DAVID O. SELZNICK had tried to bring the two talents together earlier, the composer had other obligations; Herrmann's first collaboration with Hitchcock came with *THE TROUBLE WITH HARRY*, where his score, full of whimsical woodwinds and stop-and-start rhythms, hints at the good humor that the film, a rare Hitchcock comedy, hoped to engender. He returned to score the far more serious *THE WRONG MAN* and *THE MAN WHO KNEW TOO MUCH*, where he left the pop song "Que Sera, Sera" to others but instead contributed a dramatic score (and a cameo as the conductor in the concert scene at Albert Hall).

It was followed by his three most famous movie scores for three of Hitchcock's finest films—*VERTIGO* (in which the music hints at the circular patterns and downward spirals to come); *NORTH BY NORTHWEST* (with the pounding pace of its overture preparing us for the film-long chase to come); and *PSYCHO*, in which he famously created a "black-and-white" sound by only using strings. It is perhaps Herrmann's masterwork and certainly his most imitated work, a genuine musical metaphor with slashing violins accompanying the slashing blade. Interestingly, Hitchcock had originally envisioned the scene playing without music; Herrmann forcefully disagreed, and it was a measure of the respect in which the director held him that he listened (although it helped

the composer's case that ALMA REVILLE reportedly agreed).

The two men were enough of a team that the director brought him onboard for TV's *THE ALFRED HITCHCOCK HOUR*; when Hitchcock decided that there would be no music at all in his next film, *THE BIRDS*, he still used the composer as a "sound consultant." But when their next picture together, *MARNIE*, was a box-office disappointment, Hitchcock found himself under new pressures from UNIVERSAL to find a younger composer—and, they hoped, a more commercial sound—for his next project.

"He said he was entitled to a great pop tune," Herrmann said of the music Hitchcock wanted for *TORN CURTAIN*. "I said, 'Look, Hitch, you can't out-jump your own shadow. And you don't make pop pictures. What do you want with me? I don't write pop music. It's a mistake.'" Herrmann wrote a score but the way he wanted to; the director angrily rejected it and eventually hired someone else. Herrmann never worked with Hitchcock again, although he blamed the studio, too.

"They made him very rich, and they recalled it to him," Herrmann said later. "I said to Hitchcock, 'What do you find in common with these hoodlums?' 'What are you talking about?' 'Do they add to your artistic life?' 'No.' 'They drink your wine?' 'Yes.' 'That's about all. What did they ever do? Made you rich? Well, I'm ashamed of you.'"

"There was great pressure on Hitchcock not to hire Benny Herrmann," confidante NORMAN LLOYD said later, blaming it on the studio's "so-called music department." "The reason given was that Benny Herrmann couldn't write a hit song. *Torn Curtain* was made at about the time that this vogue of having a hit song was becoming fashionable."

The never-uncertain Herrmann—who once estimated his contribution to a Hitchcock film as "40 percent"—left Hitchcock without looking back. He did not lack for work. He had already had a long association with Ray Harryhausen, writing gorgeously soaring scores for fantasy epics like *The 7th Voyage of Sinbad*; he was in demand for thrillers, too. (His music for the original *Cape Fear*, full of low, building menace, was repurposed for the remake as well.)

But the association with Hitchcock was indelible and would haunt many of his later assignments, as he worked on films for Hitchcock admirers (*Fahrenheit 451* and *The Bride Wore Black*, both for FRANÇOIS TRUFFAUT), imitators (*Sisters* and *Obsession*, both for BRIAN DE PALMA), and even former Hitchcock colleagues (*Endless Night* for SIDNEY GILLIAT, cowriter of *THE LADY VANISHES*). His last score was for Martin Scorsese's *Taxi Driver*, and—quite fittingly—the final chords it strikes are ones from *Psycho*.

He died of a heart attack in Hollywood at 64.

References

"Bernard Herrmann," *Biography*, http://www.biography.com/people/bernard-herrmann-9336913; "Bernard Herrmann," *IMDb*, http://www.imdb.com/name/nm0002136/bio?ref_=nm_ov_bio_sm; Royal S. Brown, "An Interview with Bernard Herrmann," http://www.bernardherrmann.org/articles/an-interview-with-bernard-herrmann; Patrick McGilligan, *Alfred Hitchcock: A Life in Darkness and Light* (New York: HarperCollins, 2003), 506–7; Stephen Rebello, *Alfred Hitchcock and the Making of Psycho* (New York: Harper Perennial, 1991), 138–39; Steven C. Smith, "For the Heart at Fire's Center: Norman Lloyd," *Bernard Herrmann Society*, http://folk.uib.no/smkgg/midi/soundtrackweb/herrmann/articles/smith/lloyd; Donald Spoto, *The Dark Side of Genius: The Life of Alfred Hitchcock* (New York: Da Capo Press, 1999), 420, 460, 491; David Thomson, *The New Biographical Dictionary of Film* (New York: Knopf, 2002), 394–95.

HICKS, SEYMOUR (1871–1949)

British-born performer from the isle of Jersey, who began his theatrical career at 16. He was an early hit in revues, music halls, musical comedies, pantomimes, and literary adaptations, with *A Christmas Carol* being a particular public favorite and Scrooge becoming an iconic role. He wrote his own material and eventually owned two theaters.

By the '20s, Hicks had branched into films as well and was starring in his own production, the comedy short *ALWAYS TELL YOUR WIFE*, based on his play. When the original director, Hugh Croise, was unable to finish filming—it is unclear whether he was sick or Hicks was simply sick of him—assistant director Alfred Hitchcock was told to take over. (It is, arguably, Hitchcock's debut as a director; his own first film, *NUMBER 13*, was abandoned.) The extent of Hitchcock's input and influence here is difficult to say; only about half of the 40-minute film is known to survive, and it's impossible to be sure who shot what.

Hicks continued to act onstage and -screen, reprising his role as Scrooge in the first talkie version of the story in 1935's *A Christmas Carol* and appearing with ROBERT MONTGOMERY in the Lord Peter Wimsey mystery *Haunted Honeymoon* in 1937. He died in Hampshire at 78.

References

Sydney Higgins, "The Golden Age of British Theatre, 1880–1920: Seymour Hicks," *The Camerino Players*, http://www.the-camerino-players.com/britishtheatre/

SirSeymourHicks.html; "Seymour Hicks," *IMDb*, http://www.imdb.com/name/nm0382957/bio?ref_=nm_ov_bio_sm.

HIGH ANXIETY (US 1977)

DIRECTOR: Mel Brooks.
SCREENPLAY: Mel Brooks, Ron Clark, Rudy De Luca, Barry Levinson.
PRODUCER: Mel Brooks.
CINEMATOGRAPHY: Paul Lohmann.
EDITOR: John C. Howard.
ORIGINAL MUSIC: John Morris.
CAST: Mel Brooks (Richard H. Thorndyke), Madeline Kahn (Victoria Brisbane), Cloris Leachman (Nurse Diesel), Harvey Korman (Dr. Charles Montague).
RUNNING TIME: 94 minutes. Color.
RELEASED THROUGH: 20th Century Fox.

Having already lampooned Broadway musicals (*The Producers*), westerns (*Blazing Saddles*), classic horror films (*Young Frankenstein*), and the silents (*Silent Movie*), Mel Brooks now narrowed his focus to satirize, not an entire genre, but a single director, and so this farce—while combining large parts of *SPELLBOUND* and *VERTIGO*—also includes references to *THE BIRDS*, *NORTH BY NORTHWEST*, *PSYCHO*, and other classics.

"I wrote a letter saying, basically, 'Dear Mr. Hitchcock, I do genre parodies and in my estimation you are a genre,'" Brooks later told National Public Radio about his preproduction work on the film. "'I don't mean that you're overweight. I mean that you've done every style and type of movie, and that you're just amazing, and I would like to do a movie dedicated to you, based on your style and your work.'" According to Brooks, Hitchcock—who'd liked *Blazing Saddles*—not only approved but also contributed ideas to the script, including the one of the birds attacking the hero by defecating on him. After the film came out,

Hitchcock sent Brooks a case of wine as a thank-you gift.

As it's parodying a career and an approach rather than a specific film or genre, *High Anxiety* is a little more diffuse than the earlier Brooks films. There is, for example, a Frank Sinatra–style ballad stuck in the middle, simply inserted to give Brooks a chance to burlesque a lounge act. And the supporting cast, padded out with some of Brooks's old pals and cowriters, isn't as sharp as it could be (although Madeline Kahn makes a fine, funny "Hitchcock BLONDE"). But it's all done with affection and, impressively, a real insider's knowledge. Any fan, for example, can spoof the *Psycho* shower scene. But casting Hitchcock's longtime matte painter ALBERT WHITLOCK as the film's own living MACGUFFIN, a kidnapped industrialist? That's an act of genuine, hardcore movie love—not surprising for a film that carried a dedication to the "Master of Suspense."

References
"Mel Brooks: 'I'm an EGOT, I Don't Need Any More,'" *National Public Radio*, December 27, 2013, http://www.npr.org/2013/12/27/256597762/mel-brooks-im-an-egot-i-dont-need-any-more; James Robert Parish, *"It's Good to Be the King": The Seriously Funny Life of Mel Brooks* (Hoboken, NJ: John Wiley and Sons, 2008), 221.

HIGHSMITH, PATRICIA (1921–1995)

Texas-born novelist, short-story writer, and the child of two artists and survivor of an unhappy childhood. After graduating from Barnard College, she took a job writing for comic books, contributing stories to such early series as *Spy Smasher* and *Captain Midnight*, as well as writing western strips, romances, and illustrated biographies of famous men.

She published her first novel, *STRANGERS ON A TRAIN*, in 1950; it was successful, although it was the movie adaptation the following year (which made Guy far more sympathetic while providing a simpler, more dramatic finale) that made her famous. Her next novel, *The Price of Salt*, was about a lesbian love affair; most controversially, it dared to have a happy ending rather than assigning its characters to the "well of loneliness" other gay novels had previously invoked. It was published under a pseudonym and is the basis of the 2015 film *Carol*.

Most of the rest of Highsmith's works were crime thrillers but only in the sense that *The Stranger* or *Crime and Punishment* are, too; chiefly they are stories about people who become criminals out of clumsiness or expedience. GUILT is usually absent in her callow characters, as is regret; the amoral thief and murderer Tom Ripley remains her most famous creation (albeit one usually misunderstood by filmmakers). Not surprisingly, Highsmith much preferred animals to people; the titles of two of her short-story collections, *Little Tales of Misogyny* and *The Animal Lovers Book of Beastly Murder*, were well-chosen. She enjoyed her own company, tobacco, and strong drink.

Highsmith spent the last 32 years of her life in Europe, first in England and then in Switzerland, where her love of privacy was respected and her eccentricities more accepted although still commented on. (She could make appallingly racist remarks and once attended a cocktail party with a handbag full of snails, which she kept as pets.) She died at 74 in Locarno of cancer. She left her entire estate to the artists' colony at Yaddo, where she had finished the final draft of *Strangers on a Train*.

References
Michael Dirda, "This Woman Is Dangerous," *New York Review of Books*, July 2, 2009, http://www.nybooks.com/articles/archives/2009/jul/02/this-woman-is-dangerous; Kim Morgan, "The Gnarly Allure of Patricia Highsmith," *Daily Beast*, December 5, 2015, http://www.thedaily beast.com/articles/2015/12/05/the-gnarly-allure-of-patricia-highsmith.html; Gerald Peary, "An Interview with Patricia Highsmith," *Sight and Sound* (Spring 1988), 104–5, http://www.geraldpeary.com/interviews/ghi/highsmith.html.

HITCH
The director's favored nickname but also a persona—rotund, precise, slyly witty—and a practically trademarked brand, marked by his own minimalist self-drawn caricature and eventually growing to encompass television shows, children's books, anthologies, comics, magazines, record albums, and almost anything else you (or his agent) could think of.

Hitchcock began the creation and feeding of this character early, hiring a publicist after *THE LODGER* debuted and contributing articles to publications from *Film Weekly* ("My Screen Memories," 1936) to *Good Housekeeping* ("The Enjoyment of Fear," 1949). The result was that—bolstered by his witty cameos—he became recognizable in a way few working directors had been since the era of D. W. Griffith. Unless they acted, too, like Erich von Stroheim, filmmakers were rarely celebrities to American audiences. Hitchcock always was. When the television show *ALFRED HITCHCOCK PRESENTS* began in the '50s, it not only fleshed out that teasing, avuncular persona but also provided a personal theme song in "Funeral March for a Marionette." He had become as famous as many of the actors he cast in his films.

There was, in some circles perhaps, a downside to this; self-promotion has its limits, even in Hollywood, and in the '60s, as Hitchcock became more of a trademark, undoubtedly some thought of him as less of an artist. Yet ultimately his branding drew many people to see the "new Hitchcock" in a way they never would have consciously looked forward to see the "new Huston" or the "new Hawks," to name two of his contemporaries; it may have narrowed people's image of him, but it also focused it.

And in some ways, the playful public persona of "Hitch" himself—darkly humorous but never morbid, teasing but never terrorizing, risqué but never vulgar—may have been his most clever creation.

Reference

Donald Spoto, *The Dark Side of Genius: The Life of Alfred Hitchcock* (New York: Da Capo Press, 1999), 73, 102–4, 418.

HITCHCOCK (US 2012)

DIRECTOR: Sacha Gervasi.
SCREENPLAY: John J. McLaughlin, based on the book *Alfred Hitchcock and the Making of 'Psycho'* by Stephen Rebello.
PRODUCERS: Alan Barnette, Joe Medjuck, Tom Pollock, Ivan Reitman, Tom Thayer.
CINEMATOGRAPHY: Jeff Cronenweth.
EDITOR: Pamela Martin.
ORIGINAL MUSIC: Danny Elfman.
CAST: Anthony Hopkins (Alfred Hitchcock), Helen Mirren (Alma Hitchcock), Scarlett Johansson (Janet Leigh), James D'Arcy (Anthony Perkins), Danny Huston (Whitfield Cook), Michael Wincott (Ed Gein).
RUNNING TIME: 98 minutes. Color.
RELEASED THROUGH: Fox Searchlight.

A docudrama based chiefly on the Stephen Rebello book *Alfred Hitchcock and the Making of 'Psycho,'* with some details interpolated from PATRICK MCGILLIGAN's *ALFRED HITCHCOCK: A LIFE IN DARKNESS AND LIGHT*; taking a late-in-life creative peak in the filmmaker's life, it focuses on the time put in on finding, developing, and filming *PSYCHO*, despite the difficulties with PARAMOUNT and Hollywood CENSORSHIP.

It is a good story and one told both in Rebello's book and in JANET LEIGH's own memoirs of the production, *Psycho: The Classic Thriller.* Yet for some reason, the filmmakers seem unconcerned about getting simple facts right. Some of these are minor (the movie was not filmed on the Paramount lot, as the film suggests, but at UNIVERSAL); some are rather more serious. (The early death of the story's heroine wasn't an invention of ALMA REVILLE's but in the original novel by ROBERT BLOCH.)

Worse, the movie seems intent on creating conflict where in fact there was none. Hitchcock is portrayed as being dangerously delusional. (He has long, disturbing, hallucinatory conversations with the real-life inspiration for Norman Bates, the serial killer ED GEIN.) And apparently thinking Alma wasn't interesting enough in her own right (and she was), the script has her actually directing part of *Psycho* (which is simply untrue) while in the midst of a complicated emotional affair with the screenwriter WHITFIELD COOK (which is, to say the least, arguable).

The Hitchcock estate seemed determined to primly ignore the film, and—perhaps because Leigh, Cook, ANTHONY PERKINS, and most of the other onscreen characters were already dead—the movie did not attract the criticism that *THE GIRL* had, although *Time* criticized it for having a "happy ending that no one can believe" and proclaimed it "fine for anyone who prefers their Hitchcock history tidied up, absent the megalomania, the condescending cruelty and tendency to sexual harassment."

References

Mary Pols, "'Hitchcock'—To Psycho, with Love," *Time*, November 20, 2012 http://entertainment.time.com/2012/11/20/hitch

cock-to-psycho-with-love; Stephen Whitty, "'Hitchcock' Review: 'Psycho,' Analyzed," *NJ.com*, http://www.nj.com/entertainment/index.ssf/2012/11/hitchcock_review_psycho_analyz.html.

HITCHCOCK, ALFRED (1899–1980)

The following is a timeline of major events in Hitchcock's life. For further details on specific films or colleagues, see individual entries. Some dates are approximate; unless specified, films are dated by their initial release.

August 13, 1899. Alfred Joseph Hitchcock born in London, the youngest of three children. (His sister is Ellen Kathleen; his brother is William John.) His father, William, is a greengrocer.

August 14, 1899. ALMA REVILLE born in London.

c. 1904. William Hitchcock delivers his son to the local police to be locked up as a "naughty boy." Although the child is only left alone in a cell for a short while, the memory stays with him forever.

1910–1913. Alfred Hitchcock enrolled at the Jesuit school St. Ignatius College. Later, Hitchcock continues at a local council school to take courses in draftsmanship and commercial art.

1914. Hitchcock takes junior job at W. T. Henley's Telegraph Works Company. William Hitchcock dies.

1914–1919. Works on technical drawings, diagrams at Henley's, eventually rising to a position in the advertising department. Exempted from draft due to "obesity." Contributes short stories often featuring unreliable narrators, love triangles, or twist endings to Henley's employee magazine. Takes art classes at night.

Finds freelance art work with local film productions.

1921. Begins full-time employment at Famous Players-Lasky, designing intertitles. Progresses to working on sets and scripts.

1923. First directing jobs, on *NUMBER 13* (unfinished) and codirecting the short *ALWAYS TELL YOUR WIFE* (partially lost).

1923–1925. Codirects and/or cowrites five films, including *THE WHITE SHADOW* for GAINSBOROUGH PICTURES, which has taken over from Famous Players-Lasky. Begins courting film editor and assistant director Alma Reville.

1925. Directs his first solo feature for SIR MICHAEL BALCON at Gainsborough Pictures, *THE PLEASURE GARDEN*, shot in Germany. Directs *THE MOUNTAIN EAGLE*. (Both films will have their releases delayed until 1927 by disappointed distributor C. M. WOOLF.)

1926. Directs *THE LODGER: A STORY OF THE LONDON FOG*. Film's release again held up by Woolf; recut, it is previewed to an enthusiastic press. Hitchcock marries Reville in December.

1927. *The Lodger* finally released to popular acclaim. *THE RING*, another hit, and *DOWNHILL* for BRITISH INTERNATIONAL PICTURES. *EASY VIRTUE.*

1928. *THE FARMER'S WIFE. CHAMPAGNE.* Daughter PATRICIA HITCHCOCK born.

1929. *THE MANXMAN. BLACKMAIL*, his first talkie and his second thriller.

1930. *JUNO AND THE PAYCOCK*, episodes of revue *ELSTREE CALLING* and *MURDER!*, another hit thriller.

1931. THE SKIN GAME. Release of *MARY*, a German-language version of *Murder!* shot simultaneously with original film.

1932. NUMBER 17. RICH AND STRANGE.

1933. Directs *WALTZES FROM VIENNA*, a picture he will consider a particular low point. It will be released the following year.

1934. Hitchcock leaves British International Pictures, resumes collaboration with Balcon at GAUMONT-BRITISH. *THE MAN WHO KNEW TOO MUCH* revives career, firmly establishes Hitchcock's reputation as the "Master of Suspense."

1935. THE 39 STEPS. Reemphasizes themes and details first seen in *The Lodger*—a wrong man on the run, questions of GUILT and innocence, BONDAGE, theaters, BLONDES—to be explored for the rest of his career.

1936. SECRET AGENT. SABOTAGE.

1937. YOUNG AND INNOCENT.

1938. THE LADY VANISHES. Wins best director award from NEW YORK FILM CRITICS CIRCLE. Biggest success since *The 39 Steps*, it increases Hitchcock's and Hollywood's mutual interest. Hitchcock takes meetings with both Samuel Goldwyn and DAVID O. SELZNICK. Hitchcock's agent—Myron Selznick, David's brother—advises him to turn down Goldwyn.

1939. JAMAICA INN, last Hitchcock feature to be shot in Great Britain for a decade. Leaves with his family and assistant JOAN HARRISON for America and a contract with Selznick.

1940. REBECCA. Film wins best picture at the ACADEMY AWARDS, Hitchcock loses best director prize to John Ford for *The Grapes of Wrath*. Buys country home in Santa Cruz mountains. *FOREIGN CORRESPONDENT.*

1941. SUSPICION, first film with CARY GRANT. Film wins best actress Oscar for JOAN FONTAINE. *MR. AND MRS. SMITH.*

1942. SABOTEUR. Buys home in Los Angeles. Hitchcock's MOTHER dies.

1943. SHADOW OF A DOUBT. Hitchcock's brother dies of complications from alcoholism.

1944. LIFEBOAT. Nominated for best director, loses to Leo McCarey for *Going My Way*. Shoots two propaganda shorts in Great Britain for the British Ministry of Information, *BON VOYAGE* and *AVENTURE MALGACHE.*

1945. SPELLBOUND, first film with INGRID BERGMAN. Nominated for best director, loses to Billy Wilder for *The Lost Weekend*. Helps supervise editing of Holocaust documentary footage, eventually shown as *MEMORY OF THE CAMPS.*

1946. NOTORIOUS. Forms independent production company with producer SIDNEY BERNSTEIN, TRANSATLANTIC PICTURES.

1947. THE PARADINE CASE. Last film under the Selznick contract.

1948. ROPE. First film with JAMES STEWART. First of the Transatlantic productions.

1949. Returns to England to shoot *UNDER CAPRICORN*, his first film in COLOR and last with Bergman. Its financial failure hastens end of Transatlantic Pictures.

1950. Signs contract with WARNER BROS. *STAGE FRIGHT.*

1951. STRANGERS ON A TRAIN is released, his first hit since *Notorious*. First film with cinematographer ROBERT BURKS.

1953. I CONFESS.

1954. DIAL M FOR MURDER, his only film in 3-D—it ends up being released to most theaters "flat"—and his first film with GRACE KELLY. *REAR WINDOW,* another hit, also with Kelly and his first film with screenwriter JOHN MICHAEL HAYES. Is nominated for best director, loses to Elia Kazan for *On the Waterfront.*

1955. TO CATCH A THIEF. THE TROUBLE WITH HARRY, first film with composer BERNARD HERRMANN. *ALFRED HITCH-COCK PRESENTS* begins on television. Becomes a US citizen (retaining dual citizenship with Great Britain).

1956. THE MAN WHO KNEW TOO MUCH. THE WRONG MAN. Signs VERA MILES to a personal contract.

1957. First book on Hitchcock's art, *HITCHCOCK* by ERIC ROHMER and CLAUDE CHABROL, published in France.

1958. VERTIGO. Last film with Stewart.

1959. NORTH BY NORTHWEST. Last film with Grant.

1960. PSYCHO. Nominated for fifth and last time as best director. Loses to Billy Wilder for *The Apartment.*

1961. Signs TIPPI HEDREN to a seven-year contract.

1962. Offered and declines the Companion of the British Empire award. Begins extensive INTERVIEWS for *HITCHCOCK/TRUFFAUT. Alfred Hitchcock Presents* replaced by *THE ALFRED HITCHCOCK HOUR.* It will run until 1965.

1963. THE BIRDS.

1964. MARNIE. Last film with Herrmann. Last film with Hedren. Last film with Burks.

1966. TORN CURTAIN.

1968. Receives Irving Thalberg Memorial Lifetime Achievement award.

1969. TOPAZ.

1971. Alma Reville suffers a stroke. She largely recovers, although other strokes and health issues will follow in later years.

1972. FRENZY.

1974. Hitchcock suffers a heart attack and is implanted with a pacemaker.

1976. FAMILY PLOT.

1977. THE SHORT NIGHT is announced as Hitchcock's next film. Early work begins on the script.

1978. The Short Night continues in development with new writers.

1979. Hitchcock's sister Ellen Kathleen dies. *The Short Night* project is quietly abandoned. In ill health, Hitchcock finally closes his office at UNIVERSAL in May. His knighthood is announced as part of the Queen's New Year Honours list.

1980. Dies at home of renal failure on April 29. His body is cremated and his ashes scattered at sea. (Alma Reville will die two years later. Her body will be cremated and her ashes scattered at sea.)

References

"Hitchcock Chronology," *Hitchcock Zone,* http://the.hitchcock.zone/wiki/Hitchcock _Chronology; Patrick McGilligan, *Alfred Hitchcock: A Life in Darkness and Light* (New York: HarperCollins, 2003); Donald Spoto, *The Dark Side of Genius: The Life of Alfred Hitchcock* (New York: Da Capo Press, 1999).

HITCHCOCK, PATRICIA (1928–)

The only child of Alfred Hitchcock and ALMA REVILLE, "Pat" was born in London in 1928 and moved to America with her family in 1939. At 12, she got her first professional acting part—in the short-lived Broadway play *Solitaire*—and, after graduation from a CATHOLIC girls' school in 1947, enrolled in the Royal Academy of Dramatic Art in London, where she lived with relatives.

Hitchcock used her in several of his films, but if there was some nepotism involved, there was no favoritism; the parts were always small, generally comic, and not particularly flattering. She is "Chubby" Bannister in *STAGE FRIGHT* and morbid Barbara Morton in *STRANGERS ON A TRAIN*; in *PSYCHO*, she is Caroline, Marion Crane's gabby, slightly nasal coworker. Pat Hitchcock married in 1952—to the grandnephew of the Boston archbishop, much to her father's pride—and gradually stepped away from her career. She appeared, mostly briefly, in ten episodes of *ALFRED HITCHCOCK PRESENTS*—"I played more English maids than you will ever know!"—and had a few bit parts in other films. *Skateboard*, a 1978 comedy, was her last credit.

Since then, she has enjoyed her home in California, her family, and horses, and if she herself hasn't carried forward the Hitchcock name in films, then she has protected it as best she can, donating his papers to the Margaret Herrick Library, appearing in many authorized documentaries, and coproducing her own movie about his longtime production designer ROBERT F. BOYLE (*The Man on Lincoln's Nose*). She also cowrote a book about her mother, *Alma Hitchcock: The Woman behind the Man*, which denied that her father played cruel practical JOKES, reprinted her mother's recipes and luncheon menus, and described her parents' marriage and collaboration in glowing terms.

Pat Hitchcock has also over the years given interviews, although her answers were always brief. Her favorite film of his? "*NOTORIOUS*." His own favorite? "*SHADOW OF A DOUBT*." Her childhood? "We were a very close family." The various books detailing stories of his poor treatment of actresses or his cruel practical jokes? "Hurtful" and "untrue." His dark, obsessive films? "He was a brilliant filmmaker and he knew how to tell a story, that's all." Over the years, the interviews became more reluctant, even combative—there was the feeling of a dutiful daughter being forced to perform for company when she didn't wish to simply because it was an occasion. (A 2005 interview with the *Times* of London—with the headline "Even Scarier than *Psycho*"—seems to have been the last long one for print.) Her children have now taken over as the keepers of the family flame.

"People will think what they want to think, that's what my father always said," Pat Hitchcock observed once. "They pay their money, they are entitled to. Anyway, I don't care what they think." If that's really true, then she is happier than most.

References

Helena de Bertodano, "Even Scarier than Psycho," *Times*, April 5, 2005, http://www.thetimes.co.uk/tto/life/article1718836.ece; Pat Hitchcock O'Connell and Laurent Bouzereau, *Alma Hitchcock: The Woman behind the Man* (New York: Berkeley Trade, 2004), 3, 153, 233–55; Suzie Mackenzie, "The Woman Who Knew Too Much," *Guardian*, August 27, 1999, http://the.hitchcock.zone/wiki/The_Guardian_%2828/Aug/1999%29_-_Pat_Hitchcock:_The_woman_who_knew_too_much; "Pat Hitchcock," *IMDb*, http://www.imdb.com/name/nm0386877/bio?ref_=nm_ov_bio_sm.

HITCHCOCKIAN

Decades before the idea of "personal branding" became commonplace, Alfred Hitchcock very cannily promoted himself in the

'20s and '30s—hiring a personal publicist, doing rounds of INTERVIEWS, writing bylined articles for popular magazines, and even endorsing products. His reputation of the "Master of Suspense" began while he was still in England, and within a few years of his arrival in America, he himself became not only a celebrity but also a kind of genre all his own—one would go see the "new Hitchcock" the way you would buy tickets to "that new horror picture."

But eventually the more famous he became, the more diluted his name grew. He went beyond being an honored trademark to being a loosely defined adjective—"Hitchcockian"—that could be applied to (and was soon eagerly sought by) other filmmakers. Although Hitchcock's films actually cover a wide variety of genres (though they were frequently unsuccessful, he did do straight dramas, comedies, even a musical), his imitators concentrate on only two: the serial-killer shocker and the romantic international thriller. They tend to miss the point of each.

Hitchcock did a number of films about lethal lunatics; the most obvious ones are *THE LODGER, SHADOW OF A DOUBT, ROPE, STRANGERS ON A TRAIN, PSYCHO,* and *FRENZY.* In almost all of them (we never actually meet the killer in *The Lodger*), the killer is suave, even charming; in most of them, the victims are STRANGLED; in all of them, the simple message is that the villain may look just like you—might even be you, given just a few dark twists or turns.

Unfortunately, these aren't the things that most of his admirers choose to imitate. Instead, the so-called Hitchcockian murder mystery puts the emphasis on surprise rather than suspense. The IDENTITY of the killer is often kept a secret until the end (something Hitchcock really doesn't do; it's not his fault if we choose to believe our eyes and Norman Bates's protestations).

The murders in these films are often particularly gory, and the "twist" ending generally involves a split personality or another showy bit of madness. It's as if the only Hitchcock film they saw were *Psycho,* and all they took away from it was the scene with the psychiatrist.

Some of these films are successful on their own terms; the deliberately over-the-top *Homicidal* from William Castle features a shock beheading and some genuinely Hitchcockian gender bending. But most of Castle's other similar killer-thrillers—*Strait-Jacket, I Saw What You Did*—copy not Hitchcock's style but only his flair for publicity and personal iconography. (Like Hitchcock, Castle appeared in his own trailers.)

There were many other serial-killer films in the wake of *Psycho,* most of them quickly identified by their titles—*Paranoiac, Fanatic, The Psychopath*—some of them even based on stories by *Psycho* scribe ROBERT BLOCH and some of them, like *The Texas Chainsaw Massacre,* based on old ED GEIN himself. (There were many more films, too, such as *Taste of Fear,* which the uninformed called Hitchcockian but were actually imitating his French rival, HENRI-GEORGES CLOUZOT and his *LES DIABOLIQUES.*) But although some had a few genuine thrills, their interests were not Hitchcock's, and his obsessions were beyond them. And then *Halloween* came out and then *Friday the 13th* and then cruder slasher films, which did away with any remaining subtleties.

The other kind of Hitchcock film sometimes imitated is the couple-on-the-run film, a sort of thriller he pretty much invented in *THE 39 STEPS* and returned to with *SABOTEUR* and, finally setting out to top himself, *NORTH BY NORTHWEST.* And after that film, there was another miniflurry of Hitchcock imitators, centering on mismatched male-female couples in jeopardy and often bearing a one-word title: *Charade, Mirage, Arabesque, Gambit*. None of them fully explored the themes—corrupting ruling-class conspiracies, flawed heroes, GUILT—that made his own films so resonant.

True, most featured Hitchcock veterans (CARY GRANT in the first, GREGORY PECK in the next two, SHIRLEY MACLAINE in the last), as well as complicated puzzles, beautiful costars, unusual chase scenes, and interesting backgrounds; best is the charming *Charade*, which had Grant and Audrey Hepburn looking for looted fortune while evading the clutches of some odd character actors and running through Paris to a percussive Henry Mancini score. (Like many Hitchcock thrillers, it ends in a theater, too.) But even it is slightly off—its humor a bit too broad, its thrills a bit too comic.

In any case, eventually the James Bond movies made the Hitchcock international thrillers obsolete; playing baldly for a broader audience, they made the quips more obvious, the sex more voluptuous, the climaxes more cataclysmic. The days of quaint MACGUFFINS—spies chasing after a statue with a belly full of microfilm—were gone. Now nothing less than a megalomaniac out to destroy the planet would do.

Yet the ultimate irony was that—even before the knockoff Hitchcockian thrillers themselves gave way to big-budget spy movies or the ersatz Hitchcockian serial-killer films were superseded by slice-and-dice gore pictures—none of Hitchcock's imitators had ever really, truly understood what they were imitating. They thought "Hitchcockian" meant surprise endings, Cary Grant, mad killers, European capitals. They didn't realize it meant guilt and innocence, BONDAGE and duty, responsibility and regret. Which is what had made him the "Master of Suspense" all along.

References

Landon Palmer, "Culture Warrior: What Is Hitchcockian Suspense," *Film School Rejects*, http://filmschoolrejects.com/features/culture-warrior-what-is-hitchcockian-suspense-lpalm.php; Donald Spoto, *The Dark Side of Genius: The Life of Alfred Hitchcock* (New York: Da Capo Press, 1999), 73.

HITCHCOCK'S FILMS

Seminal English-language study by ROBIN WOOD, first published in 1965. The work, which had begun with a close reading of *PSYCHO* for the magazine *CAHIERS DU CINEMA*, followed in that journal's tradition of AUTEUR THEORY and careful analysis and was an early and essential look at the director's movies, with a strong emphasis on his American work.

The initial essay on *Psycho* had first been rejected by the English film magazine *Sight and Sound* because editor Penelope Houston felt Wood was taking seriously a film that had been only meant as a JOKE. Indeed, Wood's book-length critical history came out at a time when his first sentence—"Why should we take Hitchcock seriously?"—was still a popular query. It was one Wood's book then clearly, cogently answered, with separate chapters carefully analyzing *STRANGERS ON A TRAIN, REAR WINDOW, VERTIGO, NORTH BY NORTHWEST, PSYCHO, THE BIRDS, MARNIE,* and *TORN CURTAIN*. He found much to praise in each.

In 1989, Wood—who had not only since come out as a gay man and declared himself a Marxist but also had time to reconsider his feelings about auteurism and criticism in general—published a new version of his book, *Hitchcock's Films Revisited*, with the original material not only annotated and corrected but also accompanied by much new material. If it is less clear cut and concise than the first, then it is no less valuable.

References

William Grimes, "Robin Wood, Film Critic Who Wrote on Hitchcock, Dies at 78," *New York Times*, December 22, 2009, http://www.nytimes.com/2009/12/22/ arts/22wood.html?_r=0; Armen Svadjian, "A Life in Criticism: Robin Wood at 75," *Your Flesh*, January 1, 2006, http:// yourfleshmag.com/books/a-life-in-film -criticism-robin-wood-at-75/am; Robin Wood, *Hitchcock's Films* (New York: Paperback Library, 1969), 7–15.

HITCHCOCK/TRUFFAUT

Along with *HITCHCOCK'S FILMS* by ROBIN WOOD, perhaps the one essential book on the director's work.

Before he became a great director in his own right, FRANÇOIS TRUFFAUT had been a critic and one of Hitchcock's most fervent admirers, hailing him as one of cinema's greatest AUTEURS. Although by 1962 Truffaut was now making personal films of his own, he still thought critics did not take Hitchcock seriously (partly because of the director's own jocular attitude toward INTERVIEWS), and he "felt the imperative need to convince."

So a series of long interviews began. It would stretch, Truffaut said, to 50 hours of recorded tapes; after 4 years of transcription, editing, fact-checking, and illustration research, the book was published in France in 1966 and in America the following year. (Portions of the original tapes can be heard online at various sites, including http:// www.filmdetail.com/2011/02/14/the-hitch cock-and-truffaut-tapes.) A revised edition—with some additional thoughts from Hitchcock on *FRENZY* and Truffaut's own thoughts on *FAMILY PLOT*, the TIPPI HEDREN controversy, and Hitchcock's final decline—was published after Hitchcock's death and just before Truffaut's.

The original volume is easy to criticize now. Truffaut was an unabashed and

sometimes uncritical devotee; he occasionally fails to follow up on Hitchcock's own allusions, functioning chiefly as a highly intelligent stenographer, carefully taking down every humorous anecdote and how-I-got-that-shot story. But that stenography is important, too; Hitchcock was relaxed and expansive with his young admirer, and if some of the stories here are familiar, then they are also filled with unequaled detail. The book remains a vital work of scholarship and a primary source for many volumes that followed, including this one.

References

"Alfred Hitchcock and François Truffaut (Aug/1962)," *Hitchcock Zone*, http://the.hitchcock.zone/wiki/Alfred _Hitchcock_and_Fran%C3%A7ois _Truffaut_%28Aug/1962%29; "The Hitchcock and Truffaut Tapes," *Film Detail*, http://www.filmdetail.com/2011/02/14/ the-hitchcock-and-truffaut-tapes; François Truffaut, *Hitchcock/Truffaut*, rev. ed. (New York: Touchstone, 1985), 11–12.

HITCHCOCK/TRUFFAUT
(US 2015)

DIRECTOR: Kent Jones.
SCREENPLAY: Kent Jones, Serge Toubiana.
PRODUCERS: Charles S. Cohen, Oliver Mille.
CINEMATOGRAPHY: Nick Bentjen, Daniel Cowen, Eric Gautier, Mihai Malaimare Jr., Lisa Rinzler, Genta Tamaki.
EDITOR: Rachel Reichman.
ORIGINAL MUSIC: Jeremiah Bornfield.
CAST: Alfred Hitchcock, François Truffaut, Paul Schrader, Martin Scorsese, David Fincher, Wes Anderson.
RUNNING TIME: 80 minutes. Color.
RELEASED THROUGH: Cohen Media Group.

Film historian and festival programmer Kent Jones INTERVIEWS filmmakers who talk about how the famous book-length interview influenced their life and work. A film that salutes not only the original book (while hinting, tantalizingly, at some of the anecdotes Hitchcock insisted be off the record) but also the filmmakers themselves, with many current directors talking about their creative debts and analyzing various classic films.

Reference

"Hitchcock/Truffaut," *IMDb*, http://www.imdb.com/title/tt3748512.

HODIAK, JOHN (1914–1955)

Pittsburgh-born performer who grew up in Michigan and began acting in plays at his local Ukrainian Catholic Church. Proudly working class, with an awkward and pronounced accent, he caddied and toiled in an auto plant while dreaming of acting and laboring on his elocution; by 1939, he was in Chicago, playing the title role in the *Li'l Abner* radio show.

The daily serial lasted little more than a year, but by 1942, he had an MGM contract. They loaned him out for Fox's *LIFEBOAT*, where he played the hunky sailor on whose bare chest TALLULAH BANKHEAD's Connie adds her own, lipsticked icon. After a few more good films—*A Bell for Adano*, *Command Decision*—Hodiak's career faltered, but he made a strong stage comeback on Broadway in the role of Lt. Maryk in *The Caine Mutiny Court Martial*. After its two-year run, Hodiak—recently divorced from wife ANNE BAXTER—returned to Hollywood and movie work.

He died in the home he had bought his parents of a sudden heart attack at 41.

References

Paul Guggenheimer, "One Hundred Years of John Hodiak," *Pittsburgh Post-Gazette*, April 16, 2014, http://www.post-gazette.com/ae/movies/2014/04/16/ One-hundred-years-of-John-Hodiak/stories/201404160030; "John Hodiak," *IMDb*, http://www.imdb.com/name/nm0388303/bio?ref_=nm_ov_bio_sm.

HOMOLKA, OSCAR (1898–1978)

Viennese performer who, after classical training, began a serious career on the German stage, working for Max Reinhardt, playing in Shakespeare, appearing in the first German productions of O'Neill, and starring in everything from Edgar Wallace thrillers to plays by Brecht and Shaw.

Given his association with Brecht, and the fact that his first wife, actress Grete Mosheim, was Jewish, Homolka wisely left for England shortly after Hitler came to power, where he resumed his film career. In 1936, he starred as the vaguely foreign bomber in *SABOTAGE*. By 1940, he was in Hollywood, where he began playing supporting parts, sometimes as eccentric old-world relatives (*I Remember Mama*, for which he won an Oscar nomination) but more often as villainous Communists or suspicious servants (*Mr. Sardonicus*). He was busy on TV and appeared on three episodes of *ALFRED HITCHCOCK PRESENTS*.

He died at 79 in Sussex.

References

"Oscar Homolka," *IMDb*, http://www.imdb.com/name/nm0393028/bio?ref_=nm_ov_bio_sm; Alfred E. Twomey and Arthur F. McClure, *The Versatiles: Supporting Character Players in the Cinema, 1930–1955* (New York: Castle Books, 1969), 116.

HOMOSEXUALITY

In many Hitchcock films, the character of the gay man and woman follows the same stereotypical, homophobic impulses as most of noir. The lesbian is obsessed and predatory (*REBECCA*). The gay man is effeminate, neurotic, slightly pretentious, and fatally fixated on straight men (*ROPE, STRANGERS ON A TRAIN, NORTH BY NORTHWEST*). And both are perhaps at least better off than the cross-dresser, who is simply, unpredictably violent (*MURDER!, PSYCHO*). Yet these clichés stand somewhat apart from how Hitchcock viewed homosexuality in real life.

Even during his extremely naïve 20s, he was comfortable around gays, even slightly intrigued by them; he deeply admired F. W. MURNAU, collaborated happily with IVOR NOVELLO, and explored the after-hours world of Berlin. Occasionally, close associates speculated—very quietly—about his own orientation. (Rodney Ackland, who was gay and worked with Hitchcock on *NUMBER 17*, said that the director once confessed, "I think I would have been a poof if I hadn't met Alma at the right time"; SAMSON RAPHAELSON, who liked the couple, still described them as "this odd, weird, little faggish man and this sweet little boyish woman.")

Later on, many of Hitchcock's male STARS—MICHAEL REDGRAVE, JOHN GIELGUD, CHARLES LAUGHTON, MONTGOMERY CLIFT, RAYMOND BURR, FARLEY GRANGER, JOHN DALL, and ANTHONY PERKINS, among others—were either gay or bisexual; the director's willingness to insert beefcake shots of Novello, CARY GRANT, JOHN GAVIN, and other male stars suggests a certain awareness of homoerotic imagery. Despite his rigid CATHOLIC upbringing, Hitchcock welcomed gay and bisexual actors socially (Granger remembered many family dinners with his lover ARTHUR LAURENTS at the Hitchcock home); in spite of the times, Hitchcock cast these actors in a variety of roles and encouraged freedom in their performances (the way Perkins sashays up the STAIRCASE in the old dark *Psycho* house).

Hitchcock's films can't be said to be gay friendly in the way that other films of the time by gay directors, such as James Whale or George Cukor, are; the regular rough equation of homosexuality with emotional disturbance seems to be, on the surface, a clear and hurtful one. Yet the line Hitchcock draws most often isn't between homosexuality and homicide but between MOTHER obsession and murder—Bruno in *Strangers on a Train* may be gay, but Norman Bates really isn't meant to be, and neither is Bob Rusk in *FRENZY*. The homosexuality is beside the point; it's their twisted relationship to mother, not to men, that made them what they are.

So perhaps that's not homophobia. Perhaps it's misogyny (or, more accurately, gynophobia—not so much hatred of women as terror of them). Or perhaps it's just that this complicated artist contained several competing impulses at once, both an awe of women and a fear of them, both an impulse to put them high up on a pedestal and an urge to pull them down into the mud, both a desire to see them tortured and a need to decry that torment.

"I think the best of Hitchcock films continue to fascinate me because he's obviously right inside them, he understands so well the male drive to DOMINATE, harass, control and at the same time he identifies strongly with the woman's position," gay critic ROBIN WOOD said in 2000. They're a "kind of battleground between these two positions."

And in the midst of that fighting—sometimes as collateral damage—are Hitchcock's gay characters.

References
Peter Ackroyd, "Alfred Hitchcock Was an Overgrown Schoolboy," *Daily Mail*, March 21, 2015, http://www.dailymail.co.uk/home/event/article-3002550/Alfred-Hitchcock-overgrown-schoolboy-schoolboy-s

-obsession-sex.html; Farley Granger, interview with the author, April 2007; William Grimes, "Robin Wood, Film Critic Who Wrote on Hitchcock, Dies at 78," *New York Times*, December 22, 2009, http://www.nytimes.com/2009/12/22/arts/22wood.html?_r=0; Donald Spoto, *The Dark Side of Genius: The Life of Alfred Hitchcock* (New York: Da Capo Press, 1999), 86; John Russell Taylor, "The Lady Appears," *Times*, September 6, 2008, http://the.hitchcock.zone/wiki/The_Times_%2806/Sep/2008%29_-_The_lady_appears; François Truffaut, *Hitchcock/Truffaut*, rev. ed. (New York: Touchstone, 1985), 39.

"THE HORSE PLAYER" (US; ORIGINALLY AIRED MARCH 14, 1961)

DIRECTOR: Alfred Hitchcock.
SCREENPLAY: Henry Slesar, from his story.
PRODUCERS: Joan Harrison, Norman Lloyd.
CINEMATOGRAPHY: John L. Russell.
EDITOR: Edward W. Williams.
ORIGINAL MUSIC: Joseph E. Romero.
CAST: Claude Rains (Father Amion).
RUNNING TIME: 30 minutes with commercials. Black and white.
ORIGINALLY BROADCAST BY: NBC.

An elderly priest discovers the source of the sudden influx of cash into the collection plate—an inveterate gambler. Is it wrong to pray for his continued luck? A slight story that mostly gave the director the chance to reunite with one of the STARS of *NOTORIOUS*, while playfully wrestling with a few CATHOLIC themes.

References

Tim Brooks and Earle Marsh, *The Complete Directory to Prime Time Network TV Shows*, 8th ed. (New York: Ballantine Books, 2003), 29; Jack Edmond Nolan,

"Hitchcock's TV Films," *Film Fan Monthly* (June 1968), 3–6.

HULL, HENRY (1890–1977)

Cultured, Louisville-born performer from a theatrical family (his father was a drama critic) who moved between stage and film. He first appeared on Broadway in 1911, made his movie debut in the D. W. Griffith melodrama *One Exciting Night* in 1922, and may be best known for playing Hollywood's first lycanthrope in *Werewolf of London* in 1935. He was in *LIFEBOAT* as Charles J. Rittenhouse Jr., a millionaire and the film's symbol of capitalism; generally, however, Hollywood cast him as various hardscrabble pioneers and struggling ranchers. (He had actually, after his Broadway debut, taken some time off to go prospecting for gold; it didn't pan out.)

He died at 86 in Cornwall after a stroke.

References

"Henry Hull," *IMDb*, http://www.imdb.com/name/nm0401434/bio?ref_=nm_ov_bio_sm; Alfred E. Twomey and Arthur F. McClure, *The Versatiles: Supporting Character Players in the Cinema, 1930–1955* (New York: Castle Books, 1969), 119.

HUNTER, EVAN (1926–2005)

New York author, born Salvatore Lombino, who began writing pulp fiction and had his first literary success with *Blackboard Jungle* in 1954, a novel about juvenile delinquency and public schools, based on his own brief experience teaching in the Bronx, and later turned into a popular movie. Although he would write in a variety of genres, including science fiction, his greatest and long-lasting success came with police procedurals, most published under the name Ed McBain, starting with *Cop Hater* in 1956.

He contributed two stories to *ALFRED HITCHCOCK PRESENTS* and wrote one episode and in 1963 was asked to write the screenplay for *THE BIRDS*. Hunter enjoyed the story conferences but was later dismayed to see that his script had not only been cut but also rewritten; an entirely new scene between ROD TAYLOR and TIPPI HEDREN had been added, in which she talks about her childhood; to Hunter, it sounded like bad ad-libbing. (In actuality, Hitchcock had hastily written it himself.)

Later, Hunter would be harshly critical of the film and its STARS. "Since Hedren and Taylor could not handle the comedy at the top of the film, the audience became bored," he claimed. "They had come to see birds attacking people, so what was all this nonsense with these two people, one who can't act and the other who's so full of machismo you expect him to have a steer thrown over his shoulder?"

Still, the collaboration continued, with Hunter working on the screenplay for the director's next film, *MARNIE*. When Hunter persistently argued against the marital rape scene Hitchcock insisted on, however, he was fired and replaced by novice JAY PRESSON ALLEN. (Hunter described his experiences working with the director in the short, candid 1997 memoir *Me and Hitch*.)

Hunter continued to occasionally write for television and the movies but found more success and less stress in novels, sometimes publishing three or four a year under a variety of pen names; in 2000, two of his pseudonyms even collaborated on a book, which sounds like its own pitch for a potential Hitchcock picture.

A heavy smoker, he died at age 78 of laryngeal cancer.

References

Kyle B. Counts and Steve Rubin, "The Making of 'The Birds,'" *Cinemafantastique* 10, no. 2 (Fall 1980), http://the.hitchcock.zone/wiki/Cinemafantastique_%281980%29_-_The_Making_of_Alfred_Hitchcock%27s_The

Birds; *Ed McBain: The Official Site*, http://www.edmcbain.com/default.html; "Evan Hunter," *IMDb*, http://www.imdb.com/name/nm0402805/bio?ref=nm_ov_bio_sm; Bill Peschel, "Me and Hitch: Evan Hunter Remembers Alfred Hitchcock," *Planet Peschel*, http://planetpeschel.com/2010/04/me-and-hitch-evan-hunter-remembers-alfred-hitchcock; Marilyn Stasio, "Evan Hunter, Writer Who Created Police Procedural, Dies at 78," *New York Times*, July 7, 2005, http://www.nytimes.com/2005/07/07/books/evan-hunter-writer-who-created-police-procedural-dies-at-78.html?_r=0; *The Trouble with Marnie*, directed by Laurent Bouzereau (2000), documentary, http://the.hitchcock.zone/wiki/The_Trouble_with_Marnie_%282000%29_-_transcript.

HUNTER, IAN (1900–1975)

South African performer who made his stage debut in England in 1919 and remained busy in British and American films and on London and Manhattan stages. He made his first movie appearance in 1924 in *Not for Sale* and has good parts in Hitchcock's *THE RING* and *DOWNHILL* and a smaller one in *EASY VIRTUE*; by the mid-'30s, he was in Hollywood, where he was Richard the Lionheart in *The Adventures of Robin Hood*. Twenty years later, he was still playing in *Robin Hood*, although this time in the British TV series. (A few of the scripts were, coincidentally, written by Ian McLellan Hunter, no relation but an American screenwriter who had been blacklisted during the McCarthy era.) The actor retired in the early '60s and died at 75 in London.

References

"Ian Hunter," *IMDb*, http://www.imdb.com/name/nm0402842/bio?ref_=nm_ov_bio_sm; Thomas Staedeli, "Portrait of the Actor Ian Hunter," *Cyranos*, http://www.cyranos.ch/sphunt-e.htm.

I

I CONFESS (US 1953)

DIRECTOR: Alfred Hitchcock.
SCREENPLAY: George Tabori, William Archibald, from the play *Nos Deux Consciences* by Paul Anthelme.
PRODUCERS: Uncredited (Alfred Hitchcock, Sidney Bernstein).
CINEMATOGRAPHY: Robert Burks.
EDITOR: Rudi Fehr.
ORIGINAL MUSIC: Dmitri Tiomkin.
CAST: Montgomery Clift (Father Michael Logan), Anne Baxter (Ruth Grandfort), Brian Aherne (Willy Robertson), Karl Malden (Inspector Larue), O. E. Hasse (Otto Keller), Dolly Haas (Alma Keller).
RUNNING TIME: 92 minutes. Black and white.
RELEASED THROUGH: Warner Bros.

Father Michael Logan is in his church late one night in Quebec City when an agitated Otto Keller, his own caretaker, comes in for confession. He tried to rob a lawyer named Villette, the man reveals; he ended up killing him instead. Keller, who had been Villette's gardener, left the crime scene disguised by wearing a priest's cassock.

Keller leaves the church and later tells his wife all that's happened—but declares he feels safe, as all priests are forbidden from revealing the secrets of the confessional. The next day, Keller goes back to Villette's house, returns the stolen money, and notifies the police of this "mysteri-ous" murder. As the investigation begins, a haunted Logan watches from the street, where he catches the attention of one of the investigators.

The police then hear reports of a priest leaving Villette's house the night of the murder—and Logan arouses their suspicions further when he refuses to give an alibi for the night in question. The reason is that he had agreed to meet Ruth that night, a woman he loved before he was ordained; Villette had been trying to blackmail her with old and scurrilous rumors.

The police arrest Logan and, in a search of his room, find the blood-smeared cassock that Keller has placed there; Logan is charged with murder and put on trial, where he refuses to break the seal of the confessional and Ruth's testimony is twisted to make it look as if she and the priest are still having an affair. Although Logan is acquitted for lack of evidence, no one believes he is innocent; as he leaves the courtroom, an angry mob forms.

Distraught by this injustice, Keller's wife tries to turn her husband in to the police; panicked, Keller shoots her and runs away. With the police and Logan in pursuit, Keller hides in the Chateau Frontenac; when he sees Logan, he accuses him of betraying his vows and revealing his crime—thereby handing his own confession to the police. When he tries to kill

I Confess was problematic for Alfred Hitchcock, chiefly due to his strained relationship with star Montgomery Clift. *Warner Bros./Photofest © Warner Bros.*

Logan, he himself is shot; he just has time to make his final confession before he dies.

One of those Hitchcock's films beloved chiefly by the French and those intrigued by its CATHOLICISM. Although some of the early AUTEURISTS, particularly ERIC ROHMER and CLAUDE CHABROL, praised *I Confess* as one of the director's most Christian works and, in some ways, an "allegory of the Fall," Hitchcock remained far less enamored of it, as its production had been fraught with troubles with the studio and his STAR, and in the end, it had failed to attract an audience, always in his eyes the one truly unforgivable sin.

The troubles began early. There were a long series of unsuccessful scripts (at one point, without avail, he had tried to get GRAHAM GREENE to try his hand), including some complete revisions (a favored but finally abandoned version had the priest fathering an illegitimate child and being wrongly executed). There were casting difficulties (the studio vetoed his original leading lady, Anita Bjork, when it was discovered she was an unmarried mother). There were problems on the set (MONTGOMERY CLIFT arrived with an on-set acting coach and a heavy drinking problem). And after all that effort, when it was all done, from the general American public came only—indifference.

Hitchcock suspected one of the problems was that he had been, quite literally, preaching to the choir. "We Catholics know that a priest cannot disclose the secret of the confessional," he said later, "but the Protestants, the atheists, and the agnostics all say, 'Ridiculous! No man would remain silent and sacrifice his life for such a thing.'" The majority of moviegoers never accepted the central premise, he maintained, and the film itself was too dour and humorless; it should have been, he second-guessed, a "serious story told with tongue-in-cheek."

It's hard to say exactly where Hitchcock would have inserted the humor in a tale of murder and blackmail that depended so heavily on issues of GUILT, sin, penance, and a priest's unbreakable vows or that a slightly ironic approach would have helped the film find any more viewers, who seemed split on whether the whole thing was distasteful or simply dull; as it was, the movie was banned in Ireland, where it was judged an insult to the clergy.

And actually, if anything, the brooding seriousness helps this story. In fact, everything about *I Confess* is deeply grim, from the rainy, real-life Canadian locations to the thickly shadowed BLACK-AND-WHITE CINEMATOGRAPHY to Clift's performance, both anguished and alone, as he stalks the streets with his handsomely furrowed brow. Deeply personal perhaps, too, from its Catholic emphasis to the fact that the one other person who knows the killer's dirty secret—his wife, Alma—has the same name as Hitchcock's spouse.

Some sequences stand out. The early, opening shots of Quebec City and Keller's confession in church; the frustratingly unfair courtroom scene; Logan's halting harrowing exit from the court, surrounded by angry accusing faces, making his way through the crowd like Jesus carrying his cross through the streets. The very first shots of traffic signs, seeming to point the way to the murder scene, underlie the relentless, one-way march of guilt and penance that lie ahead; the Gothic architecture looms menacingly over the characters like accusers. (Only the flashbacks—full of airy balconies and STAIRCASES and shot in a focus so soft it almost glows—offer any sense of hope and freedom.)

For someone often hailed as a Catholic artist, there are not many scenes of self-sacrifice in Hitchcock's work; still, this one surely registers as his greatest. And while many of his films play with notions of guilt and innocence, this is one in which the TRANSFERENCE of sin is quite real; Father Logan not only takes on the knowledge of his parishioner's evil deeds but also seems fated to take on their responsibility as well, even to the point of assuming the civil punishment. It is expiation by proxy.

Yet, as Hitchcock himself knew, there could be no real grandeur in the priest's act because it's really one of spiritual self-preservation; Logan is not so much protecting Keller from punishment as he is safeguarding his own immortal soul. To break the seal of the confessional—to go back on his vows—would make any of his own, youthful indiscretions pale by comparison. It would be a grievous, deliberate sin—and so Logan's story is really a drama of inaction, of a character who refuses to speak up or move forward, who becomes mired in martyrdom not because of noble self-sacrifice but only because the other choice is his own damnation.

Like *SECRET AGENT* years before, it's a melodrama of endurance, of passivity, of impotence. And even a master of storytelling like Alfred Hitchcock could find no way to make that fully entertaining.

References

Paula Marantz Cohen, *Alfred Hitchcock: The Legacy of Victorianism* (Lexington: University of Kentucky Press, 1995), 97; "I Confess," *Irish Film Institute*, http://www.ifi.ie/film/i-confess; Eric Rohmer and Claude Chabrol, *Hitchcock: The First Forty-Four Films*, translated by Stanley Hochman (New York: Frederick Ungar, 1979), 112–18; Donald Spoto, *The Dark Side of Genius: The Life of Alfred Hitchcock* (New York: Da Capo Press, 1999), 335–41.

IDENTITY

In the standard, cozy British mystery, the only real question is, Who done it? The perpetrator is unknown, but everyone else is clearly delineated—dowager, debutante, inspector from "the Yard"—and the sole identity left to be fixed is that of the murderer's.

Those sort of guessing games interested Hitchcock hardly at all. Although the identity of the villain is kept a secret in some Hitchcock films, in many more, it's given away right at the start. There's never any doubt who the agents are in *SABOTEUR* or *SABOTAGE*, what Uncle Charlie is really up to in *SHADOW OF A DOUBT*.

It goes directly to his beliefs about SUSPENSE VS. SURPRISE. What would often be a third-act climax in another person's film—the lord of the manor is actually a foreign spy!—is, in a Hitchcock movie like *THE 39 STEPS*, only the beginning. Besides, in Hitchcock films, identity is a far more serious topic and a far more fluid thing.

Occasionally, someone will assume an identity for a prank, like the practical JOKES the director himself used to play—Melanie Daniels pretending to be a pet shop clerk in *THE BIRDS*. At other times, it's merely for a quick advantage and a step up socially—like brash crime reporter Johnny Jones transforming himself into Huntley Haverstock, an American newspaper's esteemed *FOREIGN CORRESPONDENT*.

And the curious thing about identity is Hitchcock's films is that sometimes, when we dress ourselves in borrowed robes, they change to fit us—or we somehow grow into them. Because, outfitted with a serious name and a sober hat, the former Johnny Jones actually does becomes a successful *Foreign Correspondent*; once he gives in and accepts his new life as George Kaplan, successful American spy, Roger O. Thornhill actually becomes a successful American spy. Mistaken for a political speaker, Richard Hannay gives a rousing political speech in *The 39 Steps*; once a man introduces himself as Dr. Edwardes, even the psychiatrists of *SPELLBOUND* will assume he is Dr. Edwardes and listen to him with respect.

Sometimes, to become a thing, all that is necessary is to give ourselves the name of that thing. Maxim de Winter's new wife in *REBECCA* is a frightened little mouse, unsure of her place, her role, her name. (We never hear her Christian one spoken.) But once she tells Mrs. Danvers, firmly, "I am Mrs. de Winter now," she finally begins to become her.

The danger arises, of course, when we not only tell a lie to others but also begin to believe it ourselves, when we lose grasp on our own identity. Who really is KIM NOVAK at any single moment in *VERTIGO*? Is she really Judy only pretending to be the tough, no-illusions Madeleine? Is she Madeleine pretending to be the fragile, romantic Judy? Is she both, always, at once? Is she ever really sure?

Or in Hitchcock's most complex meditation on identity, *PSYCHO*, in which a quiet clerk in an office becomes an embezzler, a hardware store owner plays private detective, and Norman Bates is his own MOTHER. Or, more accurately, his idea of his own mother. Because Norman not only hides his own GUILT at murdering her by resurrecting her (the murder never happened!) but also by TRANSFERRING his guilt to her—she's the one who cuts hotel guests to ribbons, who slashes private detectives across the face. He's no killer. He never gave anyone strychnine, no, not he. He's the faithful son, the janitor with bucket and mop, the one who always cleans up the mess.

"He was never all Norman," the psychiatrist smugly observes at the end. "But he was often only Mother." Except he wasn't. He was never one person. He was always both, together, at the same time—his mother's mannerisms but his moods, her voice but his own pathological jealousy and deeply secret incestuous lust. And because no one can really be two people at the same time, Norman, when forced to realize the duality, retreats into one. And Judy/Madeleine, unable to be either one or the other, has to kill both.

Hitchcock did not direct many classic, by-the-book mysteries. But that's because the mystery in most of his films isn't who the villain will turn out to be but who the protagonist has really been all along.

Reference

François Truffaut, *Hitchcock/Truffaut*, rev. ed. (New York: Touchstone, 1985), 73.

"INCIDENT AT A CORNER" (US; ORIGINALLY AIRED APRIL 5, 1960)

DIRECTOR: Alfred Hitchcock.
SCREENPLAY: Charlotte Armstrong, from her story.
PRODUCERS: Joan Harrison, Norman Lloyd.
CINEMATOGRAPHY: John L. Russell.
EDITORS: Edward W. Williams.
ORIGINAL MUSIC: Frederick Herbert.
CAST: Jack Albertson (Harry), Vera Miles (Jean Medwick), George Peppard (Pat Lawrence), Philip Ober (Malcolm Tawley).
RUNNING TIME: 60 minutes with commercials. Black and white.
ORIGINALLY BROADCAST BY: NBC.

A school crossing guard is dismissed after anonymous accusations of molestation begin; a variety of conflicting motives and testimonies arise. An episode of *Ford Startime*, this is one of only two TV shows directed by Hitchcock for a series not under his own imprimatur (the other being "FOUR O'CLOCK" for the series *SUSPICION*); he had his regular cameraman, though, and JOAN HARRISON producing, as well as VERA MILES in a supporting role. The parallels not just to *Rashomon* but HENRI-GEORGES CLOUZOT's *Le Corbeau* are interesting.

References

Ivan Butler, *Horror in the Cinema* (New York: A. S. Barnes, 1970), 104–8; Jack Edmond Nolan, "Hitchcock's TV Films," *Film Fan Monthly* (June 1968), 3–6.

INSANITY

"We all go a little mad sometimes."

—Norman Bates

That's a loyal son's defense of his mother in *PSYCHO*, but do any directors' characters go mad quite as often as Hitchcock's? From the compulsive, twitchy vigilante of *THE LODGER* (who is, do not forget, the movie's hero) to the homicidal thief of *FAMILY PLOT* (which is, remember, one of the director's lighter films), Hitchcock's work is studded with sociopaths, schizophrenics, and outright psychotics.

The director was, of course, forgiving of quirks; he had enough of his own. He had a fixation on precision and order. (He memorized TRAIN timetables as a boy and was unforgiving of tardiness all his life.) He found eggs of any sort revolting, was deeply afraid of BIRDS and policemen, and of course fascinated by BLONDES. After using the bathroom, he would carefully wipe it down with clean towels so not a drop of water was left behind. His tastes in clothes and in meals could seem almost petrified.

But in Hollywood, such behavior isn't considered neurotic; in fact, it barely rises to the level of colorful. Directors—particularly good ones—have long been known to be short on social skills, long on detail. Once, at most, they'd be called "temperamental"; today, they're usually said, sometimes with affection and always with understanding, to have a "little bit of OCD" or even be "on the spectrum."

And just as Hitchcock was quite aware of—even JOKED drolly about—his own phobias, he was fascinated with the way in which quirks could take root and grow and twist the minds and actions of others. He was a frequent visitor to museums of vice and criminality, an avid reader of true-crime stories, particularly of serial killers. The more outré the case, the more it drew him.

It is reflected in his films, where—unlike his television shows—murder was rarely for gain or even done out of passion. It was an act of pure madness. The stalking killer in *The Lodger*, Uncle Charlie in *SHADOW OF A DOUBT*, Bob Rusk in *FRENZY*—these are not men who murder for profit. Rusk absentmindedly rifles one victim's purse; in *Psycho*, Norman Bates unknowingly sinks Marion's $40,000 with her in the swamp. It's not about money, nor is it really—even in *Frenzy*—about sex. It's about these men's hatred of women and linked to their twisted relationships to the woman who looms largest in their lives, Mom. But Hitchcock doesn't try to thoroughly diagnose their disorders, much less offer any answers.

There's a suggestion that Uncle Charlie may have suffered a head injury as a child, but no doctor shows up with X-rays to talk about head traumas or lesions on the temporal lobe; when the state psychiatrist shows up to "explain" Norman at the end of *Psycho*, he really explains nothing. Although he never went into analysis himself, Hitchcock took FREUD seriously—*SPELLBOUND* was one of the first Hollywood movies to take him seriously—but what Freud chiefly provides Hitchcock is a helpful vocabulary for talking about a subject that otherwise remains a mystery.

Perhaps that's because, in some deeply old and Christian way, Hitchcock's smiling villains aren't so much suffering from a mental illness as a sickness of the spirit; they have no humanity, no conscience, no soul. (The hero in a Hitchcock film proves his goodness by feeling guilty; the villain, by feeling no regret at all.)

In our modern world, we talk about psychoses and dose them with chemicals; in another time, we would talk about demons and bless them with holy water. In Hitchcock's world there are devils; they are dangerous, and they are everywhere, as the films' own cinematography constantly underlines—just look across your rear courtyard at the right apartment window, and you'll see a murder. And they are in us, too, waiting, the way Hitchcock's Jesuit teachers told him that Satan always is, bid-ing his time, weighing our weaknesses, knowing his chance will come. After all, "We all go a little mad sometimes," as Norman observed.

Before adding, with a nervous laugh, "Haven't you?"

References

Patrick McGilligan, *Alfred Hitchcock: A Life in Darkness and Light* (New York: HarperCollins, 2003), 448, 465; Donald Spoto, *The Dark Side of Genius: The Life of Alfred Hitchcock* (New York: Da Capo Press, 1999), 16, 38, 115.

INTERVIEWS

"Actors come and actors go," Alfred Hitchcock pronounced in 1925, "but the name of the director should stay clearly in the mind of the audiences." And that was before he even truly had a career. By the time *THE LODGER* was officially released in 1927, he was already working with a publicist; by the time of his first sound film, *BLACKMAIL* in 1929, he was sitting for long profiles; by the '30s, he was writing his own essays and think pieces for film magazines and newspapers.

He was never not conscious of image. Interviews became an important part of that effort, and he was not alone in this. John Huston, for example, had worked on newspapers; he wrote and liked writers and was friendly with several, including JAMES AGEE and Lillian Ross, whose profiles did much to fill out our image of the man. Huston, however—particularly with Ross, whose work became the excellent book *Picture*—gave the writers access and left them to it. That sort of surrender—here, watch whatever you want, say whatever you want, I'm a big boy—was absolutely impossible for the controlling Hitchcock.

So his interviews—while frequent and often lengthy—were done very much under his own rules. He would host lavish press events but avoided all but the briefest press conferences. His preferred field of engagement was his own office, into which the reporter—invariably younger and usually intimidated—would be politely ushered. And then Hitchcock would begin to speak, as if a "Play" button had been pressed, repeating the ANECDOTES he had told a thousand times before.

If the question was about an early film, then he'd talk a little nostalgically of technical troubles they'd had during those days and how he'd found a way to overcome them. If the writer suggested a subtext or theme to his work, then he might accept it or shrug or JOKE, but he would rarely want to explore it further, as that might lead to exploring him.

Old, occasionally risqué jokes were trotted out, drawled in that Cockney accent made for music hall fun; some gossip would be indulged in (and if the STAR were someone he never wanted or expected to work with again—like TALLULAH BANKHEAD, like KIM NOVAK—grow quite pointed). And then at the end of an hour or two—he was generous with his time and so bored on the set that he would sometimes give interviews during shooting—it would be over, and the young reporter would go away with his tape recorder, convinced he had a wonderful interview. Until he transcribed it and realized he merely had the same wonderful portrait of HITCH that a dozen other journalists had drawn.

Occasionally people pushed back. In the 1950s, ANDRE BAZIN—who had already charged the director with trying to hide behind anecdotes—took a more argumentative approach ("Traditional criticism often reproaches you for brilliant but gratuitous formalism" is how he began his own one-on-one); for his book-length interrogation, FRANÇOIS TRUFFAUT took a more sympathetic, gently persistent one.

In fact, Truffaut—quite rightly—saw that the lack of respect given Hitchcock in some quarters was partly due to the lack of respect he gave any inquiries into his art. "It was obvious," Truffaut declared, that the director had "been victimized in American intellectual circles because of his facetious response to interviewers and his deliberate practice of deriding their questions." Truffaut decided that his book, *HITCHCOCK/ TRUFFAUT*, would move beyond that.

Except as entertaining and invaluable as that book is—as much as you can hear the director's rich voice in every definitive answer—it is often essentially the same Hitchcock interview, full of talk about MACGUFFINS and process shots. It is a thorough and thoroughly readable book. But it is still an interview in which Hitchcock is thoroughly in charge. And he controls what we hear—and learn—as rigidly as he policed every frame of every one of his films.

References
Andre Bazin, "Hitchcock vs. Hitchcock," in *Focus on Hitchcock*, edited by Albert LaValley (Englewood Cliffs, NJ: Prentice Hall, 1972), 60–69; Donald Spoto, *The Dark Side of Genius: The Life of Alfred Hitchcock* (New York: Da Capo Press, 1999), 73, 95, 418; François Truffaut, *Hitchcock/Truffaut*, rev. ed. (New York: Touchstone, 1985), 11–12.

IRVINE, ROBIN (1901–1933)
London-born performer and vague relative of Robert Louis Stevenson, who made his stage debut in 1918 and by the early '20s was a leading man in London theater. He made his first film appearance in 1925 and had several strong parts in early Hitchcocks, including playing the young cad who gets his friend expelled in *DOWNHILL* and the rich young eligible in *EASY VIRTUE*. On a springtime vacation in Bermuda with his wife, actress Ursula Jeans, he caught an unseasonable chill; it only worsened quickly. He died of pleurisy at the age of 32.

References
"Obituary: Robin Irvine," *Times*, May 2, 1933, http://the.hitchcock.zone/wiki/The _Times_%2802/May/1933%29_-_Obitu ary:_Robin_Irvine; "Robin Irvine," *IMDb*, http://www.imdb.com/name/nm0410216/ bio?ref_=nm_ov_bio_sm.

"I SAW THE WHOLE THING" (US; ORIGINALLY AIRED OCTOBER 11, 1962)

DIRECTOR: Alfred Hitchcock.
SCREENPLAY: Henry Slesar, from a story by Henry Cecil.
PRODUCERS: Joan Harrison, Gordon Hessler.
CINEMATOGRAPHY: Benjamin H. Kline.
EDITOR: Edward W. Williams.
ORIGINAL MUSIC: Lyn Murray.
CAST: John Forsythe (Michael Barnes), John Fiedler (Malcolm Stuart), Philip Ober (Col. Hoey).
RUNNING TIME: 60 minutes with commercials. Black and white.
ORIGINALLY BROADCAST BY: NBC.

Accused of causing a fatal accident, mystery writer JOHN FORSTYHE defends himself in court and proves the eyewitnesses unreliable—but also enables a conviction he will regret. Hitchcock's last work for television returns to his old themes of innocence and GUILT.

References
Tim Brooks and Earle Marsh, *The Complete Directory to Prime Time Network TV Shows*, 8th ed. (New York: Ballantine Books, 2003), 29; Jack Edmond Nolan, "Hitchcock's TV Films," *Film Fan Monthly* (June 1968), 3–6.

J

JACK THE RIPPER

Also known as "Saucy Jack," "Leather Apron," "Spring-heeled Jack"—and the first modern serial killer. There are, of course, stories of repeat thrill-killers going back to ancient China, and Gilles de Rais prowled 15th-century France—but those were before the days of cheap newspapers and a (just barely) literate working class. The arrival of both played an enormous part in building the iconography of the Whitechapel butcher. The area—full of gin, poverty, and prostitutes—was already riddled with crime and stained with violence. But five crimes in the late summer and early fall of 1888 seemed to be linked, both in their methodology and their brutality, and journalists sensationalized (and in some cases fictionalized) the events to attract a rabid reading public.

Not that the murders needed much embellishing. In each case, the woman's throat was cut—in one, hastily (suggesting the murderer had been interrupted), and in the last one, down to the spine, but generally with two slashes, from left to right. In most cases the uterus and other organs had been removed, and there were other savage mutilations to the body. There was never a sign of sexual assault. There were other brutal crimes in the area in the era—there were many—but these five immediately seized the public's imagination. No one was ever caught.

Coming at a time of both early criminology and popular journalism, the "Jack the Ripper" case, as it came to be known, established many archetypes. First, there were the crazed killer's boastful letters to the papers—copied by modern madmen from the Zodiac Killer to Son of Sam. In this early instance, the killer supposedly signed them "Saucy Jacky" or addressed them "From Hell." One letter came accompanied by a human kidney; the writer claimed to have fried and eaten its mate. And there were the early, psychological profiles—inspiring not only a science but also fictional characters from Clarice Starling in *Silence of the Lambs* to Fox Mulder in *The X-Files*. At the time, London police surgeon Robert Bond hypothesized that the killer did not have medical training but was a loner, "revengeful or brooding," possibly a religious zealot, and liable to fits of "homicidal or erotic mania."

The case, however, proved difficult from the beginning. The immediate problem was that journalists were not above fabricating letters to drive their papers' circulation, nor were copycat killers unknown. Newspapers claimed to receive many boastful confessions, but of the three most famous—the "Dear Boss," "From Hell," and "Saucy Jacky" missives—the timelines can be wrong, the details vague, and the penmanship inconsistent. (Of the three, the "From Hell" letter—the one

Louis Jourdan, a David O. Selznick discovery, was cast despite Hitchcock's reservations in *The Paradine Case*. *Selznick Releasing Organization/Photofest © Selznick Releasing Organization*

accompanied by a kidney—is most widely assumed to be genuine.)

The biggest problem was that criminal investigations were themselves crude. Fingerprint identification did not gain acceptance in Scotland Yard until the turn of the century, and the preservation of crime scenes was not yet observed. (In at least one instance, what seemed to be an anti-Semitic graffito left near one murder was erased by order of the police commissioner to fend off any anti-Jewish violence.)

And the final hurdle to solving the Ripper cases was simply that the Ripper stopped. Although violence in the East End slums would continue—it would always continue—these murders, with their signature throat slashings and mutilations, came to an abrupt end, as mysteriously as they had begun. Had the killer simply stopped? Unlikely. Had he—or she—immigrated to another country? Killed themselves? Died in an accident or as a result of someone else's act of violence? Or simply, finally, been diagnosed and locked away by their family in an institution?

No one knew. No one will probably ever know. Which has not stopped—in fact, which has clearly fueled—more than a century of hypotheses (The Ripper was a mad doctor! A butcher! The Duke of Clarence! A syphilitic aristocrat! An occultist!) and popular fiction.

The most famous was *THE LODGER*, written 25 years after the fact by novelist MARIE BELLOC LOWNDES, in which the Ripper—under the absurd name "Mr. Sleuth"—takes a room in a cheap lodging house run by a former butler and maid. The author (who had originally begun the novel as a short story) was no elegant stylist, but she creates a strong female character in the landlady and a sense of suspense, and the ending in Madame Tussaud's prefigures Hitchcock's fondness for climaxes against famous backdrops.

Hitchcock, already a true-crime devotee as a teenager, obviously knew well the story of the killer who had prowled familiar London streets, as well as the recently published best seller; Belloc Lowndes's story became one of his first features and stands as the first typically "Hitchcock" film. His adaptation added more ambiguity to the story, however, as well as layers of GUILT; while future movies (*PSYCHO*, *FRENZY*) would evoke the smiler with the knife, the mythology most clearly surfaces

again in *SHADOW OF A DOUBT*, in which a charming amiable houseguest turns out to be a misogynist murderer.

Of course the character turns up in other films as well; in addition to various remakes of *The Lodger* (including the 1944 one with Laird Cregar, made after Hitchcock couldn't get his own remake project off the ground, and 1953's *Man in the Attic* with Jack Palance), the real Jack the Ripper has made villainous guest appearances in many films, including 1924's *Waxworks*, 1929's classic *Pandora's Box*, 1979's *Time after Time*, and 2001's *From Hell*; he is also the subject of ROBERT BLOCH's most famous work, after *Psycho*, the frequently anthologized short story "Yours Truly, Jack the Ripper."

And despite some 100 published book-length hypotheses and a miniseries or two, he has never been completely, convincingly identified.

References
"Jack the Ripper," *FBI*, https://vault.fbi.gov/Jack%20the%20Ripper; "Jack the Ripper," *Metropolitan Police*, http://content.met.police.uk/Site/jacktheripper; "Jack the Ripper Timeline," *Whitechapel Murders History Resource*, http://www.jack-the-ripper.org/timeline.htm; Donald Spoto, *The Dark Side of Genius: The Life of Alfred Hitchcock* (New York: Da Capo Press, 1999), 33–34, 232; Elyssa Warkentin, "Marie Belloc Lowndes Rewrites the Ripper," *Nineteenth Century Gender Studies* (Spring 2011), http://www.ncgsjournal.com/issue71/warkentin.htm.

JAMAICA INN (GB 1939)

DIRECTOR: Alfred Hitchcock.
SCREENPLAY: Sidney Gilliat, Joan Harrison, J. B. Priestley, Alma Reville, from the novel by Daphne du Maurier.
PRODUCERS: Erich Pommer, Charles Laughton.

CINEMATOGRAPHY: Bernard Knowles, Harry
Stradling.
EDITOR: Robert Hamer.
ORIGINAL MUSIC: Eric Fenby.
CAST: Charles Laughton (Sir Humphrey
Pengallan), Maureen O'Hara (Mary Yel-
len), Robert Newton (Jem Trehearne),
Leslie Banks (Joss Merlyn), Emlyn Wil-
liams (Harry the Peddler), Wylie Wat-
son (Salvation Watkins).
RUNNING TIME: 108 minutes. Black and white.
RELEASED THROUGH: Associated British Pic-
ture Corporation.

Having recently lost her MOTHER, young
single Irishwoman Mary Yellen is headed
to 1819 Cornwall to stay with her Aunt
Patience, who runs the lodging house
Jamaica Inn with her husband, Joss. The
carriage driver, however, refuses to take her
there and leaves her in the road; she finds
shelter at the manor house of the eccentric
squire Sir Humphrey Pengallan, who sees
that she gets to the inn the next day.

What Mary soon learns, however, is
that her Uncle Joss is part of a gang of murderers, who deliberately wreck merchant
ships on the rocky coast and then kill the
sailors and plunder the cargo. What she will
not learn until later is that Sir Humphrey is
secretly behind the entire operation.

That night, the gang turns on one of
their own, Jem, whom they suspect of stealing from them; Mary helps him escape, and
the two flee. They take refuge at Sir Humphrey's mansion, where Jem reveals his real
IDENTITY as an undercover officer of the
law, there to investigate the ship wreckers.
Sir Humphrey, still concealing his own
identity as the gang's mastermind, pretends
to join his fight; Mary, worried about her
aunt being arrested, rushes back to Jamaica
Inn to warn her.

Sir Humphrey and Jem arrive at the
inn in pursuit, with Sir Humphrey still pretending to be on Jem's side; the gang ties

them up and goes to wreck another ship.
Once they depart, Sir Humphrey reveals his
true nature to Patience and leaves to pack
his things and flee the country; after he
goes, Jem persuades her to let him go, too.

At the coast, Mary relights a warning
beacon, and the ship sails safely away; when
the gang turns on her, Joss helps her escape
and is fatally shot. He manages to get them
back to Jamaica Inn, where Sir Humphrey,
having returned, shoots Patience as well
and kidnaps Mary, intending to take her
with him to France. But Jem and British
troops board his ship in the harbor, and Sir
Humphrey, his mind unhinged, leaps to his
death from the top of the mast.

Based on a 1936 DAPHNE DU MAURIER
novel (itself based on a real inn in Cornwall said to be haunted and known to have
once been a smugglers' base), *Jamaica Inn*
was Hitchcock's last film in Great Britain
before leaving for Hollywood, DAVID O.
SELZNICK, and *REBECCA*. It all went
famously wrong.

Hitchcock, who didn't much like
period pictures to begin with, felt uncomfortable with the material and helpless
with CHARLES LAUGHTON, who, as
STAR and coproducer, dictated the casting
(including his discovery, the novice MAU-
REEN O'HARA), demanded that his role
be built up (he had originally been set to
play Joss), and then delayed production so
he could work on his approach to the part.

Meanwhile, du Maurier was so
enraged by the liberties taken with her
book (her villain was a parson—something
the filmmakers had changed out of fear
of offending American CENSORS) that
she threatened to withdraw the rights to
Rebecca, leading Selznick to take a particularly hard line with Hitchcock on any of the
changes he and the screenwriters proposed
for that picture. Although *Jamaica Inn*
turned out to be a hit at home, Hitchcock

himself later dismissed the film as one of his worst. To a true follower, though—and a careful viewer—like its lightning-lit landscapes, its blood-and-thunder melodrama occasionally shows flashes of interest.

The script, for example, assembles a fine cast of characters for the criminals—one a religious zealot, another a dandy, and the third a vaguely fey sociopath. He's played by EMLYN WILLIAMS, just one of the many fine character actors on hand, including ROBERT NEWTON (playing Jem and still in possession of his later-ruined-by-drink looks), and, as Joss, LESLIE BANKS, a far more forbidding presence than he'd been in the 1934 THE MAN WHO KNEW TOO MUCH.

O'Hara, still a teenager and only in her third film, is a little uncertain as Mary, although she has lovely eyes, and the film shows off her figure by conspiring to get her soaking wet as often as possible. The two wrecking scenes that bracket the film are well done and particularly brutal, with the criminals clubbing the stranded sailors to death as the victims mercifully sink out of frame.

And then, of course, there is Laughton, sashaying through the film to his own unheard music (literally—he told Hitchcock he was basing his walk on a particular German waltz) and lasciviously coveting every beautiful object he sees, be it horse or orphan—until he finally, albeit a bit abruptly, descends into pure madness.

Hitchcock loathed working with this "extremely difficult" man (although he would bring him back in less than a decade for a part in THE PARADINE CASE) and derided the "completely absurd" film for the rest of his life. (As a symbol, perhaps, of his contempt for it at the time, he didn't even bother to include a CAMEO for himself.) That it was cut to 98 minutes for its American release and had until recently been seen only in shoddy, public-domain prints hasn't helped its reputation.

Yet it remains important for summing up an insular British movie world Hitchcock was now consciously leaving behind. And for suggesting, with its continued interest in some familiar themes—particularly slightly effeminate villains and the hypocrisy of powerful men whose fine clothes conceal traitorous hearts—that there might be some ideas he was taking with him.

References
Mark Duguid, "Jamaica Inn," *BFI Screenonline*, http://www.screenonline.org.uk/film/id/441604/index.html; "Jamaica Inn, Cornwall," *Cornwall Calling*, http://www.cornwall-calling.co.uk/culture/jamaica_inn.htm; Jim McDevitt and Eric San Juan, *A Year of Hitchcock: 52 Weeks with the Master of Suspense* (Lanham, MD: Scarecrow Press, 2009), 113; Patrick McGilligan, *Alfred Hitchcock: A Life in Darkness and Light* (New York: HarperCollins, 2003), 222–25; Donald Spoto, *The Dark Side of Genius: The Life of Alfred Hitchcock* (New York: Da Capo Press, 1999), 180–86; François Truffaut, *Hitchcock/Truffaut*, rev. ed. (New York: Touchstone, 1985), 121–23.

JEANS, ISABEL (1891–1985)
Elegant London-born performer who began her theatrical career in 1908 as a protégée of Herbert Beerbohm Tree and soon was busy on the stage in everything from Shakespeare to Sheridan. Once married to CLAUDE RAINS—he divorced her when, scandalously, she became pregnant by another man—she made her movie debut in 1917 in *The Profligate* and appeared in a popular film series starring IVOR NOVELLO as the underworld character "The Rat."

Her very public divorce from Rains in 1915—the pregnancy itself had ended in a miscarriage—may have typed her a bit in films; she would also appear with Novello in Hitchcock's *DOWNHILL* in 1927, playing an unfaithful actress, and, the next year, play the lead in his adaptation of *EASY VIRTUE* as the wife suspected of adultery.

Jeans was always busiest on the stage, appearing frequently on both Broadway and the West End, where she was particularly acclaimed for her work in plays by Oscar Wilde and Chekhov. Later, the sophisticated older woman became her specialty, a part she essayed for Hitchcock in *SUSPICION*, playing one of Johnnie's friends, Mrs. Newsham; her most famous movie role was probably as Aunt Alicia in *Gigi*. Continuing to work into her 70s, Jeans also played the mother of Lord Peter Wimsey on British television and appeared—along with half of London it seemed—in the all-star hallucination *The Magic Christian*.

Offstage, Jeans married the man Rains divorced her over and enjoyed a more-than-40-year union with him; a lively social presence, she was particularly fond of poker games and horse races. She died at 93 in London; she is not to be confused with her sister, Ursula Jeans (who, to muddy things even further, was the wife of one of the STARS of *Downhill*, ROBIN IRVINE).

References

"Isabel Jeans," *IMDb*, http://www.imdb.com/name/nm0419978/bio?ref_=nm_ov_bio_sm; "Isabel Jeans," *Stars of British Films*, http://www.britishpictures.com/godfrey/card30.htm.

JOKES

The product of two cultures—Cockney and Irish CATHOLIC—that admire flavorful language, colorful word play, and humor, Hitchcock grew up with an enormous sense of humor and a fondness for practical jokes (although it should be pointed out that two of the crueler gags attributed to Hitchcock by DONALD SPOTO—tying a string of fireworks to a schoolmate's bottom and leaving his daughter stranded for hours at the top of a Ferris wheel—have been denied by the alleged victims).

Hitchcock's jokes could be practical ones, either charmingly surreal (the horse he had delivered to Gerald du Maurier's dressing room one night) or strangely cruel (secretly dosing a crew member's drink with laxative and then daring him to sit in the studio all night chained to the camera—where, predictably, he dirtied his own trousers). They could be silly ones done for the camera, like many of his CAMEOS (particularly the weight-reduction one in *LIFEBOAT*), his introductions to his own TV show, or the gag photos he would occasionally pose for, wearing a chamber pot as a helmet or got up in full drag as Queen Victoria. They could be verbal ones, ANECDOTES polished over literally decades of retelling, that he'd trot out in INTERVIEW after interview—the definition of MACGUFFIN or his reply to the reader whose wife would no longer take baths after *LES DIABOLIQUES* and now, after *PSYCHO*, refused to take showers ("Send her to the dry cleaners.")

But much of his humor is in the movies themselves. Often they're actual jokes, witty retorts or double entendres, arriving fully developed in the screenplay or devised in conferences with the scriptwriters—MICHAEL REDGRAVE explaining "I went to Cambridge" after he suddenly knocks out an Oxford man in *THE LADY VANISHES* (which always got a huge response in British theaters), the sharp and sexy dialogue JOHN MICHAEL HAYES delivered so expertly for *REAR WINDOW* and *TO CATCH A THIEF*, the constant puns and joking plot clues sneaked into *ROPE* and *Psycho*.

And then there is a kind of jocularity that's actually part of the film's DNA and an integral part of Hitchcock's filmmaking. Sometimes it's a playfulness—the way he allows us to only hear parts of a conversation or trial by having doors open or closed (or drowns out the conversation entirely, as in *NORTH BY NORTHWEST*, because he knows it's something only the character really needs to hear). Sometimes it's a mere quick, sick joke—like the inspector's wife breaking a breadstick in *FRENZY*, just as he's described the snapping of the dead victim's rigor-mortis fingers. Or sometimes it can be a sort of philosophical shrug at the pure arbitrary nature of life, an acknowledgment of the jokes that the universe plays on us all the time—like Norman unknowingly throwing away the $40,000 in *Psycho* that had once meant everything to Marion. Or the way the two separate stories of *FAMILY PLOT* connect, just like the meandering but ultimately intersecting paths in the local cemetery.

Hitchcock did not often make outright comedies—*MR. AND MRS. SMITH* and *THE TROUBLE WITH HARRY*, both disappointments, were the only two he made in America. But he rarely made a film without humor. And when he did—in *VERTIGO*, in *I CONFESS*, in *THE WRONG MAN*—it was always a sign that the themes he was exploring were far too serious for him to even begin to joke about.

References

Pat Hitchcock O'Connell and Laurent Bouzereau, *Alma Hitchcock: The Woman behind the Man* (New York: Berkeley Trade, 2004), 153; Patrick McGilligan, *Alfred Hitchcock: A Life in Darkness and Light* (New York: HarperCollins, 2003), 20, 148–49; Donald Spoto, *The Dark Side of Genius: The Life of Alfred Hitchcock* (New York: Da Capo Press, 1999), 32, 109–12, 325–26.

JONES, CAROLYN (1930–1983)

Texan-born performer with wideset eyes and a nicely offbeat, slightly bohemian persona; an acting prodigy, she joined the Pasadena Playhouse at 15 and by 22 was under contract at PARAMOUNT. One of her most memorable early roles was Vincent Price's "model" for Joan of Arc in *House of Wax*; she was also Theodora in the first *Invasion of the Body Snatchers*.

Always busy on TV, she was in an episode of *ALFRED HITCHCOCK PRESENTS* ("The Cheney Vase") in 1955 and the next year appeared in *THE MAN WHO KNEW TOO MUCH* remake in a small part as Cindy; she was nominated for a supporting Oscar for *The Bachelor Party* and had her greatest, if perhaps limiting, success as the coolly erotic Morticia on TV's *The Addams Family* from 1964 through 1966.

The movie work disappeared after that, and her television appearances were mostly limited to guest spots, although she had a role in the miniseries *Roots* and a one-season nighttime soap *Capitol*. It was while she was appearing on that show that she was diagnosed with colon cancer; she died from it in West Hollywood at age 53.

References

"Carolyn Jones," *Cult Sirens*, http://cultsirens.com/jones/jones.htm; "Carolyn Jones," *IMDb*, http://www.imdb.com/name/nm0427700/bio?ref_=nm_ov_bio_sm.

JOURDAN, LOUIS (1921–2015)

Impeccably elegant son of a Marseille hotelier, whose early career in films was cut short by the war. When the German occupiers tried to put him to work making Nazi propaganda, he fled and joined the Resistance (although he would later typically, modestly, say only, "I was given work to do and I did it.") After the war, DAVID O. SELZNICK signed him to a contract; his first film for Selznick was, oddly, Hitchcock's last, *THE PARADINE CASE*, as the servant ALIDA VALLI falls in love with. (Hitchcock thought him badly miscast; he told FRANÇOIS TRUFFAUT the story would have had much more power if this great lady had fallen for some rough piece of trade like ROBERT NEWTON, "with horny hands, like the devil!")

The sleek, suave, cosmopolitan lover was pretty much all that Jourdan was offered for the next few decades. Privately, he much preferred croquet and his childhood sweetheart, to whom he was married for 68 years; publicly, he accepted the typecasting. "Any actor who comes here with an accent is automatically put in roles as a lover," he explained. Still, Jourdan was much better in his next American film, *Letter from an Unknown Woman*, and in 1954 made his Broadway debut in *The Immoralist* (a play that his erratic young costar James Dean quit after opening night). Jourdan had a classic role in the 1958 film *Gigi*, however; in later years, he played *Count Dracula* for the BBC and was a suave villain in silly films from *Octopussy* to *Swamp Thing*.

He died in Beverly Hills at 93.

References

"Louis Jourdan," *IMDb*, http://www.imdb .com/name/nm0431139/bio?ref_=nm_ov _bio_sm; David Thomson, *The New Biographical Dictionary of Film* (New York: Knopf, 2002), 448; François Truffaut, *Hitchcock/Truffaut*, rev. ed. (New York: Touchstone, 1985), 173, 177.

JUNO AND THE PAYCOCK (GB 1930)

DIRECTOR: Alfred Hitchcock.
SCREENPLAY: Alfred Hitchcock and Alma Reville, based on the play by Sean O'Casey.
PRODUCER: Uncredited (John Maxwell).
CINEMATOGRAPHY: Jack E. Cox.
EDITOR: Emile de Ruelle.
ORIGINAL MUSIC: Uncredited.
CAST: Sara Allgood (Juno Boyle), Edward Chapman (Captain Boyle), John Laurie (Johnny Boyle), Kathleen O'Regan (Mary Boyle), Barry Fitzgerald (the Orator).
RUNNING TIME: 85 minutes. Black and white.
RELEASED THROUGH: Wardour Films.

In the slums of Dublin, Juno Boyle slaves away to feed her family, while her preening husband, Captain Boyle—"the paycock"— lives in a world of laziness and pints at the pub. Their daughter Mary is unmarried and on strike; their son Johnny, who lost an arm in the Irish war for independence, has turned informer.

Mary finds a suitor in Charlie Bentham, though, a lawyer who proclaims that the family is due a large inheritance; borrowing against it, the captain purchases new furniture and a record player and invites all and sundry to a great party.

But Bentham, it seems, is mistaken; there will be no windfall. He disappears, leaving behind a pregnant Mary; their new furniture is all repossessed, and Johnny is seized by the IRA, taken away, and shot. "There is no God," Mary declares. Juno begins to pray.

One of Hitchcock's early play adaptations for BRITISH INTERNATIONAL PICTURES and material that spoke to him, with its Irish working-class characters and theme of a family split by war; "It's an excellent play," he later said to FRANÇOIS TRUFFAUT. "I liked the story, the mood, the characters and the blend of humor and tragedy very much. As a matter of fact, I had O'Casey in mind when I showed a bum in a café announcing the end of the world in *THE BIRDS*."

The problem, Hitchcock later decided, was that there was not much he could— or even should—do with this material to put his stamp on it. He and his wife kept as closely to O'Casey's play as they could. They used most of the original Abbey Theatre cast (although Barry Fitzgerald took on a different part), and Hitchcock inventively got around the primitive sound technology by "mixing" the soundtrack on the set, staging background noises or gunshots in different relations to the one microphone.

But in the end, what had he truly done as a director except turn the camera on and make sure of the blocking? What visual invention had he brought to O'Casey's words? Despite his efforts, it remained a filmed play, the camera keeping a respectful distance. "The film got very good notices, but I was actually ashamed, because it had nothing to do with cinema," he said later. "The critics praised the picture and I had the feeling I was dishonest, that I had stolen something."

He had made a film, and it had even been a hit. But it had not been truly a "Hitchcock film."

Reference

François Truffaut, *Hitchcock/Truffaut*, rev. ed. (New York: Touchstone, 1985), 69.

KAEL, PAULINE (1919–2001)

Petaluma-born daughter of chicken farmers, a writer (and briefly movie executive) who influenced generations of not only journalists but also filmmakers. Possibly it's because she studied neither journalism nor film at the University of Berkeley but literature and philosophy.

After leaving school, she lived a defiantly bohemian lifestyle on both coasts, complete with artist friends, menial jobs, and an out-of-wedlock daughter she had with the gay poet and experimental filmmaker James Broughton; later, she would start selling pieces on movies to small magazines and even program films for a Berkeley revival house. Eventually she landed at the *New Yorker*, where she raised banners (Paul Schrader, BRIAN DE PALMA) and burned bridges (David Lean, Michael Moore) for more than two decades.

Unlike ANDREW SARRIS, her frequent literary duelist, Kael did not push the AUTEUR THEORY or even write from a particular critical point of view; she was as likely to give actors the credit for a film's success as she was a director, and her *The Citizen Kane Book* insists that screenwriter Herman Mankiewicz had at least as much to do with that classic as Orson Welles. Her write-ups spent far less time on a movie's visual appeal than on its characters and emotions and how it made you feel. (Kael was very insistent—bullying, some even said—about how you were supposed to react to a movie.)

These tendencies didn't necessarily endear her to scholars, but they did gain her readers and many acolytes; even when she was writing about radical documentaries or French classics, her style was insistent, informal, slangy. Read her reviews aloud, and they sound like a scene at a Manhattan bar as someone puts down their second drink and launches into a diatribe about Kubrick's misanthropy. They're monologues, but they're incredibly entertaining monologues.

By the time Kael was being widely read, however, Hitchcock was winding down; he only had a few films left in him by the time she officially joined the *New Yorker*'s staff in 1968. (And the best of them, *FRENZY*, she dismissed in an aside as "rancid, mechanical" and "obviously engineered.") But she also wrote hundreds of capsule reviews for films in repertory, though, and those notices show a more appreciative eye. She said the original *THE MAN WHO KNEW TOO MUCH* had the "director's ingenuity and flair and sneaky wit," wrote about the "breathtaking" murder sequence in *SABOTAGE*, and called *THE 39 STEPS* "one of the three or four best things Hitchcock ever did." And if she seemed to show a partiality for the British thrillers—well, many did at the time, par-

Grace Kelly costarred with James Stewart in *Rear Window*, the darkest of her three films for the director. *Paramount Pictures/Photofest © Paramount Pictures*

ticularly as *REAR WINDOW* and *VERTIGO* had been kept out of circulation for years after their release.

Kael struggled with ill health in the 1980s after being diagnosed with Parkinson's; in 1991, she announced her retirement from regular reviewing. Did she think she had made a difference in the movies, someone asked her? Her nonanswer? "If I say yes, I'm an egotist, and if I say no, I've wasted my life."

She died in Great Barrington, MA, at 82.

References

Susan Goodman, "She Lost It at the Movies," *Modern Maturity* (March/April 1998), https://sites.google.com/site/raysawhill/home/interviews/pauline-kael; Pauline Kael, *5001 Nights at the Movies: A Guide from A to Z* (New York: Holt, Rinehart, and Winston, 1982), 361, 508, 594–95; Pauline Kael, *Reeling* (New York: Warner Books, 1976), 78; A. O. Scott and Manohla Dargis, "Mad about Her: Pauline Kael, Loved and Loathed," *New York Times*, October 14, 2011, http://www.nytimes.com/2011/10/16/movies/pauline-kael-and-her-legacy.html.

KAFKA, FRANZ (1883–1924)

A voice of the modern age and one of its crucial influences, Kafka was born in Prague in what was then Bohemia and raised in an upper-middle-class, largely secular German-Jewish family. His father was a successful merchant, and although their eldest son showed an early interest in art and literature, he received a degree in law and went to work for a large insurance company. It was assumed he would later take over the family business in "fancy goods."

Away from the office and his mundane duties of processing compensation claims and compiling annual reports, Kafka—who had developed interests in philosophy, Judaism, cinema, and other pursuits—dedicated himself to fiction, writing short stories, novels, and a play, although there were often long gaps between their composition and publication. His story *The Metamorphosis* was published in 1915, his novel *The Trial* in 1925.

In 1917, Kafka was diagnosed with tuberculosis; the progression of the disease was rapid, and in 1918, he left the insurance company with a disability pension. He spent much of the rest of his life in and out of health care facilities while continuing to write. Final complications of the disease left him unable to eat; he died essentially of starvation at 40.

It was FRANÇOIS TRUFFAUT, perhaps, who first linked the two artists, calling Hitchcock an "artist of anxiety, like Kafka, Dostoevsky and Poe." But the connections are perhaps not so much in the nature of intersecting influences as in parallel developments. Like Kafka, Hitchcock grew up with a strict father and a painful disappointment in his own appearance; like Kafka, too, his works frequently feature severe (yet ultimately unknowable) authority figures suddenly, mysteriously tormenting mild and unremarkable protagonists.

For the writer, the underpinnings of his theme were psychological and at times political; for the director, they were much more personal. At the age of four or five, Hitchcock had been brought down to the police station by his father, who told them to lock his son up as a "naughty boy"; his particular sin was never specified and his release, a short time later, just as unexplained. Perhaps his father had meant it only as a JOKE (and if so, one can see where the son's sometimes cruel sense of humor began). But it left Hitchcock with his own fear of authority and his own suspicion that there are powerful institutions that operate according to their own ever-changing rules and may arbitrarily persecute the innocent and GUILTY alike.

Often these mistakes by shadowy figures form the start of one of Hitchcock's lighthearted entertainments—Roger Thornhill calls over a lobby boy at the wrong time and is mistaken for a spy in *NORTH BY NORTHWEST*—but in *THE WRONG MAN* they are dealt with at painful length, as Manny finds himself arrested, jailed, and finally put on trial for a crime he didn't commit. Manny fights back, but every motion he makes just seems to draw him deeper into trouble, like the man in quicksand whose struggles only pull him further in; as in the tribulations of Josef K. in *The Trial*, what had begun first as some sort of bureaucratic mistake, some annoying inconvenience, only escalates into disaster the more strenuously the hero tries to extricate himself.

Unlike Kafka, who populates his story with surreal incidents, Hitchcock's story is hyperrealistic; also unlike Kafka, Hitchcock provides a (relatively) happy ending, in the literal form of a deus ex machina; in answer to Manny's prayers, the real culprit is arrested, and Manny is exonerated. Yet of all of Hitchcock's films, this is the most Kafkaesque. But there is something lurking just underneath the surface of all of Hitchcock—that steady expectation of sudden and utterly unfair "justice"—that spoke to Kafka, too.

And, in the Englishman's case, may have had its beginnings in that small boy, brought to the police station by his father, to be locked up for some mysterious, never specified indiscretion.

References

"Franz Kafka," *Biography*, http://www.biography.com/people/franz-kafka-9359401; "Franz Kafka Biography," *Franz Kafka Online*, http://www.kafka-online.info/franz-kafka-biography.htm; Patrick McGilligan, *Alfred Hitchcock: A Life in Darkness and Light* (New York: HarperCollins, 2003), 7–8; François Truffaut, *Hitchcock/Truffaut*, rev. ed. (New York: Touchstone, 1985), 20.

KALEIDOSCOPE

One of the projects toyed with during Hitchcock's fallow period in the mid-'60s, this idea got further than most, with an assortment of new and veteran Hitchcock collaborators—including the novelist Howard Fast, thriller writer Hugh Wheeler, SAMUEL A. TAYLOR, ALEC COPPEL (both of whom had worked separately on *VERTIGO*), ALMA REVILLE, and even BENN W. LEVY, who had worked on *BLACKMAIL* and *LORD CAMBER'S LADIES*—brought in to develop the script.

The essential idea, as sketched out by Hitchcock, would be to focus on a serial killer whom the police try to catch by sending a female officer undercover; typical of the director's approach to story development, he had already decided on three visuals, and so the screenwriters would have to incorporate scenes by a waterfall, aboard an abandoned ship, and at an oil refinery.

The project promised to employ an undefined "experimental" approach (Hitchcock had just seen *Blow-Up* and been much impressed) and proceeded far enough for some test footage. (A few stills and less than a minute of film survives, including fragments of a nude bedroom scene.) Like much of his material at this point, it was overtly SEXUAL and violent; UNIVERSAL refused to fund it, even after Hitchcock suggested using lesser-known actors and a modest budget.

Eventually it was abandoned, although one of its alternate titles—*FRENZY*—would be used when Hitchcock returned to the serial-killer theme in 1972.

References

"Alfred Hitchcock's 'Kaleidoscope'—Footage (No Audio)," *Flickr*, https://www.flickr.com/photos/49597617@N02/4629223639; Patrick McGilligan, *Alfred Hitchcock: A Life in Darkness and Light* (New York: HarperCollins, 2003), 676–83, 686–88; Donald Spoto, *The Dark Side of Genius: The Life of Alfred Hitchcock* (New York: Da Capo Press, 1999), 496.

KELLY, GRACE (1929–1982)

Fashion icon, fairy tale princess, muse.

Grace Kelly was in some ways the American dream made not just real but also extraordinary—from steerage to royalty in three generations. Her paternal grandfather arrived from County Mayo in 1869; her father, Jack, born 20 years later, was a Philadelphia bricklayer.

A champion sculler though, too, and an Olympic gold medalist who eventually turned his masonry business into a million-dollar company and married a model, his daughter would be raised in proper, Main Line luxury (and go to private convent schools). But Grace was no scholar, and with the help of her black-sheep uncle, George Kelly—ostracized by the family for being gay but renowned for winning the Pulitzer for his play *Craig's Wife*—she would get a spot at the American Academy for Dramatic Arts (AADA) in Manhattan.

AADA was not impressed with her at first, and perhaps to overcompensate, Kelly may have studied too hard—in losing her natural, slightly nasal accent, she took on the chilly, slightly too-proper tones of former academy graduates Gene Tierney and Jennifer Jones. She made her movie debut in 1951 in *Fourteen Hours* and, the next year, got a more prominent part in *High Noon*. Star Gary Cooper praised her work ethic, and when he saw how the camera loved her, director Fred Zinnemann gave her extra close-ups. Kelly was not so impressed with herself. "When I saw the first cut of that picture," she confessed later, "I raced back to New York from Hollywood and begged (drama coach) Sandy Meisner for acting lessons."

John Ford liked her in the movie, though, and when Gene Tierney was unable to do *Mogambo*, he cast Kelly in the part. It built on a screen persona she'd hinted at in *High Noon*—the calm, cultured lady with heated emotions held barely in check—and also drew on Kelly's own private life (who, despite her youth and cool demeanor, already had a history of affairs with her older leading men).

She was the real-life image of that fantasy woman Hitchcock called a "snow-covered volcano"—and she soon became the next, and perhaps the most famous, "Hitchcock BLONDE."

Mogambo had yet to be released when, in June 1953, the actress and director met in a meeting set up by Kelly's agent. Kelly—who was still only 23—was petrified. "I could not think of anything to say to him," she recalled later. "In a horrible way it seemed funny to have my brain turned to stone." But the silence spoke volumes to a director who once remarked, "I've never wanted to have the obvious blonde, the one who has sex hanging around her neck like jewelry." He offered her a one-picture deal.

The picture was *DIAL M FOR MURDER*, which immediately introduced Kelly to the director's meticulous preproduction planning—her wardrobe drew his usual fastidious attention, based on a COLOR palette that would gradually change from bright romantic colors at the beginning of the film to drab neutrals as her troubles deepen and her hopelessness grows.

Kelly, innocently enough, dared to disagree with him on one of his ideas. For the film's central scene, the late-night assault, he wanted her to wear a plush velvet dressing gown; Kelly insisted that, as the character was rushing from bed, she wouldn't have stopped to put it on and should still be in her nightgown. Her suggestion was correct—and it gave the gruesome attack an even more obvious SEXUAL undercurrent—but, when accepted, was also surprising: Hitchcock was not in the habit of taking suggestions from performers.

After the film—which had included an affair with costar RAY MILLAND that nearly ended his marriage—Kelly returned to New York and new offers, including the part of Edie in *On the Waterfront*. But Hitchcock wanted her, too, for his next film, *REAR WINDOW*, and while it didn't offer the obvious challenge the other film's character did—transforming herself into a drab, working-class Jersey girl—that was chiefly because it had been so obviously tailored to her.

Kelly took the *Rear Window* assignment and once again found a director very intent on how she looked and would be photographed onscreen, with particular attention to the cut and color of her clothes; green would be a significant color, as would the filmy negligee—almost as sheer as *REBECCA*'s—that she pulls from her tiny overnight case.

As an actress, the film gave her more to do than *Dial M for Murder* had; her relationship to her leading man, JAMES STEWART, is more complex and ambiguous than her failed marriage in the other film, and the dialogue has more humor and meaning. She gives a bit of bounce to every line, and her slow-motion lean in to kiss Stewart has all the power of a dream. But *Rear Window* is also significant in the way it seems to so cruelly crystallize Kelly and Hitchcock's relationship in the scene where Lisa prowls around the murderer's apartment while Jeff watches her from across the courtyard: A beauty, framed in a perfect rectangle, vulnerable but untouchable, watched by a man, seated and physically powerless, through an enormous lens.

Her third film with Hitchcock would be a romp; unlike *Dial M for Murder*, with its marriage turned sour, or *Rear Window*, with its undercurrents of GUILT and innocence and VOYEURISM and loneliness, *TO CATCH A THIEF* would be bright and lively, a cat-burglar-and-mouse tale, with CARY GRANT as the former jewel thief and Kelly (and perhaps her diamonds) as the treasure he's tempted to steal. But it would also be the strongest portrayal yet of that "snow-covered volcano" Hitchcock always idolized, the woman who was a proper lady at the gala and then something quite else in the back of the taxi on the ride home. It was the old Madonna/whore dichotomy but instilled in one person, not just the realization of that common "Nordic blonde" fetish he acknowledged but the product of long-ago years of CATHOLIC teaching on female saints and filthy seductresses.

In *To Catch a Thief*, it's best captured in a single, lightly done scene as Kelly very properly allows Grant to escort her back to her hotel room and then leans forward with unexpected sensuality to kiss him goodnight; it also runs throughout JOHN MICHAEL HAYES's winking yet seemingly proper dialogue, as the couple go for a polite picnic ("Leg or breast") or kiss in her room, as the camera cuts away from their embrace to seaside fireworks.

The film is charming, although not much more than that—none of Kelly's three movies for Hitchcock would give her quite the range she was allowed in *The Country Girl* (for which she won an Oscar). But no other filmmaker so effortlessly caught her porcelain beauty, her sterling determination, or her own innate elegance. That Hitchcock adored her—completely, chastely, achingly—is apparent in both every scene he shot and the absolute absence of any scandalous gossip from the three sets.

It was while she was shooting *To Catch a Thief*, however, that Kelly fell in love with Monte Carlo; later that year, returning to Europe to represent the United States at the Cannes Film Festival, she fell in love with its bachelor ruler, as well. She wore Prince Rainier's engagement ring while filming *High Society* and, after finishing *The Swan*—and her family finished negotiating a $2 million dowry to the monarchy—she retired from films. She was 26.

After her marriage, there were occasional rumors of Kelly's return to motion pictures; early in its development, Hitchcock offered her the lead in *MARNIE*, and it seemed—in his mind, at least—that she would return to the screen and him. But there was opposition—from the prince, from her subjects, reportedly even from the Vatican, where this Catholic royal was also a "Princess of the Church." Kelly had to decline. According to one biographer, afterward she cried for a week.

Hitchcock eventually went back to *Marnie*, which he made with TIPPI HEDREN, while Kelly returned to her royal duties. She supported beautification efforts, promoted Monte Carlo tourism, encouraged the performing arts, and raised the royal heirs. Although there would be other offers—the script for *The Turning Point* was briefly considered—she never acted again. And then in 1982, she went for a drive . . .

The specious gossip began almost immediately. The crash had come, tragically, on the same spot where she'd shot a famous romantic scene from *To Catch a Thief*. Her teenage daughter, Princess Stephanie, had actually been driving, and it had all been hushed up. In fact, it wasn't even the same road as that movie scene, and Kelly had been behind the wheel. She'd suffered a stroke while making a sharp turn, it seemed, and lost control of the car. She died the next day in the hospital. She was 52.

Less than two months before, she'd granted a rare sit-down to Pierre Salinger, John F. Kennedy's old press secretary. It's an awkward interview—Salinger was a dreadful interviewer—but it's her last one, and seen today, it has a certain bittersweet power, particularly when Salinger asks her how she'd like to be remembered. "I suppose mostly in terms of my children and their children," she says, nervously twisting the rings on her fingers. "I would like to be remembered as trying to do my job well, being understanding and kind. . . . I don't

feel as if I achieved enough in my career to stand out more than many other people. I was very lucky in my career and I loved it but I don't think I was accomplished enough as an actress to be remembered."

Of everything that Grace Kelly said or did, it was the only time that she was spectacularly, clumsily wrong.

References

"Grace Kelly," *IMDb*, http://www.imdb.com/name/nm0000038/bio?ref_=nm_ov_bio_sm; Patrick McGilligan, *Alfred Hitchcock: A Life in Darkness and Light* (New York: HarperCollins, 2003), 609–10, 614; Pierre Salinger, "Interview with Grace Kelly," *20/20*, September 1982, http://www.beyondgracekelly.com/princess-grace-last-interview; Donald Spoto, *The Dark Side of Genius: The Life of Alfred Hitchcock* (New York: Da Capo Press, 1999), 343–44, 398, 414; Donald Spoto, *Spellbound by Beauty: Alfred Hitchcock and His Leading Ladies* (New York: Harmony Books, 2008), 203–6, 210; David Thomson, *The New Biographical Dictionary of Film* (New York: Knopf, 2002), 464; Thilo Wydra, *Grace: A Biography* (New York: Skyhorse, 2014), 103–36, 165–84, 241–56.

KENDALL, HENRY (1897–1962)

London-born performer who made his stage debut at 17 and then—after heroic service in the Royal Air Force during the First World War—returned to the stage, usually in light comic roles. He was particularly known for his versatile work in revues and often directed as well. His film work was less notable, chiefly consisting of cheap comedies and mysteries—low-budget "quota quickies" made during the '30s strictly to satisfy a government edict that every English movie theater show a certain percentage of British productions.

Hitchcock's *RICH AND STRANGE*, made in 1931, was more ambitious; Kendall starred as the husband who gets taken in by a lovely swindler, and the drama showed off some of Hitchcock's skill with large sets and clever shots. But the movie was not a success, either in England or in America (under the more exotic title *East of Shanghai*); Hitchcock went back on the hunt for ideas, and Kendall returned to the stage.

He died in London of a heart attack at 65.

References

"Henry Kendall," *IMDb*, http://www.imdb .com/name/nm0447597/bio?ref_=nm_ov _bio_sm; Patrick McGilligan, *Alfred Hitchcock: A Life in Darkness and Light* (New York: HarperCollins, 2003), 121.

KILLERS

"The more successful the villain," Hitchcock told FRANÇOIS TRUFFAUT during their epic INTERVIEW, "the better the picture."

This was a credo Hitchcock stood by. While his hero could be—in fact, should be—an everyman (albeit, preferably, one played by the biggest available STAR), the villain had to be physically and socially impressive.

Although there had to be a few exceptions (the portly traveling salesman of *REAR WINDOW*, the shy motel owner of *PSYCHO*), Hitchcock's villains are often handsome, usually rich, and truly formidable. They may be smarter than the hero; they're certainly more devious. It gives his films that extra layer of drama, of suspense—the hero is so clearly overmatched that, even though we know he'll triumph in the end, we can't quite see how.

Raising the stakes even higher, with only a few exceptions (the "real" thief in *THE WRONG MAN*, Mrs. Danvers in *REBECCA*), most of Hitchcock's villains are killers, too. And they kill without a moment's hesitation and walk away from the corpse without a second's worth of GUILT.

Some kill for a cause (pretty much all the spy pictures, including *NORTH BY NORTHWEST*, *THE LADY VANISHES*, and *THE 39 STEPS*). Some kill out of psychosis (*Psycho*, of course, but *FRENZY* and *SHADOW OF A DOUBT*, too). But all of them are pleasant, polite, and socially acceptable people. None would draw a second look, unless perhaps it was one of admiration. They don't twitch or stare. They have nice smiles and good manners. They seem like the right sort.

Some of Hitchcock's heroes are killers, too, though. And they're not nearly as successful at it. That's because, unlike his sociopaths, they have a conscience; they're full of doubt and self-criticism, hesitation and clumsiness. In *DIAL M FOR MURDER*, death comes at the end of a pair of the heroine's desperately grabbed and awkwardly wielded household scissors; in *Shadow of a Doubt*, it's from the twisting to and fro on a speeding TRAIN. In *TORN CURTAIN*, the murder of the Communist spy requires an accomplice, a knife, a blunt object, and finally a gas oven; in *LIFEBOAT*, the death of the German comes at the hands of a mob, in Hitchcock's words, a "pack of dogs." These are not the almost elegant acts of professional murderers, and that's one of the ways we know these people can still be saved.

Far more often, they can't even bring themselves to do the killing. They set the trap, unwittingly or not, and someone else steps in—the Nazis who turn on Sebastian at the end of *NOTORIOUS*, the police sharpshooter who takes out the murderer in *I CONFESS*, the nun who frightens Judy to her death in *VERTIGO*. The heroes are blameless—at least legally—although the endings of *Vertigo* and *I Confess* hardly leave them without guilt.

But those who can kill without guilt—who can do it with a smile and then go back to their college reunion dinner or business meeting or afternoon by the pool—those are the truly successful killers. And they are the hard, black, beating heart at the center of every Hitchcock film.

Reference

François Truffaut, *Hitchcock/Truffaut*, rev. ed. (New York: Touchstone, 1985), 107, 156, 191.

KNIGHT, ESMOND (1906–1987)

Surrey-born performer who made his stage debut in 1925 and his film debut in 1928. He was in JOHN GIELGUD's legendary 1930 production of *Hamlet* and appeared in all 3 Shakespearean films directed by LAURENCE OLIVIER and, a kind of good luck charm, in 11 of the films made by Michael Powell and Emeric Pressburger. "A sulky, handsome young man with a mane of black hair and magnetic eyes," Powell called him, "almost too romantically handsome to be true."

Although Knight had, perhaps unwisely, taken a job in Nazi Germany in the mid-'30s starring in the anti-Communist film *Schwarze Rosen*, he served heroically in the English Navy in World War II; when the German warship *The Bismarck* attacked his vessel, he was badly wounded in the face by shrapnel. He lost one eye and remained blind for two years. He acted though, even when sightless, and eventually resumed his career fully after the war, appearing in *Black Narcissus*, *The Red Shoes*, *Robin and Marian* (minus his glass eye), and even—ironically—*Sink the Bismarck!* in which he played the captain of his own, real-life ship. His last film was *Superman IV: The Quest for Peace* in 1987.

Knight's only film for Hitchcock was the disastrous *WALTZES FROM VIENNA*, in which he played Johann Strauss, the Younger. Knight later said that Hitchcock realized early in the production that

the film wasn't working; his reaction was to harangue the cast, calling their acting "deplorable," lamenting the high salary being paid to STAR JESSIE MATTHEWS, and referring to Knight as the "Quota Queen" due to his work in those low-budget British pictures. Practical JOKES—of Hitchcock's preferred, embarrassing sort—were also common. "I was continually on the *qui vive* for some elaborate legpull at my expense," Knight wrote, "which automatically produced a feeling of nervousness, and I soon developed a hopeless inferiority complex under his direction."

The film opened to poor reviews and worse box office, and both men were happy to try to forget it and their association with it and each other. Knight continued to act and paint; he died in London at age 80.

References

"Esmond Knight," *IMDb*, http://www.imdb.com/name/nm0460874/bio?ref_=nm_ov_bio_sm; "1933–1935: An Encounter with Hitch," *Esmond Knight*, http://www.esmondknight.org.uk/hislife04.htm; Donald Spoto, *The Dark Side of Genius: The Life of Alfred Hitchcock* (New York: Da Capo Press, 1999), 135–36.

KNOTT, FREDERICK (1916–2002)

China-born son of English missionaries who received his law degree from Cambridge and served seven years in the British Army before turning his hand to writing. His first credit was the screenplay for the Hammer noir *Man Bait* in 1952, but the same year, the BBC used his teleplay for *DIAL M FOR MURDER*; it later became a hit play in both London and New York, and Knott adapted it for the screen for the Hitchcock film in 1954.

His other credits include the plays *Write Me a Murder* and a variation on *Volpone* called *Mr. Fox of Venice* (which he later adapted into the film *The Honey Pot*);

his other great success was the play *Wait until Dark*, which—like *Dial M for Murder*—also featured an attack on a vulnerable woman in her own apartment and was adapted into a successful film.

Knott died in New York at 86. "He wrote only for money," his wife said frankly after his death. "He hated writing."

References

"Frederick Knott," *IMDb*, http://www .imdb.com/name/nm0461425; Douglas Martin, "Frederick Knott, Playwright, Dies at 86," *New York Times*, December 20, 2002, http://www.nytimes .com/2002/12/20/arts/frederick-knott-play wright-dies-at-86.html.

KNOWLES, BERNARD (1900–1975)

Manchester-born photographer who emigrated to America while barely out of his teens and worked for the *Detroit News*. Returning to Britain in the early '20s, he took a job as an assistant cameraman at GAINSBOROUGH PICTURES, quickly working his way up to director of cinematography on the 1927 drama *Mumsie*.

By 1935, he had begun his association with Hitchcock; together they would make *THE 39 STEPS, SECRET AGENT, SABOTAGE, YOUNG AND INNOCENT,* and *JAMAICA INN*. Knowles was a smart craftsman with a wide range; he could capture soft, shifting shadows (*Jamaica Inn*); pull off a difficult camera movement (*Young and Innocent*); or pack detail into a close-up (*The 39 Steps, Sabotage*). His flexible, effortless style was a vital component of Hitchcock's mid-'30s successes.

Like many cinematographers, though, Knowles yearned to direct; despite an impressive debut with the moody mystery *A Place of One's Own*, however, his work as a filmmaker was less successful, and he spent most of his latter career working in budget-strapped British TV. His final credit was his most interesting failure: the Beatles' bizarre *Magical Mystery Tour* in 1967.

He died in Buckinghamshire shortly before his 75th birthday.

References

"Bernard Knowles," *Britmovie*, http:// www.britmovie.co.uk/directors/Bernard -Knowles; "Bernard Knowles," *IMDb*, http://www.imdb.com/name/nm0461497/ bio?ref_=nm_ov_bio_sm.

KONSTAM, PHYLLIS (1907–1976)

London-born stage performer, she made her movie debut in Hitchcock's *CHAMPAGNE* in a bit part and had another small role the next year in his *BLACKMAIL*. Larger roles were to follow in *MURDER!* as the inquisitive Doucie and *THE SKIN GAME* as the scandalous Chloe. In 1931, while sailing to New York to appear on Broadway, she met tennis star Henry "Bunny" Austin; they married within the year, and she effectively retired from films, only making four more features over the next 40 years, while joining her husband in devoting much of her time to the Moral Re-Armament movement. She died in Somerset of a heart attack at 69.

References

"Phyllis Konstam," *IMDb*, http:// www.imdb.com/name/nm0042496/ bio?ref_=nm_ov_bio_sm; "Phyllis Konstam (1907–1976)," *UK Initiatives of Change*, http://uk.iofc.org/phyllis-kons tam-1907-1976.

KONSTANTIN, LEOPOLDINE (1886–1965)

Moravia-born performer who made her Berlin stage debut in 1907, launching a career marked by performances in works by Shakespeare and Schiller and under the direction of Max Reinhardt. She appeared in a production of Franz Wedekind's scandalous *Spring Awakening* and made a brief American tour in 1911. She added films to her repertoire in 1912 and had the title role in the 1918 version of *Lola Montez.*

Her career slowed after motherhood and marriage, and a divorced Konstantin left for England in 1938 with her son; tragically, he died in a bombing during the early days of the London blitz. Leaving for America but unable to speak English, the middle-aged performer took a factory job. It was German director and actor Reinhold Schuenzel, already cast in *NOTORIOUS* as Dr. Anderson, who suggested her to Hitchcock for the part of the coldhearted matron; ETHEL BARRYMORE had already turned down the role, and the studio's suggestion, MILDRED NATWICK, then 41, was far too young to be playing the MOTHER of CLAUDE RAINS, then 57.

As it was, Konstantin was only three years older than Rains and had only recently, laboriously, mastered English; she was perfect, however, as the mother who sets out to calmly murder her disloyal daughter-in-law. ("My very first part and they made in me this monster!" the actress exclaimed later.)

Notorious was one of Hitchcock's first truly adult love stories, but it was also his first in-depth exploration of smother love, and Konstantin was its archetypal embodiment—Madame, the mother who sees her son as both a child and a partner and every younger woman as a rival and a threat. It's particularly effective here because the performance is so deliberately underplayed; few scenes in Hitchcock are as chilling as Konstantin sitting up in bed, calmly lighting a cigarette as she discusses how to murder Alicia.

Sadly, it would be Konstantin's only American movie. She made three appearances on American TV dramas—always playing European nobility—then returned to Austria, where she continued to work occasionally onstage and on the radio. She died in Vienna at 79.

References
"Leopoldine Konstantin," *IMDb*, http://www.imdb.com/name/nm0465369/bio?ref_=nm_ov_bio_sm; Donald Spoto, *The Dark Side of Genius: The Life of Alfred Hitchcock* (New York: Da Capo Press, 1999), 287; Thomas Staedeli, "Leopoldine Konstantin," *Cyranos*, http://www.cyranos.ch/smkons-e.htm.

KOSLECK, MARTIN (1904–1994)

Pomeranian-born performer who studied with Max Reinhardt, made his film debut in 1923, and had a busy stage and club career in Berlin. His first sound film was the early German sci-fi classic *Alraune.* Already a committed antifascist, he prudently left Germany as the Nazi movement surged; his name was later said to be on the Gestapo's enemies list.

Eventually arriving in America, Kosleck—whose English was excellent—migrated between Broadway and Hollywood before playing Joseph Goebbels in the film *Confessions of a Nazi Spy* in 1940, the same year he appeared as one of the villains in Hitchcock's *FOREIGN CORRESPONDENT.* Like Conrad Veidt and other refugees, the actor would specialize in Axis spies and Nazis for years; he portrayed Goebbels onscreen five times.

Kosleck, a slight man with an intense stare, soon became a regular presence in low-budget horror films as well, particularly after the war ended, appearing in *House of Horrors* and *The Flesh Eaters*, among others. In between roles, he amused himself—and eventually supported himself as well—by painting. During the Cold War, he found a new source of employment; now, on television, he played mostly Communist villains.

He died following abdominal surgery in Santa Monica at 89.

References
"Martin Kosleck," *IMDb*, http://www.imdb.com/name/nm0467170/bio?ref_=nm_ov_bio_sm; "Martin Kosleck: Actor, 89," *New York Times*, January, 30 1994, http://www.nytimes.com/1994/01/30/obituaries/martin-kosleck-actor-89.html.

KRASNA, NORMAN (1909–1984)

Queens-born writer who went to law school but dreamed of journalism. He dropped out of St. John's University to join the *New York World* as a copy boy in 1928, rising rapidly to become, however briefly, a drama critic at the *New York Evening Graphic*. In the early '30s, he left papers and New York to go to Hollywood as a studio publicist. Krasna reportedly taught himself playwriting by retyping BEN HECHT and Charles MacArthur's *The Front Page* 20 times; his first, a derivative effort, *Louder, Please!* was a Broadway flop but garnered him a new job at Columbia as a screenwriter.

He would go to work on the scripts for Jean Harlow's *Bombshell* and *Reckless*; contribute the story for FRITZ LANG's *Fury*; and do the screenplays for *Hands across the Table*, *Wife vs. Secretary*, and *Bachelor Mother*. His plays *Dear Ruth*, *John Loves Mary*, and *Kind Sir* later all became films as well, the last under the title *Indiscreet*. He specialized in wisecracking marital comedies and farces turning on MISTAKEN or assumed IDENTITIES.

The script for 1941's *MR. AND MRS. SMITH* was his, although it went through many title changes—from the horrendous *Who Was That Lady I Seen You With* to the more elegant *Slightly Married*—and was at the time said to be a favorite of both CAROLE LOMBARD and, DONALD SPOTO says, Alfred Hitchcock (although later, Hitchcock would dismiss the film as something he did only as a favor to the actress, whom he'd become friendly with). The film was a solid hit, if an artistic disappointment.

Krasna won the best screenplay Oscar two years later for *Princess O'Rourke* and continued to write and occasionally direct; his last movie credit was for the 1964 Sandra Dee movie *I'd Rather Be Rich*. Krasna died in 1984 in Los Angeles.

References
Patrick McGilligan, *Alfred Hitchcock: A Life in Darkness and Light* (New York: HarperCollins, 2003), 267–68, 276–77; "Norman Krasna," *IMDb*, http://www.imdb.com/name/nm0469915/bio?ref_=nm_ov_bio_sm; Donald Spoto, *The Dark Side of Genius: The Life of Alfred Hitchcock* (New York: Da Capo Press, 1999), 236–38; François Truffaut, *Hitchcock/Truffaut*, rev. ed. (New York: Touchstone, 1985), 139–40.

KRUGER, ALMA (1871–1960)

Pittsburgh-born performer (some sources cite an 1868 birthdate) who made her Broadway debut in 1907 and was kept busy over the next quarter-century appearing in many Shakespearean productions as well as *Hedda Gabler* and *Camille*. She made her movie debut in 1936 in *These Three*.

Kruger regularly played matriarchs, including head nurse Molly Byrd in the Dr. Kildare and Dr. Gillespie movie series. In *SABOTEUR*, she plays the wealthy woman (and Nazi collaborator) whose charity auction goes awry; she was no relation to fellow cast member OTTO KRUGER. Alma Kruger's last screen appearance was in *Forever Amber* in 1947; she died at age 88 in Seattle.

References
"Alma Kruger," *IMDb*, http://www.imdb.com/name/nm0472557/bio?ref_=nm_ov

_bio_sm; Hal Erickson, "Alma Kruger Biography," *Fandango*, http://www.fandango.com/almakruger/biography/p39465.

KRUGER, OTTO (1885–1974)

Musically gifted Toledo-born performer who made his Broadway (and movie) debuts in 1915 and whose early stage credits included a steady diet of romances and comedies, including the original production of George S. Kaufman and Edna Ferber's *The Royal Family*. By the early '30s, he was chiefly working in Hollywood, where he played the hero in *Dracula's Daughter* and also appeared in *Dr. Ehrlich's Magic Bullet* and *Another Thin Man*.

Kruger was often cast as wealthy villains or unscrupulous businessmen; in *SABOTEUR* he is Tobin, the Nazi agent who enjoys a rich and respectable American life. (He was no relation to fellow cast member ALMA KRUGER.) Otto Kruger continued to play less-than-heroic characters, including the duplicitous Jules Amthor in *Murder, My Sweet* and the judge who tries to send away Will Kane in *High Noon*; he worked until the early '60s, when a number of strokes left him unable to memorize lines. He died of another stroke on his 89th birthday in Woodland Hills, CA.

References

"Otto Kruger," *IMDb*, http://www.imdb.com/name/nm0472603/bio?ref_=nm_ov_bio_sm; Alfred E. Twomey and Arthur F. McClure, *The Versatiles: Supporting Character Players in the Cinema, 1930–1955* (New York: Castle Books, 1969), 137.

KULESHOV EFFECT

A filmmaker since his teens, the Russian-born Lev Kuleshov (1899–1979) was a leading cinema theorist and a driving force behind the world's first cinema academy, the Moscow Film School. His disciples included directors Sergei Eisenstein and Vsevolod Pudovkin. Kuleshov was a particular proponent of MONTAGE, the joining together of separate shots to tell a story or especially create an emotional effect; in his most famous example of this, he took a single expressionless close-up of pre-Revolutionary matinee idol Ivan Mosjoukine and intercut it with various close-ups: a dead infant, a bowl of soup, a woman sitting on the couch.

The close-up of Mosjoukine remained the same, yet when shown to audiences, viewers always ascribed to it an emotion based on the subject the actor was supposedly looking at; after "seeing" the lifeless child, the food, or the beauty, the star's expression was successively interpreted as grief, hunger, or lust—even though the actual reaction shot was always identical. Some audiences even praised the breadth and subtlety of his acting.

The sequence—referred to as the "Kuleshov experiment" or "Kuleshov effect"—was cited by Pudovkin as an example of the power of editing; by combining two completely separate shots, a filmmaker can create an entirely new feeling based on the images and the way they are joined and juxtaposed. Through this editing, the director—not the actor, not the writer—creates the film's ultimate message (and can constantly change it by recombining the same images in an almost limitless number of ways).

This is the power of montage, and it is significantly specific to film itself; it is the bedrock of what Hitchcock used to enthusiastically call PURE CINEMA. It is an important part of many of his movies and, as he described it to FRANÇOIS TRUFFAUT, underpins most of *REAR WINDOW*. "In the same way, let's take a closeup of Stewart looking out of the window at a little dog that's being lowered in a basket," Hitchcock said, after recounting the initial Kuleshov sequence. "Back to Stewart, who has a kindly smile. But if in the place of the little dog you show a half-naked girl exercising in front of her open window, and you go back to a smiling Stewart again, this time he's seen as a dirty old man!"

Of course, the power of the Kuleshov effect not only empowered the director (and his editor) but also greatly decreased the control of the performer; as *Rear Window* proved, it was what Hitchcock cut to that made the point, not any expression on JAMES STEWART's face. In fact, this philosophy led to Hitchcock often insisting that his actors—DIANE BAKER, TIPPI HEDREN, KAREN BLACK, GREGORY PECK—provide him with a blank canvas, giving as bland and noncommittal an expression as possible in close-ups; Hitchcock would provide the emotion himself later in the editing. For actors like MONTGOMERY CLIFT, for whom motivation was everything, this was endlessly frustrating, turning them into mere mannequins; for others, like CARY GRANT, it provided their underplayed performances with layers of teasing ambiguity.

Hitchcock was a firm believer in and skilled practitioner of Kuleshov's theories for his entire career, but the aesthetic breakthrough was less helpful to its discoverer; during the Stalinist era, when heroic realism became the style, the tricks of montage were viewed as somehow suspect. Kuleshov's own directing work slowed during the '30s and ended during World War II, although he continued to teach. He died in Moscow at age 71.

But his influence—whether in the Odessa Steps sequence of *Battleship Potemkin* or the shower scene of *PSYCHO*—continues. And will always continue, as long as any filmmaker anywhere takes two separate pieces of film and, putting them together, makes 1 + 1 = 3.

References

Lev Kuleshov, *Kuleshov on Film*, translated, edited, and with an introduction by Ronald Levaco (Berkeley: University of California Press, 1974), 183–95; David Shipman, ed., *Movie Talk: Who Said What about Whom in the Movies* (New York: St. Martin's Press, 1988), 36; François Truffaut, *Hitchcock/Truffaut*, rev. ed. (New York: Touchstone, 1985), 214–15.

L

THE LADY VANISHES (GB 1938)

DIRECTOR: Alfred Hitchcock.
SCREENPLAY: Sidney Gilliat and Frank Launder, based on the novel *The Wheel Spins* by Ethel Lina White.
PRODUCER: Uncredited (Edward Black).
CINEMATOGRAPHY: Jack Cox.
EDITOR: R. E. Dearing.
ORIGINAL MUSIC: Louis Levy, Charles Williams.
CAST: Margaret Lockwood (Iris Henderson), Michael Redgrave (Gilbert), Dame May Whitty (Miss Froy), Paul Lukas (Dr. Hartz), Basil Radford (Charters), Naunton Wayne (Caldicott), Cecil Parker (Mr. Todhunter).
RUNNING TIME: 96 minutes. Black and white.
RELEASED THROUGH: Metro-Goldwyn-Mayer Ltd.

In tiny Bandrika, an avalanche has stopped regular train service and stranded an assorted crew of English tourists—a young engaged woman, a whimsical music student, an adulterous couple, a pair of cricket fans, and a slightly dotty English governess. Also, it seems, a killer—a street singer is murdered one night, and the next morning a flowerpot pushed off a windowsill almost kills the governess, Miss Froy. It glancingly strikes the young woman, Iris, instead, though—and the motley crew boards the next train out of Bandrika. But then two more mysteries develop: Miss Froy vanishes. And when Iris reports her disappearance, everyone onboard tells her she's imagining the entire thing.

But Iris isn't hallucinating, even though that's the explanation of a traveling doctor; Miss Froy was there, and her fellow passengers simply have their own selfish reasons for not wanting to get involved. Gilbert, the music student, believes her, though—and together the two set out to find the truth.

It turns out to be fantastic—Miss Froy is actually an undercover English agent, and the doctor, the leader of a group of spies who've kidnapped her and plan to sneak her off the train at the next stop with the aid of the secret police. But with pluck, ingenuity—and the help of those two surprisingly heroic cricket fans—Iris and Gilbert take control of the train and escape to safety and England.

Where Iris discovers she no longer wants to get married—at least, not to anyone but Gilbert.

For those who know Hitchcock well, this is often the film they love the most purely.

At one point, FRANÇOIS TRUFFAUT claimed to watch it at least twice a week in hopes of uncovering its filmmaking secrets—and yet found himself so blissfully caught up in its plot and characters every time that he could do nothing but enjoy it. And pioneering Hitchcock scholar ROBIN

Janet Leigh gave *Psycho* its humanity and its most shocking moment. *Paramount Pictures/Photofest* © *Paramount Pictures*

WOOD admitted, "If there is no chapter on *The Lady Vanishes* in my book on Hitchcock, this is purely because it is too perfect, so transparent that there is little to say."

It is, of all his entertainments, perhaps the most beautifully balanced. *NORTH BY NORTHWEST* is a little long, *SABOTEUR* a little serious—but *The Lady Vanishes*,

notwithstanding the STRANGULATION of that poor anonymous singer early on, remains speedy and lighthearted. Even at the end, as hero and heroine escape, all the villain can manage is a rueful smile as he wishes them, "Jolly good luck!"

That Hitchcock is so perfectly in control of the mood and effects throughout is doubly impressive, as it hadn't originally been his project at GAINSBOROUGH PICTURES; Roy William Neill (who gets an assistant director credit here) was supposed to make the film earlier and had even gone to Yugoslavia to do some shooting. Then the authorities saw what the film was about and kicked the crew out.

Hitchcock, looking for a movie, took on the aborted project a year later but had the script rewritten to give it a sharper, funnier beginning and a more exciting end. MARGARET LOCKWOOD, a raven-haired change from the usual Hitchcock BLONDE, was cast as Iris, and MICHAEL REDGRAVE (at JOHN GIELGUD's urging, despite the troubles Gielgud had on *SECRET AGENT*) made his movie debut as Gilbert. BASIL RADFORD and NAUNTON WAYNE played the cricket fans (and so beautifully that they soon reprised the characters in the screenwriters' *Night Train to Munich* and became a bit of a comedy team in British films).

Hitchcock sets the mood early, as his camera moves over a charmingly childish miniature set of the mountain village—it feels almost deliberately unreal—to settle in at the inn. And at this point in his career, with Hitchcock already planning a move to America, the scenes mix both of his worlds: The characters may still be charmingly, eccentrically English (daffy spinsters, here-here cricket fans), but the situations (sexy starlets in negligees, some mildly HOMO-SEXUAL innuendo, a meet-cute trick out of *Top Hat*) already look to Hollywood.

The Wheel Spins was the name of the original (loosely adapted) novel, and circles and revolutions recur in the film—the moving faces of Iris's friends after she's struck on the head, the wheels of the TRAIN, the spinning mechanism inside a magician's "disappearing" cabinet. It is not just a visual device but also a metaphoric one, pointing us to the character reversals

the film is crammed with—in *The Lady Vanishes*, a Cambridge scholar will turn out to be a decent pugilist; a boring tourist, a crack shot; a kindly doctor, a ruthless spy; and a mild-mannered pensioner, a plucky British agent. It is a movie where that horribly scarred accident victim hasn't been in an accident at all, where that mute European nun is actually a sharp-tongued English lady in high heels.

Working again with cinematographer JACK E. COX, Hitchcock gets accomplished visuals throughout, from the process work of speeding trains to the sly shifts in focus and careful compositions meant to draw our attention to a drugged glass of wine or a character's furtive worry. The sound has been carefully thought out, too, with most of the movie played in silence except for the music the characters bring to it—bits of folkloric dancing, Gilbert's "Colonel Bogey March," Miss Froy's incessant humming (which turns out to be the MACGUFFIN on which the entire movie's plot depends).

And yet, for all its lightness, there is still a serious, political side to the film with the characters—as they would later in *Casablanca* and in Hitchcock's own *LIFE-BOAT*—stand for the nations of the world, delaying or dithering in the face of the Nazi threat. The Eastern Europeans we meet in Bandrika are gentle victims, the ones who comprise the doctor and his gang are crafty villains (and the Italians—at least in the personage of the magician—their willing if not particularly competent accomplices).

But who are the English? Some of them, like the nun, are willing traitors; some, like the cricket fans, wish only to remain determinedly uninvolved. Some, like Iris, are sounding the alarm about the present danger, while others, like Gilbert, insist on the need for more information. And then there is the appeaser, the cheating lawyer Mr. Todhunter, who only wants a quick and convenient truce—and is shot dead, even as he waves the white handker-chief of surrender.

Hitchcock would soon be leaving for America—and soon be attacked by old mentor SIR MICHAEL BALCON for deserting England in its hour of need. But whatever his reasons for going to Hol-lywood (and they were chiefly to enlarge and enhance his career), you cannot doubt that Hitchcock suspected what dangers lay ahead for everyone. Or that—even in the lighthearted *The Lady Vanishes*—he was saying that it was time for everyone to act.

References

Frank Miller, "The Lady Vanishes," *TCM*, http://www.tcm.com/tcmdb/title/80706/ The-Lady-Vanishes; Donald Spoto, *The Dark Side of Genius: The Life of Alfred Hitchcock* (New York: Da Capo Press, 1999), 172–76; François Truffaut, *Hitch-cock/Truffaut*, rev. ed. (New York: Touch-stone, 1985), 116–18; Michael Wilmington, "The Lady Vanishes," *Criterion*, https:// www.criterion.com/current/posts/26 -the-lady-vanishes; Robin Wood, "The Lady Vanishes Revisited," *Criterion*, https://www.criterion.com/current/ posts/997-the-lady-vanishes-revisited.

"LAMB TO THE SLAUGHTER" (US; ORIGINALLY AIRED APRIL 13, 1958)

DIRECTOR: Alfred Hitchcock.
SCREENPLAY: Roald Dahl, from his story.
PRODUCERS: Joan Harrison, Norman Lloyd.
CINEMATOGRAPHY: John L. Russell.
EDITOR: Richard G. Wray.
ORIGINAL MUSIC: Uncredited.
CAST: Barbara Bel Geddes (Mary Maloney), Harold Stone (Lieutenant Jack Noonan), Allan Lane (Patrick Maloney).
RUNNING TIME: 30 minutes with commer-cials. Black and white.
ORIGINALLY BROADCAST BY: CBS.

BARBARA BEL GEDDES is a careful and economical homemaker—so much so that, after she kills her cheating husband with a frozen leg of lamb, she cooks it and then serves it to the police as they fruit-lessly search for the murder weapon. One of the most famous of the series' episodes, marked by a typically restrained perfor-mance by Bel Geddes (until the very end), and the reappearance of Hitchcock's typical conflation of FOOD and emotions.

References

Tim Brooks and Earle Marsh, *The Com-plete Directory to Prime Time Network TV Shows*, 8th ed. (New York: Ballantine Books, 2003), 29; Jack Edmond Nolan, "Hitchcock's TV Films," *Film Fan Monthly* (June 1968), 3–6.

LANDAU, MARTIN (1928–)

Brooklyn-born performer who studied art at the Pratt Institute and landed a job early on as a cartoonist's assistant for the New York *Daily News*. In 1950, though, he quit to pursue an acting career, study-ing with Lee Strasberg at the Actors Stu-dio and eventually making his Broadway debut in 1957. Alfred Hitchcock saw the play and later cast him as Leonard, JAMES MASON's murderous assistant and close confidante, in *NORTH BY NORTHWEST*.

"I chose to play Leonard as a gay char-acter," Landau said later. "It was quite a big risk in cinema at the time. My logic was sim-ply that he wanted to get rid of EVA MARIE SAINT with such a vengeance, so it made sense for him to be in love with his boss, Vandamm, played by James Mason. Every one of my friends thought I was crazy, but Hitchcock liked it. A good director makes a playground and allows you to play."

Landau mostly played on smaller play-grounds after that—he did a great deal of TV, including an episode of *THE ALFRED HITCHCOCK HOUR*, and runs on both

Mission: Impossible and *Space: 1999*—and his career cooled during the 1980s. Good parts in *Tucker: The Man and His Dream* and *Crimes and Misdemeanors* helped resurrect it, though, and in 1994, he won the best supporting actor Oscar for playing Bela Lugosi in Tim Burton's *Ed Wood*. He is still acting, still teaching, still active.

References
Tim Burrows, "Martin Landau: I Chose to Play Leonard as Gay," *Telegraph*, October 12, 2012, http://www.telegraph.co.uk/cul ture/film/starsandstories/9601547/Martin -Landau-I-chose-to-play-Leonard-as-gay .html; "Martin Landau," *Biography*, http:// www.biography.com/people/martin -landau-212185; "Martin Landau," *IMDb*, http://www.imdb.com/name/nm0001445/ bio?ref_=nm_ov_bio_sm.

LANDIS, JESSIE ROYCE (1896–1972)

Chicago-born performer whose first and busiest career was on the New York stage. She made her Broadway debut in 1926; played Jo in *Little Women*, Althea in *Merrily We Roll Along*, and Queen Elizabeth in Jose Ferrer's *Richard III*; and replaced DAME JUDITH ANDERSON as Delia in *The Old Maid*.

She had some small and intermittent parts in the movies but made an impression as GRACE KELLY's worldly, weary MOTHER (and CARY GRANT's potential mother-in-law) in *TO CATCH A THIEF* in 1955; three years later, she played Grant's less-than-impressed mother in *NORTH BY NORTHWEST*. (Although JOKES were made about Landis being a year younger than Grant, she was actually seven years older; earlier in her career, she had shaved eight years off her age.)

Landis continued to work on stage, screen, and television, including an episode of *ALFRED HITCHCOCK PRESENTS*; her final appearance was on a *Columbo* episode. She died at 75 in Danbury, CT.

References
"Jessie Royce Landis," *IBDb*, http://ibdb .com/person.php?id=15358; "Jessie Royce Landis," *IMDb*, http://www.imdb.com/ name/nm0484829/bio?ref_=nm_ov_bio _sm; "Jessie Royce Landis: What a Character," *Once Upon a Screen*, http://auro rasginjoint.com/2013/11/09/jessie-royce -landis-what-a-character.

LANE, PRISCILLA (1915–1995)

One of five daughters of a small-town Indiana dentist and a stage-struck mother. Baby Priscilla and older sister Rosemary took dance lessons from an early age; two of their sisters, Leota and Lola, were busy onstage in New York and in movies from 1929, respectively. (The fifth daughter seems to have passed through life as a happy, nearly anonymous nonprofessional.)

In 1932, Rosemary and Priscilla signed as vocalists with bandleader Fred Waring ("The Sweetest Music This Side of Heaven"); when his band went to Hollywood to make *Varsity Show* in 1937, the two sisters went along and soon won movie contracts. Big sister Lola joined them for *Four Daughters* in 1938, the big debut of John Garfield, and Priscilla was groomed for stardom, with important parts in *Brother Rat* and *The Roaring Twenties*.

Although she was sometimes compared to Barbara Stanwyck and could meet costars with the same direct gaze, Priscilla's natural warmth and baby face softened that image. Still, her screen persona suggested she knew more of the world than Indiana; she was amiable, but she was nobody's fool, an alert and suspicious attitude she brings to *SABOTEUR*.

It was Stanwyck, however, whom Hitchcock really wanted for that picture (he had previously hoped to cast Stanwyck in *FOREIGN CORRESPONDENT*); another choice was Margaret Sullavan (who had been one of his early ideas for *REBECCA*). Instead, the studio prevailed upon him to use Lane in *Saboteur* (and, as the male lead, ROBERT CUMMINGS in place of JOEL MCCREA or Gary Cooper).

Already peeved at making the film on loan-out to the budget-conscious UNIVERSAL, Hitchcock resented not having the A-list STARS he now considered essential to his Hollywood work; later he would say Lane "simply wasn't the right type for a Hitchcock picture," with FRANÇOIS TRUFFAUT agreeing that she was "hardly a sophisticated woman" and "too familiar." This is, inarguably, unfair; whatever strength *Saboteur* has is wrapped up in the very real, young, and middle-class appeal of its stars. Substitute bigger names, and you dilute its charm.

Impulsive in love, Lane had already one annulment behind her when she broke her engagement to one man to marry another, an Army Air Corps lieutenant, in 1942; after her marriage, she only made a few more pictures (including *Arsenic and Old Lace*) before retiring for good in 1948 to raise a family in her husband's native New England. She had four children—none of whom followed her into show business.

Lane died of a heart attack at 79 in Andover, MA.

References

Patrick McGilligan, *Alfred Hitchcock: A Life in Darkness and Light* (New York: HarperCollins, 2003), 300–301; "Priscilla Lane," *IMDb*, http://www.imdb.com/name/nm0485509/bio?ref_=nm_ov_bio_sm; David Shipman, "Obituary: Priscilla Lane," *Independent*, April 10, 1995, http://the.hitchcock.zone/wiki/The_Independent_%2810/Apr/1995%29_-_Obituary:_Priscilla_Lane; François Truffaut,

Hitchcock/Truffaut, rev. ed. (New York: Touchstone, 1985), 145–46.

LANG, FRITZ (1890–1976)

Vienna-born filmmaker, the son of a respected architect who himself was interested in art and design from an early age. His enormous visual sense was obvious early, particularly in his science-fiction classic *Metropolis* and in *The Testament of Dr. Mabuse*, and can be glimpsed in later films with their stark urban lines, sharp angles, and deep shadows.

After service during the First World War—in which he was wounded three times—Lang turned full time to filmmaking. (He had already sold several screenplays while convalescing in military hospitals.) He had a popular hit with *The Spiders* in 1919 and followed that with *Die Nibelungen*, *Dr. Mabuse the Gambler*, and *Metropolis*—and although the ancient spectacle of *Siegfried* awed, it was the latter films, with their dark conspiracies and megalomaniac villains, that would course through much of Lang's work.

"He stole from Fritz Lang," historian David Thomson once said of Hitchcock, and certainly Hitchcock studied Lang when he was working in Germany in the '20s (and looked to F. W. MURNAU, too); it was one of the reasons SIR MICHAEL BALCON had sent him, to see if could pick up any Teutonic tricks. The Englishman incorporated some (EXPRESSIONISM) and discarded others (multipart epics). And he added a photographic effect to his toolbox—the Schüfftan process, used to double-expose scenes and thereby fake massive sets, one Lang had used brilliantly in *Metropolis*.

More to the point, though, there were things that Hitchcock saw in some German films that validated feelings he already had. After all, like Hitchcock, Lang was a CATHOLIC artist (although his mother was Jewish—enough to stain him in the books of the Nazi record-keepers); like Hitchcock, his work, too, is wracked with GUILT and often twists our emotions, asking us to forgive the unforgivable.

Who, after all, are we to sympathize with in *M*? The desperate child murderer, who wrestles guiltily with his sin? Or the impassive cops and criminals, who so coldly join forces in order to eliminate him? And the wrenching scene of pudgy, perspiring PETER LORRE, trapped, pleading "I can't help myself"—how far is this from the image of stolid, sweating RAYMOND BURR, asking JAMES STEWART, "What do you want?" in *REAR WINDOW*? The line between guilt and innocence, the despised and the pitied, is ever shifting. If there were a difference, then it was that genre mattered less to Lang. What was important was the cold, damp air of despair that wafted through them all, the feeling that even an innocent man had forces arrayed against him that he couldn't comprehend, and that the fix was already in. Lang's characters fight, they flail—but their fate is already set.

This defeatism is part of Lang, and it was a large part of noir—it's why he was always more identified with the genre than Hitchcock was (and never the popular entertainer the "Master of Suspense" strove to be). Yet they meet at points. You can imagine Hitchcock directing *The Ministry of Fear*; you can imagine Lang directing *THE WRONG MAN*. (And what a fascinating double feature their twin, separate studies of SEXUAL obsession—*Scarlet Street* and *VERTIGO*—would make.)

What you can't quite do is imagine the world of American thrillers without them.

References
Peter Bogdanovich, *Who the Hell's in It* (New York: Knopf, 2004), 170–234; "Fritz Lang," *IMDb*, http://www.imdb.com/name/nm0000485/bio?ref_=nm_ov_bio_sm; Patrick McGilligan, *Alfred Hitchcock: A Life in Darkness and Light* (New York: HarperCollins, 2003), 63–64; David Thomson, *The New Biographical Dictionary of Film* (New York: Knopf, 2002), 490–92; François Truffaut, *Hitchcock/Truffaut*, rev. ed. (New York: Touchstone, 1985), 26.

LATHAM, LOUISE (1922–)
Texan-born performer on Broadway since 1956. She had gone to school with screenwriter JAY PRESSON ALLEN, who recommended her to Hitchcock for *MARNIE*. Although she was only eight years older than TIPPI HEDREN at the time, Latham convincingly played her MOTHER; their lifelong disconnect of GUILT, sublimated anger, and repressed memory makes for one of the saddest parental relationships in all of Hitchcock's films.

Marnie was Latham's screen debut; her work following that was mostly on TV (including an episode of *ALFRED HITCHCOCK PRESENTS*), although she was also in Steven Spielberg's first feature, *The Sugarland Express*, and Thomas McGuane's own *92 in the Shade*. She retired in 2000 and lives in California.

References
"Louise Latham," *IMDb*, http://www.imdb.com/name/nm0490103/bio?ref_=nm_ov_bio_sm; *The Trouble with Marnie*, directed by Laurent Bouzereau (2000), documentary, http://the.hitchcock.zone/wiki/The_Trouble_with_Marnie_%282000%29_-_transcript.

LAUGHTON, CHARLES (1899–1962)
Yorkshire-born performer whose appetites—for food and pleasure but chiefly for daring, delicious play—made him one of the greatest of actors of the '30s and a reli-

able (if reliably hammy) character STAR for the rest of his life.

The Catholic son of innkeepers, Laughton was expected to go into the family business but was always interested in drama. After serving in the trenches of World War I (during which he was gassed) and briefly helping out at the family establishment, he enrolled at the Royal Academy of Dramatic Art in 1925; within a year, he was on the London stage. By the late '20s, he was being acclaimed (and married to costar Elsa Lanchester); by the early '30s, he had made his first foray into film acting, playing characters—Nero in *The Sign of the Cross*, Dr. Moreau in *Island of Lost Souls*, the serial husband of *The Private Life of Henry VIII*—with all the amoral glee of decadent babies, guiltlessly giggling in their own mess. The last role won him an Oscar, and his blustering Bligh in the 1935 *Mutiny on the Bounty* carried him into movie immortality.

Returning to England, he formed Mayflower Pictures with exiled German producer Erich Pommer, who knew Alfred Hitchcock from the silents; one of their productions became *JAMAICA INN*, based on a DAPHNE DU MAURIER best seller, with Laughton discovery MAUREEN O'HARA in the lead and Hitchcock directing.

It was a miserable experience for star and director, but chiefly for Hitchcock. He had never been fond of period pictures, a dislike intensified by the failure of *WALTZES FROM VIENNA*; he only wanted to be done with this one so he could leave for America and his new contract with DAVID O. SELZNICK. And then there was Laughton, who turned out to be precisely the sort of actor who would soon drive the director to distraction, full of sudden ideas and whimsies and questions. At one point he told Hitchcock that filming would have to be delayed until he figured out how his character walked; there needed

to be a certain music in his step, he confided, like a German waltz.

"You can't direct a Laughton picture," Hitchcock said later. "The best you can hope for is to referee." But as Laughton was also a producer, Hitchcock had little choice but to soldier on—perhaps why so much of the film, apart from its shipwreck scenes, has a bit of a rushed feel. Afterward, the two men parted company and went on to separate, immediate, and much greater successes—Laughton with *The Hunchback of Notre Dame* and Hitchcock with *REBECCA*.

Laughton's career slowed in the '40s as Hitchcock's picked up speed, but they both (possibly) worked on *FOREVER AND A DAY* in 1943, and reteamed for *THE PARADINE CASE* in 1947, with Laughton playing the lascivious judge. It was the beginning of a rich period for Laughton, who would turn ambitiously to directing (the uniquely poetic *The Night of the Hunter*, a collaboration with JAMES AGEE, was his only film) and play a number of delightful old rascals, including senators of both the ancient empire (*Spartacus*) and the modern (*Advise and Consent*).

Although he always had a tendency to pad out a thin script with thick slices of ham, at his best Laughton was a deeply committed, emotionally honest movie actor full of marvelous looks and superb invention; watch again in *Island of the Lost Souls*, as he hops coquettishly on top of an operating table and casts an eye over the latest castaway sailor.

Laughton had no illusions about his own attractiveness; he had a face, he once proclaimed, that "could stop a sundial." (Alternately, he compared it to the "back end of an elephant" and claimed he had quit *David Copperfield* because every close-up made it look as if he wanted to molest Freddie Bartholomew; W. C. Fields took over the part.)

But he was not only one of the talkies' first great actors; he also remains one of its most modern. And while Hitchcock might have grumbled about things being delayed because of some inaudible tune, it's that sort of music that runs through every Laughton performance—and that the actor alone could hear and so brilliantly dance to.

He died of kidney cancer at 63 in Hollywood.

References

"Biography," *Official Charles Laughton Website*, http://charleslaughton.freeservers.com/bio.htm; "Charles Laughton," *IMDb*, http://www.imdb.com/name/nm0001452/bio?ref_=nm_ov_bio_sm; Patrick McGilligan, *Alfred Hitchcock: A Life in Darkness and Light* (New York: HarperCollins, 2003), 222–25; Donald Spoto, *The Dark Side of Genius: The Life of Alfred Hitchcock* (New York: Da Capo Press, 1999), 184; David Thomson, *The New Biographical Dictionary of Film* (New York: Knopf, 2002), 498–99; François Truffaut, *Hitchcock/Truffaut*, rev. ed. (New York: Touchstone, 1985), 121–23.

LAUNDER, FRANK (1906–1997)

Hertfordshire-born author who left an office job for work with a repertory company in Brighton. When a play he wrote won him more praise than any acting job he'd undertaken, he decided to switch careers, landing a staff job with BRITISH INTERNATIONAL PICTURES in 1928. By 1936, he had teamed with SIDNEY GILLIAT; their fifth effort, THE LADY VANISHES, became (after briefly gaining the interest of another director and then being rewritten) Alfred Hitchcock's 1938 hit and the first to feature the director's name on theater marquees.

Launder and Gilliat would do a sort of spin-off of *The Lady Vanishes*, *Night Train to Munich*, for Carol Reed, but as Hitchcock had already observed, the screenwriters were not happy seeing directors get most of the credit; the duo eventually turned to producing and directing their own scripts, including *Captain Boycott*, *Green for Danger*, and the St. Trinian's comedies, many of them marked by their sly humor and strong female characters.

Launder died at 91 in Monte Carlo.

References

Alan Burton, "Frank Launder," *BFI Screenonline*, http://www.screenonline.org.uk/people/id/460455; David Cairns, "Individual Pictures: The Cinema of Launder and Gilliat," *BritMovie*, http://www.britmovie.co.uk/2008/08/26/individual-pictures-the-cinema-of-launder-and-gilliat; "Frank Launder," *IMDb*, http://www.imdb.com/name/nm0490950/bio?ref_=nm_ov_bio_sm.

LAURENTS, ARTHUR (1917–2011)

Brooklyn-born lawyer's son and Cornell grad who fatefully took a night class at New York University in radio writing. When the teacher declared no script should ever begin with a character answering the phone, Laurents promptly wrote one—and sold it to CBS. He was 22. He got a job at the network writing for various shows and stayed with them until World War II, when the army assigned him a job in Queens working on training films. His first play for the theater, *Home of the Brave*, was staged in New York in 1945; it was bought for the movies (he would do the adaptation in 1949), and he went out to Hollywood as a screenwriter. Although Laurents was denied credit for his first film effort, *The Snake Pit*, his work won him an assignment adapting the play ROPE for Alfred Hitchcock.

Hitchcock's choice of Laurents may have been motivated partly by wanting a playwright on the project, as his plans for the film consisted of long, deliberately "uncinematic" takes; it might also have been wanting a gay writer with an understanding of its characters and of HOMOSEXUALITY (which nervous executives referred to only as "it"). Laurents (who was actually dating STAR FARLEY GRANGER at the time) had the difficult job of both weaving in that subtext and keeping it from attracting the CENSORS' wrath—a trick he pulled off deftly. (So deftly, Laurents wrote later, that JAMES STEWART never seemed to notice that his character was supposed to be gay, too.)

"We never discussed the homosexual element of the script, but Hitchcock knew what he wanted to be able to get away with," Laurents wrote later in his memoirs. "He was as intrigued by varieties of SEXUAL life and conduct as he was by the varieties of moviemaking—in fact, he was like a child who's just discovered sex and thinks it's all very naughty. . . . He thought everyone was doing something physical and nasty behind every closed door—except himself: he withdrew, he wouldn't be part of it."

Laurents would go on to write the Max Ophuls noir *Caught* and Otto Preminger's *Bonjour Tristesse*, as well as *The Way We Were* and *The Turning Point*; he never worked for Hitchcock again, although the director sounded him out about *UNDER CAPRICORN* and reportedly turned to him again in the early stages of both *TORN CURTAIN* and *TOPAZ*. (Laurents smartly turned down all three after reading the source material.)

The McCarthy era meant trouble for Laurents in '50s Hollywood—but also his greatest triumphs, as he returned to New York and Broadway; he wrote the books for *West Side Story* and *Gypsy* and directed *I Can Get It for You Wholesale*, which made a star of Barbra Streisand. Later, he would direct the original *La Cage Aux Folles*, too, and successfully revisit some of his own material, staging several essential revivals

of *Gypsy* and a new bilingual production of *West Side Story*.

He died at 93 in New York.

References

"Arthur Laurents," *IBDb*, http://ibdb.com/person.php?id=4307; "Arthur Laurents," *IMDb*, http://www.imdb.com/name/nm0491306/bio?ref_=nm_ov_bio_sm; Christopher Hawtree, "Arthur Laurents: Obituary," *Guardian*, May 6, 2011, http://www.theguardian.com/stage/2011/may/06/arthur-laurents-obituary; Arthur Laurents, *The Rest of the Story* (Milwaukee, WI: Applause, 2012), 35, 39–41; Patrick McGilligan, *Alfred Hitchcock: A Life in Darkness and Light* (New York: HarperCollins, 2003), 403–8; Donald Spoto, *The Dark Side of Genius: The Life of Alfred Hitchcock* (New York: Da Capo Press, 1999), 304–5.

LAWRENCE, GERTRUDE (1898–1952)

London-born performer and legendary interpreter of the works of Noel Coward. The daughter of a determined mother and an often drunken opera singer, she made her stage debut in an amateur contest at age 6 and by 10 was appearing professionally in Christmas pantomimes. The bulk of her career and her brilliance was on the stage; she was in the Gershwins' *Oh, Kay!* on Broadway; appeared with Coward in *Tonight at 8:30*; won raves in *Lady in the Dark*; and concluded her career with the original *The King and I*, for which she won a Tony.

Lawrence's career in cinema was far more sporadic and far less acclaimed; her work in the film of *The Glass Menagerie* was roundly panned by Tennessee Williams. She had a lead role in *LORD CAMBER'S LADIES*, the sole film Hitchcock produced but did not direct. In the film, she appeared opposite Gerald du Maurier, one of her lovers; it was rumored she later had an affair with his daughter, DAPHNE DU MAURIER, as well.

Lawrence died in New York at age 54 of liver cancer during the run of *The King and I*; her last wish from her deathbed was that costar Yul Brynner's name be finally added to the marquee.

References

"Gertrude Lawrence," *IMDb*, http://www.imdb.com/name/nm0492775/bio?ref_=nm_ov_bio_sm; Michael Thornton, "The Rumbustious Life of Gertrude Lawrence," *Daily Mail*, April 30, 2009, http://www.dailymail.co.uk/femail/article-1175140/The-rumbustious-life-Gertrude-Lawrence—Hollywoods-maneater.html.

LEE, CANADA (1907–1952)

New York performer—and welterweight boxer, jockey, classical violinist, radio DJ, and civil rights champion—whose life was cut criminally short and who remains cruelly underappreciated today.

Running away from home in his early teens, Lee began a horseracing career, switching to boxing after a growth spurt. He fought professionally until his mid-20s, when a detached retina forced his retirement; although he later ran a Harlem nightclub, by 1934, he was broke. Looking for handyman work and stumbling on an open audition at the YMCA for a new play, Lee won a part, his first; two years later, in 1936, he was playing Banquo in Orson Welles's historic Haitian-themed production of *Macbeth*. "I never would have amounted to anything in the theatre if it hadn't been for Orson Welles," Lee told the *Los Angeles Tribune* in 1943. "Suddenly, the theatre became important to me. I had a respect for it, for what it could say. I had the ambition—I caught it from Orson Welles—to work like mad and be a convincing actor."

Lee joined the national tour of *Macbeth* and then scored another success in *Native Son*, winning a rave from the *New York Times* as the "greatest Negro actor of his era and one of the finest actors in the country." Lee would return regularly to Broadway throughout his career, landing parts in *Anna Lucasta*, *The Tempest*, and *The Duchess of Malfi*. Hollywood was less open to black talent, and Lee found few roles, however, although he is a boxer in *Body and Soul* and played a minister in the British-made, South African–shot *Cry the Beloved Country*. (In order to sneak into the apartheid state, Lee had to pretend to be director Zoltan Korda's servant.)

His best-remembered part was as Joe, one of the shipwrecked sailors in *LIFEBOAT*—and the only survivor who holds back as the mob turns on the German to beat him to death. It's a quiet, sensitive performance and one Lee himself constructed; when he saw the "Negro dialect" the part had been written in, he simply changed it. (Hitchcock, in a sign of respect he rarely afforded actors, let him—although some slights remain, and the white passengers still sometimes cheerfully refer to Joe as "Charcoal.")

Lee had never been afraid to speak his mind, though, decrying segregation in the armed forces even as he worked to sell war bonds. An early barrier-breaker (he was the first African American to have his own network radio show), he remained a consistent voice for equal rights; in 1949, the *New York Times* quoted Lee's attack on American broadcasting for keeping blacks in a "concentration camp" of stereotypes, consistently portraying them as "cannibals, dehumanized monsters, clowns, menials, thieves and liars."

By this time, however, Lee was already being denied work because of his leftist politics; his right to travel outside the country was restricted, costing him the lead in an

Italian-made film of *Othello* and a South American production of *Native Son*. The FBI told him the trouble would go away if Lee would simply name Paul Robeson as a Communist; Lee refused. The House Un-American Activities Committee announced it would subpoena him.

Before he had to face them, Lee dropped dead in New York of a heart attack. He was 45.

References

"Canada Lee," *IBDb*, http://ibdb.com/person.php?id=21398; "Canada Lee," *IMDb*, http://www.imdb.com/name/nm0496938/bio?ref_=nm_ov_bio_sm; "A Distinguished Actor, Canada Lee," *African American Registry*, http://www.aaregistry.org/historic_events/view/distinquished-actor-canada-lee; Kenneth Kilfara, "Canada Lee: Man Out Front," http://www.canadaleedoc.com; "Portrait of Canada Lee," *CanadaLee.org*, http://www.canadalee.org/portrait.htm.

LEHMAN, ERNEST (1915–2005)

New York–born author who was considering a career in chemical engineering until he took a writing class at the City University of New York. Although he soon began sending out short stories, he supported himself by working for a press agent feeding juicy "items" to gossip columnists, an experience he later drew on for *The Sweet Smell of Success*.

That story had begun as a novella, "Tell Me about It Tomorrow," in *Cosmopolitan* magazine; it was the success of short fiction like that which first caught Hollywood's interest and brought Lehman a contract at PARAMOUNT. He began strong with screenplays for *Executive Suite* and (with SAMUEL A. TAYLOR) *Sabrina* in 1954; in 1956, he wrote *Somebody Up There Likes Me* and adapted *The King and I*. Those early credits formed the basis of

his success and his well-deserved reputation as a versatile screenwriter: Lehman was the man you went to if you needed a cinematic adaptation of a popular play, a well-constructed drama, or a cleverly engineered comedy. His dialogue was memorable, and his plotting came free of holes.

He was originally approached by Alfred Hitchcock to do the script for *THE WRECK OF THE MARY DEARE*, but after weeks of meetings—and talking about wine, gossip, FOOD, and everything but the script—Lehman realized that neither of them had an idea of how to adapt the novel. (It was eventually written for the screen by JOAN HARRISON's new husband, author Eric Ambler, and directed by Michael Anderson.) Realizing he and Lehman were still under contract to MGM for a movie, Hitchcock calmly suggested they try something else.

"I want to do a Hitchcock picture to end all Hitchcock pictures," Lehman blurted out. The challenge appealed to the director—he was always in competition with himself anyway—and the two men kicked around ideas, situations, locales. ("I've always wanted to do a chase sequence across the faces of Mount Rushmore," Hitchcock confessed.) Then Hitchcock left Lehman to write it and went off to shoot *VERTIGO*. Lehman's script, originally titled *Breathless* and constructed as a breakneck chase across the United States, eventually became *NORTH BY NORTHWEST*.

It had taken a year to reach its final draft and a great deal of work—Lehman scouted locations himself, even clambering up Mount Rushmore; wrestled with writer's block; and often thought about simply quitting. Yet it was Lehman's great talent that the hard work never shows; *North by Northwest* is light, lively, playful, perfect. It is exactly what the screenwriter had said he wanted to do: the Hitchcock picture to end all Hitchcock pictures.

But the work was also exhausting—Lehman later said he was writing new pages in Bakersfield, even as CARY GRANT was fleeing the crop duster—and when Hitchcock told Lehman he wanted him to write his next film as well, *NO BAIL FOR THE JUDGE*, Lehman tendered his regrets.

It opened a deep rift between the two men—Hitchcock did not like being refused, particularly by writers—but it was a wise call. Although the film had already tentatively been cast, Audrey Hepburn ended up hating Samuel Taylor's *No Bail for the Judge* script when it was finally presented to her (it included a rather grim rape scene), and the project was ultimately abandoned after $200,000 had been spent on preproduction costs.

Lehman's successes continued without Hitchcock for a while; with a typical demonstration of his versatility, he wrote the screenplay adaptation for *The Sound of Music* and then turned around and did the same for *Who's Afraid of Virginia Woolf*, which he also produced. (He also rather disastrously wrote and directed *Portnoy's Complaint*.)

In 1973, Hitchcock approached Lehman again, this time to adapt a novel by Victor Canning called *The Rainbird Pattern*. The writer was surprised, not so much by the rapprochement as by the decline in the filmmaker's health and energy; over five months of conferences and rewrites, Hitchcock often spoke about abandoning the project entirely; he grew increasingly testy with Lehman's suggestions and, by the end of the process, would only communicate with him by mail. But by the end of it, they had a screenplay—once *Deception*, then *FAMILY PLOT*—ready to go.

The screenplay showed off Lehman's old strengths (witty dialogue, a carefully engineered plot) and Hitchcock's signature interests (questions of IDENTITY, parallel characters, narrative sleight of hand), but the film's mood—sometimes comic, sometimes dark—seemed to confuse audiences, and there were no STARS in the cast to attract them. Still, Hitchcock was already optimistically planning his next film and asked Lehman to write it for him, too. It was to be called *THE SHORT NIGHT*.

Hitchcock's inspiration for the story came from a real-life British prison escape, but Lehman said, "he was in love—in fact obsessed—with the idea that the leading man would rape and kill a woman at the outset of the picture." Lehman was as opposed to this idea as EVAN HUNTER had been to the marital rape in *MARNIE*, but "I always stayed on because I didn't want *Family Plot* to be his last picture," Lehman wrote later. "I didn't think it was good enough to be his last picture."

But it was his last picture. After Lehman turned in his final contracted draft to Hitchcock, the director—unsatisfied or perhaps stalling—approached other screenwriters, commissioned other drafts. But his health was failing rapidly. Eventually *The Short Night* came to an end.

"He never stopped wanting to delight us, to manipulate us and excite us and tantalize us and move us and fascinate us and enthrall us and fill us with dread and laughter and curiosity," Lehman wrote later, in a Hitchcock elegy for *American Film*. "He was a mischievous child clothed in the black serge garb of a world-weary sophisticate, and he took marvelous enjoyment in playing his games and letting us watch."

Lehman continued his own games for only a short while longer; after *Family Plot*, he did the screenplay for the terrorist thriller *Black Sunday* and wrote a novel, before retiring. He died of a heart attack at 89 in Los Angeles.

References

"Ernest Lehman," *IMDb*, http://www.imdb.com/name/nm0499626/bio?ref_=nm_ov

_bio_sm; Ernest Lehman, "Lehman at Large: Hitch," *American Film* (July 1980), 18; Patrick McGilligan, *Alfred Hitchcock: A Life in Darkness and Light* (New York: HarperCollins, 2003), 717–20, 732–33; Donald Spoto, *The Dark Side of Genius: The Life of Alfred Hitchcock* (New York: Da Capo Press, 1999), 388–89, 391–93.

LEIGH, JANET (1927–2004)

Merced, CA–born performer famously discovered when a vacationing Norma Shearer saw her photo at a ski resort where her parents worked. Offered an immediate contract at MGM, the cheerful psychology major dropped out of college and moved to Los Angeles. She was 19.

Leigh had never acted in her life, but she had an exuberance (and even more exuberant figure), which brought her a number of ingénue roles, particularly in period pictures; marriage to Tony Curtis (with whom she appeared in a half-dozen movies) increased her visibility. Orson Welles's *Touch of Evil*—with Leigh playing Charlton Heston's wife and the target of some nastiness in a motel—should have been a breakthrough for her as a serious actress, but the picture was recut and dumped by the studio.

PSYCHO—with Leigh again facing an odd innkeeper and an unpleasant overnight stay—was a true step forward, though, and the sign of a change in Leigh. There was something sharp, even a little hard, in her look now; with the arch of her eyebrow, a very careful catch in her voice, she made Marion Crane worldly, wary, smart. Marion may be in her early 30s, unmarried, and stuck in a dull job in Phoenix, but she does not give in to self-pity, and when she sees an opportunity, she grabs it. She is nobody's victim—until, of course, she is.

Years later, Leigh would cowrite a book about her experiences shooting the film, *Psycho: Behind the Scenes of the Classic Thriller*, and in it, she remembers a calm, pleasant set where Hitchcock let the actors interpret the parts as they chose, as long as they hit their marks. "He couldn't have been more considerate, or thoughtful, or respectful, or agreeable or companionable," she wrote. Leigh admitted, though, that "there have been legions of words written about Mr. Hitchcock's treatment of his leading ladies" and agreed that—as she was married, established in her career, and not under personal contract to him—her experiences might have been different.

Still, she said, shooting *Psycho* was "one of the most delicious adventures of my forty-eight years in Hollywood." (She still referred to him as "Mr. Hitchcock," and when an early galley of the as-told-to book contained a slighting reference to his ego, she had it struck out by hand from every copy sent to reviewers.) She also wanted to clear up something else: It was Hitchcock, not SAUL BASS, who shot that shower sequence.

Psycho brought an ACADEMY AWARD nomination for Leigh (which she didn't win—it went to Shirley Jones for *Elmer Gantry*) and a Golden Globes one (which she did); she followed up the movie with a strong, enigmatic part in *The Manchurian Candidate* and a joyous one in *Bye Bye Birdie*. But by this time her marriage to Curtis had ended, and she had two children; Leigh scaled back her movie work (although years later she was always available for a cameo in daughter Jamie Lee Curtis's movies).

And, if she could help it, she stayed out of showers. "If there is no other way to bathe, then I make sure all of the doors and windows in the house are locked, and I leave the bathroom door open and the shower curtain or stall door open so I have a perfect clear view," she wrote years later. "I face the door no matter where the showerhead is. The room, I might add, gets very wet."

Leigh died at home in Los Angeles of a heart attack at 77.

References

"Janet Leigh," *Biography*, http://www.biography.com/people/janet-leigh-9542160; "Janet Leigh," *IMDb*, http://www.imdb.com/name/nm0001463; Janet Leigh with Christopher Nickens, *Psycho: The Classic Thriller* (New York: Harmony Books, 1995), 48, 131; Stephen Rebello, *Alfred Hitchcock and the Making of Psycho* (New York: HarperPerennial, 1991), 107–12.

LEIGH-HUNT, BARBARA (1935–)

Somerset-born performer whose work has centered on the stage, including stints with the Royal Shakespeare Company and the Old Vic. She is also a regular on British television, where her many series and miniseries have included *The Brontës of Haworth*, *Wagner*, *Ruth Rendell Mysteries*, and the Colin Firth *Pride and Prejudice*.

Although she had started appearing on TV in 1965, *FRENZY* was her first film; Hitchcock, she remembered later, told her that he wanted to use stage actors, as he knew they would arrive well prepared and would allow him to "play with his camera" without having to spend time directing them.

"I adored Hitch and making *Frenzy* was a wonderful time," she said years later. "He went out of his way and was kindness personified, he knew I was exceedingly nervous. If I had a question he would always courteously explain something to me." Part of Leigh-Hunt's nervousness came not only from the medium but also the scene—early in the film she is brutally raped and murdered, with every degradation detailed and the final shot that of her corpse's staring EYES and open mouth. It is the ugliest scene in all of Hitchcock—and a great deal of its power comes from Leigh-Hunt's

own innate grace and spots of unexpected pathos (the moment in which, in the midst of this violent assault, the victim tries to modestly cover her bare breast is particularly heartbreaking).

Leigh-Hunt's other movie assignments were not quite as provocative or prominent, although she is in *Henry VIII and His Six Wives* with Keith Michell and *Billy Elliot*; her last screen credit to date is in 2004's *Vanity Fair*.

References

"Barbara Leigh-Hunt," *IMDb*, http://www.imdb.com/name/nm0500317/bio?ref_=nm_ov_bio_sm; Donald Spoto, *The Dark Side of Genius: The Life of Alfred Hitchcock* (New York: Da Capo Press, 1999), 513–14.

LEIGHTON, MARGARET (1922–1976)

Worcestershire-born performer with graceful elegance and haunting features. She made her stage debut in Birmingham at 16 and her London debut at 22 and was soon earning plaudits at the Old Vic. She was Roxane to Ralph Richardson's lauded *Cyrano de Bergerac* in 1946 and won two Tonys for her Broadway performances in *Separate Tables* and *Night of the Iguana*.

Her busy stage career had left her little time for movies; apart from some very early TV work, *UNDER CAPRICORN* was her third picture. It would be a difficult one. Only Hitchcock's second film in COLOR, it was also his second experimenting with long, single takes; breakaway sets were required, filmmaking was slow, and STAR INGRID BERGMAN complained bitterly to the director about the difficulties and delays.

Leighton played a variation on the Mrs. Danvers part—the housekeeper who wants her mistress out of the way so she can have the master for herself—and is striking in the role, although Hitchcock later claimed the "British critics thought it was terrible to take a lovely actress like Margaret Leighton and make her into an unsympathetic character." The film was a financial disaster and helped end his independent venture, TRANSATLANTIC PICTURES.

Leighton continued to make movies (and made two more appearances for Hitchcock, on *ALFRED HITCHCOCK PRESENTS* and *THE ALFRED HITCHCOCK HOUR*), but the stage remained her chief arena. Still, she had a good part in *Lady Caroline Lamb* and made a fine Miss Havisham in the Michael York version of *Great Expectations* in 1974, turning her fragile, somewhat birdlike beauty to haunting use.

Married to MICHAEL WILDING, a costar of *Under Capricorn*, she was diagnosed with multiple sclerosis in the early '70s; she continued acting, even when she couldn't walk, until her death in Sussex from complications of the disease. She was only 53.

References

"Margaret Leighton," *IMDb*, http://www.imdb.com/name/nm0500364/bio?ref_=nm_ov_bio_sm; François Truffaut, *Hitchcock/Truffaut*, rev. ed. (New York: Touchstone, 1985), 187.

LEOPOLD, NATHAN (1904– 1971), AND LOEB, RICHARD (1905–1936)

Rich Chicagoans, they grew up brilliant and spoiled. Although they knew each other slightly, when they were reunited at the University of Chicago, they realized they also shared a fascination with true-crime stories. After Leopold introduced a new element to the mix, Friedrich Nietzsche and his theory of the *Übermensch*—the superman who was so superior he existed outside all moral laws—they conceived their one awful idea: to prove their own perfection by committing the perfect crime.

After a series of petty thefts and vandalisms, the two moved on to the idea of murder; they planned it over more than a half-year, deciding to seize and kill a child and then use a ransom note to try to disguise it as a kidnapping. Loeb volunteered his own second cousin, the 14-year-old Bobby Franks, as the victim. They picked the boy up near his home on May 21, 1924; hit him in the head with a chisel; gagged him with an old rag; and then, after they had dumped the body in rural Indiana, poured acid over it to slow identification. Then they sent the ransom note.

Their perfect plot unraveled almost immediately. Leopold, it seemed, couldn't help talking to police and reporters (and talking bitterly about how much he disliked Franks); even more stupidly, he'd dropped his glasses at the murder scene. The police found the spectacles when they found the body, and a quick investigation revealed that only three pairs like them had been sold in all of Chicago, one to Nathan Leopold. The police picked up the duo, whose alibi quickly fell apart under questioning. Each rushed to blame the other for the actual killing.

Both men pled guilty and were put on trial for murder; lawyer Clarence Darrow concentrated all his efforts on simply seeing they weren't executed, an uphill effort climaxing in a 12-hour summation. In the end, the defendants were each given 99 years for kidnapping and life for murder. Loeb died in prison, slashed to death by a fellow inmate; Leopold was eventually released in 1958, after which he moved to Puerto Rico, married, worked for various charities, and wrote a book about birds. He died of a heart attack at 66. The man whose lost eyeglasses had sent him to prison donated his corneas.

At times called the "Crime of the Century," the Leopold and Loeb case inspired copious coverage and eventually the play *ROPE*, first performed in 1928. It was done a decade later for the BBC and a decade later as the Alfred Hitchcock film, which explicitly eroticized the men's relationship (or as explicitly as the CENSORS of the time would allow) while also suggesting that the characters' influential teacher shared in their GUILT. (The case also inspired other films, including *Compulsion* and *Swoon*.)

The themes of shared guilt and HOMOSEXUALITY as a seeming signifier of instability occur in other Hitchcock films, particularly *STRANGERS ON A TRAIN*; that movie also features a pair of bantering and somewhat superior men, the idea of certain human beings as being inconvenient or expendable, and eyeglasses dropped at a remote murder scene. But PATRICIA HIGHSMITH and Hitchcock managed to give that story some stylish ambiguity and moral weight; the real case was far more sordid. And—perhaps the most frustrating thing to Loeb and Leopold of all—not only senseless but also stupid.

References

Simon Baatz, "Leopold and Loeb's Criminal Minds," *Smithsonian*, http://www .smithsonianmag.com/history/leopold -and-loebs-criminal-minds-996498/?no -ist; Douglas O. Linder, "The Leopold and Loeb Trial: A Brief Account," http://law2 .umkc.edu/faculty/projects/ftrials/leoploeb/ Accountoftrial.html.

LEVY, BENN W. (1900–1973)

London-born, Oxford-educated playwright who served in both world wars. His stage hits included *Accent on Youth*, *Springtime for Henry*, and *Topaze* (not to be confused with the later Hitchcock film *TOPAZ*).

As a screenwriter, he worked on the dialogue for Hitchcock's *BLACK-*

MAIL and wrote the adaptation for James Whale's film of *Waterloo Bridge*. He also directed his own script for *LORD CAMBER'S LADIES*, which Hitchcock unhappily produced, slightly put out that Levy wouldn't take his suggestions. (Still, when in the early '60s Hitchcock was desperately struggling with the treatment for *KALEIDOSCOPE*, Levy was one of the former collaborators he called for help.)

After World War II, Levy entered politics; as a member of Parliament, he was a strong supporter of the Zionist movement and of ending government CENSORSHIP. Married to actress Constance Cummings for more than 40 years, he died at age 73 in Oxford.

References

"Benn W. Levy," *IMDb*, http://www.imdb .com/name/nm0506349; "Benn W. Levy," *Playwright's Database*, http://www.doollee .com/PlaywrightsL/levy-benn-w.html.

LIFEBOAT (US 1944)

DIRECTOR: Alfred Hitchcock.
SCREENPLAY: Jo Swerling, from a story by John Steinbeck.
PRODUCERS: Kenneth McGowan (Alfred Hitchcock, uncredited).
CINEMATOGRAPHY: Glen MacWilliams.
EDITOR: Dorothy Spencer.
ORIGINAL MUSIC: Hugo W. Friedhofer.
CAST: Tallulah Bankhead (Constance Porter), John Hodiak (John Kovac), Henry Hull (Charles S. Rittenhouse), Walter Slezak (Willy), Hume Cronyn (Stanley "Sparks" Garett), William Bendix (Gus Smith), Canada Lee (George "Joe" Spencer).
RUNNING TIME: 96 minutes. Black and white.
RELEASED THROUGH: Twentieth Century Fox.

An American ship and a German U-boat simultaneously destroy each other in the

North Atlantic, and the sole seaworthy lifeboat slowly fills with a few, oil-smeared survivors—a wealthy writer, an industrialist, an army nurse, some sailors, and the German captain.

As the others quarrel over left- and right-wing politics; mourn their lost possessions; or succumb to madness, thirst, exhaustion, and gangrene, the German slowly, methodically takes charge, sipping from a secret stash of water, gulping energy pills, and using his own compass to try to steer the lifeboat back to a German supply ship.

When one of the American sailors catches him, the German pushes him overboard and lets him drown. When the rest of the survivors finally grasp what's happened—and realize the German has been cleverly outwitting them all along—they beat him half to death and throw him overboard.

Just as a German supply ship approaches, it's sunk by an arriving Allied warship, and the lifeboat's passengers are rescued—along with another young German sailor who's just fled the destroyed ship and whose life the British and Americans hesitantly spare.

Although he had been brought to America as a famous director of thrillers, Hitchcock regularly tried to push past that genre in the '40s; various other projects, such as a modern-dress *HAMLET* or the romantic fantasy *MARY ROSE*, were occasionally proposed, and he took stabs at romantic comedies (*MR. AND MRS. SMITH*), courtroom dramas (*THE PARADINE CASE*), and period melodramas (*UNDER CAPRICORN*). It was actually only after several financial disappointments that, in the 1950s, he fully committed to thrillers, a genre he would stick with to the end.

The wartime drama *Lifeboat* was one of those attempts at another type of film and one Hitchcock was eager to begin; during 1943, he had approached several novelists, including Ernest Hemingway, for original stories before getting this one from JOHN STEINBECK. The challenges of a single set appealed to him as well (a challenge he would pursue again in *ROPE* and *REAR WINDOW*).

Steinbeck's original treatment was rewritten by several screenwriters, including uncredited work by Hitchcock's wife ALMA REVILLE, BEN HECHT, and PATRICIA COLLINGE; a furious Steinbeck wrote to the studio, protesting the changes, insisting that his original work hadn't included "slurs against organized labor, nor was there a stock comedy Negro." The latter particularly bothered him; while he had created a "Negro of dignity, purpose and personality," he insisted, the rewrite had merely substituted the "usual colored travesty."

It seems likely that Steinbeck was actually more infuriated by the rewriting of Kovac, his heroic leftist sailor, now criticized by the other characters as a Communist. Although the African American sailor is still occasionally called "Charcoal" by the whites, he is (thanks to CANADA LEE, who rewrote the part) the most human person on the boat and in the finished film, even though he's the worst treated back on land. ("Do I get to vote too?" he asks dryly, when the survivors are taking a poll on their next course of action.) Of all of them, Joe knows best what ideals they're really fighting for, even if they're often little more than ideals; when the rest of them turn into a mob and overwhelm the German, Joe is the only one who hangs back from the virtual lynching.

If Joe holds true to a core of strength and humanity throughout his time at sea, the other characters embark on journeys. For Sparks, the radio man, and Alice, the nurse, it'll be a slow move toward romance; for Rittenhouse the millionaire industrialist, a realization of how little real power he has. And for Connie, the elegant writer, it will be a gradual stripping away of her accumulated tokens of success—her typewriter, her mink, her jewels—until she's back to being the poor kid from Chicago she always was.

Although *Lifeboat* is a character-driven story—and one obviously lacking in scenery—Hitchcock made sure it was full of incident and imagery. (He used toy boats to work out all his camera angles in pre-production, like a little boy staging battles with tin soldiers.) The process shot of the German supply ship bearing down on the little boat like an enormous plow is stunning; the entire sequence of the emergency amputation, with a close-up of the survivors crudely sterilizing a pocket knife over a flickering flame, is memorably gruesome.

TALLULAH BANKHEAD gets special treatment, too, poking her finger through Kovac's newspaper and then teasingly leaning into him, her face swiping across the screen in a tight left-to-right close-up; another close shot, of her bare, high-arched foot slowly rubbing against his, is a small erotic jolt. (The role, her first film lead in 12 years, won her the best actress prize from the NEW YORK FILM CRITICS CIRCLE.)

Production, though, was difficult, as Hitchcock insisted on shooting in sequence, and the cast seemed to be plagued by accidents and illness; the first director of photography became sick, HUME CRONYN was injured on set, and Bankhead had a persistent bout of pneumonia. (Perhaps she caught a chill by being underdressed; the actress famously insisted on going without underwear, much to the dismay of the other cast members and the delight of the crew.) The delays helped run the budget up to more than $1.5 million. When it was released, it ran into further troubles, as it was heavily criticized for portraying the German as calmer and more capable than the British and Americans who'd hauled him onboard.

This was, of course, Hitchcock's point. Like *THE LADY VANISHES*, *Lifeboat* was a metaphor for the world; if the first film criticized English prewar appeasement, then this one suggested that the Allies needed to be resolute, even a little ruthless, if they were going to prevail against the Third Reich. Besides, the Nazi had to be a sort of superman; as the director had always said, the stronger the villain, the stronger the picture.

The German was too strong, however, for conservative columnists, who quickly turned on the movie. The syndicated Dorothy Thompson accused the film of being a "Nazi morale-builder" and demanded it be scrapped or at least seriously changed before it went into wide release. Reviewer for the *New York Times* Bosley Crowther called it "insidious" and "appalling." Hitchcock, now accused of being anti-American, called the charge "so preposterously untrue that it is a trifle irksome. If I disliked Americans, I should scarcely betray my dislike in such an unsubtle fashion."

None of this, however, was quite the sort of patriotic reception the studio had been hoping for. Faced with this sort of passionate opposition—and Hitchcock's typically too-droll denials—a frightened Twentieth Century Fox blinked, pulling back on advertising and bookings. The film ended up losing money—not something Hitchcock was accustomed to.

References

"Anti-U.S. Charge Denied," *Gloucestershire Echo*, March 16, 1944, http://the.hitchcock.zone/wiki/Gloucestershire_Echo_%2816/Mar/1944%29_-_Anti-U.S._Charge_Denied; Patrick McGilligan, *Alfred Hitchcock: A Life in Darkness and Light* (New York: HarperCollins, 2003), 328–42; Donald Spoto, *The Dark Side of Genius: The Life* of *Alfred Hitchcock* (New York: Da Capo Press, 1999), 265–70; Emily Temple, "John Steinbeck Wanted His Name Taken Off Hitchcock's 'Lifeboat,'" *Flavorwire*, http://flavorwire.com/256717/john-steinbeck-wanted-his-name-taken-off-hitchcocks-lifeboat; Dorothy Thompson, "A Film That Could Aid German Morale," *Amarillo Globe*, January 31, 1944, http://the.hitchcock.zone/wiki/Amarillo_Globe_%2831/Jan/1944%29_-_A_Film_that_Could_Aid_German_Morale.

LLOYD, NORMAN (1914–)

Jersey-City born performer whose mother thought he should take speech classes. That led to coaching in singing and dancing and gigs working the local ladies clubs. His father hoped he'd grow up to be a lawyer; instead Lloyd dropped out of New York University to go on auditions. "This was the Depression; the lawyers I saw were all driving cabs," Lloyd explained later. "So I thought, well, if I'm going to be badly off anyway, I might as well be badly off in the theater, where you get used to it."

He connected early with Orson Welles and the Mercury Theatre, playing Cinna in their famous production of *Julius Caesar*; when Welles went to Hollywood, Lloyd followed. He missed out on *Citizen Kane*, although he was soon cast as the title villain in Hitchcock's *SABOTEUR*.

"Hitch would never call this a 'political' picture," Lloyd said decades later. "He did not believe in 'political pictures.' His whole feeling was, 'I don't like social content in movies. I make entertainment.' To use GRAHAM GREENE'S phrase. But . . . if you look at *Saboteur* again, you've got a political picture. Not only the fact that it's on the Statue of Liberty that the villain finally falls."

Hitchcock called him back to play one of the inmates in *SPELLBOUND*. ("He actually loved actors. That whole thing—

'I never said actors were cattle; I said they should be treated like cattle'—he said that because he knew it would get in the papers. He understood the business.") And for a while, Lloyd continued to work, for Jean Renoir in *The Southerner*, for Lewis Milestone in *A Walk in the Sun*.

But clouds were gathering in Hollywood. Lloyd worked with John Garfield on *He Ran All the Way*, with Joseph Losey on *M*, with Chaplin on *Limelight*—and saw all three men blacklisted for their political opinions, either hounded to death or sent into exile. Then the blacklisters came for Lloyd.

It was a long road back, but he was helped by friends—first by John Houseman from the old Mercury Theatre days, who gave him a place to stay, and then by Hitchcock, who gave him a job. Lloyd was the associate producer for 184 episodes of *ALFRED HITCHCOCK PRESENTS*; when that ended its run, he moved over to *THE ALFRED HITCHCOCK HOUR* as the producer or executive producer.

"Hitchcock was a total pro," Lloyd said. "And he brooked no nonsense. I don't mean that he'd shout and carry on; he'd just walk off the set, he wouldn't put up with it. You toed the line with Hitch. But if you watched him, as I did starting with *Saboteur*, you could learn so much. I just tried to absorb it all."

The first and most crucial lesson, he says, was planning. "You would sign on for a Hitch picture and he'd tell you the story first, shot for shot—'Well, a door opens, and a foot comes through, and then a hand, and then we cut to . . .'—and he'd go on like that, telling you the whole picture, shot by shot!" Lloyd marvels. "He had it all planned out. 'If you can tell it, you can shoot it,' he used to say, 'and if you can't tell it, you can't shoot it.' They should print that out and put it up in every film school. But really, you watched him and you learned everything about telling a story. His whole head was a reel of film."

Lloyd directed some of the episodes and slowly resumed his acting career, as well, on other TV shows and movies and having a late-in-life success on the series *St. Elsewhere*. And he's still at it, having—at 100—just recently had a new picture in theaters, *Trainwreck*. He confesses he'd probably do more if he didn't spend so much time playing tennis.

References

Norman Lloyd, interviews with the author, November 2007, July 2015; "Norman Lloyd," *IMDb*, http://www.imdb.com/name/nm0516093/bio?ref_=nm_ov_bio_sm; Alex Ross, "The Magnificent Memory of Norman Lloyd," *New Yorker*, December 4, 2015, http://www.newyorker.com/culture/culture-desk/the-magnificent-memory-of-norman-lloyd.

LOCATION FILMING

In the earliest days of cinema, all filming was location filming, with the cameras catching fragmentary documents of trains entering stations and workers leaving factories; it took the pioneering Thomas Edison and George Melies to popularize the idea of the studio, in which lighting could be controlled and special effects more easily introduced.

Yet even then, location filming continued, at first giving audiences the extra value of a travelogue (the pleasant paradise of Catalina, the bustle of Coney Island). Though the claustrophobic studio days of the '30s and '40s often reduced it to second-unit work introduced via back-screen projection, after the war, lightweight cameras (and the influence of the Neorealists) brought the practice back, where urban landscapes gave noirs a gritty realism and exotic locales allowed the movies to provide something television could not.

As someone whose career ranged over a half-century, Hitchcock had a complicated and somewhat changeable attitude toward filming on location. A director who meticulously planned every shot in advance, the idea of shooting outside a studio—where the variables included everything from unpredictable weather to uncontrollable passersby—was nerve-racking. Some directors praise the miracles of happy accidents. Hitchcock was not among them.

Yet at the same time, Hitchcock had an edifice complex. There was something deep within him that loved the drama of famous landmarks and still felt the child-like thrill of seeing something historic loom in front of him. And as he grew as an artist, he also began to use iconic, real-life locations for metaphor and irony: an American traitor falls from the top of the nation's Statue of Liberty: an American hero, a pawn of his own government, runs for his life as the giant stony faces of dead presidents look implacably on.

Sometimes Hitchcock introduced locations via second-unit work that grabbed long shots, even stills, that could be repurposed later as backgrounds (as in, for example, his careful faking of the British Museum in *BLACKMAIL*); sometimes it required an actual trip (as in the beautiful and elegant COLOR travelogue that makes up much of the slight *TO CATCH A THIEF* or the small-town details that give such richness to *SHADOW OF A DOUBT*).

But even when the locations were somewhat faked (like the interiors of the United Nations for *NORTH BY NORTHWEST*), they were as real as Hitchcock could make them, based on reporting and careful photographs. And never were they arbitrary. For Hitchcock, place was a part of plot; if the film was set in Holland, as in *FOREIGN CORRESPONDENT*, then there must be windmills; if you were driving cross-country, as in *SABOTEUR*, then you must take a side trip to Hoover Dam. What your story was and where it took place were always intertwined.

Of course there were other benefits to shooting on location (advantageous tax situations, all-expenses-paid trips for Hitchcock and his family). And there were some old studio habits Hitchcock could never break; he stuck with back-projection even after technology allowed for other approaches, even when the results (as in the outboard boat scenes in *THE BIRDS* or the horse riding scenes in *MARNIE*) were far from realistic. Perhaps his eyes had grown accustomed to seeing the effect as just a different kind of realism.

But whether they were using stock footage, faked sets, or shot-on-location sequences, his films always constructed a perfect, living world. And took us there—and held us—until he was willing to let us go.

References

George Perry, "Hitchcock on Location," *American Heritage* (April 2007), http://the.hitchcock.zone/wiki/American_Heritage_%282007%29_-_Hitchcock_on_Location; Donald Spoto, *The Dark Side of Genius: The Life of Alfred Hitchcock* (New York: Da Capo Press, 1999), 351, 407; Joseph A. Valentine, "Using an Actual Town Instead of Movie Sets," *American Cinematographer* (October 1942), http://the.hitchcock.zone/wiki/American_Cinematographer_%281942%29_-_Using_an_Actual_Town_Instead_of_Movie_Sets.

LOCKWOOD, MARGARET (1916–1990)

Karachi-born performer—her British father ran a railroad—who returned to England with her mother and brother at the age of four. She began taking serious drama lessons in England not long after that, first appearing in cabarets at 10; further school-ing at the Royal Academy of Dramatic Art followed, and by 1934, she was appearing regularly onstage and on film.

She beat out Lilli Palmer and NOVA PILBEAM for the lead in *THE LADY VANISHES* in 1938 and brought a great deal of independence and charm to the part, as well as some genuine chemistry to her scenes with MICHAEL REDGRAVE, then making his film debut. (They reteamed two years later for *The Stars Look Down*.) Lockwood was an economical choice (she was already under contract to the studio) but a smart one, too, who firmly placed the role right in the sweet spot between Palmer's European worldliness and Pilbeam's girlish innocence.

"I suppose what surprised me most about Hitchcock was how little he directed us," she wrote later. "I had done a number of films for Carol Reed, and he was quite meticulous by contrast. Hitchcock, however, didn't seem to direct us at all. He was a dozing, nodding Buddha with an enigmatic smile on his face."

The '40s gave Lockwood's career a boost, as she starred in a number of period melodramas, often playing—as one of them was indeed titled—*The Wicked Lady*. (Her costumes in that film were so risqué—to American eyes—that several scenes had to be reshot for export.) By the end of the war, Lockwood was perhaps the most popular of British actresses, a sort of proto–Elizabeth Taylor, known for her fiery characters and perfectly applied beauty mark.

As the interest in passionate epics faded after the war, though, so did Lockwood, who returned to popular plays and television. Although she had one late-career success with the TV series *Justice*, there were long periods without work, and she spent the last decade of her life in seclusion, seeing only her family and a few close friends. She died in London at 73.

References

Michael Brooke, "Margaret Lockwood," *BFI Screenonline*, http://www.screenon line.org.uk/people/id/446975; "Margaret Lockwood," *IMDb*, http://www.imdb.com/ name/nm0516994/bio?ref_=nm_ov_bio _sm; Donald Spoto, *The Dark Side of Genius: The Life of Alfred Hitchcock* (New York: Da Capo Press, 1999), 174–75.

LODER, JOHN (1898–1988)

London-born performer, the son of British general W. H. M. Lowe, who had accepted the surrender of the Irish rebels in 1916. Loder went to Eton and the Royal Military College and was an officer in the First World War, serving in the Gallipoli Campaign and fighting in the Battle of the Somme, where he was taken prisoner by the Germans. He stayed in Germany after the war and eventually opened a pickle factory.

Clearly he was not interested in a military career, but sour vegetables had no lasting charm for him, either; Loder began to pursue acting, picking up some small parts in German pictures and later Hollywood. He did better on his return to England, where he played the plodding hero in *SAB- OTAGE*. (Hitchcock had wanted ROBERT DONAT for the film, as he had for *SECRET AGENT*, and once again Donat's ill health forced the director to grudgingly accept his second choice.)

Another shot at Hollywood in the '40s won Loder a role playing one of Roddy McDowall's many brothers in *How Green Was My Valley* and Bette Davis's disappointed suitor in *Now, Voyager*; tall, dark, and dependably dull, he was generally cast as sober doctors and inspectors from Scotland Yard, although the B-movie thriller *The Brighton Strangler* gave him a lead as a mad actor.

"Why is it that I'm not able to get the roles they give Clark Gable?" he complained around this time. "They always say, 'You have no name. But when you have one, come again.' By that time I'll be old and stiff. A kind of poor man's Aubrey Smith."

Loder was married five times, once to Hedy Lamarr; his last marriage was to a wealthy Argentine cattle heiress. After they divorced, he returned to England and wrote his memoirs, *Hollywood Hussar*. He died in London at 90.

References

C. Gerald Fraser, "John Loder, 90, British Actor, 90," *New York Times*, January 19, 1989, http://www.nytimes.com/ 1989/01/19/obituaries/john-loder-90-british -actor.html; "John Loder," *IMDb*, http:// www.imdb.com/name/nm0517058/ bio?ref_=nm_ov_bio_sm; Patrick McGilligan, *Alfred Hitchcock: A Life in Darkness and Light* (New York: HarperCollins, 2003), 187.

THE LODGER: A STORY OF THE LONDON FOG (GB 1927)

DIRECTOR: Alfred Hitchcock.
SCREENPLAY: Eliot Stannard, based on the novel *The Lodger* by Marie Belloc Lowndes.
PRODUCERS: Uncredited (Sir Michael Balcon, Carlyle Blackwell).
CINEMATOGRAPHY: Gaetano di Ventimiglia.
EDITOR: Ivor Montagu.
CAST: Ivor Novello (the Lodger), June Tripp (Daisy Bunting), Malcolm Keen (Joe), Marie Ault (Mrs. Bunting), Arthur Chesney (Mr. Bunting).
RUNNING TIME: 80 minutes. Black and white.
RELEASED THROUGH: W. & F. Film Service.

A BLONDE woman screams for her life, newspaper reporters scurry into action, and soon the news is out—the Avenger, a serial killer of blondes, has claimed yet another. Although many young Londoners react to the news with fear and horror, the flaxen-haired Daisy refuses to worry, even as her parents—and her police-officer boyfriend—obsess over the details of the case.

She is not even particularly concerned when her parents take in a lodger—a mysteriously quiet young man who keeps to himself, seems to have a strong aversion to blondes, and goes out for long walks late at night. Although her MOTHER begins to suspect this stranger is, in fact, the Avenger, Daisy not only accepts him but also feels an attraction.

Her possessive boyfriend, however, is less accepting—particularly as he sees the bond growing between Daisy and his new rival. He brings fellow officers and a warrant to the house, and they search the lodger's rooms, finding a gun and a map of the murder scenes. They handcuff him, but the lodger escapes, trailed by Daisy, who believes in his innocence.

The lodger blurts out his story to her—his sister was the killer's first victim, and he was really searching for the Avenger himself—when a mob begins to form, convinced they've found the killer. They are close to murdering him in the street when a paperboy announces the latest headline: the real Avenger has been caught. The lodger is set free and embraced by Daisy.

The first "real" Hitchcock film—and it was almost never seen at all.

SIR MICHAEL BALCON had the rights to MARIE BELLOC LOWNDES's novel and gave it to Hitchcock to direct; there was something in its tale of swirling mystery and mist that he thought was well suited to the young director, who had already drawn notice (and criticism) at the studio for the heavily Germanic, EXPRESSIONISTIC influence he'd shown in *THE PLEASURE GARDEN*.

Hitchcock gave the film the meticulous care in preproduction he would give all his later productions. The script was painstakingly worked out. The cast was assembled. Shots were designed so they carried not only factual information but emotional signifiers as well—the heads of policemen swaying back and forth in the back of a van's window like inquisitive eyes, the ceiling of a parlor turning into plate glass so we can see the feet of the lodger as he paces, nervously, back and forth.

True, Hitchcock also had his first run-in with the STAR system—told that matinee idol IVOR NOVELLO's lodger simply could not be the killer, the director had to abandon his original, more ambiguous ending. And his old boss, GRAHAM CUTTS, was already spreading rumors that the picture was a disaster. But Hitchcock got on well with Novello, and the production went smoothly.

The filmmaker's confidence is clear from the start. The first shot is of a screaming woman, lit brightly from behind to turn her hair into a halo; "Golden Curls To-Night," a sign flashes. From there we go to a newspaper office, where the story of the murder is being reported, set in type, printed, and disseminated—the methodical, engineering side of Hitchcock always had a fascination with process and often spoke of shooting potential sequences that would follow FOOD, champagne, or an automobile along its journey to consumers.

Now, in the third sequence, it's time to begin introducing main characters, with Daisy—and not surprisingly, the number 3 occurs again and again in this film. It's a film of triangles, in fact—the three-cornered symbol that the killer leaves as his calling card, the borders of the neighborhood in which he prowls, and the awkward relationship that soon arises among Daisy; her boyfriend, Joe; and the lodger.

"The lodger" is how he enters the film—on the doorstep, with just his EYES shining between his scarf and hat—and it's the lodger he remains; he has no other name, just as "the Avenger" remains similarly anonymous. But he also has a parallel in Joe, the policeman, who also has a fetish for blondes and an interest in Daisy.

In a standard film, Joe would be the hero, but Hitchcock is already disinterested in the world of sniveling villains and muscular saints. Right from the start, the lodger is seen as polite, educated, upper class; the rough-edged Joe makes awkward jokes about marriage (drawing a parallel between handcuffs and wedding rings) and seems to see the lively Daisy (who has her own career as a model) as his property.

The attractiveness of evil, the painful banality of good. It is a cynical point Hitchcock makes in other films—who doesn't prefer JOSEPH COTTEN to MACDONALD CAREY in *SHADOW OF A DOUBT*, ROBERT WALKER to FARLEY GRANGER in *STRANGERS ON A TRAIN*, ANTHONY PERKINS to JOHN GAVIN in *PSYCHO*? Hitchcock would have made the point even more clearly here had he been allowed to leave some question as to Novello's innocence. But the star system and the CENSORS would not allow that.

Still, the film is remarkably successful, full of energy and accomplishment and layers of meaning. (The crucifix shown in Daisy's home, for example, is later mirrored in the shot of the handcuffed lodger with his arms above him, as if he were crucified.) It's a strong, career-making debut.

Except it was almost the end of Hitchcock's career. Cutts's envious criticisms had caught the ear of mogul C. M. WOOLF; Woolf had found Hitchcock's previous films artistically pretentious, and after screening his latest, he proclaimed it unreleasable. ("Your picture is so dreadful," he told the filmmaker, "that we're just going to put it on the shelf and forget about it." He said it as if he expected Hitchcock to thank him.)

Desperate to save the movie, Balcon appealed to IVOR MONTAGU of the London Film Society. Montagu was only 22 but both cultured and connected. (He had already written about German cinema for the *Times* and was the son of prominent financier Lord Swaythling.) Could Montagu take a look at the film and give his opinion? Montagu did, and his opinion was that the film was a stunning achievement; he suggested that the title cards have a new design that underlined the triangular motif, that they be drastically cut down (Montagu later claimed there were hundreds), and that a few scenes be slightly reshot to make them clearer.

Although Hitchcock resented the second-guessing (and would, for the rest of his life, minimize Montagu's contribution—as he later would with his various screenwriters), he took the suggestions. (He took them to heart, too, probably—for an artist as purely visual as Hitchcock was to be told that his silent film was too wordy must have stung.) The titles were cut down and reshot, and some scenes were clarified and tightened. Balcon set up a press screening for September 1926, and the raves quickly began.

The good publicity finally convinced Woolf to release the other Hitchcock pictures he'd had so little faith in. *The Pleasure Garden* reached theaters in January 1927, followed by *The Lodger* (as its title was almost invariably shortened to) in February, and *THE MOUNTAIN EAGLE* in May. But before that happened, Hitchcock had already signed with another studio—and wed his occasional assistant, ALMA REVILLE. His life was launched.

References

Patrick McGilligan, *Alfred Hitchcock: A Life in Darkness and Light* (New York:

HarperCollins, 2003), 77–89; Ivor Montagu, "Working with Hitchcock," *Sight and Sound* 49 (Summer 1980), 189–93; Donald Spoto, *The Dark Side of Genius: The Life of Alfred Hitchcock* (New York: Da Capo Press, 1999), 84–89; François Truffaut, *Hitchcock/Truffaut*, rev. ed. (New York: Touchstone, 1985), 42–51.

LOEB, RICHARD (1905–1936)
See LEOPOLD, NATHAN (1904–1971), and LOEB, RICHARD (1905–1936).

LOMBARD, CAROLE (1908–1942)
Indiana-born performer who moved to California with her mother after her parents divorced. She was discovered at 13 by director Allan Dwan, who saw her playing a ferocious game of baseball and cast her in a small part in the drama *A Perfect Crime.* Enjoying the experience, she auditioned for other movies, including *The Gold Rush*; she didn't land the parts but by 16 had a small contract with Fox. Dropped after a year— and unemployed for another—she finally signed with Mack Sennett in 1927, where she was billed as one of his "Bathing Beauties" and kept busy in slapstick comedies.

She had moved to PARAMOUNT and feature films (and a brief marriage to William Powell) by the beginning of the '30s; stand-out performances in *Twentieth Century, My Man Godfrey,* and *Nothing Sacred* established her as not only one of the great Hollywood beauties but also a skilled screwball comedian. It was then that she caught the attention of Hitchcock, who—while still in England—spoke of how much he'd like to show another side of her by casting her in a more dramatic role.

"I should like to cast Lombard not in the type of superficial comedy which she so often plays but in a much more meaty comedy-drama, giving her plenty of scope for characterization," he told *Film Weekly* in 1938. "I believe that, imaginatively

treated, Lombard is capable of giving a performance equal to that of any of the best male actors, like Muni and Leslie Howard."

In fact, Lombard was about to try more serious parts, in *In Name Only* and *Made for Each Other*; soon, she'd even be briefly mentioned as a possible lead for Hitchcock's upcoming *REBECCA* (for which she would have been rather seriously miscast). When the director and actress finally met, they became fast friends; when she married Clark Gable, the Hitchcock family rented her old home in Bel Air.

The athletic, one-of-the-guys Lombard—who could look elegant in satin onscreen and swear like a stevedore off— definitely fit Hitchcock's type, and the two looked for a project. Although Hitchcock later dismissed their film, *MR. AND MRS. SMITH*, as something he'd done merely as a favor to Lombard ("She asked me to do it," he told PETER BOGDANOVICH. "The script was already written, and I just came in and did it"), he had been enthused about the project at first, which also fit his own urge to expand beyond the thriller genre.

Although the actual production bored Hitchcock even more than usual, the film was a hit—ironically because it was Lombard's first out-and-out comedy in three years after a string of the sort of dramas Hitchcock himself had urged her to take on. It was also, tragically, the last film she would ever see released; while her follow-up project, *To Be or Not to Be*, was in postproduction, a plane she was taking back from a war-bond rally crashed into a Nevada mountain, killing everyone onboard. She was 33.

References
Peter Bogdanovich, *Who the Devil Made It* (New York: Knopf, 1997), 509; "Carole Lombard," *Biography*, http://www.biography.com/people/carole-lombard-9385324; "Carole Lombard," *IMDb*,

http://www.imdb.com/name/nm0001479/ bio?ref_=nm_ov_bio_sm; Donald Spoto, *The Dark Side of Genius: The Life of Alfred Hitchcock* (New York: Da Capo Press, 1999), 210, 220, 237–38; David Thomson, *The New Biographical Dictionary of Film* (New York: Knopf, 2002), 529–31; J. Danvers Williams, "What I'd Do to the Stars," *Film Weekly*, March 4, 1939, http://the.hitchcock.zone/wiki/Film _Weekly_%281939%29_-_What_I'd_Do _to_the_Stars.

LONG TAKES

From his earliest days as a filmmaker, Hitchcock was primarily influenced by the filmmakers working in Germany, with their EXPRESSIONIST shadows and oblique camera angles, and the Soviet Union, with their reliance on quick cuts and powerful MONTAGE. Composition and editing— this was the foundation of what he called PURE CINEMA. Anything else was filmed theater.

You can see this preference in his early movies. The few times when he did feel he had been hired to film theater—such productions as *JUNO AND THE PAYCOCK*, where he felt his primary responsibility was to record performances—he let the camera run long without interruptions.

But unless a shot required a long and deliberate camera movement—such as the crane shot in *NOTORIOUS*, which slowly swoops down to reveal the key in Alicia's hand—Hitchcock preferred his takes to be short and his scenes made up of a variety of often very quick cuts. (It was one of the things in his style that annoyed ANDRE BAZIN, an outlier among the Hitchcock worshippers at *CAHIERS DU CINEMA*; he much preferred the stately rhythms of William Wyler.)

Hitchcock seemed to briefly reconsider his approach, though, in the mid-'40s while supervising a British documentary on the Holocaust (later broadcast as *MEMORY OF THE CAMPS*); even with the war still fresh in people's minds, the director realized that many people and not just the conquered Germans would still deny the facts. He told the editors to use wide shots and long takes whenever possible; the fewer cuts in the film, the less that trickery would be suspected.

It's a philosophy he began to experiment with in *THE PARADINE CASE* (much to DAVID O. SELZNICK's annoyance, who merely cut some of the longer takes) and brought to fruition in his next two projects, *ROPE* and *UNDER CAPRICORN*, both of which used extremely long takes (in the first film, as long as an entire reel of film).

Rope, of course, was adapted from a play, and sometimes with those adaptations (*DIAL M FOR MURDER*, *THE SKIN GAME*), Hitchcock could allow a certain staginess to creep in. And the period costume drama of *Under Capricorn* seemed better suited to a slower, less frenetic style.

Yet there was a philosophical and emotional component behind this new choice as well. In *Rope*, the long takes mean the drama unfolds very much in real time, thereby increasing the suspense, as the unknowing dinner guests circulate around a body in a box; in *Under Capricorn*, the leisurely shots lend an extra bit of realism to a story set in a distant land and a long-ago time, full of hidden motives, melodramatic flourishes, and secrets held tightly for years. (In both cases, they also drove the actors crazy, with both JAMES STEWART and INGRID BERGMAN railing against the process.)

Of course, long takes held another, far more personal attraction for the director— a logistical challenge, however arbitrary, and a way to stay interested in two projects that otherwise didn't seem to hold much for him. He had always had an engineer's

LORRE, PETER ■ 241

happy interest in solving technical problems, and designing breakaway sets or coming up with a way to "invisibly" cut long takes together into a seemingly unceasing film amused him for awhile.

But neither film truly connected with audiences—*Under Capricorn* was in fact a bit of a disaster—and Hitchcock soon returned to his normal manner of shooting, full of dramatic angles and emotional jolts.

References

Ingrid Bergman and Alan Burgess, *My Story* (New York: Delacorte Press, 1980), 177–78; Donald Spoto, *The Dark Side of Genius: The Life of Alfred Hitchcock* (New York: Da Capo Press, 1999), 302–3, 305–6.

LORD CAMBER'S LADIES (GB 1932)

DIRECTOR: Benn Levy.
SCREENPLAY: Benn Levy, Edwin Greenwood, Gilbert Wakefield, based on the play *The Case of Lady Camber* by Horace Annesley Vachell.
PRODUCER: Alfred Hitchcock.
CINEMATOGRAPHY: James Wilson.
EDITOR: Uncredited.
ORIGINAL MUSIC: Uncredited.
CAST: Gerald du Maurier (Dr. Napier), Gertrude Lawrence (Lady Camber), Benita Hume (Janet King), Nigel Bruce (Lord Camber).
RUNNING TIME: 80 minutes. Black and white.
RELEASED THROUGH: Wardour Films.

A rather free adaptation of a hit British play, revised to star Gerald du Maurier in the story of an adulterer planning to murder his wife, a former entertainer. The themes (a love triangle, an unhappy marriage, show business) were favorites of Hitchcock; he had worked with director BENN LEVY and was friendly with du Maurier and owed another film under his contract to BRITISH INTERNATIONAL PICTURES, so he took on the role of producer. He was a little put out, however, when it became clear on the set that Levy wasn't interested in his input; it would be the only film Hitchcock would ever produce for anyone else.

References

Patrick McGilligan, *Alfred Hitchcock: A Life in Darkness and Light* (New York: Harper-Collins, 2003), 148–49; François Truffaut, *Hitchcock/Truffaut*, rev. ed. (New York: Touchstone, 1985), 82.

LORRE, PETER (1904–1964)

Hungarian-born performer whose father, a bookkeeper and army reservist, wanted him to go into business. Lorre took some classes and a job as a bank teller in Vienna, but he had been drawn to acting since he was a teen; he was soon very busy as an improv performer at the city's Theater of Spontaneity and later became a fixture in Berlin, where—after acquitting himself in farces, light comedies, musicals, and dramas—he became a particular favorite of Bertolt Brecht, who praised the complex duality of his performances.

In fact, Lorre was playing onstage in a comedy when he also shot the grim *M* for FRITZ LANG; it was one of cinema's first serious portrayals of a serial killer, and Lorre's performance as the terrible yet terrified child murderer both made him a STAR and typecast him as a villain. It also made the newly famous Jewish actor an obvious target for the growing Nazi menace; two days before the Reichstag Fire in 1933, Lorre and his wife, Celia Lovsky, left for Paris.

His name came up a few months later in London, where Hitchcock and producer IVOR MONTAGU were casting *THE MAN WHO KNEW TOO MUCH*. "We wanted him at once," Montagu said later.

"There was never any question about his coming over to be inspected or tested—even his English was not in question, for a German accent was no obstacle in the part. He came over, not to be approved, but to be engaged."

The truth was, however, that Lorre didn't speak English with a German accent; he didn't speak much English at all beyond "yes" and "no." But Lorre said, sympathetic producer SIDNEY BERNSTEIN "put me wise to the fact that Hitchy likes to tell stories, so I used to watch him like a hawk and whenever I thought the end of a story was coming and that was the point, I used to roar with laughter and somehow he got the impression that I spoke English. . . . I got the part."

He learned the role phonetically but also pushed himself to master the language; soon he was able to trade dirty stories on the set with Hitchcock. The two men bonded over their taste for not only the risqué but also practical JOKES (when Lorre complained the studio cleaners had shrunk his costume, Hitchcock had a new one made up for him in toddler size), and as the leader of the kidnappers, Lorre gave a charmingly sinister performance, suggesting simultaneously—as Brecht had first observed—several opposite emotions at once.

After *The Man Who Knew Too Much* was a success, Lorre went to Hollywood—where he made both *Crime and Punishment* and the superb *Mad Love*—before returning to Hitchcock and England for *SECRET AGENT*, once again playing a foreign agent. It's an odd part (accompanied by an even odder wig), and Lorre seems more intent on amusing himself than interacting with the other performers, but in one of Hitchcock's lesser thrillers, he provides the most consistent bits of entertainment, even if his addiction to morphine was already obvious on the set.

Lorre returned to Hollywood after this—and briefly to the bizarre assignment of playing the Japanese detective Mr. Moto in a series of cheap mysteries. Then John Huston, who always had an eye for eccentric talent, picked Lorre for the fastidious Joel Cairo in *The Maltese Falcon* and gave him a second career—playing the wheedling, whining, and somewhat sadly regretful criminal hovering around the edge of '40s noirs.

Lorre made much of little—he was indelible in *Casablanca*, with only a few minutes of screen time, punctuating his lines with a shrug, putting several meanings into a mutter—but he grew tired of playing villains. And typecasting was the least of his worries. He still had substance abuse problems; his friendship with Brecht and outspoken politics risked the serious attention of the Hollywood witch hunters. Work began to disappear. His contract at WARNER BROS. wasn't renewed, and eventually he went bankrupt.

Slowly, over the decade, Lorre climbed back. He returned to Germany to direct, cowrite, and star in the film *The Lost One* about the country's Nazi past; he rejoined Huston and Humphrey Bogart for the cultishly beloved (but financially disastrous) *Beat the Devil*. He took on a supporting part in Walt Disney's *20,000 Leagues under the Sea* and became a busy television guest star, where he appeared in the first small-screen adaptation of *Casino Royale* and dominated two episodes of *ALFRED HITCHCOCK PRESENTS*, including—in the Peter Lorre part to end all Peter Lorre parts—Carlos, the degenerate gambler in "Man from the South."

By the 1960s, the roles were mostly in beach-blanket movies and horror films (although *The Raven* and *The Comedy of Terrors* let him indulge his old skills at improvisation and farce). Bouts of ill health, exacerbated by a thyroid condition (and the attendant weight gain), grew increasingly common and severe. He died in Los Angeles of a stroke. He was 59.

References
Patrick McGilligan, *Alfred Hitchcock: A Life in Darkness and Light* (New York: Harper-Collins, 2003), 161–62, 181–83; Teresa and Tracy Murray, *Peter Lorre: Hollywood's Sinister Star*, http://www.eviltwin.velvet sofa.com/Lorre/peter.html; "Peter Lorre," *IMDb*, http://www.imdb.com/name/ nm0000048/bio?ref_=nm_ov_bio_sm; Donald Spoto, *The Dark Side of Genius: The Life of Alfred Hitchcock* (New York: Da Capo Press, 1999), 142, 152; David Thomson, *The New Biographical Dictionary of Film* (New York: Knopf, 2002), 532–33; Stephen D. Youngkin, *The Lost One: A Life of Peter Lorre*, http://www.peterlorrebook .com.

LOVE SCENES
At the AFI tribute to Alfred Hitchcock, FRANÇOIS TRUFFAUT saluted the director for filming his love scenes like murders and his murders like love scenes. It's a neat description but a bit pat; Hitchcock's approach changed as the CENSORS grew more powerless and his own obsessions more violent—there are few love scenes in his later films, and the murders take on the mood of not sex but SEXUAL assault. Yet for most of Hitchcock's career, Truffaut's observation remained broadly true: The violence in his films would always be strangely intimate, the romance oddly menacing.

Sometimes, of course, romance is merely the prelude to violence, a hypnotically seductive glance merely the first weapon of a poisonous snake. Uncle Charlie's dapper flirtations in *SHADOW OF A DOUBT*, Bruno's exaggerated masculine strut in *STRANGERS ON A TRAIN*, Bob's slippery solicitousness in *FRENZY*—all are

merely lures, soft words meant to coax the trembling prey not into bed but into their graves.

But even when there is—supposedly—no other agenda at work, no love scene in Hitchcock is ever simply that. Most are shot through with undercurrents of disappointment and DOMINATION—Sam and Marion's postcoitus conversation in *PSYCHO* is crammed with talk of debts and alimony, Joe's teasing of Daisy in *THE LODGER* immediately conflates the symbol of a wedding ring with handcuffs and the hangman's noose.

Pure, idealistic love is something for cheaper, less challenging movies; in Hitchcock's world, Devlin and Alicia may embrace tenderly in *NOTORIOUS*, John and Frances may set off fireworks in *TO CATCH A THIEF*, but both scenes inevitably end in recriminations and regret. And then there is *MARNIE*, a film whose single love scene begins as a honeymoon night on a romantic ocean liner—and ends in rape and a suicide attempt.

For all the fantastic situations in Hitchcock, about love he remains coldly realistic—if not actually pessimistic. It is about not complete and utter honesty but deception and betrayal, based not on the equal sharing of two souls but on a struggle for dominance. Like diplomacy, it is just war by other means. And afterward, the field is littered with the wounded.

Reference
Stuart Jeffries, "Actors Are Cattle: When Hitchcock Met Truffaut," *Guardian*, May 12, 2015, http://www.theguardian.com/ film/2015/may/12/when-hitchcock-met -truffaut-hitchcock-truffaut-documentary -cannes.

LUKAS, PAUL (1891–1971)
Hungarian-born performer who made his film debut in 1915. Within a decade, he was

a busy silent-screen STAR, often playing rakes or romantic heroes in films with titles like *Three Sinners* and *Two Lovers*; he was the playboy in the film version of Preston Sturges's hit play *Strictly Dishonorable* and the kindly German scholar in the Katharine Hepburn version of *Little Women*.

He had a change of pace in *THE LADY VANISHES* as Dr. Hartz, the concerned physician who turns out to be a ruthless agent; it led to more villainous roles, as a German provocateur in *Confessions of a Nazi Spy*, a suspicious lawyer in *The Ghost Breakers*, and a mob boss in *The Monster and the Girl*. His career seemed to be on a downward trend, but the Broadway run of *Watch on the Rhine* revived it, and when he reprised his heroic antifascist part for the movies, he won an Oscar.

Lukas continued to act onstage, in films, and eventually on television; he died of a heart attack at 80 in Tangier while on the search for a retirement home.

References
"Paul Lukas," *IMDb*, http://www.imdb .com/name/nm0510134/bio?ref_=nm_ov _bio_sm; David Thomson, *The New Biographical Dictionary of Film* (New York: Knopf, 2002), 540–41.

MACGUFFIN

The thing that the characters—chiefly the antagonists—care deeply about in a thriller and for which the audience does not give a damn. Whether it's jewels, evidence of a murder, or the "secret clause" to a peace treaty is utterly unimportant; it is merely the spark that sets the story in motion. MacGuffins in Hitchcock films probably begin with the glove in *BLACKMAIL* and continue to include the necklace in *NUMBER 17*, the musical code in *THE LADY VANISHES*, the uranium in *NOTORIOUS*, the house key in *DIAL M FOR MURDER*, the microfilm in *NORTH BY NORTHWEST*, the diamonds in *FAMILY PLOT*, and many more.

IVOR MONTAGU credits screenwriter ANGUS MACPHAIL with the term, and Hitchcock's earliest public mention of it seemed to come in 1939, when he described it in a lecture at Columbia University as the "mechanical element that usually crops up in any story. In crook stories it is almost always the necklace and in spy stories it is most always the papers." Five years later, he described it in *Time* as the "thing the hero chases, the thing the picture is all about."

As to its etymology, *Time* first went into detail in 1944, crediting a "hoary British joke" about two strangers meeting on a TRAIN. One has a package, and when the second one asks what's inside, he describes it as a "McGuffin," an animal used for "hunting tigers in New York."

But there are no tigers in New York, the second gentleman responds.

"Ah," says the first, "but this isn't a real McGuffin."

Hitchcock would later give a similar explanation to FRANÇOIS TRUFFAUT and all other INTERVIEWERS, although in his version, it's usually described as a Scottish JOKE (a nod to MacPhail perhaps?), and instead of an animal and New York, the "MacGuffin" is an "apparatus" used in the "Scottish Highlands." The punchline, however, remains the same.

As does the explanation: The only one who really needs to know what the MacGuffin is, is the scriptwriter.

References

"Bourgeoisie," *Time*, December 18, 1944, http://the.hitchcock.zone/wiki/TIME_%2818/Dec/1944%29_-_Bourgeoisie; Kenneth Mogg, "Frequently Asked Questions on Hitchcock: What's a MacGuffin?" http://www.labyrinth.net.au/~muffin/faqs_c.html#Answer%201.

MACLAINE, SHIRLEY (1934–)

Before the indie-movie explosion of "manic pixie dream girls"—those colorful iconoclasts who seemed to exist in stories only to save the poor dull hero from himself—there

Marnie, with Tippi Hedren, seemed to spotlight its director's most complicated feelings about women and his star. *Universal Pictures/Photofest © Universal Pictures*

was Shirley MacLaine. The difference was the independent, melancholy heroines she played sometimes couldn't even save themselves.

Born in Virginia and named after Shirley Temple, Shirley Beaty—kid brother Warren kept the family name but added a *T*—moved to New York after high school to pursue a career in musical comedy. When star Carol Haney broke her ankle, understudy MacLaine went on for her in *The Pajama Game*. It was the night Herbert Coleman, Hitchcock's assistant producer, was in the house, and MacLaine quickly found herself with a PARAMOUNT contract. She was 20.

Her first film was to be *THE TROUBLE WITH HARRY* for Alfred Hitchcock, and it was a bit of a mismatch all around, with a clear and very wide generation gaping between the bohemian redhead eager to explore a role and the Victorian Englishman intent on asserting control. The shooting was plagued with various difficulties, from miscasting to weather, and on its release, the film was not embraced.

But MacLaine was launched—she won a Golden Globe for it as the best new female star of the year—and, after a quick comedy or two, expanded her range with *Some Came Running* and the bittersweet *The Apartment*. The rest of the decade was filled with far too many lackluster comedies, but she is iconic as the dime-a-dance girl in *Sweet Charity* (although the movie is egregiously overlong), terrific in *The Turning Point*, and quietly moving in *Being There*. She finally won her much-wanted Oscar for *Terms of Endearment*.

Since then, she has largely played variations on that part as the crusty, cantankerous old lady. She sees some missed opportunities in her career. ("I turned down two things I wish I had done: *Alice Doesn't Live Here Anymore* and *Breakfast at Tiffany's*," she said. "I have no desire whatsoever to play Shakespeare unless I want to go to the movie theater and laugh at myself, but I think I have yet to do a real heart-searing drama.") But she is still working, still outspoken, and still a proponent of a variety of spiritual beliefs, including reincarnation. Although why anyone who's put as much into life as she has needs yet another one is hard to say.

References

Shirley MacLaine, interview with the author, December 1996; Donald Spoto, *The Dark Side of Genius: The Life of Alfred Hitchcock* (New York: Da Capo Press, 1999), 354–55; David Thomson, *The New Biographical Dictionary of Film* (New York: Knopf, 2002), 546–48.

MACPHAIL, ANGUS (1903–1962)

London-born, Cambridge-educated author who entered filmmaking in the mid-'20s as an uncredited script doctor. Often working with IVOR MONTAGU, they would re-edit and rewrite titles for troubled silent films, speeding up the action, and sometimes changing the plots. His skills soon caught the attention of SIR MICHAEL BALCON, who put him in charge of the story department at GAUMONT-BRITISH studios; no film could be put into production, Balcon ordered, until the screenplay had MacPhail's approval.

MacPhail loved puns and JOKES (according to Montagu, he was the one who first came up with "MACGUFFIN" to describe the arbitrary engine of a thriller's plot) and was an important part of script conferences during the British years of Hitchcock's career; his first sizable screen credit on a Hitchcock film (he worked on the director's two wartime shorts, *AVENTURE MALGACHE* and *BON VOYAGE*) came in 1945 with the treatment for *SPELLBOUND*, although the actual screenplay was written by BEN HECHT.

MacPhail's many other credits included the Christmas party ghost story in *Dead of Night* and the delightful *Whiskey Galore!* but by the 1950s, the writer's alcoholism had reached a final, debilitating stage. Hitchcock, citing the writer's past work with British intelligence, brought him on as "consultant" for the 1956 *THE MAN WHO KNEW TOO MUCH*, but when he tried to give him a screenplay credit, screenwriter JOHN MICHAEL HAYES rebelled and successfully petitioned the Writers Guild to award him sole authorship.

That led to a break between Hayes and Hitchcock that never healed; meanwhile, the director gave MacPhail a second job afterward, taking over the writing of THE WRONG MAN after Maxwell Anderson's early drafts had been judged too poetic. Managing to keep his drinking in relative check (with some supervision by associate producer Herbert Coleman), MacPhail produced the final, grittily realistic screenplay.

It was his last screen credit; although he did some early work on VERTIGO, he begged off, telling Hitchcock he simply wasn't up to it. His health worsening, he grew more reclusive, keeping up with friends through what the London Times described as "always amusing and sometimes outrageous letters." He died two weeks after his 59th birthday.

References

"Angus MacPhail," IMDb, http://www.imdb.com/name/nm0534191/bio?ref_=nm_ov_bio_sm; Patrick McGilligan, Alfred Hitchcock: A Life in Darkness and Light (New York: HarperCollins, 2003), 508–11, 529–32; "Obituary: Angus MacPhail," Times, April 28, 1962, http://the.hitchcock.zone/wiki/The_Times_%2828/Apr/1962%29_-_Obituary:_Angus_MacPhail; Donald Spoto, The Dark Side of Genius: The Life of Alfred Hitchcock (New York: Da Capo Press, 1999), 141, 271; Martin Stollery, "Angus MacPhail," BFI Screenonline, http://www.screenonline.org.uk/people/id/447569/index.html.

MALDEN, KARL (1912–2009)

Chicago-born performer who began acting in Serbian-language plays at the local church and worked in the Indiana steel mills after graduating high school. Eventually he made it to drama school and to New York, where he first encountered the Group Theatre and Elia Kazan. World War II interrupted his career, but Malden returned to the stage, where he landed important roles in Truckline Café, All My Sons, and A Streetcar Named Desire.

When the play was filmed for Hollywood, Malden—who had already had a handful of movie roles going back to 1940—repeated the part and won the Oscar for it. Two years later, he costarred in I CONFESS and became an important part of Hitchcock's on-set team, serving as an intermediary between the emotionally fragile METHOD-actor MONTGOMERY CLIFT and the remote, results-oriented director. (Hitchcock's thank-you, Malden later said, came in an edit that favored Malden with more close-ups.)

Malden's honest, uncluttered style and rough-hewn features—he'd taken a few elbows to the face as a high school basketball player—left him at ease in both heroic and villainous roles, although his name was usually down among the supporting players. He is the crusading priest in On the Waterfront, the disappointed suitor in Gypsy. Only with his hit '70s TV series The Streets of San Francisco did he really become the sympathetic lead.

Malden—who was born Mladen Sekulovich and tried to work his family name into his movies' dialogue when he could—had his last onscreen role in an episode of The West Wing in 2000. He died in Los Angeles at 97.

References

"Karl Malden," IMDb, http://www.imdb.com/name/nm0001500/bio?ref_=nm_ov_bio_sm; Patrick McGilligan, Alfred Hitchcock: A Life in Darkness and Light (New York: HarperCollins, 2003), 460–62; Donald Spoto, The Dark Side of Genius: The Life of Alfred Hitchcock (New York: Da Capo Press, 1999), 338–41; David Thomson, The New Biographical Dictionary of Film (New York: Knopf, 2002), 551–52.

THE MALE GAZE

First named and described at length by Laura Mulvey in her 1975 article "Visual Pleasure and Narrative Cinema," this theory begins with the assumption that, as heterosexual men control the cinema, the camera stands in for them and the male viewer by looking at women in frankly and purely SEXUAL ways. Its gaze is aggressive, objectifying, diminishing.

Like many powerful ideas, the male gaze is easy to dismiss as being both obvious (of *course* movies present women as sexual objects) and full of exceptions (How does the camera's relationship to actresses change if the director is a gay man or a straight woman or a gay woman?). Yet it has survived those objections and possible exceptions to become an important tenet of feminist and cultural criticism.

It is also a central—and acknowledged—part of Hitchcock's work. From his earliest days as a filmmaker studying the early Soviet directors and the KULE-SHOV EFFECT, he knew that cinema was about looking and about not only what we saw but also how we saw it. And in his best films, watching is not just an act but also a complicated relationship: The audience watching Hitchcock watching a man watching a woman. It stretches back almost into infinity, like a hall of mirrors.

"Air, stare," the heroine declares in *MARNIE*, angrily free-associating as her husband-turned-amateur-shrink watches. "And that's what *you* do."

The clearest examples of the male gaze are the admiring or lustful ones Hitchcock's male characters (or his camera) have for the film's heroines. *THE PLEASURE GARDEN*, his first film, begins with a man in a music hall checking out the legs of chorus girls; *THE LADY VANISHES*, one of his last English movies, features a hotel worker surrounded by the bare legs of female tourists; *Marnie*, one of his last pictures, has the camera admiring the heroine's taut calves as she strides down a TRAIN platform.

This is the simplest, most classic example of the gaze with an onscreen character or the camera itself—and, behind each, the director—standing in for the men in the movie house and serving up a woman reduced, quite starkly, to her parts. (Chiefly legs, it seems; Hitchcock always seemed to find breasts and décolletage a bit vulgar, complaining about actresses whose sex appeal "hangs around their neck, like jewelry.")

It reaches a deeper, darker level in other films though, where it moves from leering to stalking. Scottie's careful shadowing of Madeleine in *VERTIGO* begins as a job; his following of Judy is evidence of his obsession. Norman's peeping on Marion in *PSYCHO* is not just the prelude to violence but also its excuse; seen through a hole in the wall, she's just an arm, a back, a flash of breast, a collection of parts. She's a body, not a being.

And then there is Bruno's fixated look at Guy in the midst of a tennis match in *STRANGERS ON A TRAIN*; here is the HOMOSEXUAL male gaze, twisted; Bruno's stare reveals not only an intensity of attraction but also a determination to bend this person to his will, to "turn" the unwilling Guy to his ends.

In some films, the gaze itself becomes the entire subject. Observing, snooping, spying—Hitchcock films are full of them, although often the spies (*SECRET AGENT*, *SHADOW OF A DOUBT*) can't bring themselves to act, and sometimes the witnesses (*THE WRONG MAN*) are mistaken.

Seeing is believing, but those beliefs aren't always right, and they don't always lead to justice. Scottie sees Madeleine fall to her death in *Vertigo*—or does he? Tourists watch Roger Thornhill stab that man at the United Nations in *NORTH BY*

NORTHWEST—don't they? We are always watching, Hitchcock says, but what are we really seeing?

REAR WINDOW—his practically feature-length meditation on the Kuleshov effect—is all about gazing. Jeff is housebound, stuck in a wheelchair, but what really imprisons him is his insistence on remaining a spectator—he looks at Lisa but cannot commit to her; he obsessively watches neighbors he never seems to have met. Jeff looks at people through his huge, phallic camera lens but remains impotently removed; unable to enter their lives, he makes up names and situations for them. He reduces them to nicknames and clichés. He does in reality what the male gaze does in relationships; he strips people of their humanity and turns them into a collection of obvious things.

It is a cold VOYEURISTIC existence, but it bears one white-hot moment of shock—when Thorwald feels his eyes on him and looks back across the courtyard, when the watched watch back. That moment was in Hitchcock's first film, too, when the chorus girl caught the letch staring, but it's not played for a wry smile here. It's presented as a startling turn-the-tables reminder—those we look at have eyes, too. Of course the genius of *Rear Window* is that the film takes it a step further, as we watch the director watching Jeff watching them—Hitchcock was always aware that going to the movies, sitting in the dark, peering at people's private lives, was a voyeuristic act as well.

It's why so many of his films (*The Pleasure Garden*, *THE LODGER*, *MURDER!*, *THE 39 STEPS*, *SABOTAGE*, *SABOTEUR*, both versions of *THE MAN WHO KNEW TOO MUCH*, and *STAGE FRIGHT*, among them) are set in theaters or concert halls, where violence breaks out and nobody can do anything but watch. Life is a show, but most of us are simply ticketholders stuck in the cheap seats.

References
Sidney Gottlieb, ed., *Alfred Hitchcock: Interviews* (Jackson: University Press of Mississippi, 2003), 195; Laura Mulvey, "Visual Pleasure and Narrative Cinema," *Screen* (Autumn 1975), 6–18; George Ritzer, ed., *Encyclopedia of Social Theory* (Thousand Oaks, CA: SAGE, 2004), 467–68.

MALLESON, MILES (1888–1969)

Surrey-born, Cambridge-educated performer who studied drama with Herbert Beerbohm Tree and made his stage debut in 1911. An educated and versatile actor, he also wrote plays, often about historical subjects or political topics. (One of his dramas, the pacifist *Black 'Ell*, was banned in England.) He cowrote the 1940 film *The Thief of Baghdad*, in which he appeared as the sultan; he also did an early script, never filmed, for a life of T. E. Lawrence and in 1931 cowrote *Sally in Our Alley* with ALMA REVILLE.

For Alfred Hitchcock, Malleson had a bit part in *THE 39 STEPS* as the manager of the Palladium and a larger one as Mr. Fortescue in *STAGE FRIGHT*; for other directors, he made a fine Canon Chasuble in *The Importance of Being Earnest*, presided over the charnel house in the ALASTAIR SIM *Scrooge*, looked forward to hanging Dennis Price in *Kind Hearts and Coronets*, and ghoulishly advertised "Room for one more!" in *Dead of Night*.

Already in his 70s, he got a second career boost with Hammer, which frequently cast him in its period horror films as cabbies and clerics; he had to retire only when his eyesight became too poor for him to continue. He died at 80 in London.

References
Catherine De La Roche, "Miles of Characters," *Picturegoer*, October 1, 1949, http://www.powell-pressburger.org/Reviews/Miles/Miles01.html; "Miles Malleson," *IMDb*, http://www.imdb.com/name/nm0539942/bio?ref_=nm_ov_bio_sm.

MANNHEIM, LUCIE (1899–1976)

Berlin-born performer who became a star in 1920s theater, film, cabaret, and operettas. She played in productions of *A Doll's House* and *Romeo and Juliet*, nearly got the MARLENE DIETRICH part in *The Blue Angel*, and had a contract with the State Theater. That all ended when the Nazis came to power in 1933; Mannheim, who was Jewish, fled, eventually landing in London. Her first film was Hitchcock's *THE 39 STEPS*; she plays the mysterious and colorfully named Annabella Smith.

She continued to act in England and made anti-Nazi broadcasts, but when the war ended, she happily returned to Germany and her career there, although she occasionally came back to Britain for a part; her last film was Otto Preminger's slightly HITCHCOCKIAN *Bunny Lake Is Missing* in 1965.

She died at 77 in Lower Saxony.

References

"Lucie Mannheim," *IMDb*, http://www.imdb.com/name/nm0543169/bio?ref_=nm_ov_bio_sm; Thomas Staedeli, "Lucie Mannheim," *Cyranos*, http://www.cyranos.ch/smmanl-e.htm.

THE MAN WHO KNEW TOO MUCH (GB 1934)

DIRECTOR: Alfred Hitchcock.
SCREENPLAY: Charles Bennett, D. B. Wyndham-Lewis, Edwin Greenwood, A. R. Rawlinson, Emlyn Williams.
PRODUCERS: Ivor Montagu (Sir Michael Balcon, uncredited).
CINEMATOGRAPHY: Curt Courant.
EDITOR: H. St. C. Stewart.
ORIGINAL MUSIC: Arthur Benjamin.
CAST: Leslie Banks (Bob Lawrence), Edna Best (Jill Lawrence), Peter Lorre (Abbott), Nora Pilbeam (Betty Lawrence).
RUNNING TIME: 75 minutes. Black and white.
RELEASED THROUGH: General Film Distributors.

Bob and Jill Lawrence are British tourists in Switzerland, where their young daughter frolics on the slopes. Jill does some sharpshooting, and they meet another amiable vacationer, Louis Bernard. But then Bernard is murdered—and, before dying, whispers details of a conspiracy centering on a dangerous plot in England.

When the Lawrences' daughter is kidnapped—to ensure their silence—they keep the plot to themselves and return to England. There, afraid to involve the authorities, Bob tracks the kidnappers to a chapel in Wapping, where he learns they plan to assassinate a diplomat during a concert at the Royal Albert Hall. He manages to get the information to Jill but is caught and locked away along with their daughter.

Jill foils the assassination by screaming just as the shooter is taking aim, and the police converge on the Wapping chapel. The spies are all killed (except for their leader, who kills himself); Jill herself takes out the assassin as he holds her daughter hostage with one perfectly aimed shot.

One of Hitchcock's greatest successes in Britain (much to the shock of his regular bête noire C. M. WOOLF, who first pronounced it "rubbish") and the only film that the director remade in America—improving it further, he thought. "The first version is the work of a talented amateur," he told FRANÇOIS TRUFFAUT, "and the second was made by a professional." This is uncharacteristically modest.

It is true that the second *The Man Who Knew Too Much* has several, purely budgetary advantages over the first—it's longer, in wide-screen and COLOR, with bigger STARS and real LOCATION work. It also has a slightly darker, more ambiguous tone. But the first film is hardly the work of a novice.

It is the work, though, of a filmmaker in need of a jolt; coming off *WALTZES FROM VIENNA*, Hitchcock was dispirited and without a contract. Producer SIR MICHAEL BALCON approached him about working together again, this time at GAUMONT-BRITISH. Did he have any ideas? Hitchcock suggested a Bulldog Drummond story he had been trying to adapt that revolved around an assassination plot and a child kidnapping.

Balcon and Hitchcock signed the deal, and over many story conferences, the script changed. Drummond dropped out, to be replaced by a typical English couple; a title, *The Man Who Knew Too Much*, was lifted from a G. K. Chesterton book Hitchcock had the rights to. An overly complicated MACGUFFIN—a spy's code traced in ice by figure skater—was changed to a dying man's message.

The opening was set in St. Moritz—where the Hitchcocks had honeymooned—and indeed, the film has a much sunnier view of marital relations than later Hitchcock stories. Bob and Jill Lawrence are devoted spouses and unquestioning equals; their union is solid, and the usual gender roles are fluid. (At the climax, it's the husband who is helpless and held captive; it's the wife who saves the day with her calm marksmanship.)

Although there are one or two uncertain moments—the rather abruptly edited skiing accident at the beginning—most of the film is masterful. Hitchcock once again used the Schüfftan process he'd used in *BLACKMAIL*, this time to expertly fake shots of the Royal Albert Hall; the final shootout at the spy's hideout is done at a breakneck pace.

There are some lovely touches, too, like the shots of EDNA BEST after the couple returns home without their daughter, Hitchcock lighting her scenes so shadows seem to close in on her from every corner. Or the close-up of NOVA PILBEAM as the kidnapped girl, all muffled mouth and wide shining EYES, as she's borne away on a sleigh with tinkling bells.

The Man Who Knew Too Much is very definitely a popular entertainment, and it has some marvelous set pieces, like LESLIE BANKS's struggle with a murderous dentist (or the battle of the folding chairs at the chapel or the assassination during a classical music concert, scenes so successful Hitchcock kept them in the remake).

Yet it also has hints of the more serious Hitchcock, too, and his favorite themes. There are bits of travelogue in between the murders and that violent event at a theater, death as mere diversion. There's also the specter of GUILT, as the British agent cruelly criticizes the parents for giving in to the kidnappers' demands ("Well, if there is any trouble, I hope you remember you're to blame," he says bluntly. "Not a very nice thing to have on one's conscience.")

And it has one of his signature touches—the charming, cultivated, cold-hearted villain—in PETER LORRE, who, sporting a dramatic scar, a strange streak in his hair, and an almost constant chuckle, is Abbott, the gang's leader. What are his real motivations? What, if anything, is his relationship to the dour woman and coconspirator at his side?

We are never sure. But Lorre—who learned his lines phonetically—is the dry, black heart of this picture. And this picture heralded another huge leap forward in Hitchcock's art.

References

Patrick McGilligan, *Alfred Hitchcock: A Life in Darkness and Light* (New York: HarperCollins, 2003), 156–69; Ivor Montagu, "Working with Hitchcock," *Sight and Sound* 49 (Summer 1980), 189–93; Donald Spoto, *The Dark Side of Genius: The Life of Alfred Hitchcock* (New York: Da Capo Press, 1999), 136–44; François Truffaut, *Hitchcock/Truffaut*, rev. ed. (New York: Touchstone, 1985), 88–94.

THE MAN WHO KNEW TOO MUCH (US 1956)

DIRECTOR: Alfred Hitchcock.
SCREENPLAY: John Michael Hayes, based on a story by Charles Bennett and D. B. Wyndham Lewis.
PRODUCERS: Herbert Coleman (Alfred Hitchcock, uncredited).
CINEMATOGRAPHY: Robert Burks.
EDITOR: George Tomasini.
ORIGINAL MUSIC: Bernard Herrmann.
CAST: James Stewart (Ben McKenna), Doris Day (Jo McKenna), Daniel Gelin (Louis Bernard), Reggie Nalder (Rien).
RUNNING TIME: 120 minutes. Color.
RELEASED THROUGH: Paramount.

Ben and Jo McKenna are American tourists in Morocco with their son, Hank. There, they meet another amiable vacationer, Louis Bernard, who helps them navigate Muslim customs and taboos. But then Bernard is murdered—and, before dying, whispers details of a conspiracy, centering on a dangerous plot in England.

When the McKennas' son is kidnapped, though—to ensure their silence—they keep the plot to themselves and go to England. There, Ben tracks the kidnappers to a chapel, where he learns they plan to assassinate a diplomat during a concert. Unable to find Ben but learning that the police have gone to the Royal Albert Hall, Jo hurries there.

There, recognizing a sinister acquaintance from Morocco, she realizes that the murder has been scheduled to happen during the concert. Ben escapes from the chapel and rushes to the hall; Jo's screams disrupt the assassination plot, and when Ben struggles with the gunman, the assassin falls to his death.

Feted at the diplomat's embassy, Jo and Ben realize that the plotters are there, too, along with Hank. When Jo sings a favorite song, Hank whistles along from upstairs—and Ben runs upstairs to rescue him.

The second version of *The Man Who Knew Too Much* isn't, on first viewing, one of Hitchcock's most interesting films. But it's fascinating to see how he approached the same material more than 20 years later and what he changed because of how he'd changed.

He had first wanted to redo the material in America for DAVID O. SELZNICK; an early memo dating back to 1941 suggested beginning the remake in Sun Valley, ID, staging the near-fatal concert at New York's Metropolitan Opera, and then crossing the Hudson to the spies' redoubt in New Jersey. It didn't happen.

But it wasn't until the mid-'50s that Hitchcock circled back, entrusting regular collaborator JOHN MICHAEL HAYES with the script (Hitchcock reportedly told him the basic story but warned him not to watch the earlier version) and quickly casting the film with JAMES STEWART and DORIS DAY, an actress he'd liked very much in the thriller *Storm Warning*.

There was LOCATION shooting in Morocco before the production returned to California, and while Stewart was used to Hitchcock at this point, Day found his remoteness disturbing. (She was also upset by the way she saw the North Africans treating their beasts of burden, an experience that only intensified her lifelong commitment to animal welfare.)

Day was so rattled on the set, in fact, that finally she told Hitchcock she would quit if he were unsatisfied. To her surprise, he not only told her he approved of her performance but also that he was far more insecure than she could ever be. "He said he was more frightened—of life, of rejection, of relationships—than anyone," she recalled later. "He told me he was afraid to walk across the lot to the PARAMOUNT commissary because he was so afraid of people. I remember feeling so sorry for him when he told me this, and from that point on I felt more relaxed about working for him."

Yet, returning to a story that he'd first done in England in 1934, you can feel Hitchcock luxuriating in his hard-won power and capabilities. The moody BLACK AND WHITE is replaced by gorgeous COLOR (fully utilized in the souk sequence, with a trail of blue dye instead of crimson blood marking a victim's final stagger). The wide-screen is well used, too (although it's the close-ups that linger emotionally), and he has not only two major STARS but also a soon-to-be hit song, "Que Sera, Sera" (albeit one sung at a somewhat painful volume).

Yet in some ways, this is a rather darker, riskier film than the first. In the first The Man Who Knew Too Much—set in the Hitchcocks' own posh honeymoon destination of cool St. Moritz—the English couple is devoted, attentive. In this one—set in uncomfortable, sticky North Africa—they're quarrelsome, a little moody.

Throughout the first half hour or so, in fact, Ben and Jo seem just a drink or a day away from what she characterizes as one of their "monthly" quarrels. She wants another child. He doesn't. She's beginning to chafe at having given up her singing career to be a midwestern doctor's wife. He doesn't understand. They're on an exotic vacation, and all he can think about are the various unpleasant surgeries he did to pay for it.

The contrast with the first film is striking. In the 1934 version, the duo shares the bad news of their child's kidnapping together and supports each other. In the 1956 one, Ben secretly slips her a sedative before telling her the truth. In the first film, it's the wife who literally saves the day by

first foiling the assassination and then by killing the assassin. In the second, it's the husband who has to arrive and finish the job both times. The first The Man Who Knew Too Much is about a happy marriage surviving a crisis. The second The Man Who Knew Too Much is about an unhappy marriage surviving a crisis because the man has the primary role in the relationship and reasserts it.

Hitchcock said that the second film was the better, "professional" one, but modern audiences may not share his preference. Still, Day gives a lovely performance—particularly in the slowly building scenes of hysteria as she realizes that her child has been kidnapped. There are some nice faces among the supporting players, including CAROLYN JONES as a friend and BRENDA DE BANZIE as the most conflicted of the kidnappers. (Although PETER LORRE is badly missed, REGGIE NALDER is a frightening presence as the actual assassin, but the spy ring here doesn't have the color and character it did in the original film.)

Is the 1956 version of The Man Who Knew Too Much a better film than the 1934 one? No. But it's a far more intriguing one—as an illustration both of the blandishments that Hollywood had provided Hitchcock and of his own movies' increasingly dark view of marriage and women.

References
Quentin Falk, *Mr. Hitchcock* (London: Haus, 2007), 132; A. E. Hotchner, *Doris Day: Her Own Story* (New York: William Morrow, 1975), 152; Patrick McGilligan, *Alfred Hitchcock: A Life in Darkness and Light* (New York: HarperCollins, 2003), 515–22; Patrick McGilligan, ed., *Backstory: Interviews with Screenwriters of the 60s* (Berkeley: University of California Press, 1997), 174–92; Donald Spoto, *The Dark Side of Genius: The Life of Alfred Hitchcock*

(New York: Da Capo Press, 1999), 359–67; François Truffaut, *Hitchcock/Truffaut*, rev. ed. (New York: Touchstone, 1985), 227–33.

THE MANXMAN (GB 1929)

DIRECTOR: Alfred Hitchcock.
SCREENPLAY: Eliot Stannard, based on the novel by Hall Caine.
PRODUCER: Uncredited (John Maxwell).
CINEMATOGRAPHY: Jack Cox.
EDITOR: Emile de Ruelle.
CAST: Carl Brisson (Pete Quilliam), Anny Ondra (Kate Cregeen), Malcolm Keen (Philip Christian).
RUNNING TIME: 110 minutes. Black and white.
RELEASED THROUGH: Wardour Films.

Two young friends on the Isle of Man grow up to take different paths, Pete becoming a fisherman and Philip, an attorney. Pete asks local beauty Kate to marry him, but her father is opposed; leaving the island to make a success of himself, Pete asks Philip to keep an eye on his girl.

Of course Philip and Kate soon fall in love, but just as they've begun plans to wed and Philip to take over the job of chief magistrate, Pete returns, a wealthy man. With her father now approving of the match, Kate agrees to marry Pete instead, but her heart is torn, and she holds a guilty secret— she is already pregnant with Philip's child.

One child and a year later, she decides to leave Pete for Philip—but Philip, concerned about his position in the town, won't have her. A hysterical Kate tries to kill herself but fails. Finally, Philip relents, and he, Kate, and their baby leave the isle; Pete is left alone, robbed of everything.

Hitchcock's last silent is both a farewell and a sort of summing-up; like *THE RING*, it features a love triangle, and like *DOWN-HILL*, it highlights the contrasting fortunes

of two friends. And it looks ahead a bit to films to come; like *THE SKIN GAME*, it's about class differences, and unlike JAMAICA INN, which was merely set in Cornwall, *The Manxman* was filmed there and makes full use of its rough seascapes. And, of course, like so many of Hitchcock's films—at the time and to come—it centers on GUILT.

The Victorian melodrama is a little too obvious (the original novel, billed as the "famous story" in the credits, had been a best seller in the 1890s), but Hitchcock used a small cast, including CARL BRISSON, who had been in *The Ring*, and Malcolm Keen, who had been in *THE MOUNTAIN EAGLE* and *THE LODGER*. (Best is ANNY ONDRA, unencumbered here by her Czech accent; she would work for Hitchcock again in *BLACKMAIL*.)

The cinematography by loyal collaborator JACK COX is fine, too, and Hitchcock's sense of visuals and editing is clear and economical—as in a scene played without titles, where Pete joyfully returns and Kate and Philip have to conceal their own guilty feelings. Sin and its consequences are really the main characters in the piece; although, when Pete is thought dead and Kate exclaims to Philip, "We're free!"—as Ruth does to Logan in *I CONFESS*—there is no escape from punishment; the reckoning is at hand. (As Hitchcock emphasizes with occasional cuts to a giant millstone, grinding away.)

Like almost all of Hitchcock's early English films, it seems, this one had a producer (this time John Maxwell at BRITISH INTERNATIONAL PICTURES) convinced it would be a failure; in fact, the film was a solid hit and earned Hitchcock strong reviews for his handling of the material. But the director never really warmed to the project; it was done as a piece of work, begun only two weeks after the birth of his daughter, and he was already looking forward eagerly to what might come next.

References

Patrick McGilligan, *Alfred Hitchcock: A Life in Darkness and Light* (New York: HarperCollins, 2003), 106; François Truffaut, *Hitchcock/Truffaut*, rev. ed. (New York: Touchstone, 1985), 61.

MARMONT, PERCY (1883–1977)

London-born performer and longtime leading man whose career encompasses both the first silent-film version of *Lord Jim* and Hammer's first sci-fi picture, *Four-Sided Triangle*; in between, he costarred with Clara Bow in *Mantrap* and played small parts in three films for Hitchcock as the lover in *RICH AND STRANGE*, as the father in *YOUNG AND INNOCENT*, and as the unlucky Caypor in *SECRET AGENT*. He died in London at 93.

References

Hal Erickson, "Percy Marmont," *Silent Hollywood*, http://silenthollywood.com/percymarmont.html; "Percy Marmont," *IMDb*, http://www.imdb.com/name/nm0549385/bio?ref_=nm_ov_bio_sm.

MARNIE (US 1964)

DIRECTOR: Alfred Hitchcock.
SCREENPLAY: Jay Presson Allen, from the novel by Winston Graham.
PRODUCER: Uncredited (Alfred Hitchcock).
CINEMATOGRAPHY: Robert Burks.
EDITOR: George Tomasini.
ORIGINAL MUSIC: Bernard Herrmann.
CAST: Tippi Hedren (Marnie Edgar), Sean Connery (Mark Rutland), Alan Napier (Mr. Rutland), Diane Baker (Lil Mainwaring), Louise Latham (Bernice Edgar), Martin Gabel (Sidney Strutt).
RUNNING TIME: 130 minutes. Color.
RELEASED THROUGH: Universal.

Cold and calculating—and yet still desperate for her aging mother's love—Marnie Edgar is a professional thief who moves from office job to office job, changing her name and hair color, using false references and a fake social security number, and then absconding with the company funds. When she applies for a job at Mark Rutland's publishing company, however, he recognizes her as the same woman who recently embezzled money from an acquaintance, Sidney Strutt. Rutland finds Marnie's duplicity intriguing, and so the handsome widower hires her.

She steals from him, too, of course, but Rutland finds where she's hiding—and reveals that he knows about her previous crimes, too. He blackmails her into marrying him, much to the disgust of his former sister-in-law. It's clearly an unhealthy relationship and only grows unhealthier—in addition to her compulsive thievery and phobias about thunderstorms and the color red, Marnie declares she can't bear to have men touch her. When Rutland rapes her on their wedding night, she tries to kill herself.

After their return home, Marnie only grows more disturbed, finally having a breakdown during a foxhunt when she finds herself surrounded by the color red—and, due to its broken leg, is forced to shoot her own beloved horse. Finally, Rutland insists on taking her back to her hometown of Baltimore to confront her mother.

They do, and eventually, the truth comes out. Marnie's mother's self-righteousness stems from her shame over her own past as a prostitute. Marnie's phobias arise from the repressed memory of a childhood trauma, when she killed one of her mother's clients during a thunderstorm. And Marnie's kleptomania is merely a way to replace the love she never felt she got with "things."

The couple leaves together under slowly brightening skies.

One of Hitchcock's greatest films or greatest failures? More than 50 years after its premiere, *Marnie* continues to spur controversy and, like its heroine, strong passions.

Its beginnings were convoluted. Hitchcock bought the rights to the WINSTON GRAHAM novel about a compulsive thief (and the man who yearns for her) in 1961, hoping to use it to lure GRACE KELLY away from her throne and back to acting, at least for one movie. Having had a congenial collaboration with JOSEPH STEFANO on *PSYCHO*, he asked him to write up a script.

Stefano, who was interested in psychology, dove in, turning in a treatment that he felt combined some aspects of *SPELLBOUND* (a psychiatrist who treated Marnie was a central character) and of *NOTORIOUS*. (Marnie formed the apex of a romantic triangle, with two men, already rivals in real life, rivals for her romantic attentions, as well.)

But then Kelly ruled out a return to the screen, and without her, Hitchcock lost interest. Stefano went on to his own project, the TV anthology series *The Outer Limits*, and Hitchcock began to develop *THE BIRDS* with screenwriter EVAN HUNTER.

It was while working on that film, however, that Hitchcock suddenly imagined its STAR, his discovery TIPPI HEDREN, as Marnie. Another script was commissioned, this time from Hunter, but the writer worried about a central scene in which the SEXUALLY repressed heroine is raped on her wedding night by the hero. Hitchcock was very insistent on it being in the picture and talked at length about the shots he'd already planned out; Hunter thought the sequence was not only offensive but also unworkable. No male character, Hunter declared, could retain the audience's sympathy after such an act.

Hunter ended up writing the scene under protest but also wrote his own version of the honeymoon, without the rape, and sent them both to Hitchcock with a note, asking him to read both and consider the alternative pages. Hitchcock simply fired him and hired another screenwriter, JAY PRESSON ALLEN, to do yet another script.

Although it seemed like an odd choice after the first two writers had failed—Allen was a novelist and a successful playwright whose grasp of screenwriting was tenuous—it could also be seen as doubly pragmatic. As a newcomer, Allen was unlikely to argue with Hitchcock over what the script did or didn't need; as a woman, she gave him cover in case there were any critical objections over the rape scene. (Allen herself had no objections; years later, she blithely asserted that she'd never seen it as a scene of a sexual assault but merely of a couple going through a "trying marital situation.") Script finally in hand, and with more pliant collaborators than Kelly and Hunter onboard, Hitchcock could finally proceed.

Yet the film's production—due to start on November 25, 1963—was delayed by the national days of mourning over John F. Kennedy's assassination, and the rest of the shoot remained shadowed by a dark mood. Although Hitchcock and star SEAN CONNERY seemed to get on relatively well—the director always liked leading men who simply got down to business—he was alternately brusque and overfamiliar with costar DIANE BAKER and MARIETTE HARTLEY, who had a small part as Marnie's coworker. At one point, Baker said, he even approached her in her dressing room and unexpectedly kissed her.

Everyone who was present noted his relationship with Hedren, his once heralded discovery, had changed; he grew more and more controlling (forbidding her, for example, to attend an award ceremony), and she grew more and more resistant. Eventually they stopped speaking to each other entirely, although the reason was unclear. The most that Hitchcock would ever say was that she had committed the unforgivable sin of cruelly referring to his weight; years later, Hedren would publicly state that he had demanded she become his mistress and, when she refused, told her that he would ruin her career.

Although many people, including Baker, back up parts of Hedren's story, others disagree; what no one disputes is that it was an unhappy set by the end of filming, and Hitchcock seemed even more removed from the actual day-to-day filmmaking than usual. Fifty years later, though, what remains—most clearly, most vividly—is the film itself. And in some ways, it is as open for interpretation—or even angry argument—as the circumstances under which it was made.

Marnie was meant, as Hitchcock always stated, as a film about a FETISH and, outside of the director's films, probably a very rare one: hybristophilia, in which the fetishist is sexually attracted to criminals. In many of Hitchcock's films, this is treated lightly—for example, in the chase films (*THE 39 STEPS*, *SABOTEUR*), in which the woman has a love/hate attraction for the suspicious man on the run, or the caper films (*FAMILY PLOT*, *TO CATCH A THIEF*), in which the bad-boy criminal exerts a certain sexual fascination. In the pitch-dark *Marnie*, though, the very core of the film is, as Hitchcock frankly told FRANÇOIS TRUFFAUT, the "fetish idea. A man wants to go to bed with a thief because she is a thief, just like other men have a yen for a Chinese or a colored woman. Unfortunately this concept doesn't come across on screen. . . . To put it bluntly, we'd have to have Sean Connery catching the girl robbing the safe and show that he felt like jumping at her and raping her on the spot."

He didn't include that scene but only because he found it dramatically implausible; the film, though, very much shows

that Mark Rutland is sexually obsessed with Marnie (he remembers her, months after a chance meeting, as the "brunette with the legs") and particularly excited by her slippery deviousness. And she knows it. "You don't love me," she says, as he begins blackmailing her into marriage. "I'm just something you've caught. You think I'm some sort of animal you've trapped!" "That's right, you are," Mark answers. "And I've caught something wild this time, haven't I? I've tracked you and caught you and by God I'm going to keep you!"

That animalistic theme is braided through the movie. Before he took over the family publishing business, Mark was a zoologist; the only thing Marnie is passionate about is horses ("Oh Florio," she says to hers, "if you want to bite somebody, bite me!") His father, Marks says, believes in "animal lust"; even the names of the characters—Strutt, Rutland—suggest swaggering males and the mating season. All of which could lead to a very easy reading of the film as an endorsement of rape culture and brutal male privilege—Marnie is a neurotic, frigid little girl, and what she needs is a real man to snap her out of it.

Except.

Except that Marnie's troubles began with the lusts of men and the constant paying parade of sailors to her MOTHER's flat—including, finally, the slightly drunken, awkwardly violent customer that led to Marnie killing him and embarking on decades of crippling neurosis, partial amnesia, horrible phobias, and sexual repression.

Except that our sympathies, clearly, are with Marnie throughout. She's very much still a child—so much so that, when she visits her mother, she's jealous of the little girl she babysits, that, when Mark finally pulls off her nightgown, she can only answer him with the shocked catatonic gaze of the abused innocent. She is a naïf, a lover of pretty things and animals. She is more sinned against than sinning.

Hitchcock builds that sympathy slowly, introducing us to Marnie as a dark femme fatale, walking away from the camera (and leaving the scene of her latest crime). She is merely a collection of parts at first—arm, legs, hands, hair. But then she washes the black—the GUILT—out of her hair, and with a swell of music, we get her first close-up and see her shining face at last, clean and young and innocent.

Of course, Marnie is not innocent—not really—but she is a bit of a child, emotionally frozen back at that first moment of long-ago crisis, and Hitchcock reinforces that over the course of the movie with her love of animals, with her irrational panics, with her unmet yearning to simply put her head in her mother's lap and have the cold, crabby woman slowly brush her hair.

It's what makes Mark's marital assault on her all the more upsetting; it seems not just a rape but also an act of child abuse. (Bolstered, perhaps, by Hitchcock's own fetishes, as well as the CENSORS of the time—we see nothing womanly of the naked Marnie, only her bare, vulnerable legs.) How can we not sympathize with Marnie when Mark says things like "I'm fighting an impulse to beat the hell out of you"? The complication at the heart of *Marnie* is that, however Hitchcock intended it, whatever issues he may have been confronting by making it, however much the movie details the complete brutalization of a woman, it always remains firmly on her side.

It is easy to not see that, just as it is easy to focus on the movie's supposed technical flaws. There are some scenes of back projection that fail to convince; the sequence of Marnie horseback riding is flagrantly unreal, with odd editing and a fake horse (borrowed from the special-effects department at Disney); the set for Marnie's childhood neighborhood is dominated by an obvious matte painting; and the final theft is punctuated with the sort of flashy zooms that less talented directors were soon to embrace.

But it was ROBIN WOOD who first argued that the falsity of these effects were intentional, and while that may seem like the most flimsy of apologias, there is a strong, demonstrable support for that. After all, Hitchcock had often and rightly used unrealistic, even EXPRESSIONIS-TIC, effects to mirror a character's disturbed mental state—the spinning lights that Jill sees before passing out in the first *THE MAN WHO KNEW TOO MUCH*, the spinning faces that haunt Iris after her accident in *THE LADY VANISHES*, the disorienting perspectives that bedevil Scottie in *VERTIGO* (and are reprised, briefly here at the end, as we slip back into the past for Marnie's flashback memory, and the apartment seems to shift in size and dimensions before our eyes). Isn't it just as likely that *Marnie* looks unreal because Marnie herself has lost grip with reality?

Look again to the honeymoon sequence, with Marnie and Mark taking a very long Pacific voyage. From the moment they board the ship to the moment they leave, we barely see one other person—not a passenger, not even a steward. When, on the morning of Marnie's suicide attempt, Mark runs down the ship's decks, they are absolutely empty. Is this the unintentional mistake of a director who was too bored or distracted or sexually frustrated to bother hiring extras? Or is this just a very deliberate effect from a filmmaker who wanted to show just how alone, and ultimately how codependent, these two suddenly married people were?

Certainly *Marnie*, like Marnie, has its problems. Connery is absurdly unbelievable as a Philadelphian preppie (with ALAN NAPIER as his British-accented father, to boot), and although Hedren manages the hysteria well, her calmer moments are flat and forced, her line readings ranging from amateurish to arch. Despite a few bravura sequences—such as Marnie's second robbery, as she tries to slip out of an office past a charwoman—the film is slowly paced.

And yet there's a duality to the film that fascinates and is a part of all of Hitchcock's films. It's just that, in much of his other work, that tension—guilt and innocence—is embodied in one character. Here, it's in the film—and perhaps the filmmaker—as *Marnie* struggles with both tormenting its heroine and grieving over the indignity she suffers. The film is about abuse, yes—but also the abuser's conscience.

References

Jay Presson Allen, interview with the author, June 1999; Diane Baker, interview with the author, September 2015; Patrick McGilligan, *Alfred Hitchcock: A Life in Darkness and Light* (New York: HarperCollins, 2003), 635–49; Patrick McGilligan, ed., *Backstory: Interviews with Screenwriters of the 60s* (Berkeley: University of California Press, 1997), 15–42; Donald Spoto, *The Dark Side of Genius: The Life of Alfred Hitchcock* (New York: Da Capo Press, 1999), 468–76; Donald Spoto, *Spellbound by Beauty: Alfred Hitchcock and His Leading Ladies* (New York: Harmony Books, 2008), 261–77; *The Trouble with Marnie*, directed by Laurent Bouzereau (2000), documentary, http://the.hitchcock.zone/wiki/The_Trouble_with_Marnie_%282000%29_-_transcript; François Truffaut, *Hitchcock/Truffaut*, rev. ed. (New York: Touchstone, 1985), 300–307; Robin Wood, *Hitchcock's Films* (New York: Paperback Library, 1969), 163–95.

MARSHALL, HERBERT
(1890–1966)

London-born performer who came from a theatrical family—and, having seen the cold hotel rooms and meager meals that went with playing the provinces, vowed early not to follow his parents into the profession. Instead, he went to college to study business and after graduation got a job as an accountant. He was so bad with numbers, though, that his employer fired him; his next position, through a family friend, was as the assistant business manager of an acting company. Eventually, he was lured onstage to take a part or two and, realizing he was better at acting than accounting, decided to commit.

He left the stage to enlist in World War I; sent into the trenches, he was shot in the knee, and after a series of badly botched operations, the doctors finally amputated his right leg. Marshall fell into a depression—a condition he would battle all his life—but eventually decided to return to the stage outfitted with an artificial limb. He soon had a series of successes on the West End and Broadway, where he put his beautifully modulated voice to use in everything from Noel Coward to Shakespeare. (His Jacques in *As You Like It* was supposed to be particularly fine.)

Marshall's mellow delivery made him a prized property when sound films came in, and his blasé manner was adaptable to amused bystanders, tender lovers, detached narrators, betrayed husbands, or even (rarely) cold killers. He is the hero in Hitchcock's *MURDER!* and, a decade later, returned to play the villain in the director's *FOREIGN CORRESPONDENT*; in between, his wife at the time, EDNA BEST, costarred in the original version of *THE MAN WHO KNEW TOO MUCH*. (Their daughter, Sarah Marshall, also went on to appear in three episodes of Hitchcock's television shows.)

The gentlemanly Marshall had a strong attraction for and to women—he was married five times and, after relocating to Hollywood, played opposite almost all of the era's female stars, from Greta Garbo and Bette Davis to Joan Crawford and MAR-

LENE DIETRICH. (Undoubtedly his genuine modesty—he was dependable, professional, and loathe to upstage—helped.) That he had a wooden leg was something he worked hard to conceal with the help of his directors; when necessary, scenes (such as his famous death in *The Little Foxes*) were carefully choreographed to keep his disability hidden.

To his immense great credit, though, during the war, he spent a great deal of time traveling to military hospitals, where he spoke to wounded veterans, particularly amputees, giving nonpitying, practical advice (even showing one worried young man how, even with a prosthesis, he could still take his sweetheart dancing). Marshall never publicized the visits—he was angry when a movie magazine finally did—and paid for his own travel and expenses.

After the war, Marshall—like many members of Hollywood's ENGLISH COLONY—found the sort of suave gentleman they used to specialize in less in demand. Unlike many, though, he stayed, finding roles in period films, sci-fi pictures, and television shows. He is in two episodes of *ALFRED HITCHCOCK PRESENTS*; he played the inquisitive inspector in the Vincent Price film *The Fly* (a script so absurd, Price later said, that he and Marshall sometimes had to be shot separately; every time they made eye contact, they burst into laughter).

Marshall had always been emotionally sensitive, and his war injury had left him in constant discomfort and occasional pain; in 1965, he checked himself into the Motion Picture Relief Fund Hospital for depression. He stayed until January 1966; barely a week after his release, he had a fatal heart attack in Beverly Hills. He was 75.

References

"Herbert Marshall," *Hollywood.com*, http://www.hollywood.com/celebrities/herbert-marshall-57294374; "Herbert Marshall," *IMDb*, http://www.imdb.com/name/nm0003339/bio?ref_=nm_ov_bio_sm; David Thomson, *The New Biographical Dictionary of Film* (New York: Knopf, 2002), 566–67.

MARY (GB 1931)

DIRECTOR: Alfred Hitchcock.
SCREENPLAY: Alma Reville, Herbert Juttke, George C. Klaren, based on the novel *Enter Sir John* by Clemence Dane and Helen Simpson.
PRODUCERS: Uncredited.
CINEMATOGRAPHY: Jack Cox.
EDITOR: Uncredited.
ORIGINAL MUSIC: Uncredited.
CAST: Alfred Abel (Sir John Menier), Olga Tchechowa (Mary Baring).
RUNNING TIME: 78 minutes. Black and white. In German.
RELEASED THROUGH: Sud-Film.

During the very early days of talkies, before the intricacies of postproduction dubbing had been worked out, occasionally two versions of the same film would be shot in shifts, the second using the identical sets but with a translated script and a foreign cast and crew. This is BRITISH INTERNATIONAL PICTURES' made-for-export version of *MURDER!* done in German; as Hitchcock had studied the language in school and picked up a little more from his shoots there in the mid-'20s, he stayed on as director, working with his regular technical collaborators but imported actors. For Hitchcock—who found even shooting one film, once he'd worked it out in his head, a bore—the experience was not a happy one.

Although he spoke German well enough to make himself understood, he couldn't really grasp the nuances of the actors' performances, and while HERBERT MARSHALL had been charming on the first set,

262 ■ *MARY ROSE*

Alfred Abel, his Teutonic replacement, was humorless and argumentative, and the plot was changed to eliminate the "half-caste" element. The film, perhaps to Hitchcock's relief, was long considered to be lost; a print, however, recently resurfaced in Germany, and it is now included as an extra on some DVD editions of other Hitchcock films.

Reference

Patrick McGilligan, *Alfred Hitchcock: A Life in Darkness and Light* (New York: Harper-Collins, 2003), 136–39.

MARY ROSE

Hitchcock saw this J. M. Barrie play during its original 1920 production in London and was immediately entranced by it; a twist on the author's earlier *Peter Pan*, in this drama, the story is not about a boy who refuses to grow up but about a young woman who doesn't grow old.

The play revolves around two odd occurrences. In the first, Mary Rose is a young child vacationing with her father on a remote Scottish island when she disappears. She reappears three weeks later, unharmed but with no memory of what happened during her time away. In the second act, Mary Rose is now a wife and MOTHER who has a sudden urge to revisit that fateful island; once again she disappears. She reappears not weeks but decades later, unaged, to find her son a grown man. No explanation is ever given for the vanishings.

Hitchcock tried several times to make this into a film, first speaking to Darryl F. Zanuck at Fox about it as a follow-up to *LIFEBOAT*. The mogul wasn't interested, but almost 20 years later, Hitchcock announced that he would be doing the Barrie play under the title *The Island That Likes to Be Visited*; he had JAY PRESSON ALLEN write a script and ALBERT WHITLOCK draw up some preproduction sketches. TIPPI HEDREN was to star.

But the relationship with Hedren ended acrimoniously, and in any case, the studio was determined to keep the "Master of Suspense" churning out thrillers; a ghostly romance, Hitchcock sadly told Whitlock, "isn't what the audiences expect of me." Although the director occasionally spoke wistfully of the project—and its influence may be seen in *VERTIGO*—he was never able to get it financed. (UNIVERSAL was so opposed to the project, he sometimes swore, they'd had a specific prohibition against making the film written into his contract.)

In an odd twist of fate, 20 years after Hitchcock's death, MELANIE GRIFFITH—Tippi Hedren's daughter—bought the rights and commissioned a new screenplay. But it, too, was never made, and *Mary Rose*—like her namesake—remains maddeningly out of reach.

References

Patrick McGilligan, *Alfred Hitchcock: A Life in Darkness and Light* (New York: HarperCollins, 2003), 650–53; Donald Spoto, *The Dark Side of Genius: The Life of Alfred Hitchcock* (New York: Da Capo Press, 1999), 62, 474–76; François Truffaut, *Hitchcock/Truffaut*, rev. ed. (New York: Touchstone, 1985), 308–9.

MASON, JAMES (1909–1984)

Yorkshire-born performer, the son of a wealthy merchant, who studied architecture at Cambridge, where he began doing amateur theatricals. After graduating, he went out on some auditions for fun and by 24 was at the Old Vic, acting under the formidable influence of Tyrone Guthrie. He had yet to take an acting class and never would. Still, Mason's dark good looks and seductive voice made him successful early on, particularly in films; he came to particular prominence in the 1940s, where his satiny menace enlivened *The Wicked Lady* with MARGARET LOCKWOOD; *Fanny by Gaslight* with Phyllis Calvert; and *The Seventh Veil* with poor, brutalized ANN TODD.

By the late '40s, Mason was in *Odd Man Out* and perhaps Britain's biggest male STAR—even more of an accomplishment as, registering as a conscientious objector, he had refused to serve in World War II, a stance that could have crippled his career. But while his fans could accept that, they could not forgive him leaving for America, which he did as the next decade dawned—an act many seemed to take as a true desertion.

Still, Mason prospered in his new home, giving a fine performance as the tragic Norman Maine in the (butchered) George Cukor version of *A Star Is Born* and becoming a fantasy hero in *20,000 Leagues under the Sea* and *Journey to the Center of the Earth*. For Hitchcock, he played Vandamm, the cultured spymaster who refuses to believe that Roger Thornhill isn't George Kaplan. Elegant and respected, he's a type seen before in *THE 39 STEPS* and *SABOTEUR*, but Mason gave him an extra bit of weary humor. ("That wasn't very sporting, using real bullets.")

Director and star had a professional, if somewhat distant, relationship on the set. "You can see from the way he uses actors that he sees them as animated props," Mason said later of Hitchcock. "He casts his films very, very carefully and he knows perfectly well in advance that all the actors that he chooses are perfectly capable of playing the parts he gives them, without any special directorial effort on his part. He gets some sort of a charge out of directing the leading ladies, I think, but that's something else."

Mason worked on an episode of *ALFRED HITCHCOCK PRESENTS*, played Maxim in a TV remake of *REBECCA*, and was the best thing about Stanley Kubrick's heavily adapted *Lolita*; following this, he began to move into supporting parts, with memorable ones in *Georgy Girl*, *Child's Play*, *The Boys from Brazil*, and *Salem's Lot*. His last great role was as the unscrupulous lawyer in *The Verdict*, for which he received his third Oscar nomination. Once again, he did not win.

Mason, who had suffered a heart attack the year he made *NORTH BY NORTHWEST*, had a second, fatal one at his home in Switzerland at age 75.

References

"James Mason," *IMDb*, http://www.imdb.com/name/nm0000051/bio?ref_=nm_ov_bio_sm; Brian McFarlane, "James Mason," *BFI Screenonline*, http://www.screenonline.org.uk/people/id/447497/index.html; David Thomson, "Every Word a Poison Dart," *Guardian*, May 14, 2009, http://www.theguardian.com/film/2009/may/15/james-mason; David Thomson, *The New Biographical Dictionary of Film* (New York: Knopf, 2002), 571–72.

MASSEY, ANNA (1937–2011)

Sussex-born performer, daughter of Canadian actor Raymond Massey and British actress Adrianne Allen, who began her career with a stroke of luck. Only 17 and then concerned only with the London social scene, she was spied by playwright William Douglas Home, who thought her perfect casting for his new play *The Reluctant Debutante*. The real-life debutante accepted without reluctance and was a hit in the play both in England and on Broadway. Her film career began in 1958.

With her boyish figure and sharp, inquisitive features, Massey wasn't an obvious choice for movies, but she had fine roles in several thrillers, including the pre-*PSYCHO* psycho thriller *Peeping Tom* and Otto Preminger's HITCHCOCKIAN *Bunny Lake Is Missing*. Massey later called Preminger "one of the cruelest and most unpleasant directors that I have ever worked with," but she had a better time on FRENZY; she'd gone in to read for the smaller part of the receptionist, and Hitchcock chose her for Babs instead, the good-hearted barmaid who ends up stuffed into a potato sack.

It was a relaxed set, she remembered later, with Hitchcock beginning most scenes by telling a "dirty schoolboy JOKE" ("He did that to relax you, because it relaxed him"), at first paying attention to "every detail—clothes and COLORS and sets and dressings. But then he got slow physically. Off the set the only conversation that seemed to interest him was about FOOD—he taught me how to make a good batter—and later I realized that this was apt at a time we were making a film so crowded with food."

Despite the privilege she'd been born into, Massey's life was not untroubled; she had difficult relationships with both parents, as well as with her brother, Daniel, also an actor; her first husband, Jeremy Brett, left her for a man, and in the late '60s, she suffered a nervous breakdown. But she put her life back together and eventually resumed a busy and lauded career onstage and on television (including a new adaptation of REBECCA, in which she played Mrs. Danvers). She died in London at 73 from cancer.

References

"Anna Massey," IMDb, http://www.imdb.com/name/nm0557281/bio?ref_=nm_ov_bio_sm; "Anna Massey Obituary," Telegraph, July 4, 2011, http://www.telegraph.co.uk/news/obituaries/culture-obituaries/tv-radio-obituaries/8615826/Anna-Massey.html; Anthony Hayward, "Anna Massey, Award-Winning Actress on Stage, Film and Television," Independent, July 5, 2004, http://www.independent.co.uk/news/obituaries/anna-massey-awardwinning-actress-on-stage-film-and-television-acclaimed-for-her-subtlety-and-intelligence-2306941.html; Peter Maitland, "Anna Massey Recalls Sudden Leap to Stardom on Stage," November 23, 1956, Saskatoon Star-Phoenix, https://news.google.com/newspapers?id=16lkAAAAIBAJ&sjid=E28NAAAAIBAJ&pg=4773,3328168&dq=anna-massey&hl=en; The Story of Frenzy, directed by Laurent Bouzereau (2000), documentary, http://the.hitchcock.zone/wiki/The_Story_of_Frenzy_%282001%29_-_transcript.

MATÉ, RUDOLPH (1898–1964)

Krakow-born cinematographer, active in films since 1919. He was an assistant to Karl Freund and worked on many of director Carl Dreyer's pictures, including the starkly beautiful The Passion of Joan of Arc and the grayly nightmarish Vampyr.

Part of the vast European exodus of Jewish talent during the early '30s, Maté relocated to Hollywood, where one of his first jobs was on the hallucinatory Dante's Inferno in 1935; subsequent highlights included the deep-focus compositions of William Wyler's Dodsworth and the rain-swept assassination sequence and thrilling airplane crash in Hitchcock's FOREIGN CORRESPONDENT.

Maté continued as a cinematographer into the late '40s (including some uncredited work on Orson Welles's The Lady from Shanghai) before moving into directing; among his films are the grimy noir classic D.O.A. and the effects-heavy When Worlds Collide. He died of a heart attack in Beverly Hills at 66.

References

"Rudolph Maté," IMDb, http://www.imdb.com/name/nm0005789/bio?ref_=nm_ov_bio_sm; "Rudolph Maté," Internet Encyclopedia of Cinematographers, http://www.cinematographers.nl/GreatDoPh/mate.htm.

MATHERS, JERRY (1948–)

Iowa-born performer who began modeling as a toddler for a local department store. TV commercials soon followed and then movies, with *Son of Paleface* in 1952. His unspoiled attitude and nearly complete checklist of cute-kid clichés—cowlicks, freckles, slightly buck teeth—won him regular work in Hollywood; his first sizable part was in *THE TROUBLE WITH HARRY* in 1955 as SHIRLEY MACLAINE's son.

Two years later, he got the starring role in the *Leave It to Beaver* sitcom, which ran until 1963; almost as innocent as his onscreen character, after the show ended, Mathers graduated high school, went on to college (he got his degree in philosophy from Berkeley), and enlisted in the Air Force Reserve, serving for nearly six years. Mathers returned to show business in his 30s, first appearing in TV spinoffs of the original *Beaver* show but doing live appearances and even Broadway as well. In 1998, he published his memoirs, *And Jerry Mathers as the Beaver*. Like him, they were squeaky clean.

References
Jerry Mathers, http://www.jerrymathers .com; "Jerry Mathers," *IMDb*, http:// www.imdb.com/name/nm0558487/ bio?ref_=nm_ov_bio_sm.

MATTHEWS, JESSIE (1907–1981)

London-born performer from a large, working-class family who first went onstage as a dancer at the age of 12. She was a star by 17, soon appearing in stage hits by Rodgers and Hart and Noel Coward, introducing the Cole Porter song "Let's Do It, Let's Fall in Love," and captivating countless males, whether they were costars, royals, or even homosexuals. "No man was safe in her presence," recalled JOHN GIELGUD.

She made her movie debut in 1923 and was the (expensive) costar of *WALTZES FROM VIENNA*; according to her leading man, ESMOND KNIGHT, Hitchcock failed to hide his dislike of both actors and was particularly annoyed at the size of Matthews's salary. (For her part, Matthews later dismissed the director as an "imperious young man who knew nothing about musicals. . . . He was out of his depth.")

Dogged by scandals and emotional troubles, Matthews's career faltered after the war, with gaps bridged by work in TV and some success on radio; she died of cancer at 74 in London.

References
Roger Phillip Mellor, "Jessie Matthews," *BFI Screenonline*, http://www.screenonline .org.uk/people/id/449354; Donald Spoto, *The Dark Side of Genius: The Life of Alfred Hitchcock* (New York: Da Capo Press, 1999), 134–36; Michael Thornton, "Jessie Matthews: The Diva of Debauchery," *Daily Mail*, June 27, 2007, http://www.dailymail .co.uk/femail/article-445576/Jessie-Mat thews-The-Diva-Debauchery.html.

MAUGHAM, W. SOMERSET (1874–1965)

Parisian-born author—his father was attached to the British embassy—who lost both his parents in childhood. The death of his beloved mother was a lifelong wound. Sent to live with his nearest (albeit unwelcoming) relative, the vicar of Whitstable, Maugham had a lonely childhood, growing up with a painful shyness and debilitating stammer. At his uncle's insistence, Maugham eventually went to London to train as a doctor. He found his studies unsatisfying, but the work gave him a chance to meet a variety of people, often under highly dramatic conditions; he had always enjoyed writing, but now he turned seriously to fiction. At 23, he published his first novel, *Liza of Lambeth*, an instant best seller.

Maugham went on to become a prolific short-story writer, novelist, and traveler, as well as playwright (at one point, he had four simultaneous hits in London) and a gentleman with a surprising taste for adventure; while in his 40s, he served in the ambulance corps in World War I and undertook various espionage missions for the Crown, mostly aimed at keeping the tsarist regime in power and in the war. (During the Second World War, he would renew his relationship with the British government's spy service.) Married for a little more than a decade in early middle age, he was nonetheless gay.

Maugham, who often drew directly on other aspects of his personal life for his fiction (the first half of his greatest novel, *Of Human Bondage*, is a very direct remembrance of his young adulthood), later turned his Great War adventures into a collection called *Ashenden, or The British Agent*. Two stories, "The Hairless Mexican" and "The Traitor," plus a play by Campbell Dixon were combined to form the screenplay for Hitchcock's *SECRET AGENT*.

"We switched the two stories round completely," Hitchcock later explained. "Made (the traitorous) Caypor the innocent victim; turned the Greek into an American; introduced a TRAIN smash for dramatic purposes; and obtained the love interest from the play." (*Ashenden*, first published in 1928, also influenced several generations of British thriller writers, from Eric Ambler and GRAHAM GREENE to Ian Fleming and John Le Carre; although he never gave the character any further adventures, Maugham would occasionally use him as a narrator and stand-in for himself in other novels.)

Maugham's many works over a 65-year career include the excellent novel *The Razor's Edge*, the play *The Letter*, and the short story "Rain," all of which have been adapted multiple times for the movies; he also left behind many other works and a number of alienated family members and friends, wounded by his sharp tongue and occasional fits of spite. He died at 91 at his villa in Nice; his ashes were scattered on the grounds of his old boarding school in Kent.

References

Alfred Hitchcock, "My Screen Memories," *Film Weekly* (May 1936), http://the.hitchcock.zone/wiki/Film%20Weekly%20%281936%29%20-%20My%20Screen%20Memories; "Somerset Maugham," *IMDb*, http://www.imdb.com/name/nm0560857/bio?ref_=nm_ov_bio_sm; "W. Somerset Maugham," *Encyclopaedia Britannica*, http://www.britannica.com/biography/W-Somerset-Maugham.

MCA

Originally the Music Corporation of America, a booking agency that specialized in jazz bands (and, during the Prohibition era, often had to deal with speakeasies and the mobsters who ran them); by 1939, it had relocated to Beverly Hills and become a major talent agency, with LEW WASSERMAN (then only 26) its brightest and boldest agent. By 1950, Wasserman was president of the company, which had also launched Revue Productions, a regular supplier of TV shows to the networks. In 1958, it bought the UNIVERSAL backlot, renting it back to the studio; in 1962, it took over the studio itself.

Alfred Hitchcock, an agency client since 1945, became a major beneficiary when he sold the company various rights, including his television show, in exchange for stock; he immediately became its third-largest stockholder. Yet some colleagues, such as BERNARD HERRMANN, thought the deal a bit of a devil's bargain; the more closely Hitchcock was tied to this single studio and his fortune to its stock price, the more his artistic independence was compromised by commercial considerations.

After several mergers, the company ceased to exist as a separate entity in 2000.

References

Royal S. Brown, "An Interview with Bernard Herrmann," *Bernard Herrmann Society*, http://www.bernardherrmann.org/articles/an-interview-with-bernard-herrmann; Brian Lamb, "When Hollywood Had a King," *Booknotes*, http://www.booknotes.org/Watch/159444-1/Connie+Bruck.aspx; Dennis McDougal, "The Last Mogul: Lew Wasserman, MCA and the Hidden History of Hollywood," http://www.dennismcdougal.com/_br_the_last_mogul__lew_wasserman__mca_and_the_hidden_history_of_hollywood_24553.htm; Donald Spoto, *The Dark Side of Genius: The Life of Alfred Hitchcock* (New York: Da Capo Press, 1999), 417–18.

MCCOWEN, ALEC (1925–)

Kent-born performer onstage since 17. After years in rep (and touring India and Burma during the war with the Entertainments National Service Association), he began a long and honored career chiefly in the classics and with such groups as the Royal Shakespeare Company and the National Theatre Company.

He made his film debut in 1953 in *The Cruel Sea*; when Hitchcock decided to cast *FRENZY* with veteran stage performers, McCowen got the role of the inspector. But despite the film's success (and a follow-up role for George Cukor in *Travels with My Aunt* the same year), McCowen's primary venue remained the stage. He originated the role of the psychiatrist in *Equus*, and among his singular successes was a reading of *The Gospel According to St. Mark*. His last screen appearance was in 2002 in Martin Scorsese's *The Gangs of New York*.

References

"Alec McCowen," *IMDb*, http://www.imdb.com/name/nm0566680/bio?ref_=nm_ov_bio_sm; Peter Jacobs, "Alec McCowen," *Gay for Today*, http://gayfortoday.blogspot.com/2007/05/alec-mccowen.html.

MCCREA, JOEL (1905–1990)

South Pasadena–born performer who grew up in and around Hollywood. As a boy, he delivered Cecil B. De Mille's newspaper, and as a teenager, he helped out with the horses on Tom Mix movies. Always interested in acting, he studied drama at Pomona College and worked at the Pasadena Playhouse; by 1930, he had his first contract at RKO. Although his good looks and unintimidating charm made him an easy fit for romances and comedies, McCrea also made thrillers (*The Most Dangerous Game*) and dramas (*These Three*) and was personally fond of westerns; two early hits were *Wells Fargo* and *Union Pacific*.

Hitchcock had wanted Gary Cooper for *FOREIGN CORRESPONDENT*, but when Cooper turned it down, he took McCrea instead; the director would later complain that, in these early days of Hollywood casting, "I always ended up with the next best," pointing specifically to McCrea as an example. On the set, Hitchcock took particular delight in making the actor as wet and uncomfortable as possible during the plane crash sequence, exulting that "it was quite a show!" (For his part, McCrea was no more impressed, remembering that the director often drank so much champagne at lunch that he would fall asleep during the afternoon's work.)

McCrea had better luck with filmmaker Preston Sturges, for whom he worked several times, including the sublime *The Palm Beach Story* and *Sullivan's Travels*; after a nicely comic turn in *The More the Merrier*, the actor turned almost exclusively to westerns, including the elegiac, late-in-life *Ride the High Country* for Sam Peckinpah. Quietly modest, inherently masculine, he was the perfect movie cowboy.

"I always felt so much more comfortable in the Western," McCrea said in 1978, shortly after he retired. "The minute I got a horse and a hat and a pair of boots on, I felt easier. I didn't feel like I was an actor anymore. I felt like I was the guy out there doing it."

He died at age 84 in Los Angeles.

References

"Joel McCrea," *IMDb*, http://www.imdb .com/name/nm0566948/bio?ref_=nm_ov _bio_sm; Donald Spoto, *The Dark Side of Genius: The Life of Alfred Hitchcock* (New York: Da Capo Press, 1999), 230–31; David Thomson, *The New Biographical Dictionary of Film* (New York: Knopf, 2002), 582.

MCGILLIGAN, PATRICK (1951–)
Milwaukee, WI–born film historian and biographer. His subjects have included directors from Nicholas Ray to Clint Eastwood and actors from James Cagney to Jack Nicholson, and he has edited several volumes of the terrific series *Backstory*, which collects interviews with Hollywood screenwriters. Although he has, to date, written only one book about Hitchcock, 2003's *ALFRED HITCHCOCK: A LIFE IN DARKNESS AND LIGHT*, it is one of the few essential ones, probing deeper than FRANÇOIS TRUFFAUT's *HITCHCOCK/ TRUFFAUT* yet taking a less relentlessly critical view of the man than DONALD SPOTO's *ALFRED HITCHCOCK: THE DARK SIDE OF GENIUS*. And while the book remains in the minority in strongly doubting TIPPI HEDREN's account of her harassment at Hitchcock's hands (as well as being the only biography to suggest that ALMA REVILLE had her own affair with WHITFIELD COOK), it's exactly that minority opinion that makes McGilligan's sometimes contrarian work so valuable—

along with the varied personal interests he brings to the material, particularly regarding Hollywood's wartime propaganda, the blacklist era, and the role of the screenwriter. Not a particularly flashy writer but a strong and important voice.

References

"Discover Author Patrick McGilligan," *HarperCollins Publishers*, http://www.harper collins.com/authors/6508; Patrick McGilligan, *Alfred Hitchcock: A Life in Darkness and Light* (New York: HarperCollins, 2003), 428, 432, 647.

MCINTIRE, JOHN (1907–1991)
Spokane, WA–born performer who grew up in Montana and had a long career in radio. He tended to be cast as cowboys and ranchers in Hollywood after his late-in-life movie debut in *The Hucksters* in 1947; among his many credits were *Winchester '73*, *The Far Country*, *The Kentuckian*, and *Rooster Cogburn*; he replaced Ward Bond on TV's *Wagon Train*, where his creased face and gravelly voice were a familiar presence.

McIntire appeared on two episodes of *ALFFRED HITCHCOCK PRESENTS* and was Sheriff Chambers in *PSYCHO*, where the small-town lawman gets the memorable line "Well, if the woman up there is Mrs. Bates . . . who's that woman buried out in Greenlawn Cemetery?" The picture was, in some ways, a family effort; McIntire's longtime wife, actress Jeannette Nolan, helped dub Mrs. Bates.

He died in Los Angeles at 83 of emphysema and lung cancer.

References

"John McIntire," *IMDb*, http://www.imdb .com/name/nm0570615/bio?ref_=nm _ov_bio_sm; Stephen Rebello, *Alfred Hitchcock and the Making of Psycho* (New York: HarperPerennial, 1991), 132–33.

MEMORY OF THE CAMPS (GB/US/USSR 1945/1985)

DIRECTOR: Uncredited (Alfred Hitchcock).
SCREENPLAY: Richard Crossman, Colin Wills.
PRODUCERS: Sidney Bernstein, Sergei Nolbandov.
CINEMATOGRAPHY: Uncredited.
EDITORS: Stewart McAllister, Peter Tanner.
ORIGINAL MUSIC: Uncredited.
RUNNING TIME: 56 minutes. Black and white.
ORIGINALLY BROADCAST BY: PBS.

During World War II, many Hollywood directors contributed to the Allied effort by shooting newsreels, training films, or propaganda; some, like John Ford and William Wyler, went under fire to bring back footage. Hitchcock—perhaps stung by SIR MICHAEL BALCON's characterization of him as a deserter for leaving England—particularly felt a need to contribute. His wartime features *FOREIGN CORRESPONDENT, LIFEBOAT*, and *SABOTEUR* all feature strong patriotic messages; he shot at least two films for the British government, *AVENTURE MALGACHE* and *BON VOYAGE*, and reportedly worked on several more in the United States, uncredited.

After the war in Europe ended, he was asked by British producer SIDNEY BERNSTEIN—soon to become his partner in the short-lived TRANSATLANTIC PICTURES—to supervise a nonfiction film about Nazi atrocities made from footage shot by the Soviet, American, and British armies as they liberated the death camps. When Hitchcock arrived in London, about a half-hour of film had been already roughly assembled.

The movie bore only the official title *German Concentration Camps Factual Survey*, and the footage was even more harrowing than most. There were many clear, unblinking shots of the naked emaciated victims, stacked like firewood; in one long sequence, we watch captured German soldiers, under the eyes of Allied soldiers, forced to drag the corpses across the empty campgrounds and toss them into mass graves. It was said that, after watching the footage, Hitchcock retreated to his London hotel room for a week.

He returned, though, and then gave some broad advice to the editors. Presciently, it seemed, he knew that people would try to minimize the horrifying details, even deny the camps' very existence. In editing the film, he said, they should try to use as many wide-angle establishing shots as possible, so the size and scope of the gruesome operation was clear. Also, he advised, cutting should be minimized, so there was no hint of trickery or manipulation.

Eventually the editing was finished and narration written. The gruesome irony, however, was that, by the time it was done, the Allies were beginning to have second thoughts; German cooperation would be needed to rebuild their own country (and resist an expansionist Soviet Union). Reminding Germans of their nation's crimes—and their own complicity—was considered unwise. The film was shelved, although not forgotten.

"At the end of the war, I made a film to show the reality of the concentration camps, you know," Hitchcock said decades later. "Horrible. It was more horrible than any fantasy horror. Then, nobody wanted to see it. It was too unbearable. But it has stayed in my mind all of these years."

It clearly influenced his films. Many of Hitchcock's following Hollywood projects—*THE PARADINE CASE, ROPE, UNDER CAPRICORN*, and *I CONFESS*—would be far darker and more despairing than his previous work and fail to find acceptance among the postwar audiences. Several would also show a different style—long, single takes; an aversion to quick cuts—from not only most of his previous films but also his central belief in the aesthetics of PURE CINEMA. Not coincidentally, perhaps, this unblinkingly realistic style was precisely the one that he had urged on the editors of the atrocity film.

Eventually Hitchcock went back to more energetically envisioned movies—and eventually, the Holocaust film was rediscovered. In 1952, about an hour of footage—the sixth reel remained in the Soviet Union—was transferred to the Imperial War Museum in London. In the '80s, the surviving footage was unearthed again and broadcast on the PBS show *Frontline*, now titled *Memory of the Camps*; a documentary about the making of the documentary, *NIGHT WILL FALL*, was shown on HBO in 2015.

It was still horrifyingly difficult to watch. Heaven help us if it ever becomes easier.

References

Richard Brody, "Hitchcock and the Holocaust," *New Yorker*, January 9, 2014, http://www.newyorker.com/culture/richard-brody/hitchcock-and-the-holocaust; Patrick McGilligan, *Alfred Hitchcock: A Life in Darkness and Light* (New York: HarperCollins, 2003), 372–75; David Parkinson, "Night Will Fall: The Story of File Number F3080," *BFI*, http://www.bfi.org.uk/news-opinion/news-bfi/features/night-will-fall-story-file-number-f3080.

MENZIES, WILLIAM CAMERON (1896–1957)

New Haven–born, Yale-educated artist who began his work in silent movies and became famous for his elaborate and exotic production designs. He created the gorgeous backdrops for Douglas Fairbanks's *The Thief of Baghdad*, made perhaps the first music videos, and directed the alternately striking and stultifying *Things to Come*.

His work impressed producer DAVID O. SELZNICK, who gave him full visual reign over the look of *Gone with the Wind* and had him supervise the construction of the sets for *REBECCA*. Annoyed by the SALVADOR DALI dream sequence of *SPELLBOUND*, the mogul had Menzies supervise a reshoot; ultimately, no one— Menzies, Hitchcock, or particularly Dali— was pleased with the result.

Menzies, who won best art direction for *The Dove* and *Tempest* at the first Academy Awards, did much to increase the power and prestige of his profession; he even created the title of "production designer" to better define its myriad duties. One of his most striking works, though, was the low-budget *Invaders from Mars*, which wed its nightmarish story of mind control with surreally stripped-down sets and a tiny, tentacled alien in a fishbowl. Even Dali would have been delighted.

References

David Bordwell, "William Cameron Menzies: One Forceful, Impressive Idea," *David Bordwell's Website on Cinema*, http://www.davidbordwell.net/essays/menzies.php; Patrick McGilligan, *Alfred Hitchcock: A Life in Darkness and Light* (New York: HarperCollins, 2003), 258, 363; "William Cameron Menzies," *IMDb*, http://www.imdb.com/name/nm0580017/bio?ref_=nm_ov_bio_sm.

MERCHANT, VIVIEN (1929–1982)

Lancashire-born performer onstage since her early teens. By the '50s, she was a mainstay on the London stage, even more so after her husband, Harold Pinter, whom she married in 1956, became an important playwright. She received particular plaudits for her roles in his *The Homecoming* and *Old Times*; among her other important productions were *The Maids*, opposite Glenda Jackson, and Peter Hall's 1967 *Macbeth*, with Paul Scofield.

Merchant was a regular presence on British TV and film, as well, bringing her winsome looks and slightly plummy voice to parts in *Georgy Girl, Accident*, and *Under Milk Wood*; she is ALEC MCCOWEN's doting wife (and dreadful would-be cook) in *FRENZY*. The public breakup of her marriage to Pinter—they divorced in 1980, and he almost immediately married his lover, writer Antonia Fraser—left Merchant bitter and deeply depressed. She died in London of complications from alcoholism at 53.

References
Herbert Mitgang, "Vivien Merchant, 53, Actress," *New York Times*, October 6, 1982, http://www.nytimes.com/1982/10/06/obituaries/vivian-merchant-53-actress .html; "Vivien Merchant," *IMDb*, http://www.imdb.com/name/nm0580357/bio?ref_=nm_ov_bio_sm.

METHOD ACTING
An approach to performance, rooted in the turn-of-the-century work of Konstantin Stanislavski, who during his work at the Moscow Art Theatre and with Anton Chekhov developed the "system," in which the actors used both their own emotional memories and a clear understanding of the characters' motivations and objectives to reach "theatrical truth." In America, the "system" was adopted and adapted by New York's Group Theatre and Actors Studio, among others, where it became known as the "Method."

Various schools later coalesced around various approaches: Like Stanislavski, Lee Strasberg and his followers stressed the importance of the actor accessing and incorporating his or her own feelings and memories, while Sanford Meisner tended to emphasize a more direct relationship with your scene partner and living "in the moment." Other acting teachers—from MICHAEL CHEKHOV and Stella Adler to Uta Hagen and Richard Boleslawski—synthesized different approaches.

"The Method means the method that works for you," explained Actors Studio member Shelley Winters.

Both hugely influential and widely misunderstood, method acting quickly became the dominant dramatic approach in postwar American theater and film—and also the target of ridicule. It is still occasionally criticized by performers coming from a more classical tradition, particularly in Britain, where there is more of an emphasis on consistent "technique." LAURENCE OLIVIER and Anthony Hopkins both made jokes at its expense, Olivier famously suggesting that its ever-anguished practitioners "just *act*."

"The Method is a blind alley and an extremely baleful influence," English actor George Rose once proclaimed. "It became a way of sidestepping structure and intelligence and of making everything personal. There is no Method that enables you to play everything from medieval morality plays to Joe Orton. In many cases, it discards art in favor of cheap psychotherapy."

For Hitchcock, method acting was at best an annoying inconvenience. At worst, it ran counter to his picture-first approach to cinema, in which it wasn't the actor but what was in the frame—and how that combined or contrasted with what was in the frame to come—that created a response in the audience. This was PURE CINEMA, and it went back to the KULESHOV EFFECT: The camera was the star. It didn't matter what the actor was feeling. All that mattered was that he looked left or right or crossed the room on cue.

There was madness in these performers' method, Hitchcock declared, and he was having none of it. "The method actor is OK in the theatre because he has a free space to move about," Hitchcock told

Bryan Forbes during a long BBC television INTERVIEW. "But when it comes to cutting (to) the face and what he sees and so forth, there must be some discipline. I remember discussing with a Method actor how he was taught and so forth. He said, 'We're taught using improvisation. We are given an idea and then we are turned loose to develop in any way we want to.' I said 'That's not acting. That's writing.'"

Most of the British actors Hitchcock worked with his whole career—from HERBERT MARSHALL to ANNA MASSEY—had no trouble with his sort of explicit do-this, look-there direction (or with his disinterest in discussing their characters). Neither did the Hollywood icons—such as CARY GRANT—who had always relied on instinct and their own personas. Some performers, such as KIM NOVAK and JANET LEIGH, remembered Hitchcock's hands-off approach to their work as rather freeing.

"I hired you because you are a talented actress," Leigh recalled the director telling her before they began *PSYCHO*. "You are free to do whatever you wish with the role of Marion. . . . But there is one rule on the set—my camera is absolute. I tell the story through that lens, so I need you to move when my camera moves, stop when my camera stops. I'm confident you'll be able to find your motivation to justify the motion. Should you have difficulty, however, I will be happy to work with you. But I will not change the timing of my camera."

Some actors accepted these rules easily. Even some method actors—such as Chekhov, a leading teacher in his own right—found a way to adapt. But for other performers, it could be a shock to see how cavalierly Hitchcock seemed to treat the art of acting. When INGRID BERGMAN would begin to agonize over how to truthfully express a character's emotion, the director blithely told her, "Fake it." When he required a certain expression from

DIANE BAKER, he reached his hands out and literally molded her face into it.

The most frustrating collaboration came, as Hitchcock would often recount, on the set of *I CONFESS*. MONTGOMERY CLIFT was not only a committed method actor but also already abusing alcohol and so deeply insecure that he brought his acting coach with him on the set for consultations; for a director who had already cut the entire film in his head—who only needed an actor to perhaps say three lines, look up, say another line, look left, and then briskly walk down a flight of stairs—all this talk of motivation was not only beside the point but also an intolerable waste of time.

"He was a Method actor, and neurotic as well," Hitchcock later said. "'I want you to look in a certain direction,' I'd say, and he'd say 'Well, I don't know whether I'd look that way.' Now immediately you're fouled up because you're shooting a precut picture. He's got to look that way because you're going to cut to something over there. So I have to say to him, 'Please, you'll have to look that way, or else.'" Eventually the relationship got so bad that Hitchcock relayed all his instructions to KARL MALDEN, who—knowing both the Method and how Hollywood worked—was able to translate them for Clift.

The irony was that, for all his criticism of these actors' approach, in many ways Hitchcock was a method director. He liked to keep his players off balance, sometimes whispering a dirty word or JOKE before a scene; it broke down barriers, prompted spontaneity, kept them from reciting lines by rote. And he would go further, if necessary, deliberately breaking down an actor's confidence if he needed them to convey uncertainty onscreen—as in the way he famously manipulated JOAN FONTAINE on the set of *REBECCA*. Although he regularly treated actors like props, Hitchcock knew that they were vulnerable human beings and realized early on that he could exploit those vulnerabilities in order to get the one thing he wanted: an emotion he could photograph. (In that way, Baker said, he was a great deal like Elia Kazan.)

Perhaps what Hitchcock really meant when he once politely objected, saying that he'd never said that actors were cattle but that they should be "treated like cattle" was not that they had no feelings but that those feelings could be exploited. And that, in the end, they were at the mercy of a man with a prod, stubbornly shocking them to get what he wants, moving them relentlessly in the direction he alone had mapped out.

References

Diane Baker, interview with the author, September 2015; Ingrid Bergman and Alan Burgess, *My Story* (New York: Delacorte Press, 1980), 150; Peter Bogdanovich, "Is That Ticking (Pause) a Bomb?" *New York Times*, April 11, 1999, http://www.nytimes .com/1999/04/11/movies/film-is-that-tick ing-pause-a-bomb.html; Mel Gussow, "The Method, Still Disputed but Now Ubiqui-tous," *New York Times*, April 14, 1987, http://www.nytimes.com/1987/04/14/ arts/the-method-still-disputed-but-now -ubiquitous.html; Alfred Hitchcock, interview by Bryan Forbes, BBC One, December 30, 1969, http://the.hitchcock. zone/wiki/Alfred_Hitchcock_and_Bryan _Forbes_%281969%29; Janet Leigh with Christopher Nickens, *Psycho: The Clas-sic Thriller* (New York: Harmony Books, 1995), 42; David Shipman, ed., *Movie Talk: Who Said What about Whom in the Mov-ies* (New York: St. Martin's Press, 1988), 36; Donald Spoto, *The Dark Side of Genius: The Life of Alfred Hitchcock* (New York: Da Capo Press, 1999), 339; Donald Spoto, *Laurence Olivier: A Biography* (New York: Harper Paperbacks, 1993), 460; Donald Spoto, *Spellbound by Beauty: Alfred Hitch-cock and His Leading Ladies* (New York: Harmony Books, 2008), 92–99.

MILES, BERNARD (1907–1991)

Middlesex-born actor who, despite his rural, working-class origins—his mother was a cook, and his father worked on a farm—went on to Oxford, a long career in theater, and eventually a peerage (on his death, he was Baron Miles of Blackfriars). He was adept at both comic, rural charac-ters and in classical plays; in 1959, he offi-cially opened the much-respected Mermaid Theatre, the first theater to open in London in roughly 300 years.

For Hitchcock, he played Drayton, the cold kidnapper in the 1956 version of *THE MAN WHO KNEW TOO MUCH*; his most beloved character may be Joe, Pip's simple guardian in David Lean's *Great Expectations*, and his most memorable one for British audiences, the Long John Silver he played in two different TV versions of *Treasure Island*, 25 years apart. He died in Yorkshire at 83.

References

"Bernard Miles," *IMDb*, http://www.imdb .com/name/nm0587061/bio?ref_=nm_ov_ bio_sm; "Bernard Miles, 83, an Actor, Peer and Founder of London Theater," *New York Times*, June 15, 1991, http://www .nytimes.com/1991/06/15/obituaries/ber nard-miles-83-an-actor-peer-and-founder -of-london-theater.html.

MILES, VERA (1929–)

Oklahoma-born, Kansas-raised performer who parlayed a long series of beauty-con-test wins (Miss Chamber of Commerce, Miss Texas Grapefruit, and finally Miss Kansas) into a series of short-lived Holly-wood contracts; as she later joked, "I was dropped by the best studios in town."

She was busy on TV however, and when Alfred Hitchcock saw her in an episode of

The Pepsi-Cola Playhouse in 1955, he called her in for an interview and offered her a personal five-year contract. He compared her to GRACE KELLY (flattery later recycled for TIPPI HEDREN and DIANE BAKER). He demanded total control over her appearance and wardrobe, even off the set, so that she didn't go around looking like a "Van Nuys housewife."

A petite, reserved brunette, Miles seemed an unlikely heir to Kelly's glamorous throne, but the calm surface she projected proved to be the perfect camouflage for emotionally troubled characters; she is excellent as the disturbed heroine of "REVENGE," the Hitchcock-directed premiere episode of *ALFRED HITCHCOCK PRESENTS*, and in her first feature for him, *THE WRONG MAN*, she gives a chilling portrayal of a woman slipping into mental illness.

But by then Miles was heading into her late 30s, with an ex-husband, a new marriage, and two children. She had plans of her own. As, in late 1956, Hitchcock moved forward into the final stages of pre-production on *VERTIGO*—the movie that, he promised, would "make Vera a major STAR, a real actress"—she announced that she was pregnant again. She quit the film.

Hitchcock recast the movie with KIM NOVAK, an actress he quarreled with on the set and occasionally belittled afterward; although he would not treat Miles with the hostility he would later treat Hedren, he did view her choice of a family over his film as a disappointment, if not an outright betrayal. "I lost interest," he confessed. "I couldn't get the rhythm going with her again." He cast Miles in a few more television roles and in the thankless part of Lila in *PSYCHO*. (Years later, she reprised the character in *Psycho II*.) When her contract lapsed, he did not renew it.

Although Miles firmly denied the director had any sort of SEXUAL designs

on her—let along acted on them—she did agree that he clearly wanted to mold her, to "create another Grace Kelly out of me," a dream that she had no intention of fulfilling. "Hitchcock had a bit of a Pygmalion Complex," she said years later. "He wanted to make me into a superstar, but I just wasn't interested. . . . It just wasn't me. I was a working mother, busy raising my children and my private life has never been discussable."

Unlike Hedren, Miles, who had worked steadily before Hitchcock—she had costarred in John Ford's *The Searchers*—worked just as regularly after. She acted for Ford again in one of his last and greatest films, *The Man Who Shot Liberty Valance*. She also guest-starred on a wide variety of television shows, including a classic episode of JOSEPH STEFANO's *The Outer Limits*, "The Form of Things Unknown," and booked several stays at that television retirement village for old Hollywood stars, *Murder, She Wrote*.

Miles retired from acting in 1995 and has not given an interview or made a public appearance since. But it's safe to say that she's never regretted turning down Hitchcock and *Vertigo*. After all, "he got his picture," she noted once. "And I got a son."

References

Richard Freedman, "'Psycho' Actress Defends Hitchcock," *Spokesman-Review*, June 25, 1983, http://the.hitchcock.zone/wiki/The%20Spokesman-Review%20%2825%2FJun%2F1983%29%20-%20'Psycho'%20actress%20defends%20Hitchcock; Donald Spoto, *Spellbound by Beauty: Alfred Hitchcock and His Leading Ladies* (New York: Harmony Books, 2008), 220–24; François Truffaut, *Hitchcock/Truffaut*, rev. ed. (New York: Touchstone, 1985), 247–48; "Vera Miles," *IMDb*, http://www.imdb com/name/nm0587256/bio?ref_=nm_ov _bio_sm.

MILLAND, RAY (1907–1986)

Welsh-born performer and a born leading man blessed with good looks and easy charm. An accomplished equestrian and expert shot, he joined the Household Cavalry, the division of the British Army devoted to protecting the royal family, and won several marksmanship trophies.

The cavalry, however, was an unpaid position—it was expected that its members would be gentlemen with private sources of income—and after several years, Milland was forced to resign. He decided to try acting on an impulse and quickly began picking up film work; by 1930, he was in Hollywood with a nine-month contract at MGM.

Milland's early career was spotty—he keenly felt his lack of training and found it hard to rise above bit parts. MGM dropped his contract, and he briefly returned to England. A second try at Hollywood seemed no more welcoming—he was about to take a job running a gas station in 1934—when suddenly a British actor dropped out of the movie *Bolero* and Milland was offered the role.

The actor was kept busy, although unchallenged, over the next decade, largely appearing in exotic romances and light comedies, but in the mid-'40s, a series of pictures—the ghost story *The Uninvited*, the FRITZ LANG thriller *The Ministry of Fear*—offered a chance to stretch. Finally, Billy Wilder's *The Lost Weekend* in 1945 provided the breakthrough and an Oscar. It also featured an emotional vulnerability, even fragility, that the actor rarely got a chance (or chose) to show, largely playing cool, even cold, sophisticates; it's that arch, arctic chilliness that characterizes his performance in *DIAL M FOR MURDER* as the unflappable murderer who—like the spymasters in *THE LADY VANISHES* and *NORTH BY NORTHWEST*—greet their climactic failure with merely a shrug and a quip.

"Milland did everything he was told and then made it better," Hitchcock said after the film was released. "He made a great movie for Billy Wilder and a very good movie for me."

Dial M for Murder turned out to be a final high point for Milland's acting career; he was nearing 50 and losing his hair, and leading parts were disappearing. He turned first to directing (*The Safecracker*, *Panic in the Year Zero*, a TV adaptation of ROBERT BLOCH's "Yours Truly, Jack the Ripper"). He dipped into genre pictures (*The Premature Burial*, *X—The Man with X-Ray Eyes*). He played in films from *Frogs* to *Love Story*. He kept working.

"He was a man who was afraid to say no," John Houseman said. "He needed work and was always afraid that his career was over after a picture was over. He should have been tougher, but he was such a pleasant man that he never pushed it. He always thought he was lucky to be working. But his best work was truly memorable."

Milland died of lung cancer at 79 in Torrance, CA.

References

Michael Blowen, "Milland's Best Work Was Very Very Good," *Boston Globe*, March 12, 1989, http://the.hitchcock.zone/wiki/Boston_Globe_%2812/Mar/1986%29_-_Milland's_best_work_was_very,_very_good; "Ray Milland," *IMDb*, http://www.imdb.com/name/nm0001537/bio?ref_=nm_ov_bio_sm; "Ray Milland Dies of Cancer; Won Fame for 'Lost Weekend' Role," *Los Angeles Times*, March 11, 1989, http://articles.latimes.com/1986-03-11/news/mn-3089_1_cancer.

MINICOTTI, ESTHER (1888–1962)

Turin-born performer, née Esther Cunico, who immigrated to America with her family in 1894; long associated with the theater in Italy, the clan became active in Italian-language drama in the United States, staging both translations of classic works and modern plays for immigrant audiences in cities across the country. In 1911, she married a costar, Silvio Minicotti; they continued as frequent onstage partners.

Based in New York, she was in her 60s when she made her English-language debut on Broadway with Katherine Cornell in *That Lady*; with the Italian-language theater in decline in America, she began working in television and appeared in a limited number of excellent films, including *Shockproof, House of Strangers, Marty*, and *Full of Life*. In THE WRONG MAN, she played Mrs. Balestrero, Manny's devout MOTHER. She died at 74 in Jackson Heights, Queens.

References

"Esther Minicotti," *IMDb*, http://www .imdb.com/name/nm0591034/bio; Alfred E. Twomey and Arthur F. McClure, *The Versatiles: Supporting Character Players in the Cinema, 1930–1955* (New York: Castle Books, 1969), 160.

MISTAKEN IDENTITY

Going back to antiquity, a favorite device of both tragedians and farceurs, allowing kings to move among commoners in disguise, husbands to flirt unknowingly with their own wives, and innocents to blunder into horrible fates. Hitchcock's films use the conceit in several very different ways.

In the first, being mistaken for someone else allows for a moment of humor or a surprising insight into the character or theme. In THE 39 STEPS, Richard Hannay runs into a meeting hall and is mistaken for a campaigning candidate. He gives a rousing speech, completely stitched together out of platitudes; it illuminates not only his easy charm but also the basic mindlessness of the politics that surround him and have

created his current predicament. In THE BIRDS, Mitch mistakes Melanie for a sales-clerk at a pet store; the character's assumption reveals not only his unconscious bias (any single woman in a store must, of course, be there to serve him) but also her fondness for foolish pranks and surrounds them with not only sarcastic metaphors (cooing lovebirds, a bird in a gilded cage) but also the eventual villains of the film.

Although Hitchcock was happy to use mistaken identity for a quick point or JOKE (as in MR. AND MRS. SMITH, where the husband assumes his wife's boss is her lover), his second and more obvious use of it becomes an important plot device. In some films, it practically becomes the whole plot: Richard Hannay is assumed to be a murderer in *The 39 Steps*, Barry Caine a traitor in *SABOTEUR*, Roger Thornhill a secret agent in *NORTH BY NORTHWEST*; it's this mistake that sets them on the run, with both the police and the real villains in pursuit.

Yet more than simply sparking the story, the device illuminates character, as well, as in their travels these protagonists also begin to take on some of characteristics of the characters they've been mistaken for. Hannay learns to elude police; Caine discovers a skill for tall tales and trickery; Thornhill, a taste for espionage. They grow into their new roles, in some ways becoming the people they're playing. They also, in so doing, develop a richer identity of their own. All of them are rather bland and somewhat rootless bachelors at the beginnings of the films, simply going through their day-to-day existences; all of them by the ends of the films have not only found a passionate love but also a new appreciation for life. Their cross-country voyages have become another kind of journey.

These sort of mistaken-identity films are among Hitchcock's most enjoyable—still, as his CATHOLIC school education would have told him, penance must often be paid for pleasure. *THE WRONG MAN* is that attempt to make amends, with Hitchcock soberly detailing what a true-life case of mistaken identity means—a slow slide into a justice system out of FRANZ KAFKA, a ruined career, a broken marriage. Grimly told, without humor or even the diversion of a real Hitchcock cameo, this is not the lighthearted romp of *The 39 Steps*, and unlike Barry Caine or Roger Thornhill, Manny discovers nothing new about himself through this mistake; in fact, he merely loses the little identity he has as a husband and musician, slowly fading into nothing more than a case number.

But in the most interesting Hitchcock films, mistaken identity isn't used for a joke or even the starting point for a plot but as a theme—with the nature of identity itself becoming the point. In these movies, who and what we are is endlessly mutable. Is *THE LODGER* just another avenger, looking for justice in his sister's death—or is he literally "the Avenger," the man who killed her? Is Uncle Charlie in *SHADOW OF A DOUBT* a beloved relative or a serial killer? Is Guy in *STRANGERS ON A TRAIN* an accomplice in his wife's death or merely a GUILTY beneficiary?

In some cases, the answer is both. In some cases, the answer remains ambiguous, even at the end. No, Maxim didn't murder *REBECCA*; John Robie is not the burglar at work in *TO CATCH A THIEF*; Johnnie is not trying to murder his new wife, despite her *SUSPICION*—in every case, their "identity" is mistaken, the label attached to them by others not correct. But none of them is truly innocent. All of them are guilty of something.

And in the most complex Hitchcock films of all, identity is at its most complicated, as well. When, in *VERTIGO*, is Judy being Madeleine, and when is Judy being Judy, and when is she Judy being Madeline

being Judy? When Norman goes *PSYCHO* and "becomes" his MOTHER, is he really being his mother—or only his own, twisted interpretation of her? "He was never all Norman," the psychiatrist glibly announces at the end. "But he was often only Mother." But was he? And how often are any of us "only" one person at any one time? What sort of multitudes do all of us really contain?

"Mother . . . what is the phrase?" Norman stammers to Marion. "She isn't quite herself today." Which is perhaps a dark film's darkest joke: No, she's not herself today; she's Norman, instead. But then, in Hitchcock, the greatest mistake we make about identity is thinking we have only one.

THE MOLIERE PLAYERS

Founded in London by actor Paul Bonifas, a member of the Free French Forces, the Moliere Theatre was a group of actors—French refugees who'd previously been with the Comedie Francaise, the Theatre Sarah Bernhardt, and other companies—who now performed the works of that titular playwright and other classics in England for the public and the armed services. They also lent their talents to several British propaganda films, including Hitchcock's *AVENTURE MALGACHE* and *BON VOYAGE*, although the first was long suppressed out of fears that it was close enough to actual events to possibly result in a libel suit. Onscreen, the actors were billed only as "the Moliere Players" chiefly to protect their families back in occupied France but included Bonifas (who years later played the stamp dealer in the HITCHCOCKIAN *Charade*), Paul Clarus, and Paulette Preney.

References
"Paul Bonifas," *IMDb*, http://www.imdb.com/name/nm0094585; Donald Spoto, *The Dark Side of Genius: The Life of Alfred Hitchcock* (New York: Da Capo Press, 1999), 270.

MONTAGE

Although it is perhaps the most modern art, in many ways, the cinema is an amalgam of other, older fields. It has the narratives of fiction and the performances of drama, the orchestral scores of music, the scenery and costumes of art and fashion—even dance enters into it, if you can consider how elaborately some action sequences are choreographed. What makes cinema its own, unique art is montage.

The careful practice of cutting between two scenes, or even among different perspectives within the same scene, and through that contrast and combination making something new—that magical math of adding one and one and somehow making three—that is something that only the movies have, and it's at the heart of Hitchcock's work.

Of course, Hitchcock did not invent montage—there are classic examples from the work of Eisenstein and D. W. Griffith—but in some ways, he rescued it. During the rise of the Hollywood studio film, for many overworked filmmakers, editing had become something more like assembling. Nervous executives usually demanded "coverage," meaning that every scene would be shot, often from start to finish from a small variety of angles. If the scene was of two people talking on a couch, there would be a long shot of the room; an occasional medium shot showing the two people clearly; and then intercut, over-the-shoulder close-ups of each.

This was the standard practice, although, of course, there were always exceptions, particularly when strong, independently minded directors were involved—from the crazed close-ups of James Whale's campy *Bride of Frankenstein* through the idiosyncratic camera movements of Orson Welles's *Citizen Kane*. Such filmmakers as John Huston and John Ford developed their own, singular styles.

For workaday directors churning out mainstream Hollywood films, however, much of the product consisted of scenes photographed with a fixed camera from several standard angles, all of which would be cut together later by the editor (often under the watchful eye of the producer, who could reorder the cuts to emphasize or minimize a performance). It was a safety measure—an insurance against some director's eccentric style or a star's unusual performance—that sought to turn art into a risk-free, assembly-line entertainment made up of interchangeable parts.

The word *montage*, meanwhile—which once covered all sorts of editing—now came to mean one specific thing: A collection of often-silent footage played over music, illustrating the passage of time. This could be as simple (and simplistic) as close-ups of various newspaper headlines and falling calendar pages, or it could be a more artful sequence of shots bridged by optical effects. (Many fine directors, such as Don Siegel and Robert Wise, began their careers in the editing room, cutting together montage sequences.) This sort of editing—often relying on old stock footage—was strictly a visual shortcut, a way of packing a certain amount of necessary but dull, exposition into a minute or so of screen time. Hitchcock objected to both ideas.

He disliked coverage, chiefly because he felt—as GRAHAM GREENE had rightly surmised he did in an early review—that there was really only one best place for the camera in every situation. Hitchcock also knew that giving the producer postproduction options was giving up control of the production, allowing someone else to ultimately impose their vision (exactly why, of course, DAVID O. SELZNICK *loved* coverage). So Hitchcock precut the film in his head and recorded those thoughts on paper, carefully sketching out each scene shot-by-shot before shooting even began.

But beyond that, he was entranced by classic montage because this—the juxtaposition of images—was at the heart of the PURE CINEMA he often spoke of and proof that movies created a singular, powerfully emotional response in viewers. It wasn't even enough to simply choose the right camera angles; you had to know how to put them together.

"There are two primary uses of cutting or montage in film," Hitchcock explained to PETER BOGDANOVICH in 1963. "Montage to create ideas, and montage to create violence and emotions. For example, in *REAR WINDOW*, where JIMMY STEWART is thrown out of the window in the end, I just photographed that with feet, legs, arms, heads. Completely montage. I also photographed it from a distance, the complete action. There was no comparison between the two. There never is. . . . It is much more effective if it's done in montage, because you involve the audience much more—that's the secret."

If it was a secret, it was one Hitchcock used again and again. The climactic scene in *SABOTEUR* as he cuts between Barry's face, Fry's anguish, and the slowly ripping sleeves; the struggles in *DIAL M FOR MURDER* and *SHADOW OF A DOUBT*, as the women's open mouths and writhing legs add a level of sick SEXUALITY to the violence; the infamous shower murder in *PSYCHO* that makes a minute feel like 30 and convinces us we've seen nudity and knife wounds when all we've seen is a blur—this is Hitchcock creating violent emotions simply by cutting together different pieces of film.

The other type of montage, Hitchcock went on to explain to Bogdanovich, was the "juxtaposition of imagery relating to the mind of the individual. You have a man look, you show what he sees, you go back to the man. You can make him react in various ways. You see, you can make him look

at one thing, look at another—without his speaking, you can show his mind at work, comparing things—any way you run there's complete freedom. It's limitless, I would say, the power of cutting and the assembly of the images."

This is, of course, the famous KULESHOV EFFECT, and it's one that Hitchcock was also adept at—the quick contrasting close-ups of Mr. and Mrs. Verloc in *SABOTAGE* that herald the murder, the slow interplay between Lila Crane's questioning face and what she sees in the Bates house in *Psycho*—these are sequences in which our feeling about the character's feelings come directly from seeing what they see. Its purest example comes, of course, in *Rear Window*. What kind of person is Scottie, anyway? We don't know as we sit there, watching him watching—until Hitchcock shows us precisely what he's looking at.

Hitchcock was too complete a craftsman to be wed to only one technique. He was nearly as skilled with moving the camera as with editing within it (the breathlessly complicated crane shots in *NOTORIOUS* and *YOUNG AND INNOCENT*, the heartbreaking reverse DOLLY in *FRENZY*). He could also lose his way—being so intimidated by the writing that he shot *JUNO AND THE PAYCOCK* like a play or being so momentarily besotted by long takes that he made *ROPE* without any real use of montage at all. (Both, he later admitted frankly, were fundamental mistakes.)

But it is his use of montage—his special brilliance in stitching together little pieces of film—that we truly remember today. And for which he'd probably most like to be remembered.

References

Peter Bogdanovich, *The Cinema of Alfred Hitchcock*, http://the.hitchcock.zone/wiki/ Alfred_Hitchcock_and_Peter_Bogda novich_%281963%29; Alfred Hitchcock, interview by Bryan Forbes, BBC One, December 30, 1969, http://the.hitchcock.zone/wiki/Alfred_Hitchcock_and_Bryan_Forbes_%281969%29; François Truffaut, *Hitchcock/Truffaut*, rev. ed. (New York: Touchstone, 1985), 110–13, 214–15.

MONTAGU, IVOR (1904–1984)

London-born son of a baron who studied zoology at Cambridge and developed a precocious interest in and appreciation of film, particularly the avant-garde. He was the first film critic hired by the *Observer* and the *New Statesman* and by 21 had cofounded the London Film Society, which championed foreign films and experimental efforts. It was his public enthusiasm for Soviet and Germanic cinema that led producer SIR MICHAEL BALCON to approach him with Hitchcock's first cut of *THE LODGER* in 1926; the studio didn't know enough to call it EXPRESSIONISTIC, but they knew they didn't want to release it.

"What was the distributor's chief grudge against the latest Hitchcock—'The Lodger' by name?" Montagu wrote later. "It was supposed to be highbrow, the most scarlet epithet in the film trade vocabulary. Hitch, indeed, was deeply suspected by the distributors of this damning fault. Had he not even been trained in an art school?"

Montagu praised the film, however, while offering some suggestions—drastically cutting back the number of title cards, for example. Although Hitchcock was initially resistant to changing the film at all, he found the ideas useful and incorporated them. The recut movie was not only approved for release but also made him a famous filmmaker.

Montagu helped edit Hitchcock's *DOWNHILL* and *EASY VIRTUE*, as well, and eventually joined Balcon at GAUMONT-BRITISH Studios, where he worked as an associate producer (some-times uncredited) on *THE MAN WHO KNEW TOO MUCH*, *THE 39 STEPS*, *SABOTAGE*, and *SECRET AGENT*.

Montagu's individual contributions to those later films, though, are difficult to ascertain; preproduction story conferences were often freewheeling affairs, and Hitchcock could be stingy with sharing praise. (Talking to FRANÇOIS TRUFFAUT decades later about *The Lodger*, Hitchcock failed to credit Montagu at all, merely saying that an amorphous "they" had recommended changes to his cut, and he had "agreed to make about two.")

Although his early association with Hitchcock was a historic one, it was not the only history Montagu was to make. He shot his own experimental comedies (often collaborating with CHARLES LAUGHTON and H. G. Wells), went to Hollywood with Sergei Eisenstein, documented the Spanish Civil War, spied for the Soviets in World War II (codename: "Intelligentsia"), cowrote *Scott of the Antarctic*, and spent decades working to promote Marxism and table tennis. He died at 80 in Hertfordshire.

References

Patrick McGilligan, *Alfred Hitchcock: A Life in Darkness and Light* (New York: HarperCollins, 2003), 190; Ivor Montagu, "Working with Hitchcock," *Sight and Sound* 49, no. 3 (1980), http://the.hitchcock.zone/wiki/Sight_and_Sound_%281980%29_-_Working_with_Hitchcock; "Obituary: Ivor Montagu," *Times*, November 7, 1984, http://the.hitchcock.zone/wiki/The_Times_%2807/Nov/1984%29_-_Obituary:_Ivor_Montagu; Tom Ryall, "Ivor Montagu," *BFI Screenonline*, http://www.screenonline.org.uk/people/id/446857; Donald Spoto, *The Dark Side of Genius: The Life of Alfred Hitchcock* (New York: Da Capo Press, 1999), 88–89; François Truffaut, *Hitchcock/Truffaut*, rev. ed. (New York: Touchstone, 1985), 49–51.

MONTGOMERY, ROBERT
(1904–1981)

New York–born performer whose comfortable life of private schools and European jaunts ended abruptly in 1922, when his bankrupt father leapt from the Brooklyn Bridge. His son was soon taking whatever jobs he could find while looking for work as a writer or actor, making his Broadway debut two years later in the farce *The Mask and the Face*. It closed after 19 performances.

It was the first in a long line of one-month wonders over the decade—Montgomery's biggest stage hit, *Dawn*, managed about eight weeks—but his good looks and unobtrusive style kept him employed and eventually won him an entrée into Hollywood and a contract at MGM.

Over his career, Montgomery was mostly cast in lightly comic roles, such as Hitchcock's *MR. AND MRS. SMITH* (he was second choice, after CARY GRANT), but he looked for darker parts, too. He won an Oscar nomination for his role as a mad killer in *Night Must Fall* and, after serving with distinction in World War II, returned to direct several films, including *Ride a Pink Horse* (produced by JOAN HARRISON) and the Raymond Chandler adaptation *Lady in the Lake*. For that picture, Montgomery—who also starred—stayed offscreen, having the camera see only what his character saw, a stylistic twist Hitchcock ridiculed years later in an INTERVIEW with PETER BOGDANOVICH.

"Young directors always come up with the idea, 'Let the camera be someone and let it move as though it's the person, and you put the guy in front of a mirror and then you see him,'" he said. "It's a terrible mistake. Bob Montgomery did that in 'Lady in the Lake'—I don't believe in it myself. What are you really doing? You are keeping back from the audience who it is. What for? That's all you are doing. Why not show who it is?"

Montgomery continued to direct and dabble in politics—he was a supporter of the hunt for Communists in Hollywood and later advised President Eisenhower on his television appearances. He directed his last film, *The Gallant Hours*, in 1960 and after directing a final Broadway play in 1962, *Calculated Risk*, quietly retired. He died at 77 in New York of cancer. One of his children was TV's beloved witch, Elizabeth Montgomery.

References

Peter Bogdanovich, *The Cinema of Alfred Hitchcock*, http://the.hitchcock.zone/wiki/Alfred_Hitchcock_and_Peter_Bogdanovich_%281963%29; "Robert Montgomery," *IMDb*, http://www.imdb.com/name/nm0599910/bio?ref_=nm_ov_bio_sm; David Thomson, *The New Biographical Dictionary of Film* (New York: Knopf, 2002), 610.

MOORE, BRIAN (1921–1999)

Belfast-born author of short fiction, novels, and screenplays, including ghost stories, mysteries, and dramas. Born and raised as a Catholic in Protestant-dominated Northern Ireland, he left for Canada after World War II, originally writing thrillers with titles like *Wreath for a Redhead* and *A Bullet for My Lady*, all published under pseudonyms. Although *The Lonely Passion of Judith Hearne* made his reputation as a novelist in 1955, Moore continued to occasionally write thrillers and, in the '60s, began doing scripts, as well. His first major assignment was *TORN CURTAIN* for Alfred Hitchcock.

Although Moore enjoyed California, he later charged that the director had a "profound ignorance of human motivation" and that working on the script was "awful, like washing floors"; after turning in his draft, he told Hitchcock that he thought neither the plot nor the characters worked and suggested the director simply write the whole thing off. The advice was not well received.

"Taking criticism or confronting disagreement was another problem for Hitchcock," Moore later said. "As with all living legends, no one had the courage to tell him anything that was wrong. That was very bad for the poor man. And because of his own personality and background—as the lonely, frightened boy—he had a horror of confrontation with people. He wasn't able to argue something out face to face. So he did things through intermediaries, or he sent someone on a vacation and then replaced him."

Which was what Hitchcock did to Moore, telling him to take some time off and then passing the script on to two other screenwriters, Keith Waterhouse and Willis Hall, asking them to liven up the dialogue. They continued those fixes even during shooting, although Moore ended up receiving sole credit for the screenplay. (Later, Moore channeled some of his anger over the incident into his novel *Fergus*.)

Moore continued to write scripts and novels, and sometimes one came from the other; his last produced screenplay was for 1991's *Black Robe*, based on his own book. Many of his works deal with religion, doubt, loneliness, and the continued strife in Northern Ireland; GRAHAM GREENE once called Moore his "favorite living author."

Moore died in Malibu at 77 of emphysema.

References

"Brian Moore," *IMDb*, http://www.imdb .com/name/nm0600972/bio?ref_=nm_ov_ bio_sm; Christopher Fowler, "Invisible Ink: Michael Moore," *Independent*, March 20, 2011, http://www.independent.co.uk/ arts-entertainment/books/features/invisi ble-ink-no-69—brian-moore-2246881

.html; Patrick McGilligan, *Alfred Hitchcock: A Life in Darkness and Light* (New York: HarperCollins, 2003), 662–65; Donald Spoto, *The Dark Side of Genius: The Life of Alfred Hitchcock* (New York: Da Capo Press, 1999), 488–90.

MORTON, MICHAEL (1864–1931)
English-born author and popular dramatist whose hits—many adapted into silent films—included *The Yellow Passport, Colonel Newcome*, and WOMAN TO WOMAN. He was the first to adapt Agatha Christie to the stage, turning her novel *The Murder of Roger Ackroyd* into the play *Alibi*, although Christie said his proposed changes—he wanted "to take about 20 years off Poirot's age, call him Beau Poirot, have lots of girls in love with him and give him a strong love interest"—convinced her to start doing her own dramatizing. The indestructible *The Mousetrap* was one of the results.

Morton had a longer and presumably more satisfying relationship with Hitchcock, who adapted *Woman to Woman* into the similarly titled film, turned Morton's novel *Children of Change* into THE WHITE SHADOW, and shared screenplay credit with him on THE PASSIONATE ADVENTURE; Hitchcock also served as the art director and assistant director on all three movies, which were directed by GRAHAM CUTTS and released between 1923 and 1924.

Morton died at 67 in London.

References

"Michael Morton," *Omics International*, http://research.omicsgroup.org/index .php/Michael_Morton_%28dramatist%29; Matthew Pritchard, "Why They Wanted to Take 20 Years Off Poirot," *Daily Mail*, July 10, 2010, http://www.dailymail.co.uk/ home/moslive/article-1293355/Agatha -Christie-Why-wanted-20-years-Poirot -girlfriend.html.

MOTHERS

"Well, a boy's best friend is his mother"

—Norman Bates

The maternal figure is a constant image in Alfred Hitchcock's work—but also a far more complicated one than in many other directors' films. Sometimes she is an ineffectual, shadowy presence. Sometimes she is a nurturer. Sometimes she is a domineering monster. And sometimes she is an even more ambiguous character—part leader, part lover. And different mothers come at different points in Hitchcock's career and life.

In his silent films, they are mostly absent, although they occasionally serve as a repository of the audience's own fears and doubts (*THE LODGER*) or authority figures who drive the plot forward with their worries about social status, suitable marriages, and what people will think. Most of these characters were created while Hitchcock was still a bachelor and living at home or newly married and childless. His own mother remained the prime template.

His treatment of maternal figures, though, changes after the arrival of his daughter, an event that made his wife, ALMA REVILLE, once simply his partner, now the newly dominant maternal figure in his life. After this, the status of mothers increases in his films. And so in *JUNO AND THE PAYCOCK*, the woman is a patient and long-suffering source of strength; in *THE MAN WHO KNEW TOO MUCH*, a fierce defender; in *THE LADY VANISHES*, a plucky symbol of British intelligence; and in *SABOTAGE*, an avenging angel. These women are far braver and bolder than the flawed and sometimes hesitant men around them. To Hitchcock, a new husband and father, mothers and older women are now genuine, unembarrassed, unironic heroes.

There is an interesting, subtle shift ahead, though. After Hitchcock went to Hollywood with his wife and daughter and he seemed to identify even more strongly with the women in his films, they, like him in this new world, become more hesitant, rootless, uncertain. The mother of *SHADOW OF A DOUBT* is the most truly pathetic—so emotionally fragile a creature that her own daughter is willing to let a murderer go free rather than risk letting her find out the truth. (Most significantly, perhaps, *Shadow of a Doubt* was made while Hitchcock was in the process of losing his own ailing parent; like the character in the film, she was named Emma.) It is in some ways a fond, teary goodbye to his mother (and, with his daughter now a teenager, in some ways to the idea of gentle motherhood itself).

And now, from here on in—apart from the second *THE MAN WHO KNEW TOO MUCH*, a remake of his own '30s film—mothers will be far more fearsome creatures in his work. The next one we meet is in *NOTORIOUS*, the formidable, old-world matriarch whose adult son troops into her bedroom to confide (much as, when he was a child, Hitchcock used to have to dutifully recount his day's adventures to his mother); her judgments of him are withering, and her plans for cleaning up his messes are coldheartedly precise. She protects her son, as you'd protect any weak thing, but she is also contemptuous of his weakness. Wrapped in satin and disapproval, she is motivated by duty, not love.

At first, the mothers who follow her in Hitchcock's '50s films aren't quite as forbidding. In fact, they may seem to be essentially comic figures—like Bruno's dithering, overindulgent mother in *STRANGERS ON A TRAIN*. But they can also be smotheringly attentive, even flirtatious, an element that now brings an uncomfortable tinge of incest to the proceedings. Jessie may be Francie's meddling mother in *TO CATCH A THIEF*, but that doesn't mean she isn't interested in John Robie herself; Clara may be Roger's mother in *NORTH BY NORTH-WEST*, but sometimes she's so weary of him that you'd think he were her husband. (Complicating matters in both films is that the actors—JESSIE ROYCE LANDIS and CARY GRANT—are, in reality, only a few years apart in age.)

The incest reaches a Grand Guignol climax in *PSYCHO*. The film is full of pushy, domineering parents—the Texas oilman who wants to buy off his daughter's unhappiness, the mother who gives Caroline tranquilizers to get through her honeymoon, the father who's left Sam in debt, the mother whose picture on the wall judges Marion's love life. None, however, quite touches Mrs. Bates, who—at least according to the state psychiatrist who examined her son Norman—was a "clinging, demanding woman" who spent years living locked away with her only son "as if there was no one else in the world." But, as her own son admits, a "son is a poor substitute for a lover," and eventually she found a real one.

And when she did—and, when stunned by this act of betrayal, the jealous Norman killed them both—his mother has her postmortem revenge by taking his life, too, bit by bit, slowly infecting his personality until she takes it over completely. Not just a controlling personality, she controls him utterly. No longer just a possessive mother, she now possesses him. There are several Mrs. Bates in *Psycho*—the one of flesh and blood and the one of Norman's memory, the one of chemicals and sawdust who sits in the fruit cellar and the one in a cheap wig and black dress who stalks the motel—and all of them are made up of love and hate. They are the figures of a son's awed worship and sublimated desire, and taken together, they are the scariest character in all of Hitchcock.

Not that there weren't more—if less melodramatic—monster mothers to come. In *THE BIRDS*, the widowed Lydia Brenner is so reliant on her son, Mitch, so terrified of being abandoned again, that—like Madame Sebastian in *Notorious*—she drives away every woman who comes near him. In *MARNIE*, Bernice Edgar is so ashamed of her own past, so determined to raise her daughter "decent," that she creates a daughter who's both starved for affection and pathologically terrified of men—and who therefore sedates herself through long horseback rides and compulsive thievery.

For a film about two bachelors, meanwhile, *FRENZY* is a film filled with mothers. True, the only real one we meet in it is the parent of the film's psychopath, and however briefly we see her, she's of a type with the moms in the director's other serial-killer movies—indulgent, jovial, overly familiar. But if she's the only flesh-and-blood parent, then it's the rest of the women in the film who, while being childless, emerge as truly maternal—Brenda (who still worries about Richard, her angry ex-husband, and slips money into his pocket when he's not looking); Babs (who stubbornly sticks up for Richard at work and believes him when nobody else will); even Mrs. Oxford, the inspector's wife, who cooks elaborate (if apparently inedible) meals for her hardworking husband.

These kind, caring, giving women feel very much like a rebuke to the horrendous harridans Hitchcock's postwar films have given us. And yet how does the world reward them for their sacrifices and worries and oversolicitous service? Mrs. Oxford is mocked behind her back. Babs is raped and killed and shoved into a sack of potatoes (only to have her body unpacked and cruelly abused again). And Brenda is raped and killed, too, in excruciating detail, and then abandoned like a half-eaten piece of fruit—much as, afterward, the killer tosses away an apple core. Even when the filmmaker seems to treat them sympathetically—they are three of the kindest characters in Hitchcock—they are ridiculed and minimized and assaulted by others. It cannot be merely a coincidence that this portrayal of the maternal figure as warm, as vulnerable, as endangered, came just at the point when Hitchcock's own wife was increasingly battling illnesses and reminding him of how yet another maternal figure might be lost to him soon; like *Shadow of a Doubt*, it is a sad, complicated tribute. It became his final and ultimately forgiving word on the subject.

And so, the story of mothers in Hitchcock's films is a complex one of both objectification and identification, of figures who are at first protective; then ineffectual; then domineering and destructive; and finally, simply, at risk. It is a love story. It is a horror story. And—most ironic of all—it is one that our greatest storyteller may not even have realized he was telling all along.

Reference

Donald Spoto, *The Dark Side of Genius: The Life of Alfred Hitchcock* (New York: Da Capo Press, 1999), 18, 260–61, 288.

THE MOUNTAIN EAGLE (GB 1927)

> DIRECTOR: Alfred Hitchcock.
> SCREENPLAY: Eliot Stannard, Max Ferner, Charles Lapworth.
> PRODUCER: Sir Michael Balcon.
> CINEMATOGRAPHY: Gaetano di Ventimiglia.
> EDITOR: Uncredited.
> CAST: Nita Naldi (Beatrice), John F. Hamilton (Edward Pettigrew), Bernhard Goetzke (J. P. Pettigrew), Malcolm Keen (John "Fear o' God" Fulton).
> RUNNING TIME: 83 minutes. Black and white.
> RELEASED THROUGH: Wolf and Freedman Film Service.

In a remote Kentucky town, bitter widower J. P. Pettigrew is incensed when he sees his son, Edward, has fallen in love with the schoolteacher, Beatrice Brent—perhaps because he desires the woman himself. But when he approaches her, she rejects him, and his son disappears.

Now even more infuriated, Pettigrew decides to have the schoolteacher arrested on moral charges. But a hermit and old rival, John Fulton—who once romanced Pettigrew's wife—saves Beatrice from jail by marrying her. Undaunted, Pettigrew then accuses Fulton of murdering his missing son and eventually has him thrown into prison.

A year later, John escapes from prison and returns to his mountain cabin to find that his child with Beatrice is deathly sick. Battling a blizzard to get back into town and find a doctor, he runs into Pettigrew again—and Edward, who has suddenly reappeared, putting an end to the murder charge.

Hitchcock's second film (although only released after his third film, *THE LODGER*, had become a hit), it was shot in Austria and Germany, with the Alps doubling for the mountains of Kentucky and famous vamp NITA NALDI trying to pass as a backwoods school marm. (According to Hitchcock, she arrived with "four-inch heels, nails like a mandarin's, and a black dog to match her black, swathed dress.")

Although Hitchcock later pronounced the finished film "awful," the melodrama was relatively well received on both sides of the Atlantic, with Britain's *Daily Mail* guardedly saying that it was "full of character though undramatic" and the *Bakersfield Californian* enthusing, "There are more than the usual number of thrills even for a Naldi picture and the picture, in addition, offers some scenic gems."

Although some stills survive, the film itself is considered lost.

References

Alfred Hitchcock, "Life among the Stars," *News Chronicle*, March 15, 1938, http://the.hitchcock.zone/wiki/News_Chron icle_%281937%29_-_Life_among_the _Stars; Patrick McGilligan, *Alfred Hitchcock: A Life in Darkness and Light* (New York: HarperCollins, 2003), 71–72; "Nita Naldi Appears in Mountain Film," *Bakersfield Californian*, February 1, 1927, http://the.hitchcock.zone/wiki/Bakersfield_Cali fornian_%2801/Feb/1927%29_-_Nita _Naldi_Appears_in_Mountain_Film; François Truffaut, *Hitchcock/Truffaut*, rev. ed. (New York: Touchstone, 1985), 39–41.

MR. AND MRS. SMITH (US 1941)

DIRECTOR: Alfred Hitchcock.
SCREENPLAY: Norman Krasna.
PRODUCER: Harry E. Edington.
CINEMATOGRAPHY: Harry Stradling Sr.
EDITOR: Uncredited (William Hamilton).
ORIGINAL MUSIC: Edward Ward.
CAST: Carole Lombard (Ann Smith), Robert Montgomery (David Smith), Gene Raymond (Jeff Custer).
RUNNING TIME: 95 minutes. Black and white.
RELEASED THROUGH: RKO.

Ann and David Smith are a generally happy but frequently contentious Manhattan couple who, three years into their union, suddenly discovers that their marriage certificate is not technically valid. A simple, second ceremony will set things right, but a planned romantic night out turns into a disaster, and when David hesitates in proposing again, Ann kicks him out.

When David goes back the next morning, he sees her with an older gentleman; jealous, he causes a scene only to find out that the fellow was Ann's new boss, and now she's out of a job. Ann declares that now she'll never remarry David, although Jeff, David's law partner, assures him he'll persuade her to change her mind.

Instead, though, Jeff and Ann begin to date—and it seems likely to grow serious, although various accidents keep the lovers apart. Finally, the two take a skiing vacation with Jeff's parents at Lake Placid—only to discover that David has rented the cabin next to theirs. Pretending to be suddenly sick, David arouses Ann's sympathies and forgiveness; realizing the two are truly in love, Jeff leaves them alone to patch up, for now at least, their marriage.

An unusual departure for Alfred Hitchcock. And yet, in retrospect, perhaps not so unusual.

Apart from certain properties (such as *MARY ROSE*, which the director tried to adapt for years), Hitchcock's true investment in a project is sometimes difficult to judge in hindsight. Typically, he was enthused about most assignments, at least through preproduction; during the shooting, though, unless a sudden technical challenge presented itself, he grew utterly bored. Afterward, his final judgment seemed directly tied to the film's success—if it wasn't a hit with audiences and critics, then he was likely to disown it, even claiming, in a bit of sour grapes, that he had never really wanted to make it in the first place.

So *Mr. and Mrs. Smith* is a difficult film to place, as far as Hitchcock's original feelings were. According to DONALD SPOTO, the director was enthused about the project early on (and indeed, it fits into his often-stymied attempt in the '40s to do different sorts of films); according to Hitchcock, who talked down the picture in later life, it was merely a movie he'd taken on as a "favor" to Lombard, a dear friend who wanted to work together.

The simple truth seems impossible to discern at this point, but it is a fact that, before leaving England, Hitchcock had said he wanted to direct CAROLE LOMBARD and that, after arriving, he spoke of making a "typical American comedy." *Mr. and Mrs. Smith*, with its marriage-license gimmick and slightly threadbare screwball antics—the carefree genre had begun to seem less funny once the war began—fit the bill. And Lombard had been doing dramas then with mixed results—a carefree comedy was what her career needed.

Although Lombard and Hitchcock weren't able to get their first choice for the male lead—CARY GRANT, by now a busy freelancer, didn't have a spare moment in his schedule—ROBERT MONTGOMERY seemed like a safe replacement, and Gene Raymond was cast as the third part of the triangle. The set was a happy one, too, with Lombard tweaking the director's already-infamous remark about actors being cattle by setting up a small pen on the set. Inside were three cows with nametags reading "Lombard," "Montgomery," and "Raymond."

A happy set but hardly a thrilling one. "I more or less followed NORMAN KRASNA's screenplay," Hitchcock told FRANÇOIS TRUFFAUT later. "Since I didn't really understand the type of people who were portrayed in the film, all I did was photograph the scenes as written."

Yet there were HITCHCOCKIAN touches throughout, from the MACGUFFIN of the technically invalid marriage license to the MISTAKEN IDENTITY of Ann's boss. The ski-resort vacation looks back to Hitchcock's own honeymoon with Alma (already referenced in *THE MAN WHO KNEW TOO MUCH*); a scene with Ann and Jeff stuck at the top of a parachute ride foretells a bet Hitchcock later had with his own daughter, briefly stranding her at the top of a Ferris wheel during *STRANGERS ON A TRAIN*.

There's also a darkly humorous scene about trying to recapture past romance; on their big night out, David and Ann revisit a favorite restaurant, only to find that it, like their marriage, has lost a great deal of its charm. It's a slightly sour view of marriage that would reoccur more regularly in Hitchcock's '50s films, particularly *DIAL M FOR MURDER* and the remake of *The Man Who Knew Too Much.*

Although *Mr. and Mrs. Smith* did well on release, it—like the Smiths' favorite restaurant—hasn't aged well. The situations feel forced, and the characters aren't very likable. (There's no real reason, beyond wishing for an end to the movie, to even want the Smiths to reunite.) Although it has a number of Hitchcock moments (like his naughty-boy teasing of the CENSORS with a bathroom scene and another sequence when someone gets unexpectedly drunk), the moments don't add up to a film.

Yet it was, nonetheless a hit—and sadly the last of Lombard's films released before her death in a plane crash.

References

Patrick McGilligan, *Alfred Hitchcock: A Life in Darkness and Light* (New York: HarperCollins, 2003), 276–78; Donald Spoto, *The Dark Side of Genius: The Life of Alfred Hitchcock* (New York: Da Capo Press, 1999), 236–40; François Truffaut, *Hitchcock/Truffaut*, rev. ed. (New York: Touchstone, 1985), 139–40; J. Danvers Williams, "What I'd Like to Do with the Stars," *Film Weekly*, March 4, 1939, http://the.hitchcock.zone/wiki/Film _Weekly_%281939%29_-_What_I%27d _Do_to_the_Stars.

"MR. BLANCHARD'S SECRET" (US; ORIGINALLY AIRED DECEMBER 23, 1956)

DIRECTOR: Alfred Hitchcock.
SCREENPLAY: Sarett Rudley, based on a story by Emily Neff.
PRODUCER: Joan Harrison.
CINEMATOGRAPHY: John L. Russell.
EDITOR: Edward W. Williams.
ORIGINAL MUSIC: Stanley Wilson.
CAST: Mary Scott (Babs Fenton), Robert Horton (John Fenton), Dayton Lummis (Mr. Blanchard).
RUNNING TIME: 30 minutes with commercials. Black and white.
ORIGINALLY BROADCAST BY: CBS.

ALFRED HITCHCOCK PRESENTS's low-key, lightly comic twist on *REAR WINDOW*, with an inquisitive (and increasingly suspicious) mystery writer who becomes convinced her neighbor is up to no good.

References

Tim Brooks and Earle Marsh, *The Complete Directory to Prime Time Network TV Shows*, 8th ed. (New York: Ballantine Books, 2003), 29; Jack Edmond Nolan, "Hitchcock's TV Films," *Film Fan Monthly* (June 1968), 3–6.

"MRS. BIXBY AND THE COLONEL'S COAT" (US; ORIGINALLY AIRED SEPTEMBER 27, 1960)

DIRECTOR: Alfred Hitchcock.
SCREENPLAY: Halsted Welles, based on the story by Roald Dahl.
PRODUCERS: Joan Harrison, Norman Lloyd.
CINEMATOGRAPHY: John L. Russell.
EDITOR: Edward W. Williams.
ORIGINAL MUSIC: Frederick Herbert.
CAST: Audrey Meadows (Mrs. Bixby), Les Tremayne (Dr. Bixby), Stephen Chase (the Colonel).

RUNNING TIME: 30 minutes with commercials. Black and white.
ORIGINALLY BROADCAST BY: NBC.

Another cynical take on marriage for *ALFRED HITCHCOCK PRESENTS*, in which, given a mink by her lover, a married woman tries to figure out a way to bring it home without arousing suspicion.

References

Tim Brooks and Earle Marsh, *The Complete Directory to Prime Time Network TV Shows*, 8th ed. (New York: Ballantine Books, 2003), 29; Jack Edmond Nolan, "Hitchcock's TV Films," *Film Fan Monthly* (June 1968), 3–6.

MURDER! (GB 1930)

DIRECTOR: Alfred Hitchcock.
SCREENPLAY: Alfred Hitchcock, Walter C. Mycroft, Alma Reville, based on the novel *Enter Sir John* by Clemence Dane and Helen Simpson.
PRODUCER: Uncredited (John Maxwell).
CINEMATOGRAPHY: Jack E. Cox.
EDITOR: Rene Marrison.
ORIGINAL MUSIC: John Reynders.
CAST: Herbert Marshall (Sir John Menier), Norah Baring (Diana Baring), Esme Percy (Handel Fane).
RUNNING TIME: 98 minutes. Black and white.
RELEASED THROUGH: Wardour Films.

The police arrive at a cheap hotel to find a young actress dead on the floor, beaten to death, and another actress, Diana Baring, still in the room, dazed, a poker at her feet and blood on her clothes. She has no memory of the murder, but as she and the other woman had been quarreling—and she refuses to explain about what—she is quickly arrested and charged with murder.

At the trial, most of the jurors vote "guilty," with only Sir John Menier—an actor and impresario who knew the young woman slightly—resisting. But the others browbeat him, and finally he goes along. The woman is sentenced to death and sent to jail to await the hangman.

But Menier begins to feel he acted too hastily. Tracking down members of Baring's stock company, he investigates the murder himself. Eventually he begins to suspect another actor in the troupe, Handel Fane. He's a female impersonator and occasional high-wire artist but also—and this is the secret he's desperate to conceal—only half white.

Taking a tip from *HAMLET*, Menier asks Fane to audition for a play he's written based on the actual crime, in which he plays a murderous "half-caste"—but although shaken, Fane refuses to confess and leaves. Menier follows him to the circus where he is currently working, and—seeing him waiting in the audience—a despairing Fane ties a rope around his neck and leaps from the high wire, killing himself.

Baring is released from jail, and we next see her embracing Menier—but only onstage, where they are now costars.

A return to genre, if not to outright greatness.

Just as *BLACKMAIL* had seen Hitchcock getting back to the thrills of *THE LODGER* after six straight dramas, *Murder!* was another attempt at a mystery done after the less-than-dramatic adaptation of *JUNO AND THE PAYCOCK*, some work on the revue *ELSTREE CALLING*, and the comedy short (now presumed lost) *An Elastic Affair*, done in conjunction with a studio talent search. *Murder!* however, never earns its exclamation mark.

The BRITISH INTERNATIONAL PICTURES film begins strongly, with a welter of overlapping dialogue and sound effects and a pan across a rooming-house wall, as heads pop out of windows—a small foreshadowing of the images to come in *REAR WINDOW*. And the jury room sequence—introducing a variety of comical types and, artfully staging through a succession of close-ups and repeated lines, their bullying of Sir John Menier—works very well.

But Menier's investigation of the murder is improbable (although not quite as impossible as being a juror at the murder trial of a young woman he already knew and had mentored). And instead of the chase through the British Museum that climaxed *Blackmail*, *Murder!* ends with a talky scene at Menier's home and then the villain's suicide. It's dramatic, but it's not great drama.

Yet the film does incorporate several HITCHCOCKIAN touches and stylistic flourishes. There is, for example, the EXPRESSIONISTIC use of spinning lights and imagined faces that haunt Fane, the murderer, just before he leaps to his death. The marvelously surreal—truly silent comedy—touch when a lowly stage manager visits Menier and his feet literally sink into the plush carpets. And an ongoing visual motif of frames-within-frames, as we see people in mirrors or hanging out of windows or a prop door continually obscures half of the action we see onstage—always reminding us that there are things hidden from view and our understanding.

And thematically, there is, of course, the wrong man—although here, it's the wrong woman—and both Hitchcock's attention to pertinent detail (we follow the police along on their investigation, see the testimony at the trial) and occasional ironic disinterest (as the death sentence is about to be read, the camera decides to stay in the jury room instead and watches the porter sweep up).

But there are more subtle subtexts, too, interests that would only become clearer with the films to come. Such as the work of FREUD, which the director seemed both intrigued and suspicious of (one of the jurors, a fatuous upper-class woman, has a variety of theories about the defendant's "fugue" state). There is also a nod to GUILT (Menier blames himself for Baring's conviction) and, if not outright HOMOSEXUALITY, then certainly a sort of SEXUAL exoticism (a cross-dressing trapeze artist?).

But what also runs through the film—as it does in so many Hitchcock films to come—is an awareness of actors and audiences, of PLAYS WITHIN PLAYS and the shows we all put on in public. Here, it's rooted in the plot—the characters are performers, the police conduct their interviews during a performance, the story climaxes at the circus, and it all ends up back onstage. Yet Hitchcock also draws deeper parallels between spectators. (The jurors at the trial, their heads swiveling back and forth, are no different from the folks in the stalls at the circus.) Connections between performances on- and offstage, too. Onstage, Diana Baring is the sweet, young ingénue; offstage; is she perhaps something else? Onstage, Fane is a man pretending to be a woman; offstage, a murderer pretending to be innocent. Everything is an act, and everyone is an actor; all that ever changes is the crowd we play to.

Concurrent with filming the English *Murder!* Hitchcock also directed a German-language version, shot with a different cast and eventually released under the title *MARY*. It was not a successful effort, the director confessed; he spoke German but not well enough to judge the nuances in the actors' performances, and the STAR, Alfred Abel, was particularly stiff and stubborn. (While there had been the announcement of a third version to be done in French, the film was never made.)

Although Hitchcock later claimed the original English-language film was "too sophisticated for the provinces," it was a hit

in the cities, with the London *Times* hailing it as "not simply a brilliant exercise in mystery melodrama" but a serious character study and the sort of film "of which any country might be proud"; Hitchcock's status as the country's brightest young director was once again affirmed. It would be something he would have to remind himself of as the next few years would bring only such commercial disappointments as *THE SKIN GAME, NUMBER 17*, and *WALTZES FROM VIENNA*.

References

Patrick McGilligan, *Alfred Hitchcock: A Life in Darkness and Light* (New York: HarperCollins, 2003), 133–39; "Murder!" *Times*, September 23, 1930, http://the.hitchcock.zone/wiki/The_Times_%2823/Sep/1930%29_-_%22Murder%22; Donald Spoto, *The Dark Side of Genius: The Life of Alfred Hitchcock* (New York: Da Capo Press, 1999), 126–28; François Truffaut, *Hitchcock/Truffaut*, rev. ed. (New York: Touchstone, 1985), 73–77.

MURNAU, F. W. (1888–1931)

Westphalian-born filmmaker and child prodigy who was reading Nietzsche and Schopenhauer while still in grammar school and studied philology and literature in Berlin and Heidelberg. After valiant service with the German Air Force in World War I, he began a film career, starting a studio with Conrad Veidt.

Many of Murnau's most famous early films were fantasies—*Der Janus-Kopf, Faust*, and the classic *Nosferatu*, an unauthorized adaptation of *Dracula* (which was suppressed—though not successfully destroyed—by Bram Stoker's widow). His style was marked by EXPRESSIONIST techniques—exaggerated shadows, askew angles, and effects that more closely mirrored the characters' inner feelings than any objective reality.

Murnau was not wed to genre, however. His *The Last Laugh*—which, on one of his trips to Germany, Hitchcock had watched him shoot—was the story of a man who is humiliated when he is demoted from hotel doorman to bathroom attendant; *Sunrise*, one of the most beautiful silents, tells a story of true love and corrupting seduction. Both films avoid an excess of titles—*The Last Laugh* has only one—to tell their stories visually.

From 1926 on, Murnau worked in Hollywood, where he was respected—*Sunrise* won a special Oscar as a "unique and artistic production"—but his films were not huge commercial successes. His last film, *Tabu*, was an impressionistic documentary of life in Polynesia. A week before its opening in 1931, Murnau was killed in a car crash. He was 42.

Murnau was, along with FRITZ LANG, one of Hitchcock's few directing models—the "German filmmakers of 1924 and 1925," he remembered, who were "trying very hard to express ideas in purely visual terms." When he went to Germany as a young filmmaker, Hitchcock visited their studios in hopes of watching them on the set; later, when he finally had control over his own productions, he would recall being inspired by their inventive imagery and their championing of emotional truth over mere factual recording—their church of PURE CINEMA.

References

"F. W. Murnau," *Biography*, http://www.biography.com/people/fw-murnau-20717047; "F. W. Murnau: Biog.," *Lenin Imports*, http://www.leninimports.com/murnau_fw.html#partone; Donald Spoto, *The Dark Side of Genius: The Life of Alfred Hitchcock* (New York: Da Capo Press, 1999), 67–71; David Thomson, *The New Biographical Dictionary of Film* (New York: Knopf, 2002), 619–21.

N

NALDER, REGGIE (1907–1991)
Viennese-born performer, the son of (in his own words) a "celebrated courtesan" and an operetta star. During the war, he played clubs and cabarets, finally ending up in occupied Paris, working as an Apache dancer. After the war, he began getting small parts in movies, where his oddly hard, masklike features—partly the result of disfiguring burns, although Nalder was always vague on the circumstances—won him roles as a villain, including that of the assassin in the 1956 *THE MAN WHO KNEW TOO MUCH.*

"Hitchcock never gave actors any real direction," he told David del Valle in 1989. "I was a bit put off at first. You really didn't know where you stood with him. He told very crude and dirty stories like a schoolboy. He knew exactly what he wanted from you, and once you were there he felt it was up to you not to disappoint him." The only guidance he ever gave Nalder, the actor remembered, was "to regard the man I was going to assassinate as if he were a beautiful woman."

After the success of the Hitchcock film, Nalder began to work steadily in America, mostly on television (*Thriller, Star Trek*—where he sported antennae on "Journey to Babel") and in genre pictures, including *The Bird with the Crystal Plumage*, the infamous *Mark of the Devil*, and TV's *Salem's Lot*, in which he plays a very *Nosferatu*-inspired vampire. He died in Santa Monica at 84 of bone cancer.

References
David del Valle, "The Face That Launched a Thousand Trips," *Kinoeye*, http://www.kinoeye.org/03/02/delvalle02.php; "Reggie Nalder," *IMDb*, http://www.imdb.com/name/nm0620513/bio?ref_=nm_ov_bio_sm.

NALDI, NITA (1894–1961)
New York performer and working-class Irish girl named Mary Dooley, who had to go to work to support her brother after her father abandoned the family and her mother died. Early work as an artist's model led to a vaudeville act and parts in Broadway choruses. When she was picked to be a Ziegfeld girl, she changed her name.

Hollywood offers soon followed, with Naldi starting out strong costarring in *Dr. Jekyll and Mr. Hyde* with John Barrymore (a lifelong friend) and Cecil B. De Mille's first version of *The Ten Commandments*; costarring with Rudolph Valentino in *Blood and Sand*, *A Sainted Devil*, and *Cobra* established her as Hollywood's premiere "vamp." Offscreen, Naldi added to the iconography with her heavy drinking, frank language, and rumored bisexuality.

That femme fatale image, though, began to pale by the mid-'20s, along with Naldi's career; playing a small-town schoolteacher in Hitchcock's *THE MOUNTAIN*

North by Northwest featured Cary Grant in a celebration of Hitchcock's classic man-on-the-run thrillers. MGM/Photofest © MGM

EAGLE was supposed to be a chance to take on a different sort of part, although the director was initially horrified to see her arrive at the European set done up in extravagant Hollywood style.

"However," he had to admit, "Nita turned out to be a grand person. For all her entourage, there was nothing high-hat about her. She talked to everybody in her heavy New York drawl. The Germans, accustomed to the starchiness of the Hohenzollerns, fell hard for this American royalty."

The film, though, failed to reestablish her stardom, nor did the few that followed. Naldi retired before the talkies came in, but her investments didn't survive the crash; by 1932, she was bankrupt. She never acted in films again, although she did appear onstage—usually summer stock—and always showed a ready wit. When impresario Billy Rose congratulated her on her successful engagement at his Diamond Horseshoe Nightclub, reciting Kipling's "A Fool There Was," she waved the praise away. "Don't be a fool," she said. "It's curiosity. They think I'm dead."

She died alone of a heart attack in a rented hotel room subsidized by generous friends and the Actor's Fund; it was two days before the maid found her. Naldi was 66.

References

Donna L. Hill, Joan Myers, and Christopher S. Connelly, *Nita Naldi*, http://nitanaldi.com; Alfred Hitchcock, "Life among the Stars," *News Chronicle*, March 15, 1938, http://the.hitchcock.zone/wiki/News_Chronicle_%281937%29_-_Life_among_the_Stars; "Nita Naldi," *IMDb*, http://www.imdb.com/name/nm0620519/bio?ref_=nm_ov_bio_sm.

NAPIER, ALAN (1903–1988)

Worcestershire-born performer who trained at the Royal Academy of Dramatic Art and performed with the Oxford Players. He spent much of the '30s in West End theaters before leaving for Hollywood. Tall, lean, and confident, he was often cast as doctors in such films as *Madame Curie*, *The Song of Bernadette*, *The Uninvited*, and *Ministry of Fear*.

He was in three episodes of *ALFRED HITCHCOCK PRESENTS* (including the three-part show "I Killed the Count") and two episodes of *THE ALFRED HITCHCOCK HOUR*; in *MARNIE*, he plays SEAN CONNERY's father, the two of them portraying two of cinema's least likely Philadelphians. He was, however, much to his surprise, best known for playing Alfred, Bruce Wayne's butler, on TV's *Batman*.

He died in Santa Monica of pneumonia at 85.

References

"Alan Napier," *IMDb*, http://www.imdb.com/name/nm0621002/bio?ref_=nm_ov_bio_sm; Alfred E. Twomey and Arthur F. McClure, *The Versatiles: Supporting Character Players in the Cinema, 1930–1955* (New York: Castle Books, 1969), 170.

NARCEJAC, THOMAS (1908–1998)

Rochefort-sur-Mer-born author who taught philosophy at Nantes for more than 20 years and wrote several novels about sailors and the sea. He is best remembered, though, for his partnership with PIERRE BOILEAU, with whom he wrote dozens of thrillers, young-adult mysteries, and authorized sequels to Maurice Leblanc's novels about the jewel thief Arsene Lupin.

Hitchcock, who was scouting constantly for new stories to adapt, had originally tried to buy the rights to the duo's *Celle Qui N'Etait Plus*; they went instead to HENRI-GEORGES CLOUZOT, who made it as *LES DIABOLIQUES* in 1955. (Prefiguring *PSYCHO*, the film had a nasty scene inside a bathroom—and an advertising campaign that warned audiences not to give away the twist.) Hitchcock then bought one of the pair's subsequent books, *D'Entres Les Morts*, and began transforming it into *VERTIGO*.

The director and his screenwriters made a significant change, however; whereas, in the novel, you only learn about Judy's masquerade at the end, Hitchcock had a scene put in toward the last third, when she writes a letter confessing everything. It was a bold move, and Hitchcock doubted the wisdom of it himself; until the film's final release, he tried cuts both with and without the scene. But ultimately he left it in as the clearest proof of his strongest storytelling belief: Surprise is a simple shock; suspense is the anticipation of one.

Although Boileau died in 1989, Narcejac continued to credit his new mysteries to Boileau-Narcejac. He died of a heart attack in Nice at 89.

References
Patrick McGilligan, *Alfred Hitchcock: A Life in Darkness and Light* (New York: HarperCollins, 2003), 563–64; "Thomas Narcejac," *Encyclopaedia Britannica*, http://www.britannica.com/biography/Thomas-Pierre-Ayraud-Narcejac.

NATWICK, MILDRED (1905–1994)
Baltimore-born performer who attended Bryn Mawr School and made her Broadway debut in 1932. She was a particular hit onstage in George Bernard Shaw's *Candida* and Noel Coward's *Blithe Spirit* and in her film and television work was frequently cast as flustered but well-mannered eccentrics. There had been talk about (mis)casting her in *NOTORIOUS*, as CLAUDE RAINS's MOTHER; that luckily did not come to pass, but Hitchcock later signed her for *THE TROUBLE WITH*

HARRY for Miss Gravely. She was, he thought, one of the few in the cast who got the dry, slightly British tone of the humor absolutely right.

Later, Natwick was busy on television (including two episodes of *ALFRED HITCHCOCK PRESENTS*); won an Oscar nomination for the genteel mother-in-law in *Barefoot in the Park*; and had her own mystery series, *The Snoop Sisters*, with Helen Hayes. Natwick died of cancer in her Park Avenue apartment at 89.

References
"Mildred Natwick," *IMDb*, http://www.imdb.com/name/nm0622450/bio?ref_=nm_ov_bio_sm; Donald Spoto, *The Dark Side of Genius: The Life of Alfred Hitchcock* (New York: Da Capo Press, 1999), 287; Alfred E. Twomey and Arthur F. McClure, *The Versatiles: Supporting Character Players in the Cinema, 1930–1955* (New York: Castle Books, 1969), 171.

NESBITT, CATHLEEN (1888–1982)
Cheshire-born performer who, after finishing her education at the Sorbonne, began a career on the stage after Sarah Bernhardt, a family friend, urged her on. She was in the cast of *The Playboy of the Western World* when its Broadway performance nearly caused a riot (as it had in Dublin); was John Barrymore's first leading lady in the John Galsworthy play *Justice*; and was courted by Rupert Brooke, who wrote her ardent love poems (but died in World War I of blood poisoning from a mosquito bite).

In movies since 1919, her first American film was *Three Coins in the Fountain* in 1954; although she was already 66, she would act for another three decades, appearing in films from *An Affair to Remember* to the original *The Parent Trap*. In *FAMILY PLOT*, she played Julia Rainbird, the wealthy—and GUILT-ridden—eccentric, whose desire to find a lost heir sets the entire plot in motion.

She died in London at 93.

References

"Cathleen Nesbitt," *IMDb*, http://www.imdb.com/name/nm0626350/bio?ref_=nm_ov_bio_sm; Chris Hastings, "Letters Reveal Rupert Brooke's Doomed Love," *Telegraph*, October 14, 2007, http://www.telegraph.co.uk/news/uknews/1566128/Letters-reveal-Rupert-Brookes-doomed-love.html.

NEWMAN, ALFRED (1901–1970)

New Haven–born musician and child prodigy who played in theaters, restaurants, and eventually the vaudeville circuit as the "Marvelous Boy Pianist." By 20 he was a regular fixture in the orchestra pit of Broadway theaters, conducting the scores for musicals by Jerome Kern and George Gershwin.

Going out to Hollywood to conduct the score for Irving Berlin's *Reaching for the Moon*, he soon found steady work at studios, eventually settling in at Fox (for whom he wrote the signature, triumphant fanfare accompanying their logo). Credited with more than 200 scores—including that of *FOREIGN CORRESPONDENT*—some of his most memorable work included the dreamy romanticism of *Wuthering Heights* and the rousing, Copland-esque *How the West Was Won*.

Newman died at 68 in Los Angeles. Of his four children, three work in music, with daughter Maria being an accomplished soloist, and David and Thomas both writing for films. Other musically inclined Newmans include his brothers, Lionel and Emil, and his nephew Randy.

References

"Alfred Newman," *IMDb*, http://www.imdb.com/name/nm0000055/bio?ref_=nm_ov

_bio_sm; "Alfred Newman," *mfiles*, http://www.mfiles.co.uk/composers/Alfred-Newman.htm.

NEWMAN, PAUL (1925–2008)

Ohio-born performer who, after service in World War II, earned a degree in drama at Kenyon University and then got some practical experience with touring stock companies. A year's study at the Yale School of Drama followed and then work on the "METHOD" at the Actors Studio in Manhattan; in 1953, he made his Broadway debut in *Picnic*.

By the following year, Newman was in Hollywood, starring in the faux-biblical epic *The Silver Chalice*. (When it appeared on television years later, he publically apologized for it in a newspaper ad.) In 1956, though, he got a break with *Somebody up There Likes Me* (originally intended for James Dean, who died before filming); within five years, the hits *Cat on a Hot Tin Roof*, *Exodus*, and *The Hustler* had established him as a top STAR. Although his popularity was partly based on his chiseled torso and sky-blue eyes, Newman always had more to offer; like Dean, he projected a rebelliousness and vulnerability. But his best parts also showed a core of inner strength, too; unlike Dean, who often seemed on the edge of hysterics, Newman always showed a steely sense of self.

It was his red-hot fame, though, that made UNIVERSAL insist Hitchcock cast Newman as a rocket scientist in *TORN CURTAIN*. Hitchcock had wanted CARY GRANT, but Grant told him he was retiring, and the studio felt a bankable star was necessary after the director's last two films with TIPPI HEDREN. As added insurance, JULIE ANDREWS would be cast as Newman's wife.

Hitchcock resented the imposition (and the stars' huge salaries) and was put off when Newman, arriving at the Hitchcocks' for a dinner party, promptly doffed his jacket and asked for a beer; the fact that Newman was also one of those dreaded Method actors, like MONTGOMERY CLIFT, also drew his distrust. When the actor persistently questioned Hitchcock about the part, the conflict-averse director considered it bad manners and simply withdrew. "I think Hitch and I could have really hit it off, but the script kept getting in the way," Newman said later.

The film, which had cost $5 million to make, made only a disappointing $7 million in its initial release and led to another frustrating lull in Hitchcock's career; Newman, however, was unscathed and went on to one of his biggest hits, *Cool Hand Luke*.

Newman's star would continue to rise, as his antiestablishment individualism proved to play just as well in the '60s and '70s as it had in the '50s; the work would continue to deepen and broaden, too, having room for entertainments like *Butch Cassidy and the Sundance Kid*, *The Sting*, and *Slap Shot* and more serious dramas like *The Verdict*, *Absence of Malice*, and *The Color of Money*, for which he finally won an Oscar.

Happily married to actress Joanne Woodward for 50 years and an avid race car driver and dedicated philanthropist, Newman died at his Connecticut home of lung cancer at 83.

References

Patrick McGilligan, *Alfred Hitchcock: A Life in Darkness and Light* (New York: HarperCollins, 2003), 664, 672; "Paul Newman," *IMDb*, http://www.imdb.com/name/nm0000056/bio?ref_=nm_ov_bio_sm; "Paul Newman," *Paul-Newman.com*, http://www.paul-newman.com/bio.htm; Donald Spoto, *The Dark Side of Genius: The Life of Alfred Hitchcock* (New York: Da Capo Press, 1999), 490; David Thomson, *The New Biographical Dictionary of Film* (New York: Knopf, 2002), 630–31.

NEWTON, ROBERT (1905–1956)

Dorset-born performer from an artistic family—his great-grandfather had cofounded the Winsor and Newton art supply company, and his father was an esteemed landscape painter. Newton was onstage since his early teens and followed the roles wherever they took him, filling in the gaps between engagements with odd jobs—waiting tables in New York's Hell's Kitchen, working on a cattle ranch in Canada. By the '30s, he was back in England and an established stage star, and by the late '30s, he began to concentrate on movie work; in Hitchcock's *JAMAICA INN* he is Jem, the thief who turns out to be an undercover agent.

He was a romantic hero in that picture, but Newton was a prodigious drinker, and his looks began to go quickly; it's hard to see the soft, almost feminine features of Jem in his Bill Sykes in *Oliver Twist*, a part Newton played less than a decade later. (It was around this time that Hitchcock thought of using the now-dissipated Newton again as the lover in *THE PARADINE CASE*, but DAVID O. SELZNICK insisted on LOUIS JOURDAN.)

Newton continued to work—his portrayals of *Blackbeard, the Pirate* and Long John Silver in *Treasure Island* made him particularly popular among schoolboys and fans of pirate impressions, and he would appear on an episode of *ALFRED HITCHCOCK PRESENTS*—but he had a tendency to both chew the scenery and drink everything in sight; even Richard Burton was said to be appalled by his excesses. "I had a great weakness for Bobbie Newton," director David Lean confessed. "[But] he used to drink far too much. And when he had a couple of drinks, he would speak the absolute truth, which could be horrifying."

Newton died in Beverly Hills, in his wife's arms, of a heart attack. He was 50.

References

Susan Dauenhauer Ciriello, *A Tribute to Robert Newton*, http://www.mooncove .com/newton/index.htm; "Robert Newton," *IMDb*, http://www.imdb.com/name/ nm0628579/bio?ref_=nm_ov_bio_sm; Alfred E. Twomey and Arthur F. McClure, *The Versatiles: Supporting Character Players in the Cinema, 1930–1955* (New York: Castle Books, 1969), 172.

NEW YORK FILM CRITICS CIRCLE

The oldest critics organization in the United States, founded in 1935 as a corrective to the ACADEMY AWARDS. In 1938, it gave its best director honors to Alfred Hitchcock for *THE LADY VANISHES*, an early and important start in establishing his critical reputation in America. In years to come, GRACE KELLY, INGRID BERGMAN, TALLULAH BANKHEAD, and JOAN FONTAINE would all win prizes for their appearances in his films, although none of his movies would ever win best picture.

Reference

New York Film Critics Circle, http://www .nyfcc.com/awards.

NIGHT WILL FALL (GB/US 2014)

DIRECTOR: Andre Singer, Lynette Singer.
PRODUCERS: Brett Ratner, Sally Angel.
CINEMATOGRAPHY: Richard Blanshard.
EDITORS: Arik Lahav, Stephen Miller.
ORIGINAL MUSIC: Nicholas Singer.
CAST: Helena Bonham Carter (Narrator).
RUNNING TIME: 75 minutes. Black-and-white and color.
RELEASED THROUGH: British Film Institute.
ORIGINALLY BROADCAST BY: HBO.

Nonfiction film about the making and rediscovery of *MEMORY OF THE CAMPS*, the Hitchcock-supervised documentary on the Holocaust mixing old and new footage. Not to be confused with the 1985 restoration of the original film broadcast on public television or *Night Must Fall*, the 1937 thriller with ROBERT MONTGOMERY.

References

Richard Brody, "Hitchcock and the Holocaust," *New Yorker*, January 9, 2014, http:// www.newyorker.com/culture/richard -brody/hitchcock-and-the-holocaust; Patrick McGilligan, *Alfred Hitchcock: A Life in Darkness and Light* (New York: HarperCollins, 2003), 372–75; David Parkinson, "Night Will Fall: The Story of File Number F3080," *BFI*, http://www.bfi.org.uk/news -opinion/news-bfi/features/night-will-fall- story-file-number-f3080.

NO BAIL FOR THE JUDGE

Long-gestating project based on the novel of the same name by wry British author Henry Cecil. The plot centers on a respected jurist who is accused of murdering a prostitute; determined to clear him, his loving daughter inveigles a charming thief into helping her investigate the crime. Hitchcock was interested in the story and Cecil's darkly humorous approach and, starting in the mid-'50s, began to develop a script.

There were difficulties from the start, however, both with the material (prostitution was still a problematic subject for the CENSORS) and the screenwriters; although Hitchcock first approached JOHN MICHAEL HAYES, the two had a falling out after *THE MAN WHO KNEW TOO MUCH*. He then went to ERNEST LEHMAN during the production of *NORTH BY NORTHWEST*, but Lehman turned him down.

Hitchcock finally called in SAMUEL A. TAYLOR, who had worked on *VERTIGO*, and engaged him to write a treatment; in Hitchcock's preferred telling of the story, the daughter would be a barrister herself and the villain a respected woman, the unsuspected head of a major prostitution ring. Audrey

Hepburn, who had long wanted to work with the director, would play the lawyer; Laurence Harvey, her larcenous ally; and old dependable JOHN WILLIAMS, the judge.

Ultimately, though, Hepburn turned down the project, although the reason is somewhat in dispute. Several scholars, quoting Hitchcock's associate producer Herbert Coleman, insist it was because of a brutal scene in which—while disguised as a prostitute—Hepburn's character is abducted and assaulted in a park; writer Stephen DeRosa insists Hepburn loved the script and only withdrew because she became pregnant.

In any case, after Hepburn refused him, too, Hitchcock—who could be temperamental when denied—decided to abandon the film completely. Although PARAMOUNT had spent at least $200,000 developing the project, he told them to write it off, saying it would be better to lose that money now rather than the entire budget after an obviously flawed film flopped.

References

Steven DeRosa, "No Bail for the Judge," *Writing with Hitchcock*, http://www.writingwithhitchcock.com/nobailforthejudge.html; Patrick McGilligan, *Alfred Hitchcock: A Life in Darkness and Light* (New York: HarperCollins, 2003), 571, 576–78; Donald Spoto, *The Dark Side of Genius: The Life of Alfred Hitchcock* (New York: Da Capo Press, 1999), 409–12.

NOIRET, PHILIPPE (1930–2006)

Lille-born performer who decided to study theater after a bumpy time in school. He toured with a theatrical troupe for seven years and also developed a satirical stand-up act, in which he came onstage as Louis XIV and discussed current politics. His film career began in earnest in Louis Malle's *Zazie Dans le Metro* in 1960, and he rarely stopped acting after.

Acclaimed in French cinema, he had less luck with his American films, often appearing in misfires like *Night of the Generals, The Assassination Bureau,* and *Who Is Killing the Great Chefs of Europe?* In Alfred Hitchcock's muddled *TOPAZ,* he is the duplicitous Jarre.

Noiret found better parts in better movies in Europe, where he made *La Grande Bouffe, Coup de Torchon, Cinema Paradiso,* and *Il Postino* among many others. That he was able to find steady work at all in the movies with his hangdog face sometimes amused and perplexed him. "At the beginning, I was just doing it for the money, and because they asked me to do it," he told critic Joe Leydon. "But after two or three years of working on movies, I started to enjoy it, and to be very interested in it. And I'm still very interested in it, because I've never really understood how it works. I mean, what is acting for the movies? I've never really understood."

He died in Paris of cancer at 76.

References

Ronald Bergen, "Philippe Noiret," *Guardian,* November 24, 2006, http://www.theguardian.com/news/2006/nov/25/guardianobituaries.france; Joe Leydon, "R.I.P. Philippe Noiret, 1930–2006," *Moving Picture Blog,* November 23, 2006, http://www.movingpictureblog.com/2006/11/rip-philippe-noiret-1930-2006.html.

NORTH BY NORTHWEST (US 1959)

DIRECTOR: Alfred Hitchcock.
SCREENPLAY: Ernest Lehman.
PRODUCER: Uncredited (Alfred Hitchcock).
CINEMATOGRAPHY: Robert Burks.
EDITOR: George Tomasini.
ORIGINAL MUSIC: Bernard Herrmann.
CAST: Cary Grant (Roger O. Thornhill), Eva Marie Saint (Eve Kendall), James Mason (Phillip Vandamm), Leo G. Carroll (the Professor), Martin Landau (Leonard), Jessie Royce Landis (Clara Thornhill).
RUNNING TIME: 136 minutes. Color.
RELEASED THROUGH: MGM.

Successful, staid, and utterly boring Manhattan executive Roger O. Thornhill is having a drink at the Plaza when he is accidentally mistaken by foreign agents for George Kaplan, an American spy; kidnapped and interrogated by the villainous Phillip Vandamm, Thornhill barely escapes—only to have no one—including his own mother—believe him.

Thornhill tracks Kaplan to a New York hotel—the room is empty, but when he unthinkingly answers the phone, the agents become only more convinced that he's their target. And when, after visiting the United Nations, he becomes the suspect in the death of an American diplomat, the police join the chase.

Knowing that Kaplan had a hotel reservation in Chicago, Thornhill takes a train, where he meets the flirtatious Eve Kendall. She offers to help him—without revealing that she's secretly working for Vandamm. When they arrive in Illinois, she sends him to a meeting with Kaplan—but the location turns out to be an empty field, and Thornhill is almost killed by a dive-bombing plane.

Thornhill tracks Eve to an auction house, where she's with Vandamm, busily bidding on a primitive statue. When he sees he's not meant to leave alive, Thornhill causes a scene, bringing the police. They take him away but instead of rushing him off to jail take him to the Professor, an American spymaster who explains that George Kaplan is a fiction meant to distract Vandamm from their real agent—Eve.

Realizing she's been put in jeopardy, Thornhill agrees to one more bit of playacting—he will follow the agents to their next stop, Mount Rushmore, where he will demand custody of Eve to have his revenge; instead Eve pretends to kill Thornhill, thereby proving her loyalty to Vandamm and eliminating "Kaplan" from the plot.

When Thornhill realizes, however, that Eve remains in danger, scheduled to fly away with Vandamm, he eludes the Professor and his men and sneaks into Vandamm's house. There he discovers that the statue has a belly full of stolen microfilm—and they're already onto Eve. Grabbing the statue and Eve, he makes his escape, fleeing over the heads of the Mount Rushmore monument with Vandamm's men in pursuit. Only a well-aimed bullet from a park ranger saves them.

The film ends with Roger and Eve back on the rails but now married, preparing to share an upper berth while the TRAIN hurtles into a tunnel.

They had spent fruitless weeks meeting about adapting *THE WRECK OF THE MARY DEARE*—but mostly talking about wine and movie-industry gossip—when screenwriter ERNEST LEHMAN finally told Alfred Hitchcock he hadn't the foggiest idea of how to tackle the script. Hitchcock told him not to worry about it, and when Lehman protested that they'd still owe a film to MGM, Hitchcock told him they'd simply do something else.

"I want to do a Hitchcock picture to end all Hitchcock pictures," Lehman blurted out. That caught the old AUTEUR's attention because *North by Northwest* is certainly that—both a summing-up and a kind of finale, bidding farewell to his mischievous man-on-the-run films with their mix of lighthearted travelogue and how-far-can-we-push-it SEXUAL tension. From now on—until that final wink at the audience in *FAMILY PLOT*, also scripted by Lehman—the movies would be darker, grimmer, more despairing.

North by Northwest is huge and elegant fun, although getting to that point was even harder work than usual, as Lehman found himself under deadline and in the usual position of the Hitchcock screenwriter, stitching together different, somewhat disconnected ideas.

There would be the central gimmick of a "pretend" secret agent put in place to distract attention from the real spy (an idea Hitchcock bought from a journalist). There would be some moments borrowed and bettered from other Hitchcock films (the knife-in-the-back murders from *THE 39 STEPS* and the second *THE MAN WHO KNEW TOO MUCH*). And then there would be the pet ideas that the director had always wanted to get onscreen—such as the chase across the carved, impassive faces on Mt. Rushmore.

Lehman worked frantically, and the process dragged on—which actually suited Hitchcock's purposes. He had already vaguely discussed the project with JAMES STEWART; now he realized that CARY GRANT was the better choice, but Hitchcock, characteristically loath of any confrontation, shrank from telling Stewart he was no longer wanted. Finally, the deadline for *Bell, Book and Candle* loomed, and the actor had to withdraw; Hitchcock could counterfeit his polite regret while quickly signing up the ever-charming, ever-unknowable STAR the project really needed.

EVA MARIE SAINT, meanwhile, was brought onboard as double agent Eve Kendall (over the objections of MGM, which would have preferred contract star Cyd Charisse); the supporting cast was filled out with JAMES MASON (Yul Brynner had actually been first choice), New York theater actor MARTIN LANDAU, JESSIE ROYCE LANDIS (who'd previously sparred lightly with Grant onscreen in *TO CATCH A THIEF*), and favorite Hitchcock supporting actor LEO G. CARROLL.

Trusted cinematographer ROBERT BURKS and composer BERNARD HERRMANN were hired, as well; SAUL BASS was asked to design the titles; and Hitchcock personally took Saint on a shopping spree at Bergdorf's for her costumes. It was the only time, she later said, she felt like she had a "sugar daddy," as she watched his obvious delight in spending money on her expensive clothes.

"He was a gentleman, he was funny, he was so attentive to me, with the character, and he cared about everything Eve Kendall wore," she said. "He had an eye for the specifics of the character." (But, she pointed out, he was always strictly polite and professional—if, perhaps, because he also knew she was happily married and with a new baby at home.)

The hard work continued during production. Denied permission to film on the grounds of the United Nations, Hitchcock had to "steal" the wide shot of Grant walking up the steps and into the building by hiding his camera in a hired van parked across the street. (So in a way, Hitchcock, terrified of the police since childhood, finally got to face his secret fear and commit a crime.) The complicated picture went an extra $1 million over budget, and more than a month into shooting, Grant complained to Hitchcock that he still didn't understand the story. Hitchcock told him that was perfect, as his character wasn't supposed to be able to make heads or tails of it, either.

There was one more problem, too, after the film was finished; the studio felt it was too long. Couldn't Hitchcock trim it back to something closer to two hours? Perhaps cut the scene in the woods between Grant and Saint after she "shoots" him? Hitchcock not only resented the intrusion but also disagreed strongly—the scene is the first honest one between the two characters and the core of their deepening romance. But then he found a lovely fact; his contract included the right of final cut without exception. The scene stayed in.

Despite the cost overruns and occasional second thoughts from star and studio, *North by Northwest* was a success with audiences and critics. And if it wasn't quite the Hitchcock picture to "end all Hitchcock pictures"—*PSYCHO, THE BIRDS,* and *MARNIE* would all follow and go deeper and darker—then it did serve as a sort of Hitch's greatest hits, showcasing his artistry and, even with the framework of a light entertainment, his most consistent themes and favorite aesthetic approaches.

The craftsmanship throughout the movie is evident right from Bass's titles, in which a grid of intersecting lines eventually turns into the façade of a typical midcentury skyscraper. It's a design that works on several levels, immediately setting the start of the story in modern Manhattan and suggesting (along with the actual title, with its directions from *Hamlet*) the grid of the map the hero will traverse.

It's also, though, the foreshadowing of a compositional form that continues throughout the film—the tall vertical and the broad horizontal. It's a combination that appears again in *Psycho* with the mansion and the motel, but in *North by Northwest*, we see it several times—in that stolen wide shot of the United Nations buildings; in the running man and the chasing plane; in the tall pines and low cars in Eve and Roger's meeting in the woods; and finally in the sheer, modernist planes of Vandamm's house in South Dakota.

It is, indeed, a contrast that's "quite pleasing to the eye," as FRANÇOIS TRUFFAUT later called its use in *Psycho*, but here, it also suggests opposites and intersections—a world in which people pretend to be exactly what they aren't, in which utterly different worlds violently collide.

Also strongly used in the film is sound, not only with Herrmann's score (even better in its quietly insinuating moments than its loudly percussive ones), but also without it; the famous crop-dusting sequence has only a few lines of dialogue and no music at all and delivers its effects purely through cutting and composition (which is why, no doubt, Hitchcock first thought of having the shower murder in *Psycho* played in silence, too—until Herrmann talked him out of it).

The film also shows Hitchcock's brilliance at getting the casting absolutely right and then turning the actors loose. Grant is perfectly at ease in the role of the shallow Madison Avenue ad man who believes a lie is just an "expedient exaggeration" until he gets caught in a thicket of them. (He gets to show off his old acrobatic grace, too, as he takes several falls, making one of them, into an irrigation ditch, almost balletic.) Saint is cool and graceful as Eve; Mason, silkily menacing as Vandamm; and as his trusted aide Leonard, Landau adds more than a touch of homoerotic obsessiveness.

The gay subtext—and sometimes outright text—between Leonard and Vandamm is another Hitchcock theme; at their worst, his films seem to conflate HOMOSEXUALITY and emotional instability (if not outright insanity). But it's only one part of a movie that serves as a virtual checklist of HITCHCOCKIAN subjects; domineering maternal figures (hauled in by the police, Thornhill's first call isn't to his lawyer but his MOTHER); icy BLONDES who are really "snow-covered volcanoes" (the chilly Eve propositions Roger over lunch); villains who move easily through society (like the traitors of *The 39 Steps* and *SABOTEUR*, Vandamm is a well-respected man); and the violent climax played out against the famous backdrop of a national landmark.

More than that, though, *North by Northwest*, like so many Hitchcock films, is a film about IDENTITY. Who is Roger O. Thornhill? The *O*, he tells Eve, stands for nothing (as it did for the self-inventing DAVID O. SELZNICK). He doesn't seem to stand for much either. Twice divorced ("They said I led too dull a life"), he makes his living in advertising, selling people things they don't need, taking business meetings with people who don't hear him, basically slipping through Manhattan without leaving a trace.

He is a man who figuratively isn't there—until he's confused with George Kaplan, a man who literally isn't there, a fictional construct who is (in actual truth) an empty suit, moved around from vacant room to vacant room. And the curious thing is that, by being confused with Kaplan, Thornhill, who isn't really present for anyone or anything in his life, suddenly becomes real and of vital importance. He is pursued by villains, he pursues a lovely woman, he takes action. He is alive, and he has an identity at last—and only because his own identity was MISTAKEN for someone else's and his own life was taken over by a man who never lived.

The strange, shifting idea of who we are and how we see ourselves and how others see us—it's a constant in Hitchcock's works, and in his darkest films (*VERTIGO*, *Psycho*), it's a black and bottomless hole. Who we are changes with any moment, crumbles under every stress.

But in his lightest films, the subject of identity takes on a slightly more optimistic tinge. Who are we, really? Only who we really want to be. And no one knew that better than the poor abandoned son from Bristol who reinvented himself as the world's most sophisticated lover and the fearful fat boy from London who became cinema's coldblooded master of suspense. If *North by Northwest* is not the greatest Hitchcock film ever made, then it is undeniably his most American because it validates its central promise in every frame: Here, you can be anyone you want to be.

References

Destination Hitchcock: The Making of North by Northwest, directed by Peter Fitzgerald (2000), documentary, http://the

.hitchcock.zone/wiki/Destination_Hitchcock:_The_Making_of_North_by_Northwest_%282000%29_-_transcript; Patrick McGilligan, *Alfred Hitchcock: A Life in Darkness and Light* (New York: HarperCollins, 2003), 548–49; Eva Marie Saint, interview with the author, November 2009; Donald Spoto, *The Dark Side of Genius: The Life of Alfred Hitchcock* (New York: Da Capo Press, 1999), 406–9; François Truffaut, *Hitchcock/Truffaut*, rev. ed. (New York: Touchstone, 1985), 248–57, 269; Barbara Vancheri, "Film Emissary Eva Marie Saint Plays Role Well," *Pittsburgh Post-Gazette*, November 4, 2012, http://www.post-gazette.com/movies/2012/11/14/Film-emissary-Eva-Marie-Saint-plays-role-well/stories/201211140179.

NOTORIOUS (US 1946)

DIRECTOR: Alfred Hitchcock.
SCREENPLAY: Ben Hecht.
PRODUCER: Uncredited (Alfred Hitchcock).
CINEMATOGRAPHY: Ted Tetzlaff.
EDITOR: Theron Warth.
ORIGINAL MUSIC: Roy Webb.
CAST: Ingrid Bergman (Alicia Huberman), Cary Grant (T. R. "Dev" Devlin), Claude Rains (Alexander Sebastian), Madame Leopoldine Konstantin (Madame Sebastian), Louis Calhern (Paul Prescott).
RUNNING TIME: 101 minutes. Black and white.
RELEASED THROUGH: RKO.

After the Second World War and the conviction of her traitorous father, Alicia Huberman slips into a self-loathing haze of parties, alcohol, and casual affairs. She's pulled out of her tailspin by T. R. Devlin, an American agent who offers her a chance to strike back at her father's old Nazi circles by helping the government infiltrate a group of Germans who have already fled to South America.

The Americans' plan is to have Alicia seduce the leader of the group, Alex Sebastian, an old admirer of hers, and Devlin—who has begun to fall in love with her—assumes she'll refuse. But he presents the scheme to her anyway without voicing any objections, and she glumly agrees—and so they both proceed, each disappointed in the other.

In Rio, Alicia not only contrives to catch Sebastian's eye but soon wins a proposal from him, as well. She agrees to marry him and, ensconced in his house, begins reporting back to Devlin about the men who come there for meetings and something that seems to be hidden in the wine cellar—to which only Sebastian has a key.

Devlin convinces her to get Sebastian to throw a huge party and steal the key; at the party as a guest, Devlin sneaks down to the cellar with Alicia, where they accidentally discover that many of the wine bottles seem to be filled with a mineral ore. Sebastian almost discovers them, and Devlin quickly covers up by embracing Alicia and letting her husband think they slipped away for a kiss—but soon Sebastian finds out the truth (so does Devlin—the mineral ore is enriched uranium).

Sebastian's mother is horrified when he tells her he's married an American spy; if he tells his cohorts, they'll kill him for his stupidity. They must murder Alicia first, she proclaims, and soon she begins slipping poison into her daughter-in-law's coffee. When Alicia shows up at her scheduled meeting with Devlin appearing ill, he assumes she's hungover, but when she misses another one, he grows concerned. He goes back to Sebastian's house and, realizing she's being poisoned, carries her out to a hospital—leaving Sebastian behind to deal with his suddenly, murderously suspicious colleagues.

One of Hitchcock's greatest films began two decades apart in the minds of three different men.

The first was John Taintor Foote, a sometimes-outdoors writer (and eventual screenwriter—he did *The Mark of Zorro*) who, in 1921, had his two-part story "The Song of the Dragon" published in the *Saturday Evening Post*. It was the tale of a young Broadway ingénue who, to help the American war effort, agrees to seduce one of the Kaiser's enemy agents; afterward, a letter from the president himself helps convince her fiancé's family that, despite this, she is still worthy of marriage. It's an absurd melodrama, but something in it appealed to DAVID O. SELZNICK, who bought the rights and filed them away.

More than 20 years later, Hitchcock was finishing up *SPELLBOUND* and eager to find another project for INGRID BERGMAN. He began to rough out a story about a woman who becomes part of a big confidence game; to pull it off, she has to marry a wealthy man. Hitchcock thought the story might be set in South America, Argentina perhaps, and suggested it to Selznick, Bergman, and RKO. (He also may have been reminded of two colleagues—CHARLES BENNETT and Reginald Gardiner—who had both been asked by the British government to "befriend" women thought of aiding the Nazi cause.) Selznick recalled the story he had bought (and vaguely thought about turning into a project for Jennifer Jones). Slowly, all the disparate ideas began to come together.

Turning them into a screenplay fell to BEN HECHT, who had already written *Spellbound* and had helped to anonymously punch up several other Hitchcock scripts (and would continue to). He and Hitchcock hashed out the basic outline over long story conferences; then Hecht would quickly turn the ideas into pages. There were additional conferences with Selznick, which Hitchcock particularly dreaded, as they were always scheduled for late at night and never began on time. (Selznick had one perfect idea, though, on casting: for Sebastian, no to Clifton Webb, yes to CLAUDE RAINS.)

Selznick had his own troubles, though, with *Duel on the Sun* and his mounting debts; eventually, reluctantly, he sold *Notorious*, its director, script, and STARS to RKO as a complete package. He would take the "A Selznick Release" credit but would have no further involvement; for Hitchcock, who had suffered the mogul's constant supervision and second-guessing (even recutting his scenes on *Spellbound*) it was a welcome relief (albeit a short-lived one; Selznick would be back to his meddling on their next and last film together, *THE PARADINE CASE*).

Not that Hitchcock's troubles ended there. The CENSORS raised objections to the material, primarily to the portrayal of Alicia as a "loose" woman (rewrites made her more drunken than promiscuous, although slighting allusions to her being "not a lady" and a reference to her "playmates" still remained); Hitchcock worried about the ending (at one point, a far more violent one was considered, with Sebastian's MOTHER shooting her son and trying to kill Alicia and Devlin stopping her only by wrecking their car).

And Hitchcock later said that he himself was followed by government agents, alarmed by his making a movie about nuclear material—although, this may be another instance of him preferring a slightly embroidered anecdote to the plain truth. (By the time *Notorious* went into production, the bomb had already been dropped.)

Yet, as many talents had been involved in *Notorious*, the final product was very clearly—very brilliantly—a Hitchcock film. Like many of the great Hollywood studio films, the performances are based on personas, with the stars both playing to (and playing off our expectations of) their onscreen iconography. CARY GRANT is a fantasy figure, impossibly gorgeous and elegantly tailored. (When he's introduced,

all we see for the longest time is the back of his perfectly groomed head.) But he is also unobtainable, unknowable, and coldly cruel; his hard-boiled words to Alicia are like slaps in the face. ("Dry your eyes, baby, it's out of character.")

As Alicia, Bergman is full off the yearning vulnerability we saw in *Intermezzo: A Love Story* and *Casablanca*. But she is no virgin here, and as PAULINE KAEL noted, it was those "fallen woman" performances (in *Saratoga Trunk*, in *Dr. Jekyll and Mr. Hyde*) that were often Bergman's most interesting. The pain she shows at Devlin's bitter insults is palpable; the whispered urgency of her lovemaking is thrilling.

Rains is the third part of the triangle; always one of Hollywood's greatest voices (he was an instructor at the Royal Academy of Dramatic Art when JOHN GIELGUD was a pupil) and a versatile character actor, he brought the part, as Selznick knew, the sort of smooth sympathy Webb would have had to strain for. But here also is Rains showing his own vulnerability, the short old man in love with a vital young woman, the DOMINATED son still in thrall to Mommy.

The maternal instinct is a strong subtext in *Notorious*, and for the first time, it begins to take on a darker tone. The mother in *SHADOW OF A DOUBT*, made after Hitchcock's own mother had died, is a loving one, if somewhat vulnerable and in need of protection; in *Spellbound*, made directly after, Dr. Petersen takes on a sort of no-nonsense mothering role with Ballantyne, not unlike the parentally protective relationship ALMA REVILLE had with Hitchcock himself (a role Bergman tries unsuccessfully to assume again in *Notorious* with Grant, referring to herself as "Mama").

But by *Notorious*, that maternal character has hardened; Madame Sebastian (and "Madame" was the way Hitchcock always referred to Alma in public) is coldly practical and guiltlessly domineering. Like Hitchcock with his own mother, Sebastian meekly goes to her bedroom to give her the news of the day; like Hitchcock with his own wife, he listens carefully while she gives him no-nonsense advice on how to protect himself from the envious people around him, all jockeying for position.

In *Notorious*, however, this guidance comes with a price; although Alma understood a director had to have leading ladies, Madame Sebastian will have no other woman in her son's life. (As Sebastian protests bitterly, "You've always been jealous of any woman I've ever shown any interest in.") She is the first example of the clinging, demanding mother—more spurned lover than loving parent—who we see in later, even darker Hitchcock films like *PSYCHO* and *THE BIRDS*. Madame Sebastian had no hand in her son's wedding, but she is quite happy to take charge of the events leading up to her daughter-in-law's funeral.

But if Madame Sebastian has a twisted view of a mother's love, then few people love simply in *Notorious*; it's a film of faulty images and unmet expectations, of ugly doubts and unspoken obligations. Devlin falls for Alicia, even though her past disturbs him; a prisoner of a sexist double standard, it's hard for him to be with her knowing that other men got there first.

"You're sore because you've fallen for a little drunk you tamed in Miami and you don't like it," Alicia tells him. "It makes you sick all over, doesn't it? People will laugh at you, the invincible Devlin, in love with someone who isn't worth even wasting the words on." She's right, and so even though he stands up for her in private (turning quickly on a colleague who refers to her as a "woman of that sort"), Devlin constantly tortures them both, testing her by setting up situations—Will you sleep with Sebastian? Will you marry Sebastian?—to see if she's still the woman he knows she was. He hopes she'll refuse. She, needing some definite proof of his love, hopes he'll forbid her first.

And when he doesn't tell her no, she knows he doesn't love her, and when she says yes, he knows she's doesn't love him—both equally convinced, both equally wrong.

The irony, of course, is that they so clumsily misread and misunderstand each other in a film that is in love with and attentive to detail—from the precise title card that begins the drama, telling us where we are and when it is (something reprised later in *Psycho*) to the very careful close-ups of seemingly innocent, suddenly significant objects—a bottle of wine, champagne in an ice bucket, a key clutched in a hand, dirt on a cellar floor.

They are tiny details that Hitchcock's camera, wielded by TED TETZLAFF, captures expertly, particularly in a complicated crane shot (which required the construction of an on-set elevator) that swoops down and across a formal entryway to capture the key in Alicia's hand or the nicely edited moment (cleanly cut by Theron Warth, usually stuck on B movies) in which Devlin accidentally smashes a bottle in the wine cellar.

And, best of all, there is the kiss—a stunning sequence in which (cheekily getting around censorship restrictions) Hitchcock has Grant and Bergman prolong the moment by locking lips, breaking off, nuzzling some more, cuddling a bit, going back for another session—all the while talking about a chicken dinner while the camera itself, hanging close, seems to join them in an embrace à trois.

Full of romance and regret, passion and GUILT, *Notorious* remains one of Hitchcock's signature accomplishments—and his last great film until *STRANGERS ON A TRAIN* five years later.

References

Ingrid Bergman and Alan Burgess, *My Story* (New York: Delacorte Press, 1980), 160; Patrick McGilligan, *Alfred Hitchcock: A Life in Darkness and Light* (New York: HarperCollins, 2003), 374–81; Donald Spoto, *The Dark Side of Genius: The Life of Alfred Hitchcock* (New York: Da Capo Press, 1999), 283–90; Donald Spoto, *Spellbound by Beauty: Alfred Hitchcock and His Leading Ladies* (New York: Harmony Books, 2008), 147–60; Bob Thomas, *Selznick* (New York: Pocket Books, 1972), 209; François Truffaut, *Hitchcock/Truffaut*, rev. ed. (New York: Touchstone, 1985), 167–72.

NOVAK, KIM (1933–)

Chicago-born performer whose early beauty-contest title—"Miss Deepfreeze"—seemed to presciently signal both the good looks and slightly cool persona that would mark (and sometimes hamper) her time in Hollywood, where shyness is so often mistaken for hauteur.

Her first love as a student had been art, but modeling paid the bills and won her a contract at Columbia, where the bullying mogul Harry Cohn would micromanage her career, trying to make her over into the next Rita Hayworth or Marilyn Monroe "or, better yet, a composite of both," Novak said later. "That always was amazing to me in Hollywood. They hire you because they think you have something special. Yet they feel the need to make you over into what they want, into something else."

Novak resisted, though, and after a strong debut in the B movie *Pushover* (made even more remarkable by the free-spirited Novak's obvious refusal to wear a bra), she had a string of hits with *The Man with the Golden Arm*, *Pal Joey*, and the achingly romantic *Picnic*.

She was not Hitchcock's first choice for *VERTIGO* (VERA MILES had been scheduled to do it until she became pregnant and withdrew), and the relationship may have been further strained when shooting was held up due to her salary fight with Cohn. In fact, in many ways—frankly voluptuous, creatively independent, intellectually questing—Novak was precisely the sort of leading lady Hitchcock usually avoided. But even if the director never quite warmed to his STAR, then his star never lost her affection for the part, and his typical refusal to engage her questions about motivation actually ended up giving her a kind of freedom.

"I was so used to being told what I was supposed to be thinking," she said. "But when I went to him to talk about how to play the part, he said, 'That's what you're supposed to do, my dear.' And that's when I started enjoying it. 'This is incredible,' I thought, 'I'm going to be able to work this out myself.' And who could identify with this more than I could, because of what I was dealing with at Columbia Pictures and with Harry Cohn? I really identified with the fact of someone who was being made over, who was saying 'Please, see who I am. Fall in love with *me*.'"

Audiences seemed to have, but Novak struggled to express herself, and while there were still fine films ahead—including the delightful *Bell, Book and Candle* with *Vertigo* costar JAMES STEWART—there were many other poor films and some bad business decisions. She felt betrayed by directors—with Robert Aldrich redubbing her in *The Legend of Lylah Clare* and Mike Figgis drastically recutting *Liebestraum*—and finally retired from films in the early '90s to paint and putter.

Private life suits her. Novak seems to have found a kind of peace with her husband, her art, and her pets, yet her occasional brave returns to the spotlight have sometimes felt uncomfortable (an appearance at a film festival, where she spoke tearfully for the first time about her bipolar disorder) if not outright cruel (a spot at the 2014 Academy Awards, where her suspiciously "youthful" looks were harshly scrutinized). But the woman who stood up to Harry Cohn isn't going to hide. And when it comes to her love for *Vertigo*, she isn't going to be quiet.

References

Kim Novak, http://www.kimnovakartist .com; Kim Novak, interview with the author, October 1996; "Kim Novak," *Biography*, http://www.biography.com/peo ple/kim-novak-9425476; "Kim Novak," *IMDb*, http://www.imdb.com/name/ nm0001571/bio?ref_=nm_ov_bio_sm; *Obsessed with Vertigo: New Life for Hitchcock's Masterpiece*, directed by Harrison Engle (1997), documentary, http://the .hitchcock.zone/wiki/Obsessed_with_Ver tigo:_New_Life_for_Hitchcock's_Master piece_%281997%29_-_transcript; David Thomson, *The New Biographical Dictionary of Film* (New York: Knopf, 2002), 640–41.

NOVELLO, IVOR (1893–1951)

Welsh-born performer, whose mother was a well-known vocal coach. She encouraged his interest in music, and Novello went from being a child prodigy to singing in the choir at Oxford, to which he'd won a scholarship. At 21, he wrote the lyrics to "Keep the Home Fires Burning," an extraordinarily popular song during World War I.

Novello's songwriting continued, although after the war, he began to act, as well; blessed with dark, matinee-idol looks, he made his film debut in 1920 and his stage debut the next year. He starred in Hitchcock's THE LODGER (although his stardom required a rewrite so that he was not exposed as the murderer) and in the movie version of his own play *DOWNHILL*, which he cowrote with CONSTANCE COLLIER (who'd used the penname "David L'Estrange").

Novello was not particularly a subtle actor, and in films, he tended to specialize in shy, tortured types or honorable young prep-school boys. That made him fine for *The Lodger* and even *Downhill* (which also exploited his appeal among female and gay male audiences by having him strip to the waist) but led to smirks from British critics, who saw him as Cardiff's poor answer to Rudolph Valentino (and just as suspiciously "unmanly").

Novello, who also wrote some lyrics for *ELSTREE CALLING*, went to Hollywood in the early '30s but found few parts and was mostly employed as a rewrite man on other people's movies. (Reportedly, he penned the "Me Tarzan, you Jane" exchange for *Tarzan, the Ape Man*.) Pronouncing his own efforts in America "rubbish," he returned to England and to a long and successful career as a composer and stage performer.

Novello died at age 58 in London of a coronary thrombosis; he is perhaps best remembered today through the British songwriting award established in his name in 1955.

References

"Ivor Novello," *IMDb*, http://www.imdb .com/name/nm0637040/bio?ref_=nm_ov _bio_sm; Geoffrey Macnab, "Homme Fatal," *Guardian*, January 9, 2004, http://www.the guardian.com/film/2004/jan/10/1.

NUMBER 13 (GB 1922)

DIRECTOR: Alfred Hitchcock.
SCREENPLAY: Anita Ross.
PRODUCERS: John Hitchcock (Alfred Hitchcock, Clare Greet, uncredited).
CINEMATOGRAPHY: Joe Rosenthal.
CAST: Clare Greet (Mrs. Peabody), Ernest Thesiger (Mr. Peabody).
RUNNING TIME: Unfinished. Black and white.
RELEASED THROUGH: Unreleased.

A comedy short about a wealthy American couple who build a low-income housing project in Britain. This was slated to be Hitchcock's first film as a director, but the financing abruptly disappeared; although friends and relatives contributed funds—as did the lead actress, Clare Greet—filming eventually had to stop.

"A rather chastening experience," the director later confessed; production never restarted, and whatever footage was completed was written off as lost long ago. Yet although he may have chosen to forget this picture, rarely mentioning it in INTERVIEWS, he did not forget Greet's generosity; he continued to cast her in his films, even in bit parts, until the end of her life.

References

Patrick McGilligan, *Alfred Hitchcock: A Life in Darkness and Light* (New York: HarperCollins, 2003), 54–55; "Number Thirteen," *BFI*, http://explore.bfi.org.uk/4ce2b74ea4923; François Truffaut, *Hitchcock/Truffaut*, rev. ed. (New York: Touchstone, 1985), 27–29.

NUMBER 17 (GB 1932)

DIRECTOR: Alfred Hitchcock.
SCREENPLAY: Alfred Hitchcock, Alma Reville, Rodney Ackland, based on the play by Jefferson J. Farjeon.
PRODUCERS: Leon M. Lion (John Maxwell, uncredited).
CINEMATOGRAPHY: Jack Cox.
EDITOR: A. C. Hammond.
ORIGINAL MUSIC: Adolph Hallis.
CAST: John Stuart (Barton), Leon M. Lion (Ben), Anne Grey (Nora), Donald Calthorp (Brant), Ann Casson (Miss Ackroyd).
RUNNING TIME: 66 minutes. Black and white.
RELEASED THROUGH: Wardour Films.

Investigating an abandoned house in London, an undercover police detective finds a comical hobo, Ben—and an unidentified dead body. They are soon joined by a woman, Miss Ackroyd, who falls through the skylight—and by three mysterious people who are thieves, there to retrieve a diamond necklace they've hidden in a toilet.

After a protracted struggle, the thieves escape, with the rest in pursuit and a wild chase ensuing by bus and freight TRAIN. When a stray bullet kills the engineer, the train speeds out of control and crashes into a departing ferry. Everyone is rescued from the water, and the necklace is safely recovered.

Told that his next directing project for BRITISH INTERNATIONAL PICTURES would be *Number Seventeen* (identified on some contemporary posters as *Number 17*), Hitchcock was annoyed. Not only had the script he really wanted to direct, *London Wall*, been given to another director, but also he thought this property (based on a play, first a novel, by Joseph Farjeon) was hackwork full of old-dark-house clichés. Then he had an idea: Why not play the whole thing for laughs as a satire of mystery thrillers? And, indeed, it might have worked as a comedy—if Hitchcock and his coscenarists had thought of including any jokes. But *Number 17* only plays like a parody with all the funny bits taken out.

The completed film—which runs barely over an hour—splits into two unequal parts. In the first, a variety of people converge on the abandoned house, getting into various fights and, occasionally, revealing their surprise true IDENTITIES. A long, dull slog, it has most of the action taking place on a dimly lit flight of STAIRS and only Leon M. Lion, who originated the role of the tramp onstage—he served as producer, too—showing any life. The second half then turns into an exaggerated chase, ending in an almost childish orgy of destruction. It briefly wakes up the film, thanks to its frantic crosscutting (and prefigures some of the more adult work to come in *THE LADY VANISHES*), but the deliberately hyperbolic nature of the action doesn't induce the gales of laughter Hitchcock assumed it would.

There are a few Hitchcock touches, such as a SUBJECTIVE shot of a fist coming straight at the camera, followed by a reaction shot of a man falling backward—a set-up the director would repeat several times in years to come, even as late as *NORTH BY NORTHWEST*. There are also a few Hitchcock obsessions, such as a fondness for scenes set in bathrooms and touches of BONDAGE. But the plot is a muddle, the characters uninteresting, the acting undistinguished, and the comedy never really connects. "A disaster" Hitchcock called it years later, and it would be difficult to argue with him.

References

Patrick McGilligan, *Alfred Hitchcock: A Life in Darkness and Light* (New York: HarperCollins, 2003), 146–48; Donald Spoto, *The Dark Side of Genius: The Life of Alfred Hitchcock* (New York: Da Capo Press, 1999), 129; François Truffaut, *Hitchcock/Truffaut*, rev. ed. (New York: Touchstone, 1985), 81–82.

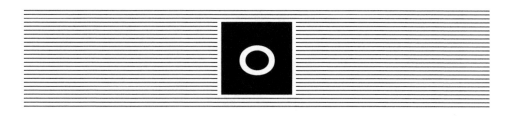

OAKLAND, SIMON (1915–1983)

Brooklyn-born performer—some sources list his birth date as 1922—and the son of a laborer, who began his career in the arts as a violinist; later, after World War II, he turned to the stage instead, making his debut in 1948 and getting his big break when he took over from Paul Muni in the original Broadway production of *Inherit the Wind.*

He had made his screen debut in a bit part in *The Desperate Hours* in 1955 and tended to play stern authority figures—doctors, newspaper editors, policemen. Alfred Hitchcock cast him as the psychiatrist in *PSYCHO* who's called upon to "explain" Norman Bates; that it's a gratingly dull scene says less about Oakland than it does, perhaps, about Hitchcock's suggestion that all explanations of character are pointless.

Oakland would appear in *West Side Story, The Sand Pebbles, Bullitt,* and many TV episodes; he was a regular on several series, including the cult fantasy show *The Night Stalker.* He died at 68 of cancer in Cathedral City, CA.

References

"Simon Oakland," *IMDb,* http://www.imdb.com/name/nm0643000/bio?ref_=nm_ov_bio_sm; "Simon Oakland, 61, Actor Who Starred in 3 TV Series, Dies," *New York Times,* September 1, 1983, http://www.nytimes.com/1983/09/01/obituaries/simon-oakland-61-actor-who-starred-in-3-tv-series-dies.html.

O'HARA, MAUREEN (1920–2015)

Dublin-born performer who yearned to act from an early age and was in music and dance classes from the age of six, including dramatic studies with the Abbey Players. She made a screen test at 18 under her own name, Maureen FitzSimons. CHARLES LAUGHTON, who was then beginning his own company, Mayflower Productions, signed her to a seven-year contract; pronouncing her name too long for marquees, he changed it.

Her first major role was with Laughton as the spirited orphan girl who finds her uncle's Cornish house is a nest of cutthroats and smugglers in *JAMAICA INN;* although Hitchcock seemed to take his usual perverse interest in getting his leading lady as wet and uncomfortable on the set as possible, O'Hara had no problem with his direction and wrote later in her memoirs that she "never experienced the strange feeling of detachment with Hitchcock that many other actors claimed to have felt."

"Hitchcock was fabulous to work with," she said another time. "But he couldn't help it. He had the gift of genius from the heavens and gave the world wonderful stories and movies."

Laurence Olivier escorts Joan Fontaine into Manderley in *Rebecca*, as Edward Fielding looks on. *United Artists/Photofest © United Artists*

She reteamed with Laughton in America for *The Hunchback of Notre Dame*, in which she played the gypsy Esmerelda; this led to a long career in Hollywood, where her flaming hair and Junoesque stature kept her busy in costume dramas, although her favorite films were *Miracle on 34th Street*; *How Green Was My Valley*; and, of course, *The Quiet Man*.

"Every STAR has that certain something that stands out and compels us to notice them," she said once. "As for me I have always believed my most compelling quality to be my inner strength, something I am easily able to share with an audience. I'm very comfortable in my own skin."

She died at 95 in Boise, ID, one year after being awarded an honorary Oscar for a lifetime of performances that "glowed with passion, warmth and strength."

References
"Actress Maureen O'Hara Dies at 95," *USA Today*, October 25, 2015, http://www.usa today.com/story/life/people/2015/10/24/actress-maureen-ohara-dies-at-age-95/74536318; Ronald Bergen, "Maureen O'Hara: Obituary," *Guardian*, October 24, 2015, http://www.theguardian.com/film/2015/oct/25/maureen-ohara; "Maureen O'Hara," *IMDb*, http://www.imdb.com/name/nm0000058/bio?ref_=nm_ov_bio_sm; Nick Thomas, "Oscar-Winning Maureen O'Hara Speaks about Her Life as a Hollywood Legend," *Irish Central*, September 25, 2015, http://www.irishcentral.com/culture/entertainment/Oscar-winning-Maureen-OHara-speaks-about-her-life-as-a-Hollywood-legend.html#.

OLIVIER, LAURENCE
(1907–1989)
Surrey-born performer who came from a long line of clergymen. His father was a little too extravagantly "high church" to find regular employment (he styled himself as "Father Olivier") but was a good speaker who had once dreamed of his own career on the stage and encouraged his youngest son to explore drama professionally.

A precocious star, Olivier drew attention even in grammar-school plays; actress Ellen Terry raved about his Brutus in *Julius Caesar* when the boy was only 10. Olivier went on to Oxford and then won a scholarship to the Central School of Speech Training and Dramatic Art. (PEGGY ASHCROFT was a classmate.) By 1925, he was appearing regularly on the London stage,

frankly modeling his casual style after actor Gerald du Maurier.

"If I wasn't an actor, I think I'd have gone mad," Olivier said years later. "You have to have extra voltage, some extra temperament to reach certain heights. Art is a little bit larger than life—it's an exhalation of life and I think you probably need a little touch of madness."

Slowly establishing himself, Olivier married actress JILL ESMOND in 1930 and—although denigrating the medium—took a stab at films, which paid better than the stage. ("You've no artistic integrity, that's your trouble," Noel Coward told him.) It proved unsuccessful, though—the studios suggested he change his name to "Larry Oliver"—and ended with him being fired from *Queen Christina*, in which he was to have appeared with Greta Garbo.

Returning to England and the stage, Olivier joined the Old Vic, although his naturalistic reading of Shakespeare's lines was often compared (unfavorably) with the more poetic style of older actors, such as JOHN GIELGUD. By the late '30s, though, Olivier had finally drawn acclaim for his performance in *Coriolanus*—and begun his affair (later to blossom into marriage) with the gorgeous, erratic Vivien Leigh.

A second try at Hollywood was more successful, with Olivier's performance in *Wuthering Heights*—a difficult one, with director William Wyler pushing him toward an even smaller, more cinematic style—winning him an Oscar nomination for best actor and no doubt getting him the lead in Alfred Hitchcock's *REBECCA* (based, oddly enough, on a novel by DAPHNE DU MAURIER, the daughter of his old idol).

Olivier was too young for the role—a problem only exaggerated by the obviously fake gray streaks in his hair—but he caught the character's arrogance and quicksilver moods. Not all of that was strictly acting, either; Olivier was furious that Leigh hadn't been cast as his costar (producer DAVID O. SELZNICK, who had already put her in *Gone with the Wind*, wanted the STARS kept separate until Olivier's divorce came through), and the actor frequently took out his anger on the skittish JOAN FONTAINE, mocking her mercilessly.

It was a difficult working relationship—Olivier would occasionally spray her with spittle during their close-ups, then upbraid her for complaining—made deliberately more difficult by Hitchcock, who, even as he encouraged Fontaine, took pains to remind her that no one else liked her. The psychological torture was cruel but effective; Fontaine ended up projecting precisely the sort of wounded uncertainty that the role and her director required.

After *Pride and Prejudice*—in which again, much to Olivier's anger, Leigh was not cast—the couple got the chance to appear onstage in a production of *Romeo and Juliet* they helped finance. The play flopped, but another pairing, in the movie *That Hamilton Woman*, was more successful. Following its release, the now-married couple returned to England, where Olivier volunteered his services for the war effort. It was with the encouragement of the Ministry of Information that he made his rousing version of *Henry V*.

Olivier would follow this after the war with his acclaimed (and Oscar-winning) film of *Hamlet*—an obligation that prevented him from starring in *THE PARADINE CASE*—and racked up further stage successes; Leigh was by now sadly battling both alcoholism and manic depression. (The couple would finally divorce in 1960; in 1961, he married his last wife, actress Joan Plowright.)

Critics who had first been suspicious of his more naturalistic approach to the classics now acclaimed his work for its modern vigor and unforced physicality; in some ways, Olivier—despite his technical prowess and disdain for METHOD ACTING—served as the perfect bridge between the prewar British classicists and the postwar acolytes of the Actors Studio, bringing to his parts both accomplished technique and visceral immediacy.

Unlike his friends and compatriots Gielgud and Ralph Richardson, however, Olivier maintained a healthy appreciation for stardom and its iconography. Personally, like Orson Welles, he had an enormous love for wigs, costumes, and putty noses, always feeling a bit naked onstage without them; privately, like almost everyone, he stood in enormous awe of CARY GRANT, who seemed to exist so perfectly easily onscreen.

In the '50s, Olivier appeared with Leigh for the last time in *Titus Andronicus*, a performance that brought him more raves, and then dazzled in the gritty *The Entertainer*, a role he later repeated on film. Throughout the '60s, he would move between the screen and the stage, excelling in *Spartacus*, the HITCHCOCKIAN *Bunny Lake Is Missing*, and *Oh! What a Lovely War* and helping found the National Theatre, where he served as director for 10 years.

By the '70s, his health had grown too frail to encourage long theatrical runs, but he continued to appear regularly in films and television, with memorable roles in ANTHONY SHAFFER's *Sleuth*, *Marathon Man*, *The Boys from Brazil*, and *A Little Romance*—admitting, without a touch of guilt, that he did the vast majority of his movie roles for the money, although in 1983 he rallied to do a fine *King Lear* for television. Knighted in 1947, he was made a peer of the realm in 1970; unlike many others, he resisted using the titles in his film and stage credits.

He died of renal failure at 82 in West Sussex.

References

"Biographies: Laurence Olivier," *History*, http://www.history.co.uk/biographies/laurence-olivier; "Laurence Olivier," *IMDb*, http://www.imdb.com/name/nm0000059/bio?ref_=nm_ov_bio_sm; Patrick McGilligan, *Alfred Hitchcock: A Life in Darkness and Light* (New York: HarperCollins, 2003), 249–50, 391; Donald Spoto, *The Dark Side of Genius: The Life of Alfred Hitchcock* (New York: Da Capo Press, 1999), 212–19; Donald Spoto, *Laurence Olivier: A Biography* (New York: Harper Paperbacks, 1993), 170–71; Donald Spoto, *Spellbound by Beauty: Alfred Hitchcock and His Leading Ladies* (New York: Harmony Books, 2008), 87–99; David Thomson, *The New Biographical Dictionary of Film* (New York: Knopf, 2002), 647–49.

ONDRA, ANNY (1903–1987)

Galicia-born performer who by 17 was already appearing onstage and making films. To engage in such a disreputable profession brought her a beating from her father, an army officer, but the free-spirited woman redoubled her efforts, soon becoming a leading lady in first Czech and then German cinema; as language was no barrier in the silent era, by the late '20s, she was lending her BLONDE good looks to British films as well.

In 1929, Alfred Hitchcock cast her in *THE MANXMAN*, as the third part of the triangle, and then in *BLACKMAIL*. Her Czech accent, however, proved to be a problem when the decision came to shoot the film with sound; the director had actress JOAN BARRY stand offscreen and speak the lines while Ondra mouthed them. (Ondra's first, giggly sound test, with the portly director making risqué remarks, survived and can be found online.)

With the talkies ending her international career, Ondra returned to Germany, where in 1933 she married boxer Max Schmeling; she continued to make films, mostly light comedies and musicals under the direction of her mentor and former lover Carl Lamac. Although Ondra and Schmeling were of formidable propaganda value to the Nazi regime—at least until the boxer lost his second fight with Joe Louis—they also quietly resisted it, even briefly hiding two Jewish children in their Berlin apartment.

Ondra essentially retired in 1943, although she returned for two more films in the 1950s. She died in Hollenstedt of a stroke at 83.

References

"Anny Ondra," *IMDb*, http://www.imdb.com/name/nm0648565/bio?ref_=nm_ov_bio_sm; "Anny Ondra Screentest," *BFI*, https://www.youtube.com/watch?v=7Z8mSwzSQQk; Tim Bergfelder, "Anny Ondra," *BFI Screenonline*, http://www.screenonline.org.uk/people/id/460529.

"ONE MORE MILE TO GO" (US; ORIGINALLY AIRED APRIL 7, 1957)

DIRECTOR: Alfred Hitchcock.
SCREENPLAY: James P. Cavanagh, from a story by F. J. Smith.
PRODUCER: Joan Harrison.
CINEMATOGRAPHY: John L. Russell.
EDITOR: Edward W. Williams.
ORIGINAL MUSIC: Stanley Wilson.
CAST: David Wayne (Sam Jacoby), Steve Brodie (Motorcycle Cop).
RUNNING TIME: 30 minutes with commercials. Black and white.
ORIGINALLY BROADCAST BY: CBS.

After accidentally killing his wife, Sam puts her in the trunk of his car and decides to dump the body in a lake; on the drive there, however, he's stopped by a motorcycle cop who notices his broken taillight and insists on helping him fix it. A simple story whose long periods of silence and basic situations—the nerve-racking drive, the suspicious policeman, the body to be sunk and disposed of—seems to prefigure *PSYCHO*, which the same cinematographer would shoot three years later.

References

Tim Brooks and Earle Marsh, *The Complete Directory to Prime Time Network TV Shows*, 8th ed. (New York: Ballantine Books, 2003), 29; Jack Edmond Nolan, "Hitchcock's TV Films," *Film Fan Monthly* (June 1968), 3–6.

ORMONDE, CZENZI (1906–2004)

Tacoma, WA–born writer—née Gladys Snell—whose family relocated to Los Angeles while she was a teenager. In her 20s, she began working for various studios as a secretary, writing short stories in her spare time. She sold to a number of slick magazines, including *Collier's*, *Liberty*, and the *Saturday Evening Post*; some of the stories she wrote for *Cosmopolitan* were reworked and published as her first novel, *Laughter from Downstairs*, in 1947.

When Alfred Hitchcock was looking for a new screenwriter for *STRANGERS ON A TRAIN*—he already had a treatment from WHITFIELD COOK and several screenplay drafts he deemed unusable from RAYMOND CHANDLER—he turned to various "name" writers, including his old collaborator BEN HECHT. Here the facts grow a little fuzzy. According to several sources, Hecht turned him down but recommended Ormonde, his extravagantly named assistant; according to her son, however, Ormonde was already working for Hitchcock as an assistant when she was approached with the assignment.

In any case, Hitchcock gave her the writing job with the instructions she read neither the novel nor Chandler's script; instead, he told her the story and then sent her off to write. Working under the supervision of his associate producer, Barbara Keon, and ALMA REVILLE and with the start of production looming, she did the final script in less than a month. (Chandler—who actually didn't want any credit—still shared it, as the studio wanted to trade on his fame.)

Ormonde wrote several television episodes over the next decade, another novel, and two movies—the crime picture *Step Down to Terror* and the Mr. Magoo cartoon feature *1001 Arabian Knights*—but later retired to live quietly in Idaho. When *Once You Meet a Stranger*, a gender-switched TV remake of *Strangers on a Train* was done in 1996, Ormonde once again got screenplay credit—and once again had to share it with Chandler.

She died in Hayden, ID, at 98 of complications from a fall.

References

"Czenzi Ormonde," *IMDb*, http://www.imdb.com/name/nm0650262; Carl Gidlund, "Czenzi Ormonde: A Private Person, a Prolific Writer," *Spokesman Review*, August 14, 2004, http://www.spokesman.com/stories/2004/aug/14/czenzi-ormonde-a-private-person-prolific-writer; Patrick McGilligan, *Alfred Hitchcock: A Life in Darkness and Light* (New York: HarperCollins, 2003), 443, 445–49; Donald Spoto, *The Dark Side of Genius: The Life of Alfred Hitchcock* (New York: Da Capo Press, 1999), 324, 328, 332.

P

THE PARADINE CASE (US 1947)

DIRECTOR: Alfred Hitchcock.
SCREENPLAY: David O. Selznick, Alma Reville, James Bridie, from the novel by Robert Hichens.
PRODUCER: David O. Selznick.
CINEMATOGRAPHY: Lee Garmes.
EDITOR: Hal C. Kern.
ORIGINAL MUSIC: Franz Waxman.
CAST: Gregory Peck (Anthony Keane), Alida Valli (Maddalena Paradine), Charles Laughton (Judge Horfield), Ethel Barrymore (Sophie Horfield), Louis Jourdan (Andre Latour), Ann Todd (Gay Keane).
RUNNING TIME: 125 minutes. Black and white.
RELEASED THROUGH: Selznick Releasing Organization.

The beautiful, coolly reserved—and recently widowed—Mrs. Paradine is arrested one night at her London home, charged with murdering her blind, older husband at their country estate. She is quickly taken to prison, where she is greeted by her solicitor, Sir Simon, who brings the barrister who will argue her case, Anthony Keane.

Keane, though happily married, is almost immediately besotted by his client, whom he endeavors to defend. And the more he investigates, the more suspicious he is of the dead man's handsome young valet, who seems to have had a more intimate relationship with his mistress than he should. Over Mrs. Paradine's objections, Keane determines to defend her by suggesting that the servant might have committed the murder in order to collect a bequest.

During the trial, though, the misogynist Judge Horfield is clearly biased against Keane's client, and Mrs. Paradine is furious when Keane tries to cast suspicion on the valet. After a day of angry testimony, the servant kills himself—and the distraught Mrs. Paradine confesses on the stand to having been in love with him and having poisoned her husband to extricate herself from the marriage.

Defeated, Keane slinks home to his forgiving wife.

A picture only its producer wanted to make.

DAVID O. SELZNICK had first read Robert S. Hichens's novel *The Paradine Case* in the '30s (he would later adapt Hichens's novel *The Garden of Allah*) and tried three times over the decade to get a production up and running. Each time, though, the screenplay—with its central story of adultery—ran afoul of the CENSORS. By the mid-'40s, though, Selznick decided to take another pass at it. His seven-year contract with Alfred Hitchcock was about to lapse, and the director had shown no real interest in renewing;

Anthony Perkins found huge success as Norman Bates in *Psycho* but also a typecasting that followed him for years. *Paramount Pictures/Photofest © Paramount Pictures*

as he was still on the payroll at $5,000 a week—and his last project had been sold off to RKO as a package deal—Selznick was determined to squeeze at least one more movie out for his own studio. Once again, *The Paradine Case* was dusted off.

No one apart from Selznick—who had to buy back the rights from MGM—really warmed to the idea. Although the "Master of Suspense" had already done a comedy (*MR. AND MRS. SMITH*) and a straight drama (*LIFEBOAT*) since his arrival in America, courtroom thrillers were one of Hitchcock's least favorite genres; in fact, his films generally cut away from trials entirely or reduced them to a few lines of overheard dialogue. Nor were STARS clamoring to perform in it. LAURENCE OLIVIER turned down the lead role—he was already busy preparing *HAMLET*—and the all-important female lead was a question mark. (Reportedly, Greta Garbo had been approached and refused it with a simple, firm "No murderesses.")

Eventually GREGORY PECK was set for the lawyer, and two new Selznick discoveries—Italian actress ALIDA VALLI (billed here simply as "Valli") and French actor LOUIS JOURDAN—were cast as Mrs. Paradine and her lover. Neither was Hitchcock's choice. The raven-haired Valli was far more in line with Selznick's taste in leading ladies, and Jourdan was simply too handsome for the role; for the story to have any power, Hitchcock insisted, the lady should be having an affair with someone crude, like ROBERT NEWTON, big and rough and "with horny hands, like the devil." (Clearly the director knew, from his personal connections to the famous EDITH THOMPSON murder case, the way the flouting of social taboos could add fire to any obsessive romance.)

Nor did the story conferences go smoothly. Hitchcock, who was already not-so-secretly planning a break with Selznick and preparing for his new venture, TRANSATLANTIC PICTURES, delegated work on the script to others. An old friend, James Bridie, did an initial treatment without conferring with the director; after a number of screenwriters turned down the assignment, ALMA REVILLE took charge. Although she ended up getting an "adaptation" credit (BEN HECHT lent an invisible hand, too), Selznick thought even this too generous; he insisted on writing the screenplay himself, although often his pages would arrive only as the day's shooting was about to begin.

The difficulties continued during the shoot, which lasted a grueling four months

(a record for Hitchcock) and cost $4 million, or nearly as much as *Gone with the Wind*—and this for a film in black and white, with no spectacular crowd scenes or special effects. Some of this was Hitchcock's fault (his first, laborious, time-consuming experiments with long takes and elaborate tracking shots), some was Selznick's (constant on-the-set and in-the-editing-room meddling), and some simply bad luck (a stretch of bad weather that complicated the exterior sequences).

All would have been forgiven and forgotten if the film worked. But there was little life to the performances. *The Paradine Case* is supposed to be—like *VERTIGO*, like *MARNIE*—a story of SEXUAL obsession, in this case both Keane's for Mrs. Paradine and Mrs. Paradine's for the servant. Peck, however, remains too sensible and polite throughout and—Hitchcock was right—Valli's adultery too understandable for the mad act of passion it's supposed to be. (Who but a saint wouldn't cheat on a bitter old blind man with a handsome young Louis Jourdan?)

There are flashes of some interesting themes that a better script (or a more involved director) might have drawn out. There is the implication (cut by the censors) that Judge Horfield gets a singular sexual frisson out of sentencing women to death; there are also the three unhappy marriages (the Paradines, the Keanes, the Horfields) that fill the film. But there are no explicit comparisons drawn between them, and Mrs. Keane is made so blandly, selflessly understanding—perhaps serving as Selznick's wish-fulfillment version of his own wife, as the entire film seems to plug into the obsession with Jennifer Jones that wrecked Selznick's marriage—that the tension dissipates.

And while there are the usual Hitchcock subtexts of GUILT and innocence, IDENTITY and performance, another deeper layer—as in, for example, the possibility that the valet's relationship with his master was more erotic than dutiful—is never explored or given even the vague hints Hitchcock sneaked past the censors in ROPE and STRANGERS ON A TRAIN. Frankly, Hitchcock seemed to find the story dull—and as he always did when a film failed to arouse his deeper interests, he diverted himself with technical challenges.

Visually, the film is certainly very rich. Director of photography LEE GARMES—who had immortalized MARLENE DIETRICH a decade before—gave both Jourdan and Valli the full star treatment; a jailhouse scene between Peck and Valli is a symphony of slowly shifting lighting, as if clouds were passing by just out of sight. There are also some interesting long takes (an idea Hitchcock possibly brought back from his work on MEMORY OF THE CAMPS) and some nicely, subtly angled shots in the courtroom in which the camera consistently looks up to emphasize CHARLES LAUGHTON's status and looks down to emphasize Peck's lack of power. In another bravura sequence, we stay tight on Valli's face as Jourdan enters behind her and see her intense awareness of the man, as if she can almost smell him.

But despite these flourishes, *The Paradine Case* is still more a Selznick movie than a Hitchcock picture. The relationship between director and producer had always been its own mix of power and status and hard-won compromise, but with Hitchcock already distracted by future projects and clearly uninterested in any further collaborations, Selznick grew more forceful and less likely to compromise than ever. He had already rewritten the script; in postproduction, he took over the editing and scoring. None of this was for the better. Long, complicated camera movements were abruptly cut into separate, mismatched shots; entire scenes were lost, as what reportedly had been close to a three-hour film was

trimmed by nearly a third. (Among the missing: the scenes that, in the film's early engagements, had probably helped ETHEL BARRYMORE win an Oscar nomination.) An intrusive FRANZ WAXMAN score only played up the jarring shifts in mood between domestic tranquility and illicit obsession; worse, it shamelessly recycled a theme from Waxman's work on REBECCA.

In the end, Selznick's interferences only took a middling film and muddled it; the movie became Hitchcock's biggest financial failure to that date (only *TOPAZ* eventually surpassed it), and Peck later said it was the only film he'd made that he'd like to take out and burn. Although one can speculate as to what the director's cut would have looked like, speculation is what it must remain; reportedly all the alternate footage was lost in a 1980 flood.

References

Rudy Behlmer, ed., *Memo from David O. Selznick* (New York: Viking Press, 1972), 374, 377–79; Patrick McGilligan, *Alfred Hitchcock: A Life in Darkness and Light* (New York: HarperCollins, 2003), 384–96; "The Paradine Case: Notes," *TCM*, http://www.tcm.com/tcmdb/title/86212/The-Paradine-Case/notes.html; Donald Spoto, *The Dark Side of Genius: The Life of Alfred Hitchcock* (New York: Da Capo Press, 1999), 293–302; Donald Spoto, *Spellbound by Beauty: Alfred Hitchcock and His Leading Ladies* (New York: Harmony Books, 2008), 163–73; Bob Thomas, *Selznick* (New York: Pocket Books, 1972), 242–43; François Truffaut, *Hitchcock/Truffaut*, rev. ed. (New York: Touchstone, 1985), 173–77.

PARAMOUNT

The second-oldest American film studio, after UNIVERSAL, and the last one to still have its base in Hollywood, Paramount Pictures grew out of Adolph Zukor's Famous Players Film Company, which tried to broaden the motion picture audience by offering better-educated customers more literary offerings; "Famous Players in Famous Plays" was their slogan. Two years later, the company was reconstituted as Paramount, although much of Zukor's mind-set held fast and would continue—well into the 1930s and 1940s, Paramount had a reputation for literate, slightly naughty sophistication. It was also known as being more of a writers' haven than most, with some of their best screenwriters—Preston Sturges, Billy Wilder—ascending to the director's ranks.

As government antitrust regulations hurt Paramount badly in the 1950s—more than most studios, it had relied heavily on aggressive "bloc-booking" practices and maintained an extensive chain of theaters—Hitchcock's arrival there in 1954 was welcome. (Coincidentally, his first studio job had been at a British subsidiary of Paramount, British Famous Players-Lasky, Ltd.) And the relationship was mutually beneficial, with Hitchcock doing his best work for the studio—*REAR WINDOW*, *TO CATCH A THIEF*, *THE TROUBLE WITH HARRY*, *THE MAN WHO KNEW TOO MUCH*, and *VERTIGO*.

It was *PSYCHO*, though, that was the breaking point—dismayed by the subject matter, the studio refused to fund it, even to let it be shot on their lot, although they grudgingly agreed to distribute it. Hitchcock left shortly thereafter for UNIVERSAL and with his own, very nice parting gift; thanks to the contract LEW WASSERMAN had negotiated for him, the rights to all his Paramount films reverted back to him eight years after their initial release dates.

References

Ivor Davis, "Return of the Missing Hitchcocks," *Times*, November 15, 1983, http://the.hitchcock.zone/wiki/The_Times_%2815/Nov/1983%29_-_Return_of_the_missing_Hitchcocks; "History," *Studios at Paramount*, http://www.paramountstudios.com/ working-on-the-lot/general-info/history.html; Patrick McGilligan, *Alfred Hitchcock: A Life in Darkness and Light* (New York: HarperCollins, 2003), 47–50.

PARKER, CECIL (1897–1971)

Sussex-born performer who, after service in the First World War, began his stage career in London. Although his first successes were in Shakespeare, he soon became best known for his light, comic performances (or at least his comical characters—even his villains were never as important or impressive as they thought they were). For Hitchcock, he was the craven Mr. Todhunter in *THE LADY VANISHES* and the blustering governor in *JAMAICA INN* and later dropped by for an episode of *ALFRED HITCHCOCK PRESENTS*; a regular presence in Ealing comedies, he was particularly delightful in *The Man in the White Suit* and *The Ladykillers* and had a long and successful stage run in *Blithe Spirit*. He died at 73 in Brighton.

References

"Cecil Parker," *IMDb*, http://www.imdb.com/name/nm0662116/bio?ref_=nm_ov_bio_sm; Bruce McFarlane, "Cecil Parker," *BFI Screenonline*, http://www.screenonline.org.uk/people/id/448873.

PARKER, DOROTHY (1893–1967)

New Jersey–born, ultra-Manhattan writer who brought her sharp and extremely focused wit to everything she did; although some lamented the fact that she never wrote a novel or even her memoirs, her talent was best lit by flashes of lightning, glimpsed quickly in short stories; brief poems; and the brisk, rude dialogue of screenplays.

She began her writing career during World War I, working at the "slick" magazines, including *Vogue* and *Vanity Fair*; she was fired from the latter when her wickedly negative reviews began to annoy too many Broadway producers, but she found a more congenial home at the *New Yorker*. Her moving "Big Blonde" won the O. Henry Prize as best short story of 1929, and she published several best-selling collections of poetry.

In 1934, she and new husband Alan Campbell moved to Hollywood, where they found, as BEN HECHT had said, that writers worked in teams, "like piano movers"; the duo wrote the original *A Star Is Born* and worked on friend Lillian Hellman's *The Little Foxes*, but many of their other contributions went uncredited or survived only as stray bits and pieces.

Alfred Hitchcock, for example, who remembered her as an "extraordinary woman" recalled her contributing "some very funny lines to *SABOTEUR*, including the quarrel between the thin man and the midget" but feared many of her touches were too subtle for most audiences. (In a sign of how much he enjoyed her company, he offered her the rare invitation to join him in his cameo in the picture, playing the older couple who spot ROBERT CUMMINGS and PRISCILLA LANE on the road; in the end, other actors were used, and Hitchcock appeared alone in a different scene.)

Parker had always been prone to suicidal depressions, and a growing drinking problem—and a difficult marriage to Campbell, who apparently cheated on her with either sex—made it hard for her to concentrate on her screenwriting. The advent of the McCarthy era made that unnecessary, as her leftist politics led to her being blacklisted in 1950; her last produced screenplay was *The Fan* for Otto Preminger.

Returning to New York permanently after a brief divorce and then remarriage to Campbell (who committed suicide in 1963), she moved into a residential hotel, occasionally writing book reviews or doing television appearances. Of the Jazz Age—and her central spot at the famed Algonquin Round Table—she had no fond memories. "These were no giants," she said of her old New York friends. "Think who was writing in those days—Lardner, Fitzgerald, Faulkner and Hemingway. Those were the real giants. The Round Table was just a lot of people telling jokes and telling each other how good they were. Just a bunch of loudmouths showing off."

She died of a heart attack in New York at 73. A lifelong champion of civil rights, she left her entire estate to the Rev. Martin Luther King.

References

"Dorothy Parker," *Academy of American Poets*, http://www.screenonline.org.uk/people/id/448873; "Dorothy Parker," *Biography*, http://www.biography.com/people/dorothy-parker-9433450; "Dorothy Parker," *IMDb*, http://www.imdb.com/name/nm0662213/bio?ref_=nm_ov_bio_sm; Roger Ebert, "Never Mess Around with a Dead Body," *Chicago Sun-Times*, December 14, 1969, http://www.rogerebert.com/interviews/hitchcock-never-mess-about-with-a-dead-body-you-may-be-one; Dorothy Herrmann, *With Malice toward All: The Quips, Lives and Loves of Some Celebrated 20th-Century American Wits* (New York: G. P. Putnam's Sons, 1982), 78.

THE PASSIONATE ADVENTURE (GB 1924)

DIRECTOR: Graham Cutts.
SCREENPLAY: Alfred Hitchcock, Michael Morton, based on the novel by Frank Stayton.
PRODUCERS: Sir Michael Balcon.
CINEMATOGRAPHY: Claude L. McDonnell.
EDITOR: Uncredited.
CAST: Alice Joyce (Drusilla), Marjorie Daw (Vicky), Clive Brook (Adrien), Lillian Hall-Davis (Pamela), Victor McClaglen (Herb).
RUNNING TIME: 68 minutes. Black and white.
RELEASED THROUGH: Gaumont British.

"A thrilling dramatic story," according to its ads, "of a West End husband who sought an East End sweetheart and revolutionized his wife." Perhaps sowing the seeds of the GRAHAM CUTTS–Alfred Hitchcock enmity, the *Times* pointedly differentiated between the contributions of the director and the screenwriter, praising an "interesting production" that had been "rather spoiled by a poor plot." Only incomplete versions of the film survive.

References

Advertisement, *Hammond Lake County Times*, September 11, 1926, http://the .hitchcock.zone/wiki/Hammond_Lake_ County_Times_%2811/Sep/1926%29 _-_The_Passionate_Adventure; "The Film World: The Passionate Adventure," *Times*, August 18, 1924, http://the.hitchcock.zone/ wiki/The_Times_%2818/Aug/1924%29 _-_The_Film_World.

PECK, GREGORY (1916–2003)

San Diego–born performer whose long, lean figure; dark good looks; and sonorous voice made him a leading man for three decades. The son of a pharmacist, he was pre-med at the University of California, Berkeley; the director of the school's drama program, however, encouraged him to try out for productions, and Peck ended up appearing in five plays during his senior year alone.

After graduation, Peck moved to New York, studying with acting coach Sanford Meisner and taking whatever work he could find. (He was briefly an NBC page.) He made his Broadway debut in 1942 and by 1944 was in Hollywood and very busy; unlike many young actors, he was exempt from the draft, having injured his back taking a dance class with Martha Graham. (Although, Peck later said, the studio publicists claimed it was from an old sports injury, believing fans wouldn't find a dance-class deferment "macho enough.")

Although he was nominated for an ACADEMY AWARD for his second film, *The Keys to the Kingdom*, there was a certain wooden righteousness to Peck's performances that narrowed his range; unlike other Hitchcock leading men, such as CARY GRANT, HENRY FONDA, or (especially) JAMES STEWART, he had few shadows to him and was best at playing stalwart heroes who never questioned themselves or their cause. He was excellent as the crusading journalist in *Gentleman's Agreement* or the committed lawyer in *To Kill a Mockingbird*, less compelling as the sociopaths of *Moby Dick* or *The Boys from Brazil*.

On *SPELLBOUND*—only his fourth film, and a complex, multilayered part—an uncertain Peck appealed to his director for guidance. Hitchcock, faced perhaps with the first of the METHOD actors he would meet in Hollywood, merely told him to make his face a blank; the camera would do all the work. Peck left unsatisfied. "I wanted more than that; the business was so new to me," the actor confessed later, noting that the filmmaker seemed distracted, even depressed. "I had the feeling that something ailed him," Peck said, "and I could never understand what it might be."

Someone who knew Hitchcock's obsessions with his leading ladies might have given him a hint; *Spellbound* was the director's first picture with his beloved INGRID BERGMAN, but it was Peck, not him, with whom she would soon be having a brief affair. It was not enough that Hitchcock had to direct them in their love scenes on the set; now he had to imagine their real ones after the lights were turned off.

Peck returned to work for Hitchcock again on *THE PARADINE CASE* and professed himself once again perplexed at the director's apparent unhappiness ("He was obviously suffering terribly about something during the shooting"); most likely it was due to DAVID O. SELZNICK's constant interfering, which, Peck admitted, was "so foreign to (Hitchcock's) method of working" and "created an unavoidable tension between them." Although director and STAR got along well enough, the film was a low point for both; later in life, Peck proclaimed it the only film of his he wished he could burn.

The '50s, however, brought Peck the delightful comedy *Roman Holiday* and a part with some shading in *The Man in the Gray Flannel Suit*; *Cape Fear* was a prickly noir, and *To Kill a Mockingbird*, of course, an instant classic, the perfect melding of character and actor. "I put everything I had into it—all my feelings and everything I'd learned in 46 years of living, about family life and fathers and children," he said. "And my feelings about racial justice and inequality and opportunity."

Peck went on to star in two of the better HITCHCOCKIAN thrillers—*Mirage* and *Arabesque*—as well as the horror hit *The Omen* and remained busy in films, philanthropy, and progressive causes throughout the '90s. He died of bronchopneumonia in Los Angeles at age 87.

References

Ronald Bergen, "Gregory Peck Obituary," *Guardian*, June 13, 1993, http://www.theguardian.com/news/2003/jun/14/guardianobituaries.film; Brad Darrach, "Gregory Peck," *People*, June 15, 1987, http://www.people.com/people/archive/article/0,,20096523,00.html; "Gregory Peck," *IMDb*, http://www.imdb.com/name/nm0000060/bio; Patrick McGilligan, *Alfred Hitchcock: A Life in Darkness and Light* (New York: HarperCollins, 2003), 357–60, 391; Donald Spoto, *The Dark Side of Genius: The Life of Alfred Hitchcock* (New York: Da Capo Press, 1999), 276, 298; David Thomson, *The New Biographical Dictionary of Film* (New York: Knopf, 2002), 670–71.

THE PERFECT CRIME

As a child and teenager, Alfred Hitchcock had been fascinated by the careful interlocking details of TRAIN timetables and had been a neat and precise artist. From the time he was a young adult, he had a passion for true-crime stories—often personal INTERVIEWS set up to promote his most recent films would be interrupted by his happy recitations of the "acid bath" murders or exactly how Dr. H. H. CRIPPEN had been caught. And the two obsessions combined neatly, nicely—and profitably—in his lifelong interest in the "perfect crime" and how seemingly mild men (almost always men) might get away with it.

The morbid fantasy receives its most thorough working-out in *SHADOW OF A DOUBT*, in which old friends Joseph Newton and Herbie Hawkins gleefully discuss—in a purely theoretical fashion, of course—how they'd set out to kill each other and get away with it. It's a sort of game they indulge in over dinner or sitting on the porch. How to do it? Fast-acting poison? Blunt object?

"Well, if I was gonna kill you, I wouldn't do a dumb thing like hitting you on the head," Herbie protests after Joseph brings up the lead-pipe solution. "First of all, I don't like the fingerprint angle. Of course, I could always wear gloves. Press your hands against the pipe after you were dead and make you look like a suicide. Except it don't seem hardly likely that you'd beat yourself to death with a club. I'd murder you so it didn't look like murder."

Joseph's daughter, Charlie, grows disgusted by their bloodless after-dinner chats—but by then, she knows there's a real killer in the house, an uncle who seems to have already racked up several perfect crimes. But she also doesn't realize the sort of vicarious joy that these mild men—and Hitchcock, too, perhaps—took in these deadly daydreams, utterly safe ways of dissipating anger or frustration without cops or consequences.

In Hitchcock's films, of course—mostly thanks to the CENSORS and the audience expectations they had engendered—there were no perfect crimes; the criminal, no matter how carefully he plotted, would be killed or caught by the end. Yet you can feel the chilly delight the director must have taken in the story conferences leading up to the filming, as the murderer's perfect plans were carefully devised.

There are several fatal ideas, of course, in SUSPICION—including the untraceable poisons Johnnie is so interested in—although in the final, unsatisfying version of the film, Johnnie's urges turn out to be suicidal rather than murderous in nature. More straightforward is STRANGERS ON A TRAIN, in which Bruno has a novel insight into committing the perfect crime—simply have two men switch murders, each killing the other's intended victim, thereby removing the police's usual starting point, motive.

Details are, of course, the usual stumbling blocks in any attempt at perfection, and Hitchcock—so wed to routine that he meticulously planned out not only his art but also his daily life—enjoyed having his criminals bedeviled by unforeseen, tiny, but suddenly crucial circumstances. The lighter that Bruno drops down a storm drain in *Strangers on a Train*, the car that Norman can't quite get to sink in *PSYCHO*, the monogrammed stickpin that Bob Rusk needs to retrieve in *FRENZY*—all threaten to keep them from success. And it is Hitchcock's manipulative mastery that we identify with these characters and want them to succeed—even though they are the stories' villains and we know they must fail.

And yet, not always. The villains on Hitchcock's television shows often seemed to get away with it—even if the director returned after what seemed to be their final triumph to quickly (if not convincingly) assure us that they were eventually caught and sent to prison. In fact, the cen-

sors demanded a similar scene at the end of *VERTIGO*, explaining that the murderer had been tracked to Europe—and to shut them up, Hitchcock dutifully shot a few minutes of Scottie and Midge listening to a news report of it on the radio—but he never included it in the film, making *Vertigo* one of the very rare studio pictures in which a murderer goes unpunished.

It seems that, complicated as it was—and the murder plot in *Vertigo*, if you make the mistake of thinking about it too much, is the most preposterous in Hitchcock—the killing of the real Madeleine really was the perfect crime. Although not, perhaps, as perfect as the film that surrounds it.

References

Patrick McGilligan, *Alfred Hitchcock: A Life in Darkness and Light* (New York: HarperCollins, 2003), 562; Donald Spoto, *The Dark Side of Genius: The Life of Alfred Hitchcock* (New York: Da Capo Press, 1999), 20, 32–34, 115.

"THE PERFECT CRIME" (US; ORIGINALLY AIRED OCTOBER 20, 1957)

DIRECTOR: Alfred Hitchcock.
SCREENPLAY: Stirling Silliphant, based on the story by Ben Ray Redman.
PRODUCER: Joan Harrison.
CINEMATOGRAPHY: John L. Russell.
EDITOR: Edward W. Williams.
ORIGINAL MUSIC: Stanley Wilson.
CAST: Vincent Price (Charles Courtney), James Gregory (John Gregory).
RUNNING TIME: 30 minutes. Black and white.
ORIGINALLY BROADCAST BY: CBS.

Devastated when an attorney tells him his work once sent an innocent man to his execution, an egotistical criminologist vows to cover up his mistake—by killing the attorney and disposing of the body in a kiln. Not a particularly new murder method for Vincent Price, who had not long ago starred in *House of Wax* and *The Mad Magician*, nor for *ALFRED HITCHCOCK PRESENTS*, in which the signature puzzle was often not how to kill someone but how to dispose of the body.

References

Tim Brooks and Earle Marsh, *The Complete Directory to Prime Time Network TV Shows*, 8th ed. (New York: Ballantine Books, 2003), 29; Jack Edmond Nolan, "Hitchcock's TV Films," *Film Fan Monthly* (June 1968), 3–6.

PERJURY

Another unproduced project, although this one progressed further than some; designed as a follow-up to *YOUNG AND INNOCENT*, press releases boasted it would have a screenplay by Hitchcock, ALMA REVILLE, and JOAN HARRISON (inspired by a short story by Marcel Archard) and star NOVA PILBEAM. Originally called *False Witness* or *The False Witness*, by 1938 it had been given a new title (probably to evoke the earlier *BLACKMAIL*, *MURDER!*, and *SABOTAGE*) and was said to revolve around a con man and his daughter—but then Hitchcock moved on to *THE LADY VANISHES* instead and then to *JAMAICA INN*, and whether there ever truly had been a finished script or not, the idea was dropped.

Reference

Patrick McGilligan, *Alfred Hitchcock: A Life in Darkness and Light* (New York: HarperCollins, 2003), 202.

PERKINS, ANTHONY (1932–1992)

Manhattan-born performer and only son of actor Osgood Perkins, who had been a leading man in the silents and a character actor in such talkies as *Scarface* but died when his son was five years old. Anthony Perkins, who had always had a vivid, oedipal connection to his mother, remembered the relationship growing even unhealthier after his father's death. "She was constantly touching me and caressing me," he said years later. "Not realizing what effect she was having, she would touch me all over, even stroking the inside of my thighs right up to my crotch."

At sleepaway camp, Perkins discovered acting could be a release from his unhappy home life; by 14, he was playing in summer stock and at 20 was cast by George Cukor in *The Actress*. For the rest of the '50s, Perkins, although determinedly presented by publicists as a teen heartthrob, tended to be at his best playing SEXUALLY uncertain, emotionally fragile young men: The boy "saved" from HOMOSEXUALITY in Broadway's *Tea and Sympathy*, the fearful father-dominated baseball player in *Fear Strikes Out*.

Perkins hesitated taking the role in *PSYCHO*, knowing that appearing onscreen in a dress was an enormous career risk. (Playing a mad serial killer was far less of a gamble, as leading men from ROBERT MONTGOMERY to Robert Mitchum had already proven; it wasn't onscreen psychosis that ever hurt your career but effeminacy.) But Hitchcock urged him on and repaid Perkins's faith with his own confidence; although he typically bristled at actors' involvement, he incorporated many of Perkins's suggestions—slightly overlapping some dialogue, compulsively gobbling candy—into the film. Hitchcock even let him pick his wardrobe (ultimately, Perkins wore his own clothes).

Perkins's Norman Bates—flashing from boyish grins to steely-eyed anger within the space of a few minutes of conversation, walking with a softly hip-swaying femininity or contorting his face into a mad rictus of pain—is complex and original, one of the great, enduring characters of cinema. Hitchcock was right to pick him. But Perkins's doubts were right, too—the twisted Norman was so indelible that he got conflated with the actor, and for most of the rest of the '60s, Perkins could only find work outside Hollywood. Although some of those movies were outstanding— Orson Welles's *The Trial*, the darkly moody *The Fool Killer*, the cynical thriller *Pretty Poison*—most never played beyond a small cult of admirers.

The '70s, though, saw a middle-aged Perkins reestablishing himself as a character actor (albeit one who often played slightly unhinged people and would occasionally give his lines an unexpected, artificially staccato twist). He starred in *Equus* on Broadway. He cowrote the clever thriller *The Last of Sheila* with longtime friend Stephen Sondheim. He even—after years of literally running away from interested actresses like Jane Fonda and Brigitte Bardot—had his first heterosexual experience, with Victoria Principal, while shooting *The Life and Times of Judge Roy Bean*.

As the '80s began, now married to photographer Berry Berenson and with two sons, Perkins finally returned to the part of Norman with *Psycho II*. "It is the Hamlet of horror roles," he said later, as the franchise continued. "You can never quite get enough of playing Norman Bates. It's always interesting. . . . He's a character who has really emerged in a dimensional way. And of how many characters, how many screen characters can that be said? You know it's a great compliment to the original concept by Hitchcock."

Now firmly typecast—and resigned to it—Perkins worked almost exclusively in horror films as the decade went on, eventually playing Norman his fourth and final time in a made-for-TV movie in 1990; by

that time the actor had been diagnosed with AIDS, and his next few, flawed projects were more about providing for his family than personal achievement. He died at his Los Angeles home at 60 of AIDS-related pneumonia; almost exactly nine years later, Berenson was murdered when the plane she was on was flown into the World Trade Center.

References
"Anthony Perkins," *Biography*, http://www.biography.com/people/anthony-perkins-9437779; "Anthony Perkins," *IMDb*, http://www.imdb.com/name/nm0000578/bio; Steve Biodrowski, "Interview: Psycho Star Anthony Perkins," *Cinefantastique Online*, http://cinefantastiqueonline.com/2008/09/interview-psycho-star-anthony-perkins; Brad Darrach, "Return of Psycho," *People*, June 13, 1983, http://www.people.com/people/archive/article/0,,20085251,00.html; Stephen Rebello, *Alfred Hitchcock and the Making of Psycho* (New York: Harper Perennial, 1991), 59–60, 88–89.

PICCOLI, MICHEL (1925–)
Paris-born performer, the product of a musical family—his mother was a pianist; his father, a violinist—he made his film debut in 1945, although he perhaps only grew truly prominent in 1963 in Jean-Luc Godard's *Contempt*. Following that success, he would work with many of the great directors, including Agnes Varda, Costa-Gavras, Louis Malle, Jacques Demy, and—especially—Luis Bunuel, with whom he made seven films, including *Belle du Jour*.

Unfortunately, his collaboration with Hitchcock was on the lackluster *TOPAZ*, in which he played spymaster Jacques Granville, a partnership made even more difficult by the fact that when the film was previewed—and its ending greeted with catcalls—the busy Piccoli was unavailable for reshoots. Hitchcock desperately cobbled together a new ending in which Piccoli's character returned home and shot himself offscreen; that the only usable footage he had of a man entering the house was a long shot of another actor, PHILIPPE NOIRET, was something he had to pray audiences wouldn't notice. (As they stayed away in any case, the worry was unfounded.)

Sixty years after his debut, Piccoli continues to appear regularly onscreen and challenge himself by working with difficult scripts and young directors.

References

"Michel Piccoli," *IMDb*, http://www.imdb .com/name/nm0681566/bio?ref_=nm_ov _bio_sm; Donald Spoto, *The Dark Side of Genius: The Life of Alfred Hitchcock* (New York: Da Capo Press, 1999), 502–3; James Travers, "Michel Piccoli," *Films de France*, http://www.filmsdefrance.com/biography/ michel-piccoli.html.

PILBEAM, NOVA (1919–2015)

London-born performer and daughter of actor Arnold Pilbeam who made her stage debut at five in a charity performance. By 12, she was a trained actress, appearing onstage regularly. She made her first movie, the marital drama *Little Friend*, at 15 and was quickly signed by GAUMONT-BRITISH to a 7-year contract. Her next movie was the 1934 version of *THE MAN WHO KNEW TOO MUCH*.

She was a small, alert, terrified presence in that film, all curls and wide, frightened EYES, and she also impressed the next year in the period film *Tudor Rose*; Hitchcock cast her again in 1937's *YOUNG AND INNOCENT*, and although he could be brusque on the set—sometimes using a stopwatch to get the actors to speed up the dialogue—he remained particularly solicitous of Pilbeam, who was 18 and appearing in her first somewhat adult role. (Although

Hitchcock also considered casting her in his next film, *THE LADY VANISHES*, he ultimately opted for the rather more sophisticated MARGARET LOCKWOOD; other Hitchcock-Pilbeam collaborations, including *PERJURY*, were announced but never made.)

"Hitch had everything in his head before he went to the set; therefore one was rather moved around and manipulated a lot," Pilbeam said of her films with him. "Having said that, I liked him very much. For instance, in *Young and Innocent*, there was a dog that both Hitch and I adored; there came a time that we had finished the sequences with the dog and he was supposed to go back. We were both so upset that Hitch decided to write him another sequence so we could keep him around for another five or six days."

The British film industry was still economically unstable in the late '30s—one of the reasons Hitchcock happily left for Hollywood—and just as Pilbeam was transitioning to adult roles, it seemed there were fewer of them to be found. DAVID O. SELZNICK, who of course had screened Hitchcock's British work and noticed her in *Young and Innocent*, thought she might be right for *REBECCA*; although DONALD SPOTO says Hitchcock was "bitterly" opposed to casting her, the director had even floated her name himself in INTERVIEWS as a possible STAR, opposite Ronald Colman. But Pilbeam's advisors were leery of signing a long contract, and Hitchcock—perhaps because he had such strong memories of her as a child—eventually decided she was too young for the part. She stayed in Britain.

In 1939, Pilbeam married Pen Tennyson, a great-grandson of the poet who had met her when she was 15 and he was a very young assistant director on *The Man Who Knew Too Much*; he joined the navy in 1940 and died the next year in a plane crash. Pilbeam continued to act, mostly onstage, including a season with the Old Vic, and married BBC journalist Michael Whyte in 1951; after the birth of their daughter in 1952, she officially retired and successfully avoided most interviewers. She died at 95 in London.

References

Philip Hoare, "Nova Pilbeam: Alfred Hitchcock's Star Who Vanished from View," *Independent*, July 21, 2015, http://www.independent.co.uk/news/obituaries/nova-pilbeam-alfred-hitchcocks-star-who-vanished-from-view-10402905.html; "Interview with Actress Nova Pilbeam," *Hitchcock Zone*, June 1990, http://the.hitchcock.zone/wiki/Interview:_Nova_Pilbeam_%28Jun/1990%29; "Nova Pilbeam," *Classic British Cinema*, http://www.wickedlady.com/films/ladies/Pilbeam Nova/index.html; "Nova Pilbeam," *IMDb*, http://www.imdb.com/name/nm0683345/bio?ref_=nm_ov_bio_sm; Donald Spoto, *The Dark Side of Genius: The Life of Alfred Hitchcock* (New York: Da Capo Press, 1999), 163, 176, 217.

THE PLAUSIBLES

Hitchcock's dismissive nickname for the nitpickers in the audience who, rather than being swept away by the drama onscreen, often poked holes in the narrative, wondering, for example, why the endangered hero and heroine didn't simply go to the police. ("Because it's boring," was the director's often-stated riposte, although in actuality his scripts usually provided a solid reason the authorities couldn't be trusted either.)

Frankly, the idea that a storyteller had to follow the rules of everyday life annoyed Hitchcock. "In the fiction film, the director is the god," he insisted to FRANÇOIS TRUFFAUT. "We should have total freedom to do as we like, just as long as it's not dull." Yet while Hitchcock could be bedeviled by people who demanded logic out

of films that were, in many ways, waking dreams—after all, how plausible is it that a spy ring would try to assassinate a man by dispatching a crop duster?—he also took pains to head them off early. During preproduction, assistants would fact-check the details in the script; photographers would be sent out, not only to document the real locations, but also the fictional ones.

"Film should be stronger than reason," Hitchcock insisted. But he always grounded his cinematic emotions in hard reality, trying to answer an audience's questions before they were even raised. "Hitchcock had what he called the 'icebox theory,'" said Brian Moore, who worked with him—unhappily—on TORN CURTAIN. "A man goes to a film with his wife, comes home. They take a piece of chicken out of the icebox and start talking about the film, and she says, 'You know, the bus doesn't run from Oxford to Ireland on Thursdays.' And they sit down and destroy your movie, because they find all the other things that are wrong with it."

Hitchcock worked hard to avoid those postmovie postmortems by doing nearly endless and precise preplanning, from scouting locations to researching the script to casting extras. What sort of domestic staff would a foreign embassy have in London? How easy is it to sell a car in a hurry? How would a middle-class man be booked in a New York police station? What sort of neighbors might you have in a modest, slightly artistic West Village neighborhood? One of the reasons we don't stop to ask ourselves these questions watching THE MAN WHO KNEW TOO MUCH or PSYCHO or THE WRONG MAN or REAR WINDOW is that Hitchcock had already asked them and made sure he had the answers.

And that we believe him when he shares them with us makes it easier to believe him when he tells us far more interesting things.

References

"Moore: Ireland's Runaway, Rebel Son," *Vancouver Sun*, June 9, 1990, http://the.hitchcock.zone/wiki/Vancouver_Sun_%2809/Jun/1990%29_-_Moore:_Ireland's_runaway_rebel_son; François Truffaut, *Hitchcock/Truffaut*, rev. ed. (New York: Touchstone, 1985), 99–103.

PLAYS WITHIN PLAYS

"The play's the thing," boasts *HAMLET*, "wherein I'll catch the conscience of the king," and so he has the traveling players put on a deliberately, painfully inappropriate work—hoping that its obvious parallels to a real-life crime will shock his murderous uncle into confessing. It's a theatrical trick and so, not surprisingly, one that actor Sir John Menier explicitly turns to in *MURDER!* as he hopes to startle his prime suspect into confessing.

It doesn't work for Menier (nor did it provide a quick and painless solution for Hamlet), but even when it doesn't figure in the plot, it is a part of many Hitchcock films—the person who assumes another IDENTITY, the performance within the performance, the pretty polished entertainment into which real life suddenly intrudes. (Hitchcock actually considered doing a modern-dress version of *Hamlet* with CARY GRANT, until other considerations and a nuisance lawsuit intruded.)

Show business—with its mad mix of assumed roles, ever-changing poses, and purposefully accepted lies—is a large part of Hitchcock right from the beginning. His first film, *THE PLEASURE GARDEN*, is set in the cheap and brittle world of the theater; his first thriller, *THE LODGER*, begins against the backdrop of a stage show's flashing sign. The smooth falsity of fantasy contrasted with the rough lies of life: This is a contrast made clearer in *Murder!* as we see the police awkwardly interviewing suspects backstage as the actors constantly interrupt themselves to rush out onstage to applause. (Nor is it just the theater he's concerned with; public performances of all kinds appear regularly as backdrops in Hitchcock, whether it's the auction in *NORTH BY NORTHWEST* or the ballet in *TORN CURTAIN*.)

The boisterous world of the music hall figures largely in *THE 39 STEPS* (in which the story begins and ends with the spies' pathetic catspaw, Mr. Memory) and in *THE LADY VANISHES* (where a magician has helped make more than rabbits disappear). The imagery is pushed further in *SABOTAGE* and *SABOTEUR*, in which some of those films' crucial action unfolds in theaters while other, more comic films are being shown; like a distorting hall of mirrors, the audience for these movies watches another audience watching other movies, as the merry onscreen laughter of the fictional viewers mocks the worries of the real ones.

Sometimes—as in *STAGE FRIGHT*—the world of the theater and the drama of actors assuming roles is a quite literal one. More often—most interestingly—in Hitchcock, players and playacting are a more flexible metaphor for real life. Barry in *Saboteur*, Alicia in *NOTORIOUS*, Judy in *VERTIGO*, Eve in *North by Northwest*, the titular *MARNIE*, and the bumbling George in *FAMILY PLOT*—all are playing parts. (So are John in *SPELLBOUND* and Norman in *PSYCHO*—they just don't know it.) All of then perform their own plays within the play—pretending to be different people with different agendas from the ones they truly are.

Which, the movies suggest, we all do, every day—while trying hardest not to catch the "conscience of the king" but perhaps to disguise or ignore our own. And while all the world is, indeed, a stage, it's the amateur players who are the most likely to find the curtain ringing down early.

References

"Filming Hamlet," *Aberdeen Journal*, September 5, 1945, http://the.hitchcock .zone/wiki/Aberdeen_Journal_%2805/ Sep/1945%29_-_Filming_Hamlet; Caroline Moorehead, *Sidney Bernstein: A Biography* (London: Jonathan Cape, 1984), 173–74.

THE PLEASURE GARDEN
(GB 1925)

DIRECTOR: Alfred Hitchcock.
SCREENPLAY: Eliot Stannard, based on the novel by Oliver Sandys.
PRODUCERS: Sir Michael Balcon, Erich Pommer.
CINEMATOGRAPHY: Gaetano di Ventimiglia.
EDITOR: Uncredited.
CAST: Virginia Valli (Patsy Brand), Carmelita Geraghty (Jill Cheyne), Miles Mander (Levett), John Stuart (Hugh Fielding).
RUNNING TIME: 93 minutes. Black and white.
RELEASED THROUGH: Woolf & Freedman Film Service.

Jill, a young actress, comes to London to pursue a career and is almost immediately robbed; Patsy, a slightly worldlier chorus girl, takes her under her wing and finds her a job at a theater called the Pleasure Garden. Jill soon finds her new job brings her far more interesting men than her attentive boyfriend, Hugh; Patsy, meanwhile, is attracted to Hugh's friend and business colleague, Levett.

Hugh is sent by his company to "the East"; Levett, after marrying Patsy, follows. Jill, meanwhile, begins to enter into a serious romance with a foreign nobleman and grows distant from Patsy.

Levett writes Patsy to tell her that he is ill, but when Patsy borrows the money to join him, she finds him living with a "native woman." She leaves, heartbroken; infuriated, he murders the woman, and then goes in search of Patsy. When he finds her with Hugh, he accuses his friend of seducing her; when Levett turns on Patsy in a rage, he is shot dead.

Hugh and Patsy return to London, where the newspapers report that Jill and her noble fiancé are to be married.

Hitchcock's first film and a very bumpy debut.

What actually should have been his first feature, *NUMBER 13*, had been abandoned in 1922 when the money ran out; three years later, producer SIR MICHAEL BALCON was going to give the 26-year-old director another, better chance. With a screenplay by the busy ELIOT STANNARD—who would write eight more scripts for Hitchcock—*The Pleasure Garden* had a strong, melodramatic plot and international appeal; its leading ladies had been imported from Hollywood, there would be LOCATION shooting in Italy, and studio space had been reserved in Munich.

Problems arose immediately. Traveling from Germany to Italy, cinematographer GAETANO VENTIMIGLIA advised the novice director to hide the film stock and camera equipment to save money on the obligatory import duties; the authorities missed the camera, but when they discovered the smuggled film at the Austrian border, it was confiscated. (As bad as the financial blow was, the emotional cost to Hitchcock—morbidly afraid of the police—must have been even worse.)

Money troubles continued in Genoa, where Hitchcock's hotel was robbed—the thieves getting away with much of his ready cash. New film stock had to be purchased, with the director now forced to borrow from Ventimiglia and his leading man, Miles Mander. (Meanwhile his leading ladies, used to Hollywood budgets, were quickly running through money as well; traveling separately with ALMA REVILLE, who was working as

Hitchcock's assistant, they demanded first-class accommodations.)

Nor did things go any more smoothly when actual shooting began; an important scene at Lake Como had to be delayed when another actress confessed she couldn't get in the water because she was menstruating. Hitchcock—then almost 26 and still living with his mother—hadn't heard the word before, and the cinematographer had to take him aside and provide a crash course in the female reproductive cycle. (Hitchcock recounts the production disasters at length—with the philosophical equanimity only eventual triumph can bring—in the book *HITCHCOCK/TRUFFAUT*.)

Once the location work was out of the way, though, and cast and crew had reassembled at the studios in Munich, things went better, as Hitchcock—once again back on a soundstage—found himself in his element. He began the film with a shot in a theater of chorus girls coming down a spiral STAIRCASE, while a patron spies on one dancer's legs through his opera glasses; as critic Dave Kehr remarked, that opening sequence alone functions as a sort of "clip reel" of Hitchcock themes and images—VOYEURISM, spirals, PLAYS WITHIN PLAYS—that he would return to for the rest of his career.

The story (although typically melodramatic, complete with a hallucinatory mad scene, and marked by some obvious performances) also featured the love triangles, personal betrayal, romantic cynicism, and exotic locations that his films would continually rely on, as well as a fondness for visual symbolism; when Patsy awakes from her honeymoon night, the camera lingers on an apple, a bite taken out of it. We are in the pleasure garden indeed, where the forbidden fruit has been tasted.

Balcon was pleased with the film, remarking on how "American" it seemed—a compliment, considering how flat and cheap most British filmmaking looked at the time—and planned a 1926 release. The stodgy distributor C. M. WOOLF, though—who had been getting critical reports back from Hitchcock's old mentor, GRAHAM CUTTS—disagreed. To him it appeared "German"—in other words, arty, confusing, and definitely noncommercial. He demanded it be put on the shelf—and so it was, even though Balcon had thought enough of it to give Hitchcock his next assignment, *THE MOUNTAIN EAGLE.*

Only after the success of *THE LODGER* in 1927 would *The Pleasure Garden* find wide distribution and, even then, often in crudely truncated form; recent efforts have restored some once-scissored footage.

References

Sarah Kaufman, "Hitchcock's Restored First Film Shows Roots of Fascination with Dance," *Washington Post*, August 2, 2012, http://www.washingtonpost.com/ entertainment/theater_dance/hitchcocks -restored-first-film-shows-roots-of-fasci nation-with-dance/2013/08/01/cdb47ece -f95c-11e2-b018-5b8251f0c56e_story.html; Dave Kehr, "Hitchcock: Finding His Voice in Silents," June 19, 2013, *New York Times*, http://www.nytimes.com/2013/06/23/mov ies/silent-hitchcock-films-come-to-the -harvey-theater-in-brooklyn.html?_r=0; Patrick McGilligan, *Alfred Hitchcock: A Life in Darkness and Light* (New York: HarperCollins, 2003), 69–71; Donald Spoto, *The Dark Side of Genius: The Life of Alfred Hitchcock* (New York: Da Capo Press, 1999), 77–84; François Truffaut, *Hitchcock/Truffaut*, rev. ed. (New York: Touchstone, 1985), 31–39; Holly Williams, "Alfred Hitchcock: Dial R for Restoration," *Independent*, June 27, 2012, http://www .independent.co.uk/arts-entertainment/ films/features/alfred-hitchcock—dial-r-for -restoration-7893106.html.

PLESHETTE, SUZANNE (1937–2008)

Brooklyn-born performer who attended New York's High School of the Performing Arts and Finch College before delving into classes with Sanford Meisner at the Neighborhood Playhouse. She made her television debut in 1957 and also landed a part in the Broadway production of *Compulsion*, a play about the LEOPOLD AND LOEB case.

She remained busiest onstage and in television at first, including an episode of *ALFRED HITCHCOCK PRESENTS*; her first sizable movie role came in 1962 in *Rome Adventure*, a romance with Tab Hunter (to whom she was very briefly married). The next year, she appeared in *THE BIRDS* as Annie, the slightly wounded, lightly sardonic teacher who'd once loved Mitch and stuck around Bodega Bay afterward.

Pleshette brought her own confident SEXUALITY and husky Scotch-and-cigarettes voice to the part, making Annie one of Hitchcock's more memorable supporting characters, although the director didn't seem to appreciate her at the time. "Hitch didn't know what to do with me," Pleshette said in a 1999 *Literature Film Quarterly* interview, remarking that her METHOD training threw him. "He regretted the day that he hired me."

It was mostly back to movie romances and TV episodes after that, although her wicked wit on talk shows won her fans; after seeing her banter with Bob Newhart on *The Tonight Show*, sitcom producers cast her as his wife in *The Bob Newhart Show*, which became a deadpan hit. When its six-season run ended, she starred or guest-starred on several more mostly short-lived television shows. After battling lung cancer for several years, she died in Los Angeles at 70 of respiratory failure.

References

Greg Garett, "Hitchcock's Women on Hitchcock," *Literature Film Quarterly* 27, no. 2 (1999), http://the.hitchcock.zone/wiki/ Literature_Film_Quarterly_%281999%29 _-_Hitchcock's_women_on_Hitchcock; Anita Gates, "Suzanne Pleshette, 70, 'Newhart' Actress, Dies," *New York Times*, January 21, 2008, http://www.nytimes.com/ 2008/01/21/arts/21cnd-pleshette.html?_r=0; "Suzanne Pleshette," *Biography*, http:// www.biography.com/people/suzanne- pleshette-265943; "Suzanne Pleshette," *IMDb*, http://www.imdb.com/name/ nm0687189/bio?ref_=nm_ov_bio_sm.

"POISON" (US; ORIGINALLY AIRED OCTOBER 5, 1958)

DIRECTOR: Alfred Hitchcock.
SCREENPLAY: Casey Robinson, based on the story by Roald Dahl.
PRODUCERS: Joan Harrison, Norman Lloyd.
CINEMATOGRAPHY: John L. Russell.
EDITOR: Edward W. Williams.
ORIGINAL MUSIC: Uncredited.
CAST: James Donald (Harry Pope), Wendell Corey (Timber Woods).
RUNNING TIME: 30 minutes. Black and white.
ORIGINALLY BROADCAST BY: CBS.

A reworking of a classic Roald Dahl story, in which James Donald wakes in the middle of the night to discover a poisonous snake has slithered into his bed and is now curled up asleep on his chest. Does he move and risk its fangs or just—wait? Veteran screenwriter Casey Robinson's changes to Roald Dahl's spare tale softens the focus somewhat (and eliminates its racial angles), although his teleplay's new twist has a nice sting.

References

Tim Brooks and Earle Marsh, *The Complete Directory to Prime Time Network TV Shows*, 8th ed. (New York: Ballantine Books, 2003), 29; Jack Edmond Nolan, "Hitchcock's TV Films," *Film Fan Monthly* (June 1968), 3–6.

POLICE

It is a story Hitchcock told many times over many years. This is how he told it to FRANÇOIS TRUFFAUT.

"I must have been about four or five years old," he said. "My father sent me to the police station with a note. The chief of police read it and locked me in a cell for five or 10 minutes, saying 'This is what we do to naughty boys.'" It's a brief ANEC-DOTE, and the usual lesson taken from it is that this is why Hitchcock protagonists are so often bedeviled by the law and often end up arrested, handcuffed, or confined.

But it was not the claustrophobic image of the cell that truly seemed to linger with Hitchcock (although many of his films, including *PSYCHO* and *THE BIRDS*, feature people trapped in confined spaces). Nor was it even the loss of liberty (although the elements of BONDAGE—handcuffs, keys, ropes, and locked doors—occur again and again in his films, many of which also carefully detail the dehumanizing process of arrest). No, what truly struck the boy—and lingered with him—was the utter, inexplicable arbitrariness of it.

Did he know why he was being punished, Truffaut asked the director, some 60 years after the fact. "I haven't the faintest idea," Hitchcock said. "As a matter of fact, my father used to call me his 'little lamb without a spot.' I truly cannot imagine what it was I did." And it's that detail that's the important one and was to color all the decades of work to come.

Because it's not merely the sudden arrival of authority that interests Hitchcock nor the way it's able to rob someone of liberty and control. More than the loss of freedom, it's the complete KAFKA-esque capriciousness of it that terrifies—that the punishment that comes may have nothing to do with justice or even the facts, that it can simply arrive and catch you up without warning or even any kind of logic.

The fear of arrest was not a fake one, either. Writer CZENZI ORMONDE, while working on *STRANGERS ON A TRAIN*, was also given the job of chauffeuring Hitchcock around; once when they were on the highway, their car was stopped by a policeman. Apparently he'd spotted them leaving the studio and only wanted to tell the director how much he liked his films, but when Ormonde looked to the backseat, she saw Hitchcock in a kind of trance. "He didn't care what was said, perhaps had not heard it," she said. "Fists were clenched, face was pale, his eyes stared ahead. Visibly this was a very frightened man."

Hitchcock, of course, used all his fears to fuel his films. But while they are sometimes necessary to knit up the loose threads of the plot and arrest the villain at the end—as in *DIAL M FOR MURDER*, *REAR WINDOW*, *TO CATCH A THIEF*, or *FRENZY*—police officers are never the main characters in Hitchcock films and are almost always ineffectual. Ted Spencer and Jack Graham can poke around all they like in *SABOTAGE* and *SHADOW OF A DOUBT*, but in the end, the heroines are the ones who bring the cold killers to rough justice; not only does the local sheriff in *Psycho* see nothing odd when he goes out to interview Norman—even after searching the place—but he's apparently ignored several local missing-persons cases, too.

Sometimes Hitchcock's policemen actively make things worse. In *THE LODGER*, Joe's jealousy of the upstairs tenant hampers his own investigation; in *THE 39 STEPS* (and all the innocent-man-on-the-run films to come), the officers stubbornly refuse to listen to the hero's protestations of innocence, blindly (and often clumsily) pursuing him based on circumstantial evidence alone. They make up their minds quickly and turn all their attention to punishment—like the parents who, seeing a broken window, don't need to waste time listening to their child's tearful denials.

And sometimes—often most interestingly—the police are more malevolent forces, using their power to hurt and harass. The highway patrolman who, EYES hidden behind his mirrored sunglasses, stops Marion Crane on her way to the Bates Motel—What's really going on inside his head? Scottie Ferguson, so carefully tailing Madeleine and Judy in *VERTIGO*, masking his obsessiveness with the excuse that he's just on a job—What's his true motivation? We'll know soon enough, but in these films, the police aren't just plot devices—they're also sinister forces, characters who seem to appear out of nowhere.

Like the sergeant who so blandly, blithely locked little Alfred away. Like the universe that suddenly—as in *The Birds*—one day simply turns itself upside down.

References

Patrick McGilligan, *Alfred Hitchcock: A Life in Darkness and Light* (New York: HarperCollins, 2003), 448; François Truffaut, *Hitchcock/Truffaut*, rev. ed. (New York: Touchstone, 1985), 25.

POLITICS

"Hitchcock has never been a 'serious' director," filmmaker LINDSAY ANDERSON—then a critic—wrote dismissively in *Sequence* in 1949. "His films are interesting neither for their ideas nor for their characters. None of the early melodramas can be said to carry any sort of a 'message'; when one does appear, as in *FOREIGN CORRESPONDENT* and *LIFEBOAT*, it is banal in the extreme—'You'll never conquer them,' ALBERT BASSERMAN [*sic*] wheezes on his bed of torture, 'the little people who feed the birds.'"

Obviously, Anderson was not a particular admirer of the director. (Although he praised many of the early British pictures, he felt Hitchcock too often settled for purely commercial ventures and proclaimed *NOTORIOUS* one of the "worst of his career.") And admittedly, this was written during a particular lull in Hitchcock's filmmaking; in 1949, he had just finished *THE PARADINE CASE* and *ROPE*, and fans had only *UNDER CAPRICORN* and *STAGE FRIGHT* to look forward to. Even if one felt it necessary to defend Hitchcock as a great artist, for many it would take the 1950s, with its long string of complicated films, to prove the case.

But to a committed, politically engaged filmmaker like Anderson, what clearly kept Hitchcock out of the ranks of "serious" directors is what seems like his total disinterest in the great conflicts of the century. For Hitchcock, it seemed, politics was just a tool that provided a ready villain—Nazis in the '40s, Communists in the '60s. Although he worked regularly—and without pay—throughout the '40s to contribute propaganda films to the war effort, for Hitchcock, it seemed, ideologies were just another MACGUFFIN.

Yet Hitchcock was still more quietly, personally political than Anderson—or many others—gave him credit for.

Born on the edge of the Victorian era, he was raised in an extravagantly class-conscious Britain with several marks against him—he was Anglo-Irish; he was CATHOLIC; and his father, who sold vegetables and poultry, was "in trade." Hitchcock did not go to university, and (although his elaborately slow drawl sometimes disguised it from American ears) his speech was thick with Cockney inflections. Once he began to make movies, he began to move in a very different circle—actor Gerald du Maurier was a knight, screenwriter IVOR MONTAGU the son of a baron—in which he knew he did not fit.

"I think he felt a bit uncomfortable with all these established stage actors,"

JOAN FONTAINE said of his attitude on the set of *REBECCA* and his general disconnect from Hollywood's expat ENGLISH COLONY. "I think that there was also a social thing there," she remembered. "Hitchcock's origins were within the sound of Bow bells, so he didn't get around much socially."

Beyond his social unease with the industry's C. AUBREY SMITHS, Hitchcock's own class consciousness comes through in his films. Although there are exceptions, most of Hitchcock's heroes are working class or part of the genteel poor: the "second Mrs. de Winter" in *Rebecca*, Richard Hannay in *THE 39 STEPS*, Barry Caine in *SABOTEUR*, Richard Blaney in *FRENZY*, George Lumley in *FAMILY PLOT*. His characters work as bank clerks and own run-down hardware stores, drive cabs, and tend bar; dance in chorus lines or quietly labor as "paid companions" to bullying older women.

There are exceptions, of course, people in his films with careers and advanced degrees; some of them are even heroes. Yet often, there's something a little wobbly in their character, something unprofessional in their professional demeanor. Dr. Constance Petersen lets herself fall in love with a dangerous patient in *SPELLBOUND*; Dr. Ben MacKenna secretly sedates his own wife in the second *THE MAN WHO KNEW TOO MUCH* (while in the first version, a dentist turns out to be a murderous traitor). Education is no guarantee of common sense, let alone morality, among the elite.

As a predictor of bad behavior, though, money seems to be a reliable one in Hitchcock films. Sometimes the rich are merely shallow and a little careless—Roger Thornhill in *NORTH BY NORTHWEST*, Jessie and Frances Stevens in *TO CATCH A THIEF*, Melanie Daniels in *THE BIRDS*. But they're just as regularly pompous and ineffectual, like Rittenhouse in *LIFEBOAT*,

or cold and callous, like Mark in *MARNIE*. They are rarely people to depend on.

Often, they are people to fear. Although Hitchcock's films featured many foreign enemies—from the vague fascists of the '30s British films to the Third Reich agents of the '40s ones to the undefined Cold War villains of the '50s—there is one clear point throughout: Rarely are they acting alone. And when they need reliable collaborators in an unsuspecting land, they choose from among that country's upper classes. (It is not a coincidence that the two survivors who most quickly befriend the German sailor in *Lifeboat* are the two richest passengers, Rittenhouse and Connie.)

This theme of upper-class treachery is not a point that Hitchcock emphasizes, yet it's not an unimportant one because it sets him apart from many of his contemporaries—British spy fiction, from the days of JOHN BUCHAN to the heyday of Ian Fleming, was always shot through with xenophobia, touched by nasty paranoid suspicions that there were traitors among us, nasty and duplicitous foreigners whose real allegiance was to another land.

In Hitchcock, though, it's our own upper classes that we have to watch out for, people who've been given everything and still want more. In films like *The 39 Steps*, *Saboteur*, and *North by Northwest*, the villains aren't men with heavy accents and greasy overcoats but wealthy, well-dressed, and respected natives. They give parties. They hold charity balls. And when a beloved wife comes in to check on them—and finds them holding a gun on someone—she merely quietly retreats, closing the door behind her. Unlike the spies at work in their own countries, in *TORN CURTAIN* and *TOPAZ*—unlike the Soviets and Cubans who are risking their lives for a cause—these men don't even have the excuse of idealism. They're in it for profits, not patriotism.

"You're one of the ardent believers—a good American," Tobin sneers at Barry in *Saboteur*. "Oh, there are millions like you. People who play along, without asking questions. I hate to use the word stupid, but it seems to be the only one that applies. The great masses, the moron millions. Well, there are a few of us unwilling to troop along.... A few of us who are clever enough to see that there's much more to be done than just live small complacent lives, a few of us in America who desire a more profitable type of government. When you think about it, Mr. Kane, the competence of totalitarian nations is much higher than ours. They get things done." It's a long speech in a fast-moving movie, and Hitchcock's choice to stop things for a bit and let Tobin give it—on top of the speeches he's already given and with the treasonous dowager's charity gala already going on downstairs—shows how important the director thought it was.

Of course Hitchcock had already become a wealthy and respected man, with rich California property and an extensive wine cellar; later, he would add an impressive art collection and a fortune in MCA stock. He was no strident foe of capitalism, and the proof of his outwardly apolitical nature is that even as many of his collaborators—DOROTHY PARKER, ARTHUR LAURENTS, NORMAN LLOYD—were being caught up in the witch hunts of the McCarthy era, Hitchcock continued working, uncontroversial and unscathed. (Yet when he could, he quietly defied the blacklist and reached out to its victims—he hired Lloyd as a producer on his television shows over network objections and personally contacted other actors and directors, such as Paul Henreid, to ask them to contribute as well.)

That Hitchcock himself was never suspected of "subversive" ideas—at least, not since *Lifeboat* brought charges of being "un-American"—doesn't mean he didn't hold onto his own, lifelong suspicions. That he didn't make movies about "serious" issues doesn't mean that, from childhood, he had been taught to treat class and money and power very seriously—and with a certain degree of distrust. He knew who the enemy was. And that often that villain was living in the loveliest house in town.

References

Lindsay Anderson, "Alfred Hitchcock," *Focus on Hitchcock*, edited by Albert LaValley (Englewood Cliffs, NJ: Prentice Hall, 1972), 48–59; "Anti-U.S. Charge Denied," *Gloucestershire Echo*, March 16, 1944, http://the.hitchcock.zone/wiki/Gloucestershire_Echo_%2816/Mar/1944%29_-_Anti-U.S._Charge_Denied; Norman Lloyd, interviews with the author, November 2007, July 2015; Patrick McGilligan, *Alfred Hitchcock: A Life in Darkness and Light* (New York: HarperCollins, 2003), 526; Donald Spoto, *The Dark Side of Genius: The Life of Alfred Hitchcock* (New York: Da Capo Press, 1999), 218; Dorothy Thompson, "A Film That Could Aid German Morale," *Amarillo Globe*, January 31, 1944, http://the.hitchcock.zone/wiki/Amarillo_Globe_%2831/Jan/1944%29_-_A_Film_that_Could_Aid_German_Morale.

THE PRUDE'S FALL (GB 1924)

DIRECTOR: Graham Cutts.
SCREENPLAY: Alfred Hitchcock, from the play by May Edginton and Rudolph Besier.
PRODUCER: Michael Balcon.
CINEMATOGRAPHY: Hal Young.
EDITOR: Uncredited.
CAST: Jane Novak (Beatrice), Julanne Johnston (Sonia), Warwick Ward (Andre), Miles Mander (Sir Neville).
RUNNING TIME: 70 minutes, estimated. Black and white.
RELEASED THROUGH: Wardour Films.

A French naval officer tests a widow's character by asking her to be his mistress. The theme of cruelly testing a true love's character hints perhaps at *NOTORIOUS*, while the report that BETTY COMPSON appeared in an unbilled part is intriguing—but the film opened to poor reviews ("Not of first-rate quality") and survives today only in fragments.

References

Iris Barry, "The Prude's Fall," *Daily Mail*, November 23, 1925, 6; "The Prude's Fall," *BFI Screenonline*, http://explore.bfi.org.uk/4ce2b6bf19466.

PSYCHO (US 1960)

DIRECTOR: Alfred Hitchcock.
SCREENPLAY: Joseph Stefano, from the novel by Robert Bloch.
PRODUCER: Uncredited (Alfred Hitchcock).
CINEMATOGRAPHY: John L. Russell.
EDITOR: George Tomasini.
ORIGINAL MUSIC: Bernard Herrmann.
CAST: Anthony Perkins (Norman Bates), Janet Leigh (Marion Crane), John Gavin (Sam Loomis), Martin Balsam (Milton Arbogast), Vera Miles (Lila Crane).
RUNNING TIME: 109 minutes. Black and white.
RELEASED THROUGH: Paramount.

In love with Sam Loomis, a man too poor to marry her, desperate Marion Crane steals $40,000 from the company safe and drives off to see him. After a nerve-racking and rainy drive, she pulls in for the night at a nearly deserted motel, where Norman Bates, the shy young owner, makes her a sandwich. They talk a little about themselves—Norman mostly about his demanding mother, who "goes a little mad sometimes"—and Marion turns in, determining to return the money the next day.

Then, as she's taking a shower, a shadowy figure enters the motel bathroom and stabs her to death. Minutes later, Norman arrives and cleans up the bloody mess that he knows his maniacal mother has left behind, dumping Marion's body (and, unknowingly, the $40,000) in a nearby swamp. But Marion's disappearance and her theft have been noticed. A private detective, Arbogast, traces her as far as the motel—but when he tries to sneak inside the house to talk to Mrs. Bates, he's killed as well.

Finally, Loomis and Marion's sister, Lila, team up to try to find Marion themselves. They get as far as Arbogast did, but this time, while Loomis tries to keep Norman busy, Lila gets inside the house to try to talk to his mother. She finds a strange, frozen-in-time home—and, in the fruit cellar, the mummified corpse of the long-dead Mrs. Bates. Norman appears, dressed in her clothes and wielding a knife but is quickly disarmed by Loomis.

Later, at the police, a psychiatrist gives his explanation: A pathologically jealous Norman killed his mother years ago when she began to see another man and then, unable to face his own guilt, dug up her corpse, stuffed it, and finally began to speak for her, eventually giving her his own murderous personality. Meanwhile, in a holding cell, the now completely mad, completely "Mother" killer only sits and smiles, insisting she wouldn't even hurt a fly.

Hitchcock's darkest, sickest JOKE—and his most heart-wrenching cry of despair.

The director's morbidly funny, blackly bitter masterpiece began, though, as a different kind of technical challenge. The mid- to late '50s had seen an explosion in horror films, from Britain's Hammer studios, the tiny American International Pictures, and the loudly attention-grabbing producer William Castle. All were shot very cheaply (usually, apart from the Hammer efforts, in BLACK AND WHITE), and most made a great deal of money.

What, Hitchcock mused, if you took the same building blocks—a gruesome story leavened by sardonic humor, a cheap production pushed by sensationalistic advertising—and asked a really good director to construct something out of it? Then what would you get? Something like *Psycho*, he decided.

The book had already been read and dismissed by the story department at PARAMOUNT. "Too repulsive for films, and rather shocking even to a hardened reader," went the memo. But Hitchcock read the book himself on the recommendation of his assistant Peggy Robertson and bought it anonymously through an agent at MCA. When he brought it back to Paramount, however, announcing it as his next project, they were horrified. They refused to fund it. They even refused to let him shoot it on their lot.

So Hitchcock announced that he would pay for it himself and shoot it at UNIVERSAL, where he did his television show. All Paramount had to do was distribute it. He'd take all the risk—he'd even waive his director's fee—in return for a 60 percent stake. The studio agreed (something they'd regret later—the film turned out to be Hitchcock's biggest hit, making roughly $32 million theatrically before it ended its years-long run). Budgeting the production at a lean $800,000, the director cast it economically (ANTHONY PERKINS still owed a film to Paramount, VERA MILES was under personal contract, and JOHN GAVIN was on salary at Universal) and assembled much of the crew from his television show, where people knew how to work fast.

There were some tensions and second thoughts before and during shooting. Some of JOSEPH STEFANO's ideas, including making the incestuous relationship between Norman and his MOTHER explicit, would never have gotten past the CENSORS; Hitchcock struggled with a crew that was quick but perhaps not quite as polished as his usual feature-film technicians. Perkins remained worried about what such an extreme role would do to his career; JANET LEIGH, whose previous parts had been largely decorative, wondered if she could tackle such a tough complex heroine. Hitchcock assuaged their doubts and encouraged them to add their own touches to their roles—as long as they knew their lines and hit their marks.

The shower scene—storyboarded by "pictorial consultant" SAUL BASS, who later claimed to have directed it as well—took a week of shooting a nearly nude Leigh, along with body doubles for both her and Perkins. (Hitchcock, who usually had little patience for surprise endings, was intent on keeping this one intact; a female body double for Norman-as-Mother was extra insurance, so no one recognized Perkins's broad shoulders.) Other scenes—such as the state psychiatrist's literally anticlimactic summation—were handled more briskly.

Eventually Hitchcock wrapped the picture, edited it, and added the score. (BERNARD HERRMANN's music was very nearly the opposite of the modern jazz the director had requested—he had also wanted silence for the shower scene—but so delighted Hitchcock that he raised Herrmann's fee and gave him a prominent place in the opening credits.) After some more squabbles with the censors—there is a brief blurry flash of body double Marli Renfro's breasts as Marion pulls open the curtain that stayed in and one clear shot of the corpse's buttocks, which Hitchcock cut, probably having always meant it as a bargaining chip—the picture was sent out to theaters.

It was sent out with two more marketing innovations meant to preserve its secrets: Critics weren't given advance screenings, and no one was admitted after the picture began (a promotional trick stolen from rival HENRI-GEORGES CLOUZOT's *LES DIABOLIQUES* but also a way of ensuring that latecomers didn't come in after the shower scene and wonder where Janet Leigh was). Unless they'd already read the novel, people wouldn't know what they were in for.

They soon did. The critics were largely unimpressed—"A blot on an honorable career," declared the *New York Times*—but audiences got the film and the joke. Hitchcock and Stefano had layered the film with tiny quips and inside references, some of which would only be apparent on a second or third viewing—Norman's apology that his mother wasn't "quite herself" that day—but audiences roared nonetheless, partly to dispel the tension, partly because the film seemed to tap into the sick humor then coming into vogue. The crowds were so vocal, in fact, that Hitchcock considered pulling the prints and remixing the soundtrack; people might be laughing too loud to hear some of the dialogue. (As the picture was already in wide release, the plan was abandoned.)

But *Psycho* is more than just a dark joke. Yes, there are many bits of grim foreshadowing and knowing nudges throughout the sneakily sardonic film, which sometimes plays like a live-action Charles Addams cartoon. Within a few minutes of the opening, Marion will be joking to Sam about cheap hotels that don't care when you check in, but "when your time is up . . . "; moments after Marion's corpse is sunk into a swamp, a customer enters Sam's store looking for poison, insisting that "death should always be painless."

But there's also bravura filmmaking. There's beautifully realized imagery and extended metaphors. And, more than anything, there's an almost palpable sense of existential dread.

There are also some superb performances, particularly from Leigh and Perkins, who go deep into their characters and themselves. Leigh had been in Hollywood since the late '40s, but she had finally aged out of her ingénue roles into a less certain future—*Psycho* captures a hard, adult determination here that other movies hadn't. And Perkins gives Norman so many qualities—flashes of madness, yes, but also humor and bashfulness and even touches of effeminacy—that, when the film demands we switch allegiances and identify with him instead of Marion, we immediately oblige.

Not every actor's performance is quite as interesting—yet their flatness works for the parts they've been asked to play. MARTIN BALSAM is dull, methodical, conscientious—just what you'd expect from a private detective working a case. Gavin is handsome enough to imagine a woman willing to commit a crime to be with him—and dull enough to push her to have second thoughts. SIMON OAKLAND's psychiatrist is smug and glib—but isn't that the point? Each actor serves the film perfectly.

But Hitchcock is the real STAR here, and the cinematic flourishes are many. In some ways the most audacious is the simplest—getting rid of Leigh's character early in the picture. Although that may not resonate as strongly with contemporary audiences, at the time, her dismissal was nearly as shocking as the form it took. Hollywood movies simply didn't write a major star out of a script like this; if Hitchcock was willing to do that, then clearly *Psycho* was willing to do anything. (And it was—among the many taboos the movie broke was the prohibition against seeing a toilet, let alone a flushing one.)

Then, of course, there was the shower murder itself, the KULESHOV EFFECT gone mad—knife, mouth, knife, abdomen, drain, mouth, knife, showerhead, all cut together by GEORGE TOMASINI into an orgy of near-subliminal images, so deliberately fast and sometimes intentionally blurred that the audience never knew what it was seeing and always remained convinced it had seen more than it had.

But there were quieter, more elegantly formal sequences, too. Like the opening, starting with the Phoenix skyline, then picking out a building, then slowly going inside the window of one room, a complicated move Hitchcock had vainly tried to do in a single shot; even assembled out of several separate ones, it still silently grounded the story, at least for now, in dully recognizable reality. Or the ending, with Norman/Mother sitting against that blank featureless wall, thinking, thinking—and then his/her smile dissolving into a corpse's skeletal grin. All of this was beautifully shot and edited, but what also filled *Psycho* with meaning were the symbols within those images.

It's a movie filled with EYES—the ones a highway patrolman hides behind glasses, the "cruel" ones studying you that Norman imagines in the madhouse, his own as he peeps at his pretty guest, Marion's dead staring pupils as she lies on the cold bathroom floor, the sightless sockets of the lifeless Mrs. Bates, the unseen ones that are "probably watching" Norman at the end.

It's a movie filled with BIRDS, too—Marion Crane from Phoenix, to begin with, but also the pictures of pretty songbirds that fill the murder cabin, Cabin 1 (and only Cabin 1), and the stuffed predators that look down on Norman in his parlor, and Marion, as she pecks at her sandwich "like a bird."

And it's a movie filled with domineering parents who still rule their adult children's lives—the dead father whose debts Sam fights to pay off, the daddy who's giving his "sweet baby girl" a $40,000 wedding gift, the mother who gives Marion's friend tranquilizers for her honeymoon, the departed mom whose picture looks down on Marion and Lila, the possessive Mrs. Bates who finally, literally, possesses her own son.

But more than anything, *Psycho* is a movie filled with a kind of silent-scream anguish, a Munch painting come to life. It begins in the harsh, pitiless light of the desert and ends in the dank muck of a swamp, and nothing in between seems to happen according to any plan or any sense of justice. A sinning woman determines to make amends and takes a shower to wash herself clean—and is murdered anyway. A young man comes across enough money to help him start over—and unthinkingly throws it away.

No one gets what they want in *Psycho*, and to some extent that includes the audience. You like the heroine? Too bad. *Psycho* kills her in the first act. You have hopes for the detective? Good. *Psycho* kills him off, too. You think, well, maybe now Marion's boyfriend and her sister will fall for each other? No, they won't. Whatever your expectations were, *Psycho* ignored them at every turn. A happy ending? There's only one person smiling at the end of the movie, and it's dear dead Mom.

The universe is random, *Psycho* said; movies can be just as capricious. Ironically, it took Hitchcock, the most meticulous of directors, to embrace the modern moral chaos—and throw down that artistic gauntlet. Very few filmmakers since have dared pick it up.

But still, thanks to *Psycho*, that possibility exists onscreen—that the good people will not win, that the bad people will win our hearts, that nothing will turn out right or even conclusively. For Marion Crane may have lost her life when she stepped into that shower. But the American movie audience lost its innocence forever.

References

Patrick McGilligan, *Alfred Hitchcock: A Life in Darkness and Light* (New York: HarperCollins, 2003), 578–601; Donald Spoto, *The Dark Side of Genius: The Life of Alfred Hitchcock* (New York: Da Capo Press, 1999), 413–21; François Truffaut, *Hitchcock/Truffaut*, rev. ed. (New York: Touchstone, 1985), 266–83; Stephen Whitty, "A Psycho Analysis," *NJ.com*, http://www.nj.com/entertainment/movies/index.ssf/2010/10/a_psycho_analysis_alfred_hitchcocks_spookiest_movie_brought_with_it_the_end_of_hollywood_innocence.html.

PSYCHO (US 1998)

DIRECTOR: Gus Van Sant.
SCREENPLAY: Joseph Stefano, based on the novel by Robert Bloch.
PRODUCERS: Brian Grazer, Gus Van Sant.
CINEMATOGRAPHY: Christopher Doyle.
EDITOR: Amy E. Duddleston.
ORIGINAL MUSIC: Bernard Herrmann.
CAST: Vince Vaughn (Norman Bates), Anne Heche (Marion Crane), Viggo Mortensen (Sam Loomis), William H. Macy (Arbogast), Julianne Moore (Lila Crane).
RUNNING TIME: 105 minutes. Color.
RELEASED THROUGH: Universal.

It's an idea best suited perhaps for an academic paper or maybe a late-night dorm discussion: What would a classic movie look like if you took the shooting script and remade it precisely, shot for shot, but with different actors and in COLOR instead of BLACK AND WHITE? Well, it might look a bit like Gus Van Sant's redo of *PSYCHO*—although, one would hope, more interesting.

Van Sant's inexplicable remake—he has since called it an "experiment" and a "prank"—follows the Hitchcock film pretty slavishly but in color and with a different cast, with Vince Vaughn, Anne Heche, Julianne Moore, Viggo Mortensen, and William H. Macy taking over, respectively, for ANTHONY PERKINS, JANET LEIGH, VERA MILES, JOHN GAVIN, and MARTIN BALSAM. Few are improvements.

Macy is a little livelier than Balsam, and Mortensen more interesting than Gavin. But Moore has nothing to add to what was always a minor role, and Heche lacks Leigh's weary warmth. And Vaughn's Norman—big, beefy, slightly lunkish—strikes a definite off-note. And with the cinematography and editing basically aping the first, nearly shot for shot, the movie seems less like an aesthetic exercise than a waste of time; it's as pointless (and appalling) as colorizing a classic, and the few touches Van Sant adds feel like mistakes.

In the first film, for example, we saw Norman spying on Marion as she undressed, then retreating silently to his house; here, he masturbates while he watches. The change is not only crude but contradictory; part of the point and power of the shower murder is that the mad Norman can't express his SEXUALITY in any other way. To allow him this sort of physical release removes some of the reason for his attack.

For all its careful copying, Van Sant's *Psycho* feels like a movie made by someone who watched the original a hundred times and yet never really saw a thing.

Reference

Scott Tobias, "Gus Van Sant," *AV Club*, http://www.avclub.com/article/gus-van-sant-13800.

PSYCHOANALYSIS

Although *SPELLBOUND* is rightly credited with being one of the first Hollywood films to take psychoanalysis seriously—and often noted as being a personal project for DAVID O. SELZNICK, who had his own analyst hired and credited as a consultant—Hitchcock's interest in the subject predates it by more than a decade with a rather fatuous FREUDIAN showing up as one of the jurors in *MURDER!* Even when psychiatry isn't explicitly mentioned, its theories and diagnoses are often a part of his early thrillers—the temporary traumatic amnesia that Diana suffers in *Murder!*, the combination of GUILT and vengeance that drives the tenant in *THE LODGER*.

Although many of Hitchcock's villains are clearly disturbed, if not outright mad—Charlie in *SHADOW OF A DOUBT*, Brandon in *ROPE*, Norman in *PSYCHO*, Bob in *FRENZY*—it's unlikely the curdled MOTHER fixations and thwarted sexual desires that drive them to kill could ever have been defused with a rigorous application of talk therapy. In fact, the few Hitchcock characters who do seek out professional help for problems—Scottie in *VERTIGO*, Rose in *THE WRONG MAN*—find it provides little immediate relief.

In the end, Hitchcock remains a romantic, not a clinician, and only in those cases when the therapy comes from a lover—Constance in *Spellbound*, Mark in *MARNIE*—is there any sort of breakthrough. All of our relationships are marked by assumed IDENTITIES, willful dishonesty, deeply hidden shames, his films insist. Only being honest with one another—utterly, emotionally naked—is there ever any hope for change.

Reference

Patrick McGilligan, *Alfred Hitchcock: A Life in Darkness and Light* (New York: HarperCollins, 2003), 356.

PUBLICITY

From the start of his directing career, Alfred Hitchcock was very conscious of advertising, public relations, and the as-yet-unnamed "branding"—he hired personal publicists almost as soon as *THE LODGER* gave him a name to push, and his actual signature (and later his own minimalist caricature of his profile) became a part of film titles, posters, and merchandizing tie-ins. He wrote a number of bylined articles for both film-oriented and general-interest magazines and newspapers and sat for countless INTERVIEWS.

His personal involvement grew even stronger once he escaped the ego of DAVID O. SELZNICK and became his own producer; he would not only pose drolly for preproduction publicity photos but also eventually appear in the advertising trailers, presenting the same sort of sarcastic, gleefully morbid character he had used on his television show.

Right from the start, Hitchcock's point of view was "You make pictures for the press," his old British colleague IVOR MONTAGU remembered. "This, he explained quite frankly, was the reason for 'the Hitchcock touches'—novel shots that the critics would pick out and comment upon—as well as those flash appearances that gradually became a trademark in his films. He went on to explain that, if you made yourself publicly known as a director—and this you could only do by getting mention in the press in connection with your directing—this would be the only way you became free to do what you wanted."

Particularly elaborate—and instructive—was the campaign for *PSYCHO*. The trailer (with Hitchcock giving a tour of the empty set and even giving away some important plot points) ran 6½ minutes; a separate, 11-minute "press book on film" about the film's admittance policies was made and shown to distributors to explain the special marketing. The requirements—"No one—*but no one*—will be admitted after the start of each performance of *Psycho*" read the signs posted outside theaters and in their lobbies—were similar to ones used for the release of HENRI-GEORGES CLOUZOT's *LES DIABOLIQUES*. They also brought to mind some of the ballyhoo beloved of producer William Castle, whose 1958 *Macabre*, a self-styled B-movie, had offered every audience member an insurance policy guaranteed to pay out if they died of fright during a screening. (No one ever collected.)

There was a practical purpose for these admission requirements; at the time, movies in major cities ran nearly continuously, with some fans wandering in after a picture had started and simply staying until the next showing. Hitchcock knew this would be disastrous for a film with huge surprises in both its first and third acts, and so he insisted on people seeing it from the beginning or not at all, even suggesting theater owners hire extra security to keep order. But beyond the obvious benefits of preserving the secrets of *Psycho*—an unusually crucial matter to Hitchcock, who generally avoided classic whodunits—this approach ensured that other patrons would see people lining up for the next screening. The film would definitely be talked about, before and afterward. (Along with his other demands to theater owners came the insistence that, after the final title, the room go dark for a half-minute before the house lights came up; "Never, never, never will I permit *Psycho* to be followed immediately by a short subject or newsreel," he added.)

It was the sort of advertising campaign that Castle—who by now was hiding plastic skeletons in the rafters (*House on Haunted Hill*) and electric buzzers in the seats (*The Tingler*) could only dream of, and it clearly worked; after its long run in theaters (including a 1965 re-release), *Psycho* had earned back more than 40 times its budget and made Hitchcock millions.

All of this was more than a way to publicize a film, though. It was a way to publi-cize the filmmaker. Hitchcock had always suspected, right from the beginning, that the director was the true star of the movie; for years, all he had been attempting to accomplish, with his interviews, his image, his inescapable appearances, was to ensure audiences recognize that top billing. *Psycho* gave it to him forever.

References

Stephen Rebello, *Alfred Hitchcock and the Making of Psycho* (New York: Harper-Perennial, 1991), 147–57; Donald Spoto, *The Dark Side of Genius: The Life of Alfred Hitchcock* (New York: Da Capo Press, 1999), 85–87.

PURE CINEMA

Although the term dates back to at least the 1920s and early debates among French critics on the nature of film as art, Alfred Hitchcock had been using the phrase in the early '60s, and in his 1963 monograph for an upcoming Museum of Modern Art retrospective, PETER BOGDANOVICH tried to pin him down: How would you define *pure cinema*?

"Pure cinema," Hitchcock replied, "is complementary pieces of film put together, like notes of music make a melody." He then went on to describe two slightly different examples of MONTAGE, both from *REAR WINDOW*, in which an action sequence is broken down into different shots (arms, legs, faces) or, as with the KULESHOV EFFECT, a static shot of someone looking is broken up and defined by an insert shot of what he is looking at. The way you put the different pieces of film together, he suggested, is what moviemaking was all about.

But pure cinema is more than editing, although editing is perhaps the only thing that the movies can claim as their own. For Hitchcock, "pure cinema" was very simply visual storytelling—the way that an artist used composition, imagery, planes of action, focus, and lighting within a single shot to express an idea and then multiplied that idea by joining that shot to another.

"The screen rectangle must be charged with emotion," he insisted to FRANÇOIS TRUFFAUT, and it is a theme Hitchcock returns to throughout their long conversations: Cinema is an emotional medium, and the director's job is to consciously use visual methods—the size of the image, the contrast between shots—to incite unconscious feelings in his audience.

Hitchcock's first work in films came during the silent era (and his first job, designing title cards, was more visual still), so using pictures, not dialogue, to tell a story was always important to him. "In many of the films now being made, there is very little cinema," he complained in the '60s. "They are mostly what I call 'photographs of people talking.' When we tell a story in cinema, we should resort to dialogue only when it's impossible to do otherwise."

The idea, after all, was to make a film, not a radio show; if, as Hitchcock said another time, you could close your eyes and still follow a movie perfectly, then the director wasn't doing his job. It was not merely because of age or stubbornness that he still most often referred to his chosen medium not as "films" or "movies" but "the pictures."

To list the moments of pure cinema in Hitchcock's work is, essentially, to list the most memorable sequences from his movies, but they would probably begin with the shot of THE LODGER pacing his room upstairs—a fact we know only because the director dissolves from the ceiling, with its slightly wobbly light fixture, to the heavy pane of plate glass that IVOR NOVELLO is treading. It is not a rational moment; it is a purely visual and emotional one.

And it is using imagery to convey complex situations—even slightly indescribable emotions—that Hitchcock always

excelled at. The way that the cleaning lady's scream fades into the noise of a locomotive in THE 39 STEPS and immediately hurtles us along into the action; the careful cutting between a ticking bomb, the innocent child carrying it, and the clocks surrounding him that almost unbearably ratchets up the tension in SABOTAGE; the simple stare into the camera that Uncle Charlie gives in SHADOW OF A DOUBT, a breaking of the fourth wall that both invites us to join him in his madness and makes us shrink back.

Rarely merely visual flourishes, Hitchcock's choices almost invariably advance the plot or deepen our relationship to the characters. He could use an inexorably long shot, moving from a vast crowd into a single detail, to stress the narrative importance of a facial twitch (YOUNG AND INNOCENT) or a simple key (NOTORIOUS); he could pull the camera up high for a static bird's-eye view to encourage us to dispassionately view humans in turmoil (DIAL M FOR MURDER, THE BIRDS); or he could use the SUBJECTIVE CAMERA to bring us close and have us feel the impact of a punch (STRANGERS ON A TRAIN, NORTH BY NORTHWEST) or identify with a character's horrible actions (PSYCHO, FRENZY).

Yet while Hitchcock always remained first and foremost a visual storyteller—the strongest evidence of his brilliant, early career in silent film—he was always a complete filmmaker. Although he insisted that motion pictures should, naturally enough, use motion and pictures to tell their stories, he respected the written word; he not only worked with outstanding screenwriters, such as BEN HECHT, but frequently collaborated with acclaimed authors, too, from THORNTON WILDER to (less felicitously) RAYMOND CHANDLER and JOHN STEINBECK. The dialogue in Shadow of a Doubt, in Notorious, in VERTIGO, in Psycho is always beautiful and sometimes even poetic.

His reliance on actors was less obvious; as someone who never tired of quoting the lessons of Kuleshov, he knew that, given a simple close-up of an actor's face, he could create any effect he wanted later in the editing room (the reason he so often advised—and frustrated—uncertain actors by telling them not to show any emotion at all).

Yet Hitchcock had a strong respect for the power of a STAR's persona; the complex, self-doubting JAMES STEWART was right for certain roles; the ultimately unknowable CARY GRANT, perfect for others. And if he had no patience for actors inquiring after their motivation—that was their job, and he preferred they had figured all that out before they arrived on his set, delaying his schedule—as long as they hit their marks, he was perfectly open to them improvising and making their characters their own. He may have enjoyed insulting actors or pretending to—he certainly did not enjoy their demands on his budgets—but the number of remarkable performances in his films refutes any suggestion that he didn't appreciate acting.

For someone who had begun in silents, he adapted to sound easily, too. Both *BLACKMAIL* and *MURDER!* are experimenting with aural montage and layered soundtracks at a time when many directors were still wondering how to hide the microphone; by the time he had arrived in Hollywood, with its wealth of talented composers, Hitchcock was ready to add music to his visuals in a way that he hadn't really been able to in Britain. BERNARD HERRMANN, with his brilliant ear for orchestration (and shared appreciation of Wagner), turned out to be the perfect pair of ears for his eyes; the sinuous repetitions of his score for *Vertigo*, the stabbing strings of the music in *Psycho*, both emphasize and elaborate on those movies' moods and meanings.

This was always Hitchcock's firmest belief: A movie is not just story and action, actor and dialogue; it's also imagery, editing, and sound. And it was Hitchcock's innate ability to keep all those different elements separate in his head yet find a way to join and juxtapose them onscreen, that made him one of the movies' greatest proponents of pure cinema—and one of its purest cinematic geniuses as well.

References

Peter Bogdanovich, *The Cinema of Alfred Hitchcock*, http://the.hitchcock.zone/wiki/Alfred_Hitchcock_and_Peter_Bogdanovich_%281963%29; Alfred Hitchcock, interview by Bryan Forbes, BBC One, December 30, 1969, http://the.hitchcock.zone/wiki/Alfred_Hitchcock_and_Bryan_Forbes_%281969%29; François Truffaut, *Hitchcock/Truffaut*, rev. ed. (New York: Touchstone, 1985), 61, 110–13, 214–15.

QUAYLE, ANTHONY
(1913–1989)

Lancashire-born, classically trained actor who joined the Old Vic in 1932 and the army in 1939. After serving with distinction (and behind enemy lines in Albania with Special Operations) during World War II, he returned to the theater, specializing in the classics, his efforts as a director and actor leading to the establishment of a vital theater scene at Stratford-on-Avon and the eventual birth of the Royal Shakespeare Company.

Quayle had made his film debut in 1938 in a small part in *Pygmalion*; little more than character work ever followed for the strapping actor with the fine voice and the moon face. "I wasn't asked to be a handsome young man in films because I wasn't a handsome young man," he declared later, noting that his film work was mostly paycheck parts. "I was in the Tarzan films and *Fall of the Roman Empire* and one dreary thing after another," he said.

He was, characteristically, being modest. Quayle's natural, authoritative bearing let him play noble Romans, stern British officers, or men of the church; among his better films were *Laurence of Arabia*, *The Guns of Navarone*, and *Anne of the Thousand Days*. In addition to his stage work, he also did a great deal of television, including *Moses the Lawgiver*, *Masada*, and the 1981 remake of *DIAL M FOR MURDER*, in which he played the inspector.

Quayle had only a small part in Hitchcock's *THE WRONG MAN*, but one of his scenes was particularly memorable; as the defense lawyer, he meets with Manny and Rose in his office to go over new developments in the case. But as Hitchcock's camera slowly circles him, Quayle's quietly inquisitive look shows us what Manny is oblivious to; although the news is guardedly hopeful, Rose is already unresponsive and sinking into a dangerous depression.

He died of cancer at 76 at his London home.

References

"Anthony Quayle," *IMDb*, http://www.imdb.com/name/nm0703033/bio?ref_=nm_ov_bio_sm; Glenn Collins, "Sir Anthony Quayle, British Actor and Theater Director, Dies at 76," *New York Times*, October 21, 1989, http://www.nytimes.com/1989/10/21/obituaries/sir-anthony-quayle-british-actor-and-theater-director-dies-at-76.html?sec=&spon=&pagewanted=2; Roger Phillip Mellor, "Anthony Quayle," *BFI Screenonline*, http://www.screenonline.org.uk/people/id/491735.

R

RADFORD, BASIL (1897–1952)

Chester-born performer and minister's son who fought in the brutal trenches of World War I—emerging with that shocking scar across one cheek—and then came home to enroll in the Royal Academy of Dramatic Art. He made his London debut in 1924 and spent most of the next few years abroad on the stages of New Zealand, Canada, and California.

Radford made his movie debut in 1929 and did several films for Hitchcock, including *YOUNG AND INNOCENT*, in which he plays Erica's uncle, and *JAMAICA INN*, in which he shows up as one of Sir Humphrey's unnamed dinner guests. In between, though, he nabbed his most famous role, playing Charters in *THE LADY VANISHES*, the slightly fuddy-duddy Englishman whose only interest is the cricket results (until, hang it all, old man, the Fascists attack and one simply has to pick up a revolver and pitch in).

It's a cheekily satiric yet, in the end, quietly approving portrayal of English values, and—often partnered with NAUNTON WAYNE, who played his traveling companion, Caldicott—Radford would continue to milk the character for much of the rest of his career, particularly in *Night Train to Munich* and *Crook's Tour* (which gave the characters new adventures) and such classics as *Dead of Night* and *Whiskey Galore!*, which basically continued the partnership under different names.

Although he did other, more properly prestigious films, sometimes solo (such as *The Winslow Boy*), it was his playing sweetly dim, impossibly stalwart types that won him the hearts of many Britons, in the movies and on the BBC; he died in London at 55 while rehearsing for a new play with Wayne. Reportedly, the heart attack hit him as he was in the pub, reaching for a pint—precisely as you might have expected Charters to go.

References

"Basil Radford," *IMDb*, http://www.imdb com/name/nm0705509/bio?ref_=nm _ov_bio_sm; "Obituary: Basil Radford," *Times*, October 21, 1952, http://the .hitchcock.zone/wiki/The_Times_%2821/ Oct/1952%29_-_Obituary:_Basil_Radford; Matthew Sweet, "Mustard and Cress," *Guardian*, December 29, 2007, http://www .theguardian.com/film/2007/dec/29/film.

RAINS, CLAUDE (1889–1967)

London-born actor (and son of a struggling actor) who grew up with a lisp, a stammer, and a rough Cockney accent. Performing, nonetheless, since childhood, he was discovered by fabled actor/manager Sir Herbert Beerbohm Tree, who paid for the vocal coaching Rains needed—which would help turn him into one of the most mellifluous actors of his generation.

A veteran of World War I (where a gas attack left him permanently, partially

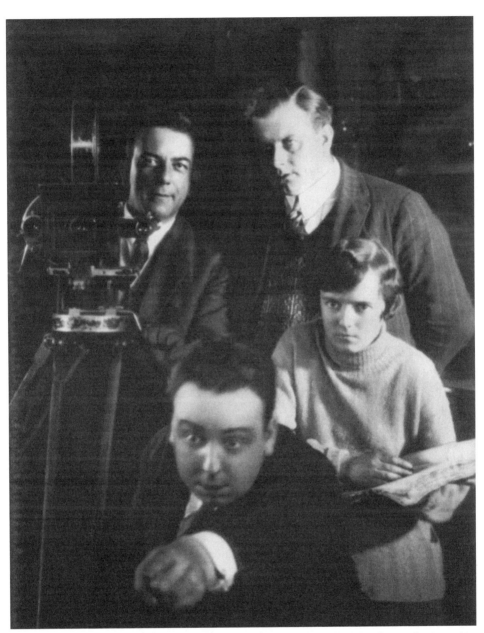

Alfred Hitchcock and Alma Reville at the beginning of their personal and professional partnership, on the set of *The Mountain Eagle* with two unidentified crew members. *Photofest*

blinded) and of the Royal Academy of Dramatic Art (where, as a star pupil, he later returned to teach, numbering JOHN GIELGUD among his students), Rains made his talkie debut in James Whale's *The Invisible Man* in 1933; although bandages or special effects left him faceless until the end, his sterling-silver voice made the most of the witty dialogue and made him a movie favorite.

Short and already middle-aged, Rains was an unlikely leading man. And so he settled comfortably into a long reign as one of the art's most dependable character actors, nominated four times for the best supporting actor prize (he never won) and leaving an indelible mark on *Casablanca*; *The Adventures of Robin Hood*; *Mr. Skeffington*; *Now, Voyager*; *Mr. Smith Goes to Washington*; *Laurence of Arabia*; and many others.

For Hitchcock, his by far finest work—despite five separate appearances on *ALFRED HITCHCOCK PRESENTS*— would be in *NOTORIOUS* as Nazi collaborator Alex Sebastian. Hitchcock had originally thought of Clifton Webb, who had previously scored in a similar role—the older, beauty-obsessed murderer in *Laura*. But Webb's delicate archness would have deprived Sebastian of the warmth that this villain nonetheless needed to have, and at DAVID O. SELZNICK's insistence, Rains was cast.

Selznick had never been shy about meddling, but this suggestion may have been his best; Sebastian is a villain working secretly with fugitive Nazis to develop an atomic weapon and, eventually, plotting to poison his wife—yet Rains shows us, not a monster, but a MOTHER-DOMINATED weakling, who, at this late date in his life, has finally taken over running the family business (no doubt disappointingly, in his mother's eyes) and at last dared to fall in love.

His scenes with INGRID BERGMAN's Alicia are full of soft words and crackling energy—she does, indeed, clearly affect him "like a tonic"—and Rains never fails to convince us that this short older man has fallen completely, adoringly for this tall slim goddess (much as, perhaps, a certain fat older man already worshipped the actress playing the part). Arguably, Sebastian deserves Alicia more than Devlin does—he loves her more completely, unashamedly, unreservedly. And it's a love that never fades, even as he's coolly watching her drink her coffee full of arsenic.

Rains received his last best supporting actor nomination for *Notorious* (and lost again) and continued to work regularly, although the rebellious, youth-oriented '50s were not a congenial time for 60-ish British character actors with beautiful speaking voices. He still kept busy, though, starring in everything from the kiddie-matinee remake of *The Lost World* to playing Herod in *The Greatest Story Ever Told*; in between, he retreated to his sprawling farm in New England. He died at 77 from an abdominal hemorrhage in New Hampshire. No one has ever sounded quite like him since.

References

"Claude Rains," *Encyclopaedia Britannica*, http://www.britannica.com/biography/Claude-Rains; "Claude Rains," *IMDb*, http://www.imdb.com/name/nm0001647/bio?ref_=nm_ov_bio_sm; Donald Spoto, *The Dark Side of Genius: The Life of Alfred Hitchcock* (New York: Da Capo Press, 1999), 287; David Thomson, *The New Biographical Dictionary of Film* (New York: Knopf, 2002), 709–10.

RAPHAELSON, SAMSON (1894–1983)

New York–born playwright and screenwriter who first worked in advertising. Encouraged by his secretary, he turned his short story "Day of Atonement" into the play *The Jazz Singer*; it became not only the Broadway hit but also Hollywood's first talkie smash. Raphaelson continued to produce hit plays but by the '30s was an in-demand Hollywood screenwriter, where his work ranged from *Trouble in Paradise* and *The Shop around the Corner* to *The Last of Mrs. Cheyney* and *The Harvey Girls*, and he was known for his tight construction and sparkling, sophisticated dialogue.

For Hitchcock, he worked—along with JOAN HARRISON and ALMA REVILLE— on *SUSPICION* (which, before the director had come onboard, already had a script from Nathaniel West and Boris Ingster that apparently Hitchcock discarded). Based on the excellent Francis Iles novel *Before the Fact*, it is the story of a born victim—an insecure woman who remains besotted with her husband, even as it becomes clear he's planning to poison her.

The screenplay follows the book faithfully enough, but the central idea of the story posed a problem, not just for the CENSORS but also the studio—How could leading man CARY GRANT play a murderer? DONALD SPOTO insists that Hitchcock had known of this problem from the beginning and was, in fact, more interested in the study of a wife's paranoia; Hitchcock himself claimed the objection was only raised later.

The effect, though, remained the same—a novel about a plotting sociopath of a husband now became a movie about a morbidly distrustful wife. Even Hitchcock's and Raphaelson's skills can't sell that switch (although the movie remains entertaining for the most part and won JOAN FONTAINE the best actress Oscar).

Raphaelson and his wife enjoyed the company of the Hitchcocks (although he once remarked, quite intriguingly, that in private they seemed like a slightly gender-switched couple—Hitch a bit effeminate, Alma a trifle mannish). Raphaelson, who turned down a later offer to write *I CONFESS*, began to curtail his screenwriting in the '50s but continued to write and teach and discovered a new love for photography. He died in New York at age 89.

References

Patrick McGilligan, *Alfred Hitchcock: A Life in Darkness and Light* (New York: HarperCollins, 2003), 280; "Samson Raphaelson," *Encyclopaedia Britannica*, http://www.britannica.com/biography/Samson-Raphaelson; "Samson Raphaelson," *IMDb*, http://www.imdb.com/name/nm0710723/bio?ref_=nm_ov_bio_sm; Donald Spoto, *The Dark Side of Genius: The Life of Alfred Hitchcock* (New York: Da Capo Press, 1999), 243–46.

REAR WINDOW (US 1954)

DIRECTOR: Alfred Hitchcock.
SCREENPLAY: John Michael Hayes, based on a story by Cornell Woolrich.
PRODUCER: Uncredited (Alfred Hitchcock).
CINEMATOGRAPHY: Robert Burks.
EDITOR: George Tomasini.
ORIGINAL MUSIC: Franz Waxman.
CAST: James Stewart (L. B. "Jeff" Jefferies), Grace Kelly (Lisa Fremont), Thelma Ritter (Stella), Raymond Burr (Lars Thorwald), Wendell Corey (Det. Thomas Doyle).
RUNNING TIME: 112 minutes. Color.
RELEASED THROUGH: Paramount.

After breaking his leg running after the perfect shot of a racetrack crash, photojournalist L. B. "Jeff" Jefferies is stuck in a cast, in a wheelchair, and in his stifling Greenwich Village apartment. To pass the time, he sits by his window overlooking the back courtyard, using his telephoto lens to spy on the little dramas unfolding in his neighbors' apartments—a pastime that amuses neither the prickly Stella, his visiting health aide, nor Lisa, the socialite fashion model to whom he refuses to commit.

Jeff gives his neighbors nicknames—the leotard-clad "Miss Torso," who energetically does her dance routines; "Miss Lonelyhearts," who is dateless and dejected—but finds his attention increasingly drawn to one apartment, where the quarreling Mrs. Thorwald has suddenly vanished and Mr. Thorwald disappears for long stretches of time in the middle of the night. Convinced that a homicide has happened, Jeff tells his suspicions to Stella and

Lisa, who begin to share them, and a friend in the police department (who remains unconvinced).

Lisa volunteers to be Jeff's legs and investigate and, finally slipping into the Thorwalds' apartment, finds the wife's wedding ring—strong proof that the woman has not, as her husband claims, simply gone on a long trip. But the police arrive and arrest Lisa for burglary, and Stella has to go post bail, leaving Jeff alone and defenseless in the apartment.

Thorwald, who has realized his across-the-courtyard neighbor has been spying on him, goes over to Jeff's apartment to end the surveillance permanently. Jeff temporarily blinds Thorwald by setting off flash-bulbs, but the burly man rushes forward and manages to push Jeff out the window before the police arrive and arrest him. Jeff, however, survives the fall—albeit now with two broken legs—and is soon recuperating at home, with Lisa in hovering attendance.

An essential Hitchcock film and an insight into the essence of Hitchcock himself as a man and an artist.

"If someone were to ask 'What are the movies of Alfred Hitchcock like,'" filmmaker Curtis Hanson says in the documentary *'Rear Window' Ethics*, "someone who knew nothing about movies, you could show them *Rear Window* and in a sense touch on everything in Hitchcock."

Rear Window marked a new studio for Hitchcock (after the less-than-thrilling union with WARNER BROS., LEW WASSERMAN had arranged for a multipicture deal at PARAMOUNT) and a new screenwriting collaborator in JOHN MICHAEL HAYES (who would turn out to be one of his best). It also definitively marked the '50s as Hitchcock's greatest, most creative decade—an era that would also include such masterpieces as *STRANGERS ON A TRAIN*; *VERTIGO*; *NORTH BY NORTH-* *WEST*; and, not to stretch the point, *PSYCHO* (which would begin filming in November 1959).

Preproduction went smoothly. Hayes's initial treatment—based on a CORNELL WOOLRICH story Hitchcock had the rights to—was polished enough that JAMES STEWART agreed to star even before the script was written and GRACE KELLY turned down *On the Waterfront* to play Lisa. After having a massive set constructed on the Paramount lot comprising more than two dozen apartments—all with windows and fire escapes and at least a dozen completely furnished—Hitchcock then turned his attentions to Kelly, conferring with her and EDITH HEAD to make sure her wardrobe was precisely correct, right down to the strappy sandals. It was like dressing a doll (or, as Head said later, with perhaps unintentional insight, like "putting a dream together").

Filming was typically precise but without problems, with journalists coming by to wonder at the impressive set—one of the largest ever built at Paramount, Hitchcock bragged. Refining and advancing the techniques he'd used to create a realistic city backdrop in *ROPE*, Hitchcock had steam rising from rooftop pipes and, in one brief shot, even a few pigeons on a roof. Rather than mix the sound carefully, artificially, later, much of it was played and re-recorded live, so that the street noises would have depth and distance. Apart from FRANZ WAXMAN's jittery, jazzy theme, most of the music was deliberately diegetic, too, sourced to onscreen radios or pianos. The film was a deserved and enormous hit and, as the rights eventually reverted to Hitchcock, a huge financial success for him, as well.

Certainly it was a film full of fine performances. Stewart projects just the right mixture of painful boredom, helpless anguish, and slightly sweaty obsession.

(The last two would come in handy again in *Vertigo*.) And Kelly does indeed look like a dream, a metaphor Hitchcock underlines by giving her a pale green outfit (always an otherworldly COLOR for him), and having the camera slip briefly into stuttering slow motion when she leans in to give the lightly dozing Stewart that first kiss. Although Kelly's socialite line readings are occasionally a trifle too affected—as an acting student, she had worked perhaps a little too hard to lose her Philadelphia accent—it ends up working with her character, and the street-corner snap of THELMA RITTER and WENDELL COREY are always there to bring the film back to earth.

Excellent, too, is RAYMOND BURR as Thorwald, whom we barely get to know in the film—like Jeff, until the end we've only seen him from afar. But when we do meet him, he's hesitant, halting. "What do you want from me?" he asks, and Jeff has no answer. Yes, ostensibly, Jeff is doing his duty as a citizen, helping to bring a murderer to justice. But there has been a kind of sadism to Jeff's investigation, too, a kind of harassment in his anonymous notes and phone calls that brings to mind HENRI-GEORGES CLOUZOT'S *Le Corbeau*. How many other Thorwalds are out there, some of them inconveniently innocent, being prodded by neighbors? How many are victims of this kind of prying gossip?

Thorwald is a complex character enriched by the way that Burr, a deeply closeted gay man in real life, was able to put so much persecuted pain in that single line: "What do you want from me?" (And also perhaps by Hitchcock's wicked sense of humor: Thorwald, who sells junk by day and then butchers at night, is—with his silver hair, rimless glasses, and imposing bulk—a veritable stand-in for the meddling mogul DAVID O. SELZNICK.)

Rear Window is inarguably Hitchcock's most formally perfect film. He had

often spoken of the KULESHOV EFFECT to critics, used it to dismiss the honest worries of actors: All you needed to create a feeling, he insisted, were two close-ups, with an insert shot stuck between them. It didn't matter what the actor was trying to convey; in fact, it might be better if he remained emotionless. What you cut to is what created the emotion.

That three-shot sequence is the primary visual code of *Rear Window* endlessly repeated. We see Jeff, we see what he is looking at, and then we cut back to him. Stewart is, of course, too emotional an actor not to react—he doesn't give Hitchcock the utterly blank slate that the director might have demanded from others. But it is always the object of his gaze—"Miss Torso," "Miss Lonelyhearts," Thorwald—that allows us to interpret his gaze.

The constant cutting in *Rear Window* is important to provide not only information but also pace—apart from Jeff's brief fall to the courtyard, we never really leave his apartment, and its own small environs prohibit any fancy camera movements (beyond that lovely pan at the beginning, which quickly tells us—in simple, discrete images—that his name is J. B. Jefferies, that he's a photographer, and that he was injured taking photos of a tremendous race car accident).

That sort of storytelling approach—stingy with words, lavish with visuals—is not only part of Hitchcock's love of PURE CINEMA, but it also harkens back to his silent days, when information was always best conveyed through pictures. (It still is, Hitchcock would argue later; it's just that filmmakers got lazy once sound came in.) That simple love of imagery is part of *Rear Window*, too; in some ways, the apartments across the courtyard all function as separate, silent movies. We rarely overhear more than shred of dialogue; the action is almost always confined within the single rectangle—screen—of their windows.

And yet, wordlessly—just as he had in the '20s—Hitchcock tells complete little vignettes just through pictures. The honeymooning couple who eventually wake from the blush of first love. The artist struggling with a composition, who finally discovers inspiration. The lonely woman fighting off depression, who finds hope at last. Even the bouncy "Miss Torso" gets her own tiny tale—and like everyone besides the Thorwalds, her own happy ending. (The idea of all those small stories, the screenwriter later said, was Hitchcock's contribution.)

Yet *Rear Window* is, for all its clockwork precision and old-school mastery, one of his darkest films. Hitchcock's movies had touched on the MALE GAZE before, that cold, hard objectifying look turned on pretty women out of lust (*THE PLEASURE GARDEN*) or jealousy (*NOTORIOUS*). This was an entire movie based on it, as Jeff sits impotently in his wheelchair and "plaster cocoon" of a cast and turns his EYES, then his binoculars, and then finally his huge phallic telephoto camera lens on his neighbors across the empty courtyard.

"The New York State sentence for a Peeping Tom is six months in the workhouse," snaps Stella, his no-nonsense nurse, and there's certainly no denying that pure prurience is the initial spur to Jeff's snooping (brought home by the—uncharacteristically obvious for Hitchcock—admiring shot of "Miss Torso" as she bends over to look in her refrigerator). Jeff may defend himself later by saying he's trying to solve a crime—but it's the sex and soap operas he sees that really catches his attention.

And because Jeff has derived pleasure out of this VOYEURISM, according to the rough CATHOLICISM of Hitchcock's films, there must be pain, too—so he has to sit there in his chair and writhe uselessly, only watching while across the way Lisa is manhandled by the murderous Thorwald (just as movie audiences—voyeurs, too—must sit in their seats and watch helplessly, as characters we've grown to identify with walk into danger and far away from any chance of our help).

But in the end, what Jeff is seeing isn't just sex and violence. He's also seeing life, or at least many different versions of it. Sitting there in his apartment, staring across into other people's homes, he and Lisa are catching glimpses of possible futures. Will they be like the lusty honeymoon couple or the fatally battling Thorwalds? Will Jeff be like the angry, frustrated pianist or the aimlessly puttering artist? Is Lisa, as he suggests, like the overly popular "Miss Torso"? Or, as she fears, like the forgotten "Miss Lonelyhearts"?

Hitchcock's pictures had always shown unhappy marriages, unions built out of expedience or sundered by betrayals, and in *Rear Window*, the timeless questions are ones of compatibility and compromise. Jeff wants to get back to trotting around the Third World and doesn't think Lisa is tough enough to keep up with him. She insists she is—but frankly would much rather he took a safe, posh job in New York. Yet she will win him over by proving herself by climbing up fire escapes in heels and fighting off murderers (and then win again when he ends up with two broken legs and has to stay home, and she—despite the dressed-down outfit of loafers and cuffed jeans—can go back to reading *Vogue* when he's not looking).

It is a slightly sardonic ending—the final shot of her pulling out that fashion magazine only after she sees he's asleep suggests that, while she's remained true to herself, she's perfectly happy to keep that secret from him for now. Will he bend to her will in the end, or she to his? But then the film ends, and the shades—not just metaphorically but also literally—come down. The peeping into other people's lives has ended. For now.

References

Patrick McGilligan, *Alfred Hitchcock: A Life in Darkness and Light* (New York: Harper-Collins, 2003), 480–90; Patrick McGilligan, ed. *Backstory: Interviews with Screenwriters of the 60s* (Berkeley: University of California Press, 1997), 174–92; *'Rear Window' Ethics*, directed by Laurent Bouzereau (2000), documentary, http://the.hitchcock.zone/wiki/Rear_Window_Ethics:_Remembering_and_Restoring_a_Hitchcock_Classic_%282000%29_-_transcript; Donald Spoto, *The Dark Side of Genius: The Life of Alfred Hitchcock* (New York: Da Capo Press, 1999), 345–49; Donald Spoto, *Spellbound by Beauty: Alfred Hitchcock and His Leading Ladies* (New York: Harmony Books, 2008), 209–12; François Truffaut, *Hitchcock/Truffaut*, rev. ed. (New York: Touchstone, 1985), 213–23.

REBECCA (US 1940)

DIRECTOR: Alfred Hitchcock.
SCREENPLAY: Joan Harrison, Robert E. Sherwood, Phillip MacDonald, Michael Hogan, based on the novel by Daphne du Maurier.
PRODUCER: David O. Selznick.
CINEMATOGRAPHY: George Barnes.
EDITOR: Uncredited (W. Donn Hayes).
ORIGINAL MUSIC: Franz Waxman.
CAST: Laurence Olivier (Max de Winter), Joan Fontaine (Mrs. de Winter), Judith Anderson (Mrs. Danvers), George Sanders (Jack Favell), Leo G. Carroll (Dr. Baker), C. Aubrey Smith (Col. Julyan), Florence Bates (Mrs. Van Hopper).
RUNNING TIME: 130 minutes.
RELEASED THROUGH: United Artists.

While working as the paid companion and social secretary to a demanding old dowager, a young woman is quickly, impetuously romanced by the dashing widower Max de Winter—married within weeks, they return together to Manderley, his enormous manor in Cornwall.

The house is full of memories of his beautiful late wife, Rebecca—and run by an imperious housekeeper, Mrs. Danvers, who remains loyal to her former mistress. Shy and unsophisticated, the new Mrs. de Winter begins to doubt her husband's love—a fear Danvers happily feeds.

Then, during a storm, Rebecca's capsized ship is recovered from the ocean floor—and signs point to "foul play." Max confesses the truth to his new bride—he did not worship Rebecca but loathed her. When she taunted him that she was pregnant by another man, he struck her; she fatally hit her head, and to conceal the body, he deliberately sank the boat.

At the inquest, Favell, one of Rebecca's old lovers, tries to blackmail de Winter by revealing the pregnancy. A trip to her doctor reveals, however, that it was a fatal cancer she was carrying, not a child; her mockery of Maxim was a clever way of both committing suicide and blaming him for her death. De Winter will not be prosecuted.

Flavell calls Danvers to tell her the news; tipped into madness, she sets fire to Manderley. The new Mrs. de Winter and the rest of the staff flee, while the mansion—and Danvers—are destroyed.

It was supposed to be *TITANIC*.

That was DAVID O. SELZNICK's original plan for Alfred Hitchcock's first picture, and as in everything Selznick, the scale was grandiose: The mogul would buy the *Leviathan*—a World War I–era German passenger ship seized by the Americans and currently docked in Hoboken—tow it to Santa Monica, and then film the entire disaster picture aboard. The actual sinking of the vessel would serve as climax.

When that plan fell apart (even if he could have purchased the ship, which was being sold for scrap, his assistants were told it would cost $2 million just to get it to California), Selznick went to his second choice: Hitchcock would adapt the best-selling gothic romance *Rebecca*.

There were arguments for and against this. On the positive side, all of Hollywood was currently taken with Selznick's ongoing efforts to adapt another best seller, *Gone with the Wind*, and DAPHNE DU MAURIER's *Rebecca* was a property that Hitchcock had tried (and failed) to buy while he was back in England. On the negative side, he had already managed to make a film of du Maurier's, *JAMAICA INN*—and she had loathed it. And when Hitchcock presented the producer with his first, quite cavalier adaptation of this novel—he began it on an ocean liner with everyone getting seasick—Selznick responded with an angry, even more verbose memo than usual. ("I just finished reading it," Hitchcock deadpanned some 30 years later.) The short version of Selznick's thunderous ultimatum: "We bought *Rebecca* and we intend to make *Rebecca*, not a distorted and vulgarized version of a successful work."

Although being called vulgar by a Hollywood producer must have stung a director as class-conscious as Hitchcock, a new, more faithful script was devised (with Selznick, as he had with *Gone with the Wind*, insisting on screenwriters using the original novel as their Bible). Most of the work was done by increasingly trusted Hitchcock colleague JOAN HARRISON; playwright ROBERT E. SHERWOOD got an inordinate share of the credit but contributed the crucial work-around that made Rebecca's death an accident and thereby slipped it past the CENSORS.

Thinking again of spectacle, Selznick dispatched a staff headed by WILLIAM CAMERON MENZIES to find a grand mansion where they could shoot the film on LOCATION; as it was becoming increasingly clear that Britain would soon be at war, estates were scouted throughout the United States and Canada. When no property could be found that matched both requirements—immensely baronial and geographically convenient—Selznick reluctantly agreed to the use of miniatures, which Hitchcock was accustomed to anyway. Manderley was re-created on the scale of one inch to one foot.

Casting was a thornier problem. Selznick suggested both David Niven and William Powell, neither of whom Hitchcock really wanted; another possibility, Ronald Colman, whom Hitchcock favored, begged off, seeing it correctly as the woman's picture. (Apparently unmentioned was CARY GRANT, who would have been perfect as the irresistible, unknowable Max—but he hadn't yet really shown the shadows he would when Hitchcock finally began to work with him the next year, on *SUSPICION*.)

Finally, LAURENCE OLIVIER was cast—although part of the appeal for him was that Selznick agreed to consider casting Olivier's then-love, Vivien Leigh, as his costar. Eventually, Selznick demurred, saying that he didn't want to give their affair—an open secret—any possible publicity, but the choice was the right one artistically, as well. Leigh's screen test, done with Olivier, survives, and she's far too confident, he far too solicitous; for *Rebecca* to work, de Winter needs to be cold and withdrawn; his wife, nervous and unsure.

Many other actresses were tested—with Selznick deliberately trying to gin up the same enthusiasm he had before finally choosing Leigh for Scarlett in *Gone with the Wind*—and some were clearly unsuitable. ANNE BAXTER, still a teenager, was deemed too young; Selznick, who had a mogul's hunger for signing up new talent, pushed for NOVA PILBEAM, whom Hitchcock had worked with twice before and had originally suggested himself. But the director—perhaps still remembering the actress as a teen—ended up vetoing the choice. Finally, after many screen tests, JOAN FONTAINE was picked.

Fontaine was only 22 and lacking in confidence; she had always been second-best at home, behind older sister Olivia de Havilland, and things had settled into the same pecking order in Hollywood. (When she began acting, her mother had even forbidden her from using the family name in case she did anything to detract from her sister's starry standing.) If she was naturally a bit vulnerable, then she found little on the set to give her confidence; most of the supporting actors were cool to her, and Olivier—still bitter that he was not playing opposite Leigh—was openly hostile.

And Hitchcock—brilliantly, coldly—used that, controlling the actress with small, passive-aggressive insinuations. It was true, he told her sadly, nobody else liked her. But he did, and if she only relied on him . . .

"He was a Svengali," Fontaine remembered later. "He wanted control over me and he seemed to relish the cast not liking one another. . . . It kept him in command and it was part of the upheaval he wanted. He kept me off balance, much to his own delight." It seemed sadistic, but it was also effective; as Fontaine would also admit, "Of course this helped my performance, as I was supposed to be terrified of everyone."

Fontaine gives a lovely, delicate performance, and while it was definitely helped by Hitchcock's manipulation (during and after filming, with more-than-usual care taken in shaping her performance in the editing room), she perfectly embodies the part of a hesitant, sheltered, virginal bride. She completely wins us to her side—which is what makes her eventual, assertive "I am Mrs. de Winter now" (a bit of a nod to the "I am Mrs. Norman Maine" from Selznick's 1937 A Star Is Born) so satisfying.

Olivier is less effective as Max; he seems more imperious than confident, more paternal than romantic, someone who looks at his bride and muses, "It's a pity you have to grow up." Of course, the script doesn't help him ("I'm asking you to marry me, you little fool" is hardly the most romantic of proposals), nor do the obvious silver streaks applied to his hair, but it's still a less romantic performance than the film requires (or that he had just given, under William Wyler's stern and constant direction, in Wuthering Heights).

The supporting parts, however, drawn chiefly from the ENGLISH COLONY of ex-pat actors—including LEO G. CARROLL, soon to become a Hitchcock favorite—are all filled nicely. GEORGE SANDERS is evasive and insinuating as Flavell, and JUDITH ANDERSON is extraordinary as Mrs. Danvers. Rarely seen in motion, often holding her head at a bit of an angle like a hungry BIRD regarding a worm, she is a consistently unsettling presence, with her cold jealousy of the new Mrs. de Winter surpassed only by her passionate devotion to the old, as she wanders Rebecca's bedroom or longingly strokes her sheer negligee. (Although years later, Anderson denied that there were any overtones of HOMOSEXUALITY, Hitchcock, as always, knew precisely what he was suggesting—as had the censors, who'd warned him to be careful.)

Given a large budget and a capacious soundstage, Hitchcock gives Rebecca a glossier look (and a slower pace) than he had given his English pictures. GEORGE BARNES's camera prowls the (deliberately oversized) sets, using deep focus to draw our eyes to every detail; there is more movement here than in earlier Hitchcock films and less editing.

Less action, too, as Rebecca is really a mood piece. Although it's still mischaracterized as noir, in fact it is Gothic and owes so much to *Jane Eyre*—the forbidding mansion, the Byronic hero, the naïve working-girl-turned-lover, the mysterious first wife—it's good for du Maurier that Charlotte Brontë's copyright had long lapsed (which hadn't prevented a Brazilian author from claiming that du Maurier had plagiarized *her* when the novel first appeared).

True, that dark-and-stormy-night moodiness doesn't necessarily play to Hitchcock's strengths. He works hard at using cross-cutting to ratchet up tension in an early scene—Will Max propose marriage before the heroine has to leave with her hated boss?—but his skill at creating jangling moments of suspense chiefly goes unused in a movie built on slow revelations and done under the watchful eye of a literal-minded producer who wouldn't allow for the invention the director would bring to other sinister character pieces, such as *SHADOW OF A DOUBT*.

Nonetheless, the film is marked by HITCHCOCKIAN touches. The upper classes and their empty morality continue to underwhelm him; death does not end people's control over others, nor does legal innocence assuage people's painful GUILT. And *Rebecca* is, even more than many of his films, about IDENTITY and performance; literally anonymous (the film never calls her by name), the heroine is first one woman's hired friend and then another man's bullied wife. But who is she really? Yes, "I am Mrs. de Winter now," she proclaims at last, but even that sign of independence is one of dependence; even that role is one another person has already played, and better.

"This is turning out to be a Selznick picture," Hitchcock groused during filming, and that was true, although those signs had come early and only grown more pronounced. Right from the start, the cringe-worthy opening title—"Selznick International presents its picturization of Daphne

du Maurier's celebrated novel"—had put the director's art and ego firmly in their place; later, when it won best picture, it was Selznick as producer who would, of course, collect the prize, his second in a row. This was not quite London, where for most of the last decade, it had been Hitchcock's name up on the movie marquee.

But it was his start in America, and a successful one. And it didn't even begin to hint at the successes to come.

References

Rudy Behlmer, ed., *Memo from David O. Selznick* (New York: Viking Press, 1972), 259–97; Gerald Gardner, *The Censorship Papers: Movie Censorship Letters from the Hays Office, 1934–1968* (New York: Dodd, Mead, 1987), 84–86; Patrick McGilligan, *Alfred Hitchcock: A Life in Darkness and Light* (New York: HarperCollins, 2003), 237–43, 248–53; Harrison Smith, "Was 'Rebecca' Plagiarized?" *Saturday Review of Literature*, November 29, 1941, http://www.unz.org/Pub/SaturdayRev -1941nov29-00003; Donald Spoto, *The Dark Side of Genius: The Life of Alfred Hitchcock* (New York: Da Capo Press, 1999), 212–19; Donald Spoto, *Laurence Olivier: A Biography* (New York: Harper Paperbacks, 1993), 170–71; Donald Spoto, *Spellbound by Beauty: Alfred Hitchcock and His Leading Ladies* (New York: Harmony Books, 2008), 87–99; Bob Thomas, *Selznick* (New York: Pocket Books, 1972), 186–92; François Truffaut, *Hitchcock/Truffaut*, rev. ed. (New York: Touchstone, 1985), 127–33.

REDGRAVE, MICHAEL (1908–1985)

Bristol-born performer from an acting family. His mother told him frankly that, at 6'4", he was "too tall to make a success" as a stage actor, and so after graduating Cambridge, he took a job teaching modern languages at a boys' school. But he spent much of his three years there staging Shakespeare's tragedies, always saving the leads for himself, and by 1934 had begun his dramatic career in earnest.

After two years with a Liverpool company (during which he met and married his wife, actress Rachel Kempson), he moved on to the Old Vic in London, where he played Laertes to LAURENCE OLIVIER's *Hamlet* and scored a particular hit as Orlando in *As You Like It*. Elegant in bearing, with a quick and sensitive understanding of the text and a naturally soft and musical voice, he became a stage favorite.

Redgrave looked down on film acting—his father, who had deserted the family shortly after his birth and run off to Australia, had been in silent films—but his friend JOHN GIELGUD urged him to do more movie work (even though Gielgud was currently having a rough time on *SECRET AGENT*). So when Hitchcock offered him the lead in *THE LADY VAN-ISHES*, Redgrave thought about it and finally agreed—albeit with a reluctance he didn't bother to hide. "I suppose I was something of an intellectual snob at the time," he wrote later.

Always sensitive to slights, particularly from the upper classes, Hitchcock got his back by trying the sort of direction-by-intimidation he would practice later on JOAN FONTAINE, bluntly telling Redgrave he'd been his second choice, after ROBERT DONAT. Redgrave shrugged it off. ("I suppose it was meant to make me feel a little unwelcome, but it didn't.") Besides, the actor noted, any criticism was probably deserved. "I really wasn't trying very hard anyway," he said (as his costar PAUL LUKAS agreed and pointed out acidly on the set).

What neither Redgrave nor Hitchcock quite realized at first was that it was exactly that sort of casual carelessness—Oh, for heaven's sake, it's only a movie!—that made Redgrave's performance in the film

so enormously appealing. Ironically, by not thinking very much of the job, Redgrave ended up giving the best sort of onscreen performance—the one that never seemed like acting. He's fresh, funny, and insouciantly charming throughout.

Hitchcock soon saw that Redgrave's "throwaway" style was exactly what the picture needed. But although Redgrave admired Hitchcock's unerring instincts for camera angles and audiences (Redgrave thought the line in the script about Cambridge was silly, and yet in theaters it always got the biggest laugh), he found Hitchcock's taste for practical JOKES rather cruel, and it was very clear the filmmaker wasn't interested in working closely with performers. The stage actor returned happily to the stage.

Redgrave's triumphs there were many, including leading roles in most of the great Shakespearean tragedies; he also wrote (and starred in) his own adaptation of Henry James's *The Aspern Papers* and directed many plays, in addition to writing a novel and several books, two of them on acting. He was knighted by the queen and, of course, became the patriarch of another generation of actors, Vanessa, Corin, and Lynn (whose own children have continued the tradition further).

And, despite his early indifference to screen acting, Redgrave gave a number of indelible and widely varied performances in films; he stars in the best version of Oscar Wilde's *The Importance of Being Earnest* and in the coal-mining drama *The Stars Look Down*; he is the cold and emotionally awkward teacher in *The Browning Version* and the memorably mad ventriloquist in the classic *Dead of Night*.

Always adept at playing emotionally vulnerable heroes, Redgrave's personal life was sadly equally fragile; despite his long and apparently happy marriage to Kempson, Redgrave was bisexual, and while some of his relationships were of long standing, he was also drawn compulsively to rough, anonymous pickups (which he later reviled himself for). Then, in the mid-'60s, he began to have problems remembering lines onstage, and people whispered that he was drunk. It would be another decade before he was finally diagnosed as having Parkinson's disease.

"I'm not going to pretend that this is an easy or especially happy time for me," he said a few years later while being interviewed for his 70th birthday. "For a long time nobody understood the Parkinson's condition and doctors thought I was just forgetful or drunk, and even now the work isn't easy." But he kept working, kept trying, and, he said, continued to look back "almost always in amazement and gratitude at the way my career has gone and the people I've been allowed to know."

He died at 77 in Buckinghamshire.

References

Lynn Barber, "His Necessary Degradations," *Telegraph*, April 28, 2004, http://www.tele graph.co.uk/culture/books/3616047/His -necessary-degradations.html; Brian McFarlane, "Michael Redgrave," *BFI Screenonline*, http://www.screenonline.org.uk/people/ id/460508; "Michael Redgrave," *IMDb*, http://www.imdb.com/name/nm0714878/ bio?ref_=nm_ov_bio_sm; Donald Spoto, *The Dark Side of Genius: The Life of Alfred Hitchcock* (New York: Da Capo Press, 1999), 152, 175–76; Matt Wolf, "Obituary: Sir Michael Redgrave," *Boston Globe*, March 22, 1985, http://the.hitchcock.zone/wiki/Boston _Globe_%2822/Mar/1985%29_-_Obitu ary:_Sir_Michael_Redgrave.

REMAKES BY HITCHCOCK

Like many great stylists, Alfred Hitchcock was not particularly reverent of his source material. Films like *JAMAICA INN* and *REBECCA* rework their novels' plots and characters, and others, such as *THE BIRDS*, throw out nearly everything but the title. *FOREIGN CORRESPONDENT*, based on a reporter's memoirs, is entirely a work of fiction, *SUSPICION* completely subverts the book's theme, and many of Hitchcock's movies—from *THE LADY VANISHES* to *REAR WINDOW*—introduce romances not present in the books or stories that inspired them.

Naturally, a filmmaker so liberal in his adaptations wouldn't care that a property had been adapted before, either; what mattered, as always, was the stamp that he would put on it. So early in his career, Hitchcock calmly turned out new versions of *THE MANXMAN* (already made 13 years before in 1916) and *THE SKIN GAME* (previously made 11 years before in 1920). And he remade himself, helming the German-language adaptation of *MURDER!* (*MARY*) and filming a Hollywood version of THE MAN WHO KNEW TOO MUCH 22 years after he'd done the first in England. (Although he had also wanted to remake *THE LODGER* in the '40s, spending his own money to acquire the rights, it was eventually made by someone else.)

Then, of course, in addition to remakes, he indulged in redos—lines of dialogue and bits of business that reoccur in several films, as well as wholesale situations that repeat—there could have been no *NORTH BY NORTHWEST* without *SABOTEUR* and no *SABOTEUR* without *THE 39 STEPS*. In some ways, you could argue that he was constantly plagiarizing himself—GUILTY hero, frosty heroine, treacherous authority figures, panicky flights from justice. But as the director was fond of pointing out, true plagiarism is actionable. Self-plagiarism is style.

Reference

"25 Remarkable Alfred Hitchcock Quotes," *Magical Quotes*, http://www.magicalquote

.com/25-remarkable-alfred-hitchcock
-quotes.

REMAKES OF HITCHCOCK

With their well-known titles and finely honed plots, Hitchcock's films offer a charming enticement to filmmakers. A daunting challenge as well: If Hitchcock already made a hit out of the material, then your film will suffer hugely by comparison. And if he couldn't do something with the story, then what on earth makes you think you'll manage any better?

Still, some directors have made the attempt. The most successful have been the various versions of THE LODGER, possibly because Hitchcock's British silent films aren't as well known as his American sound movies, probably because he had to take liberties with MARIE BEL-LOC LOWNDES's novel to keep the hero from being the murderer that later versions could forgo. The most atmospheric version was probably the lushly produced 1944 film with Laird Cregar as the killer undertaken after Hitchcock couldn't get his own new remake up and running; a further 1953 remake with Jack Palance has a certain grimy power. Another modern, L.A.-set version followed in 2009.

Equally as popular is STRANGERS ON A TRAIN, although the instinct is often to switch the characters' genders. *Once You Kiss a Stranger* tried that in 1969, and *Once You Meet a Stranger* took another stab at it for television in 1996; it fell to Danny DeVito to burlesque the entire idea in *Throw Momma from the Train* in 1996. In 2015, yet another version was announced, with David Fincher set to direct.

DIAL M FOR MURDER has also been remade for television in 1981 and as a movie in 1998 under the title *A Perfect Murder*, but then it had already been a play (and first a BBC film) before Hitchcock got to it; *SHADOW OF A DOUBT* unwisely

became *Step Down to Terror* in 1958 and was then remade for TV in 1991 under its original title, with TIPPI HEDREN cast—largely for publicity value—in a small part.

REAR WINDOW also had a small-screen outing in 1998 (in a genuinely inventive rethinking that made Jeff paralyzed and cast real-life quadriplegic actor Christopher Reeve in the role). It was also the obvious, if uncredited, inspiration for the 2007 teen-oriented film *Disturbia*, which brought an unsuccessful lawsuit from the copyright holders to CORNELL WOOLRICH's original short story; Woolrich's tale has also given rise recently to a play that follows his original short story more closely.

Other popular Hitchcock projects include THE 39 STEPS (remade twice in Britain and later turned into a successful comic play), REBECCA (remade several times for British television and planned for but never produced as a Broadway production), and THE LADY VANISHES, remade badly in 1979 and again for television in 2013. (In addition, that film's cricket-loving Charters and Caldicott have popped up in other movies of their own.)

There have also been various, less prominent versions—chiefly for television—of JAMAICA INN, SUSPICION, LIFEBOAT, and NOTORIOUS, as well as a sequel to THE BIRDS, titled unimaginatively *The Birds II: Land's End* and featuring Hedren in a small part. When ALFRED HITCHCOCK PRESENTS was briefly revived for TV, it, too, recycled some old scripts from the original show (and found another bit part for Hedren, as well).

The most fertile property, however, still remains PSYCHO. It gave birth eventually to *Psycho II* and *Psycho III*, both of which are at least true to the spirit of the story; *Psycho IV: The Beginning* was a prequel made for television, which also gave a home to the 1987 TV movie *Bates Motel* and the unrelated TV prequel series *Bates Motel*, which began its run in 2013. There was also Gus Van Sant's slavishly faithful, completely unnecessary COLOR remake in 1998 and any number of films that steal the story's twist or find their own inspiration in the crimes of ED GEIN. It remains the most enduring of all of Hitchcock's films and, for merchandisers, certainly the most profitable: Paying visitors to UNIVERSAL Studios can snap photos of the old Bates place and buy all the overpriced souvenirs—from posters to bars of soap—that their budgets, or MOTHERS, will allow.

Reference
Donald Spoto, *The Dark Side of Genius: The Life of Alfred Hitchcock* (New York: Da Capo Press, 1999), 248.

"REVENGE" (US; ORIGINALLY AIRED OCTOBER 2, 1955)

DIRECTOR: Alfred Hitchcock.
SCREENPLAY: Francis Cockrell, from a story by Samuel Blas.
PRODUCERS: Alfred Hitchcock, Joan Harrison.
CINEMATOGRAPHY: John L. Russell.
EDITOR: Edward M. Williams.
ORIGINAL MUSIC: Stanley Wilson.
CAST: Vera Miles (Elsa Spann), Ralph Meeker (Carl Spann).
RUNNING TIME: 30 minutes with commercials. Black and white.
ORIGINALLY BROADCAST BY: CBS.

When a man returns home from work, his traumatized wife tells him she was SEXUALLY assaulted; when she points out the assailant later on the street, her husband follows him and beats him to death. Only as they drive away does he realize that his wife is delusional—she sees rapists everywhere.

This was the first episode of Hitchcock's new *ALFRED HITCHCOCK PRES-*

ENTS, and it set the tone, with Hitchcock drily insulting the sponsors and the ending providing a nasty little jolt. That Hitchcock cast VERA MILES in this important role—good preparation for her breakdown scene in *THE WRONG MAN* the following year—showed how highly he thought of her and her prospects and helped underline how bitterly disappointed he would be when she then dropped out of *VERTIGO*.

References
Tim Brooks and Earle Marsh, *The Complete Directory to Prime Time Network TV Shows*, 8th ed. (New York: Ballantine Books, 2003), 29; Jack Edmond Nolan, "Hitchcock's TV Films," *Film Fan Monthly* (June 1968), 3–6.

REVILLE, ALMA (1899–1982)
Devoted wife and nearly lifelong creative partner of Alfred Hitchcock who was born in Nottingham. Her parents worked in the lace business, but after the family moved to Twickenham, her father found a new job at a film studio, working on costumes. Tiny, tomboyish Alma—who had already missed several years of school due to ill health—joined him in the industry while still a teenager, getting a position in the company's editing department.

Her title was "cutter" and the work was—at the time—more detail oriented than artistic, but Reville's career progressed quickly. Although she appeared onscreen briefly in the 1918 film *The Life Story of David Lloyd George*, this was due more to the studio's lack of actors than any desire on her part to perform; behind the scenes was where she preferred to be (and indeed, after her marriage to Alfred Hitchcock, her influence would become even more invisible).

But Reville took on many jobs at Islington Studios, quickly moving on to assistant director. When Hitchcock met her, in fact, she was already a valued staffer, while he was still only a part-time title designer; later, a 1925 story in the movie magazine *The Picturegoer* would profile her as a rising young filmmaker who, alas, has "never had time to get married!" It was only after Hitchcock had not only established his own career but also surpassed hers that he felt bold enough to propose. (He did it during an ocean voyage while she was seasick because, he JOKED, he knew she'd be too weak to resist.)

"I had wanted to become, first, a movie director and, second, Alma's husband—not in order of emotional preference, to be sure, but because I felt the bargaining power implicit in the first was necessary in obtaining the second," Hitchcock explained in an article for *McCall's* in 1956. "I had met her a few years before at the PARAMOUNT studios in London when I was only an editorial errand boy told by everybody to keep out of the way. She was already a cutter and producer's assistant and seemed a trifle snooty to me. I couldn't notice Alma without resenting her, and I couldn't help noticing her."

They had worked together before the marriage—she took on a variety of roles during the disastrous LOCATION SHOOT of *THE PLEASURE GARDEN*—and remained a team afterward, although she was not always credited. (She reportedly appears unbilled in *THE LODGER*, for example, as a woman listening to the radio.) An extremely observant viewer, she worked continuity on many of his films, sometimes receiving credit—her name appears on some of his best British films—and often not. She was always the last pair of eyes on every finished production; famously it was Reville who noticed that a supposedly dead JANET LEIGH either blinked or gulped—sources

disagree—during her final onscreen moment in *PSYCHO*. (It was fixed in editing.)

Hitchcock had a habit of minimizing other people's contributions to his films, and in 1974, when an author suggested including Reville in a book about female screenwriters, the director declined on her behalf, insisting that she was "never a creative writer in the sense we know it today." Perhaps he felt he was protecting a shy and ailing woman from reporters. Certainly two decades before, in his article for *McCall's*, he had been far more generous about her contributions (if, at the same time, a little defensive).

"She does read for me and I rely on her opinion," he wrote then. "She helped work out on paper the chase scene in *TO CATCH A THIEF*. She tries to be on the set the first day we begin shooting a film, sometimes goes to rushes, and always gives me her criticisms. They're invariably sound." Although he said he suspected he was "accused a lot of overshadowing her," he protested, "it isn't my fault, really, that Alma has stayed so much out of sight of the public."

"He listened to everything she said," said NORMAN LLOYD, who knew the couple for 40 years and has always objected to portrayals of the director as a misogynist or the Hitchcocks' marriage as anything but supportive. "His admiration for her was enormous."

In fact, Reville was Hitchcock's favorite collaborator; she has more than a dozen credits, ranging from continuity to screenplay, on his films from *THE RING* in 1927 through *STAGE FRIGHT* in 1950—and that can't begin to account for whatever suggestions she made to him privately as to possible projects, solutions to thorny script problems, or music. (It was her advice to keep BERNARD HERRMANN's score for the shower scene in *Psycho* rather than have it play out in silence, as Hitchcock had originally wanted.) She kept an eye on casting, too; DIANE BAKER, among other actresses, remembered her taking a serious interest in their careers and their potential.

Although Reville was thoroughly involved in her husband's work—and at times seemed to have few friends of her own—she had her own professional interests, as well. She had doggedly pursued her career before meeting Hitchcock and, even after their marriage, continued to write scripts for other directors; her filmography counts nearly a dozen extracurricular efforts, her last one—the Jack Benny farce *It's in the Bag!*—coming in 1945. She kept her name professionally after marriage and her own boyish style; for a long time, she favored pants suits made for her in London by a men's tailor. Yet she also very carefully catered to "Mr. H," worrying about what to serve for dinner, making sure that nothing disrupted his obsessive devotion to routine.

Postmortem biographies and various movies have speculated wildly on Reville's real relationship with her husband, her opinion of his alleged SEXUAL transgressions, and her own private life. DONALD SPOTO's study describes a marriage that was basically sexless and often contentious, with a director who was "terrified" of his spouse; PATRICK MCGILLIGAN's biography suggests Hitchcock merely deeply respected her opinion (and that she, for her part, had her own affair, or at least emotional dalliance, with screenwriter WHITFIELD COOK). The film *HITCHCOCK* presents Reville as a take-charge character who actually directed part of *Psycho*; *THE GIRL* portrays her as, at best, a meek helpmate and enabler of her husband's abuses of other women.

As for daughter PATRICIA HITCHCOCK, the protector of the family legacy, her 2004 book *Alma Hitchcock: The Woman behind the Man*, takes a far homier approach to her MOTHER—emphasizing

not only her art but also her entertaining (complete with recipes), while studiously avoiding any talk of domestic disagreements or extramarital rumors.

What really happened inside their marriage is ultimately unknowable. What's inarguable is that Hitchcock was a man compulsively dedicated to routine—from his preproduction plans to his identical dark-blue suits—and the greatest, most emotional part of that routine was his more-than-50-year marriage to Alma Reville, whom he almost invariably referred to in public, with formal respect, as "Madame." Her role seemed to change throughout their marriage—going from his lover to Pat's mother to (after his mother's death) his own maternal figure. Yet he was always almost childishly dependent on her, and when—late in their lives—she began to have serious health problems, he was often frantic with worry.

In 1979, an ailing Hitchcock was given a lifetime achievement award from the American Film Institute. Although he was known for being flippant in public and rude if he thought the prize was less than he deserved—he picked up his Irving Thalberg Award at the ACADEMY AWARDS a decade before with only the briefest of thank-yous—this time he spoke at some length, at least when it came to her.

"I beg to mention by name only four people who have given me the most affection, appreciation and encouragement," he said. "The first of the four is a film editor, the second is a scriptwriter, the third is the mother of my daughter Pat, and the fourth is as fine a cook as ever performed miracles in a domestic kitchen—and their names are Alma Reville. Had the beautiful Miss Reville not accepted a lifetime contract, without options, as 'Mrs. Alfred Hitchcock' some 53 years ago, Mr. Alfred Hitchcock might be in this room tonight—not at this table, but as one of the slower waiters on the floor. I share my award, as I have my life, with her."

Alma Reville died in Bel Air at 82.

References

"Alma in Wonderland," *Picturegoer* (December 1925), http://the.hitchcock .zone/wiki/Picturegoer_%281925%29 _-_Alma_in_Wonderland; "Alma Reville," *IMDb*, http://www.imdb.com/name/ nm0720904; John Anderson, "Alfred Hitchcock's Secret Weapon Becomes a Star," *New York Times*, November 16, 2012, http://www.nytimes.com/2012/11/18/ movies/hitchcock-and-the-girl-remem ber-alma-reville.html?_r=1; Diane Baker, interview with the author, September 2015; Josephine Botting, "Will the Real Mrs. Hitchcock Please Stand Up?" *BFI*, February 11, 2014, http://www.bfi.org.uk/ news-opinion/bfi-news/features/will-real- mrs-hitchcock-please-stand-up; Nisha Lilia Diu, "Mrs. Alfred Hitchcock: The Unsung Partner," *Telegraph*, February 8, 2013, http://www.telegraph.co.uk/culture/ film/film-news/9832084/Mrs-Alfred-Hitch cock-The-Unsung-Partner.html; Alfred Hitchcock, "The Woman Who Knows Too Much," *McCall's* (March 1956), http:// the.hitchcock.zone/wiki/McCall's%20 %281956%29%20-%20The%20Woman%20 Who%20Knows%20Too%20Much; Pat Hitchcock O'Connell and Laurent Bou- zereau, *Alma Hitchcock: The Woman behind the Man* (New York: Berkeley Trade, 2004), 1–5; Norman Lloyd, interviews with the author, November 2007, July 2015; Pat- rick McGilligan, *Alfred Hitchcock: A Life in Darkness and Light* (New York: Harper Collins, 2003), 427–28, 439; Stephen Rebello, *Alfred Hitchcock and the Making of Psycho* (New York: HarperPerennial, 1991), 118; Donald Spoto, *The Dark Side of Genius: The Life of Alfred Hitchcock* (New York: Da Capo Press, 1999), 340, 485, 507.

RICH AND STRANGE (GB 1931)

DIRECTOR: Alfred Hitchcock.
SCREENPLAY: Alfred Hitchcock, Alma Reville, Val Valentine, based on a story by Dale Collins.
PRODUCER: John Maxwell.
CINEMATOGRAPHY: Jack E. Cox.
EDITOR: Winifred Cooper, Rene Marrison.
ORIGINAL MUSIC: Adolph Hallis.
CAST: Henry Kendall (Fred Hill), Joan Barry (Emily Hill), Percy Marmont (Com- mander Gordon), Betty Amann (the Princess).
RUNNING TIME: 93 minutes. Black and white.
RELEASED THROUGH: Wardour Films.

A bored and quarrelsome married couple, Fred and Emily Hill, are startled by a tele- gram from a rich uncle who offers to give them an advance on their expected inheri- tance so they can enjoy their lives while they're young; quickly, Fred quits his dull office job, and they board a ship bound for Ceylon.

The Hills aren't very experienced world travelers; Fred gets seasick before they're even out of sight of England, and both of them are a bit shocked by Paris. Back onboard, though, they begin to give in to temptation—Fred starts a romance with a pretty German princess, and Emily falls for a handsome bachelor. The flirtations soon turn serious.

After the ship reaches Ceylon, though, Emily learns that the "princess" is in fact a con artist. She returns, too late, to warn Fred, who's already lost most of his money. The couple cobbles together enough funds to book a passage back to London on a freighter.

Their troubles, however, are not yet at an end—the ship crashes in the fog and is abandoned. Fred and Emily are rescued by Chinese looters and make their way back to England—definitely poorer and perhaps no wiser, as once again they fall into an argument.

Poor and dull.

Hitchcock developed the material with Dale Collins (an Australian journalist and novelist who specialized in maritime adventures) about experiences he and his wife had (including a rambunctious evening they'd enjoyed long ago in Paris with NITA NALDI). In fact, Hitchcock told FRANÇOIS TRUFFAUT, he and his wife had taken a round-the-world trip before filming in order to "do some preliminary research" for the film—which included a surprising detour one night when, thinking they were going to see a belly dancer, they ended up in a bordello. "We had been behaving exactly like the couple in the book—two innocents abroad!" he exclaimed. (Hitchcock, at least by his own accounts, had an odd habit of accidentally wandering into suggestive situations.)

Hitchcock cast music hall performer HENRY KENDALL as Fred and, for want of a better option, the BLONDE but bland JOAN BARRY; PERCY MARMONT and Betty Amann were to play their dalliances. The production itself gave Hitchcock the chance to indulge in both miniatures and detailed sets (Fred's office, with the clerks lined up in soulless rows, is particularly good), as well as to incorporate some definitely risqué material. And the film, like many of his to come, centers on a marriage that is far from perfect; Fred is impulsive and selfish, and it's only Emily's steadying hand that keeps him on his feet.

But while the theme was interesting, the actors weren't engaging, and some performances were off-puttingly exaggerated; meanwhile, Hitchcock's later, masterful touch at alternating comedy and drama was still underdeveloped, and although the concept is full of wry sophistication, some of the supposedly lighter scenes fall flat or flirt with bad taste (including a rather grisly scene on the Chinese junk).

Contemporary audiences and critics agreed, with the film failing in both England and America (where it was given the more exotic title *East of Shanghai*). "The story moves slowly and disconnectedly," opined the London *Times*, "and the dialogue is not even broadly funny. Mr. Hitchcock is clearly out of form. And Mr. Henry Kendall and Miss Joan Barry are as clearly out of luck." Later critics have been somewhat kinder, however, finding autobiographical touches in the story—with Fred and Emily Hill standing in for Alfred and Alma Hitchcock—and hints of his marital-discord movies to come.

As for Hitchcock, he had clearly invested something of himself in the movie, and while he was often quick to disown his commercial failures, he always remained a little fond of this one. "I liked the picture," he told Truffaut more than 30 years later. "It should have been more successful."

References
"New Films in London: Rich and Strange," *Times*, December 14, 1931, http://the.hitchcock.zone/wiki/The_Times_%2814/Dec/1931%29_-_New_Films_in_London:_Rich_and_Strange; François Truffaut, *Hitchcock/Truffaut*, rev. ed. (New York: Touchstone, 1985), 78–81.

THE RING (GB 1927)

DIRECTOR: Alfred Hitchcock.
SCREENPLAY: Alfred Hitchcock.
PRODUCER: Uncredited (John Maxwell).
CINEMATOGRAPHY: Jack E. Cox.
EDITOR: Uncredited.
CAST: Carl Brisson ("One-Round" Jack Sander), Lilian Hall Davis (the Girl), Ian Hunter (Bob Corby).
RUNNING TIME: 89 minutes. Black and white.
RELEASED THROUGH: Wardour Films.

At a small country carnival, swaggering fighter "One-Round" Jack Sander takes on all challengers, while his girlfriend takes the tickets. His supremacy is challenged on several fronts, though, when he's beaten by a fairgoer who turns out to be Australian champ Bob Corby, who collects the prize money and promptly spends it on a bracelet for Jack's girl.

When she seems responsive to Corby's attentions, Jack decides to take more aggressive action, finally asking his girlfriend to marry him and going to the city to pursue his career as a prizefighter. He quickly rises in fame and formidability, but his marriage grows strained, and she begins to seek outside consolation with Corby.

Enraged, Jack quarrels violently with her and then challenges Corby to meet him in the ring. Jack is, once again, getting the worst of it, until his wife rushes to him between rounds, assuring him, "I'm in your corner." Jack rallies to win the fight and goes off with his wife, who takes off Corby's bracelet and drops it on the floor.

A winner.

Shortly after the success of THE LODGER, Hitchcock signed a new contract with BRITISH INTERNATIONAL PICTURES, starting his career there as England's most famous—and, undoubtedly to the moguls' displeasure, highest-paid—director. He had not yet turned 28.

Although BIP would soon frustrate him by assigning uninteresting or unsuitable projects, to start off their association, they asked the young director what he'd like to work on; he surprised them by announcing it would be the story of two boxers, The Ring, based on his own screenplay. This was the first (and last) time Hitchcock would have sole credit on a script (although frequent collaborator ELIOT STANNARD reportedly helped with some ideas here). Yet while the box-ing milieu seemed like an odd one for him, the story's real focus—an unsatisfying marriage and a dangerous romantic triangle—was one he had already explored and would turn to again.

Danish CARL BRISSON—blue-eyed, curly-haired, and a trained boxer—was cast as Sander, with beefy South African IAN HUNTER getting one of his first film roles as Corby. "The Girl"—she doesn't seem to be named in the film, although some sources identify her as "Nelly"—was played by the tragic LILLIAN HALL-DAVIS. Brisson is given to popping his eyes a bit, but Hall-Davis—still spelling her name as "Lilian" here and forgoing the posh hyphen—is much better, affecting an insolent slouch in her early scenes and a hungry, appraising look.

Budget worries and salary disagreements left Hitchcock without a top cameraman, so he worked for the first time with JACK E. COX as his cinematographer; it was perhaps to his advantage, as this was an even more ambitious film visually than THE LODGER, and Cox, who specialized in "trick" work, was unlikely to balk at any of Hitchcock's shots as being impossible or confusing.

And The Ring is perhaps the most interesting looking of all of Hitchcock's silents. It begins with an almost surreal, very F. W. MURNAU, sequence of the fair—all rides and legs and giant gaping mouths (although it is hard to tell whether they are open in laughter or terror). Once again, as in THE PLEASURE GARDEN—and as in many Hitchcock films to come—a parallel is drawn between public amusements and secret dangers.

From there, we move on to the tent where the boxing exhibition is—and the film's first metaphor, a bit of DOUBLING that presents the tent as a kind of stand-in for the movie theater where another audience is watching. Standing outside, the girl even lifts a flap to peer inside at the bouts—creating a rectangle of action in the middle of the photographed square we're already watching. It is, if not a hall of mirrors, then a series of lenses.

Hitchcock, beginning here and continuing throughout the film, uses many clever devices to tell the story wordlessly. (Ironically, for a filmmaker who'd begun as a designer of intertitles, he uses very few of them here.) The rarity of a second-round fight for "One-Round" Jack is illustrated by the appearance of a brand-new, never-used "Round 2" card; the slow deflation of romantic joy is suggested by a glass of champagne going flat.

Champagne occurs again and again in the film—poured over the fighters' heads in the ring to revive them, cast aside in a nightclub when Sander has his final quarrel with Corby—but the most extended metaphor comes from the title itself. It is the squared circle in which the boxers compete; it is also the circular bracelet, shaped like a viper, that Corby gives to this story's untrustworthy Eve, Jack's girl. Jack then twists it small, into the size of a ring, when he proposes; later, she restores it to its original shape and wears it high up on her arm as a symbol of Corby's hold on her. Rings and cycles, circles and snakes—the world goes round and round.

Add to this a gallery of grotesques (from the carnival sideshow performers who attend Jack's wedding, in a sort of dry run for *Freaks*, to his not-much-more-presentable ringside entourage of grinning, oafish friends) and some stunning, impressionistic work with distorting lenses (turning backgrounds into a dizzy blur or piano keys into a row of slashing vertical lines), and you have a movie that, however melodramatic its storyline, is full of visual invention and thematic sophistication.

The picture opened in Great Britain to the sort of raves that might turn any filmmaker's head, praised as the "greatest production ever made in this country" and Hitchcock being touted as the industry's savior. "You have set the standard not only for your own company, but for every British producer," ran one notice in *Bioscope*. "Our first hope is that you will long continue to make films in this country, because the producing industry—which owes you a debt of gratitude—can ill afford to be without your talent."

It was only his sixth film, and already English film lovers were worried about losing him to Hollywood. They were right, but it would take another dozen years—and at least another cycle of disappointments and successes.

References

"Great British Film: The Ring," *Daily Mail*, October 1, 1927, http://the.hitchcock.zone/wiki/Daily_Mail_%2801/Oct/1927%29_-_Great_British_Film:_The_Ring; Patrick McGilligan, *Alfred Hitchcock: A Life in Darkness and Light* (New York: HarperCollins, 2003), 94–98; Tom Ryall, *Alfred Hitchcock and the British Cinema* (London: Continuum International, 1996), 93–94; François Truffaut, *Hitchcock/Truffaut*, rev. ed. (New York: Touchstone, 1985), 52–55.

RITCHARD, CYRIL (1897–1977)

Sydney-born performer who fell in love with the theater during a childhood performance of *Peter Pan*; although his parents had hopes he would follow a career in medicine, he was squeamish at the sight of blood and dropped out of school, finding work as a chorus boy in comic operettas. He ascended to stardom fairly rapidly and danced and sang his way through a number of revues and musicals in Sydney, New York, and London; the titles—*Bubbly*; *Puzzles of 1925*; *Oh, Lady! Lady!*—give some of their flapper flavor.

He had only made one other feature, the excellent *Piccadilly*, when Hitchcock cast him as the attempted rapist in *BLACK-MAIL*; considering Ritchard was an elegant musical-comedy star at the time, it was an interesting bit of casting and one that Hitchcock couldn't help trumpeting with a small visual trick: setting up the scene so that a light fixture cast a shadow, like a Victorian villain's curling moustache, along Ritchard's upper lip. It was, Hitchcock said later, a "sort of farewell to silent pictures."

Ritchard continued to work chiefly onstage and later on TV; in the 1950s, the two combined (along with his earlier stab at villainy and his first theatrical memory) in a much-beloved portrayal of Captain Hook in *Peter Pan* with Mary Martin, first done on Broadway and later as an oft-repeated TV special. The show gave Ritchard an entirely new career as a children's performer, which—in between more adult work—he kept alive with appearances in *Hans Brinker* and *The Dangerous Christmas of Red Riding Hood* and by providing voices for *The Daydreamer* and an early animated version of *The Hobbit*.

He died in Chicago of a heart attack at 80 while touring with a Stephen Sondheim revue.

References

"Cyril Ritchard," *IMDb*, http://www.imdb.com/name/nm0728509; *Cyril Ritchard: 1897–1977*, http://users.bestweb.net/~foosie/cyril.htm; François Truffaut, *Hitchcock/Truffaut*, rev. ed. (New York: Touchstone, 1985), 69.

RITTER, THELMA (1902–1969)

Brooklyn-born performer and an indispensable character actress for 20 years of roles on stage, screen, and television. Ritter studied at the American Academy of Dramatic Arts and had begun a career as a stage actress and radio performer when she retired to raise her two children; she returned to her career in her mid-40s with bit parts in *Miracle on 34th Street* and Joseph Mankiewicz's *A Letter to Three Wives*. The latter didn't get her an onscreen credit, but it got the director's attention; the next year he cast her as Birdie, Bette Davis's dresser, in *All About Eve*, and Ritter's sardonic, streetwise performance won her the first of what would be six Oscar nominations.

Ritter's no-nonsense, don't-kid-a-kidder delivery made her a fan favorite, particularly in comic roles, where she punctured pretensions so easily you'd think she was armed with a dozen hatpins: *The Mating Season*; *The Model and the Marriage Broker*; *With a Song in My Heart*, *A Hole in the Head*. But she had more serious parts in *The Incident* and *The Misfits* and brought frantic life to Moe, the police informant in *Pickup on South Street*.

REAR WINDOW was very much in Ritter's wheelhouse—as Stella, Jeff's visiting nurse, she dispatched salty wisdom and alcohol rubdowns with equal verve. Although it was clearly a supporting role, it was also central: while Jeff may intellectualize everything and Lisa lose herself in romantic idealism, Stella is not only the voice of reason but also the movie's humorous moral center, unafraid to call people out for their foolishness (or dangerous obsessions).

"The humor that Thelma Ritter brought to *Rear Window* was absolutely wonderful," PATRICIA HITCHCOCK said. "My father loved that, because he knew that you couldn't keep going. You had to give the audience a break. You had to have them laugh at something. His whole life was the importance of having a sense of humor in whatever you do."

Although Ritter never won an Oscar— "Now I know what it feels like to be the bridesmaid and never the bride," she said after being nominated and losing for the fourth time in a row—she did get a Tony for best actress in a musical for *New Girl in Town* (sharing it that year, in an unusual tie, with her costar, Gwen Verdon) and was a steady and welcome presence on television.

She died in New York of a heart attack at 66.

References

'Rear Window' Ethics, directed by Laurent Bouzereau (2000), documentary, http://the.hitchcock.zone/wiki/Rear_Window_Ethics:_Remembering_and_Restoring_a_Hitchcock_Classic_%282000%29_-_transcript; "Thelma Ritter," *IMDb*, http://www.imdb.com/name/nm0728812/bio?ref_=nm_ov_bio_sm; Alfred E. Twomey and Arthur F. McClure, *The Versatiles: Supporting Character Players in the Cinema, 1930–1955* (New York: Castle Books, 1969), 195.

ROHMER, ERIC (1920–2010)

Tulle-born filmmaker born Maurice Scherer, who studied history in college and later worked as a teacher before becoming a freelance writer and journalist. Although he had used other pen names, he eventually settled on "Eric Rohmer"—saluting filmmaker Erich von Stroheim and pulp novelist Sax Rohmer—to hide his career from his disapproving family. (In fact, they never found out—even after he started making films.)

An early and important critic, Rohmer began his own film journal in 1950, later joining ANDRE BAZIN's *CAHIERS DU CINEMA*, where he became a central figure, serving as a somewhat conservative counterbalance to Jean-Luc Godard and a tireless advocate for American directors, particularly Howard Hawks, and Alfred Hitchcock. In 1957, with CLAUDE CHABROL, he published *Hitchcock*, the first full-length study of the director's films. (The book was later translated into English and reprinted as *Hitchcock: The First Forty-Four Films.*)

Rohmer and Chabrol took Hitchcock seriously as a CATHOLIC artist; that focus has been occasionally criticized or ignored by subsequent writers who've chosen to analyze the director's work from Marxist, feminist, or other viewpoints. But most importantly, the two critics took Hitchcock seriously as an *artist*—still somewhat daring during a time when America's own intellectuals reflexively derided Hollywood "product" and routinely worshipped at the thrones of foreign AUTEURS like Bergman and Fellini. Years later, Rohmer and Chabrol's book remains essential, and its emphasis on the director's obsession with GUILT and innocence, prescient.

Rohmer himself remained at *Cahiers* as an editor for some time, even as younger colleagues were establishing their filmmaking careers; although he made his first feature, *Sign of Leo*, in 1959, it would be another decade before he began the long string of successes that started with 1969's *My Night at Maud's* and would include *Claire's Knee*, *Love in the Afternoon*, and *Pauline at the Beach*. Filled with bright sunshine and personal shadows, his unique films turn on issues of morality, hypocrisy, and self-knowledge.

He died at 89 in Paris.

References

"Eric Rohmer," *IMDb*, http://www.imdb.com/name/nm0006445/bio?ref_=nm_ov_bio_sm; Dave Kehr, "Cahiers Back in the Day," *Film Comment* (September/October 2001), http://www.filmcomment.com/article/cahiers-back-in-the-day; Derek Schilling, "Eric Rohmer," *New Wave Film*, http://www.newwavefilm.com/french-new-wave-encyclopedia/eric-rohmer.shtml.

ROMAN, RUTH (1922–1999)

Massachusetts-born performer who grew up in straitened circumstances. Her father, a carny, died when she was still a child, and her mother had to wait tables and work in a laundry to support them. For a while, they moved monthly—always just before the rent came due.

Roman stayed optimistic. "When you start out poor, you don't know what you're missing," she said later, and after dropping out of high school, the teenager soon started getting work with local theaters. By the early '40s, she was in Hollywood, living in a boarding house with Linda Christian and five other would-be stars; they called their place, Roman joked, "The House of the Seven Garbos."

She had gotten mostly small parts in bad movies and serials when Stanley Kramer cast her in *Champion* in 1949, not a flashy role but a good movie; WARNER BROS. signed her to a contract and began pushing her as a STAR, which is how she came to be cast in *STRANGERS ON A TRAIN*. Because she was mogul Jack Warner's idea, not Hitchcock's, his attitude toward her ranged from disinterest to cordial dislike; as costar FARLEY GRANGER observed, "He had to have one person in each film he could harass."

Roman survived the memorable experience (and the frankly unmemorable part) to do other movies, including *The Bottom of the Bottle*, Anthony Mann's *The Far Country*, and a great deal of television, including an episode of *THE ALFRED HITCHCOCK HOUR*; her most memorable performance, however, undoubtedly came at sea in 1956, when she grabbed her three-year-old son and fled the sinking *Andrea Doria*. (Both survived, albeit on separate lifeboats.)

Roman died at 76 in Laguna Beach, CA.

References

William H. Honan, "Ruth Roman, Glamorous and Wholesome Star, Dies," *New York Times*, September 11, 1999, http://www.nytimes.com/1999/09/11/movies/ruth-roman-75-glamorous-and-wholesome-star-dies.html; "Ruth Roman," *IMDb*, http://www.imdb.com/name/nm0738746/bio; Donald Spoto, *The Dark Side of Genius: The Life of Alfred Hitchcock* (New York: Da Capo Press, 1999), 325.

ROPE (US 1948)

> DIRECTOR: Alfred Hitchcock.
> SCREENPLAY: Arthur Laurents, Hume Cronyn, based on the play by Patrick Hamilton.
> PRODUCERS: Uncredited (Sidney Bernstein, Alfred Hitchcock).
> CINEMATOGRAPHY: Joseph Valentine, William V. Skall.
> EDITOR: William H. Ziegler.
> ORIGINAL MUSIC: Uncredited (David Buttolph).
> CAST: James Stewart (Rupert Cadell), Jon Dall (Brandon), Farley Granger (Philip), Sir Cedric Hardwicke (Mr. Kentley), Constance Collier (Mrs. Atwater).
> RUNNING TIME: 80 minutes. Color.
> RELEASED THROUGH: Warner Bros.

To prove their superiority to the common man, roommates Brandon and Philip strangle a friend in their Manhattan apartment, hide his body in a trunk, and then host a dinner party to celebrate their execution of a perfect murder and clear status as intellectual "supermen."

Among the guests are the victim's father, aunt, and fiancée; also in attendance is Rupert Cadell, now a publisher but once Brandon and Philip's teacher and a great advocate of Nietzsche's theories of the *Übermensch*, that man who is above conventional morality. Certainly, Brandon and Philip feel, their murder is proof of his theory.

As the evening goes on, though, Brandon overconfidently begins to drop hints and taunts, and the more guilt-ridden Philip gets drunk and argumentative. The party eventually breaks up, but as Rupert leaves, the housekeeper mistakenly hands him the dead boy's monogrammed hat; his suspicions growing, Cadell returns to confront the two murderers and, after discovering the body, summons the police.

A story of emotional BONDAGE and a production of self-imposed artistic constraints—which ironically marked the start of Hitchcock's true Hollywood freedom.

He had, for seven years, chafed under his contract with DAVID O. SELZNICK— a business arrangement that often brought him larger budgets and STARS but also saw him loaned out to other studios and, worst of all, gave Selznick the final say on everything from casting to cutting. Before *THE PARADINE CASE* had even finished, Hitchcock was in busy consultation with SIDNEY BERNSTEIN—who had worked with him on the Free French films and the Holocaust documentary—and preparing what would be the first project for their new TRANSATLANTIC PICTURES venture, *UNDER CAPRICORN.*

When INGRID BERGMAN was unavailable to star, however, the men decided to postpone the production and embark instead on *Rope,* an adaptation of the 1929 PATRICK HAMILTON play (which itself had obviously been inspired by the LEOPOLD AND LOEB case). Hitchcock assigned old friend HUME CRONYN to do the initial treatment; later, ARTHUR LAURENTS was hired to turn it into a screenplay. It would be the first feature-film writing credit for both.

CENSORSHIP, they knew, would be a problem; word was, Laurents later said, that the story was about HOMOSEXUALITY (or "it," as the topic was referred to). There could be no suggestion of "it" in the script, Laurents was told, and so he went carefully through the original play's dialogue, eliminating all the antique British-isms—"Oh, my dear boy"—that were already drawing unwelcome, if mistaken, American attention. But Laurents sharpened the rest of it, so much so that—without ever mentioning the word *homosexual*—there was no doubt that its two main characters, single men sharing a lush New York apartment, were in a relationship (as, at times, were Laurents and star FARLEY GRANGER; indeed, *Rope* was decidedly the most "it" movie Hitchcock had ever made, with costar JOHN DALL—and even Francis Poulenc, the composer whose piano piece Granger is practicing—gay as well).

Laurents also added the sort of black humor that Hitchcock loved; throughout the story, there are lines with DOUBLE meanings ("One guest who must be gotten rid of," "like the grave," "knock 'em dead") that comment surreptitiously on the story and provide more evil laughs than any film until *PSYCHO.* "These hands will bring you great fame," says a dotty psychic, as she examines the fingers of the young pianist; unknown to her, he's a young STRANGLER, too, and it's only infamy that's ahead for him.

After the script came casting, a tricky thing for a film whose subject was still "it," no matter how subtly. Hitchcock wanted CARY GRANT for the young men's influential teacher, but he was unavailable—according to DONALD SPOTO, because he was under contract to RKO; according to Laurents, because he refused to play a gay character. MONTGOMERY CLIFT was approached and demurred, too, for the same skittish reasons, and so Hitchcock signed JAMES STEWART to play the teacher—his first role for the director—and Granger and Dall to play the two killers. SIR CEDRIC HARDWICKE and CONSTANCE COLLIER rounded out the cast.

Even more than usual, however, the real star of the film would be Hitchcock and his camera. Determined to make a splash with his new company's debut production, Hitchcock decided that *Rope* would not only be his first film in Technicolor—inspired by the LONG TAKES he'd tried to do in *The Paradine Case* (which had been butchered by Selznick), he also would go even further this time, telling the story in 80 minutes of "real time" and letting single shots literally run as long as there was still film left in the camera. There would be no editing in the traditional sense; instead, the camera would be constantly on the move, and at the end, the various single-take, 10-minute-long scenes would merely need to be quickly spliced together.

Hitchcock had been interested in this approach for a while, spurred on possibly by his work supervising the documentary on the Nazi death camps, in which he urged the editors to do as little cutting as possible in order to head off any charges of trickery; if long, uninterrupted takes gave a feeling of truthfulness to a documentary, then they might add a heightened sense of realism to a feature, as well. It was, like the choice to shoot in Technicolor, a modern approach and a chance for a filmmaker on the edge of 50 to show that he was still as comfortable on the cutting edge as he'd ever been.

Yet this style of editing also ran contrary to everything Hitchcock had ever preached about the art of MONTAGE—the cumulative, dramatic effect of joining together short, separate images—and it would provide endless headaches on the set, where walls had to suddenly roll away on casters and a single muffed line could require an entire 10-minute retake. INGRID BERGMAN and other stars would drop by to see the shoot (which required incredibly complicated lighting cues to create a gathering dusk through the apartment windows), but despite Hitchcock's typical pride in the size and scope of his self-imposed challenges, he didn't always succeed at them; a great deal of Technicolor footage had to be reshot when it came back from the lab too garishly COLORED, and even in the final print, some of the DOLLY SHOTS are noticeably wobbly.

After the shoot, Stewart grumbled that Hitchcock had rehearsed his camera, not his actors, and it's true that the performances are inconsistent. Collier—whom Hitchcock knew since the '20s, when she had written the play *Down Hill* with IVOR NOVELLO—gave the film some gentle humor as the daffy dowager, and Hardwicke provided the story's real heart as the victim's worried father (as well as a bit of an implicit lecture to the heartless audience: You might find murder mysteries amusing, but in real life, there is loss and misery).

But Dall is even more affected than the part calls for, and Granger is a bit uncertain. As for Stewart, he never truly convinces as a professor of Nietzsche. (It's also doubtful that Hitchcock ever told him that his character was supposed to be gay, as Laurents said he was always intended to be.)

Nor does his third-act speech really ring true; "You've given my words a meaning I never dreamed of," Stewart protests when he realizes he's inspired two murderers, but this is a self-serving dodge. His character may gild his philosophy in small jokes and cynical asides, but his talk of "superior" men and "inferior" victims is the talk of bigots and fascists, and that the two impressionable preppies he raised on it would later use it to justify their own cruelties shouldn't be such a surprise; giving Stewart's character this easy way out weakens the sense of GUILT that Hitchcock's best work addresses. (Also underdeveloped is the metaphor of bondage itself—Brandon and Philip strangled David with a rope, but the couple is tied together as well, bound not only by their shared guilt but also by their corrosive and unequal relationship.)

Stewart was right, of course; more than most of Hitchcock's films, it's the camera that's the real actor here, and often it's a worthy star. Although usually on the prowl, it sometimes gets its most dramatic effects by simply standing still and watching—action revealed through a now-open, now-closed swinging door or a long static shot in which the maid prepares to open up the trunk where the body is hidden as characters talk unconcernedly offscreen. There's also a nice SUBJECTIVE shot (copying one in *REBECCA*) in which Stewart's character theorizes about the murder; as he describes what must have happened, the camera's eye moves about the room, imagining.

Yet despite a few moments—the stark, onscreen murder, his most shocking since *THE LODGER*, the heart-rending shot of Hardwicke looking out the window, waiting for a son who'll never arrive—*Rope* is as cold as its antiheroes, a film that's mostly about its own cleverness. "It was worth trying," Stewart observed later, summing up the one-take experiment. "Nobody but Hitch would have tried it. But it really didn't work."

Except to announce that Hitchcock had finally won his independence—and was ready to use it.

References

Farley Granger, interview with the author, April 2007; Farley Granger with Robert Calhoun, *Include Me Out: My Life from Goldwyn to Broadway* (New York: St. Martin's Press, 2007), 68–71; Arthur Laurents, *The Rest of the Story* (Milwaukee, WI: Applause, 2012), 39; Patrick McGilligan, *Alfred Hitchcock: A Life in Darkness and Light* (New York: HarperCollins, 2003), 402–14; *Rope Unleashed*, directed by Laurent Bouzereau (2001), documentary; Don-ald Spoto, *The Dark Side of Genius: The Life of Alfred Hitchcock* (New York: Da Capo Press, 1999), 302–8; François Truffaut, *Hitchcock/Truffaut*, rev. ed. (New York: Touchstone, 1985), 179–84.

RÓZSA, MIKLOS (1907–1995)

Budapest-born musician raised in a wealthy family and inculcated with an appreciation of music and his country's culture, whose influence on him was "vital," he said later. "I was never a methodical folksong collector like Kodály or Bartók," he said. "I was interested only in the music, which I found strong in expression and fascinating rhythmically. I sometimes played violin with the gypsies for fun, and we might join together to serenade a certain village beauty (whose name I still remember)."

Having mastered the violin, viola, and piano as a child, Rózsa continued his musical studies in Leipzig and, after moving to Paris, began his career as a classical composer in earnest. Yet he was interested in cinema, as well, and his first film work came in London in the late '30s, where fellow Hungarian émigré Alexander Korda hired him to do the score for *Knight without Armor*; it was enough of a success that Rózsa was soon hired full time, turning out lush music for *The Four Feathers* and *Thief of Baghdad*.

In Hollywood since the early '40s, Rózsa wrote the scores for several Billy Wilder pictures, including the noir classic *Double Indemnity*; he also pioneered the use of the THEREMIN, whose eerie, electronic tones in *The Lost Weekend* and *SPELLBOUND* duplicate the heroes' disturbed emotional states. But Rózsa resented producer DAVID O. SELZNICK's interference (he always wanted more violins), and Hitchcock thought Rózsa's score was overbearing—although he may have merely resented the fact that it was the composer who won an Oscar for the picture. The partnership was discontinued.

Rózsa, though, continued as a Hollywood favorite, particularly for noir projects; among his later credits are *The Red House*, *Brute Force*, *Kiss the Blood off My Hands*, and *The Asphalt Jungle* (although, as *Ben Hur*, *King of Kings*, and *El Cid* proved, he could do epic, too). One of his last credits is for *Dead Men Don't Wear Plaid* in 1982, a pastiche that cleverly recycled clips from various Hollywood classics, including *SUSPICION* and *NOTORIOUS* (although not *Spellbound*, the one Hitchcock film Rózsa had worked on). Sadly, a severe stroke later that year ended Rózsa's regular work for films, although he continued to compose orchestral music.

He died in Los Angeles at 88.

References

Patrick McGilligan, *Alfred Hitchcock: A Life in Darkness and Light* (New York: HarperCollins, 2003), 379; "Miklós Rózsa," *IMDb*, http://www.imdb.com/name/nm0000067/bio?ref_=nm_ov_bio_sm; David Raskin, "David Raskin Remembers His Colleagues: Miklós Rózsa," *American Composers Orchestra*, http://www.americancomposers.org/raksin_rozsa.htm.

R.R.R.R.

Another aborted project from the uncertain '60s, this one had its genesis in a much older idea of Hitchcock's about a family-run hotel in which everyone but the proprietor was a crook; in this latest version, a glamorous woman (Sophia Loren was mentioned) would check into a Manhattan hotel, carrying a treasure in rare coins; the hapless manager's thieving relatives would all work overtime trying to steal them from under his nose. (The title refers to a grading system used by coin dealers; "R.R.R.R." is the finest.)

After approaching the rather wildly inappropriate Vladimir Nabokov with this idea, as well as with the germ of what would become *TORN CURTAIN*—Nabokov turned down both—Hitchcock brought his comical, coin-thief concept to the writers of the lighthearted Italian caper *Big Deal on Madonna Street*, Agenore Incrocci and Furio Scarpelli. They worked on it on and off for several months without success until Hitchcock dropped the idea to return to developing *Torn Curtain*, this time turning to BRIAN MOORE instead.

References

Steven DeRosa, "Alfred Hitchcock's Italian Connection," *Writing with Hitchcock*, http://stevenderosa.com/writingwithhitchcock/italianconnection.html; Donald Spoto, *The Dark Side of Genius: The Life of Alfred Hitchcock* (New York: Da Capo Press, 1999), 484–85.

RUSSELL, JOHN L. (1905–1967)

New York–born cameraman who, after an abortive start in the '30s, resumed his movie career following World War II; assignments included interesting but often awkwardly economical projects like Orson Welles's beleaguered *Macbeth*, Edgar G. Ulmer's *The Man from Planet X*, and the early Ray Harryhausen picture *The Beast from 20,000 Fathoms*.

Both professionally capable and aesthetically unobtrusive, Russell soon moved on to television, where he would become the busy director of photography on many series, including *M Squad*, *Thriller*, and *General Electric Theater*. He was director of photography on both *ALFRED HITCHCOCK PRESENTS* and *THE ALFRED HITCHCOCK HOUR*, overseeing nearly 100 episodes; when Hitchcock decided to use his television crew on the low-budget *PSYCHO*, Russell came along to provide the cinematography.

Like his work for the television show, Russell's work was mostly flatly lit and a little gray, although that worked for the sterility of Marion Crane's Phoenix and the ugly low-budget environs of the Bates Motel. And under Hitchcock's careful direction, other images came to life—the low angles of a looming Norman, the high bird's-eye view that obscures MOTHER as she's carried down the STAIRS, the clinical blankness of the cell at the end. And, of course, the shower scene, with the blinding whiteness of the tiles, the silver flashes of the knife, the water, and at the end the empty blackness of Marion's unseeing EYE.

Although *Psycho* was an extraordinary hit (and won Russell an Oscar nomination), he quickly returned to his typically modest work on the Hitchcock show. Apart from a few rare movie assignments—an ill-advised remake of *The Cabinet of Dr. Caligari* written by ROBERT BLOCH, the subpar HITCHCOCKIAN *Jigsaw*—the rest of his career was spent turning out episodes of TV's *McHale's Navy*, *The Virginian*, and *Run for Your Life*.

He died at 62 in Los Angeles.

References

Jim Hemphill, "DVD Playback: Psycho," *American Society of Cinematographers*, https://www.theasc.com/ac_magazine/ December2008/DVDPlayback/page3.php; "John L. Russell," *IMDb*, http://www.imdb .com/name/nm0005852.

S

SABOTAGE (GB 1936)

DIRECTOR: Alfred Hitchcock.
SCREENPLAY: Charles Bennett, Ian Hay, Helen Simpson, E. V. H. Emmett, Alma Reville, based on the novel *The Secret Agent* by Joseph Conrad.
PRODUCERS: Uncredited (Sir Michael Balcon, Ivor Montagu).
CINEMATOGRAPHY: Bernard Knowles.
EDITOR: Charles Frend.
ORIGINAL MUSIC: Uncredited (Hubert Bath, Jack Beaver, Louis Levy).
CAST: Sylvia Sidney (Mrs. Verloc), Oscar Homolka (Karl Verloc), John Loder (Ted Spencer), Desmond Tester (Stevie).
RUNNING TIME: 76 minutes. Black and white.
RELEASED THROUGH: Gaumont British Distributors.

As London grinds to a halt during a blackout, saboteur Karl Verloc quietly returns to the apartment above his cinema and carefully washes his hands. No one—not his wife or her young brother, Stevie, who lives with them—suspects that he is part of a gang of foreign terrorists. In fact, he pretends to have slept through the power failure, and when the patrons at his theater demand their money back, he tells his wife to pay them, assuring her they can afford it.

However, at a meeting with his boss at a public aquarium, Verloc finds out he's not to be paid for his latest work; rather than terrifying the city, the blackout, it seems, was merely laughed off by Londoners. Verloc is told that for his next assignment he's to plant a bomb in a busy downtown subway station.

Already suspicious of Verloc, Scotland Yard has assigned an agent, Ted Spencer, to work undercover, posing as a helper at the neighborhood greengrocer's. He befriends the family, and the obviously unhappy Mrs. Verloc responds to his attentions. Meanwhile, Verloc gets the "package" from the gang's bomb maker, who tells him it's timed to go off at 1:45. When one of Verloc's confederates identifies Spencer as a lawman, Verloc realizes he's being watched and decides to use an unknowing Stevie to deliver the bomb.

Along the way, though, Stevie is constantly delayed—by sidewalk salesmen, by a parade, by pokey traffic. The bomb goes off before he can deliver it, killing him. Hearing the news later that night, Mrs. Verloc slips into a daze, even as Verloc blames Scotland Yard for the boy's death—if he wasn't being watched, then he could have delivered the bomb himself, he says—and suggests that, perhaps now, the couple will have a child of their own. His wife fatally stabs him with a carving knife and prepares to give herself up to the police.

Scotland Yard has just arrived, however—as has the bomb maker, who is

Patricia Hitchcock looks on in horror as Robert Walker demonstrates his favorite murder method to Norma Varden in *Strangers on a Train. Warner Bros./Photofest © Warner Bros.*

worried there may be evidence in the apartment tying him to the crime. While the sympathetic Spencer stops Mrs. Verloc from confessing, the police chase the terrorist into the house. He sets off a bomb—destroying not only himself but also Verloc's body and any evidence of the murder. Mrs. Verloc is free.

A dark little movie about acts of violence, not the least of which is committed against the audience.

After finishing *SECRET AGENT*, Hitchcock turned immediately to his next project, an adaptation of a Joseph Conrad novel about anticzarist revolutionaries at work in England. That storyline would have to be changed, as would the book's title, *The Secret Agent*.

As usual, Hitchcock and his writers kept the spine of the plot while adding characters and incidents for commercial reasons (there would now be a romance for Mrs. Verloc, and she would not commit suicide at the end) or to pique Hitchcock's artistic interests. (Instead of selling pornographic books, Verloc now ran a movie theater, allowing the director to once again, as he had in *THE PLEASURE GARDEN*, *THE RING*, and *THE 39 STEPS*, contrast innocent public pleasures with private dirty secrets.)

Having failed to get him for *Secret Agent*, Hitchcock again tried to sign ROBERT DONAT for the lead—there were even ads in *Variety* prematurely announcing him as cast in the film, then called *The Hidden Power*—but the actor had to beg off due to ill health; dull JOHN LODER got the part instead. (The persistent Hitchcock would try to reteam with Donat again for *THE LADY VANISHES* and again be unsuccessful.) Although the director flirted with the idea of casting PETER LORRE again—playing a foreign agent in a Hitchcock film for the third time in three years—OSCAR HOMOLKA was given the role of Verloc, the terrorist, possibly because Lorre's morphine addiction had already caused delays on *Secret Agent*. Hollywood star SYLVIA SIDNEY was cast as Mrs. Verloc in keeping with SIR MICHAEL BALCON's fondness for American names.

The production was particularly lavish, with several city streets—the sort of rough-and-tumble East End neighborhood where Hitchcock's father had had his own green-grocer's shop—constructed on a soundstage. Even a working tram was set up, an expense that annoyed the studio—particularly producer IVOR MONTAGU—but that Hitchcock insisted on, determined to give the film every bit of urban realism he could.

His attention to this sort of detail undoubtedly helped keep up his interest in a film whose cast failed to engage him; he remained unenthused about the stolid Loder (the very opposite of the lightly charming Donat) and Sidney, who was used to carefully playing a scene all the way through and was jangled by Hitchcock's jigsaw method of short, sharp cuts—look down, grab this, look left, turn here (although it was precisely that HITCHCOCKIAN MONTAGE that provided her with her best scene, in which, much to her own apparent astonishment, she kills her husband).

Although *Sabotage* still maintains the basic idea and much of the glum mood of Conrad's work, it is also very much a Hitchcock film, not least of all because of its visual style. Short, staccato images and quick words or phrases quickly lay out the story. Verloc is identified seamlessly within the first few minutes as we see the act of sabotage, are told how it was done, and then watch him washing sand from his hands at home. The murder scene—which so frustrated Sidney—is a marvel of both editing (the flurry of close-ups as she is tempted, resists, and then gives in to the urge for revenge) and moral ambiguity. (Verloc seems to willingly thrust himself onto the knife as much as she thrusts it into him, and both give a little gasp of pain and surprise as it happens.)

There is also the film's stunning set piece, in which—almost sadistically toying with the audience—Hitchcock gives the time bomb to Stevie (played, in another touch of realism, not by a cherub but the slightly geeky, awkward Desmond Tester) and then sets him off on his way. We know that the device is set to go off at 1:45; frequently the camera cuts to clocks ticking away. But then Hitchcock delays the child with one distraction after another. And then, after fraying our nerves almost to the snapping point, he finally seats the boy on a slow-moving bus, next to a woman with an adorable puppy—and sets the bomb off, blowing bus, boy, dog, and everyone else to smithereens.

It is a remarkable sequence—remarkable most of all in its ending. (To kill not only a child onscreen but also a dog is an act few mainstream directors would try even today.) And it was a mistake, Hitchcock later felt; to build such tension and then not let it safely dissipate put the film slightly, permanently off kilter and angered audiences. "A grave error on my part," he soberly told FRANÇOIS TRUFFAUT.

Yet it's all of a piece with this dour, somewhat depressing film. Its heroine is, like so many of Hitchcock's women, a character without her own clear IDENTITY—a wife to Verloc who shows little interest in him, a sister to Stevie who acts more like his mother. She has no clear image of herself (the film doesn't even give her a first name) and no true hold on her own feelings. Minutes after mourning Stevie, she's laughing at a cartoon and then anguished again; her murder of her husband seems to surprise her more than it does him. She's emotionally confused and morally complicated in a way Hollywood CENSORS never would have allowed—not only is she a married woman clearly attracted to the single man pursuing her, but also the unresolved ending (in a borrowing from *BLACKMAIL*) literally lets her get away with murder.

Sabotage is also, like many other Hitchcock films, interested in PLAYS WITHIN PLAYS, movies within movies. When Verloc meets his boss, it's at an aquarium, with huge tanks glowing balefully like projected films; when Spencer goes to spy on Verloc, he slips behind the movie theater's screen, the image always behind him playing in reverse.

And of course it's the movies themselves that influence this movie's climax; fleeing to the theater after Stevie's death, his sister is first distracted by the comic cartoon playing there and then struck by its violence and repeated cry in *WHO KILLED COCK ROBIN?* (BIRDS are, hardly for the last time, a motif as well, from the pet shop where the bomb maker works to the birdcage where he hides the explosives to Verloc's promise to "kill two birds with one stone" to the coded "the birds will sing at 1:45" about the bomb's timing.)

Carefully constructed and rapidly and vividly told, *Sabotage* is one of the most accomplished—and certainly the bleakest—of Hitchcock's British talkies.

References

"Alfred Hitchcock: The Hidden Power," *Variety*, June 10, 1936, http://the.hitch cock.zone/wiki/Variety_%281936%29 _-_Alfred_Hitchcock:_The_Hidden_Power; Hillel Italie, "Hollywood Queen: Actress Sylvia Sidney, 80, Recalls Full Career," *Kitchener-Waterloo Record*, November 28, 1990, http://the.hitchcock.zone/wiki/Kitchener -Waterloo_Record_%2828/Nov/1990%29 _-_A_Hollywood_queen_Actress_ Sylvia_Sidney,_80,_recalls_full_career; Patrick McGilligan, *Alfred Hitchcock: A Life in Darkness and Light* (New York: HarperCollins, 2003), 184–91; Donald Spoto, *The Dark Side of Genius: The Life of Alfred Hitchcock* (New York: Da Capo Press, 1999), 155–58; François Truffaut, *Hitchcock/Truffaut*, rev. ed. (New York: Touchstone, 1985), 107–11.

SABOTEUR (US 1942)

DIRECTOR: Alfred Hitchcock.
SCREENPLAY: Peter Viertel, Joan Harrison, Dorothy Parker.
PRODUCERS: Uncredited (Frank Lloyd, Jack H. Skirball).
CINEMATOGRAPHY: Joseph Valentine.
EDITOR: Otto Ludwig (Edward Curtiss, uncredited).
ORIGINAL MUSIC: Frank Skinner.
CAST: Robert Cummings (Barry Kane), Priscilla Lane (Pat), Otto Kruger (Tobin), Alma Kruger (Mrs. Sutton), Norman Lloyd (Fry), Ian Wolfe (Robert).
RUNNING TIME: 108 minutes. Black and white.
RELEASED THROUGH: Universal.

A fire breaks out in an aircraft hangar of a US defense plant—and turns into a fatal inferno when a worker uses an extinguisher that's been secretly filled with gasoline. Barry Kane, who gave the dead man the extinguisher, tells the investigators he'd first been given it by another worker named Fry—but when they can find no one by that name in the plant's records, they assume Kane is the killer, and Kane goes on the run.

Kane tracks Fry to the California desert and a well-appointed ranch—whose millionaire owner, Tobin, turns out to be the leader of a group of saboteurs. Tobin calls the police, who arrest Kane and put him in handcuffs, but Kane escapes, finding refuge at the cabin of a blind man. When the man's niece, Pat, shows up, her uncle urges her to take Kane to a blacksmith to have the cuffs taken off, but she doesn't believe Kane's protestations of innocence and stops the car, hoping to flag down help. Kane uses the car's fan to break his handcuffs—wrecking the car in the process—and he and Pat set off on foot.

After briefly taking shelter with a circus, Kane and Pat follow the saboteurs to a ghost town. Pat hides, and Kane passes himself off as one of the gang in order to get to the bottom of their plot. Pat runs off, while he travels with them to New York, where they meet with their other members at a society ball. Pat is there, too, captive and already waiting—as is Tobin, who now exposes Kane's lie. Kane and Pat are locked up—Kane in a storeroom and Pat at the gang's headquarters in Rockefeller Center.

Kane escapes, while Pat slips a note for help out the window. Kane chases the spies to the Brooklyn Navy Yard and discovers Fry, ready to set off a bomb and blow up a new ship. Kane foils him, but Fry and the gang take him back to their office—where the police, alerted by Pat's note, are already waiting. Fry ducks inside Radio City Music Hall, with the police and Kane in pursuit—there's a shootout, and Fry flees again.

Kane, detained by the police, tells Pat to follow him—and finally Fry, Pat, and eventually Kane all converge at the Statue of Liberty. Kane and Fry fight at the top of the statue—and Fry falls to his death.

After SUSPICION, Hitchcock began developing a script for a new movie for DAVID O. SELZNICK, calling on the faithful JOAN HARRISON and young screenwriter PETER VIERTEL. The egotistic and workaholic Selznick—who found Hitchcock's lack of suitable deference and reluctance to work around the clock maddening—assigned one of his associates, John Houseman, to supervise the team's efforts.

Houseman was immediately taken by the director, a "man of exaggeratedly delicate sensibilities, marked by a harsh CATHOLIC education and the scars from a social system against which he was in perpetual revolt." Yet even as he marveled at Hitchcock's intelligence and cinematic savvy, he found the filmmaker's approach to writing a screenplay oddly scattered; various set pieces, images, and bits of business were first proposed and then strung together rather than arising logically and organically from the story. (Later, Hitchcock would agree, telling FRANÇOIS TRUFFAUT that the final screenplay had a "mass of ideas but they weren't sorted out in proper order; they weren't selected with sufficient care.")

Although the script went through rewrites, Selznick never warmed to it; after shopping it around, he sold it to another producer, Frank Lloyd, who set it up at UNIVERSAL. Hitchcock resented the outside deal—once again, Selznick would be making a fat profit off him—as well as the usual economics that smaller studios and producers were prone to; although Hitchcock hoped for Gary Cooper and Barbara Stanwyck in the leads, he was told to take ROBERT CUMMINGS and PRISCILLA LANE. (He also wanted popular cowboy star Harry Carey to play Tobin, but the actor—at the urging of his outraged wife—refused to play a traitor.)

Despite the compromises and constraints, *Saboteur* is still a smart, fast adventure—and perhaps the most purely HITCHCOCKIAN Hitchcock picture since *THE LADY VANISHES*, unencumbered by the period trappings of *JAMAICA INN* or the ostentatious "good taste" of *REBECCA*. It's propulsive and peripatetic, like *THE 39 STEPS* but a little more serious, with its hero carrying the GUILT of an innocent man's death—and, like the big new country it's set in, a movie done on a grander scale and shot through with working-class idealism.

Some of those were undoubtedly DOROTHY PARKER's touches (she was brought in for a rewrite and contributed the scene with the blind man, as well as most of the dialogue for the circus sequence); some came from that sore class resentment of Hitchcock's that Houseman had so perceptively noticed. *Saboteur* is one of Hitchcock's most proletarian pictures;

his hero is a worker in a leather jacket, its villains a gang of plutocrats who sneer at Kane's honest patriotism. *Saboteur* isn't just a trek across America but also through America, and its observations are very clear. Whenever Kane turns to a figure of wealth or authority for help, he's batted away or betrayed; whenever he appeals to one of the overlooked—a truck driver, an elderly blind man, a van full of circus freaks—he's embraced.

Hitchcock had his fun with the big set pieces. The shootout at Radio City Music Hall took an idea from *SABOTAGE* and added guns to make a mirrored image of real and onscreen violence, creating another PLAY WITHIN A PLAY; the famous climax at the top of a national monument, with the villain's life literally hanging by a thread, would later be restaged and improved in *NORTH BY NORTHWEST* (with Hitchcock correcting his "error" that time by making sure it was the hero and heroine who were in jeopardy). He also achieved some striking compositions—the black smoke of the defense plant fire slowly entering our view from the right until it practically fills the screen, the contrast between the tiny human figures at the bottom in Radio City and the enormous projected close-ups behind them.

And there are smaller pleasures, too, such as the nicely sketched-in villains— OTTO KRUGER, NORMAN LLOYD as the smirking Fry, Alan Baxter as the slightly perverse Freeman, and IAN WOLFE as a sadistic butler with a blackjack. Or another, quietly comic touch in which Pat—whom we've been told is a commercial model— keeps constantly showing up on billboards that comment on the action. Or the topical insertion of newsreel footage of the sunk *S.S. Normandie*, lightly implying that she'd been destroyed by enemy sabotage, too (a quick scene that brought angry objections from the navy).

Saboteur tends to be devalued in the Hitchcock canon, judged as having neither the originality of *The 39 Steps* nor the dazzling scale of *North by Northwest*; Hitchcock himself, while remaining proud of the Statue of Liberty shot, tended to speak slightingly of it, too, later on, complaining that neither Cummings nor Lane was up to the material. But it's exactly their regular, accessible attitudes that make the movie work as a celebration of working-class honesty and perseverance; his first film with an all-American cast, it remains his most all-American film.

References

Norman Lloyd, interviews with the author, November 2007, July 2015; Patrick McGilligan, *Alfred Hitchcock: A Life in Darkness and Light* (New York: HarperCollins, 2003), 294–306; Donald Spoto, *The Dark Side of Genius: The Life of Alfred Hitchcock* (New York: Da Capo Press, 1999), 249–55; François Truffaut, *Hitchcock/Truffaut*, rev. ed. (New York: Touchstone, 1985), 145–51.

SAINT, EVA MARIE (1924–)

Newark-born actress who was studying to become a teacher when a college play awakened a love of drama. After graduation, she moved to New York, where she pursued modeling jobs and went out on auditions. The stage and live TV presented plenty of opportunities—if not plenty of money—until 1954, when Elia Kazan cast her in *On the Waterfront*. Admittedly thrown—and kept—off balance by Marlon Brando's fresh and unpredictable performance, she gave a touching portrayal of shy, sheltered Edie Doyle and won the ACADEMY AWARD for best supporting actress.

"When he did 'Waterfront' he really was at the height of his joy in what he did," she said of Brando. "He was so observant, he would pick up on any little thing you did—doing a scene with him was like playing chamber music. . . . I don't know what happened later. That Marlon you saw—that wasn't the Marlon I knew. He almost seemed ashamed of being an actor."

Saint scored again in *A Hatful of Rain* and *Raintree County* and on television, where she was often cast in realistic, downbeat, "kitchen-sink" dramas. Enjoying the idea of casting against type, Hitchcock then chose her for the glamorous spy Eve Kendall in *NORTH BY NORTHWEST*.

"I still have no idea why he saw me as this sexy spy lady," she said. "But who doesn't want to be a sexy spy lady? He knew exactly what he wanted, too. He oversaw everything—my hair, my makeup, my shoes. And when he didn't like the costumes MGM came up with, he took me to Bergdorf's and said, 'All right, Eve, whatever you like'—that's where I found that beautiful black dress with the roses."

She is very good in *North by Northwest*, perfectly embodying the sort of fire-and-ice BLONDE that Hitchcock had made a FETISH of—dressed with prim, proper elegance yet able to calmly bat risqué double entendres back and forth over luncheon. "Externals were very important to (Hitchcock)," she said. "That was, actually, the only direction he'd give me. 'Lower your voice.' 'Don't move your hands.' 'Look Cary in the eye.' Of course, that wasn't hard! People ask sometimes, 'What was CARY GRANT really like?' And I always say, 'Just as beautiful as you think he was, inside and out.'"

The director—whom, she stresses, never said or attempted anything inappropriate with her—took a particular pleasure in the new look he'd given her and begged her to hold on to it. "I don't want you to do a sink-to-sink movie again ever," she remembered him telling her. "Women go to the movies, and they've just left that sink at home. They don't want to see you at the sink."

In fact, Saint did a variety of motion pictures after *North by Northwest*—including the modern epic *Exodus* and the rollicking farce *The Russians Are Coming! The Russians Are Coming!* as well as a few more downbeat dramas—but in the end, it wasn't the "sink-to-sink" movies that called her but the demands of her own domestic life. Married and with two children, she turned down many of the movie offers that came her way; eventually, they stopped coming as regularly, and she turned to TV roles and occasional stage work. For more than a decade, she didn't do movies at all.

She refuses to write an autobiography. ("They're all so boring! Me, me, me, me, me.") But she's still happy to appear at film festivals and retrospectives and talk about Kazan and Marlon and Hitch. She still reads scripts, too. But she says, "The characters are always grandmothers on oxygen, and while there's nothing wrong with that if you need it, I don't, yet. I'm still upright. I'm still going."

References

Destination Hitchcock: The Making of North by Northwest, directed by Peter Fitzgerald (2000), documentary, http://the.hitchcock.zone/wiki/Destination_Hitchcock:_The_Making_of_North_by_Northwest_%282000%29_-_transcript; Eva Marie Saint, interview with the author, November 2009; Barbara Vancheri, "Film Emissary Eva Marie Saint Plays Role Well," *Pittsburgh Post-Gazette*, November 4, 2012, http://www.post-gazette.com/movies/2012/11/14/Film-emissary-Eva-Marie-Saint-plays-role-well/stories/201211140179.

SANDERS, GEORGE (1906–1972)

Russian-born performer of Scottish-Estonian ancestry. When the revolution came, his family fled to England, where he went to prep school and college and cycled through several careers (he was reportedly fired from his position with a Latin American tobacco firm for drunkenness and dueling) before taking a job in advertising. It was there that a secretary, Eileen Fogelson, suggested he pursue a career on the stage. (She would be pursuing her own career soon enough under two of her middle names: Greer Garson.)

Sanders began his career as a chorus boy and a cabaret performer—he had a fine singing voice and actually recorded an album late in life, *The George Sanders Touch: Songs for the Lovely Lady*—before starting in films in the early '30s, eventually moving to Hollywood, where he landed steady work in a movie mystery series playing "the Saint."

Hitchcock cast him twice in 1940, first as the caddish Jack Favell in *REBECCA*—car salesman, adulterer, blackmailer, and all-around bounder—and then, slightly against type, as the more heroic but no less sardonic ffolliott in *FOREIGN CORRESPONDENT*. Both quickly perceptive and elegantly lazy, Sanders immediately understood Hitchcock's method of directing and incorporated it into his own understated approach. "The important thing for a STAR is to have an interesting face," the actor said later. "He doesn't have to move it very much. Editing and camerawork can always produce the desired illusion that a performance is being given."

Sanders was, however, being characteristically, coolly self-deprecating; he was, in fact, quite capable of giving a performance and gave good ones in a variety of pictures, including *The Picture of Dorian Gray*; *The Ghost and Mrs. Muir*; and, of course, his Oscar-winning turn as the bitter drama critic in *All about Eve*. And although many of his roles called for a certain smug superiority, Sanders played comedy well and showed other sides of his talent in FRITZ LANG's *While the City*

Sleeps, Roberto Rossellini's *Viaggo in Italia*, and even the sci-fi favorite *Village of the Damned*. Still, he remained typecast as a snob and a scoundrel, even calling his 1960 autobiography *Memoirs of a Professional Cad* (although, in his own mild defense, he asserted, "I was beastly but never coarse. A high-class sort of heel").

Eventually, however, even those parts stopped coming, and Sanders's personal life, always complicated—of his four wives, two were Gabor sisters—spun further out of control. There were personal tragedies— over the course of 1967, he lost his mother, his wife, and his brother, actor Tom Conway—and health issues. Sanders began to drink heavily, suffered a small stroke, and started showing signs of dementia, none of which he bore quietly. (When he became unable to play his piano, he hacked it to pieces with an axe.) He finally checked into a hotel on the Spanish coast, wrote a short suicide note—"Dear World, I am leaving because I am bored. I feel I have lived long enough. I am leaving you with your worries in this sweet cesspool. Good luck."— and swallowed five bottles of barbiturates. He was 65.

References

"George Sanders," *Hollywood's Golden Age*, http://www.hollywoodsgoldenage .com/actors/george_sanders.html; "George Sanders," *IMDb*, http://www.imdb.com/ name/nm0001695/bio?ref_=nm_ov _bio_sm; "George Sanders: Biography," *TCM*, http://www.tcm.com/tcmdb/per son/169430|59366/George-Sanders/biogra phy.html; David Thomson, *The New Biographical Dictionary of Film* (New York: Knopf, 2002), 773–74.

SARRIS, ANDREW (1928–2012)

Brooklyn-born writer and hugely influential critic who, after college and a stint in the army, moved to Paris in the early '50s. There he met FRANÇOIS TRUFFAUT and other cinephiles—still journalists then, not yet directors—and became an enthusiastic convert to the AUTEUR THEORY, which saw the director as the true author of the film and found consistent themes and interesting artistic approaches in the work of such often-underestimated Hollywood filmmakers as Nicholas Ray, Alfred Hitchcock, and Howard Hawks.

Returning to America, Sarris began writing on film for a variety of alternative weeklies or specialty publications; his first review for *The Village Voice*, of *PSYCHO*, was a rave, declaring Hitchcock the "most daring avant-garde filmmaker in America today." In 1962, his piece in the periodical *Film Culture*, "Notes on the Auteur Theory," brought the pioneering work of Truffaut and the rest of the *CAHIERS DU CINEMA* crowd to a much larger audience and established Sarris as the Church of the Director's leading American disciple.

Sarris's 1968 book *The American Cinema: Directors and Directions, 1929–1968* remains both an essential text and an endlessly debatable ranking of filmmakers; John Huston, Billy Wilder, and especially Stanley Kubrick came in for pointed criticism, but Sarris placed Hitchcock in the highest classification, the Pantheon, calling him not only the "supreme technician of the American cinema" but also a moral artist whose "reputation has suffered from the fact that he has given audiences more pleasure than is permissible for serious cinema" and whose harshest critics were clearly "intellectual puritans."

An inspiration to generations of critics—and a lively and combative counterweight to the equally acerbic and assertive PAULINE KAEL—Sarris wrote, taught, and reviewed for more than 50 years. He died in New York from complications of a fall at 83.

References

Kent Jones, "Hail the Conquering Hero: Andrew Sarris Profiled," *Film Comment* (May/June 2005), http://www.film comment.com/article/hail-the-conquer ing-hero-andrew-sarris-profiled; Michael Powell, "A Survivor of Film Criticism's Heroic Age," *New York Times*, July 9, 2009, http://www.nytimes.com/ 2009/07/12/movies/12powe.html?_r=2& pagewanted=all&; Andrew Sarris, *The American Cinema: Directors and Directions, 1929–1968* (New York: Dutton, 1968), 56–61.

SECRET AGENT (GB 1936)

DIRECTOR: Alfred Hitchcock.
SCREENPLAY: Charles Bennett, Alma Reville, Ian Hay, based on short stories by W. Somerset Maugham and the play by Campbell Dixon.
PRODUCERS: Uncredited (Sir Michael Balcon, Ivor Montagu).
CINEMATOGRAPHY: Bernard Knowles.
EDITOR: Charles Frend.
ORIGINAL MUSIC: Uncredited (John Greenwood).
CAST: John Gielgud (Richard Ashenden), Madeleine Carroll (Elsa Carrington), Peter Lorre (the General), Robert Young (Robert Marvin), Percy Marmont (Caypor).
RUNNING TIME: 86 minutes. Black and white.
RELEASED THROUGH: Gaumont British Picture Corporation.

A British captain home on leave during the First World War is surprised to see his own obituary in the newspapers—and then to be summoned to the office of a government official named only "R," who informs him that he's being given a new identity, Ashenden, and a new job as a spy. His first assignment is to go to Switzerland, where a German agent is at work.

Ashenden arrives there, along with a new colleague—a girl-chasing eccentric who calls himself "the General"—to discover another fellow agent, the attractive Elsa, already waiting for them. Their first contact is murdered before they can talk to him, but a button found at the murder scene leads them to identify another British tourist, Caypor, as the killer.

Ashenden and the General lure Caypor to the top of a mountain, and when Ashenden refuses to go through with it, the General guiltlessly pushes Caypor off the cliff. After they return to town, though, there is a coded message from headquarters telling them that Caypor is innocent. A horrified Elsa announces she is quitting the assignment, and she and Ashenden quarrel.

Ashenden and the General get a lead that the spies have been working out of a local chocolate factory; after a large bribe, one spy reveals that the real enemy agent is Marvin, a guest at the hotel who has been amiably flirting with Elsa all along—and has now left the country with her. Ashenden and the General rush off after them, and soon all four are on the same train to Constantinople. The train is attacked by British forces and crashes. A dying Marvin shoots the General, and Elsa and Ashenden resign from the secret service.

THE MAN WHO KNEW TOO MUCH had been a huge hit, and its follow-up, *THE 39 STEPS*, became Hitchcock's first truly international success. So for his next picture, he turned to another spy story—and decided to turn the genre on its head by emphasizing, not breathless intrigue and dashing heroes, but GUILT and mistakes and regret.

Based on two spy stories by W. SOMERSET MAUGHAM (with a romantic angle borrowed from the stories' previous stage adaptation by Campbell Dixon), Hitchcock and chief writer CHARLES

BENNETT developed a script that revolved around uncertainty and indecision. Their hero would be a reluctant spy, someone who didn't want the job (and, in fact, doesn't do it when the moment comes); the theme of the movie would be the shades-of-gray morality of espionage itself.

The *HAMLET*-like struggles of the hero appealed to JOHN GIELGUD, who was still uncertain about the rewards of movie work (although Hitchcock was uncertain about him, too; as usual, he would have preferred to have had ROBERT DONAT). MADELEINE CARROLL, so lovely in *The 39 Steps*, was brought back to play Elsa, and the scene-stealing PETER LORRE of *The Man Who Knew Too Much* was given the role of the General, a mysterious figure who is also known as "the Hairless Mexican" (because, "R" explains with surreal logic, he is neither hairless nor Mexican).

The story, though, would have its own HITCHCOCKIAN story logic; because part of it, like *The Man Who Knew Too Much*, would be set in Switzerland, where the Hitchcocks had honeymooned, it was important that a few Swiss details were woven into the plot. So, Hitchcock decided, one murder would take place in the Alps, and the spies' headquarters would be in a chocolate factory. Somehow cuckoo clocks were overlooked.

Production was difficult. Gielgud, who was simultaneously starring in *Romeo and Juliet* onstage at night, realized early that the beautiful Carroll was getting all the close-ups and Lorre, an inveterate ham, all the attention. It didn't help that Hitchcock, who had at first emphasized the hero's moral quandaries, now seemed to regret them, as he was stuck with the very undramatic story of a spy who didn't want to complete his assignment. (Also adding to the on-set difficulties: Lorre's mounting morphine use.)

Gielgud was right to worry; he seems cold and detached onscreen here, turning his hawklike profile left and right without ever developing any connection to Carroll—a severe problem, as the script demands that she fall in love with him practically at first sight (a problem also exacerbated by the fact that ROBERT YOUNG, playing the duplicitous Marvin, is far more smoothly charming). And Lorre—sporting not only a curly wig but also an earring—steals everything in the scenes that isn't nailed down.

And, of course, the hero's motivation was somewhat backward; his drive is not to accomplish something but to avoid it. That, Hitchcock realized too late, was fatal. "In an adventure drama your central figure must have a purpose," he told FRANÇOIS TRUFFAUT. "That's vital for the progression of the film and it's also a key factor in audience participation. The public must be rooting for the character; they should almost be helping him to achieve his goal." But, he said, as this character himself didn't want to achieve it, "it's a negative purpose, the film is static— it doesn't move forward."

The film gets off to a good start, though, with a deliberately faked funeral— an empty casket, a one-armed mourner, and a cold wit that predates the Bond films by a quarter of a century. There's also a strong scene in which Ashenden and the General enter a church for a planned rendezvous, as a long, absurdly sustained chord plays on the pipe organ; it's only when the two approach the organist that they realize he's dead, the keys pressed down by his lifeless fingers.

Also well staged is the assassination scene, with Ashenden and the General taking Caypor up into the mountains while Elsa keeps Caypor's wife busy with a request for German lessons. Hitchcock cuts between the two sequences, with

Caypor (PERCY MARMONT from *RICH AND STRANGE*) hiking happily to his death, while back at the hotel, his dog grows more and more agitated, scratching at the door, as Mrs. Caypor begins to have premonitions of disaster. It is the sort of intuitive, dreamlike effect that Hitchcock would often reach for in his silent films, and it's the best scene in the picture.

The scene in the chocolate factory, however, doesn't really exploit the potential of those endless conveyor belts, and although he daringly cuts to a completely black screen at the moment of the TRAIN crash, the miniature work is far below what he later achieved on *THE LADY VANISHES*.

And, most fatally, Carroll and Gielgud never click. "No good you standing there looking middle-aged," she snaps at him early on; "Bit fond of yourself, aren't you?" he fires back. The lines feel, not like banter, but like signs of a genuine real-life antipathy, and the romantic-comedy element of Marvin, Ashenden's supposed rival, seems like an awkward, out-of-character afterthought in a glum movie that's really about a coldhearted government, a reluctant hero, a botched mission, and the murder of an innocent man. There are some good scenes here and some typical Hitchcock concerns—GUILT and IDENTITY and grim duty. But they're never successfully integrated into a whole, or the film.

References

John Gielgud, *Early Stages: An Autobiography* (San Francisco: Mercury House, 1989), 163–65; Patrick McGilligan, *Alfred Hitchcock: A Life in Darkness and Light* (New York: HarperCollins, 2003), 178–84; Donald Spoto, *The Dark Side of Genius: The Life of Alfred Hitchcock* (New York: Da Capo Press, 1999), 152–54; François Truffaut, *Hitchcock/Truffaut*, rev. ed. (New York: Touchstone, 1985), 105–7.

SELZNICK, DAVID O. (1902–1965)

Pittsburgh-born producer who entered the business as a teenager, working for his father, pioneering mogul Lewis J. Selznick (who had actually distributed some of Hitchcock's earliest work in America). After high school let out, David would head to the Selznick office to negotiate contracts. When his father, never a cautious businessman, managed to lose his business in 1923 at the height of the silent era, his son David set out on his own quest—although whether to redeem his father's name or merely replace it with his own, writ larger, is both debatable and not necessarily contradictory. (The family saga helped inspire the hugely entertaining roman à clef film *The Bad and the Beautiful*.) David's brother, Myron, meanwhile, eventually became an agent—and was the connection that eventually brought Hitchcock and David O. Selznick together and ended up bringing Hitchcock to America.

It is easy for Hitchcock's most fervent admirers to see David O. Selznick as the epitome of the crude Hollywood mogul: good enough to buy the Hitchcock family their steamship tickets and pay the director a nice salary but no more than a money-and-marquee-names vulgarian in the end, someone whose crass and obvious tastes hampered Hitchcock's work and compromised his art until the director finally, relieved, rid himself of his contract. It would also be desperately unfair.

Selznick was full of faults. His taste in material was, if not low-, then definitely middle-brow (and, unlike Hitchcock, he then treated those properties with unearned respect). He preferred conventional filmmaking techniques—not Hitchcock's tricky MONTAGE ("Goddamn jigsaw cutting") but standard coverage, with plenty of shot choices (not just for aesthetic reasons but also to give the producer more control in the editing room). He was a poor delegator, often thinking—and often wrongly—that he could write a better script, coax out a better performance, than the veterans he'd hired to do just that. But what he was was a great producer—a man who recognized talent, who understood detail, who appreciated audiences, who remained a genius at promotion. "The way I see it," he said once, "my function is to be responsible for everything"—and it was a job he loved.

Although his 1930 marriage to Louis B. Meyer's daughter Irene was the source of plenty of snickers—"The son-in-law also rises," went the joke—Selznick had already left the MGM story department at that point, taking on executive positions first at PARAMOUNT and then at RKO, while occasionally selling story ideas. (*Dracula's Daughter* was his, credited to his pseudonym "Oliver Jeffries"—perhaps the inspiration for Hitchcock's hero in *REAR WINDOW*, "L. B. Jefferies," and another of the director's frequent tweaks of his old boss.)

The Selznick touch was evident early, as he demonstrated a fearless embrace of spectacle (the big-risk *King Kong*) all-STAR casts (*Dinner at Eight*) and the sort of leather-bound 19th-century classics he remembered from his father's library: *David Copperfield*, *A Tale of Two Cities*, *Anna Karenina*. At, first, RKO (and then back at MGM in a triumphant return), he nurtured new stars, like Katharine Hepburn; played the stern parent to unreliable talents, like John Barrymore; and worked closely with directors, like George Cukor who shared his devotion to strong stories; rich production values; and a clear, clean pictorial style.

Striking out on his own in 1935, Selznick riskily established his own studio, Selznick International Pictures (later dissolved and then reformed as the Selznick Studio). Further hits came, including *A Star Is Born*; *Nothing Sacred*; *The Prisoner of Zenda*; and, of course, *Gone with the Wind*, the most successful movie of all time. But while Selznick had space on the RKO lot and distribution initially through United Artists, he did not at first have that other important studio asset, a large list of contract players; he worked hard on signing actors to long-term deals and, at various times, had JOSEPH COTTEN, INGRID BERGMAN, and Vivien Leigh on his roster.

Occasionally frustrating to those talents, though, was that Selznick—chronically overextended, both artistically and financially—would set up a film only to sell the package to another studio or tell a star or director under contract that their next assignment would be for someone else. (He signed up, then sold off, Gene Kelly's services before he had even gotten the actor on a frame of film.) The practice gave Selznick breathing room and ready cash—he invariably pocketed the difference between what he was paying his talent and what he was renting them out for—although it left some stars dizzy.

"Of course he rented me out for large sums," said Bergman, whom Selznick had discovered working in Sweden. "A lot of my friends said, 'What an interesting agent you have. The roles are reversed. He takes ninety per cent and you get ten per cent.'" But Bergman remained practical about it; she liked to work, and however much of her loan-out fees Selznick kept for himself, she was still making far more than she would have back home.

Hitchcock was less sanguine about the situation. At first, a Selznick contract felt like a winning lottery ticket. By the mid-'30s, Hitchcock was Great Britain's most acclaimed (and highest paid) director, but he had become a very large fish in an increasingly shallow pond; British film production dropped in half from 1936 to 1937, and the films that were getting made had to contend with tight budgets and often crude special effects (Hitchcock had been particularly angry when he had to argue with producers to build a working streetcar for *SABOTAGE*). Yet negotiations with larger American studios—as Selznick was not averse to reminding him later—had not seemed promising.

Finally, in a 1938 deal brokered by brother Myron, Selznick International offered a contract with options and various bonuses (and agreed to bring over and hire Hitchcock's assistant, JOAN HARRISON, too). According to press reports, Selznick even had the director's first three films picked out: *REBECCA*, *TITANIC*, and something called *The Flashing Stream* with CAROLE LOMBARD playing a mathematician. (Later, Selznick even floated a fourth one—his remake of *Intermezzo* with Bergman, its original Swedish star and his latest "discovery.") Finally, though, *Rebecca* was chosen as the pair's premiere collaboration.

Right from the start, it illustrated the contrast and conflict between the two equally egotistical men. Temperamentally, they were simultaneously too alike and too different to get along. Both men were convinced they knew everything about making pictures; both men wanted what was up on the screen to reflect their vision and theirs alone. Yet each man also had very different ways of working. Even on the set, Hitchcock preferred to keep office hours, returning home in time for dinner with his wife. Selznick, fueled by energy, amphetamines, and around-the-clock secretaries (they were actually assigned in relays), would summon directors to his home at 10 o'clock at night and then keep them waiting for hours before calling them in for lengthy, all-night conferences.

They had a lot to confer about, too. Hitchcock had always treated story material liberally, rejiggering it for the screen as necessary; if he'd had no qualms about rewriting Joseph Conrad and W. SOM-ERSET MAUGHAM, then he certainly wasn't concerned about staying faithful to DAPHNE DU MAURIER (and, in fact, had already broadly changed her novel *JAMAICA INN*, infuriating her). Selznick, on the other hand, had a certain reverence for the published word—and the more popular the original had been, the greater his respect grew. He loathed Hitchcock's first-draft screenplay for *Rebecca* and would later worry that his script for *SABOTEUR* was emotionally cold and gimmicky. And Hitchcock's firm control of every shot left Selznick little elbow room to jump into postproduction and recut the films the way he wanted. (Not that he didn't try; toward the end of the partnership, with Hitchcock already beginning to disengage, Selznick leapt in and drastically re-edited *THE PARADINE CASE*, chopping up its long camera movements and removing nearly an hour of narrative. The results were no improvement.)

And yet, more than some moguls, Selznick truly loved the movies with a passion that went beyond profits. ("He had such enormous enthusiasm, and such enormous energy," Bergman said after his death. "He really burned his candle at both ends.") He gave Hitchcock budgets he could never have dreamed of in Britain—as astonishing as the miniatures are in *Rebecca*, the sets are even more impressive. And he understood the importance of talent, making sure that CLAUDE RAINS was cast in *NOTORIOUS* and engineering Hitchcock's important collaborations with Bergman, JOAN FONTAINE, Joseph Cotten, and screenwriter BEN HECHT. (Had composer BERNARD HERRMANN, whom Selznick had originally wanted, been free for *SPELLBOUND*, the mogul would have forged that crucial partnership, too.)

"Selznick was totally disorganized but essentially a loveable man, while Hitchcock, whose manner was not quite so lovable, was totally organized," said GREGORY PECK, who made both *Spellbound* and *The Paradine Case* with the duo. "This created an unavoidable tension between them, and it clearly affected Hitchcock's attitude during production."

Yet both men gave the other something he wanted—Selznick providing Hitchcock with resources, Hitchcock providing Selznick with popular and award-winning movies. It cannot have been easy getting a second best picture award after having just won one for *Gone with the Wind*, but Hitchcock's *Rebecca* gave Selznick that extra acclaim; five years later, *Spellbound* would bring another best picture nomination. And Hitchcock—albeit not by choice—gave Selznick the cash he needed to sink into his own lavish productions of *Since You Went Away* and *Duel in the Sun*, as the mogul banked large fees for renting Hitchcock out for pictures like *FOREIGN CORRESPONDENT* and selling off already-developed projects like *Saboteur* and *Notorious*.

Still, as mutually beneficial as the relationship was at times, it was doomed to be short-lived. Hitchcock had not borne meddling easily, even as a novice director; to be in his 40s, an internationally acclaimed filmmaker, and still have to suffer a producer's second-guessing was intolerable. And in his own, utterly self-assured conviction that every one of his suggestions could only make the picture better, Selznick simply could not get out of his own way—demanding extra violins for the *Spellbound* score (and alienating both composer MIKLOS RÓSZA as well as Hitchcock) or insisting on new discovery LOUIS JOURDAN for *The Paradine Case* (and thereby, Hitchcock was convinced, destroying the picture's theme of a degrading, obsessive love).

If only the mogul could have occasionally not sent that memo, not insisted on this change. The final irony of the famous Hitchcock-Selznick collaborations is that the less Selznick collaborated on the production and postproduction of a particular Hitchcock film—*Foreign Correspondent*, *Saboteur*, *SHADOW OF A DOUBT*, *LIFEBOAT*, *Notorious*—the better the movies were. The films on which he truly earned and took producer credit—*Spellbound*, *The Paradine Case*—are among the least interesting of their output. Even the initial, Selznick-produced *Rebecca*—while entertaining and full of Gothic style—was, its own director admitted, more a Selznick picture than a Hitchcock one.

Much to Selznick's annoyance, Hitchcock had been plotting his escape from this embrace for years; he had founded TRANSATLANTIC PICTURES with SIDNEY BERNSTEIN in 1946 and even while making *The Paradine Case* was planning what they thought would be the company's first production, *UNDER CAPRICORN*—all the while avoiding Selznick's increasingly anxious offers of a new five-picture deal. Hitchcock had had enough of Selznick's interference (and, as the mogul's choice of *The Paradine Case* seemed to prove, his taste for glossy, old-fashioned melodrama). Hitchcock wanted something new, something modern, something daring. Most of all, he wanted out.

It wasn't an easy break at first. When Bergman wasn't yet available for *Under Capricorn*, Bernstein and Hitchcock rushed into *ROPE* instead, with Hitchcock indulging his new independence by doing even longer takes and more elaborate camera movements than the ones Selznick had hated in *The Paradine Case*. The film was not a particular success, nor was *Under Capricorn*, nor *STAGE FRIGHT*, which followed; Transatlantic soon crumbled under its own weight. But *STRANGERS ON A TRAIN* at WARNER BROS. marked a return to form, and with *REAR WINDOW*—whose villain, Hitchcock colleague NORMAN LLOYD suggested, also bore a more-than-coincidental resemblance to a certain movie mogul—Hitchcock regained his stride.

Selznick never did. His last commercial success as a producer, the overheated *Duel in the Sun*, was released before he parted ways with Hitchcock; after the split, his projects grew further apart, more problematic, and increasingly primarily devoted to second-wife Jennifer Jones's career: *Portrait of Jennie*, *Gone to Earth* (which he then re-edited and re-released as the equally disappointing *The Wild Heart*), *Indiscretion of an American Wife*, and *A Farewell to Arms*.

When in 1965 the Producers Guild gave Hitchcock a testimonial dinner, Selznick—who had not made a movie in eight years—was invited to speak. Although introduced wittily by his old employee—Hitchcock JOKED that he was going to turn one of Selznick's gargantuan old memos into its own movie, *The Longest Story Ever Told*—Selznick used his time at the podium to complain endlessly about the current state of the industry. He sounded tired and bitter. He sounded, Garson Kanin said later, "like a man who was dying." Three months later, Selznick had a fatal heart attack in his lawyer's office in Los Angeles. He was 63.

"Not half a dozen men have been able to keep the whole equation of pictures in their heads," F. Scott Fitzgerald wrote in *The Last Tycoon*. He was talking about his main character, boy-wonder producer Monroe Stahr (and Irving Thalberg, the character's true inspiration). But if he wasn't also thinking about the man who'd briefly brought him on for *Gone with the Wind* rewrites, then he should have been. Few knew more about the movies than David O. Selznick—and no one was less able to keep it to himself.

References

Rudy Behlmer, ed., *Memo from David O. Selznick* (New York: Viking Press, 1972), 259–71, 336, 407; Ingrid Bergman and Alan Burgess, *My Story* (New York: Delacorte Press, 1980), 151; "David O. Selznick," *IMDb*, http://www.imdb.com/name/nm0006388/bio?ref_=nm_ov_bio_sm; "David O. Selznick, Producer of 'Gone with the Wind,' Dies," *New York Times*, June 23, 1965, http://www.nytimes.com/learning/general/onthisday/bday/0510.html; "Hitchcock to Direct Three American Films," *Dundee Evening Telegraph*, March 17, 1939, http://the.hitchcock.zone/wiki/Dundee%20Evening%20Telegraph%20%2817%2FMar%2F1939%29%20-%20Hitchcock%20to%20Direct%20Three%20American%20Films; "Ingrid Bergman," *IMDb*, http://www.imdb.com/name/nm0000006/bio?ref_=nm_ov_bio_sm; Norman Lloyd, interviews with the author, November 2007, July 2015; Patrick McGilligan, *Alfred Hitchcock: A Life in Darkness and Light* (New York: HarperCollins, 2003), 277–78, 301, 369; Donald Spoto, *The Dark Side of Genius: The Life of Alfred Hitchcock* (New York: Da Capo Press, 1999), 168–80, 277–78, 293–99; Bob Thomas, *Selznick* (New York: Pocket Books, 1972), 251, 302–3; David Thomson, *The New Biographical Dictionary of Film* (New York: Knopf, 2002), 796–98; François Truffaut, *Hitchcock/Truffaut*, rev. ed. (New York: Touchstone, 1985), 127, 165, 173.

SETS

Like so much of what went into his films, Hitchcock's sets serve two purposes, sometimes simultaneously, sometimes alternately—the creation of a plausibly real world and the illustration of the sometimes surreal things that happen within it.

Much as he enjoyed the work of the German EXPRESSIONISTS as a young man, Hitchcock had no abiding interest in re-creating the mad, nightmarish world of *The Cabinet of Dr. Caligari*—outside of the dream sequence in *SPELLBOUND*. His sets were usually rooted in a kind of hyperreality; if circumstances prohibited filming in a real LOCATION (or if, simply, the big-studio style at the time mandated a soundstage), then what Hitchcock put onscreen would look more like the real thing than the thing itself.

Interiors of famous locations, from the Old Bailey to the United Nations to Ernie's in San Francisco, were studiously documented and then later re-created to perfect scale at the studio for *THE PARADINE CASE, NORTH BY NORTHWEST*, and *VERTIGO*. Locations that did allow for a camera crew—the New York City settings of *THE WRONG MAN*, Washington landmarks for *STRANGERS ON A TRAIN*, a flower market for *TO CATCH A THIEF*—were carefully picked and prepped. The right location brought the audience into the story.

Into the character, too. What sort of apartment would a retired San Francisco detective have? What might a bohemian, middle-class West Village apartment complex look like? All of this was researched before a frame of *Vertigo* or *REAR WINDOW* was ever shot, and the ensuing realism brought the audience into these characters' lives, too; the slightly stuffy furnishings of the Newton house in *SHADOW OF A DOUBT*, the portraits of the dead father in the Brenner living room in *THE BIRDS*, and Lina's new home in *SUSPICION* say more about those families than an entire paragraph of dialogue could.

Sets served other purposes, too. In single-setting films like *ROPE* and *LIFEBOAT* (and, to some extent, *Rear Window* and *DIAL M FOR MURDER*), it was important that the backgrounds be, if not busy, then at least interesting; if we were going to be largely stuck in a single apartment, then it was important that, as the camera panned about, there were things—broken cameras, framed pictures—to catch our eyes and

convey information. And of course, the sets themselves had to be made practical—walls on wheels and disappearing furniture, so that the particularly bulky COLOR (and, for *Dial M for Murder*, 3-D) cameras could roam freely.

But apart from conveying a realistic sense of place and feeling for character and adding interest to the frame—all while allowing a major studio camera crew to move about—Hitchcock's sets could break with reality, too, using those old Expressionist tricks to convey a feeling or a mood.

It isn't logical that the first-floor ceiling of the house in *THE LODGER* would suddenly turn to plate glass—but it allowed Hitchcock to show the nervous pacing of the man upstairs. It makes little architectural sense for the doorknobs to be placed as high as they are in Manderley in *REBECCA*—but it quietly underlined the idea of the heroine as a child playing at being a grownup. The vast emptiness of the final jail cell in *PSYCHO*, the lack of any courtroom sets at all in *Dial M for Murder*—these aren't realistic choices. But they immediately help us focus on the single, abandoned character in the camera's eye. And they help Hitchcock do what he always said every director's primary job was: to fill the screen with emotion.

References

Patrick McGilligan, *Alfred Hitchcock: A Life in Darkness and Light* (New York: HarperCollins, 2003), 390, 533–34, 553–55; George Perry, "Hitchcock on Location," *American Heritage* (April 2007), http://the.hitchcock.zone/wiki/American_Heritage_%282007%29_-_Hitchcock_on_Location; Donald Spoto, *The Dark Side of Genius: The Life of Alfred Hitchcock* (New York: Da Capo Press, 1999), 70, 258–59, 325, 347; Joseph A. Valentine, "Using an Actual Town Instead of Movie Sets," *American Cinematographer* (October 1942), http://the.

hitchcock.zone/wiki/American_Cinematog
rapher_%281942%29_-_Using_an_Actual
_Town_Instead_of_Movie_Sets.

SEXUALITY

Born at the end of the Victorian age, raised
in an Irish CATHOLIC family, and given
a religious education that stressed temptation, sin, GUILT, and punishment, Hitchcock entered adulthood knowing very little
about sex and having experienced even less.

Called upon to write the screenplay for
WOMAN TO WOMAN at 24, he struggled
with its romantic melodrama of single
motherhood and lost love; "I'd never been
with a woman," Hitchcock said later, "and I
didn't have the slightest idea what a woman
did to have a child." When at 26 he was
shooting *THE PLEASURE GARDEN* and
didn't know why an "indisposed" actress
couldn't get in the water one day, someone
had to explain what menstruation was.

According to several sources, after the
birth of his daughter, Hitchcock's sex life
was basically one of abstinence, with actual
relations complicated by his obesity and,
finally, chronic impotence. Yet his interest
never waned. Late in life, Hitchcock himself recounted various tales of visiting a pair
of lesbian exhibitionists in 1920s Germany
(Hitchcock drank cognac and observed),
mentioned an "accidental" trip to a bordello (his wife in tow), and enthusiastically
recommended a Parisian museum of vice.
Like so many of his characters, he liked to
watch.

Certainly the odd pairing of Alfred
and ALMA REVILLE—one a somewhat
prissy gargantuan, the other a gamine in
custom-made men's suits—must have
occasionally raised an eyebrow, too, if not
outright questions about their own private
arrangements. Writer SAMSON RAPHA-
ELSON, who had worked amiably on *SUS-
PICION* with both of them, couldn't help
once sharply remarking about the vision

of "this odd, weird, little faggish man and
this sweet little boyish woman." Yet the two
were definitely, powerfully linked, although
whether Hitchcock worshipped her or was
DOMINATED by her is one issue biographers are still arguing over.

According to his movies, at least,
Hitchcock's own sexual interests seemed
to lie in icy BLONDES with shapely legs,
although his films also regularly touched
on such specific predilections as VOYEUR-
ISM or BONDAGE. (Asked on the set of
REAR WINDOW why he was taking such
care to shoot a close-up of GRACE KEL-
LY's feet, which would never appear in the
movie, he responded, "Haven't you ever
heard of the shoe FETISH?") The clichés of
postwar erotica—busty actresses who wore
sex "like a necklace"—left him unmoved.
Meanwhile Hitchcock's view of the sex act
itself was complex, fueled by lust and guilt,
complicated by religious prohibitions and
physical difficulties. "He was as intrigued
by varieties of sexual life and conduct as he
was by the varieties of moviemaking—in
fact, he was like a child who's just discovered sex and thinks it's all very naughty,"
ARTHUR LAURENTS wrote in his memoirs. "He thought everyone was doing
something physical and nasty behind every
closed door—except himself: he withdrew,
he wouldn't be part of it." Perhaps because
he recognized its power.

Hitchcock's films are full of sex and
sexual variations (or at least as much as he
could sneak past the CENSORS); they feature gay men and lesbians, cross-dressing,
promiscuity, adultery, and barely sublimated Oedipal urges—in addition to the
usual, garden-variety assortment of combative courtships and unhappy and unful-
filling marriages. But what they share is a
firm belief that sex is its own, life-changing
force—and that it can be a powerful and
destructive weapon in the hands of those
who wield it.

It's shown, most obviously, in his many films about sex crimes, starting with *THE LODGER* and going on to include obvious examples like *SHADOW OF A DOUBT*, *PSYCHO*, and *FRENZY* (and making room for less obvious sex criminals, like Mark, the hero—and marital rapist—of *MARNIE*). These are men driven by fetishes but often mostly by fury—a fury that, in *Psycho* and *Frenzy* at least, has its roots in smothering, sexualized relationships with their own MOTHERS.

But in Hitchcock's films, if men wield sex like an axe, often blundering about and inevitably bringing about only their own deaths, then his female characters employ it like a stiletto. *REBECCA* seduced everyone around her—her husband, her maid, her cousin, the family business advisor—and, even after her death, still holds them in her thrall. At first, in *NOTORIOUS*, Alicia used sex as a sedative for herself and a punishment against her father—but soon deploys it more carefully to ensnare Alex Sebastian in a lie of a marriage.

Yet her attraction to Devlin ensnares her, too, trapping her in an unequal, even masochistic, relationship because this is the power that sex has—we can use it against others, but if we're not careful in how we wield it, then its sharp edge can draw our blood, too. Think of Maddalena, whose calm beauty has drawn in Anthony Keane—but who, herself, is emotionally enslaved to her husband's valet in *THE PARADINE CASE*. Or of Judy in *VERTIGO*, who is the pretty bait in the trap that's been set for Scottie—but soon becomes ensnared herself.

Sex can cloud our judgment, bind us to partners in ways that are unhealthy for both—a situation, interestingly, that Hitchcock mostly explores with his HOMOSEXUAL (albeit closeted) characters. Would Philip have joined in the murder in *ROPE* if he weren't in love with the domineering Brandon? Would Guy have gone through with his crime in *STRANGERS ON A TRAIN* if he hadn't so quickly, obviously been eager to impress Guy? And what of Mrs. Danvers and her besotted worship of her mistress? Wasn't the spark for Danvers's final, mad act of arson struck the very first time her heart began to burn for Rebecca?

But this is what sex does to us—clouds our judgment, blunts our logic, leads us to martyred selflessness and senseless self-destruction. It's a primal, powerful force, and while the villains and villainesses of Hitchcock can manage it for a while, turning that energy against others, Hitchcock's heroes and heroines almost always succumb.

Think of Lina in *Suspicion*, convinced that her husband is a murderer and yet too in love to stop him. Or of Marion in *Psycho*, so desperate for Sam Loomis that she not only sneaks away for tawdry trysts but also is willing to risk prison to finance their life together. Or Anthony in *The Paradine Case* or Scottie in *Vertigo*, basically destroying their reputations, even perhaps their lives, because of their pull toward an enigmatic other. Because this is what it does. Sex blinds you. Sex wrecks you. Sex can even kill you.

No wonder that Hitchcock, as Laurents suggested, preferred to keep it shut behind a door—except for those times when he would briefly take it out and look at it in the light from a projector.

References

Patrick McGilligan, *Alfred Hitchcock: A Life in Darkness and Light* (New York: HarperCollins, 2003), 280; Donald Spoto, *The Dark Side of Genius: The Life of Alfred Hitchcock* (New York: Da Capo Press, 1999), 304–5, 348; François Truffaut, *Hitchcock/Truffaut*, rev. ed. (New York: Touchstone, 1985), 29, 34, 39, 78–80.

SHADOW OF A DOUBT (US 1943)

DIRECTOR: Alfred Hitchcock.
SCREENPLAY: Thornton Wilder, Sally Benson, Alma Reville, Gordon McDonnell.
PRODUCER: Jack H. Skirball.
CINEMATOGRAPHY: Joseph Valentine.
EDITOR: Milton Carruth.
ORIGINAL MUSIC: Dmitri Tiomkin.
CAST: Joseph Cotten (Charles Oakley), Teresa Wright (Charlotte "Charlie" Newton), Patricia Collinge (Emma Newton), Henry Travers (Joseph Newton), Hume Cronyn (Herbie Hawkins), Macdonald Carey (Jack Graham), Wallace Ford (Fred Saunders).
RUNNING TIME: 108 minutes. Black and white.
RELEASED THROUGH: RKO.

Charles Oakley is a serial killer, STRANGLING wealthy older women and pocketing their jewels—but when the police begin to close in, he flees his cheap Newark, NJ, rooming house and heads west to Santa Rosa, CA, to visit his unsuspecting sister and her family. There, he's welcomed as a favorite—particularly by his namesake niece, Charlotte "Charlie" Newton, who sees him as a bright, beautiful burst of excitement in her dull, small-town life.

He's soon followed to Santa Rosa by two detectives, however, who, posing as census takers, start interviewing and photographing this "typical American family." When Charlie learns that they're really investigating her uncle, she's outraged—then concerned when she realizes he has one of the victim's rings. When, over a casual family dinner, he goes on a rant about women as "fat, wheezing animals," she realizes he's not the eccentric charmer she thought he was.

Knowing that Charles's arrest would kill her emotionally fragile mother, Charlie resists helping the detectives, urging her uncle to simply leave town—but when another suspect is killed trying to escape, he decides there's no longer any need to run. After she insists, he attempts to kill her—once by sawing through a step on a steep staircase, another time by locking her in a garage filling up with carbon monoxide.

Charlie survives both attempts, and when Charles realizes she will now go to the detectives—with the ring as evidence—he announces his intention to leave town. As Charlie is on the train saying goodbye, though, he grabs her, intending to push her off and under the tracks. He slips instead and is killed by an oncoming train—and his body later returned to Santa Rosa, where he's given a big sentimental funeral, while Charlie and the chief detective stand in the back of the church, alone in the truth.

Hitchcock's own favorite and one of his very best.

He was looking for a project after *SABOTEUR* and was at first uncertain. DAVID O. SELZNICK's office suggested an adaptation of *Gaslight*, but Hitchcock passed, and that eventually went to George Cukor, who made it with INGRID BERGMAN (although Hitchcock would later work through the same material somewhat with Bergman in his own period drama, *UNDER CAPRICORN*). Several JOHN BUCHAN novels were suggested and batted around, including *GREENMANTLE*; Hitchcock, in turn, mentioned an idea he had for a story about a mad ventriloquist, which Selznick was not enthusiastic about.

Finally, Hitchcock came back with something provisionally called *Uncle Charlie* from writer Gordon McDonnell, the husband of a Selznick story editor. This was readily approved, albeit as a loan-out project for UNIVERSAL, and Hitchcock began working on a treatment with THORNTON WILDER, the esteemed author of *Our Town*. When Wilder was called away by the army—he ended up serving three years in intelligence in Africa and Italy—Hitchcock finished the screenplay with Sally Benson and ALMA REVILLE.

Benson—who had just published the *New Yorker* stories that would become *Meet Me in St. Louis*—added to the small-town touches that Hitchcock felt so important to the story, a picture that, following *Saboteur*, would help establish him as a truly American director. For more verisimilitude, he insisted on shooting on LOCATION in Santa Rosa (although the interiors were later done on a Hollywood soundstage).

As Uncle Charlie, the murderous misogynist who covers it all with good manners and natty clothes, Hitchcock had originally thought of William Powell (whom he'd once suggested for *REBECCA*), but the actor was unavailable. JOSEPH COTTEN, whom Selznick had under contract anyway, became a similar outside-the-box choice; TERESA WRIGHT played his opposite number, his adoring niece Charlotte. MACDONALD CAREY played the dull policeman, while veterans PATRICIA COLLINGE and HENRY TRAVERS played Charlotte's parents, and new Hitchcock confidante HUME CRONYN played their neighbor. A local girl, Edna May Wonacott, played Charlotte's bratty sister; she was the child of a local grocer, whose store reminded Hitchcock of his father's.

It's possible that the bespectacled, skinny little girl reminded him a little of his own daughter, too; family was on Hitchcock's mind a great deal at this time, as just before filming began, he received word that his mother, Emma, already in ill health, had gotten worse. Wartime restrictions and studio obligations made a trip home to see her nearly impossible; she died while the film was still being shot. She was 78. Work was perhaps a welcome distraction from her death; certainly the film shows his complete and utter focus.

In a difficult part, Cotten's performance is precise, easily turning from airy charm to baleful menace; his very controlled, utterly cold monologue on wealthy older women is chilling, its final shot of the actor breaking the fourth wall and turning to stare directly at us, as sharp and cold as an icicle. And so it is perfectly right that his DOUBLE, Wright—playing his "twin" but also his reversed, mirror image—should be so warm and easy, all soft edges and gentle, slightly MOTHERLY concern.

And perhaps the most delicate performance at all comes from Collinge, playing the mother, Emma—named perhaps after Hitchcock's own mother. "He never brought personal things into movies," his daughter protested years later in a documentary on a *Shadow of a Doubt* DVD. "This is what everybody doesn't realize. Everything came from his imagination." And it's said that many friends called Hitchcock's mother "Emily," anyway.

Yet no matter how personal it was, what he and his screenwriters imagined here was both touching and, for Hollywood movies, ahead of its time—the character of a woman who used to be a laughing girl, who used to be full of fun, but now "works like a dog," Charlotte worries. "Just like a dog." A woman who distracts herself with recipes and her women's club but can't quite escape the sense that she's lost something. Her errant brother, yes. But perhaps herself, as well, after marriage and motherhood. "You sort of forget you're you," she starts to say once, but then the camera cuts away. Those who wish to make an argument for Hitchcock as feminist should begin here, with Emma Newton.

Strong as all the characters are—perhaps the most complex of this period, along with those of *NOTORIOUS*—Hitchcock never forgets the visual or loses sight of his metaphors. Santa Rosa is a slow, even static, place, where most things stay the same, so forms of transportation represent not only motion but also literal engines of change. Uncle Charlie arrives on a TRAIN belching black smoke and gains a brief reprieve when the police's other likely suspect is killed running headlong into an airplane propeller; a train not only provides Charlie's final escape but also, he hopes, a way of eliminating his own threat, Charlotte.

Shadow of a Doubt is also, like so many Hitchcock films, a story about IDENTITY—not only the misplaced one of Emma Newton but also the shared one of Charlie and Charlotte. It's in their names, of course; it's also in their posture. (The film begins with nearly matching sequences of them both lying alone in their separate bedrooms, a continent apart, their arms above their heads.) "We're like twins," Uncle Charlie tells her; later, he'll take her to the Till Two bar and order two double brandies.

"It might seem easy to read too much into Hitchcock films but you can always prove it," Wright mused decades later over his use of symbolism. "It's always so, and I don't think it's ever an accident."

But the two characters are linked by more than that, too. Eventually, Charlotte finds out about her uncle's crimes and shrinks from him in disgust. But buried underneath that disgust, is there a bit of recognition, as well? The way he talks about the world—as a place full of "swine," of unthinking animals—isn't far from how she talks about her own disgustingly dull family. ("We eat and sleep and that's about all.") He breaks the law because he doesn't think it applies to him, but she's willing to break the law, too, and let a serial killer escape. Special rules for special people.

Shadow of a Doubt is the title, but the film has shadows, too, and that's part of its brilliance. It's easy to accept Santa Rosa as Hitchcock's idealized version of small-town America; complete with stern spinster librarian and overprotective cop, it's like a dry run for Frank Capra's *It's a Wonderful Life*. Yet on a second viewing, you realize it doesn't need a magic spell to turn into Pottersville; its dark side is right there, just barely hidden.

Look again at slatternly Louise Finch, who's been fired from restaurants all over town and now waits tables at the sleazy Till Two; watch Charlotte's painfully plain friend Catherine and how avidly she runs her EYES up and down every man she meets. What do they do when they're not at work or church? And what of Herb, the twitchy middle-aged bachelor who still lives with his mother and immerses himself in true-crime stories and murder fantasies? What happens when he draws the shades? Santa Rosa's innocence is as sweet—and about as deep—as the icing on a wedding cake. Yes, you can see why Uncle Charlie likes this town.

References

Beyond Doubt: The Making of Hitchcock's Favorite Film, directed by Laurent Bouzereau (2000), documentary, http://the.hitchcock.zone/wiki/Beyond_Doubt:_The_Making_of_Hitchcock's_Favorite_Film_%282000%29_-_transcript; Gaye Lebaron, "Film That Put Santa Rosa on the Map," *Press Democrat*, March 28, 2009, http://www.pressdemocrat.com/csp/mediapool/sites/PressDemocrat/News/story.csp?cid=2269915&sid=555&fid=181; Patrick McGilligan, *Alfred Hitchcock: A Life in Darkness and Light* (New York: HarperCollins, 2003), 306–21; Donald Spoto, *The Dark Side of Genius: The Life of Alfred Hitchcock* (New York: Da Capo Press, 1999), 256–62; François Truffaut, *Hitchcock/Truffaut*, rev. ed. (New York: Touchstone, 1985), 151–55; Joseph A. Valentine, "Using an Actual Town Instead of Movie Sets," *American Cinematographer* (October 1942), http://the.hitchcock.zone/wiki/American_Cinema

tographer_%281942%29_-_Using_an
_Actual_Town_Instead_of_Movie_Sets.

SHAFFER, ANTHONY
(1926–2001)

Liverpool-born writer who, after graduating Cambridge with a law degree, began
writing whodunits with his twin brother
Peter, published under the pen name "Peter
Anthony." Later turning to plays, he had an
enormous success with the clever mystery
Sleuth; although the first film Shaffer wrote,
Mr. Forbush and the Penguins, was a disaster, Hitchcock hired him to work on the
London-set *FRENZY*, seen as a return not
only to Hitchcock's birthplace but also the
film *THE LODGER*, which had established
him as the "Master of Suspense."

"It was a film he really had to do,"
Shaffer said later. "He had lost some of his
self-confidence, and he had no interest in
politics. Spy thrillers were out of the question because of the recent failures he'd had
but he seemed to have this excited interest
in bizarre SEXUAL crimes. So this rather
grim story of a rapist-STRANGLER was
perhaps inevitable."

After the film's success, Shaffer would
go on to adapt *Sleuth* for the movies (the
film, coincidentally, to costar Michael
Caine, who had turned down *Frenzy*, and
LAURENCE OLIVIER, who had reviled
Shaffer's original play as a "piece of piss")
and write the original script for the much-
lauded horror film *The Wicker Man*. Shaffer's successful adaptation of Agatha Christie's novel *Murder on the Orient Express*
typed him a bit; he would eventually adapt
three more Christie books for the screen.

Still, it was brother Peter Shaffer—who
wrote the plays *Equus*, *The Royal Hunt of
the Sun*, *Five Finger Exercise*, and *Ama-
deus*—who always drew most of the critical kudos; Anthony's work was often called
clever, but his works tended to be dismissed
as "just entertainment," a charge at which

he bristled. "What do you mean 'just'?" he
demanded once. "It's a bloody sight harder
to entertain than to bore."

He died in London at 75.

References
Nigel Fountain, "Anthony Shaffer,"
Guardian, November 7, 2011, http://www
.theguardian.com/news/2001/nov/08/
guardianobituaries.nigelfountain; Paul
Lewis, "Anthony Shaffer, 75, Author of
Long-Running 'Sleuth,' Dies," *New York
Times*, November 12, 2011, http://www
.nytimes.com/2001/11/12/theater/anthony
-shaffer-75-author-of-long-running-sleuth
-dies.html; Donald Spoto, *The Dark Side of
Genius: The Life of Alfred Hitchcock* (New
York: Da Capo Press, 1999), 509.

SHAYNE, KONSTANTIN
(1888–1974)

Ukraine-born actor from a family of writers and performers. After fighting a losing war against the Bolsheviks, like many
other White Russians, he went into exile,
eventually arriving in America, where—at
age 50—he made his Hollywood debut.
After five years of small parts in B movies, he began to land slightly larger roles in
better productions, including *Five Graves
to Cairo*, *None but the Lonely Heart*, *The
Secret Life of Walter Mitty*, and Orson
Welles's HITCHCOCKIAN *The Stranger*,
in which he plays the fugitive Nazi who
leads authorities to Welles's hiding place
in Connecticut. Television work followed
in the 1950s, including two episodes of
ALFRED HITCHCOCK PRESENTS;
Shayne's last film appearance was as Pop,
the bookseller and amateur historian in
VERTIGO. He died at 85 in Los Angeles.

References
"Konstantin Shayne," *IMDb*, http://
www.imdb.com/name/nm0790164/
bio?ref_=nm_ov_bio_sm; "Konstantin

Shayne: Biography," *Hollywood*, http://www.hollywood.com/celebrities/konstantin-shayne-59056412.

SHERWOOD, ROBERT E. (1896–1955)

Born in New Rochelle, NY, the son of a stockbroker and a well-known illustrator, Sherwood went to Harvard and then to war before returning to become a Manhattan journalist. By the '20s, he was reviewing movies for the first incarnations of *Life* and *Vanity Fair* and, before the end of the decade, was a successful playwright. He would win three Pulitzer Prizes for drama (a fourth for biography); his hits, many adapted into movies, included *Idiot's Delight*, *The Petrified Forest*, *Abe Lincoln in Illinois*, and *Waterloo Bridge* and often revolved around historical crises and social injustices.

Sherwood's first movie job was rewriting some of the titles for the Lon Chaney *The Hunchback of Notre Dame* in 1923; later, he would turn out the screenplays for the charming *The Ghost Goes West* with ROBERT DONAT, as well as *The Bishop's Wife* and William Wyler's powerful *The Best Years of Our Lives*, for which he won the ACADEMY AWARD. He also received credit for *REBECCA*, although that was largely a matter of DAVID O. SELZNICK trading on a famous name; reportedly Sherwood's largest contribution to the script was finding a way to work around the CENSORS' objections by making Rebecca's death an accident rather than a murder.

Sherwood left Hollywood shortly thereafter to work for the war effort and write speeches for Roosevelt; he returned to plays and screenplays afterward and died in New York at 59 of a heart attack.

References

Patrick McGilligan, *Alfred Hitchcock: A Life in Darkness and Light* (New York: Harper-Collins, 2003), 242; "Robert E. Sherwood," *Encyclopaedia Britannica*, http://www.britannica.com/biography/Robert-E-Sherwood; "Robert E. Sherwood," *IBDb*, http://ibdb com/person.php?id=8367; "Robert E. Sherwood," *IMDb*, http://www.imdb.com/name/nm0792845/bio?ref_=nm_ov_bio_sm.

THE SHORT NIGHT

One of Hitchcock's longest-gestating projects—although eventually stillborn. Plans for *The Short Night* began in 1968, when Hitchcock bought the rights to the novel by Ronald Kirkbride. Based on the prison escape of the British double agent George Blake (Hitchcock later purchased the rights to a nonfiction account of the case as well), it would be a story about treachery and deceit, a part of espionage that had fascinated Hitchcock since the defection of British spy Kim Philby in 1963.

Although Hitchcock went so far as to scout some LOCATIONS in Finland—where the bulk of the film was to be set—and discuss the script with *TOPAZ* writer SAMUEL A. TAYLOR, after the failure of that spy film, Hitchcock decided not to tackle yet another espionage picture and eventually ended up going back to the beginnings of his career and *THE LODGER*, with a story about another London serial killer in *FRENZY*.

After finishing *FAMILY PLOT*, though, Hitchcock—having briefly considered an Elmore Leonard novel, *Unknown Man No. 89*—decided to revive *The Short Night*, and in 1977, it was announced as his next film. For the rest of that year—and well into the next—preproduction continued, with EDITH HEAD, ROBERT F. BOYLE, and ALBERT WHITLOCK all reporting for duty. Yet the script never worked, even as four different writers—James Costigan, ERNEST LEHMAN, NORMAN LLOYD, and David Freeman—took their turns in the chair opposite the increasingly distracted director, going over ideas and then later trying to turn them into pages.

Costigan didn't last long. Lehman endured for a while but confessed the whole process "has bad memories for me. It's something I prefer to forget. We had a number of arguments about it. He wanted the hero to rape a woman at the beginning of the picture. . . . I just refused to do it. I've always wondered why he insisted on that."

It was like the fights with EVAN HUNTER over the SEXUAL assault in *MARNIE*, and after being denied by a writer once again, Hitchcock turned to someone he probably felt would be more compliant—this time, longtime collaborator Lloyd, whom he'd known for 35 years and who had helped produce both of his TV series. But after three months, Lloyd hadn't made any headway and advised the director to move on to something else. Hitchcock moved on to yet another screenwriter instead.

Freeman was young, with only a few credits. (He would eventually go on to write *Street Smart* and *The Border*.) Perhaps he suggested the combination of energy and malleability Hitchcock needed at that junction; certainly the director wanted no more arguments over the rape with which he was determined to start the picture. But work progressed fitfully, as Hitchcock seemed to spend most of his time reminiscing about the past and downing "brandy by the beakerful," as Freeman later wrote. Finally, after five months, they had a script.

But Hitchcock was growing increasingly frail; his wife was already basically an invalid. The idea that he could rally to direct a picture—let alone one that still called for location work in Scandinavia—was beginning to resemble the sort of fantasy even his own films couldn't make plausible. Finally, in the spring of 1979, Hitchcock himself realized the physical

effort of filmmaking was at last beyond him. He told LEW WASSERMAN he was retiring—actually, still shrinking from any overt emotional engagement, he asked someone else to relay the message—and gave orders for the office to be packed up and his personal effects moved to his home.

He was dead within a year.

References

"North by Northwest," *Creative Screenwriting* (November 2000), http://the.hitchcock.zone/wiki/Creative_Screenwriting_%282000%29_-_%22North_by_Northwest%22:_An_Interview_with_Ernest_Lehman; Donald Spoto, *The Dark Side of Genius: The Life of Alfred Hitchcock* (New York: Da Capo Press, 1999), 509, 537–38, 541–44, 732–34, 742.

SIDNEY, SYLVIA (1910–1999)

Bronx-born performer, the daughter of a seamstress and a clothing salesman. Her parents divorced when she was five, and her mother later married a dentist, who adopted her. Sylvia, a bashful teenager with a stutter, took some acting classes as a way of overcoming her shyness; she began appearing in plays and at 16 was discovered by a Hollywood talent scout.

Her first important film was the proto-Hollywood gangster film *City Streets* in 1931; it was followed by *Fury* and *You Only Live Once* for FRITZ LANG, and William Wyler's *Dead End*. In between the last two films, and a little tired of the parts being offered, she went to London to do *SABOTAGE*; English studios were convinced Hollywood STARS broadened their box office, and SIR MICHAEL BALCON had jumped at the chance to sign her.

Yet Sidney, who had trained as a theater actress, didn't understand Hitchcock's PURE CINEMA of quick cuts and contrasting images; it seemed abrupt even by Hollywood standards, a new kind of direction in which the actor became just another prop. She had to admit, once she saw the famous kitchen sequence in which she stabs her husband, that it worked; still, she said, "It was all Hitchcock. It had nothing to do with people acting."

"She could not piece together in her mind what Hitchcock was after," producer IVOR MONTAGU remembered. "She had always acted a scene right through, and she badly needed words, a single sentence or even a phrase, to start a mood off for her, as a singer needs a note to find the key."

Sidney returned to Hollywood but continued to buck at the parts she was given, complaining the studios always cast her as the "girl of the gangster, then the sister who was bringing up the gangster, then later the mother of the gangster, and they always had me ironing somebody's shirt." She brought real life to those people—a real wounded sense that happiness was fleeting and life was fragile—but she was also said to be difficult to work with, and from 1956 to 1973, she made no films at all.

She worked on television, though, and in 1973 won an Oscar nomination for her comeback movie role in *Summer Wishes, Winter Dreams*; her last movie was in *Mars Attacks!* in 1996, and two years later, she notched her last TV job, joining the cast of the reboot of *Fantasy Island*. Working until the end, the diminutive actress smoked like a fiend, turned out endless works of needlepoint (she wrote two books on the craft), and told Hollywood exactly what she thought of it; she died at 88 from esophageal cancer in New York.

References

Hillel Italie, "Hollywood Queen: Actress Sylvia Sidney, 80, Recalls Full Career," *Kitchener-Waterloo Record*, November 28, 1990, http://the.hitchcock.zone/wiki/Kitchener-Waterloo_Record_%2828/Nov/1990%29_-_A_Hollywood_queen_Actress_Sylvia_Sidney,_80,_recalls_full_career; Patrick McGilligan, *Alfred Hitchcock: A Life in Darkness and Light* (New York: HarperCollins, 2003), 187–90; Donald Spoto, *The Dark Side of Genius: The Life of Alfred Hitchcock* (New York: Da Capo Press, 1999), 156; Alyssa Gallin Steinberg, "Sylvia Sidney," *Jewish Women's Archive*, http://jwa.org/encyclopedia/article/sidney-sylvia; "Sylvia Sidney," *IMDb*, http://www.imdb.com/name/nm0796662/bio?ref_=nm_ov_bio_sm; "Sylvia Sidney, '30s Film Heroine, Dies at 88," *New York Times*, July 2, 1999, http://www.nytimes.com/1999/07/02/movies/sylvia-sidney-30-s-film-heroine-dies-at-88.html.

SIM, ALASTAIR (1900–1976)

Edinburgh-born performer whose parents were a tailor and a country girl who, at first, spoke only Gaelic. The daydreaming Alastair was a marked disappointment to his father. ("Mark my words, that boy will end up on the gallows," was frequently heard in the family's rooms above the shop.) When Sim announced that, rather than continuing with his college studies in chemistry, he was becoming an actor, he was turned out of the house.

Sim eventually became a teacher, instead, with a specialty in elocution—he would later be hailed as having one of the British theater's most resonant and distinctive voices—even opening a drama school for children. (Years after his death, tabloid rumors surfaced about the real nature of his mentorship of young performers; undeniable was the fact that he married one of his young pupils as soon as she turned 18. They remained married until his death.)

Finally, at the age of 30, Sim made his own stage debut. He was an understudy and a bit player in Paul Robeson's fabled production of *Othello* and, in a slightly more than year-long stint with the Old Vic, drew admiring notices for his skill with the classics, particularly his Claudius in *HAMLET*. Sim was only 32 by then, but already balding and with a natural gravity (which he was happy to tweak and tease for comedy's sake), he became a valuable supporting player, frequently playing figures of somewhat dubious authority.

He had fine film roles in *Green for Danger* and *The Belles of St. Trinians*; the latter had been meant to reunite him with a favored costar, Margaret Rutherford, but when she had to bow out, he took on her role, too, in drag. (Similarly, when he turned down the lead in *The Ladykillers*, Alec Guinness took it on—and played it as a rather mischievous impersonation of Sim, complete with lank hair and tatty cardigan.)

In 1950, Sim had a supporting role in Hitchcock's *STAGE FRIGHT*—playing the eccentric father of an actress and a sort of HITCHCOCKIAN stand-in—but his most indelible character came the next year in *Scrooge* (released in the United States as *A Christmas Carol*). It's a fully felt and beautifully cast film, down to the smallest part, and even the occasionally awkward special effects can't detract from what is not only one of Sim's best performances but also the best Scrooge ever put on the screen.

By the end of the '50s, the comfortably wry, terribly British films in which Sim made such an impression were being crowded out by movies about Teddy boys and angry young men; Sim made two pictures in 1960 and then didn't appear onscreen again until the blistering *The Ruling Class* in 1972. But he made occasional appearances on television, continued to work on the stage, and kept living as private a life as possible.

"It was revealed to me many years ago with conclusive certainty that I was a fool and that I had always been a fool," he observed once. "Since then I have been as happy as any man has a right to be."

He died in London of lung cancer at 75.

References

"Alastair Sim," *IMDb*, http://www.imdb.com/name/nm0799237/bio?ref_=nm_ov_bio_sm; Stephen Hopley, *Alastair Sim*, http://www.alastairsim.net; Geoffrey Wansell, "The Weirdo of St. Trinians," *Daily Mail*, June 30, 2008, http://www.dailymail.co.uk/tvshowbiz/article-1030063/The-Weirdo-Of-St-Trinians-New-book-claims-Alastair-Sim-scholarly-young-girls.html.

SIMPSON, HELEN DU GUERRY (1897–1940)

Sydney-born author from a prominent family whose works covered many genres—poetry, plays in blank verse, biographies, mysteries, historical dramas, and even a guide to home economics, *The Happy Housewife*. (She also decoded messages for the British Admiralty during World War I, studied music at Oxford, and was active in Australian politics.) *Boomerang* and *Saraband for Dead Lovers* were perhaps her best-received books, but *Enter Sir John*, one of three novels she cowrote with Clemence Dane, would serve as the basis for Hitchcock's *MURDER!* She also contributed some dialogue to *SABOTAGE*, and later, the director would adapt her novel *UNDER CAPRICORN*. She died of cancer in Worcestershire at 42.

References

"Helen Simpson," *IMDb*, http://www.imdb.com/name/nm0801026; Alan Roberts, "Helen du Guerry Simpson," *Australian Dictionary of Biography*, http://adb.anu.edu.au/biography/simpson-helen-de-guerry-8433.

THE SKIN GAME (GB 1931)

DIRECTOR: Alfred Hitchcock.
SCREENPLAY: Alfred Hitchcock and Alma Reville, based on the play by John Galsworthy.
PRODUCER: Uncredited (John Maxwell).
CINEMATOGRAPHY: Jack E. Cox.
EDITORS: A. Gobbett, R. Marrison.
ORIGINAL MUSIC: Uncredited.
CAST: C. V. France (Mr. Hillcrist), Helen Haye (Mrs. Hillcrist), Jill Esmond (Jill Hillcrist), Edmund Gwenn (Mr. Hornblower), John Longden (Charles Hornblower), Frank Lawton (Rolf Hornblower).
RUNNING TIME: 88 minutes. Black and white.
RELEASED THROUGH: Wardour Films.

In the bucolic British countryside, the newly rich Hornblower family has begun to assert their power by throwing tenant farmers off their land and making plans for modern, smoke-belching factories; the old-money Hillcrists are appalled but seem powerless to stop them, even as the Hornblowers begin buying up land near their own estate.

When the Hillcrists learn that Hornblowers' daughter-in-law has a past as a "professional correspondent" in drummed-up divorce cases, they threaten to expose her unless the Hornblowers sell them back the neighboring land. Mr. Hornblower reluctantly gives in to the blackmail.

The whispers have already begun, however, and realizing that his wife has been keeping a secret from him, the younger Hornblower announces his intention to divorce her. His pregnant wife drowns herself, and the once-arrogant Hornblower family stands tragically ruined—as the Hillcrists begin to wonder if they've only debased themselves.

"I didn't make it by choice," Alfred Hitchcock later told FRANÇOIS TRUFFAUT, dismissing *The Skin Game* some 30 years after he'd shot it. "There isn't much to be said about it." Loyal Hitchcock students might disagree.

Although in later life Hitchcock tended to devalue films he'd made outside his genre (as perhaps they tended to detract from his brand as the "Master of Suspense"), right into the 1940s, he had shown an openness to different sorts of films and approaches. This was particularly true during the first decade of his career in Britain, when he adapted a number of straight plays and seemed to have a particular fondness for romantic melodramas.

He was also an awed admirer of John Galsworthy and his play *The Skin Game*, which he had seen performed in London; while it's true that the film was an assignment from his bosses at BRITISH INTERNATIONAL PICTURES, and one he soon was bored with, it still has a number of striking effects, including Hitchcock's still-experimental use of sound (a traffic jam that becomes nothing but blowing horns—an aural pun on *Hornblower*; conversations that deliberately fade away into unimportant, inaudible rumbles).

The visuals are generally less interesting, with some flat and even awkward compositions. Yet there are also a few EXPRESSIONISTIC effects (as haunting images of angry faces or ugly factories appear before the characters' eyes). And an auction scene is also particularly well handled, with Hitchcock forgoing his usual MONTAGE effects in favor of swish pans, having his excited camera constantly moving from face to face as a bidding war breaks out.

The script and the cast definitely give Galsworthy's play a slightly more pointed, class-conscious emphasis, too, with EDMUND GWENN—who had already played the same part in a silent-movie version—investing Hornblower with a sort of crude vitality and C. V. France's gouty old Hillcrist appearing far more concerned with his own way of life than the tenant farmers whose hard work supports it.

The movie is stage bound and was perhaps fated to be; as the London *Times* observed on release, the "plot is too closely knit and the action too localized to make the best cinematographic material." But some of the strongest Hitchcock themes—upper-class cruelties, marriages built on deceit, "innocent" people who are nonetheless complicit in violence—are there to be seen, too.

Still, the film was a box-office disappointment, the first in a string of increasingly flat, early-'30s films—*RICH AND STRANGE, NUMBER 17, WALTZES FROM VIENNA*—that Hitchcock only finally broke free of in 1934 with *THE MAN WHO KNEW TOO MUCH*. And once he did break free of anything, as his conversations with Truffaut proved, he tried not to look back.

References

Patrick McGilligan, *Alfred Hitchcock: A Life in Darkness and Light* (New York: HarperCollins, 2003), 139–40; "New Films in London: The Skin Game," *Times*, May 4, 1931, http://the.hitchcock.zone/wiki/The_Times_%2804/May/1931%29_-_New_films_in_London:_The_Skin_Game; François Truffaut, *Hitchcock/Truffaut*, rev. ed. (New York: Touchstone, 1985), 77–78.

SKIRBALL, JACK H. (1896–1986)

Pennsylvania-born independent producer who served for years as a Reform rabbi and then began making documentary shorts in the early '30s. One of his first features was the 1940 *Birth of a Baby*, which went on to have a long life on the exploitation circuit in a variety of cut and recut versions.

Skirball's work as an associate producer on UNIVERSAL's *SABOTEUR* in 1942 was a small step down in title but a large step up in status; the next year

he would get full producer's credit on *SHADOW OF A DOUBT* and two years later would hire ALMA REVILLE to do the screenplay for *It's in the Bag!* a raucous Fred Allen comedy. (It would be Reville's last script for anyone but her husband.)

A longtime Hitchcock admirer—and always more of a mensch than a mogul—Skirball worked hard to make sure that the director, not DAVID O. SELZNICK, got any promised studio bonuses. Unfortunately, after his brief association with Hitchcock, Skirball began to quickly slide back into mostly undistinguished B pictures, a decline that continued until he pretty much retired in the mid-'50s to concentrate on real estate development; he came back for one more project, Vincente Minnelli's *A Matter of Time* in 1976.

Skirball died at 89 in Los Angeles.

References

"About Our Namesake," *Skirball Cultural Center*, http://www.skirball.org/about/about-our-namesake; "Jack H. Skirball," *IMDb*, http://www.imdb.com/name/nm0804382; Patrick McGilligan, *Alfred Hitchcock: A Life in Darkness and Light* (New York: HarperCollins, 2003), 284, 298–99, 306.

SLEZAK, WALTER (1902–1983)

Viennese-born performer, the son of an opera tenor, who made his movie debut in 1922 in the Austrian film *Sodom and Gomorrah* from director Michael Curtiz. He soon became a leading man, with many friends among Viennese society and a steady career in German film. Presciently, he left Germany in 1930 for America, where he became a popular musical comedy actor on Broadway, although his large appetites soon made leading-man parts less likely. By the end of the decade, he said, he had happily accepted his new role as a character actor.

"When I think of what leading men go through trying to look young and slim!" he exclaimed later. "I just said to myself, 'Aw, let it spread.' I got obese, married, fat and prosperous, in that order. I started playing nasty roles. With them, my disposition changed. I got fat and amiable."

By the early '40s, he was in Hollywood; an early nasty role was Willie, the German captain in *LIFEBOAT*. His eyes always alert in a baby face, a small, tight smile playing around his lips, Slezak creates a cold and cunning villain who remains truly formidable even though vastly outnumbered; the very careful, studied opposite to TALLULAH BANKHEAD's pampered, shallow Connie, he is in every way the force that drives the ship and the film. (Bankhead, no METHOD actress, nonetheless ended up conflating the actor and his role, berating him off set as a Nazi; Slezak, in self-imposed exile from Fascist Europe, bore it all with his own tolerant smile.)

Slezak would go on to play a number of villains, although there was often the touch of the outlandish about them; he was in *The Spanish Main* with Paul Henreid, *The Inspector General* with Danny Kaye, and the infamous *Bedtime for Bonzo* with Ronald Reagan. He returned to Broadway (and won a Tony) for *Fanny* in 1955 and remained active in TV throughout the '60s. Later, failing health made work and life more difficult; shortly before his 81st birthday, he committed suicide, shooting himself at his Long Island home.

References

Peter B. Flint, "Walter Slezak, Actor, Is a Suicide at 80 on Long Island," *New York Times*, April 23, 1983, http://www.nytimes.com/1983/04/23/obituaries/walter-slezak-actor-is-a-suicide-at-80-on-li.html; Patrick McGilligan, *Alfred Hitchcock: A Life in Darkness and Light* (New York: HarperCollins, 2003), 341–42; Alfred E. Twomey and Arthur F. McClure, *The Versatiles: Supporting Character Players in the Cinema, 1930–1955* (New York: Castle Books, 1969), 204; "Walter Slezak," *IBDb*, http://ibdb.com/person.php?id=60293; "Walter Slezak," *IMDb*, http://www.imdb.com/name/nm0805790/bio?ref_=nm_ov_bio_sm.

SMITH, C. AUBREY (1863–1948)

London-born performer, the son of a doctor, who went to Cambridge, prospected for gold in South Africa, and was a championship cricketer. Returning to England, he went on the stage in 1895, where one of his first important jobs was playing the hero (and his royal lookalike) in *The Prisoner of Zenda*. (Forty years later, playing one of the character roles in the Hollywood version, he dryly remarked, "In my time I have played every part in *The Prisoner of Zenda* except Princess Flavia.")

By the time he made his silent-movie debut in the late teens, Smith was already 55, yet he would have a remarkable 30 years ahead of him in films, much of them in America, where he would almost invariably play some stalwart symbol of British propriety and perseverance. Offscreen, he also served as the king's unofficial ambassador to Hollywood, where he founded a cricket club and mentored a younger generation of British actors, including David Niven, LAURENCE OLIVIER, and NIGEL BRUCE.

Dubbed THE ENGLISH COLONY or the "Hollywood Raj," the group served as a sort of microcosm of old-school, upper-class life in Los Angeles—a world in which the Hitchcocks had not moved easily even at home. Yet although he didn't turn out for their cricket games, Hitchcock did draw on the group's ranks when casting his first American pictures, particularly the very British *REBECCA*, *FOREIGN CORRESPONDENT*, and *SUSPICION*.

Smith played Col. Julyan in *Rebecca* and would go on to appear in the Spencer Tracy *Dr. Jekyll and Mr. Hyde*; *Flesh and Fantasy*; *And Then There Were None*; *Cluny Brown*; and his last film, the 1949 *Little Women*; although his range was narrow, his every screen appearance—with that huge, Easter Island head and see-here-now delivery—was strangely comforting. He died at 85 in Beverly Hills; his ashes were returned to England, the place he had never really left.

References

"C. Aubrey Smith," *IMDb*, http://www.imdb.com/name/nm0807580/bio?ref_=nm_ov_bio_sm; "The English Colony in Hollywood," *Sydney Morning Herald*, March 2, 1937, http://trove.nla.gov.au/ndp/del/article/17348532; Patrick McGilligan, *Alfred Hitchcock: A Life in Darkness and Light* (New York: HarperCollins, 2003), 243–44; Ken Robichaux, "C. Aubrey Smith: Hollywood's Resident Englishman," *Picture Show Man*, http://www.pictureshowman.com/articles_personalities_SirAubrey.cfm; Donald Spoto, *The Dark Side of Genius: The Life of Alfred Hitchcock* (New York: Da Capo Press, 1999), 210, 216; Alfred E. Twomey and Arthur F. McClure, *The Versatiles: Supporting Character Players in the Cinema, 1930–1955* (New York: Castle Books, 1969), 205.

SOUND

As someone who began in the silent cinema, image was always paramount to Hitchcock. Ideas, emotions, character—this was best conveyed visually, and he often complained that with the coming of sound, many filmmakers had forgotten how to tell a story through pictures.

"In many of the films now being made, there is very little cinema," he complained in the '60s. "They are mostly what I call 'photographs of people talking.' When we tell a story in cinema, we should resort to dialogue only when it's impossible to do otherwise." The idea, after all, was to make a film, not a radio show; if, as Hitchcock said another time, you could close your eyes and still follow a movie perfectly, then the director wasn't doing his job.

Yet as the consummate (and constantly improving) craftsman, Hitchcock was not going to ignore a new tool put before him simply because it was novel—once sound was available, he looked for ways to use it, not simply in a realistic way, but also as a way to fill the screen with emotion.

In *BLACKMAIL*, for example, the word *knife* becomes almost a leitmotif on the soundtrack; in *MURDER!* a voiceover narration serves as internal monologue. Sound meant far more than simple dialogue to Hitchcock; in fact, he often played with sound to show how unimportant someone's conversation was. In *THE SKIN GAME*, the pleas of the two poor tenant farmers fade away as a distracted Mr. Hillcrist stares out the window, obsessing over how the new order of things is going to affect him; in *NORTH BY NORTHWEST*, the professor's long (and, for the audience, unnecessary) bit of exposition is drowned out by airplane noises.

Expository dialogue is, in fact, frequently cut to the minimum in Hitchcock films with important court proceedings—in films from *Murder!* to *NOTORIOUS* often reduced to a line or two overheard through a suddenly opened door. (It is when Hitchcock actually pauses and lets this sort of explanatory dialogue unfold at length, that you realize he is either bored with the material, as in *THE PARADINE CASE*, or suggesting that perhaps you should be bored with the speaker, as in *PSYCHO*.)

He could paint with sound as he did with light and shadow, too, and for a variety of effects. Was hyperrealism indicated? Then he would carefully work with microphones and mixers to make sure that anything you heard on the soundtrack was not only diegetic but also perfectly placed in space (like the noises rising from the street in *ROPE* or the far-away music and barely overheard dialogue in *REAR WINDOW*). Was a more EXPRESSIONISTIC effect necessary? Then the sound would be emphasized to the point of distortion—the scream that turns into a TRAIN whistle in *THE 39 STEPS*, the clattering cacophony of the shower-curtain rings in *Psycho*.

As an artist who had always had a visual sense—his first job in movies, after all, had been designing title cards—pictures meant the most to Hitchcock. But when sound arrived, he embraced it—as he would later embrace COLOR—and then bent it to his will.

Reference

François Truffaut, *Hitchcock/Truffaut*, rev. ed. (New York: Touchstone, 1985), 61, 64–65.

SPELLBOUND (US 1945)

DIRECTOR: Alfred Hitchcock.
SCREENPLAY: Angus MacPhail, Ben Hecht, from the novel *The House of Dr. Edwardes* by Francis Beeding.
PRODUCER: David O. Selznick.
CINEMATOGRAPHY: George Barnes.
EDITORS: Hal C. Kern, William H. Ziegler.
ORIGINAL MUSIC: Miklos Rózsa.
CAST: Ingrid Bergman (Dr. Constance Petersen), Gregory Peck (John Ballantyne/"Dr. Edwardes"), Leo G. Carroll (Dr. Murchison), Michael Chekhov (Dr. Alexander Brulov), Rhonda Fleming (Mary Carmichael), Norman Lloyd (Garmes).
RUNNING TIME: 111 minutes. Black and white, with color insert.
RELEASED THROUGH: United Artists.

At the Vermont sanitarium Green Manors, a new director, Dr. Anthony Edwardes, arrives to take over from Dr. Murchison, who is finally, reluctantly retiring. But Edwardes seems oddly excitable and prone to fits—usually brought about by parallel lines, particularly when drawn against a bright white background. This does not, however, prevent one of his new colleagues, Dr. Constance Petersen, from falling immediately in love with him.

Soon, however, she realizes that Edwardes is not only an imposter but also an amnesiac—who, he himself admits, may have killed the real Edwardes and taken his place. He flees Green Manors, but she follows him to New York. Although "Edwardes's" secret is now out, Petersen helps him escape the police and takes him to the home of her mentor, Dr. Alexander Brulov.

After "Edwardes" has another spell—in which he wanders downstairs clutching a straight razor—Brulov and Petersen analyze one of his vivid dreams. Deciphering the symbols, they deduce that he was on a ski trip with the real Edwardes and witnessed his death. Petersen takes him back to relive his last memories, and there's a breakthrough—"Edwardes" remembers that his real name is John Ballantyne and that his true traumatic memory was of a childhood accident that caused his brother's death. He also remembers that Edwardes died when he skied off a cliff.

Petersen notifies the police, but when they find Edwardes's body—with a bullet in it—Ballantyne is arrested for murder anyway. Petersen returns to Green Manors, where—reinterpreting Ballantyne's dream—she realizes it implicates Murchison as the murderer, who followed both men on their ski trip and killed Edwardes to try to avoid being dismissed. After briefly menacing her, Murchison kills himself, and an exonerated Ballantyne and Petersen are happily reunited.

DAVID O. SELZNICK only took a producer's credit on three of the films Hitchcock made while under contract to him—*REBECCA*, *THE PARADINE CASE*, and this one—and like the other two, it was a film on which he had a larger-than-usual involvement from the start, thanks to his recent and intense interest in PSYCHO-ANALYSIS. It was not surprising, perhaps, that Selznick would have been drawn to analysis; the man liked to talk at length. But he was also, by the early '40s, facing several personal crises.

The enormous success of *Gone with the Wind* had, ironically, left the mogul depressed, feeling that all he had to look forward to was anticlimax. He had already fallen in desperate love with Jennifer Jones (which would eventually lead to an affair and the wrenching end of two marriages). And his brother Myron—with whom he had a fiercely close and contentiously fierce relationship—had become a desperate alcoholic, despite Selznick's attempts at intervention, and died in 1944 at the age of 46.

Knowing his producer's interest in the material, Hitchcock got ahead of the game by buying up the rights to *The House of Dr. Edwardes*, a modern Gothic thriller about a madhouse that, he thought, could be easily—which is to say liberally—adapted into a screenplay. Selznick approved the project enthusiastically, saying he was "desperately anxious" to do it, and Hitchcock began work on the script. Early drafts with ANGUS MACPHAIL made Dr. Murchison the villain rather than the victim and added the ski-resort denouement; subsequent work with BEN HECHT fleshed out the scenes at the sanitarium and amped up the mystery and romance.

Casting was the usual combination of Selznick's interest in promoting his own contract players (JOSEPH COTTEN for the hero, perhaps) and grabbing headlines (trying, and not for the last time, to lure Greta Garbo out of retirement to play the heroine). Eventually GREGORY PECK and INGRID BERGMAN, both of whom were signed to Selznick, got the leads, while Hitchcock cast several of his own favorites, including LEO G. CARROLL and NORMAN LLOYD, in supporting parts. In addition, Selznick saw that RHONDA FLEMING, who had just done a bit part in his *Since You Went Away*, got the flashy role of a nymphomaniacal patient; his own therapist, Dr. May E. Romm, was hired and credited as the film's "psychiatric adviser."

Production was difficult and not merely because Selznick insisted on visiting the set to see how things were progressing. Oddly, as Bergman would remember later in her memoirs, every time the producer did appear, Hitchcock would immediately announce that they were having a problem with the cameras and couldn't shoot a frame; only when the producer left would the "problem" be instantaneously corrected.

"Although I think Selznick finally guessed that it was a ruse, he said nothing," she wrote. "I think Hitchcock was one of the few directors who could really stand up to him. Selznick then left him alone after that. They were two strong men, but I think they had great respect for each other." ("I left him entirely alone on the set," Selznick demurred. "During *Spellbound* I don't think I was on the set twice during the entire film.")

The actors had their own problems. Bergman enjoyed Hitchcock's company but had trouble with the role, feeling that the love-at-first-sight conceit didn't play. ("Fake it," was her director's response.) And Peck—both trained in the Stanislavski METHOD and new to movies—was the sort of actor designed to bring out the petulant worse in Hitchcock who, whenever queried, told his leading man to simply make his face a blank. "I wanted more than that; the business was so new to me," Peck confessed later, noting that the filmmaker seemed distracted, even depressed. "I had the feeling that something ailed him," Peck said, "and I could never understand what it might be." (Possibly it was that Peck and Bergman had begun an affair—a hard thing to ignore for a director who had already formed a close attachment to his leading lady.)

Nor would the problems end with the final shot, as Selznick typically now inserted himself into the postproduction process. The deliberately outré, SALVADOR DALI–designed dream sequence—which was supposed to include a shot of Bergman covered in ants—was drastically cut by Selznick, who detailed WILLIAM CAMERON MENZIES to reshoot some of it. A chunk of footage (Selznick later claimed two reels, although that seems like an exaggeration) was trimmed from the entire movie, and composer MIKLOS RÓSZA—a Selznick second choice, after BERNARD HERRMANN was unavailable—was badgered about adding more violins to the love theme. Some dialogue was—inexpertly—relooped as well. (If Hitchcock was able to bear Selznick's changes, then it was only because he was already planning his escape route; two days after shooting wrapped, he was in London, discussing the formation of what would eventually be TRANSATLANTIC PICTURES.) The final print of the film spotlighted everyone's contributions—and proved most of everyone's worries true, too (although it turned out to be a hit with audiences).

Yes, Bergman was right—the immediate, doctor-patient romance is frankly unbelievable. Peck was correct, too—he did clearly need more direction to get past some of his awkwardness. And Selznick's hand, while heavy, wasn't always unneeded—a 20-minute dream sequence, as initially planned, may have been "really

something to put in a museum," as Bergman said, but it would have stopped the picture dead (although film writer James Bigwood has suggested that Bergman probably inflated the length of the sequence over time and that the original scene was perhaps only a minute longer than the version Selznick passed for the final cut). Yet Hitchcock was correct, too, as he used his usual craftsmanship and attention to imagery and metaphor to develop his favorite themes of GUILT, IDENTITY, and romantic obsession.

The film opens with a quote from Shakespeare, and some rather self-important stuff, thanks to Romm, about psychoanalysis's ability to "open up the locked doors"—and this is an image Hitchcock makes real, superimposing (in his old, silent-movie, EXPRESSIONISTIC fashion) an image of a long hallway, with doors opening one after another, to illustrate breakthroughs. *Breakthroughs* plural because it is not just "Edwardes" who must remember his real identity as John Ballantyne but also Constance Petersen who must discover her rightful identity as a woman.

To her colleagues, she is seen as authoritative, controlling, even dully asexual. Interestingly, these attitudes are conflated with maternity; she's told she is giving in to the "MOTHER instinct," treating Ballantyne like a child. "You're not his mama, you're an analyst," Brulov snaps at her. (The idea of domineering mothers and their submissive sons being underlined again when—in a seemingly unconnected moment—one of two investigating detectives remarks offhandedly to the other about recently being dubbed a "mama's boy" himself.)

What Petersen needs to do, the movie suggests, is unlock her real self and open her own doors to the SEXUALITY she's hidden away—a process that the script suggests involves taking off her glasses, going for a picnic, and throwing some of her professional cautions aside. Yet while these suggestions are totally of their unliberated time—all that Petersen really needs is some man to take her to bed, it seems—the film has a more feminist undertone as well. Petersen isn't treated seriously by her male colleagues, one of whom is constantly flirting with her and all of whom are repeatedly shown lined up against her in a disappointing row, like judges; although her former mentor, Brulov, praises her work as an assistant, he also flatly dismisses her ideas as feminine nonsense, warning, "You'll make a fool of yourself," while Murchison, even while praising her analytical skills, calls her "rather a stupid woman."

As accomplished as she is, no one seems to take Petersen seriously as a doctor (a house detective immediately pegs her as a lovesick schoolteacher or librarian looking for a runaway husband); as attractive as she is, no one is able to see past her eyeglasses (which, apparently, serve as enough of a disguise that those two investigating detectives never recognize her).

Ballantyne is searching for his own identity, too, and—significantly for Selznick perhaps—his crisis has its roots in his relationship with his late brother, whose death he feels responsible for. (Although Selznick had intervened to get his brother treatment for his alcoholism, the therapy didn't take.) Yet even making allowances for his distressed state, Ballantyne is hardly an overly sympathetic hero; he snaps at Petersen ("If there's anything I hate, it's a smug woman") and remains a rather passive participant in his own treatment. This is Petersen's story, not his.

Petersen's story, and one that Hitchcock tells with great visuals. The image of parallel lines—indicating not only the ski tracks at the original murder scene but also the parallel tracks on which both Petersen's and Ballantyne's breakthroughs develop—

constantly reoccurs, from the tines of a fork to the furrows that children's sleds leave in the snow. So, too, does the shining glint of a violent blade—a letter opener eyed by a Green Manors patient, the razor in Ballantyne's hand—and the blinding brilliance of white, from an overly lit bathroom to a steep ski slope. The straight lines, sharp edges, high contrasts, and crystal clarity reach their own climax in the dream sequence, which Hitchcock envisioned as drawing not only on Dali's fabled sense of imagery but on the noonday sharpness and clean angles he saw in Giorgio de Chirico's style, as well—"the long shadows, the infinity of distance, and the converging lines of perspective."

Other scenes show Hitchcock's skill at conveying complicated narrative information both quickly and obliquely—as Ballantyne's quick arrest, trial, and imprisonment are illustrated solely by successive close-ups of a pleading Petersen, with shadows indicating policemen or prison bars. They show his love of challenges and sense of playfulness, as well; for a SUBJECTIVE shot in which the villain kills himself, he had a giant hand a revolver constructed so that it could turn and face the camera and then gave instructions to tint a few frames in every print crimson to illustrate the lethal explosion.

Although it was one of the first Hollywood films to attempt to deal seriously with psychoanalysis, *Spellbound* is not a terribly serious film. As Bergman suspected, Petersen's sudden love for Ballantyne and eagerness to disregard all professional prohibitions is far-fetched at best; Ballantyne's sudden breakthrough on the ski slope (while heading toward a cliff, no less) has more melodrama than believability. Yet its STARS are gorgeous, and their attraction for each other is clearly real. And if the film sometimes has no more logic than Ballantyne's own dream, Hitchcock's craftsmanship ensures it is a dream from which we are in no hurry to wake.

References

Rudy Behlmer, ed., *Memo from David O. Selznick* (New York: Viking Press, 1972), 303, 381; James Bigwood, "Solving a Spellbound Puzzle," *American Cinematographer* 72, no. 6 (June 1991), 34; Brad Darrach, "Gregory Peck," *People*, June 15, 1987, http://www.people.com/people/archive/article/0,,20096523,00.html; Leonard Leff, "Selznick International's Spellbound," *Criterion Collection*, https://www.criterion.com/current/posts/223-selznick-international-s-spellbound; Patrick McGilligan, *Alfred Hitchcock: A Life in Darkness and Light* (New York: HarperCollins, 2003), 354–64; Donald Spoto, *The Dark Side of Genius: The Life of Alfred Hitchcock* (New York: Da Capo Press, 1999), 272–78; Donald Spoto, *Spellbound by Beauty: Alfred Hitchcock and His Leading Ladies* (New York: Harmony Books, 2008), 130–44; Bob Thomas, *Selznick* (New York: Pocket Books, 1972), 224–25; François Truffaut, *Hitchcock/Truffaut*, rev. ed. (New York: Touchstone, 1985), 163–67.

SPOTO, DONALD (1941–)

New Rochelle, NY–born, CATHOLIC-educated scholar with a doctorate in theology, who along the way turned to writing about movies and the people who make them, as well as producing more sober studies of Jesus, St. Francis of Assisi, and Joan of Arc.

His longstanding interest, however, has been in Hitchcock. *The Art of Alfred Hitchcock*, a study of the films, first appeared in 1976 (a revised edition appeared in 1999); a posthumous biography of the director, *THE DARK SIDE OF GENIUS: THE LIFE OF ALFRED HITCHCOCK*, came in 1983. The latter book was particularly controversial at the time, attacked by some for its unrelenting portrayal of the filmmaker as a deeply conflicted man who worked out his SEXUAL neuroses on film and whose obsession with his female STARS sometimes tipped over into crude sexual harassment.

Of course, some of its facts were challenged (with PATRICIA HITCHCOCK O'Connell still disputing a story that her father, as a practical JOKE, once stranded her for hours on a Ferris wheel). "Hitch Hatchet Job," ran the headline in a London *Times* review that managed to misspell Spoto's name throughout—yet never mentioned that the assigned critic, JOHN RUSSELL TAYLOR, was the author of the family's preferred, authorized biography. (O'Connell's own book on her mother, *Alma Hitchcock: The Woman behind the Man*, while avoiding any mention of the harassment stories, does at least list Spoto's books in the bibliography—but also curiously manages yet another, different misspelling of his name.)

Still, many of Spoto's most shocking assertions, particularly regarding Hitchcock's treatment of TIPPI HEDREN, have been echoed by others, and if Spoto sometimes reads the films as a little too literally biographical, then as a Catholic, he seems particularly attuned to Hitchcock's themes of GUILT and dangerous sexuality. Although his book remains debatable, it is also essential—inspiring films; a pro-Hitchcock website; and, to some extent, PATRICK MCGILLIGAN's equally important but almost consistently contrary biography *ALFRED HITCHCOCK: A LIFE IN DARKNESS AND LIGHT*, which takes a less determinedly downbeat view of the subject's life (and calls into question a few of Spoto's stories).

Although several of Spoto's books deal with Hitchcock colleagues, including GRACE KELLY, INGRID BERGMAN, and LAURENCE OLIVIER, and his *Spellbound by Beauty*, a study of the director's leading ladies, recycled much of the material from *The Dark Side of Genius*—and served as the basis for the Hitchcock biopic *THE GIRL*—recent books have turned to other subjects. Spoto lives in Denmark with his husband.

References

"Interview with: Donald Spoto—Biographer/Historian," *Writers Store*, https://www.writersstore.com/interview-with-donald-spoto-biographer-historian; "Finding Aid for the Donald Spoto Papers, 1940–1988," *Online Archive of California*, http://www.oac.cdlib.org/findaid/ark:/13030/tf6q2nb47s; Pat Hitchcock O'Connell and Laurent Bouzereau, *Alma Hitchcock: The Woman behind the Man* (New York: Berkeley Trade, 2004), 153, 287; John Russell Taylor, "Hitch Hatchet Job," *Times*, May 19, 1983, http://the.hitchcock.zone/wiki/The_Times_%2819/May/1983%29_-_Hitch_hatchet_job.

STABBINGS

Although STRANGLING is the more intimate act of violence—flesh to flesh and often face to face—knives and other sharp objects recur frequently in Hitchcock, sometimes emphasizing the anonymity of an attack (*THE 39 STEPS*, the 1956 *THE MAN WHO KNEW TOO MUCH*, *NORTH BY NORTHWEST*) but more often its SEXUAL violence. The most obvious phallic symbol in Hitchcock's films—apart, of course, from the final shot of the TRAIN in *NORTH BY NORTHWEST*—they would seem to be most suited as the weapon in a rape by proxy, as when Norman Bates attacks Marion Crane in the shower.

Yet, significantly, Norman is dressed as his MOTHER in that film, as throughout Hitchcock, sharp objects are a woman's weapon, used to defend against an aggressor—the bread knife Alice wields against her attacker in *BLACKMAIL*, the kitchen blade Mrs. Verloc turns against her husband in *SABOTAGE*, the scissors Margot impales Swann with in *DIAL M FOR MURDER*, the knife the farmer's wife attacks Gromek with in *TORN CURTAIN*.

The knife may indeed be a phallic symbol—but in Hitchcock's films, and in the hands of Hitchcock's heroines, it becomes a phallus appropriated by the threatened and turned against the threat.

STAFFORD, FREDERICK (1928–1979)

Czech-born actor who was discovered in 1964 while taking a Bangkok vacation and immediately pressed into two of the *OSS 117* spy films then popular in Europe. From there, he moved on to other obviously derivative movies, including the war adventure *Dirty Heroes* ("They go where eagles dare not!") and the *Battle of Britain* knockoff *Eagles over London*.

Hitchcock, who had bitterly resented the large salaries paid to PAUL NEWMAN and JULIE ANDREWS on *TORN CURTAIN*—especially because their STAR power hadn't seemed to draw audiences anyway—was determined to cast his next spy thriller, 1969's *TOPAZ*, more economically, populating it with European (and a few lesser-known American) actors. Stafford was assigned the lead role of the French agent, Andre Devereaux.

The picture, however, played disastrously with audiences, even after Hitchcock substituted a different, hastily assembled ending. The director's career, already slowing, seriously stalled, and Stafford returned to Europe, where he made films like the Italian tearjerker *White Horses of Summer* and the German horror *Werewolf Woman*. He died at 51 in a plane crash in Switzerland.

References

"Frederick Stafford," *IMDb*, http://www.imdb.com/name/nm0821277/bio?ref

_=nm_ov_bio_sm; "Frederick Stafford," *Journey of Life*, http://frederick-stafford.journal-of-life.com/#!biographies; Donald Spoto, *The Dark Side of Genius: The Life of Alfred Hitchcock* (New York: Da Capo Press, 1999), 488–90.

STAGE FRIGHT (US 1950)

DIRECTOR: Alfred Hitchcock.
SCREENPLAY: Whitfield Cook, Ranald Mac-Dougall, Alma Reville, based on the novel *Man Running* by Selwyn Jepson.
PRODUCER: Uncredited (Alfred Hitchcock).
CINEMATOGRAPHY: Wilkie Cooper.
EDITOR: E. B. Jarvis.
ORIGINAL MUSIC: Leighton Lucas.
CAST: Jane Wyman (Eve Gill), Marlene Dietrich (Charlotte Inwood), Michael Wilding ("Ordinary" Smith), Richard Todd (Jonathan Cooper), Alastair Sim (Commodore Gill), Sybil Thorndike (Mrs. Gill), Miles Malleson (Mr. Fortesque), Patricia Hitchcock ("Chubby" Bannister).
RUNNING TIME: 101 minutes. Black and white.
RELEASED THROUGH: Warner Bros.

In London, acting student Eve Gill gives actor (and unrequited love) Jonathan Cooper a quick lift out of town as he hurriedly explains his mortal predicament—his own love, famous musical actress Charlotte Inwood, recently murdered her husband and came to Cooper for help, her dress still red with blood. When he tried to slip into her house to get her a change of clothes, he was recognized—and now the police think he's the killer.

Eve takes him to the country home of her eccentric father, the commodore, where they share their suspicion—Charlotte tricked Jonathan into going back to the scene of the crime so as to frame him for the murder. Determined to help him, Eve decides to take on a high-stakes acting job—

pretending to be Charlotte's new backstage dresser—so that she can investigate.

There is, of course, a real investigator on the case—Wilfred Smith, with whom Eve becomes very friendly—but Eve keeps her activities and Jonathan's whereabouts a secret. When her father surprises Charlotte midperformance with a doll wearing a bloody skirt, the star is unable to finish the performance, and Eve takes it as a clear sign of her guilt.

With Smith's help and Jonathan waiting close by, Eve sets up a trap at the theater to get Charlotte to confess to the killing; instead, she only insists that, while it was her idea, Jonathan carried it out. Trapped, Jonathan decides to murder Eve as well—to commit such a senseless murder would only clinch his insanity defense, he says—but Eve runs away, and trying to escape, he's killed when the heavy, fireproof safety curtain comes crashing down.

Not so much a new production as an intermission.

After the financial disappointments of *THE PARADINE CASE, ROPE*, and *UNDER CAPRICORN*, it was essential that Hitchcock course-correct his career before it truly drifted into disaster. He had talked in the past about crises like these; the best thing to do, he always said, was to go back to something you knew, something safe. So with *Stage Fright* (a project in development for some time), he went back to the world of theater—which had given him the background to some of his earliest successes, including *THE PLEASURE GARDEN; THE LODGER*, and *MURDER!* And he went back to a London story, dominated by thoroughly English actors (and influenced perhaps by a true-crime story he personally knew something about: the EDITH THOMPSON case).

Preproduction was very much a family affair. The story—from a novel by Selwyn

Jepson—was largely adapted by ALMA REVILLE and WHITFIELD COOK, a longtime friend and the playwright behind one of PATRICIA HITCHCOCK's early New York stage appearances. The cast was headed up by JANE WYMAN (who actually looked a little like a glamorized Pat) and MARLENE DIETRICH, now to become the most forbidding of Hitchcock BLONDES.

It was Reville who—on her last credited screenplay—decided to add the theatrical setting and make the heroine an acting student, like her daughter. Befitting that, the film's supporting players would grow to include some of Britain's best character actors, including ALASTAIR SIM, SYBIL THORNDIKE, and MILES MALLESON. The film would be shot on LOCATION in England, some of it at Pat's current school, the Royal Academy of Dramatic Art (with Pat and a classmate or two given small roles). So, going into production, the feeling was already familial. But the expectations were also low—a murder mystery that didn't pose much of a mystery, and a man-on-the-run story that didn't turn into much of a chase.

Stage Fright begins with a safety curtain going up—a bit of foreshadowing there—to reveal London and to signal to audiences that this is going to be not just a film set in the world of the theater but also dealing with theatricality. Like so many of Hitchcock's films, it's about IDENTITY and PLAYS WITHIN PLAYS. Eve will pretend to be a servant, Jonathan will pretend to be innocent, and Charlotte will play "director," carefully manipulating everyone into the parts she wishes them to perform. It's Jonathan, though, who does the most daring bit of acting—as the film begins, literally in the middle of a chase, he quickly launches into a long piece of exposition, telling us what he's running from. It lasts nearly 15 minutes; it's done as a flashback. *And it's a lie.*

It is, along with the bomb that actually explodes in *SABOTAGE* and the leading lady who gets abruptly killed off in *PSYCHO*, one of Hitchcock's most daring narrative choices because it has always been a strange but unexamined rule in mainstream films that flashbacks always tell the truth. Narrators may be unreliable; public testimonies can turn out to be sheer fiction. But if someone says this is what happened—and then the director shows it happening in flashback on the screen—then the audience assumes that it really did.

Which, of course, isn't the case in *Stage Fright*—and the chief reason, the practical Hitchcock would say, that the film didn't succeed. He hadn't played fair with the audience—at least, as they understood fairness—and so they turned on him.

Actually, the lying flashback isn't the worst of the film's problems. In some ways, it's the most intriguing aspect in a rather dull film. More than a decade before, Hitchcock had fled England's weather and the English film industry's limited resources; both weigh *Stage Fright* down like a damp woolen blanket. The cinematography is dominated by wishy-washy grays; one shot of Dietrich changing while Wilding stands behind her, has been so crudely fiddled with in postproduction that she almost looks like a ghost from *A Christmas Carol*. There is some nice lighting and one or two daringly extended shots, but most of the film feels like a defeated step back.

What *Stage Fright* does have is something the director had definitely missed—an even deeper roster of character actors than Hollywood could provide. Sim is delightful as the commodore—his marvelous voice managing to pack two or three notes into a single syllable—and almost every scene boasts a strong stage performer like Thorndike or Kay Walsh. Particularly rich is Joyce Grenfell, here cast as the toothy mistress of a shooting gallery; her jolly offer to load

Sim's gun ("Shall I put it in for you?") is one that must have delighted Hitchcock's dirty schoolboy heart.

But Wyman, the Hollywood STAR who helped anchor this project, at least commercially, is its weakest point (apart from being wholly unbelievable as the progeny of Sim and Thorndike), and Wilding is so lightweight as the hero that he seems ready to blow away in a gust of London wind. Todd gets some power into his one mad scene at the end—his wide eyes shining in the dark—but the entire film is so underdeveloped and lacking in tension that Hitchcock's small jokes and quirky sideshows run away with it.

Dietrich is, of course, always watchable and steals every scene she's in. (Being fitted for her widow's weeds, she asks the seamstress to give the gown a little more décolletage.) She looks beautiful (in a rare gesture of respect, Hitchcock gave her a huge amount of leeway over her costumes, even her own lighting, as well as a Cole Porter song to sing), and the character is one of the director's few, actual femme fatales. But she's also still very much the diva—the film comes to a stop whenever she performs, Hitchcock again unsure of how to handle musical numbers—and she ends up overwhelming everything else.

Despite the bloody murder that begins the film and the awful accident that ends it, *Stage Fright* does have a quiet, almost gentle feel, with its opening curtain suggesting that what lay ahead was merely a story not to be taken too seriously. For a director reeling from several failures, it must have felt like a retreat to family and the familiar. But it was not sadly a return to form. That would have to wait for the next film—*STRANGERS ON A TRAIN*.

References
Steven DeRosa, "Alfred Hitchcock's Stage Fright," *Writing with Hitchcock*, http://stevenderosa.com/writingwithhitchcock/stagefright.html; Patrick McGilligan, *Alfred Hitchcock: A Life in Darkness and Light* (New York: HarperCollins, 2003), 432–37; Donald Spoto, *The Dark Side of Genius: The Life of Alfred Hitchcock* (New York: Da Capo Press, 1999), 314–16; François Truffaut, *Hitchcock/Truffaut*, rev. ed. (New York: Touchstone, 1985), 189–91.

STAIRCASES
Flights of steps that ascend to the better stages of our nature or descend into the depths of degradation, staircases are not only a powerful symbol but also an obvious one—decades later Hitchcock would deplore his own "naïve touch" of having the hero in *DOWNHILL*, after being thrown out of his father's house, board the "Down" escalator. Much as the director enjoyed the stark visuals of symbolism, he respected subtlety more.

So more often in Hitchcock films, stairs stand for a literal escalation—of personal emotions or life-altering stakes. In some films, they function as a barrier, as one more obstacle to be overcome or curtain to be drawn aside. In *THE LODGER* and *THE 39 STEPS*, they separate the mysterious tenants from the bustling life going on down below; in *SPELLBOUND*, they divide the public rooms of Green Manors from the private office of its not-to-be-trusted chief psychiatrist. In *SUSPICION*, they inexorably delay Johnnie's slow, slow walk to his wife with that mysterious glass of milk; in *NOTORIOUS*, they're all that stand between Alicia and Devlin and escape; in *FRENZY*, they provide a long, dark, insulating barrier between what Rush does in his apartment and the outside world.

In others, they are dangerous stages, inherently uneven settings for violence. Guy's climb up the stairs to warn Bruno's father in *STRANGERS ON A TRAIN*, Arbogast's trip to interview Mrs. Bates in *PSYCHO*, the step Uncle Charlie saws through in *SHADOW OF A DOUBT* to remove the threat of Charlotte—in every case they are a place of danger and deception, where the unwary can easily slip, literally or figuratively, and hurtle to their death.

Of course they figure most hugely in *VERTIGO*, which is all about dizzying heights—and paralyzing depths—and concludes with a painful climb up the steps of the bell tower. And most humorously in the parody thriller *NUMBER 17*, in which much of the film takes place on a stairway—a winking metaphor for all the ups and downs the characters are to face.

"Stairs are very photogenic," Hitchcock told FRANÇOIS TRUFFAUT, and he certainly knew how to photograph them (his CAMEO in *I CONFESS* is even at the top of a Quebec staircase). But more than photogenic, they were dramatic—and he squeezed every bit of emotion from them he could.

Reference

François Truffaut, *Hitchcock/Truffaut*, rev. ed. (New York: Touchstone, 1985), 51.

STANNARD, ELIOT (1888–1944)

London-born author whose mother—under the pseudonym John Strange Winter—had written a popular series of books about army life. After his father died in 1912, Stannard took over his manufacturing business; by the end of the next year, it had gone bankrupt. Following his mother's lead, he went into writing instead, concentrating on the movies; in 1914 alone, he was credited with five shorts and two features.

Stannard worked very quickly, an enormous advantage in the early, catch-as-catch-can days of British cinema; although many of his earliest films are lost, he's reported to have racked up more than 300 credits, the vast majority during the silent

era. Eight of those credits were for Alfred Hitchcock (he would have gotten a ninth, Stannard later protested, if he'd been given the credit he felt he deserved for helping on *THE RING*).

Moving easily from heavily condensed versions of Dickens, Shakespeare, and Fielding to contemporary melodramas, mysteries, and comedies, Stannard was infinitely flexible, and his work for Hitchcock was eclectic as well—he's credited with *THE LODGER* but also most of the director's love-triangle melodramas, including *THE PLEASURE GARDEN* and *THE MANXMAN*. While their work together was drawn from a variety of other sources, the same themes of thwarted romances and bitter betrayals abound.

Stannard was prolific but never thoughtless; as early as 1918, he was writing about his craft and urging would-be screenwriters to first learn everything they could about moviemaking, from cinematography to scenery. (He was also presciently complaining that writers were often forgotten when people rushed to praise a film's artistry.)

Stannard's insistence on showing things rather than describing them in title cards probably won an early ally in Hitchcock; his emphasis on structure and dislike of movies that are "comprised of a series of exciting incidents and nothing else . . . (but) improbable and often impossible situations" suggests the working relationship would not have survived once Hitchcock's own tastes in narrative grew more episodic and even dreamlike.

In any case, once sound came in, Hitchcock turned to other writers, beginning with the equally prolific CHARLES BENNETT. As for Stannard—whose personal life was far less orderly than his carefully planned scripts—the early talkies, which tended at first to the sort of dialogue-driven stories he had always avoided, turned out to be enemy territory. His last film credit was in 1932.

After that, facts grow sketchy; one trade magazine described him as a "real character" possessed of a "mordant wit" and "brutal candour"—the usual polite Anglicisms for "undependable," "nasty," and "difficult." What happened in his later years is unclear. According to PATRICK MCGILLIGAN, Stannard found a minor studio job at GAUMONT; according to SIDNEY GILLIAT, he ended up pushing papers in a motor vehicle licensing department. He died in London at 56 of a heart condition.

References

David Cairns, "Eliot Stannard," *Shadowplay*, https://dcairns.wordpress.com/tag/eliot-stannard; Michael Eaton, "Script Special: The Man Who Wasn't There," *Sight and Sound*, June 6, 2012, http://old.bfi.org.uk/sightandsound/feature/49173; Patrick McGilligan, *Alfred Hitchcock: A Life in Darkness and Light* (New York: HarperCollins, 2003), 68, 77; P. L. M., "Eliot Stannard Passes," *Kine Weekly*, November 30, 1944, http://the.hitchcock.zone/wiki/Kine_Weekly_%281944%29_-_Obituary:_Eliot_Stannard_Passes.

STARS

For the first 10 or 15 years of cinema, most movie actors were anonymous, protecting both their reputations—acting still being considered a dubious calling in some circles—and, not inconsequently, the studios' profits. Because, after all, if your leading actress was billed only as "The Biograph Girl," when she proved difficult and asked for a raise, you could always simply appoint someone else in her place. Anonymity kept actors powerless.

In 1910, though, "The Biograph Girl," Florence Lawrence, left for Carl Laemmle's Independent Motion Pictures Company, now becoming not only "The IMP Girl" but also appearing for the first time under her own name. Mary Pickford soon joined the list of credited performers, and before the decade was out, a new flickering royalty had arisen—William S. Hart, Theda Bara, the Gish sisters. And with fame, performers gained leverage.

The cult of stardom was well established by the time Hitchcock reached films in the early '20s, and already, its difficult and contradictory nature was clear. On one hand, a "name" actor could bring larger audiences and convey a certain exploitable persona; on the other, he or she would now demand a larger salary and might require that characters, even entire scripts, be extensively and arbitrarily rewritten to accommodate his or her image. Throughout his career, Hitchcock would wrestle with all of this.

As a director, he had an honest appreciation of the benefits a star could provide. Famous faces were easy to identify with, drawing an audience more quickly into the story. They had certain perceived character traits—CARY GRANT's slippery charm, GREGORY PECKS's stolid decency, ANTHONY PERKINS's uncertain boyishness—that you could draw on or sneakily subvert. (And although he would call actors "cattle," even "stupid children," many actresses—JOAN FONTAINE, INGRID BERGMAN, GRACE KELLY, JANET LEIGH—would give their very best performances under his direction.)

Yet there were artistic limitations, as well. Grant could not (or would not) play a murderer; neither he nor MONTGOMERY CLIFT would sign on for a character whose heterosexuality was even vaguely questioned. Gary Cooper turned down several roles outright simply because he didn't want to be in a thriller. Ego and vanity could create other obstacles, too. CHARLES LAUGHTON approached

JAMAICIA INN with demands that his part be expanded; NITA NALDI arrived to play the part of a rural teacher in *THE MOUNTAIN EAGLE* with long Hollywood fingernails. (The stars who arrived with their own acting approaches—and, in Clift's case, his own dramatic coach in tow—were a separate problem.)

Financially, stars posed another difficulty. In Britain, Hitchcock often had been forced to cast certain foreign performers simply because their famous names helped sell the film back in their own hometowns of Berlin or New York; in America, studio budgets might require he choose from a list of contract players whom could be had cheaply or whom some mogul was determined to promote. It was through marriages of convenience like these that PRISCILLA LANE came to *SABOTEUR*, RUTH ROMAN was cast in *STRANGERS ON A TRAIN*, and JOHN GAVIN joined *PSYCHO*—and they were shotgun arrangements that unsurprisingly never led to warm feelings on either side.

Big stars who weren't under contract, meanwhile, could be expensive—something that particularly aggravated Hitchcock later as, post-SELZNICK, he became his own producer and fixed his eyes more intensely on costs. (The largest headache turned out to be *TORN CURTAIN*, where, at the studio's insistence, a substantial part of the budget went to hire JULIE ANDREWS, whom Hitchcock didn't want, and PAUL NEWMAN, whom Hitchcock disliked.) When early attempts at creating his own stable—VERA MILES, TIPPI HEDREN—went disastrously wrong, Hitchcock finally gave up on "names" entirely. *TOPAZ* and *FRENZY* were cast largely with little-known character actors, and while he and the studio flirted briefly with attracting some marquee value to *FAMILY PLOT*, the "Jack Nicholson part" was eventually taken by BRUCE DERN.

And yet, as frustrating as the idea of stardom was to Hitchcock—partly because he believed that the director was the star, mostly because he felt the best actor was a blank canvas—he understood the concept of charisma and used it better than most. He knew a true star had something—like Gerald du Maurier, the matinee idol of his youth "who could walk on a stage, flick a speck of dust off his shoulder, study his fingernails for a whole five minutes, and do it all so dramatically and with such accurate timing that he held an audience spellbound."

And so while Hitchcock preferred Margaret Sullavan's acting in her auditions for *REBECCA*, he cast Joan Fontaine, knowing her honest uncertainty was better for the role. He saw the private-school poise of Grace Kelly—but also saw through it to the passion underneath.

Personas matter, and they matter the most in Hitchcock, where character isn't conveyed through dialogue so much as a simple look, a gesture, a mood. It's the everyman decency of JAMES STEWART that makes his neuroses in *REAR WINDOW* and *VERTIGO* more shocking initially (and yet ultimately forgivable); it's the perfectly bone-deep shallowness of Cary Grant that makes his husband in *SUSPICION* so attractively untrustworthy. (And of course, it is the simple, old-fashioned fame of Janet Leigh—It's not as if he's going to kill off the star, is he?—that made *PSYCHO* so astounding.)

Still, stars were just a particularly overgrown kind of actor, and performers so often complicated things, getting between Hitchcock and his vision, his camera and the screen. They interfered, the silly things, but what could you do? "I've always said that Walt Disney has the right idea," he told journalist Oriana Fallaci. "His actors are made of paper; when he doesn't like them, he can tear them up."

References

Oriana Fallaci, *The Egotists: 16 Surprising Interviews* (Chicago: H. Regnery, 1968), 254; Richard Griffith and Arthur Mayer, *The Movies*, rev. ed. (New York: Simon and Schuster, 1971), 46–55; Alfred Hitchcock, "Life among the Stars," *News Chronicle*, March 15, 1938, http://the.hitchcock. zone/wiki/News_Chronicle_%281937%29 _-_Life_among_the_Stars; Patrick McGilligan, *Alfred Hitchcock: A Life in Darkness and Light* (New York: HarperCollins, 2003), 239, 301, 450, 722–23; Stephen Rebello, *Alfred Hitchcock and the Making of Psycho* (New York: HarperPerennial, 1991), 65; *Rope Unleashed*, directed by Laurent Bouzereau (2001), documentary; Donald Spoto, *The Dark Side of Genius: The Life of Alfred Hitchcock* (New York: Da Capo Press, 1999), 184, 337; J. Danvers Williams, "What I'd Do to the Stars," *Film Weekly*, March 4, 1939, http://the.hitchcock. zone/wiki/Film_Weekly_%281939%29 _-_What_I'd_Do_to_the_Stars.

STEFANO, JOSEPH (1922–2006)

Philadelphia-born son of a tailor who dropped out of school and ran off to New York to become an entertainer. Performing at first in Greenwich Village clubs under the name Jerry Stevens, he sang, danced, played piano, and worked up stage material for others. A stint writing for TV's *Ted Mack Family Hour* was his first onscreen credit; his first movie credit was *The Black Orchid*, a 1958 crime drama for Martin Ritt.

MCA executives recommended him to Hitchcock as a screenwriter for *PSYCHO* after a first attempt by James Cavanagh, who'd written for *ALFRED HITCHCOCK PRESENTS*, was deemed unusable; Stefano came to the first meeting with good ideas about expanding Marion Crane's role and making Norman more likeable, and Hitchcock soon hired him for the job. Stefano, who was in analysis at the time, would also suggest a flashback fleshing out Norman's oedipal attraction to his MOTHER, something he said the director was interested in doing even though they both knew they could never get it past the CENSORS.

Working hard, Stefano took ROBERT BLOCH's original novel and made it something more than clever; he made it poetic, particularly in the long exchange in the parlor, where Norman talks to Marion about "private traps" and the "laughter, and the tears and the cruel eyes studying you"—as the sightless EYES of BIRDS of prey look down on them both. It's a scene of suddenly unmasked madness—like Uncle Charlie's monologue about "stupid women" in *SHADOW OF A DOUBT*—but it's also one of despair and one of the finest in any Hitchcock film.

But then perhaps the director, Stefano later said, "had reached a point in his professional life where he was ready for a totally different kind of picture. In his previous films, he told things about himself he thought were true, but in *Psycho*, he told more about himself, in a deeper sense, than he realized. He had been very concerned about his health. . . . [H]e was grappling with his own mortality."

Despite the apparent ease of their collaboration—and Hitchcock's reluctance to break in new writers—the two men did not really work together again. Although Stefano roughed out some early ideas for *MARNIE* when the director was still hoping to sign GRACE KELLY (and Hitchcock later approached him again for *THE BIRDS*), by 1963, the younger man was busy producing (and occasionally writing) his own TV show, *The Outer Limits*, an hour-long sci-fi anthology series that occasionally flirted with the surreal (while trying to avoid the more obvious moralizing of *The Twilight Zone*).

The series only lasted two seasons but finished the pigeonholing that *Psycho* had begun; most of Stefano's subsequent assignments were fantasies or thrillers. Although publicly critical of *Psycho II* and *III* (and the Gus Van Sant remake, which reused his old script), Stefano contributed a new script for the TV movie *Psycho IV*; one of his favorite credits, though, was the far more family-friendly (and lightly autobiographical) South Philly drama *Two Bits*, starring Al Pacino as a frail grandfather.

He died at 84 in Thousand Oaks, CA, of a heart attack.

References
Ronald Bergen, "Joseph Stefano," *Guardian*, September 13, 2006, http://www.theguardian.com/news/2006/sep/14/guardianobituaries.obituaries; Adam Bernstein, "Joseph Stefano: Key Writer for *Psycho*," *Washington Post*, August 30, 2006, http://www.washingtonpost.com/wp-dyn/content/article/2006/08/29/AR2006082901421.html; Sylvia Caminer and John Andrew Gallagher, "An Interview with Joseph Stefano," *Films in Review*, January 31, 1996, http://the.hitchcock.zone/wiki/Films_in_Review_%281996%29_-_An_interview_with_Joseph_Stefano; Stephen Rebello, *Alfred Hitchcock and the Making of Psycho* (New York: Harper Perennial, 1991), 31–50; Donald Spoto, *The Dark Side of Genius: The Life of Alfred Hitchcock* (New York: Da Capo Press, 1999), 590.

STEINBECK, JOHN (1902–1968)
Salinas-born author who grew up middle class but with a strong affinity for immigrant workers and idealistic dreamers. He dropped out of Stanford and depended on odd jobs, family handouts, and whatever fish he could catch in Monterey Bay while trying to establish himself as a writer. His first book, *Cup of Gold*, was published in 1929; his first commercial success, *Tortilla Flat*, came in 1935.

By the end of the decade, Steinbeck had made his name and his fortune with *Of Mice and Men* and *The Grapes of Wrath*, books of simple language but ringing declarations of solidarity with the poor and exploited. (Both were almost immediately made into films.) After reporting under fire in the early days of World War II, Steinbeck then returned to California, where he wrote several original treatments and scripts for Hollywood.

By 1943, Hitchcock, who preferred working with novelists and playwrights on the initial, prose treatments for his films, had already shopped his *LIFEBOAT* idea to Ernest Hemingway, James Hilton, and A. J. Cronin; Steinbeck was the first author to accept. The novelist figured he'd maximize his profits by writing (and publishing) the story first and then selling the rights to the studio.

It didn't work out that way. No one wanted to handle the novella (deemed a major falling-off from *The Grapes of Wrath*), and after Steinbeck turned in his treatment, it went through at least a half-dozen other pairs of hands. After seeing the film, Steinbeck tried (unsuccessfully) to have his name removed, complaining that the final screenplay mocked the labor movement and had turned his "Negro of dignity, purpose and personality" into a comic figure.

Both criticisms seem oversensitive today—the story's leftist worker is much more a figure of authority than the boat's squabbling capitalists, and whatever clichés had been in the character of Joe (early drafts had included some painful attempts at dialect) had largely been overcome through the patient work of actor CANADA LEE. The final *Lifeboat* screenplay may not have been the story Steinbeck turned in, but it was hardly an embarrassment.

Steinbeck, however, disowned the entire production, although he would continue to contribute some screenplays to

422 ■ STEWART, JAMES

Hollywood, including ones for his own *The Red Pony* and Elia Kazan's *Viva Zapata*. (Kazan would later bring Steinbeck's last major work, the novel *East of Eden*, to the screen.) By the 1950s, however, Steinbeck had begun to seem a little out of step with a new, postwar generation of American novelists who were seizing attention; while Jack Kerouac went *On the Road* with only another mad iconoclast for company, Steinbeck packed up his poodle and chronicled his *Travels with Charlie*.

What should have been a crowning honor—his 1962 Nobel Prize for literature—only brought controversy and criticism from those who felt it wasn't deserved (including, to be fair, Steinbeck himself). He never published another piece of fiction (although he did surprise many with a sharp turn to the right, sending back favorable dispatches from the war in Vietnam).

Steinbeck died in New York at 66 of heart failure. There are still rich old men living on California farmland who despise him.

References

"John Steinbeck," *Biography*, http://www.biography.com/people/john-stein beck-9493358; "John Steinbeck," *IMDb*, http://www.imdb.com/name/nm0825705/bio?ref_=nm_ov_bio_sm; "John Steinbeck: Biography," *National Steinbeck Center*, http://www.steinbeck.org/pages/john-steinbeck-biography; Patrick McGilligan, *Alfred Hitchcock: A Life in Darkness and Light* (New York: HarperCollins, 2003), 328–36, 350–52; Emily Temple, "John Steinbeck Wanted His Name Taken off Alfred Hitchcock's Lifeboat," *Flavorwire*, February 4, 2012, http://flavorwire.com/256717/john-steinbeck-wanted-his-name-taken-off-hitchcocks-lifeboat.

STEWART, JAMES (1908–1997)

He was born in an era when every leading man had to find a type, and some of his best friends backed into the simplest, most straightforward ones. John Wayne, the Cowboy. HENRY FONDA, the Man of Integrity. The personas fit them like tailored suits, and they wore them confidently, almost without a break, for a half-century. But Stewart was lucky enough—or smart enough—to pick the best one of all: James Stewart, American.

He was one kind of fellow at first, the young, decent, slightly naïve idealist whose wrists and ankles peeked out from last year's suit, who couldn't get through a conversation with a woman without stammering or dropping his hat (or almost any conversation without an awed "Gosh!"). He was an American, or at least what Americans wished they were, at their small-town best.

But then came the war. And when Stewart came back, he seemed, not 5 or 6 years older, but 20. The men he played were innocent no longer. They wondered what exactly they had done with their lives. They worried, they raged, they obsessed. They were impatient. They were lost. But they were Americans, too—just a different, wounded, wearier sort.

He was born in Indiana, PA, where his father ran a hardware store that Jimmy, the oldest child and only boy, was expected to take over one day. Instead he went to Princeton and studied architecture—and also joined the Triangle Club, where he appeared in plays, occasionally played the accordion, and discovered a love of performance. He did summer stock on Cape Cod and then after graduation moved on to New York, where he began going out on auditions. Unlike George Bailey, he never did go back home and take over the family business.

Although the plays he got cast in had the unfortunate habit of closing rapidly, an MGM talent scout spotted him in one and signed him to a contract in 1935. The studio wasn't sure what to do with him at first—he appeared in a musical and even as a couple of villains—but by the end of the decade, he had been firmly typed as a bashful, sincere, and genuinely decent young man in *Made for Each Other*; *Destry Rides Again*; and, of course, *Mr. Smith Goes to Washington*. *The Philadelphia Story*, in which he played a slightly more sardonic figure, won him a surprise best actor Oscar.

"I've looked upon it as a skill rather than as an art," he said once to *American Film*, describing his process—without ever, of course, using such a self-serious word as *process*. "And part of the skill, I've always thought, is to make it so the acting doesn't show. As the skill develops, the acting . . . shows less, and believability comes sneaking into the thing. This is the magic. People just can't put their finger on it, and it really drives 'em right up the wall because they can't. I hope they never can, because this is one of the fascinating things about the business."

Even after becoming a STAR, Stewart, a longtime aviator, was eager to continue his family's tradition of military service but was turned down at first—with less than 140 pounds stretched out over his 6-foot-3 frame, he was seriously underweight. With the help of some heavy meals and workouts at the studio gym (and, he later conceded, a friendly fellow reading the scales), he was inducted in March 1941, nine months before Pearl Harbor. When America entered the war, the star successfully fought to be sent overseas and into combat, where he flew bombing missions over Europe.

Like many far less famous Americans, Stewart came home from the war changed, wondering if acting was any sort of serious profession for a man to have. (For a while, he briefly considered going into commercial aviation.) But the story of Frank Capra's *It's a Wonderful Life*—and its hero, a would-be engineer who did stay home and run the family business—appealed to him, and when he seemed once to waver on the set, Lionel Barrymore gave him a stern lecture on the importance of the arts and the nobility of the actor's profession. Stewart rededicated himself to doing his best.

But it would be a different sort of Stewart who now loped across America's movie screens. The cynical reporter of *Call Northside 777*, the grizzled cowboys of *Winchester '73*, *The Naked Spur*, and *The Man from Laramie*—these were not innocents. These were men who'd known pain and compromise and disappointment—and knew that only more lay ahead.

"Gosh, *Winchester '73* was a lifesaver," he said decades later. "It rescued me from a very serious situation. The audiences weren't accepting the sort of muddled, slow-talking, vulnerable, small-town-boy, hem-and-hawer type of comedy that I had been doing before the war. After the war they just didn't accept that."

Although Anthony Mann's darkly violent westerns did much to turn Stewart's image around, the first course corrections came with Hitchcock's *ROPE*, which cast the actor—wildly against type—as a prep-school headmaster, amateur philosopher, armchair expert on Nietzsche (and very possibly a closeted HOMOSEXUAL). Stewart wasn't completely comfortable in the role, but he would get better parts—and be better in them—as, in quick succession, Hitchcock cast him in *REAR WINDOW*; the 1956 remake of *THE MAN WHO KNEW TOO MUCH*, and, ultimately, *VERTIGO*.

Hitchcock's American films are often about finding the cracks in the edifice of the perfect American male, the lie that's so carefully concealed behind the matinee-idol mask; just as the director's films with CARY GRANT emphasized the untrustworthy glibness that drove Grant's charm, his projects with Stewart found something curdling behind the actor's ice-cream grin, something slightly pervy underneath the Boy Scout wholesomeness. Hitchcock had turned Grant's smooth manners into a metaphor for deception; now he transformed Stewart's innocence into SEXUAL repression.

So in *Rope*, we have Stewart as the academic mentor and molder of young minds (who is also a creator of amoral sociopaths). In *Rear Window*, we have Stewart as a professional photographer and observer of human nature (whose profession is an excuse to peep and pry yet stay uninvolved). Even in the lighter *The Man Who Knew Too Much*, shadows loom. In the first version of the film, the couple had a marriage of equals, with LESLIE BANKS even owing his life to his wife's skills; in the second, it's a marriage of small rows and brusque abuses of power, with Stewart DOMINATING DORIS DAY at every turn.

He was very good in *The Man Who Knew Too Much*, brilliant in *Rear Window*. However, making *Rope*, Stewart said, was the "craziest, most difficult thing, it was completely new. Making it was so complicated that when I finished the picture I was talking to Hitch and I said 'You know, I think you missed the boat a little with this one-set thing. You should've built bleachers around it and soaked them five, 10 bucks to watch us do this.'"

It was *Vertigo*, though, that became both men's masterpiece. Stewart's character seems, at first, to be a standard Hollywood hero, something out of his prewar movie past—the dogged policeman-turned-private-eye. But instead of being the hero, he's the villain's stooge, chosen not because he's smart enough to solve the case but because he's damaged enough to help conceal the crime even without trying.

Everything in *Vertigo* is turned upside down, Scottie's bravery undone by phobia, his reason by passion. Then even that pas-

sion sours, so adulterated by FETISH and obsession that what had been love turns into a simple, crude need to possess. And by the time Scottie's conquered his great fear—recaptured his sense of self—it's too late, his lost masculinity returning only just in time for him to stand impotently on the edge of the abyss, while the one thing he loved lies smashed on the ground below.

The two men never worked together after that. How could they? What stories were left to tell? To be fair, Stewart wanted to, though. It was Hitchcock—who could be cold whenever commercial considerations arose—who avoided Stewart, privately blaming the modest box office of *Vertigo* on the actor's increasing age (and quietly reneging on his promise to star him in *NORTH BY NORTHWEST*—which was honestly more of a Cary Grant role, anyway). And so Stewart went on to other parts and, to some extent, went backward, retreating into the past of those aw-shucks folks he'd played in the '30s.

There is, at least, a sense of irony in those roles at first—his coolly clever attorney in *Anatomy of a Murder* is not quite the plain-old country lawyer he pretends to be, and his hero in *The Man Who Shot Liberty Valance* lives much of his life knowing he's playing a part. But that subtle self-awareness soon faded, and Stewart quickly relaxed into a long string of jobs as indulgent dads and cranky old codgers.

Stewart retired from the movies in the late '70s, when problems with his hearing and memory made acting more difficult; nonetheless, he appeared in the TV miniseries *North and South, Book II* and for a long time remained a popular guest on talk shows. When Gloria, his wife of 45 years, died in 1994, however, he retreated from public life; when it was time to have the battery in his pacemaker changed in 1996, he quietly declined. He died of a blood clot the next year; he was 89. Few obituary writers could resist the lead, "It Was a Wonderful Life." None of them was wrong.

References

"Biography," *Jimmy Stewart Museum*, http://jimmy.org/biography; Peter Bogdanovich, *Pieces of Time* (New York: Arbor House, 1973), 127–40; "James Stewart," *IMDb*, http://www.imdb.com/name/nm0000071/bio?ref_=nm_ov_bio_sm; Janet Maslin, "James Stewart Recalls Hitch," *New York Times*, October 9, 1983, http://the.hitchcock.zone/wiki/New_York_Times_%2809/Oct/1983%29_-_James_Stewart_recalls_Hitch; Joseph McBride, "Aren't You . . . Jimmy Stewart?" *American Film* 1, no. 8 (June 1976), http://the.hitchcock.zone/wiki/American_Film_%281976%29_-_Aren't_You ..._Jimmy_Stewart%3F; Patrick McGilligan, *Alfred Hitchcock: A Life in Darkness and Light* (New York: HarperCollins, 2003), 565–66; David Thomson, *The New Biographical Dictionary of Film* (New York: Knopf, 2002), 835–36.

STORY, JACK TREVOR
(1917–1991)

Hertford-born writer of humble origins—his mother was a maid, and he never met his father, killed in World War I—who was largely self-educated and, as a writer, self-taught. In the 1940s, he began publishing prodigiously in any genre that would have him: mysteries, westerns, sci-fi. Many of his books were touched by wild bits of humor; Hitchcock particularly enjoyed the black comedy of Story's THE TROUBLE WITH HARRY, although his own movie adaptation transposed the action, not successfully, from England to Vermont.

The screen sale remained a sore point for Story, who said he'd transferred all rights for only 150 pounds, but money was always a problem for the writer, who twice declared bankruptcy and whose appetites, particularly for young women, tended to rapidly deplete whatever little funds he garnered from paperback novels and TV scripts.

"Story cheerfully thumbed his nose at the conventions and, like all genuine *naïfs*, was always mildly puzzled when things—as they had a habit of doing—got out of hand," the *Independent* observed in its tart obituary. "He seemed to spend his life fleeing—from wives, not-quite-wives, responsibilities, tax inspectors—and never quite making it."

He died in Milton Keynes of a heart attack at 74.

References

Jack Adrian, "Jack Trevor Story," *Independent*, December 9, 1991, http://jacktrevorstory.com/independent_obituary.htm; Guy Lawley, *Jack Trevor Story*, http://www.jacktrevorstory.com; Michael McNay, "Jack Trevor Story: View from the Rapids," *Guardian*, December 9, 1991, http://jacktrevorstory.com/guardian_obituary.htm.

STRADLING, HARRY
(1901–1970)

Newark-born filmmaker from a movie family (his uncle, Walter, had worked in the early silents; his son, Harry Jr., would follow him into the profession) who spent years shooting shorts for Poverty Row studios in Hollywood before leaving for Europe. There he would get longer and better assignments, climaxing with Hitchcock's JAMAICA INN in 1939.

When war came to Europe, Stradling returned to Hollywood. Hitchcock wanted him for REBECCA, but producer DAVID O. SELZNICK overruled him; he would finally work for the director on MR. AND MRS. SMITH and SUSPICION, where he captured the iconic shot of CARY GRANT walking up the richly shadowed STAIRCASE carrying a luminous glass of milk (literally luminous—they'd put a tiny light bulb inside it to make it glow).

An assured and adaptable professional, Stradling changed his style to suit the mood and needs of the production—giving his Oscar-winning work in *The Portrait of Dorian Gray* a romantic richness and *A Face in the Crowd* a gritty documentary feel, conjuring up dank shadows for *A Streetcar Named Desire* and glorious COLOR for *My Fair Lady*, creating both the lurid melodrama of *Johnny Guitar* and the sunny nostalgia of *In the Good Old Summertime*.

Although the veteran clashed with novice director Mike Nichols on *Who's Afraid of Virginia Woolf* (and was eventually dismissed from the project), his ability to flatteringly light and photograph Barbra Streisand for *Funny Girl* immediately made him her favorite cameraman; she would insist on him shooting all of her films. He died in Los Angeles at 68 of a heart attack while working on the fourth, *The Owl and the Pussycat*.

References

"Harry Stradling (Sr.)," *Internet Encyclopedia of Cinematographers*, http://www.cinematographers.nl/GreatDoPh/stradling.sr.htm; "Harry Stradling Sr.," *IMDb*, http://www.imdb.com/name/nm0005889; Donald Spoto, *The Dark Side of Genius: The Life of Alfred Hitchcock* (New York: Da Capo Press, 1999), 245; François Truffaut, *Hitchcock/Truffaut*, rev. ed. (New York: Touchstone, 1985), 143.

STRANGERS ON A TRAIN (US 1951)

DIRECTOR: Alfred Hitchcock.
SCREENPLAY: Raymond Chandler, Czenzi Ormonde, Whitfield Cook, based on the novel by Patricia Highsmith.
PRODUCER: Uncredited (Alfred Hitchcock).
CINEMATOGRAPHY: Robert Burks.
EDITOR: William H. Ziegler.
ORIGINAL MUSIC: Dmitri Tiomkin.
CAST: Robert Walker (Bruno Antony), Farley Granger (Guy Haines), Ruth Roman (Anne Morton), Leo G. Carroll (Sen. Morton), Kasey Rogers (Miriam Haines), Patricia Hitchcock (Barbara Morton).
RUNNING TIME: 101 minutes. Black and white.
RELEASED THROUGH: Warner Bros.

Tennis star Guy Haines is on a train, off to ask his wife for a divorce—again—when he literally bumps into the rich, eccentric Bruno Antony. The two men drink and share their similar troubles—just as Guy can't be rid of his wife, Bruno is eager to shed his father. Wouldn't it be the perfect crime, Bruno suggests, if they each murdered the *other's* victim, thereby providing the police with no motive? Guy forces a laugh at the joke.

Except Bruno isn't joking. He follows Guy's trashy, adulterous wife to a carnival and strangles her—then seeks out Guy and calmly tells him it's his turn. The horrified Guy refuses, so Bruno begins stalking him—a threatening presence soon noticed by Guy's rich new girlfriend and her disapproving father, a US senator.

Eventually Guy halfheartedly agrees to hold up his end of the deal but instead goes to Bruno's house to warn his father. There, however, he finds Bruno waiting for him, who says he suspected this would happen. He tells Guy that now he's going to make sure the police arrest him.

With the police already focusing on Guy as a suspect—and Bruno soon on his way back to the carnival to plant Guy's lighter as evidence at the murder scene—Guy has no other choice but to elude the lawmen and confront Bruno. He follows him to the carnival, where they fight on a crazily out-of-control merry-go-round.

Bruno dies in a final, ride-wrecking accident—but in his last moments unclenches his fist, revealing the lighter to Guy and the police.

A twisting meditation on DOUBLES and one of Hitchcock's most singular and meticulously worked-out films.

It came just in time. As the decade began, Hitchcock had not had an unqualified hit since *NOTORIOUS* in 1946; his attempt at launching a new, independent production company had wrecked itself on the Great Barrier Reef of *UNDER CAPRICORN*. Although he never went into a production not expecting it to resonate with audiences, as well as with himself, this time it was vital; another failure would turn a slump into a trend.

He found it in a first novel by PATRICIA HIGHSMITH titled *Strangers on a Train*. It would obviously need a heavy rewrite to avoid CENSORSHIP and meet the demands of the marketplace; in Highsmith's book, Guy does murder Bruno's father and eventually is arrested. But it already held—in its doppelgänger characters, in its exploration of GUILTY wish-fulfillment, even in its bustling TRAIN—themes and settings that deeply appealed to him. He bought the rights cheaply and began the writing process.

The first to take a run at it was WHITFIELD COOK, who had already worked on *STAGE FRIGHT*; although that film had been a disappointment, Hitchcock always preferred to keep an amiable, if mediocre, relationship going rather than begin a new one. And Cook did some good early work in conference with the director, as they moved the action to the East Coast and made the book's brutal Bruno into a charming and SEXUALLY ambiguous villain.

Turning the lengthy prose treatment into a shooting script proved to be more difficult, however. Some writers who were approached (Dashiell Hammett and, reportedly and inexplicably, JOHN STEINBECK, who'd loudly denounced his last Hitchcock collaboration, *LIFEBOAT*) turned him down. The one who did accept, RAYMOND CHANDLER, soon regretted it, as did Hitchcock.

Although the two men were alike in some ways—sharing not only an English Victorian upbringing but also all the concomitant convictions about the necessity of duty and the dangerous mysteries of sex—they clashed almost from their first meetings (typically gossipy get-togethers that, in Chandler's opinion, dragged on for hours, and almost always uselessly). Chandler, who only wanted to hammer out a script, found Hitchcock's input distracting and often quite arbitrary ("You find yourself trying to rationalize the shots he wants to make rather than the story," Chandler wrote his British publisher. "Every time you get set he jabs you off balance by wanting to do a love scene on top of the Jefferson Memorial or something like that.") Hitchcock, who preferred talking expansively, even circuitously, before starting a project, thought Chandler abrupt and sullenly uncooperative. ("I would offer him a suggestion," Hitchcock recounted later. "Instead of giving it some thought, he would remark to me, very discontentedly, 'If you can go it alone, why the hell do you need me?'")

Chandler eventually turned in a screenplay—ending with Bruno mad and in an asylum, prefiguring the end of *PSYCHO*—only to be dismissed, without a chance for revisions or even a further word. Speeding the dismissal, perhaps, had been that, at one point, Chandler referred to the director, within his hearing, as "that fat bastard"; referring to his weight was the one insult Hitchcock could never forgive. (The real reason for his later rift with TIPPI HEDREN, he once claimed, was that she'd made a similar remark.)

With the start of production nearing, Hitchcock turned first to the fastest and most dependable of his collaborators, BEN HECHT; he was unavailable but recommended his assistant, CZENZI ORMONDE. With the help of ALMA REVILLE (and Barbara Keon, an old associate from the DAVID O. SELZNICK days), they pulled together the final script, with its consistent pattern of doubles—two men, two murders, two trips to the carnival—contributed by Hitchcock himself.

Casting had already begun. Hitchcock, typically, had wanted the biggest STAR he could get for his hero; William Holden was his first choice for Guy. But when that deal didn't happen, the director turned back to FARLEY GRANGER, the star of *ROPE*. It dissipated the conflict somewhat—apart from Holden's charisma, his forceful masculinity would have made his helplessness in the situation that much more dramatic. Yet Granger's softness added a homoeroticism to the story, making his first scene with ROBERT WALKER play like a HOMOSEXUAL pickup.

Walker was a better choice as Bruno. On some level, the casting seemed like one of Hitchcock's typically small, cruel JOKES at the expense of his old boss David O. Selznick. Walker was the ex-husband of Selznick's new wife, Jennifer Jones, and the actor's very public anguish over her initial affair with Selznick was well known; casting Walker took the last person Selznick wanted to think about and put him onscreen, front and center. But Walker, whose career had cratered since the divorce, was perfect in the role; like JOSEPH COTTEN in *SHADOW OF A DOUBT*, like ANTHONY PERKINS in *PSYCHO*, he took the easy charm that had first made him a star and twisted it into something else.

The rest of the cast was drawn mostly from old standbys—LEO G. CARROLL as Guy's prospective father-in-law, PATRICIA HITCHCOCK as Barbara, the slightly plain kid sister. Only RUTH ROMAN, the leading lady, was imposed on Hitchcock by the studio, where Jack Warner was trying to build her up as a new star (as shown by her second billing, ahead of Walker, in the credits). Hitchcock, who found her unappealing as an actress and even more distasteful as a fait accompli, remained unwaveringly cold to her throughout the shoot.

The finished film, however, shows Hitchcock triumphantly back in form after five years of mistakes and near-misses. And although Chandler had a small point—it is a movie full of eye-grabbing visuals, of Hitchcock "moments"—they're not only integrated into the story but into the theme, as in the famous shot of Bruno, the one fixed point in an audience of head-swiveling tennis fans, turning the full force of his MALE GAZE on Guy.

Strangers on a Train is, on one level, a movie about the men's attraction, a cruel parody of a romance—at first casually flirtatious over drinks, then darkened by jealousy and demands, finally torn apart in a flurry of recriminations and threats. But it is also a fable that, in a favorite Hitchcock device, mirrors the two men, right from the start, as reflecting opposites: Bruno in (practically luminous) spectator shoes, Guy in plain business ones; Bruno very carefully ordering his lunch, Guy settling for a hamburger and coffee; Bruno retreating to an indolent life of silk dressing gowns and allowances, Guy in shorts and sneakers, earning his living by sweating on the tennis court.

They are a different and yet strangely matched pair, and even more than *Shadow of a Doubt*, the film makes this parallel consistently explicit, through visuals (the opening shots of train tracks, the vertical neon lights at the carnival), through dialogue

(Bruno orders a "pair of doubles," turns on Guy for being a "double-crosser"), through narrative (Guy's panicky rush back to the carnival intercut with Bruno's delayed trek to the crime scene, Bruno's STRANGLING of Guy's wife restaged in his near-strangling of Guy's future sister-in-law). It is a complementary, contradictory film of reflections that only present distorted images, parallel lines that still eventually, brutally intersect. "Isn't it a fascinating design?" Hitchcock proudly asked FRANÇOIS TRUFFAUT decades later. "One could study it forever."

Yet if *Strangers on a Train* were only that, only offered a "fascinating design," then it would be just the sort of movie that critics (like Chandler) often accused Hitchcock of making; visually interesting, full of shots for cultists to champion, yet lacking any truly developed characters or emotional depth. But there is more to the film in that, not only in its exploration of Hitchcock's old themes of wish-fulfillment and TRANSFERRED guilt—Guy exclaims he "could strangle" his wife, and then she is strangled—but in the character of Miriam, that inconvenient woman who stands between Guy and the happiness he thinks he deserves.

Miriam should be, and could initially be taken as, a worthy sort of victim—no longer in love with Guy, pregnant with another man's child, and still happily dating several different boyfriends. ("She was a tramp," is Barbara's blunt obituary.) Even worse—according, at least, to postwar dreams of upper mobility—she's an obstacle to Guy's better, richer future. Like George in *A Place in the Sun*—also released that year—Guy has a chance at a very advantageous marriage, a union that could catapult his career. (Guy may be winning tennis matches now, but he wants to go into politics.) And like Alice in *A Place in the Sun*, Miriam—clinging, carping, and

definitely lower class—is the only barrier, a living and distasteful memory of humble backgrounds and guilty, sloppy pleasures. Won't someone, anyone, just make her go away?

Yet Hitchcock has his own doubled nature, and even as he makes Miriam into a victim, he is also able to mourn her victimization. True, we see her snapping at Guy early on, making quite clear her determination to bleed him for everything she can. But then watch her in her next scene, as she lets two boys take her to the carnival. She is flirtatious but in an almost innocently girlish way; she laughs easily, she bounces along, she incessantly gobbles snacks (her "craving" a particularly sharp touch, reminding us of her pregnancy). Without Guy, she is a different woman. Even at the moment of her death, as Bruno comes up and calls her name, her attitude is one of hopeful, even desperate, expectation. Perhaps this man—so much smoother than the local boys, so much more solicitous than her husband—will finally be the one she's been looking for.

And then he reaches out and strangles her, and her death throes are caught in the twin, distorting lenses of her eyeglasses.

For all the clever, geometric precision of *Strangers on a Train*, selfish, disorganized Miriam is its awkward, crude, yet ultimately sympathetic center. ("She was a human being," is the senator's stiff rejoinder to the flippant Barbara. "Let me remind you that even the most unworthy of us has a right to life and the pursuit of happiness.") Yes, she stood in the way of Guy's perfect new marriage and potential career—but ultimately, ironically, her murder only emphasizes his own crippling weakness and moral passivity. And even exonerated of the actual murder, what sort of political career can Guy expect? (Clearly the senator, for one, no longer trusts him.) Miriam's death no more frees Guy than

Villette's death frees Logan in *I CONFESS*; it's not a liberation but just another guilty burden.

And it is also Hitchcock's consistent, mournful reminder that, as much as we, and he, might like to gossip about true crimes and fantasize about murder (the neighbors in *Shadow of a Doubt*, the party guests here, Jeff in *REAR WINDOW*), the real thing is nasty and violent and ugly. And leaves not only a victim but also a coldly empty space.

References

Dorothy Gardiner and Kathrine Sorley, eds., *Raymond Chandler Speaking* (Boston: Houghton Mifflin, 1962), 132–35; Gerald Gardner, *The Censorship Papers: Movie Censorship Letters from the Hays Office, 1934-1968* (New York: Dodd, Mead, 1987), 90–91; Farley Granger with Robert Calhoun, *Include Me Out: My Life from Goldwyn to Broadway* (New York: St. Martin's Press, 2007), 107–10; Patricia Highsmith, *Strangers on a Train* (Baltimore: Penguin Books, 1974); Patrick McGilligan, *Alfred Hitchcock: A Life in Darkness and Light* (New York: HarperCollins, 2003), 441–53; Donald Spoto, *The Dark Side of Genius: The Life of Alfred Hitchcock* (New York: Da Capo Press, 1999), 321–31; François Truffaut, *Hitchcock/Truffaut*, rev. ed. (New York: Touchstone, 1985), 193–99.

STRANGULATION

The party conversation has turned to silly things, flights of fantasy, mad hypotheticals. Two matrons and a handsome younger man get on the subject of murder. Suppose you had a spouse who was dreadfully in the way. How to do it? One woman suggests a gun. The other, poison. The elegant gentleman is unconvinced. "I have the best way, the best tools," he proudly insists, holding up his hands. "Simple, silent and quick—the silent part being the most important. Let me show you what I mean. You don't mind if I borrow your neck for a moment, do you?"

The murder expert is Bruno Antony in Hitchcock's *STRANGERS ON A TRAIN*, and he's a trifle obsessed—so much so that a particularly garish necktie he favors features a lobster, gigantic claws ready and extended. But Hitchcock was obsessed, too. For the director—who often posed for publicity photographs mock-strangling his actresses, sometimes demonstrating a one-handed technique—it was, at least in movies sometimes, the "best way."

The very first shot in the first "real" Hitchcock movie, *THE LODGER*, is of a screaming BLONDE woman being throttled, and strangulation appears again and again in the movies to come. Sometimes, it is an offscreen event or mentioned in an aside—as in *SECRET AGENT*, where it means the death of one spy, or in *NOTORIOUS*, where it's the planned end of one of the conspirators—but more often it appears onscreen, dwelled on with sometimes lurid detail.

And when it does occur onscreen, its perpetrator's intent is often SEXUAL gratification, the execution a kind of coded sex—the no-longer-merry widows whom Uncle Charlie dispatches in *SHADOW OF A DOUBT*, the innocent boy victim of the sociopaths in *ROPE*, trashy Miriam (and very nearly one of those flirty dowagers) in *Strangers on a Train*. Margot barely escapes being strangled in *DIAL M FOR MURDER*; many women in *FRENZY* do not.

Because of the sexual connotations of the panting, spasmodic act—and Hitchcock often cuts in the middle of it to the victim's legs, writhing—sometimes, as if to mark their objectification of the victims, the murderers won't use their bare hands but an object (a scarf in *Dial M for Murder*, a necktie in *Frenzy*, the titular object in *Rope*).

For the killer in the first film, it is an extra barrier between himself and what is, after all, merely a distasteful job for hire, like being a gigolo; for the killers in the second and third movies, it illustrates their contempt for their victims (as well as serving symbolically—rough rope, club tie—to reassert their own, threatened masculinity).

Because although FRANÇOIS TRUFFAUT claimed Hitchcock shot his murders like love scenes and love scenes like murders, his movie murders aren't really love scenes—they're rapes. And unlike the violence committed by his villains with knives, guns, and poison—villains who are almost always acting surreptitiously or in disguise—these strangulations are crimes committed by people determined to assert their IDENTITIES and proclaim their DOMINANCE, killers who want their victims to feel their touch, to know everything that's happening, to be terrifyingly aware right up until the moment that they are not. There are more violent deaths in Hitchcock. There are rarely more vicious ones.

Reference
Donald Spoto, *The Dark Side of Genius: The Life of Alfred Hitchcock* (New York: Da Capo Press, 1999), 261, 331.

STUART, JOHN (1898–1979)
Edinburgh-born performer who, after typically brutal service in World War I—he enlisted with many of his friends, only to see them die next to him in the trenches—returned home to become an actor. He made his film debut in 1920; in just the next year he would make 10 films, heralding the start of a career busy even in those breakneck days. When one interviewer later asked him his approach, Stuart's summation was simple: "Keep learning, work like the devil, never relax and never be satisfied."

Handsome and athletic—he was a popular leading man through the silent era—Stuart played Hugh, the ill-treated fiancé in Hitchcock's *THE PLEASURE GARDEN*, and the detective in the muddled *NUMBER 17*; he also had a bit in *ELSTREE CALLING*. Although he had survived the advent of talkies, his fortunes fell along with that of Britain's homegrown cinema; through the '30s and '40s, most of his films had low budgets and even lower expectations, and the modest Stuart's fame began to rapidly fade.

He continued to "work like the devil," however, and television brought new opportunities, as did the British horror boom, with Stuart finding supporting parts in *Village of the Damned*, *Paranoiac*, and *The Mummy*. His last film role was as one of Krypton's elders in *Superman*. He died at 81 in London.

References
Jonathan Croall, "My Dad, the Silent Film Star," *Guardian*, February 10, 2012, http://www.theguardian.com/lifeandstyle/2012/feb/11/john-stuart-actor-silent-film-star; Nick Smurthwaite, "My Father, the Silent Film Star," https://www.thestage.co.uk/features/2013/jonathan-croall-on-john-stuart.

SUBJECTIVE CAMERA
A use of the camera to show precisely what a character is seeing, perhaps even how he or she is moving (now a cliché of a certain kind of slasher movie, in which the camera itself stalks the victims, both encouraging the audience's identification with the villain and crudely concealing his IDENTITY). Unlike the close-up/insert/reaction set-up of the KULESHOV EFFECT (which Hitchcock used extensively, particularly in *REAR WINDOW*), with the subjective technique, the camera actually "becomes" the character.

Hitchcock disliked any exaggerated use of the approach, singling out for specific criticism ROBERT MONTGOMERY, his old STAR from *MR. AND MRS. SMITH*. Montgomery used the subjective camera exclusively in his direction of *Lady in the Lake*, showing his main character's face only when he happened to stop and look in a mirror; throughout the entire film, we only saw what he saw. "A terrible mistake," Hitchcock called it in an early INTERVIEW with PETER BOGDANO-VICH.

It's not that Hitchcock didn't use the style; he did, and often. But it was always more carefully and more sparingly, with an eye toward a very specific emotional effect.

The first idea—a trick picked up perhaps from F. W. MURNAU and his EXPRESSIONISTIC approach, particularly as seen in *The Last Laugh*—was to use the approach to take the audience into a character's personal and very intense emotional state. Frequently, Hitchcock does this to show a character who's about to pass out due to alcohol (*THE RING*), stress (the first *THE MAN WHO KNEW TOO MUCH*), or a blow to the head (*THE LADY VANISHES*). Images may blur, darken, or swirl like a kaleidoscope. (It's done most famously and effectively to show Scottie's illness in *VERTIGO*, as a dizzying DOLLY zoom simultaneously seems to both bring the ground to us and thrust it away.) These are subjective shots in the most literal sense of the word, showing us not only what the character is seeing but also the heightened, even hysterical, way in which he or she is seeing it.

More frequently and realistically, however—although no less emotionally—Hitchcock also uses the subjective shot to draw us further into the story or to increase our identification with the character. Sometimes it serves a purely narrative function. In *REBECCA* and again in *ROPE*, the hero describes an event that happened earlier in a particular room; we don't get the usual flashback, but as he speaks, the camera pans from place to place, emphasizing the facts and encouraging us to "see" the peo-ple who are no longer there, whose violent actions persist only in memory. The camera becomes its own character.

Even more often, though, it encourages us to take sides. In almost too many films to count—but including *SPELL-BOUND*, *PSYCHO*, and *THE BIRDS*—it helps prolong tension, as a character climbs a STAIRCASE, getting closer and closer to danger, and we walk with them, step by step. Or it increases the violence of the assault, as in attacking the protagonist, someone seems to attack us personally—in *NORTH BY NORTHWEST*, in *STRANG-ERS ON A TRAIN*—as Hitchcock cuts from the approaching fist to the injured hero falling back. Just because we're sitting in a theater seat doesn't mean we're safe.

Or innocent. There are a number of subjective shots in *Psycho*, and each one encourages us to enter the mind of the character. Like desperate Marion, we look at the stolen money in our hands and wonder; like suspicious Lila, we climb the walk to the Bates house and worry what we're going to find. The tension becomes not just prolonged but also personal. And the method of identification is so strong, albeit subconscious, that Hitchcock's best use of it in the film may even slip by unnoticed—as, coming back to clean up the mess that MOTHER has made, Norman washes the blood off his hands. Our hands, actually, as the camera looks at them under the faucet.

Because this one shot is the precise fulcrum point of the movie where we are made, invisibly but undeniably, to shift our allegiances, to abandon our interest in Marion and identify with Norman instead, to move from merely identifying with a thief to cheering on someone who is at the very least an accessory after the fact to a murder (and, by the end of the film, has turned out to be quite a good deal more than that). It is the most daring thing in the entire movie—narratively, artistically, morally—

and Hitchcock does it with a single subjective shot. But then every kind of shot, every angle, had a specific meaning to him and a singular purpose. To do an entire movie with a subjective camera would be like writing an entire story in capital letters.

Reference
Peter Bogdanovich, *The Cinema of Alfred Hitchcock*, http://the.hitchcock.zone/wiki/Alfred_Hitchcock_and_Peter_Bogdanovich_%281963%29.

SUSPENSE
CBS radio anthology show that enjoyed a long run from 1942 to 1962; it had a try-out in 1940 with a special presentation of *THE LODGER*. Alfred Hitchcock directed the story, which he was still contemplating remaking in America as a film; EDMUND GWENN and HERBERT MARSHALL appeared. (Not coincidentally, all were also involved in *FOREIGN CORRESPONDENT*, for which the show served as a plug.) When Hitchcock's own TV anthology series began in the '50s, it would look back to this series and draw on much of the same material.

Reference
Patrick McGilligan, *Alfred Hitchcock: A Life in Darkness and Light* (New York: HarperCollins, 2003), 275–76.

SUSPENSE VS. SURPRISE
He was billed from early on in his Hollywood days as the "Master of Suspense," not as the "Master of Surprise," and the distinction was important to Hitchcock. He would often draw a firm line between the two words, as he pointed out carefully to FRANÇOIS TRUFFAUT during their famous INTERVIEW.

"We are now having a very innocent little chat," he said. "Let us suppose that there is a bomb underneath this table between us. Nothing happens, and then all of a sudden, 'Boom!'" This, he said, would result in no more than 15 seconds of surprise.

"Now," he continued, "let us take a suspense situation. The bomb is underneath the table and the public knows it, probably because they have seen the anarchist place it there. . . . The audience is longing to warn the characters on the screen: 'You shouldn't be talking about such trivial matters. There's a bomb beneath you and it's about to explode!'" And this, he pointed out, could provide a good 15 minutes of suspense.

The most important lesson from that, Hitchcock said, was that "whenever possible the public must be informed." And this, like most of the important information of his films, is best conveyed visually.

In *SABOTAGE*, we know the bomb will explode at 1:45—and so Hitchcock consistently cuts to ticking clocks. We see the gun poke out of the curtains in *THE MAN WHO KNEW TOO MUCH*, the shoe starting to fall out of a coat pocket in *MARNIE*, the murderer coming back to his apartment in *REAR WINDOW*—and always, always, before the person in danger does. This multiplies the audience's engagement because now we can anticipate the dangers ahead; it underlines (and exacerbates) our VOYEURISM because we're absolutely unable to do a thing about it.

Occasionally, Hitchcock would break his own rules. Although it's briefly prefigured, the shower attack in *PSYCHO* still owes much more to shock than suspense (and the murderer's true IDENTITY is concealed until the end); some of the attacks in *THE BIRDS* come without any warning. But Hitchcock was always on the side of drawing the audience into the story, a partnership nowhere more dramatic than in *VERTIGO*, where he gives the big "surprise" of the impersonation away. Anyone could have a shock ending in the final scene; far more interesting, Hitchcock thought, to have an entire third act of breathless anticipation: What will happen when Scottie finds out? (Even so, Hitchcock wrestled with that decision until the final cut.)

Still, even Hitchcock could sometimes make a mistake—as he felt he had in *Sabotage* by actually letting the bomb go off. "I made a cardinal error there in terms of suspense," he told PETER BOGDANOVICH. "The bomb should never have gone off. If you build an audience up to that point, the explosion becomes strangely anti-climactic. You work the audience up to such a degree that they need the relief. The critics were very angry. One woman said, "I could hit you." . . . One should have done the killing a different way, off the screen or something. I shouldn't have made a suspense thing of it."

References

Peter Bogdanovich, *The Cinema of Alfred Hitchcock,* http://the.hitchcock.zone/wiki/Alfred_Hitchcock_and_Peter_Bogdanovich_%281963%29; Patrick McGilligan, *Alfred Hitchcock: A Life in Darkness and Light* (New York: HarperCollins, 2003), 563–64; François Truffaut, *Hitchcock/Truffaut,* rev. ed. (New York: Touchstone, 1985), 73.

SUSPICION

Stretching himself a little thin, Alfred Hitchcock took on this anthology mystery series for NBC in 1957, even as he was working on films and *ALFRED HITCHCOCK PRESENTS* was airing on CBS; JOAN HARRISON produced, while he took an executive producer credit; he also directed the first episode, "FOUR O'CLOCK." The series managed 42 one-hour episodes before being cancelled.

SUSPICION (US 1941)

DIRECTOR: Alfred Hitchcock.
SCREENPLAY: Samson Raphaelson, Joan Harrison, Alma Reville, based on the book by *Before the Fact* by Francis Iles.
PRODUCER: Uncredited (Harry E. Edington).
CINEMATOGRAPHY: Harry Stradling.
EDITOR: William Hamilton.
ORIGINAL MUSIC: Franz Waxman.
CAST: Joan Fontaine (Lina McLaidlaw), Cary Grant (Johnnie Aysgarth), Cedric Hardwicke (Gen. McLaidlaw), Nigel Bruce ("Beaky"), Dame May Whitty (Mrs. McLaidlaw).
RUNNING TIME: 99 minutes. Black and white.
RELEASED THROUGH: RKO.

Johnnie Aysgarth is handsome, charming, lazy, and irresponsible—so sheltered Lina McLaidlaw can't help but fall for him. They get married, despite her rich father's disapproval, and have a lavish honeymoon—on borrowed money, Lina finds out. Although he likes to live in high style, Johnnie doesn't like to work, preferring to pawn his wife's possessions or hope for a big bet to come in at the racetrack.

Although eventually she shames Johnnie into taking a job with his cousin, an old school chum of Johnnie, "Beaky," tells her that Johnnie is a lovable scoundrel who can't quite be trusted. When Lina finds out Johnnie lost his job for embezzlement, she decides to leave him—but then her father dies, and Johnnie becomes a comfort.

Her father's will, though, provides no windfall, so Johnnie convinces Beaky to become his partner in a highly risky business proposition. When Beaky mysteriously dies, Lina becomes convinced that Johnnie killed him; when she discovers that Johnnie has been researching undetectable poisons, she's convinced she's next—particularly one night when he brings her a suspicious glass of milk.

Lina doesn't drink it and the next day announces she is going to her mother's for a while; an angry Johnnie insists on driving her. When along a mountain road she becomes convinced he's trying to push her out of the car, she becomes hysterical; Johnnie stops the car and tells her he was merely trying to keep her from falling out. In fact, he confesses, the poison was for him—he can't pay back the embezzled money and is likely to go to prison. As for Beaky's death, he had nothing to do with it.

A tearful Lina apologizes, and she and Johnnie drive back to their house—to face their future together.

Whenever he felt disappointed in the last project and uncertain about the next, Hitchcock's strategy was to retreat to the familiar. So after the boredom of *MR. AND MRS. SMITH*, Hitchcock decided to go back not only to mysteries but also to the sort of cozy tea-and-arsenic thrillers that writers like Dorothy L. Sayers and Agatha Christie had been turning out for years, with their English village settings and their determinedly conservative messages of chaos confounded and order blissfully restored.

Given that, though, *Before the Fact* by Francis Iles was in some ways an odd choice to adapt; its story was about a woman who gradually becomes convinced that her husband is going to kill her but is too in love with him to save herself. (She's right, too—he does kill her.) RKO had been trying to make a film of it since at least 1935, but the CENSORS wouldn't allow it—not because the main character was a murderer but because, by knowingly drinking the poison her husband gives her, the heroine was committing suicide.

Years later, Hitchcock would protest that he had intended to confound the censors, faithfully adapt the novel, and make a film in which the husband succeeds—

but, in the next scene, unknowingly mails a letter his wife has given him in which she denounced him as her murderer. (In some more emphatic tellings of this story, this was his plan right until the very end.) The only problem, the director said later, was that the studio or his STAR wouldn't agree, and the story had to be drastically rewritten.

According to DONALD SPOTO's *THE DARK SIDE OF GENIUS*, though, Hitchcock always intended to make a movie about a paranoid wife, and his stories about studio censorship were just him typically trying to shift the blame for a critically disparaged film; in fact, Spoto insists, Hitchcock's earliest treatments made no mention of the husband being a killer, focusing instead on the wife's delusions. Indeed, Hitchcock's own initial notes to the studio emphasize his interest in telling the story of an overly suspicious spouse.

Regardless of who first decided on that change in the novel, however, discarding the book's original ending posed a real problem. What to put in place of it? And how does Johnnie—who is definitely a wastrel, if not a killer—redeem himself? Hitchcock and his writers wrestled with a variety of endings. (In one, Johnnie atoned by going off to enlist in RAF.) Another climax, which was actually shot, had Lina drinking the "poisoned" milk—only to discover that it's a glass of plain homogenized because Johnnie is preparing to drink the real poison in the other room. (She stops him, of course.)

But a sneak preview was disastrous, and so the writers came up with yet another climax, in which Johnnie is shown to be innocent of everything except the embezzlement and Lina's worries are proven to be merely wild misinterpretations. Blaming herself, Lina vows to stand by him as he faces justice and, instead of heading to her MOTHER's as planned, steers their car home, taking an abrupt U-turn—an unwitting symbol perhaps for the film's entire awkward ending.

If the script process was headache-inducing, being back in England—or at least RKO's backlot version of the same—was comforting, as were the familiar faces. HARRY STRADLING, who had worked with Hitchcock on *JAMAICA INN*, was his cameraman again; JOAN FONTAINE, NIGEL BRUCE, and LEO G. CARROLL were held over from *REBECCA*, as was composer FRANZ WAXMAN, and many of the smaller parts were filled with old British friends. (DAME MAY WHITTY, Hitchcock's Miss Froy from *THE LADY VANISHES*, even showed up to play Lina's mother.)

And although this would be the first time Hitchcock had worked with CARY GRANT (they would do three more films together), he immediately got to the heart of the actor's dark appeal—the inherent duplicity in all that charm, the infinitely flexible morality behind that seductive smile. Johnnie is irresistible, as Beaky points out, which is his fatal danger, and drawing that quality out monopolized Hitchcock's attention during the shoot (a consideration that irked Fontaine, who had received the director's full focus on *Rebecca*). But then Fontaine had already played a version of Lina in that film—the shy, bookish romantic in sensible shoes. She could be left to her own devices, now. What Grant was doing, even if he wasn't playing an outright murderer, was very new for him and required special handling.

Yet even if on the set Hitchcock was devoting most of his attention to his male star, *Suspicion*—like *Rebecca*, like *SABOTAGE*, like *MARNIE*—is one of his most complicatedly female-oriented films, as the director both insists on tormenting his heroine (like a sadist) and identifying with her (as a feminist). Even the symbolism

throughout is feminine, rejecting his usual phallic, masculine metaphors for vaginal or maternal ones—the dark tunnel the movie begins in (daringly, in total blackness), the purse Lina snaps shut when declining Johnnie's advances, the mailbox that receives important letters (and provides Hitchcock's CAMEO), the milk that may bring death instead of life.

But those visual images are just the most obvious signifiers of a film that is told—relentlessly and almost without relief—from its heroine's point of view. It's a choice made not just to insist that this is her story (although Hitchcock actually always wanted to call the film *Johnnie*) but also to make clear that this is a story told through her eyes.

This is emphasized again visually when Johnnie and Beaky are talking about their new business venture and a trip out to see the land. We see Lina's face. We see her forming the word *MURDER* with letter tiles. We see a picture of the cliff-side property and her imagining of Johnnie pushing Beaky and the poor stooge falling (all played surreally to the real-life Beaky laughing stupidly at one of Johnnie's JOKES).

It's a smartly done sequence, and it ends with the emotionally overwrought Lina fainting. That's something she does again, and that and her generally overwhelmed attitude throughout suggest that, yes, Hitchcock's interest all along was in jumping into the dark whirlpool of paranoia and telling the story of a hysterical woman who saw criminal behavior where there was none. (A situation that so intrigued him that more than a decade later it served as the basis for the first episode of *ALFRED HITCHCOCK PRESENTS*, "REVENGE," which he directed himself.)

Because despite Fontaine's wounded feelings, she is very much the star of *Suspicion*, a fact borne out by her winning the best actress Oscar that year for her performance. (And the only Oscar ever won by a Hitchcock performer—although, honestly, Fontaine had deserved it more for *Rebecca* the year before.) And like so many of Hitchcock's greatest movies—*NOTORIOUS*, *VERTIGO*—it's a story about feminine doubt. "I thought you'd stopped loving me," Lina barely breathes at one point. And as Hitchcock knew, this worry—for someone who's only capable of seeing themselves as a reflection in their lover's EYES—could be the most existential doubt of all.

References

Patrick McGilligan, *Alfred Hitchcock: A Life in Darkness and Light* (New York: HarperCollins, 2003), 284–90; Donald Spoto, *The Dark Side of Genius: The Life of Alfred Hitchcock* (New York: Da Capo Press, 1999), 243–46; Donald Spoto, *Spellbound by Beauty: Alfred Hitchcock and His Leading Ladies* (New York: Harmony Books, 2008), 107–15; François Truffaut, *Hitchcock/Truffaut*, rev. ed. (New York: Touchstone, 1985), 140–43.

SWERLING, JO (1897–1964)

Berdichev-born author who began writing for the New York stage in the early '20s. He was at first known for his comedies and scripted *Humor Risk*, a 1921 short that marked the first appearance of the Marx Brothers. (The film is now considered lost; according to one story, Groucho hated it so much that he had it burned.)

By the dawn of the talkies, Swerling was in Hollywood, where people who could write dialogue were in high demand; he wrote several dramas for Frank Capra (*Ladies of Leisure*, *The Miracle Woman*) and such popular hits as *Pride of the Yankees* and *Blood and Sand* (in addition to being one of the many writers working piecemeal on *Gone with the Wind*). A competent veteran, he helped turn JOHN STEINBECK's treatment for *LIFEBOAT* into a workable screenplay (or into a travesty, according to Steinbeck).

Adaptable, if not particularly stylish, Swerling did the screenplay for the marvelously lurid noir *Leave Her to Heaven*, helped with some rewrites for Capra's *It's a Wonderful Life*, and cowrote the book for the Broadway hit *Guys and Dolls*. He died at 67 in Los Angeles.

References

"Jo Swerling," *IMDb*, http://www.imdb.com/name/nm0842485/bio?ref_=nm_ov_bio_sm; "Jo Swerling," *International Dictionary of Film and Filmmakers*, http://www.encyclopedia.com/doc/1G2-3406802624.html; Donald Spoto, *The Dark Side of Genius: The Life of Alfred Hitchcock* (New York: Da Capo Press, 1999), 267; Emily Temple, "John Steinbeck Wanted His Name Taken off Alfred Hitchcock's Lifeboat," *Flavorwire*, February 4, 2012, http://flavorwire.com/256717/john-steinbeck-wanted-his-name-taken-off-hitchcocks-lifeboat.

T

TANDY, JESSICA (1909–1994)

London-born performer, the daughter of a traveling salesman and an educator who worked with mentally disabled children. Outwardly pale and delicate but with a core of inner strength, Tandy made her stage debut at 18, and although some directors dismissed her as not being pretty enough for leads, "in a way it was rather good," she said later. "I didn't get the part of the young ingénue. I got more interesting parts." Soon she was being acclaimed for her work in Shakespeare, her Ophelia in JOHN GIEL-GUD's 1934 production of *HAMLET* being particularly prized.

After her marriage to actor Jack Hawkins began to end, Tandy moved to America, eventually marrying fellow actor HUME CRONYN, making her Hollywood debut in *The Seventh Cross* in 1944, and following that up with small parts in the period dramas *Dragonwyck* and *Forever Amber*. The stage, however, continued to offer her the greatest awards; her performance as Blanch du Bois in *A Streetcar Named Desire*, a role she took on at Tennessee Williams's request and played for two years, was said to be one of Broadway's greatest. (Brando, being Brando, later proclaimed that they'd both been miscast and insisted the play hadn't worked as a result.)

Tandy's work in Hollywood continued to be sporadic and somewhat less rewarding; Hitchcock, however, who appreci-ated theater actors—and had known her for years through Cronyn—was keen to have her in *THE BIRDS*. (She had already appeared on three episodes of *ALFRED HITCHCOCK PRESENTS*.) And although it may not be apparent now, at the time Tandy was one of the biggest names in a film starring newcomer TIPPI HEDREN, TV actress SUZANNE PLESHETTE, and Aussie import ROD TAYLOR in only his second leading role.

Tandy was one of its biggest assets, too. Although slightly too old to be playing the MOTHER of a grade-schooler, Tandy brought heart to the character of a lonely and clinging mother, and her performance is full of stark, wordless touches—her silent gasping horror as she flees the dead farmer's house, her barely-held-at-bay hysteria as she tidies up the house after another avian onslaught. Her later scenes with Hedren have a particularly striking, guarded tenderness—deepened perhaps by the knowledge that the veteran actress was responding not only to a character but also to a similarly unsteady young STAR.

"Working with Jessica Tandy was just celestial," Hedren said later. "I mean, consummate actress. You know, just watching her working was just thrilling. Absolutely thrilling. And what a beautiful person she was—not just physically but just, you know, really considerate and fun."

Robert Donat and Madeleine Carroll pause, but only briefly, in the fast-paced *The 39 Steps*. *Gaumont British Picture Corporation of America/Photofest © Gaumont British Picture Corporation of America*

After *The Birds*, Tandy rededicated herself to the stage, often appearing with Cronyn and racking up a long list of successes in New York and regional theater; their two-hander *The Gin Game* became a particularly sweet success. And yet as she grew older, the cinema's interest was rekindled; she had good parts in *The Bostonians*, *The World According to Garp*, and *Fried Green Tomatoes* and won the best actress Oscar for *Driving Miss Daisy*. She was already 80, and although she would soon be diagnosed with cancer, she worked right until her death in Connecticut five years later.

References

All about The Birds, directed by Laurent Bouzereau (2000), documentary, http://the.hitchcock.zone/wiki/All_About_The_Birds_%282000%29_-_transcript; Marilyn Berger, "Jessica Tandy, a Patrician Star of Theater and Film, Dies at 85," *New York Times*, September 12, 1994, http://www.nytimes.com/learning/general/onthisday/bday/0607.html; "Jessica Tandy," *IBDb*, http://ibdb.com/person.php?id=68863; "Jessica Tandy," *IMDb*, http://www.imdb.com/name/nm0001788/bio?ref_=nm_ov_bio_sm.

TAYLOR, JOHN RUSSELL (1935–)

Dover-born author who went to Cambridge, studied art, and began writing on film, theater, and television in the early '60s, becoming the movie critic for the *Times* in 1962. He has written examinations of Britain's "angry young man" dramas; critical biographies of STARS, including Alec Guinness and INGRID BERGMAN; and many more books on art and artists.

For much of the '70s, Taylor lived in California, where he taught at UCLA and became friendly with Alfred Hitchcock; he eventually became the director's official biographer, too, publishing the authorized *Hitch: The Life and Times of Alfred Hitchcock* in 1978. The book had all the advantages—and disadvantages—of the family's cooperation. On the one hand, it had many personal details, particularly of the director's childhood; on the other, it seemed to praise his work indiscriminately while studiously avoiding any questions about the films' darker meanings or the filmmaker's personal life.

As a review in *American Film* said at the time, "Obviously, (Taylor) would not have got the director's cooperation were they not relatively close personal friends, but when that friendship leads to a generally uncritical point of view, even spilling over into worshipfulness, it is unclear whether the bargain was worth the price. In biographies of famous men published while the subjects are still alive, this is almost always the case."

Later, when DONALD SPOTO's *THE DARK SIDE OF GENIUS* raised questions of personal obsession and SEXUAL harassment, particularly on the sets of *THE BIRDS* and *MARNIE*, Taylor rose to the late director's defense, heatedly denying the charges on Hitchcock's behalf. (The real reason the filmmaker had broken with TIPPI HEDREN, Taylor claimed, was because, when Hitchcock refused to give her time off during shooting to fly to an awards show, she had publicly called him a "fat pig" and badly hurt his feelings.) Taylor reviewed Spoto's book for the *Times*; unsurprisingly, he panned it.

Taylor still writes about Hitchcock occasionally, and despite history's deepening and darkening portrait of the director, his own viewpoint remains essentially unchanged. "He was possibly a monster," he says now. "But a very loveable monster."

References

"John Russell Taylor: Biography," *Fandango*, http://www.fandango.com/johnrusselltaylor/biography/p188022; John Russell Taylor, "Hitch Hatchet Job," *Times*, May 19, 1983, http://the.hitchcock.zone/wiki/The_Times_%2819/May/1983%29_-_Hitch_hatchet_job; John Russell Taylor, "A Loveable Monster," *Times*, February 16, 2008, http://the.hitchcock.zone/wiki/The_Times_%2816/Feb/2008%29_-_'A_loveable_monster'; Kenneth Turan, "Nothing Too Personal," *American Film* (Decem-

ber 1978), http://the.hitchcock.zone/wiki/
American_Film_%281978%29_-_Books
:_Nothing_Too_Personal.

TAYLOR, ROD (1930–2015)

Rugged, Lidcombe-born performer who
grew up in the Australian suburbs, the son
of a family with some artistic leanings. His
father was a draftsman, and his mother, a
prolific author of children's books. Initially
interested in art, Taylor switched to drama
after seeing LAURENCE OLIVIER on tour
in *Richard III*. Supporting himself at first
by working as a window dresser, Taylor
began landing small parts on television and
in Australian films; when a 1954 prize for
his radio work won him a ticket to London,
he impulsively hopped off the plane during
a Los Angeles layover and stayed to pursue
his chances there instead.

The handsome, virile Taylor quickly
picked up supporting parts in westerns,
dramas, even light romantic comedies;
although he failed to win the audition for
the boxing drama *Somebody up There
Likes Me*, he did get the part in *The Time
Machine*, his first lead role, which led to
more TV work (and doing the voice of
Pongo in Disney's *101 Dalmatians*). *THE
BIRDS* was only his second lead.

"I got this call out of the blue from Mr.
Hitchcock and was totally amazed," Taylor
said years after. "And I came out, and being
a brash young brat, I guess I didn't show
any kind of respect that I was supposed to,
and I think he kind of liked it. And we got
on extremely well. And I did the wrong
thing—I called him Alfred!"

Overcoming that initial, unwanted
familiarity, Hitchcock came to like the
young actor, Taylor said, particularly when
it was clear he didn't have a lot of actorly
questions about motivation. But as the
filming went on, Taylor said, he noticed
that Hitchcock began to ignore him while
being strangely possessive about leading

lady TIPPI HEDREN; the director insisted
on having tea alone with her every day and
bristled when Taylor even touched her.

"She was like a precious piece of jewelry he owned, and little by little, no one
was permitted to come physically close to
her during the production," Taylor told
DONALD SPOTO. "He was putting a
wall around her, trying to isolate her from
everyone else so that all her time would
be spent only with him." Taylor tried to
be supportive of his costar—Hedren later
called him a "great pal to me and a real
strength"—but the actor was in the middle
of a tempestuous relationship with Anita
Ekberg at the time and decidedly preoccu-
pied.

After *The Birds*, Taylor held on to his
leading-man status for a few more years—
he made two movies with DORIS DAY,
including the spy parody *The Glass Bottom Boat*, and starred in the Sean O'Casey
story *Young Cassidy*—but as the '60s grew
shaggier, his old-fashioned, square-jawed
appeal began to feel a little out of fashion.

By the '70s, Taylor was mostly doing
low-budget action thrillers in Europe; by
the '80s, he'd moved on to smaller character parts. "Pretending to still be the tough
man of action isn't dignified for me anymore," the former STAR frankly admitted.
"There comes a time when you're over the
hill and there are plenty of great looking
younger actors who can take your place.
The action stars of today are making some
wonderful films. There are no 'I could do it
better' feelings in me."

Taylor retired in 2000, only to be lured
back for two, tongue-in-cheek projects—
playing Winston Churchill in Quentin Tar-
antino's *Inglourious Basterds*, a tribute to
the sort of Euro-exploitation movies Taylor
had churned out in the past and, in a nod
to *The Birds, Kaw*, a low-budget burlesque
about lethal ravens. He died at 84, in Los
Angeles, of a heart attack. "One of the most

fun people I have ever met, thoughtful and classy," Hedren said afterward. "There was everything good in that man."

References

All about The Birds, directed by Laurent Bouzereau (2000), documentary, http://the.hitchcock.zone/wiki/All_About_The_Birds_%282000%29_-_transcript; Ronald Bergan, "Rod Taylor Obituary," *Guardian*, January 9, 2015, http://www.theguardian.com/film/2015/jan/09/rod-taylor; "Rod Taylor," *IMDb*, http://www.imdb.com/name/nm0001792/bio?ref_=nm_ov_bio_sm; "Rod Taylor, Star of 'The Birds,' Dies Aged 84," *BBC News*, http://www.the guardian.com/film/2015/jan/09/rod-taylor; Donald Spoto, *Spellbound by Beauty: Alfred Hitchcock and His Leading Ladies* (New York: Harmony Books, 2008), 250.

TAYLOR, SAMUEL A.
(1912–2000)

Chicago-born author who, after a stint in the Merchant Marine, moved to New York, where he began writing for radio comedies and serving as an anonymous script doctor for bad plays. His own Broadway career began late in life with the nostalgic *The Happy Time* in 1950. It was followed three years later by *Sabrina Fair*, and when Billy Wilder decided to turn that into the movie *Sabrina*, Taylor shared the adaptation assignment (with ERNEST LEHMAN) and began a new life in Hollywood.

He became Hitchcock's last but best choice to write *VERTIGO*. Maxwell Anderson's script had been unusable (which should not have been surprising, as Hitchcock hadn't liked his script for *THE WRONG MAN* either—but liked breaking in a new writer even less). The second script, courtesy of ALEC COPPEL, hadn't been much better, the director decided, and so he turned to Taylor, who had enjoyed several recent successes.

"In those first talks, we decided that the more emotion there was in the man, the stronger the picture would be," Taylor said of their early meetings. "And he found without even thinking about it that he was making a picture that went much deeper than most of his pictures just because the basic story—not the plot—but the basic story had a true human emotion; this obsession of a man who, for the first time in his life, had fallen deeply in love."

It would be another one of the director's close, working relationships. "I gave him the characters and the dialogue he needed and developed the story, but it was from first frame to last his film," Taylor said. "There was no moment that he wasn't there."

The two men became friends, as did their wives—the Hitchcocks attended the wedding of the Taylors' son, and the couples even occasionally vacationed together—and Hitchcock would turn to him again for help when other writers were unavailable or couldn't provide the touch he wanted. The results, though, were never as magical as *Vertigo*. *NO BAIL FOR THE JUDGE* ended up not being made when Audrey Hepburn dropped out; *TOPAZ*, which was shot, unfortunately survived and staggered into theaters.

Although they remained friends, Taylor concentrated on other projects after *Topaz*, including the soapy *The Love Machine* and Wilder's *Avanti!* Neither came to much, and a 1976 return to Broadway—the western comedy *Legend*—closed after five performances. Taylor retired shortly thereafter; knowing that Hitchcock was by then depressed and in failing health, he made a point of calling him most Sundays just to check in.

"He never really had any close friends," Taylor said years later. "It must have been very hard for him. Hitch was taken very seriously by the whole world—but not by

Hollywood until it was too late. He was a great artist, but people in Hollywood . . . thought he just told a good yarn."

Taylor died of heart failure in Blue Hill, ME, at 87.

References

Obsessed with Vertigo: New Life for Hitchcock's Masterpiece, directed by Harrison Engle (1997), documentary, http://the .hitchcock.zone/wiki/Obsessed_with_Vertigo:_New_Life_for_Hitchcock's_Masterpiece_%281997%29_-_transcript; "Samuel A. Taylor," *IMDb*, http://www.imdb.com/name/nm0853138/bio?ref_=nm_ov_bio _sm; Donald Spoto, *The Dark Side of Genius: The Life of Alfred Hitchcock* (New York: Da Capo Press, 1999), 401–2, 552.

TEARLE, GODFREY (1884–1953)

Anglo-American performer born in New York but raised in England. His father was the Shakespearean actor George Osmond Tearle, and Tearle made his stage debut at nine in his father's production of *Richard III*, continuing as a member of the company; in 1908, he made his film debut in an early, abridged version of *Romeo and Juliet*. As a young man, he would go on to play in many other classics, including a particularly acclaimed *Othello*.

Tearle's film work began to pick up in the '20s and, given his resonant voice, suffered no slowdown when the talkies arrived; his movie career got a substantial boost in 1935, when Hitchcock had the regal actor play Professor Jordan, the respectable English gentleman who is identified by part of a missing finger as the leader of a gang of enemy agents called *THE 39 STEPS*.

The roles that followed were less villainous; during the war, Tearle played a long line of valiant officers onscreen and, after the conflict ended, even impersonated Franklin Delano Roosevelt in the story of the atomic bomb, *The Beginning or the End*. In 1947, he triumphantly returned to Shakespeare in the lauded Broadway production of *Antony and Cleopatra* opposite Katherine Cornell; his last film was the gentle comedy *The Titfield Thunderbolt* in 1953. He died at 68 in London.

References

"Godfrey Tearle," *IMDb*, http://www.imdb .com/name/nm0853607/bio?ref_=nm _ov_bio_sm; "Godfrey Tearle: Biography," *Fandango*, http://www.fandango.com/godfreytearle/biography/P70160.

TETZLAFF, TED (1903–1995)

Los Angeles–born filmmaker, the son of racecar driver and early stuntman Teddy Tetzlaff. Tetzlaff (whose given name was actually Dale) began his career in the '20s photographing forgettable silent comedies. By the 1930s, his star had risen considerably, thanks largely to CAROLE LOMBARD, who declared him her favorite cinematographer; he ended up shooting 10 of her films. He shot *NOTORIOUS* for Hitchcock, and you can see some of what Lombard loved in his work with INGRID BERGMAN there—she never looked lovelier, her skin soft and supple, her golden hair giving off its own special light.

It was a beautiful achievement, and as if he knew he couldn't better that film's many memorable visuals—the long slow crane shot at the party, the never-ending kiss—Tetzlaff made that film, his 115th, his last as a cinematographer and refocused his energies on directing. Although they tended to be bottom-of-the-bill features (*Son of Sinbad*, *The Treasure of Lost Canyon*), a number of noirs, particularly the HITCHCOCKIAN *The Window*, about a boy who witnesses a murder but finds no one believes him, suggests that he would have done more had he access to better material.

After a few TV episodes and a cheap cowboy picture, *The Young Land*, in 1959, Tetzlaff quit the industry; he died at 91 in Fort Baker, CA.

References

"Great Cinematographers, Part 12: Ted Tetzlaff," *The Iron Cupcake*, https://the ironcupcake.wordpress.com/2014/03/30/ great-cinematographers-part-12-ted-tetz laff; "Ted Tetzlaff," *IMDb*, http://www .imdb.com/name/nm0005898.

TEY, JOSEPHINE (1896–1952)

Inverness author, born Elizabeth Mackintosh. An athletic young woman, originally a gym teacher at a girl's boarding school, she interrupted her career to come home and take care of her ailing mother. After her mother's death, it was simply assumed that Tey—as the eldest of three daughters and unmarried—would continue to stay on and keep house for her father. She stayed for almost 30 years.

She had always written and during the '20s began to publish poems and short stories, her first novel, the mystery *The Man in the Queue*, arriving in 1929. She never published under her real name, preferring either Tey or "Gordon Daviot," and wrote mysteries, plays, and historical novels; her drama of Richard II, *Richard of Bordeaux*, was a surprise stage hit and an early popular triumph for JOHN GIELGUD, who became a lifelong friend.

Her best-known works starred Scotland Yard inspector Alan Grant; *A Shilling for Candles*, liberally adapted, became Hitchcock's YOUNG AND INNOCENT. By far the most inventive book, *The Daughter of Time*, has a convalescing Grant "investigating" the crimes of Richard III by digging into old histories; he concludes the king was framed. Nearly as successful was her imposter-heir story *Brat Farrar*, which has been adapted several times and stolen from many times more (including for the film *Paranoiac*).

Most of her stories warn about taking things at face value, and for all the puzzles she posed, the greatest may have been Tey herself; she gave no interviews and strenuously avoided all publicity. If she had any romances, their names remained as secret as their genders; although some friends said she had lost a love in battle in World War I, modern writers have made other assumptions about her sexuality, pointing out the writer used the man's name Gordon Daviot not only for her more "serious" works but in private life, as well. She remains her own last, best mystery.

Tey survived her father by only two years; when she died at 56, she left her entire estate to the National Trust.

References

Josephine Tey: A Very Private Person, http://www.josephinetey.net; Robert McCrum, "Elizabeth Mackintosh: Woman of Mystery Who Deserves to Be Rediscovered," *Guardian*, July 30, 2011, http:// www.theguardian.com/books/2011/jul/31/ robert-mccrum-elizabeth-mackintosh -mystery.

THEREMIN

Originally developed in 1920 in the Soviet Union as a proximity sensor used to detect nearby movements, Leon Theremin's invention eventually began to garner interest from avant-garde composers; its wavering tones were singularly eerie although not quite as unique as how you played it. (Unlike other instruments, you never put your hands on the theremin; you move them near it, with one hand adjusting volume and the other regulating pitch.)

In the Soviet Union, Dmitri Shostakovich pioneered its use in film, but the instrument gained its widest exposure thanks to MIKLOS RÓZSA, who used it in *SPELLBOUND*, *The Lost Weekend*, and *The Red House* to dramatize dream-like or disorienting moments. BERNARD HERRMANN's score for *The Day the Earth Stood Still* and DMITRI TIOMKIN's for *The Thing (From Another World)* are other classic Hollywood examples.

Although the theremin never became a standard component of orchestral music, it did influence new generations of electronica; similar instruments can be heard in the movie *Forbidden Planet*, the Beach Boys song "Good Vibrations," and the many works inspired by the various inventions of Robert Moog.

References

"Leon Theremin," *Theremin Times*, http://www.theremintimes.ru/leon-theremin; *Theremin World*, http://www.theremin world.com.

THE 39 STEPS (GB 1935)

DIRECTOR: Alfred Hitchcock.
SCREENPLAY: Charles Bennett, Ian Hay, based on the novel *The Thirty-Nine Steps* by John Buchan.
PRODUCERS: Uncredited (Sir Michael Balcon, Ivor Montagu).
CINEMATOGRAPHY: Bernard Knowles.
EDITOR: D.N. Twist.
ORIGINAL MUSIC: Jack Beaver, Louis Levy.
CAST: Robert Donat (Richard Hannay), Madeleine Carroll (Pamela), Peggy Ashcroft (Margaret, the Crofter's Wife), Godfrey Tearle (Prof. Jordan), Wylie Watson (Mr. Memory).
RUNNING TIME: 86 minutes. Black and white.
RELEASED THROUGH: Gaumont British Distributors.

Richard Hannay is watching a cheap, music hall variety show—chorus girls and the astounding "Mr. Memory"—when, somewhere in the crowd, shots are fired. A mad rush to the exits ensues, and Hannay finds himself pressed up against an attractive foreigner, who gives her name as Smith and asks to come home with him. She's only looking for refuge, though—as she explains to him, she's a secret agent currently working for the British government, and there are assassins after her. Hannay lets her stay but doesn't quite believe her—until she falls, dying, into his arms the next morning, a knife in her back.

Not waiting for the assassins to come back to him, Hannay flees. Remembering a few phrases from the woman's story—a small town in Scotland, military secrets, and something called "the 39 steps"—he heads north. But the police now suspect him of the murder—and when on a train he's given away by Pamela, a beautiful stranger, he has to escape, tramping across the moors. After taking brief shelter at a dour farmer's cottage, he goes to the house of the town's leading citizen, a professor, for help—only to find out that "the 39 steps" is a gang of spies and the professor is their leader.

Hannay escapes the squire and goes to the police, where he discovers they don't believe him. Running from the station, he slips into a political meeting, where he's mistaken for the featured speaker. He improvises a rousing speech, but the authorities arrive with Pamela in tow, there to identify him. They put them both in a car and handcuff them together for security, while explaining that they have to drive to a distant police station—but Hannay, realizing they aren't policemen but the professor's spies, escapes again, this time taking the handcuffed Pamela with him.

They spend the night at a local inn, with Hannay pretending that they're a runaway couple and Pamela still sure he's a murderer. But after slipping out of her cuffs and overhearing the professor's spies arrive and talking downstairs—shortly before the landlady chases them away—she realizes Hannay is telling the truth.

The next morning, she tells him that she believes him now—also that she heard the spies talking about the London Palladium. Hannay (followed eventually by Pamela) rushes off, when he spots the professor in the stands—and oddly Mr. Memory again. Hannay realizes they are using the little man to memorize state secrets. "What are the 39 steps?" Hannay shouts during the performance, and when the performer by rote begins to announce the answer—that it is an organization of spies—the professor shoots him and tries to escape. The police close in on the real spy, and Hannay is free at least.

Hitchcock's first perfect movie and the model for many to come, as well as a beautiful distillation of all the themes and motifs he had been thinking about since *THE PLEASURE GARDEN*—our world of role playing and PLAYS WITHIN PLAYS, the fluid nature of IDENTITY, GUILT and innocence, BONDAGE both literal and emotional.

After the success of *THE MAN WHO KNEW TOO MUCH* in 1934, both the studio, GAUMONT-BRITISH, and the team, Hitchcock and CHARLES BENNETT, were eager not only to repeat but also to enlarge on their earlier triumph. The studio decided to increase the new film's budget by half and to earmark some of that extra money for signing STARS who had appeal beyond Britain's borders; the filmmakers concentrated on reprising some of the elements (foreign spies, interesting locations, a couple in jeopardy, and a climactic shootout in a public place) that had worked the first time around while expanding the drama and scope.

Hitchcock thought JOHN BUCHAN would be the perfect jumping-off point— he had been a fan of the author since boy-hood—but the globe-trotting *GREENMANTLE* seemed too ambitious a project. Eventually, they agreed on Buchan's *The Thirty-Nine Steps*—although Bennett argued that the 20-year-old novel was humorless and thin on character and would need work. Together, the two men concentrated on adding both while constructing the plot as a long series of breathlessly strung-together chases—Hannay flees the assassins, then the police, then the police again, then the professor, then the police and the assassins simultaneously, all the while hanging out of moving TRAINS, jumping through windows, or ducking behind waterfalls. (The career-long criticism that Hitchcock films are just a series of fast-paced, illogical incidents begins here—Why, to start off with, do the assassins stab "Miss Smith" in the bedroom but leave Hannay sleeping quietly in the parlor?)

Casting was a little trickier than the last film, as the studio wanted actors who could play recognizable Britishers yet also appeal to foreign audiences. ROBERT DONAT was signed to play Hannay—he was English but already known to American movie fans. So, too, was MADELEINE CARROLL, an elegant, icy beauty who'd spent time in Hollywood and, the director later judged, was the "first BLOND who was a real Hitchcock type."

The "real Hitchcock type," of course, was the "snow-covered volcano"—and when shooting began (only two days after Carroll signed her contract), Hitchcock worried that perhaps she wasn't going to warm up at all. (On an early read-through, he confessed, she read her lines "in a kind of mesmeric trance.") So, when it came time to shoot the first scene of the picture—which, as the production was typically working out of sequence, came more than halfway into the plot, when she and Donat are first manacled together—Hitchcock slipped a pair of real handcuffs on the couple. And then, pretending to have misplaced the key, he left them that way for hours.

The action can be read indulgently as one of the director's typical practical JOKES (or more sinisterly as an example of a fondness for hurting beautiful women— the forged-steel cuffs left angry welts on Carroll's pale wrists). But far more probably, and certainly practically, it was Hitchcock's way of not only breaking down Carroll's reserve but also forging a natural bond between his stars. He would play similar and often misinterpreted "pranks" in the future—whispering a dirty word into actresses' ears right before a take, slapping JOAN FONTAINE on *REBECCA*, leaping on top of ANN TODD during *THE PARADINE CASE*—but they were almost always a way of breaking down artificial barriers and eliciting real emotions. While the director may have professed to hate METHOD ACTING, he always had a method of his own.

Donat had to agree it worked. "For nearly an hour Madeleine and I shared this enforced companionship, while the hunt for the key was sustained," he later said. "There was nothing else to do, so we talked of our mutual friends, of our ambitions, and of film matters generally. Gradually our reserve thawed as we exchanged experiences. When 'Hitch' saw that we were getting along famously, he extracted the 'missing' key from his waistcoat pocket, released us, and said, with a satisfied grin, 'Now that you two know each other we can go ahead.' Had it not been for Hitchcock's little ruse, Madeleine and I would probably have taken quite a time to 'get together'—to the detriment of our work in the interim."

And the stars do have a pleasantly informal connection here, giving *The 39 Steps* an easy give-and-take that later similar pictures—*SABOTEUR, NORTH BY NORTHWEST*—had to more obviously strive for. Donat—with kind eyes and a chuckle in his voice—is one of the most charming of Hitchcock heroes, understated yet always fully present. (The director so loved his leading man's performance that he kept trying to sign him for further movies—*SECRET AGENT, THE LADY VANISHES, SABOTAGE*, even *Rebecca*— but other commitments and Donat's own fragile health always intervened.)

Carroll, meanwhile, is, as Hitchcock realized later, really the prototype for all his heroines—from her staid introduction as a stuffy, bespectacled woman reading a book (an entrance he'd reprise for Fontaine in *SUSPICION*) to the revelation of her surprising sexiness as, in the midst of her flight with Hannay, she peels off her sodden stockings and shows a glimpse of thigh and garter. The actress and her character put up with a lot—being grabbed, bound, prodded, pulled, and marched through water—yet both survive without whining.

The money spent on those two marquee stars—a decided step up from LESLIE BANKS and EDNA BEST in *The Man Who Knew Too Much*—had certainly been a good investment, as had the rest of the production budget. Comfortable as he was working with miniatures, it's clear that Hitchcock also has real trains to play with here, as well as far more detailed sets and the help of composers—Mr. Memory's little theme is particularly appropriately insistent. Although *The 39 Steps* was made three years before *The Lady Vanishes*, its production values are more polished and sophisticated.

And the studio's confidence seemed to inspire Hitchcock, too, to try some new effects. The hallucinatory, double exposures of Smith's face coming back to haunt Hannay were a standard trick, too, but Hitchcock added a deliberately distorting, mechanical quality to her voice; when the maid discovers Smith's corpse and screams, he overlaps the sound, so all that comes out of her mouth is the train whistle from the next scene. (Hitchcock was also already experimenting with long, difficult camera movements, although he had to fake his best one here: The camera starts with Hannay and Pamela inside a car in a process shot and then moves outside—at which point it very briefly cuts to black and then resumes as a LOCATION shot that pulls behind the car and watches it depart.)

More than charismatic performances and intriguing style, though, the film is suffused with a variety of themes that would later become nearly trademarked as HITCHCOCKIAN. To begin with, there is the world of theater and the drama of performance. *The 39 Steps* begins in a cheap music hall, takes a brief detour to a community center, and ends at the London Palladium—like *The Pleasure Garden, Sabotage, Saboteur, STAGE FRIGHT*, and many other of the director's films, it's a story that contrasts the glitzy artifice of public entertainments and the grim reality of private lives, while wondering if they are really that different at all. (The film's first shot is a pan across a generic marquee—Music Hall—and like the performers he is going to see, Hannay soon dons his own costumes and identities, while trying desperately to see the real people behind the parts they play.) It's a movie about roles, and its true tragic hero is WYLIE WATSON's Mr. Memory—the little man so committed to giving his best performance that, given the cue, he can't help but deliver his line, even though it means his death.

There are other touches, too—soon to become Hitchcock tropes. The "snow-covered volcano," yes, but also the innocent man pursued by both the police and the real criminals. There's the completely arbitrary MACGUFFIN, as well—the plans to a noiseless aircraft engine, it turns out.

And those little things that often pop up in Hitchcock's films—spying on someone in the theater through a pair of opera glasses (*The Pleasure Garden*, both versions of *The Man Who Knew Too Much*); characters suddenly getting knives in their backs (the second *The Man Who Knew Too Much, North by Northwest*); and, of course, handcuffs (*THE LODGER, Saboteur*).

But there is one theme that not only runs through *The 39 Steps* but also is the most carefully developed. And it's that of romantic union. Within the film's brief running time, Hitchcock and Bennett present us with a variety of models for relationships. First, we meet the milkman, a married man ("Don't rub it in!") who, when he thinks Hannay is a lover fleeing a jealous husband, gives a vicarious leer and all his help; he's not in a particularly happy union, we can assume. Later, we meet the professor and his wife, a doughty matron who worries about how many guests she has for luncheon but not the fact that her husband is holding a stranger at gunpoint; theirs is a cold, obviously practical, businesslike relationship.

And then there is the crofter and his wife. The episode—which is not in Buchan's book—comes as Hannay is trudging across the moors. He stops at the home of a crofter, a grizzled tenant farmer. The man (a stereotypical movie Scot) is judgmental, taciturn, and cheap; he's also wed to a much younger woman (a lovely performance by a fresh-faced PEGGY ASHCROFT). It is not much of a marriage, probably arranged, and although they share this tiny cottage, Hannay's arrival only shows how far apart they are: While the crofter sees the stranger as a source of quick money for a night's lodging, his wife views him as a connection to the city life she left behind.

Of course, different characters always see different things in Hitchcock's films—a point borne home in a wordless sequence that could have come from one of the director's own silents. The three are having a simple dinner while a newspaper lies on the table with a story about the escaped murderer who's fled to Scotland. Hannay looks down at the headline. The wife looks down at the headline. Their eyes meet—and in a brief exchange of glances, she expresses her fear, and he vouches his innocence. And meanwhile, her husband watches it all, and assumes the two of them are only sharing looks of lust and already making promises for an assignation.

It is done without a line of dialogue—it is done, really, completely with separate close-ups and contrasting sightlines—and it is as clear an example of the director's much-beloved PURE CINEMA as any. But although the sequence barely pushes the plot forward, it gives us the film's most negative example of a marriage, a husband and wife bound by traditional beliefs and inflexible expectations, a man and woman so constrained by their own grim silences and unspoken longings that they might as well be wearing real manacles. They are the film's saddest victims.

Marriages like these three—unhappy, unfaithful, or merely passionless—reoccur throughout Hitchcock's work, and by the time he reaches Hollywood, the most problematic unions are the ones that dominate. But this is still England and early in the director's career (and in his own marriage), and so The 39 Steps also offers a corrective, and even a model, in the relationship between Hannay and Pamela.

Played out over a few days, their relationship is a miniature of a courtship, a love affair at high speed. First, they meet as strangers on a train, and he kisses her, something that seems to please her—we see her hands twisting in a ladylike ecstasy—which, when witnessed, she then feels compelled to publicly denounce. Then they are

reintroduced and taken out on a car ride by the authorities—a sort of chaperoned date. Slipping away from their guardians but now joined together (physically as well as emotionally), they move slowly toward truth and trust. They come to depend on each other. They even spend the night together. And finally, in the film's final shot, they join hands as equals, freely—the empty handcuffs hanging uselessly from Hannay's wrist like a bad memory. Our story is over. Theirs can finally begin.

Though touched with humor and excitement, marked with visual style and subtle metaphor, and hailed as Hitchcock's first truly great thriller, the critically and commercially successful The 39 Steps is also perhaps his most hopeful romance—and a product, not coincidentally, of a time when his love for cinema was still in its first flush and nothing was larger than his optimism for what lay ahead.

References

John Buchan, The Thirty-Nine Steps (New York: Popular Library, 1963); Patrick McGilligan, Alfred Hitchcock: A Life in Darkness and Light (New York: Harper-Collins, 2003), 169–76; "Robert Donat Tells His Life Story," Courier-Mail, June 23, 1938, http://trove.nla.gov.au/ndp/del/article/40995382; Donald Spoto, The Dark Side of Genius: The Life of Alfred Hitchcock (New York: Da Capo Press, 1999), 148–50; Donald Spoto, Spellbound by Beauty: Alfred Hitchcock and His Leading Ladies (New York: Harmony Books, 2008), 48–49, 51–57; François Truffaut, Hitchcock/Truffaut, rev. ed. (New York: Touchstone, 1985), 94–99.

THOMAS, JAMESON (1888–1939)

London-born actor onstage since the turn of the century who could play drama or light comedy equally well. He starred in Hitchcock's THE FARMER'S WIFE in

1928, appeared in the excellent *Piccadilly* the next year, did a cameo in *ELSTREE CALLING*, and then followed his fame to Hollywood. Leads were harder to find there, but he notched roles in *The Phantom President*, the Colin Clive version of *Jane Eyre*, *Mr. Deeds Goes to Town*, and the Clark Gable drama *Parnell*, a movie so dreadful that CAROLE LOMBARD teased Gable mercilessly about it for years; Thomas's most memorable part was probably in *It Happened One Night*, in which he played Claudette Colbert's shallow fiancé, "King" Westley. Thomas died of tuberculosis in Sierra Madre, CA; he was only 50.

References

"Jameson Thomas," *IMDb*, http://www.imdb.com/name/nm0858977/bio?ref_=nm_ov_bio_sm; Simon McCallum, "Jameson Thomas," *BFI Screenonline*, http://www.screenonline.org.uk/people/id/463274.

THOMPSON, EDITH (1893–1923)

The London-born daughter of a clerk and amateur ballroom dancer who grew into a young woman with a head for business and great personal style. Bright and independent, she soon had a career as a buyer for a large milliner. Married but childless, both she and her husband seemed dedicated to each other and their careers—the emblem of a very modern couple.

Then in 1920, Thompson became reacquainted with Freddy Bywaters, a boyhood chum of one of her siblings; Bywaters was 18, a sailor, and hugely appealing. Eventually, Thompson and Bywaters began an affair. When Thompson's husband found out, he beat her; Bywaters went to sea. But eventually the seaman returned, and he and Thompson resumed their affections.

One night, as the married couple was coming back from the theater, Thompson's husband was knifed in the street and killed.

His wife screamed, and the attacker fled, but after the police arrived, the agitated Thompson eventually identified the killer as her lover, Freddy Bywaters. She fully expected that she would be called to testify at his trial. Instead she was indicted alongside him for murder.

The trial went badly for her. Her love letters, introduced into evidence, included scandalously erotic passages—along with claims that she had already tried unsuccessfully to poison her husband and entreaties to Bywaters to "do something." Although Bywaters swore he had acted alone, on the stand Thompson seemed alternately flirtatious and self-pitying; the appalled jury voted to convict them both. They were executed on the same day, with Thompson in hysterics; according to some reports, she had to be tied to a chair before they could get the noose around her neck.

The murder and her execution were a sensation in 1920s Britain and would have caught Hitchcock's attention under any circumstances; he was a lifelong devotee of true-crime stories. Yet he had an actual connection to the case. Before the attack, not only had Edith Thompson's sister Avis worked with Hitchcock at Henley's Telegraph Works, but also the girls' father had taught him ballroom dancing; he had even met Edith briefly, and Avis and his own sister became friends (they regularly attended and volunteered at the same church). The families exchanged Christmas cards for years—never, ever, alluding to the crime.

Hitchcock, too, never spoke publicly of the connection—even as he would wax on and on about H. H. CRIPPEN and other famous killers. But he occasionally talked about making a documentary about the case and some of the emotional undertow of the crime—the idea of a woman ruined by her own passions or caught up in her lover's—certainly figures in some of his films, most particularly in *THE PARADINE CASE* and *STAGE FRIGHT*.

Years later, JOHN RUSSELL TAYLOR handed his authorized biography, *Hitch*, to the director for approval; Taylor said Hitchcock asked for only two edits in order to spare his family any embarrassment. One was the detail that his brother William had died in part due to alcoholism. And the other was that the Hitchcocks had ever known Edith Thompson.

References
Marcel Berlins, "Presumed Guilty," *Guardian*, June 14, 2001, http://www.theguardian.com/film/2001/jun/15/artsfeatures1; Molly Cutpurse, "Edith Thompson and Frederick Bywaters," *Capital Punishment UK*, http://www.capitalpunishmentuk.org/edith.html; John Russell Taylor, "The Truth about Hitchcock and Those Cool Blondes," *Times*, April 5, 2005, http://the.hitchcock.zone/wiki/The%20Times%20%2805%5FApr%2F2005%29%20-20The%20truth%20about%20Hitchcock%20and%20those%20cool%20blondes; Patrick McGilligan, *Alfred Hitchcock: A Life in Darkness and Light* (New York: HarperCollins, 2003), 37–38.

THORNDIKE, DAME SYBIL (1882–1976)
Gainsborough-born performer whose father was a canon at Rochester Cathedral and whose older brother, Russell, wrote the "Doctor Syn" thrillers. She first trained as a classical pianist, but when chronic "piano cramp" rendered performing impossible, she switched to dramatic studies. By her early 20s, she had joined a Shakespearean company and embarked on a 4-year tour of America; at 26, returning to England, she joined the Old Vic and went on to give a long string of acclaimed performances. In 1924, she originated the role of *Saint Joan*—a part George Bernard Shaw had written for her.

Although always primarily a stage actress, she made her film debut in 1921. Most of her early appearances were in cut-down versions of her Shakespearean successes, but later on, she would have larger parts in *Major Barbara* and *The Life and Adventures of Nicholas Nickleby*; in *STAGE FRIGHT*, she is JANE WYMAN's MOTHER and the most formidable member of a cast that Hitchcock crowded with theatrical veterans. Although Thorndike would make a few more major movies, including *The Princess and the Showgirl* and *Shake Hands with the Devil*, she continued to do primarily stage work.

Married to actor Lewis Casson for more than 60 years, Thorndike was a committed progressive (touring South Africa in the 1920s, she fought to allow blacks to attend her shows) and a formidable wit; asked if, over their long marriage, she had ever thought of separating from her husband, she thundered, "Divorce, never! Murder, often!" She acted right until the end of her life—which came at age 93 in Chelsea.

References
Jonathan Croall, "Sybil Thorndike: A Star of Life," http://www.str.org.uk/events/lectures/archive/lecture0810.shtml; "Dame Sybil Thorndike," *Encyclopaedia Britannica*, http://www.britannica.com/biography/Sybil-Thorndike; "Sybil Thorndike," *IMDb*, http://www.imdb.com/name/nm0861345/bio?ref_=nm_ov_bio_sm.

THE THREE HOSTAGES
Hitchcock had been a fan of author JOHN BUCHAN and his "Richard Hannay" adventures since adolescence; he thought several times of adapting *GREENMANTLE* and did succeed with a wonderful (if hardly faithful) adaptation of the author's *The Thirty-Nine Steps*.

After the failure of *MARNIE* in 1964, Hitchcock tried—as he often did after a failure—to return to the familiar; Buchan sounded like a safe bet, and he even announced Buchan's *The Three Hostages* as his next project. But the movie rights, as they often were with Buchan, were difficult to obtain, and Hitchcock began to fear the book hadn't aged as well as he'd hoped. He was also leery of a major plot device, which depended on a blind hypnotist; hypnotism, Hitchcock asserted in INTERVIEWS, never played well onscreen (although he himself had used it to comic effect in the first *THE MAN WHO KNEW TOO MUCH*).

Although some work on a script was done—possibly by Hitchcock, and so atrociously it almost seems like an elaborate in-JOKE—the project was abandoned, as were several others during this period (*KALEI-DOSCOPE, R.R.R.R.*). Eventually, Hitchcock would decide infelicitously on *TORN CURTAIN*.

References

Steven DeRosa, "The Return of Richard Hannay," http://stevenderosa.com/writingwithhitchcock/3hostages.html; Patrick McGilligan, *Alfred Hitchcock: A Life in Darkness and Light* (New York: HarperCollins, 2003), 247–48, 264–65, 657; Donald Spoto, *The Dark Side of Genius: The Life of Alfred Hitchcock* (New York: Da Capo Press, 1999), 256, 478; François Truffaut, *Hitchcock/Truffaut*, rev. ed. (New York: Touchstone, 1985), 307–8.

TIOMKIN, DMITRI (1894–1979)

Russian-born and trained musician who grew up in the Ukraine in a prominent Jewish family. His father was a doctor and his mother a musician who pushed her son toward the piano from early childhood. Tiomkin studied at the St. Petersburg Conservatory, prepared music for early Soviet agitprop spectacles, and played in silent movie houses; by the early 1920s, though, he was slowly moving west, first to Berlin, then Paris, and finally New York. Tiomkin married ballerina Albertina Rasch, and both toured internationally; Tiomkin gave George Gershwin's Concerto in F its European premiere at the Paris Opera.

The Depression, however, soon limited the audience for classical performances, and the rising tensions in Europe made touring problematic; a broken arm in 1937 seemed to definitively end Tiomkin's career as a soloist. But by then, the couple had already relocated to Hollywood, where Rasch helped choreograph musicals, particularly period ones like *The Great Waltz*; Tiomkin, meanwhile, was scoring films, getting attention for his yearning score for Frank Capra's *Lost Horizon*. (He would continue to score many of Capra's best films, including *Mr. Smith Goes to Washington*, *Meet John Doe*, and *It's a Wonderful Life*.) It was on *Lost Horizon* that Tiomkin first began a singular innovation in movie composition; before writing, he would spend time with the actors and listen to their voices so that his music would complement the vocal tones of the dialogue.

Tiomkin worked on four Hitchcock films—*SHADOW OF A DOUBT*, *STRANGERS ON A TRAIN*, *I CONFESS*, and *DIAL M FOR MURDER*. Although the stories were more rooted in reality than some of Hitchcock's other pictures—denying Tiomkin the extravagant emotions that BERNARD HERRMANN was able to tap in *VERTIGO* and *PSYCHO* or the hallucinatory moods that informed MIKLOS RÓZSA's work for *SPELLBOUND*—Tiomkin mirrored that factual feel by interweaving well-known songs into his work to comment ironically on the action: "The Merry Widow" in *Shadow of a Doubt* with its repetitive romanticism, "And the Band Played On" in *Strangers on a Train* with its cavalier innocence.

The most successful composers in Hollywood were always the most versatile, and Tiomkin—Hollywood's most successful composer throughout the 1950s—switched easily between film genres and musical styles, always providing whatever was appropriate. For 1951's sci-fi *The Thing (From Another World)*, he brought in a THEREMIN; for 1952's *High Noon*, he composed the rangy "Do Not Forsake Me, Oh My Darlin'," a cowboy song so authentic that it already sounded generations old and a piece of music so quietly dramatic that it helped tie the film together. (It also became an independent hit; Tiomkin smartly had bought back the rights.)

Tiomkin won two Oscars for his work on that movie and would go on to win two more, for *The High and the Mighty* and *The Old Man and the Sea*; much of his film work, though, would continue to be for westerns, with him providing the scores for *Gunfight at the O.K. Corral*, *Rio Bravo*, and *The Alamo*, among others. "A steppe is a steppe is a steppe," the old Ukrainian wrote in his biography. "The problems of the cowboy and the Cossack are very similar. They share a love of nature and a love of animals. Their courage and their philosophical attitudes are similar, and the steppes of Russia are much like the prairies of America."

Tiomkin died in London at 85.

References

"Dmitri Tiomkin," *IMDb*, http://www .imdb.com/name/nm0006323; "Dmitri Tiomkin: Anyone for Westerns," *mfiles*, http://www.mfiles.co.uk/composers/Dimitri -Tiomkin.htm; "Dmitri Tiomkin," *Dmitri Tiomkin: The Official Website*, http://www .dimitritiomkin.com/biography/dimitri -tiomkin.

TITANIC

DAVID O. SELZNICK always thought big, and for a while in 1938, he entertained the idea of Alfred Hitchcock making his

American debut with a film "to be based upon and called quote *Titanic* unquote," as he cabled Hitchcock's agent (who at the time also happened to be Selznick's brother Myron). Development progressed slowly, with Selznick exploring the purchase of a genuine ocean liner, which he proposed they actually sink in the Pacific, and Hitchcock JOKING of the story that at least they knew "quite obviously what the last two reels would be." But the costs looked to be prohibitive, and Selznick, who thought of himself as a literary man, could never resist the appeal of a best seller. It was decided at the last minute to go with *REBECCA* instead.

References

Patrick McGilligan, *Alfred Hitchcock: A Life in Darkness and Light* (New York: HarperCollins, 2003), 213, 216, 228–29; Bob Thomas, *Selznick* (New York: Pocket Books, 1972), 187–88.

TO CATCH A THIEF (1955)

DIRECTOR: Alfred Hitchcock.
SCREENPLAY: John Michael Hayes, based on the novel by David Dodge.
PRODUCER: Uncredited (Alfred Hitchcock).
CINEMATOGRAPHY: Robert Burks.
EDITOR: Robert Burks.
ORIGINAL MUSIC: Lyn Murray.
CAST: Cary Grant (John "The Cat" Robie), Grace Kelly (Frances Stevens), Jessie Royce Landis (Jessie Stevens), John Williams (H. H. Hughson), Brigitte Auber (Danielle Foussard), Charles Vanel (Bertani).
RUNNING TIME: 106 minutes. Color.
RELEASED THROUGH: Paramount.

A glittering season on the Riviera is being marred by a series of jewel robberies—and the police suspect John "The Cat" Robie, a hero of the French Resistance and a former thief who swears he's retired. But no one seems to believe him—including his old friends from the Resistance, many of them similarly reformed criminals who now work at a restaurant. Robie asks the owner, Bertani, for assistance—if he knew which vacationers were carrying jewels on them, then he might be able to stake out their hotel rooms and catch the real thief in the act. Bertani agrees to help.

Dodging the police at every turn—and dealing with the attentions of Danielle, the teenage daughter of Foussard, another old friend—Robie meets Bertani's contact, an insurance investigator named Hughson. Reluctantly, he gives Robie a list of agency clients in the area and suggests he concentrate on two of them—Jessie Stevens and her daughter Frances. Posing as a lumber millionaire from Oregon, Robie meets the Stevenses, and while Mrs. Stevens is mildly flirtatious, her beautiful daughter seems icily remote—until Robie escorts her to her room and she presents him with a passionate kiss. The next morning, Danielle warns him that his old friends are out to get him, convinced not only that he's stealing again but also that his crimes will ruin them all.

Robie and Frances go for a drive together—which turns perilous when they have to elude the police—and then a picnic. Frances tells him she knows he's really "The Cat," but Robie denies it. That night, he meets her in her room—where she tries to tempt him by wearing her most expensive jewels. He refuses to rise to the bait—he also points out that her "jewels" are imitation—but later that night, her mother's gems are stolen. Frances calls the police, and he slips away.

Investigating the other clients on Hughson's list, Robie interrupts a robbery in progress and is attacked in the dark. One robber gets away, but the other—Foussard—is killed in the fall. The police arrive and pronounce the string of jewel thefts solved. But Robie protests that Foussard's accomplice escaped—and that, as Foussard had a wooden leg, he could hardly be the nimble cat burglar that the authorities have been looking for.

Working with Hughson and the Stevenses, who now believe in his innocence, Robie attends a grand costume ball, expecting the thief will strike again. Slipping away, he spies the burglar on the hotel roof and gives chase; the thief turns out to be Danielle, who was working with her father and Bertani. She confesses in front of witnesses, and Robie and Frances are free to begin a life together—a life, however, that seems fated to include her mother.

A soufflé—beautiful, airy, delicious, and not particularly filling.

It was, however, precisely what Hitchcock wanted after the darkness of *REAR WINDOW*—something sunny and filled with flowers, fresh air, and beautiful people. He had been considering adapting *To Catch a Thief* since he'd finished the bleak *I CONFESS*, and the idea of a trip to the Riviera—at the studio's expense, of course—appealed to a filmmaker who liked to travel but truly adored having someone else pay for it.

For the script, Hitchcock went back to JOHN MICHAEL HAYES, who had done such a good job on *Rear Window*; for his STARS, he immediately sought out GRACE KELLY, for what would be their third collaboration, and CARY GRANT, whom he had wanted for the part since he'd first proposed the film in 1952. Both posed problems—Kelly was already committed to three other movies, and Grant had announced his retirement. But Hitchcock was always ready to wait for Kelly, and when Grant heard who his costar would be—and that the film would be shot on LOCATION in Cannes—he decided to go back to work.

Hayes's script was light on suspense but full of the sort of double entendres that Hitchcock loved, with most of them—to his delight—falling to the elegant Kelly. "Even in this light I can tell where your eyes are looking," she tells Grant as she sits in her hotel room wearing a low-cut dress. "Look. Hold them." She is, of course, talking about her diamonds, just as earlier, on their picnic—"A leg or a breast?"—she is talking about chicken. At least, that is what the filmmakers would tell the CENSORS (who, in the end, let the movie's risqué dialogue pass—perhaps because Hitchcock's regular nemesis at the Production Code, Joseph Breen, had recently retired and America's censorship rules were beginning to loosen).

Hayes's script also made room for some typical Hitchcock themes. Though meant to be frank and colorful, Mrs. Stevens is also controlling—another pushy, meddling MOTHER (the actress, JESSIE ROYCE LANDIS, would return as much the same character in *NORTH BY NORTHWEST*). And there is, of course, another wrongly accused man as our hero and another "snow-covered volcano" as our heroine.

That those themes are never seriously developed is certainly deliberate; that so little seems to be at stake, though, drags down the film. ROBERT BURKS's Oscar-winning cinematography is gorgeous—a chase through a flower market crammed with COLOR; a race along the coastline filled with beautiful, albeit process-shot scenery; some groundbreaking helicopter shots—but there's more sensuality than suspense. Even the penultimate climax of the costume ball seems to be more about Kelly's golden dress than conflict or character.

For audiences, *To Catch a Thief* was a pretty entertainment. For Grant, it was a successful lure back to acting. (It would be another decade before he truly retired.) And for audiences, it was an elegant, enter-taining trifle. But for Hitchcock, it was ultimately a relaxing, working vacation—before he plunged into some of the darkest and most personal films of his career.

References
Tifenn Brisset, "Two Interviews about 'To Catch a Thief,'" *Film International* 11, no. 6 (2013), 13–21; Patrick McGilligan, *Alfred Hitchcock: A Life in Darkness and Light* (New York: HarperCollins, 2003), 496–502; Patrick McGilligan, ed., *Backstory: Interviews with Screenwriters of the 60s* (Berkeley: University of California Press, 1997), 174–92; Donald Spoto, *The Dark Side of Genius: The Life of Alfred Hitchcock* (New York: Da Capo Press, 1999), 349–53; Donald Spoto, *Spellbound by Beauty: Alfred Hitchcock and His Leading Ladies* (New York: Harmony Books, 2008), 211–13; François Truffaut, *Hitchcock/Truffaut*, rev. ed. (New York: Touchstone, 1985), 223–26; Thilo Wydra, *Grace: A Biography* (New York: Skyhorse, 2014), 172–83.

TODD, ANN (1909–1993)
Cheshire-born performer whose petite build and quiet beauty won her the nickname of Britain's "pocket Garbo." After studying elocution and fencing at the Central School of Speech and Drama in London, she began appearing on stage in the late '20s and made her film debut in 1931. Her early parts were mostly in "quota quickies"—cheap movies made strictly for the British market—but in 1945, *The Seventh Veil*, with Todd playing a talented pianist tormented by JAMES MASON, was a major hit and made her a STAR, at least in England.

She had not yet made an American movie, though; *THE PARADISE CASE* in 1949 would be her first. Hitchcock, who had first seen her onstage in 1930—"In the right part, she would do extremely well" he told a reporter at the time—thought the part of Gay Keane, the wife who realizes her lawyer husband has fallen in love with his client, was just the one.

The part actually is a little bland, at least to modern eyes—the character of the long-suffering spouse who forgives all her mate's transgressions sometimes seems more of a wish-fulfillment from producer and cowriter DAVID O. SELZNICK, who had recently split from his wife, than a rich and vibrant character of its own. But Todd brought her own genteel grace to the role and has a memorable scene fending off the ugly advances of CHARLES LAUGHTON.

Hitchcock liked the pale BLONDE Todd, and she got on well with him, although she ached after—in one of his odder hijinks—he saw her lying down on the set and playfully jumped on top of her. He was a "very complex man," she thought, but also "really a very sad person" who had problems dealing with people. "I think power was very important to Hitch," she said. "That was perhaps the most basic thing, beneath all the masks and veils he wore—power over his cast, power over his leading ladies, power with studio executives. Perhaps this compensated for his feeling that he was ugly and unpresentable in polite society."

Unfortunately, *The Paradine Case* did Todd's career no favors, and she went back to mostly British pictures (*The Passionate Friends*, *Madeleine*, and *Breaking the Sound Barrier*, among them, all three directed by her then-husband David Lean) and, later, occasional appearances on American TV, including an episode of *ALFRED HITCHCOCK PRESENTS*. She later turned to directing travel films and wrote her memoirs. She died in London of a stroke at 84.

References

"Ann Todd," *IMDb*, http://www.imdb.com/name/nm0002897/bio?ref_=nm_ov_bio_sm; Patrick McGilligan, *Alfred Hitchcock: A Life in Darkness and Light* (New York: HarperCollins, 2003), 391; Donald Spoto, *The Dark Side of Genius: The Life of Alfred Hitchcock* (New York: Da Capo Press, 1999), 300; Tom Vallance, "Obituary: Ann Todd," *Independent*, May 7, 1993, http://www.independent.co.uk/news/people/obituary-ann-todd-2321403.html.

TODD, RICHARD (1919–2009)

Dublin-born performer whose father was an army doctor often stationed with British regiments in India. It was expected that Todd would go into the military, as well, and he even attended Sandhurst, but he decided to pursue a career on the stage instead. The decision provoked an immediate, brutal, and long-lasting family estrangement; when his mother later committed suicide, Todd coolly insisted, he did not mourn.

He had already begun his career (and even cofounded a theater in Ireland) when the war came; Todd ended up becoming a soldier anyway, even landing on Normandy on D-Day. (He deliberately hid his acting background so he would be sent into combat rather than placed in the entertainment division.) Returning home after the war, he resumed his theatrical career and in 1948 was signed to a movie contract.

One of his first films, *The Hasty Heart*, gave him a role he'd played in both Ireland and England and eventually won him an Oscar nomination. Suddenly a top STAR in Britain, he seemed a good choice for JANE WYMAN's costar in Hitchcock's London-set *STAGE FRIGHT*, but the director's beloved character actors really run away with the film, and Todd only gets a few memorable moments at the end, when the camera catches his mad, flashing EYES.

Although *Stage Fright* was not a success, and while his costume pictures for Walt Disney, including *The Sword and the Rose*, didn't buttress his standing as a serious actor, at least *A Man Called Peter* and *The Dam Busters* were solid hits. But by the 1960s, the heroic roles had given way to character parts ("My swash began to buckle," the aging actor joked), and by the '70s and '80s, the character parts were mostly in cheap genre films: *Dorian Gray*, *Asylum*, *House of the Long Shadows*. He died at 90 of cancer in the country town of Little Humby.

References

Adam Bernstein, "Richard Todd, 90, Dies: Irish-Born Actor of 'The Longest Day,'" *Washington Post*, December 29, 2009, http://www.washingtonpost.com/wp-dyn/content/article/2009/12/04/AR2009120404344.html; "Richard Todd," *IMDb*, http://www.imdb.com/name/nm0865262/bio?ref_=nm_ov_bio_sm.

TOMASINI, GEORGE (1909–1964)

American film editor from Springfield, MA, who was orphaned as a child. He and his three sisters were split up and sent to various foster homes. When, as a teenager, Tomasini discovered that his current foster parents had decided it was time he joined the priesthood, he decided he needed a change of scenery; he ran away from home, eventually ending up in Los Angeles, where he got a job as an errand boy for a film editor.

Eventually, Tomasini landed a job as a studio projectionist at PARAMOUNT, finally progressing to the editing department, where he would stay for nearly 30 years. His reputation was clinched when the troubled Vivien Leigh had to withdraw from *Elephant Walk*; Tomasini's seamless editing allowed the studio to use much of the footage in which Leigh had appeared, even though she'd now been replaced by Elizabeth Taylor.

That skillful salvage job brought his name to Hitchcock, who quickly engaged him for *REAR WINDOW*—of all his films,

perhaps the one most reliant on the editor's art. Tomasini would edit eight more of Hitchcock's pictures; when the director embarked on *PSYCHO* and deliberately went with his faster, cheaper television crew, Tomasini was one of the few feature-film colleagues he insisted on keeping.

As Hitchcock famously, meticulously storyboarded his films in advance—could even, as many actors said, describe them before shooting, shot by precise shot—it's difficult to completely assess Tomasini's personal contribution to the final product, although several witnesses say Hitchcock trusted Tomasini implicitly and depended on him for the first assembly.

According to Tomasini's wife, actress Mary Brian, "Mr. Hitchcock always gave George first cut. He wanted to see his interpretation. Then they got down to the fine work." And TIPPI HEDREN agrees that the men worked in concert. "George would assemble the piece to what he thought it should be—or close," she remembered. "And then Hitch would come in and do the final editing. And he would edit almost . . . he would say, 'Cut one frame out of here. Cut three frames out of this scene. Cut it at the beginning, three frames.' . . . He was such a perfectionist."

Tomasini's work on Hitchcock films was a model of the editor's art and always matched perfectly to the content; unobtrusive and efficient on *THE WRONG MAN*, shockingly dramatic in *MARNIE*. And while Hitchcock was hardly the sort of director to leave the final look of his film up to anyone else, there are new things in his films with Tomasini—the flurry of almost subliminal cuts in *Psycho*, the jump cuts in *THE BIRDS*—that stand out as singular and unexpected breakthroughs in his work.

Realizing the editor's skill, the director tried to sign him to an exclusive contract early on; Tomasini agreed to always give Hitchcock's projects preference but retained the right to take other assignments in between and went on to cut *The Time Machine*, *The Misfits*, and the original *Cape Fear*, a model of taut suspense.

He died of a heart attack at 55 in Hanford, CA.

References

All about The Birds, directed by Laurent Bouzereau (2000), documentary, http:// the.hitchcock.zone/wiki/All_About_The _Birds_%282000%29_-_transcript; "George Tomasini," *IMDb*, http://www.imdb.com/ name/nm0866462; Rachel Ingel, "I'll Let the Film Pile Up for You: An Interview with Mary Tomasini," *Motion Picture Editors Guild Directory*, http://www.editors guild.com/v2/magazine/newsletter/direc tory/tomasini.html.

TOPAZ (US 1969)

DIRECTOR: Alfred Hitchcock.
SCREENPLAY: Samuel A. Taylor, based on the novel by Leon Uris.
PRODUCERS: Herbert Coleman (Alfred Hitchcock, uncredited).
CINEMATOGRAPHY: Jack Hildyard.
EDITOR: William H. Ziegler.
ORIGINAL MUSIC: Maurice Jarre.
CAST: Frederick Stafford (Andre Devereaux), Karin Dor (Juanita de Cordoba), John Vernon (Rico Parra), John Forsythe (Michael Nordstrom), Michel Piccoli (Jacques Granville), Philippe Noiret (Henri Jarre), Roscoe Lee Browne (Philippe Dubois).
RUNNING TIME: 143 minutes. Color.
RELEASED THROUGH: Universal.

In autumn 1962, a KGB official sneaks out of the Soviet embassy with his wife and daughter and defects to the Americans. Brought to Washington by CIA agent Michael Nordstrom, he reluctantly pays for his new life by providing the Americans with sensitive information: first, that the Soviets may be placing missiles in Cuba, and second, that the French government is compromised by Communist agents.

Needing further information but unable to approach any Soviet sources himself, Nordstrom asks a French spy he can trust, Andre Devereaux, to get more details. Going to New York and enlisting the help of Dubois, a Haitian agent, Devereaux gets photographs of the secret Soviet-Cuban agreements from a visiting Cuban official, Victor Parra.

Still lacking concrete proof of the missiles, Devereaux then goes to Havana, where he meets with his lover, Juanita de Cordoba. A "widow of a hero of the Revolution," she is also Parra's mistress—and working secretly against Castro's government. Juanita gets proof of the bases and passes it along to Devereaux. He escapes, and Parra—discovering Juanita's treachery—shoots her. Devereaux returns to Washington to discover that his wife has left him, having faced the truth about his affair and that his own government is recalling him for working secretly for the Americans.

Devereaux returns to Paris, now knowing that there are double agents within his own organization. His son-in-law helps him confront one of them, Jarre, who is later killed by his own men. His wife confesses that a man named Granville is the other traitor—a fact she knows because she was also having an affair with Granville and saw Jarre leave his house.

Devereaux challenges Granville to a duel to be held in an empty sports stadium. Before either man can fire, however, a shot rings out, and Granville falls dead; a Soviet marksman hidden in the stands wanted to make sure there were no loose ends. The Russian assassin escapes; Deveraux and his wife are reunited; the Cuban crisis ends.

A new low.

The late '60s found Hitchcock uncertain and in some ways unmoored. *TORN CURTAIN* had been an unhappy production and had led to a bitter and lasting split from longtime collaborator BERNARD HERRMANN; it had also, like the picture before, *MARNIE,* been a critical failure and a commercial disappointment. For much of the next year, he withdrew personally and professionally—leading ALMA REVILLE to privately approach LEW WASSERMAN at UNIVERSAL in 1967 and implore him to come up with a new project for his aimless old friend.

Eventually, Hitchcock and Universal decided on *Topaz*, a recent best seller by Leon Uris about an old Cold War spy case; the studio already had the rights and a commitment from Uris to do the first draft of a screenplay. As for casting, whether it was because he was still smarting over the paychecks for the STARS of *Torn Curtain* or merely interested in a more international feel, Hitchcock decided to do without any marquee personalities; stolid JOHN FORSYTHE is the closest thing to a name in the picture, with most of the rest of the cast drawn from European cinema.

But once preproduction began, signs of trouble arose. The self-consciously serious Uris bristled at Hitchcock's attempts to add any humor to the script; Hitchcock refused to shoot the draft the novelist turned in, and Uris wasn't obligated to write any further ones. The director reached out to ARTHUR LAURENTS for help; the screenwriter declined. Finally, with the start of shooting practically upon him, he phoned SAMUEL A. TAYLOR. As he had on *VERTIGO*, when previous screenwriters had failed to turn in a camera-ready script, Taylor jumped into action.

But this was a different experience, Taylor recalled, "because Hitchcock threw out the screenplay entirely and had me writing scenes a few days—and in many cases a few hours—before they were shot." When finished, the result was a sad patchwork. The pace was glacial, the focus kept shifting from character to character, the suspense sequences were perfunctory, and the ending—well, what was the ending?

That was the biggest and most apparent problem when the studio held a disastrous sneak preview. The response cards are preserved at the Academy of Motion Picture Arts and Sciences research library, and many of them are covered in angry scrawls, with audience members writing that the film was boring, the acting was terrible, and the dueling scene the worst of all. Some even said they refused to believe Hitchcock had directed it. One person's brusque advice? "Cut, cut, cut, cut, cut, cut, cut."

It was a painful throwback to the bad old days in Britain, when C. M. WOOLF would disgustedly pronounce the latest Hitchcock picture as unreleasable—but at least Woolf had been reliably wrong. Hitchcock feared the audience and the studio were right, and in any case, he said later that fighting it "didn't seem worthwhile." A new ending was shot to replace the dueling sequence; in this one, Granville would escape, cheekily waving goodbye as he boarded a plane to Moscow and Devereaux took one to DC.

But everyone hated that ending, too, and so finally, reaching back perhaps to the quiet defeat of Sebastian in *NOTORIOUS*, Hitchcock came up with a third ending—knowing he has been exposed, Granville goes home, shuts the door, and kills himself. (Complicating things further: The actor who'd played him, PHILIPPE NOIRET, was by now unavailable, and so the editor had to use a few frames of MICHEL PICCOLI entering the house, then freeze the image, and dub in a gunshot.) The running time was cut down to 127 minutes (mostly by shortening shots in existing scenes), the new ending was tacked on, and the film went into final wide release.

And was the failure it seemed fated to be all along. You can sense Hitchcock's disengagement almost from the start, as the film begins with stock footage of the May Day parade and a flat-footed, expository title telling us that someone is about to defect. The actual defection is handled perfunctorily, the defector turns out to be thoroughly unlikable, and the film continues with no firm point of view, no protagonist for us to identify with. The first mild bit of suspense—the photographing of the secret papers—comes nearly an hour into the story.

Forsythe is as forgettable as he nearly always was, FREDERICK STAFFORD is little better, and—outfitted with a bushy revolutionary beard—JOHN VERNON is almost laughable. ROSCOE LEE BROWNE has a sly presence as the Haitian agent, and KARIN DOR adds some passion to the fiery Juanita, but by the time Piccoli and Noiret show up, any momentum has been lost, beaten into boredom by Maurice Jarre's bland yet overwhelming score and the sort of flat photography on (mostly) back-lot sets that makes the picture look like one of the studio's cheap made-for-TV movies. Even a deliberate attempt at provocation—Hitchcock had decided to take advantage of Hollywood's new freedoms and shoot a nude love scene—came to naught when it turned out both Dor and Stafford had surgical scars that would, at best, have proved a distraction.

Every so often, the old Hitchcock seems to reappear. He cheekily stages two long bits of expository dialogue—Devereaux's speech to the Haitian agent and the agent's bribe of a Cuban official—behind glass, where we can't hear a word (because honestly we don't need to). BIRD imagery pops up. (A spy camera is hidden inside a chicken carcass, and seagulls disrupt a bit of espionage.) And there is one lovely image, when Juanita is shot and falls to the floor, her purple dress spreading like a pool of blood, or perhaps opening up like the petals of a rose—flowers being a constant image in the film. (Hitchcock, always happiest when he could solve a technical challenge, got the effect by threading her dress with wires that crew members would then pull.)

But ultimately the preview audience was right: *Topaz* is too long, and it doesn't have a proper ending. Worse, it stumbles into the same trap that Hitchcock had fallen into with *SECRET AGENT* and *I CONFESS*—his heroes are all passive. The defector only escapes because of the CIA agent, the CIA agent hands the real work over to the French spy—and the French spy then gets the Haitian to get the secret papers, his Cuban lover to get the photographic evidence, and his son-in-law to expose one of the traitors. Even when Devereaux tries to take action, picking up a gun to get the second villain, the man is shot dead by one of his own. It's a movie in celebration of passivity—perhaps a reflection of the downbeat mood in which Hitchcock took it on.

"One of the tragedies of *Topaz* was that Hitch was trying to make something as if he had INGRID BERGMAN and CARY GRANT," Taylor said afterward. "But he didn't have the story for it, and he certainly didn't have the cast."

His third failure in a row, it would—as usual—send Hitchcock running to familiar territory. And in this case, he would run all the way back to England and the material of his first iconic hit, the story of an innocent man mistaken for a serial killer.

References

Arthur Laurents, *The Rest of the Story* (Milwaukee, WI: Applause, 2012), 40–41; Patrick McGilligan, *Alfred Hitchcock: A Life in Darkness and Light* (New York: HarperCollins, 2003), 683–95; Donald Spoto, *The Dark Side of Genius: The Life of Alfred Hitchcock* (New York: Da Capo Press, 1999), 498–503; *Topaz: An Appreciation*, directed by Laurent Bouzereau (2001), documentary; François Truffaut, *Hitchcock/ Truffaut*, rev. ed. (New York: Touchstone, 1985), 328–33.

TORN CURTAIN (US 1966)

DIRECTOR: Alfred Hitchcock.
SCREENPLAY: Brian Moore.
PRODUCER: Uncredited (Alfred Hitchcock).
CINEMATOGRAPHY: John F. Warren.
EDITOR: Bud Hoffman.
ORIGINAL MUSIC: Paul Addison.
CAST: Paul Newman (Michael Armstrong), Julie Andrews (Sarah Sherman), Lila Kedrova (Countess Kuchinska), Wolfgang Kieling (Gromek), Carolyn Conwell (Farmer's Wife).
RUNNING TIME: 128 minutes. Color.
RELEASED THROUGH: Universal.

American physicist Michael Armstrong and his assistant and lover, Sarah Sherman, travel to Copenhagen to attend a scientific conference. But while there, Armstrong behaves suspiciously, and when he secretly books a flight to East Berlin, Sherman follows him. To her shock and horror, as soon as Armstrong arrives behind the Iron Curtain, he announces his defection, saying that America stands in the way of peace. Armstrong is quickly debriefed by the East German government and assigned a bodyguard, Gromek, who will be keeping a careful eye on him.

While there, Armstrong slips away to a distant farm to make contact with a US agent; Armstrong, it seems, is only pretending to defect so that he can gain vital information from an East German scientist.

Gromek, though, has followed him there and quickly realizes Armstrong's real mission. Armstrong, with the aid of a farmer's wife, brutally kills Gromek.

Armstrong continues to Leipzig, where he is to meet a prominent rocket scientist; he finally reveals his real plan to Sherman and tricks the East German scientist into giving him a valuable secret formula. But Gromek's body has been found, and Armstrong and Sherman have to flee, leaving for East Berlin on a fake municipal bus operated by an anti-Communist network.

With the East German forces on high alert, it is necessary for Armstrong and Sherman to sneak out of the country. After several close scrapes at a post office and a travel agency, they are hidden inside the costume trunks of a ballet company traveling to Sweden and sail back to the West and freedom.

The midpoint in a slow slide.

With the disappointment of *MARNIE* still fresh (and the nadir of *TOPAZ* still to come), Hitchcock decided to turn to the spy genre and a real-life story that had intrigued him for some time: The Burgess-Maclean affair, in which two British double agents had fled to the Soviet Union. What most struck Hitchcock about the defector's story was that Maclean's family had followed him the next year. It would be an interesting thing, Hitchcock thought, to tell the tale of a man's treason from his wife's point of view.

As he often did, Hitchcock began the story process by looking for a novelist or playwright to work with on the treatment; Vladimir Nabokov begged off, however, professing no facility with spy stories, and James Goldman was already busy with the screenplay for his own *The Lion in Winter*. Finally, the director settled on BRIAN MOORE; it was the heroine's point of view that was the most important, Hitchcock thought, and the Irish novelist had gotten excellent notices for the female-centric *The Lonely Passion of Judith Hearne*.

The final script showed some of that initial intention. (It actually divides neatly into three parts—the first act told from Sherman's point of view, the second from Armstrong's, and then the third from both.) But Moore protested that the characters were still weak and their interactions unbelievable; the plot was "little else than a Hitchcock compendium" of tricks and twists. Hitchcock told him to take a vacation and then gave the script to two British "kitchen-sink" writers, Keith Waterhouse and Willis Hill, for another draft. (In the end, Moore—who was never formally dismissed—got sole screen credit.)

As if to emphasize this conscious trip back to the cloak-and-dagger world of *NORTH BY NORTHWEST*, Hitchcock thought briefly of reuniting that film's STARS, but CARY GRANT had once again decided to retire (and this time was sticking to it). UNIVERSAL, still smarting from Hitchcock's attempts to make a star out of TIPPI HEDREN, insisted on the biggest marquee names available: PAUL NEWMAN and JULIE ANDREWS. Both were certainly stars—it would, in fact, be the last time that Hitchcock would work with acknowledged A-list talent—but their salaries ate into the budget, and the director later grumbled that they were miscast.

Neither certainly was quite right for a Hitchcock film. Newman was another one of the director's feared METHOD actors, always asking about motivation (and unafraid to bluntly express his opinion, which rattled the conflict-averse filmmaker). And Andrews, fresh from *Mary Poppins* and *The Sound of Music*, still maintained a prim, virginal image, even during her opening scene in bed with Newman; if Hitchcock's ideal was the "snow-covered volcano," then all Andrews conveyed was

the snow. "We all knew we had a loser on our hands with this picture," Newman said later. "During the shooting, we all wished we didn't have to make it."

The film begins with one of the director's typically droll, slightly naughty touches—the heat on Armstrong and Sherman's cruise ship isn't working, and while they're in bed together during the middle of the day, they're huddled under all their coats and blankets. (Although both are presumably topless; Hitchcock would try for onscreen nudity again in *TOPAZ* and finally break the old taboo in his next film, *FRENZY*.) And it climaxes with another Hitchcock JOKE—needing to both flee a ballet performance and slip away undetected, Armstrong literally cries, "Fire!" in a crowded theater.

In between, there is one bravura sequence, in which Gromek surprises Armstrong at the farmhouse. With the help of the farmer's wife (who is never given a name and played by Liv Ullmann lookalike Carolyn Conwell), Gromek is first disarmed and then killed. It is a slow, brutal murder (both Moore and Hitchcock said they wanted to show how ugly real violence is) and a grimly ironic one, as the tools used are emblems of domesticity: a pot of FOOD, a kitchen knife, a shovel, a gas oven. (The scene of a German being gassed to death in an oven is particularly deliberately jarring.) Adding to the discomfort is that, quickly and brilliantly edited as the sequence is, it plays out in utter silence.

That was actually a last-minute choice—music had been written for the scene, but Hitchcock decided to have it unfold only to sound effects, the way he had first wanted the *PSYCHO* shower death to be shown. There had, in fact, even been two scores he could have gone with—the first one, written by BERNARD HERRMANN, which was turned down as not "pop" enough, and the second, contributed by Herrmann's replacement, John Addison. Herrmann, a hot-tempered artist to begin with, was not just insulted but also enraged by this rejection; he (rightly) accused Hitchcock of being too in thrall to the studio and its money concerns to take a stand, and he never worked with him again. (Adding irony to injury, Addison's score isn't particularly good and failed to provide the popular movie music theme the studio had hoped for.)

Herrmann wasn't the only regular Hitchcock colleague missing. The director's trusted editor, GEORGE TOMASINI, had recently died; cinematographer ROBERT BURKS was elsewhere, too (he would die, too, tragically, in 1968), nor was title designer SAUL BASS on hand. (The opening credits would instead attempt a James Bond look, with flickering flames and slightly distorted clips from the film.) And Hitchcock's increasing reliance on back-projection and studio sets was beginning to show; although ALBERT WHITLOCK's matte work is typically gorgeous, the film-maker's reluctance to spend much time on LOCATION SHOOTING robs the film of a realism that, just a decade before, had been a hallmark of *I CONFESS, TO CATCH A THIEF, THE MAN WHO KNEW TOO MUCH*, and *VERTIGO*.

In the end, Hitchcock was sadly right; Newman and Andrews are wrong for the roles and never really connect onscreen. And Moore was right, too—the film isn't a forward-moving narrative but a collection of bits. (A long scene with actress Lila Kedrova as a Polish countess trying to get to the West obviously entranced Hitchcock, but it only slows down the film in the last third, after things have already begun to stall.)

True, the scene with Gromek is a truly brutal standout—it is the closest thing in Hitchcock's films to actual sadism until the rape in *Frenzy*—and there are some nice

compositions (a raucous press conference in which Armstrong is constantly half-obscured by jostling journalists; a strained conversation between Sherman and Armstrong in an empty, airless room). But the film never comes alive, and for many, the only curtain it brought to mind was the one it threatened to ring down on a great film-maker's long career.

References

Royal S. Brown, "An Interview with Bernard Herrmann," *Bernard Herrmann Society*, http://www.bernardherrmann.org/articles/an-interview-with-bernard-herrmann; Guy Flatley, "I Tried to Be Discreet with That Nude Corpse,' *New York Times*, June 18, 1972, http://the.hitchcock.zone/wiki/New_York_Times_%2818/Jun/1972%29_-_I_Tried_to_Be_Discreet_With_That_Nude_Corpse; Patrick McGilligan, *Alfred Hitchcock: A Life in Darkness and Light* (New York: HarperCollins, 2003), 667–74; Donald Spoto, *The Dark Side of Genius: The Life of Alfred Hitchcock* (New York: Da Capo Press, 1999), 486–92; François Truffaut, *Hitchcock/Truffaut*, rev. ed. (New York: Touchstone, 1985), 309–13.

TRAINS

Alfred Hitchcock loved the idea of transportation from childhood, although at first it was simply the cold bare facts of the municipal transit system. As soon as he was allowed to travel alone, he rode every tram line in London and most of the riverboats. He kept track of the British ships at sea and studiously committed to memory every timetable he could find. It was an all-consuming hobby. Considering that, years later, he insisted that he'd never had a childhood playmate, he had plenty of time to devote to it.

Today, perhaps, this might be diagnosed as something more than an introvert's eccentricity. Hitchcock grew up to be a man who worried about detail; obsessed over certain subjects; and was committed to routine, particularly in dress and diet. He dreaded anything that threatened conflict and sometimes misread people's emotions badly. At the time, it was dismissed as odd (or not talked about at all). Today, it might be diagnosed as a sign of Asperger's.

But back then, Hitchcock was seen as simply someone who liked trains—not at all an uncommon interest, particularly in an era when rail travel was far more common than flying. In fact, railways play a particularly important role in Hitchcock's life. When he was starting his directing career, he and the cast and crew of THE PLEASURE GARDEN took an eventful trip by rail to the LOCATION shoots in Germany and Italy; when he finally arrived in Hollywood some 15 years later, it was by pulling into Los Angeles's Union Station.

Later, of course, Hitchcock would travel by plane or ocean liner, but trains reoccur in his films, although usually for particularly logical and dramatic reasons: They ensure conflict (whatever the hero is trying to get away from is now in this enclosed space with him) and pace (whatever is going to happen must occur before the next station stop). They are what make possible a very important and basic equation for suspense: tension plus time.

Trains also provided a chance for spectacle—as in the deliberately absurd climax of NUMBER 17 or the long-delayed one in SECRET AGENT. Mostly, however, Hitchcock used them instead as a means to an end, a way of increasing suspense—and introducing into his unforgiving world just one more object that may in the end betray you. In THE 39 STEPS, the train functions first as a method of escape for Richard Hannay—and then, when he is recognized, as a trap. In SHADOW OF A DOUBT, the locomotive, belching black smoke, brings Uncle Charlie triumphantly into town—

and then at the end mangles him under its wheels after he falls on the tracks.

Trains can also—with their cramped spaces and forced conviviality—create fateful, even fatal, interactions. If Guy had rented an automobile instead of boarding a dining car, then he never would have bumped into Bruno in STRANGERS ON A TRAIN; if Roger Thornhill had hitched a ride to Chicago instead of slipping aboard a train, then Eve Kendall wouldn't have been able to arrange their "accidental" meeting in NORTH BY NORTHWEST; if Johnnie hadn't ducked into Lina's compartment in SUSPICION, then they never would have embarked on their own parallel voyages of lies and doubt. We not only travel fastest when we travel alone, but in the world of Hitchcock's films, we also travel safest.

All of those elements are put to work in THE LADY VANISHES, set almost entirely on a train, which becomes not only a setting for its many characters but also a microcosm for mid-'30s Europe. The Britishers who don't want to get involved out of personal self-interest; the untrustworthy if somewhat incapable Italian; the Eastern Europeans whose true alliances are difficult to judge—these aren't just characters in a film but also symbols of their nations. And they are bound together by Europe's borders and treaties, just as their living, breathing emblems are held together by dining-car assignments and timetables.

It is one of Hitchcock's finest films, largely because—thanks to its setting—it plausibly collects a variety of people, locks them in, and then hurtles them toward a destination. It doesn't allow for a moment's release or a distracting side trip. And yet it ensures that, when they get off, they won't be the same people who boarded.

Reference

Donald Spoto, *The Dark Side of Genius: The Life of Alfred Hitchcock* (New York: Da Capo Press, 1999), 20, 208.

TRANSATLANTIC PICTURES

Hitchcock's own, ill-fated attempt at an independent, international production company. Begun in 1946, with long-time colleague SIDNEY BERNSTEIN (an instrumental figure in Hitchcock's various wartime propaganda projects for Britain), the project got under full steam as soon as Hitchcock finished *THE PARADINE CASE*, his last film for DAVID O. SELZNICK; the new company's first project, the director announced, would be *UNDER CAPRICORN* with INGRID BERGMAN.

Bergman, however, wasn't yet available for shooting, so the company pushed forward with *ROPE*, a production that failed to excite audiences; when *Under Capricorn* finally did begin, Hitchcock realized he had overspent to acquire his STAR and didn't really have the proper costar or story to justify the project. When that film failed as well, the company quietly disappeared, with WARNER BROS.—which had distributed the two previous pictures—forging a new deal with Hitchcock alone.

Selznick might be forgiven if he cracked a small smile, watching his former director get a rude lesson in what it really meant to be a mogul. But the new Warner contract made Hitchcock the producer he had often unofficially been on his previous "loan-out films"—and with Transatlantic Pictures behind him and this deal before him, Hitchcock would soon reach new heights in both artistic control and achievement.

References

Rudy Behlmer, ed., *Memo from David O. Selznick* (New York: Viking Press, 1972), 407; Patrick McGilligan, *Alfred Hitchcock: A Life in Darkness and Light* (New York: HarperCollins, 2003), 382–83, 399–402, 467; Donald Spoto, *The Dark Side of Genius: The Life of Alfred Hitchcock* (New York: Da Capo Press, 1999), 294–95, 319.

TRANSFERENCE

GUILT is a movable feast in Hitchcock, a thing neither tied to a person nor an action. What does one have to feel guilty about? In Hitchcock's darkly brooding, extremely CATHOLIC world, sometimes it seems as if—Well, what *doesn't* one have to feel guilty about? No matter how guilty the villain is, there's always enough guilt to be transferred back to the hero.

The trope of the "wrong man," the accused innocent, is of course a constant in Hitchcock's films, from *THE LODGER* through *FRENZY*; to name all its occurrences would be to practically reprint the director's list of credits. Yet those are chiefly instances of MISTAKEN IDENTITY, not moral complexity. The far more pertinent part of Hitchcock's typically stern, traditionally Catholic worldview insists that there is no wrong man, no innocent victim—that we are all sinners, all guilty of something.

Under the Catechisms, he would have been made to learn by heart at the turn of the century "sin is an utterance, a deed or a desire contrary to the eternal law," and even if we don't commit that sin ourselves, then we share the guilt of others not only by "participating directly and voluntarily" in their sinful acts or "ordering, advising, praising or approving them" but also by "not disclosing or not hindering them." His Jesuit education, Hitchcock later said, had given him, a "consciousness of good and evil, that both are always with me." But it also left him with a conviction that evil did not always require action. There were sins of inaction, too. There were sins that you committed merely in your heart, with a single, fleeting, furtive wish.

Sometimes in Hitchcock's films, his heroes are led into sin out of fear or self-interest. In *STRANGERS ON A TRAIN*, Guy knows that Bruno is a murderer—but going to the police might only throw suspicion on him. In *I CONFESS*, Father Logan knows that Otto is the killer—yet he cannot find a way to inform the authorities without imperiling his own soul by breaking a holy vow. They end up enabling these villains, and so some of the guilt is transferred back to them—and not undeservedly so, as in both cases they've profited by the crime, as the murderer has rudely dispatched someone the protagonists had fervently wished would go away. That adds to their anguish.

In Hitchcock's films, love can also lead us into temptation, being just as likely to encourage our most self-destructive instincts—crime, obsession, deceit—as it is to bring out our better natures.

Lina is in thrall to Johnnie in *SUSPICION*, for example—and so she protects someone she knows to be a liar and embezzler and believes to be a murderer. It takes forever for young Charlie to accept that her beloved uncle is a serial killer in *SHADOW OF A DOUBT*—but when she does, rather than turn him in, she only urges him to slip away from the police. Mark knows that *MARNIE* is a compulsive thief—and is willing to pay any amount of restitution, use any influence, to make sure that she never faces a judge's justice. Everyone is complicit in their beloved's crime; in the eyes of the Church, and Hitchcock's, everyone is just as equally guilty of sin.

And if Hitchcock's heroes rarely face real punishment for their behavior in the end—there will be no charges brought, no jail time imposed, on Lina or Charlie or Mark—then they still carry that weight on their shoulders. They still bear that mark on their souls. Unluckily for them, in Hitchcock's world, there's always enough guilt to go around.

References

Richard Alleva, "The Catholic Hitchcock: A Director's Sense of Good and Evil," *Commonweal*, July 12, 2010, https://www.com monwealmagazine.org/catholic-hitchcock; "Catechism of the Catholic Church," *The Holy See*, http://www.vatican.va/archive/ccc_css/archive/catechism/p3s1c1a8 htm; Bess Twiston Davies, "Hitchcock: Monster or Moralist?" *Times*, September 5, 2008, http://the.hitchcock.zone/wiki/The_Times_%2805/Sep/2008%29_-_Hitch cock:_monster_or_moralist.

TRAP FOR A SOLITARY MAN

One of the many dead-end projects that filled the early '60s, this one based on a play by M. Robert Thomas. The story, according to an item in the London Times, "shows us a young married couple on holiday in the Alps. The wife disappears, and after prolonged search the police bring back someone they claim to be she; she says she is the man's wife, and only he denies it." The newspaper went on to confidently announce that it was to be in Cinemascope, and that while no casting had been announced, it was to be made for Fox.

It isn't hard to see how the story would have appealed to Hitchcock; the Alps had always had fond associations for him since his honeymoon in St. Moritz. The idea of the DOUBLE goes back to the old, influential days of the German silents, and the dramatic situation of the protagonist who, alone, denies that someone is who she says she is had been, of course, the core of one of his greatest films, *THE LADY VANISHES*.

Perhaps the problem was that the idea appealed to too many people; it had already inspired a 1958 movie, *Chase a Crooked Shadow* (and would go on, over the next 25 years, to be adapted at least three more times). But in any case, the announcement in the paper seemed to be as far as the project went; it joined several other aborted ideas, including *THE BLIND MAN* and *VILLAGE OF STARS* as Hitchcock moved on to *THE BIRDS* and *MARNIE*.

References

Patrick McGilligan, *Alfred Hitchcock: A Life in Darkness and Light* (New York: Harper-Collins, 2003), 609; "Mr. Hitchcock's Plans," *Times*, September 23, 1960, http://the.hitchcock.zone/wiki/The_Times_%2823/Sep/1960%29_-_Mr._Hitchcock's_plans; "Robert Thomas," *IMDb*, http://www.imdb.com/name/nm0859436.

TRAVERS, HENRY (1874–1965)

Northumberland-born performer who grew up as the son of a country doctor and studied architecture in school. By 20, though, he had committed to being an actor. He was a stage actor exclusively for nearly 40 years; one of his greatest successes was in the Broadway farce *You Can't Take It with You* (later filmed by Frank Capra, with Lionel Barrymore taking Travers's part).

By 1933, though, Travers had begun appearing in films as well—he is CLAUDE RAINS's mentor in *The Invisible Man*—and would go on to appear in many films, usually as amiable figures of authority or slightly dotty senior citizens: *Dark Victory*, *Mrs. Miniver*, *Random Harvest*, *The Yearling*. His most beloved role was, of course, as Clarence Oddbody, the sweetly uncertain "Angel, 2nd Class" of Capra's *It's a Wonderful Life*.

Hitchcock cast him, very much to type, in *SHADOW OF A DOUBT* as Joseph Newton, Charlie's father, whose favorite hobby is chatting with his neighbor Herbie about how one might murder the other. It's a deft performance that delights without overdoing the cute-old-codger twinkling; particularly good are the small, furtive looks Travers gives as JOSEPH COTTEN's Uncle Charlie visits him at work and embarrasses him in front of his boss.

Travers quietly retired at the end of the 1940s and died in Los Angeles of arteriosclerosis at 91.

References

"Henry Travers," *IMDb*, http://www.imdb.com/name/nm0871287/bio?ref_=nm_ov_bio_sm; Mieka Smiles, "Wonderful Life of Henry Travers Revealed," *Journal*, December 18, 2010, http://www.thejournal.co.uk/news/north-east-news/wonderful-life-henry-travers-revealed-4443717; Alfred E. Twomey and Arthur F. McClure, *The Versatiles: Supporting Character Players in the Cinema, 1930–1955* (New York: Castle Books, 1969), 298.

TRAVERS, LINDEN (1913–2001)

Durham-born performer whose acting career began quickly. She made her first stage appearance at 20, her London debut the following year (in an IVOR NOVELLO play), and her screen debut the year after that. In 1938, Hitchcock cast her in *THE LADY VANISHES* as the adulterous Mrs. Todhunter; as one paper noted, the greatest mystery of the film may have been what a beauty like her was supposed to have seen in a toad like Mr. Todhunter.

The British film industry couldn't seem to find room for her, though, and the parts began to shrink; "I seem to have jumped out of being mistresses to playing with the comics," she said of the farces she was soon being offered. The scandalously gruesome crime thriller *No Orchids for Miss Blandish* in 1948 was definitely more serious stuff, but Travers soon retired to concentrate on her family, taking only very occasional TV roles afterward. The Hitchcock connection continued, however; her daughter Susan Travers is Rusk's final victim in *FRENZY*.

She died in Cornwall at 88.

References

Ronald Bergan, "Linden Travers," *Guardian*, November 2, 2001, http://www.theguardian.com/news/2001/nov/02/guardianobituaries.filmnews; "Linden Travers," *IMDb*, http://www.imdb.com/name/nm0871298/bio?ref_=nm_ov_bio_sm.

TREMAYNE, LES (1913–2003)

London-born performer who emigrated to Chicago with his family at the age of four. His mother had been on the British stage, and in their new home, young Les soon began working in vaudeville, carnivals, and community theater. By 17, he was on the radio; it would be the center of his career for many decades, with long stints as both an announcer and an actor, including radio serials featuring "The Falcon" and Dashiell Hammett's Nick Charles.

In films since 1949, he is particularly remembered by genre fans for adding his deep and distinctive voice to films from *The War of the Worlds* to *The Slime People*; Alfred Hitchcock cast him in several episodes of *ALFRED HITCHCOCK PRESENTS* and *THE ALFRED HITCHCOCK HOUR*, as well as the exasperated auctioneer in *NORTH BY NORTHWEST*. Tremayne had a long career, eventually working almost exclusively as a voice actor for cartoons; he died at 90 in Santa Monica.

References

Hal Erickson, "Les Tremayne," *All Movie Guide*, http://www.nytimes.com/movies/person/71705/Les-Tremayne/biography; "Les Tremayne," *IMDb*, http://www.imdb.com/name/nm0871876/bio?ref_=nm_ov_bio_sm.

THE TROUBLE WITH HARRY (US 1955)

DIRECTOR: Alfred Hitchcock.
SCREENPLAY: John Michael Hayes, based on the novel by Jack Trevor Story.
PRODUCERS: Herbert Coleman (Alfred Hitchcock, uncredited).
CINEMATOGRAPHY: Robert Burks.
EDITOR: Alma Macrorie.
ORIGINAL MUSIC: Bernard Herrmann.
CAST: John Forsythe (Sam Marlowe), Shirley MacLaine (Jennifer Rogers), Edmund Gwenn (Captain Wiles), Mildred Natwick (Ivy Gravely), Mildred Dunnock (Mrs. Wiggs), Royal Dano (Deputy Sheriff Wiggs), Jerry Mathers (Arnie Rogers).
RUNNING TIME: 99 minutes. Color.
RELEASED THROUGH: Paramount.

Harry is dead. That much is clear. But who killed him?

Is it old Captain Wiles, a poor marksman who was out shooting and fears his stray shot killed the man? Is it the elderly, solitary Miss Gravely, who gave him a kick in the head when he grabbed her? Or is it Jennifer Rogers, once reluctantly married to Harry, who, when he began to rudely renew the acquaintance, hit him over the head with a milk bottle?

All of this is prologue to the opening moment when Harry is found dead in the Vermont woods. And the driving force behind a long series of interments, disinterments, and clumsy body snatchings as Harry's poor body is hauled around small-town Vermont.

Yet although Harry is as dead as a doornail, love is still alive. Oddball artist Sam Marlowe falls for Jennifer. Wiles and Gravely form a tentative, tender alliance. And yet, as romance blossoms, the law threatens to end it as Deputy Sheriff Calvin Wiggs gets doggedly on the case.

Eventually, though—no thanks to anyone—the facts are sorted out. Despite the various assaults to his person, Harry died of natural causes. Free of any charges, Miss Gravely and Captain Wiles and Sam and Jennifer are free to go on with their lives. And comfortably, too—a passing millionaire has decided to buy all of Sam's paintings.

A very personal film and a very public failure.

Hitchcock had no doubt about the project, having read the novel by JACK TREVOR STORY when it was published in 1950 and assigning it to JOHN MICHAEL

HAYES for a screenplay adaptation even before their *TO CATCH A THIEF* had been shot. On a practical level, the plot— How do you dispose of an inconvenient corpse?—appealed to the director's true-crime fandom. On a thematic level—Are you GUILTY of murder if you only wished the person dead?—was close to his CATHOLIC heart.

"I've always wanted to do a black comedy," he told associate producer Herbert Coleman. "This story is perfect for that. . . . A low budget film. Without high-price STARS. We'll cast it with New York stage actors."

In that approach, Hitchcock was successful. Bland, button-down JOHN FORSYTHE—who had mostly done stage and radio at that point—was cast as Sam. SHIRLEY MACLAINE made her movie debut as Jennifer. (Fortuitously for her, Coleman had caught the spritely young actress's Broadway debut in *The Pajama Game* after she had to go on for injured star Carol Haney.) The rest of the cast was filled out with older theater veterans—Mildred Dunnock; MILDRED NATWICK; and Hitchcock's old star from *THE SKIN GAME* and *FOREIGN CORRESPONDENT*, EDMUND GWENN.

Yet the production ran into trouble early. Hitchcock had told Hayes to change the setting from old England to New England; they would shoot on LOCATION during the fall, the director told PARAMOUNT, so as to catch the Technicolor beauty of the autumn foliage. But when the crew arrived, they discovered most of the leaves had already fallen in a recent thunderstorm; they were reduced to shooting mostly interiors and re-creating the Vermont exteriors back in California. The bother of a location shoot had been for nothing.

There were other problems, too. Although he was supposed to be playing a bohemian artist, Forsythe remained as Brooks Brothers bland as he always was; MacLaine was suitably quirky, but her independent and outspoken approach to the part rattled the reserved director. Actually, Hitchcock said later, only Gwenn and Natwick caught the very dry and understated flavor of what he was trying to do.

The real stumbling block, though, was that what Hitchcock was trying to do had always been misguided. The charm of Story's original book—what Hitchcock had undoubtedly responded to—was the very Englishness of it, its studied refusal to acknowledge such an embarrassing situation as a possible murder. *The Trouble with Harry* should have been an Ealing comedy, with Alec Guinness as the artist, Joan Greenwood as the single MOTHER, and perhaps BASIL RADFORD and NAUNTON WAYNE as background eccentrics. Simply transplanting it to America didn't work; the attitudes of Yankee townspeople are not those of British villagers, nor are the approaches of American actors necessarily those of English ones. Things were lost in translation.

Despite the difficulties (and inevitable compromises), ROBERT BURKS managed to deliver some striking COLOR cinematography; the film also marked the beginning of Hitchcock's collaborations with BERNARD HERRMANN, with the composer contributing his most playful score. Hayes once again slipped some sexy dialogue past the CENSORS, and there are a few striking images—mostly of poor dead Harry's big feet, rudely dominating the frame in scene after scene as his corpse is continually hidden, rediscovered, and hidden again.

And however lighthearted it's meant to be, the film is still Hitchcock's largest examination of TRANSFERENCE—in the end, no one is really guilty for Harry's death, yet almost everyone shares in that guilt because of their actions or intentions, their attempts to ignore their complicity as unsuccessful as their attempts to hide Harry himself.

While Hitchcock had deliberately kept the budget low, the film still lost money. "The distributors didn't know how to exploit it," he complained later to FRANÇOIS TRUFFAUT. "It needed special handling. They felt it was too special, but I didn't see it that way. . . . To my taste, the humor is quite rich." Indeed, he often used the film as an example of the sort of amusingly morbid mood he was going for in his television shows.

Although he often disowned projects that audiences failed to embrace—their judgment, he felt, was the final one—this was one "flawed" picture he remained stubbornly fond of. "I've always been interested in establishing a contrast, in going against the traditional and in breaking away from clichés," he told Truffaut. "With 'Harry' I took melodrama out of the pitch-black night and brought it out into the sunshine. It's as if I had set up a murder alongside a rustling brook and spilled a drop of blood in the clear water. These contrasts establish a counterpoint; they elevate the commonplace in life to a higher level."

References

Herbert Coleman, *The Man Who Knew Hitchcock: A Hollywood Memoir* (Lanham, MD: Scarecrow Press, 2007), 193; Shirley MacLaine, interview with the author, December 1996; Patrick McGilligan, *Alfred Hitchcock: A Life in Darkness and Light* (New York: HarperCollins, 2003), 502–8; Patrick McGilligan, ed., *Backstory: Interviews with Screenwriters of the 60s* (Berkeley: University of California Press, 1997), 174–92; Donald Spoto, *The Dark Side of Genius: The Life of Alfred Hitchcock* (New York: Da Capo Press, 1999), 354–56; François Truffaut, *Hitchcock/Truffaut*, rev. ed. (New York: Touchstone, 1985), 226–27.

TRUFFAUT, FRANÇOIS (1932–1984)

Paris-born filmmaker who helped popularize the AUTEUR THEORY, firmly establish the artistic reputation of Alfred Hitchcock, and emerge as one of the most talented and humanist directors of the FRENCH NEW WAVE.

Born out of wedlock (a private detective the adult filmmaker hired later traced his parentage to a Jewish dentist from Bayonne), Truffaut was raised chiefly by his arts-loving grandmother until the age of eight, when she died and he was sent to live with his chilly mother and her new husband; his unhappy childhood was one of perpetual truancy and sneaking into movie theaters. He quit school for good at 14; 2 years later, he formed a cinema club.

By 20, after a disastrous time in the army—he nearly served serious time for desertion—fellow cinephile and regular mentor ANDRE BAZIN hired him to work at his film magazine, *CAHIERS DU CINEMA*. There, in 1954, Truffaut wrote "A Certain Trend of French Cinema," an early and passionate advocacy of auteurism, which insisted that the director was the true author of a film and that his or her influence could be seen in every work.

Truffaut also, along with ERIC ROHMER and CLAUDE CHABROL, became one of the fiercest defenders of Hitchcock's work; in 1955, Truffaut and Chabrol INTERVIEWED the filmmaker for *Cahiers*, and seven years later, having established himself as a filmmaker, Truffaut reapproached the director, asking this time for a book-length interview. Hitchcock eventually sat for 50 hours of taped conversations, a translator in constant attendance; the resulting mammoth dialogue, *HITCHCOCK/TRUFFAUT*, was first published in France in 1966, coming out in America the following year and later appearing in revised and expanded editions. The two men remained close friends.

In his preface to the final revised edition in 1983, Truffaut said that he had been spurred to write the book because, 20 years before, Hitchcock was still viewed by many outside of the *Cahiers* circle as simply a very slick entertainer; in some ways, Truffaut said, this was Hitchcock's own fault. Although—or perhaps because of—the director's "genius for publicity was equaled only by that of SALVADOR DALI," he was not taken seriously by American intellectuals. They tended to see him as a showman, and "his facetious response to interviewers and his deliberate practice of deriding their questions" did not win them over.

Truffaut's book, with its attention to motif and meaning, was meant to correct that. And it did in many ways. By the late '60s, the Hitchcock reappreciation—aided by ROBIN WOOD's *HITCHCOCK'S FILMS*, first published in 1965, and ANDREW SARRIS's *The American Cinema*, published in 1968—was fully underway; the Truffaut book was its flagship.

The original volume is easy to criticize now. Truffaut was an unabashed and sometimes uncritical devotee; he occasionally fails to follow up on Hitchcock's own allusions and often functions only as a highly intelligent stenographer, carefully taking down every humorous ANECDOTE and how-I-got-that-shot story. But that stenography is important, too; Hitchcock was relaxed and expansive with his young admirer, and if some of the stories here are familiar, then they are also filled with unequaled detail. The book remains a vital work of scholarship and a primary source for many volumes that followed, including this one. (In 2015, the volume even inspired its own documentary.)

Although Truffaut's book would have been a major accomplishment on its own, with his fine feature film debut in 1959, the painfully autobiographical *The 400 Blows*, Truffaut became an accomplished and critically acclaimed filmmaker himself; as his career went on, his own reputation would only increase. Full of invention and innovation, Truffaut would later experiment with narrative and editing in *Shoot the Piano Player*, switch to science fiction (and English) for the flawed *Fahrenheit 451*, and direct several HITCHCOCKIAN thrillers of his own, including two based on COR-NELL WOOLRICH novels, *The Bride Wore Black* and *Mississippi Mermaid*. He will probably be best remembered, however, for his bittersweet meditations on the eternally perplexing challenges of art and love—*Jules and Jim*, *Day for Night*, *The Story of Adele H.*, and *The Last Metro*.

His last film was the Hitchcockian thriller *Confidentially Yours*; his last completed project was the revised edition of *Hitchcock/Truffaut*. He died the next year in Paris of a brain tumor. He was only 52.

References

"François Truffaut," *Biography*, http://www .biography.com/people/fran%C3%A7ois -truffaut-9511057; "François Truffaut," *IMDb*, http://www.imdb.com/name/ nm0000076/bio?ref_=nm_ov_bio_sm; "François Truffaut," *New Wave Encyclopedia*, http://www.newwavefilm.com/french -new-wave-encyclopedia/François-truf faut.shtml; François Truffaut, *Hitchcock/ Truffaut*, rev. ed. (New York: Touchstone, 1985), 11–20, 344–48.

UNDER CAPRICORN (US 1949)

DIRECTOR: Alfred Hitchcock.
SCREENPLAY: James Bridie, Hume Cronyn, from the play by John Colton and Margaret Linden and the novel by Helen Simpson.
PRODUCERS: Uncredited (Sidney Bernstein, Alfred Hitchcock).
CINEMATOGRAPHY: Jack Cardiff.
EDITOR: A. S. Bates.
ORIGINAL MUSIC: Richard Addinsell.
CAST: Ingrid Bergman (Henrietta Flusky), Joseph Cotten (Sam Flusky), Michael Wilding (Charles Adare), Margaret Leighton (Milly), Cecil Parker (Governor).
RUNNING TIME: 117 minutes. Black and white.
RELEASED THROUGH: Warner Bros.

In 1831, a new governor arrives in Australia from Great Britain accompanied by his chipper but callow nephew Charles, who hopes to make his fortune. Charles has no obvious talents, unfortunately, but during a trip to the bank, he meets Samson Flusky, a gruff but prosperous landowner who proposes a business venture—as he is barred from purchasing any more government land, Flusky will loan Charles the money to do so for him and then buy the property back from Charles at a profit.

Despite the governor's warnings about Flusky, who has a bad reputation, Charles pays a call on him—where he realizes that, as a boy, he knew Flusky's wife, Henrietta. Unfortunately, she seems to have had a nervous breakdown and is prone to frightening hallucinations; the house is run by Milly, the housekeeper, who terrorizes the help while quietly keeping Henrietta docile by plying her with strong drink.

Seeing the calming influence Charles has on his wife, Flusky invites him to stay with them; touched by the fragile Henrietta, Charles works hard to help her feel more like her old self. Finally, Henrietta tells Charles the real family story—when she was a wealthy young Irishwoman, Flusky was her stable boy. She ran off with him and was pursued by her brother. In the ensuing fight, she shot and killed her own brother—only it was Flusky who took the blame and the six-year chain-gang sentence in Australia. She followed him, waited for him—and now they are bound together through his love and her obligation.

Discovering them together in a tender moment, the suspicious Flusky orders Charles out of the house; there is a struggle, and Flusky accidentally shoots Charles in the arm. The governor announces that, as an ex-convict, this crime means Flusky will be returned to the chain gang; Henrietta protests that it was an accident and also confesses that it was she who was guilty of her brother's death back in Ireland. The governor warns her that if she persists in

Ingrid Bergman and Alfred Hitchcock share a momentarily carefree moment in London while shooting the nerve-racking *Under Capricorn. Photofest*

that story, then he will return her to Ireland for trial.

Returning home, Henrietta again falls prey to hallucinations—until Flusky discovers that Milly, secretly in love with him, has been engineering the scares to try and drive Henrietta mad. He dismisses Milly and is arrested for the assault on Charles. Charles, however, realizing the real love between Henrietta and her husband, swears that there was no struggle and the gun discharged accidentally. The governor frees

Flusky and declines to pursue any charges against Henrietta; Charles returns to Ireland alone, the one emigrant, he jokes, who did not find his fortune in Australia.

Underwhelming, and a rather lifeless period piece that helped end the fitful life of Hitchcock's TRANSATLANTIC PICTURES.

The idea of the independent production company had been born in the mid-'40s, even as he was working on *THE PARADINE CASE* for DAVID O. SELZNICK; Hitchcock and his new partner, SIDNEY BERNSTEIN, had—after a flirtation with a modern version of *HAMLET*—decided on *Under Capricorn* for their first production. But the director's must-have STAR, INGRID BERGMAN, wasn't yet free; *Under Capricorn* was then moved to second position, with *ROPE* chosen as the company's supposedly safe debut. As it came from a tested stage play, there would be no problem coming up with a script; with Hitchcock deciding on uninterrupted 10-minute takes, production—it was assumed—would be almost effortless.

Unfortunately, there were unforeseen problems, including a box-office reaction to *Rope* that was less than thrilling, and so it became ever more important that Transatlantic's next picture be a simple, unquestioned success. And even more unfortunately, that high-stakes second picture now became the highly problematic *Under Capricorn.*

The problems should have been evident right from the start. Hitchcock had always loathed costume pictures, and his experiences on *WALTZES FROM VIENNA* and *JAMAICA INN* had given him no reason to change his mind; they always felt fake to him. ("I couldn't understand the characters; how they bought a loaf of bread or went to the bathroom.") And although he had optioned the Australian novel himself in 1945, he later claimed he'd never

cared for it and that it was Bergman who really wanted to make it, with all its oppressive melodrama and bleak moodiness—it "suited her rather than myself."

Bergman was fine in the role, at least—it's basically an extended version of the second half of *NOTORIOUS*—but MICHAEL WILDING and JOSEPH COTTEN added little fire as her costars. Of course, the director's insistence on a camera moving through long, elaborately choreographed single takes hardly helped their performances; the cables and movable walls and furniture on wheels created an amazing clutter and soon frustrated Bergman and the rest of the stars. (Unlike *Rope*, though, Hitchcock did make concessions to the conceit, incorporating insert shots and close-ups and rarely letting a take run more than five or six minutes.)

Bergman began to protest loudly, and when she grew angrier and angrier with him—according to the hypersensitive Hitchcock, one day she became "hysterical"—he simply walked off the set. The next morning, they went back to shooting as before, each of them still utterly convinced they were right. "I think he did this to prove to himself that he could," Bergman later said. "It was a challenge only to himself, to show the movie industry that he could figure out and accomplish something so difficult—so much technique, so much to show off. . . . And of course the audience couldn't care less."

Bergman was right, though. Although in *Rope* the technique had at least added to the claustrophobic setting and the "real time" unfolding of the story, here it served no obvious artistic purpose. And while it had been another coup getting JACK CARDIFF, a wizard with COLOR, as cinematographer, Cardiff found the challenges more frustrating than fulfilling (and sadly, thanks to the film's spotty postproduction history, most of the ugly prints in circulation today give only a vague hint as to his original conceptions). "I think a film of *Capricorn* being made would have been far more successful than *Capricorn* itself," Cardiff wryly observed later.

There are hints of other Hitchcock films here and HITCHCOCKIAN themes, of course. Milly—superbly played by MARGARET LEIGHTON—is a smarter, saner Mrs. Danvers, a false MOTHER figure cleverly maneuvering herself into a vacant position of authority ("*I* run this house") or, with seemingly sincere sympathy, slyly enabling her mistress's slide into useless alcoholism. ("Don't you think you should have something to drink?" she murmurs, holding her as the scene fades to black.) It's a chilly portrait—so much so, Hitchcock claimed, that English critics grew rather cross at him for what he'd done with a favorite actress.

And true, *Under Capricorn* is, along with *I CONFESS*, one of the director's most intriguingly CATHOLIC films (and one of the commercial failures most fervently defended by the *CAHIERS DU CINEMA* crowd), with GUILT and sin and whippings and Henrietta wandering through it all barefoot like some medieval penitent. It is also one of the very few Hitchcock films to deal explicitly with self-sacrifice; many Hitchcock characters passively accept the villain's guilt, but the heroes of *Under Capricorn* take action to protect others at some cost to themselves. Flusky confesses to Henrietta's crime to save her from prison; later, Charles lies to save Flusky and then exiles himself so that the woman he loves can be alone with the man who most deserves her.

But the production design is cheap and unconvincing—the Flusky mansion a more-than-usually-obvious matte painting, the waterfront and pier a cramped mockup—and although Bergman is given a nice, dramatic entrance, there's no standout

sequence or memorable moment. It's the sort of picture that Hitchcock always said he hated—pictures of people talking—and it marks the lowest point in a dull period of halfhearted efforts that stretched from *The Paradine Case* to *STAGE FRIGHT*. More than a new beginning, it seemed to mark the end of something—beginning with Transatlantic Pictures, which could not afford this second flop. Bergman and Hitchcock never worked together again—there was first her scandalous affair with Roberto Rossellini and then his discovery of GRACE KELLY. And discounting the early-'60s setting of 1969's *TOPAZ*, Hitchcock never again made a period film.

References

Ingrid Bergman and Alan Burgess, *My Story* (New York: Delacorte Press, 1980), 175, 177–78; Patrick McGilligan, *Alfred Hitchcock: A Life in Darkness and Light* (New York: HarperCollins, 2003), 419–27; Eric Rohmer and Claude Chabrol, *Hitchcock: The First Forty-Four Films*, translated by Stanley Hochman (New York: Frederick Ungar, 1979), 97–103; Donald Spoto, *The Dark Side of Genius: The Life of Alfred Hitchcock* (New York: Da Capo Press, 1999), 308–11; Donald Spoto, *Spellbound by Beauty: Alfred Hitchcock and His Leading Ladies* (New York: Harmony Books, 2008), 175–82; François Truffaut, *Hitchcock/Truffaut*, rev. ed. (New York: Touchstone, 1985), 184–89.

UNIVERSAL

The oldest surviving American film studio, founded in 1912 by a consortium, including Carl Laemmle, who had begun in the business with nickelodeons (and gone on to start the Independent Moving Pictures Company, IMP, which pioneered the STAR system).

By 1915, Universal—now owned outright by Laemmle—was in California and not only producing films but also charging admission fees to star-struck tourists.

The studio prospered in the '20s under the supervision of production chief Irving Thalberg (later lured away to MGM), had an opulent success with Lon Chaney's 1925 *Phantom of the Opera*, and released a string of now-classic horror films in the early 1930s.

But the company was rife with nepotism—"Uncle Carl Laemmle / Has a very large faemmle," Ogden Nash quipped—did not own its own theaters, and (ironically, given Laemmle's success with IMP) had few of the sort of major stars that MGM and WARNER BROS. had signed. In 1936, the family gambled on director James Whale's massive production of *Show Boat*, borrowing—for the first time—funds to finance it. But although the film ended up being a hit, it went grievously over budget, and the lender called in the loan. The Laemmles lost the company.

When Hitchcock did his work for Universal in the early '40s, the studio was, although not poverty row, definitely second tier, relying heavily on teen musicals, Abbott and Costello comedies, and endless (and endlessly cheaper) sequels to its monster movies. *SABOTEUR* and *SHADOW OF A DOUBT* were both prestige productions for them, and Hitchcock was given far more freedom than he had under DAVID O. SELZNICK, but Universal's consistent inability to sign and keep major stars frustrated some of his casting ideas.

The studio continued to rely heavily on modestly budgeted genre films through the 1950s (and under a brief name change to Universal-International) until it was taken over by MCA, a talent agency that first bought the company's production facilities in 1958 and assumed entire control in 1962. Top MCA clients, such as Hitchcock, DORIS DAY, and CARY GRANT, signed contracts with the studio, and Universal's production facilities—and its films' production values—were noticeably increased.

The Hitchcock deal, however, was complicated and full of conflicting interests. MCA head LEW WASSERMAN, who had been Hitchcock's wily agent, was now head of the studio and essentially his boss; Hitchcock, who received a large bloc of Universal shares in exchange for his TV show and film rights, became both an employee at Universal and, as the company's third-largest stockholder, one of his own employers.

The deal gave the director both freedom and unforeseen limitations; while the studio backed the risks of *THE BIRDS* (and of his new discovery TIPPI HEDREN), it vetoed many of his pet projects, while pushing others. The director's much-adored *MARY ROSE* was one it specifically vetoed; the dreary *TOPAZ*, one it thrust upon him. Other specific dictates were handed down, with the studio insisting not only on JULIE ANDREWS and PAUL NEWMAN for *TORN CURTAIN* but also on a pop score, resulting in a permanent rift between the director and longtime collaborator BERNARD HERRMANN.

"They made him very rich, and they recalled it to him," Herrmann said later. "I said to Hitchcock, 'What do you find in common with these hoodlums?' 'What are you talking about?' 'Do they add to your artistic life?' 'No.' 'They drink your wine?' 'Yes.' 'That's about all. What did they ever do? Made you rich? Well, I'm ashamed of you.'"

Universal was the director's home for 15 years. And yet sometimes, it seemed as if he was really only an honored but very well-paying boarder, whose luxurious accommodations came at a cost.

References

"About Universal," *Universal Studios Hollywood*, http://www.universalstudioshollywood.com/auditions/about-universal; Royal S. Brown, "An Interview with Bernard Herrmann," *Bernard Herrmann Society*, http://www.bernardherrmann .org/articles/an-interview-with-bernard -herrmann; Richard Griffith and Arthur Mayer, *The Movies*, rev. ed. (New York: Simon and Schuster, 1971), 46–55; Brian Lamb, "When Hollywood Had a King," *Booknotes*, http://www.booknotes.org/ Watch/159444-1/Connie+Bruck.aspx; Dennis McDougal, "The Last Mogul: Lew Wasserman, MCA and the Hidden History of Hollywood," http://www.dennismcdou gal.com/_br_the_last_mogul__lew_wasser man__mca_and_the_hidden_history_of _hollywood_24553.htm; Steven C. Smith, "For the Heart at Fire's Center: Norman Lloyd," *Bernard Herrmann Society*, http:// folk.uib.no/smkgg/midi/soundtrackweb/ herrmann/articles/smith/lloyd; Donald Spoto, *The Dark Side of Genius: The Life of Alfred Hitchcock* (New York: Da Capo Press, 1999), 417; "Universal Studios," *Encyclopaedia Britannica*, http://www.bri tannica.com/topic/Universal-Studios.

VALENTINE, JOSEPH A. (1900–1948)

New York–born cameraman who began his career as a still photographer and then switched to cinematography in 1924. Early films include Frank Borzage's dreamily romantic silent *7th Heaven*. Later credits were less impressive, with Valentine eventually settling in at the unambitious UNIVERSAL, where he nonetheless worked hard to capture the comic improvisations of W. C. Fields on *My Little Chickadee* and made the most of the expansive interiors and fog-bound woods of *The Wolfman*.

His crisp style and calm professionalism were a good match for Hitchcock, and he was a solid director of photography on the director's two pictures for Universal, capturing some fine images in *SABOTEUR*—the billowing clouds of smoke at the burning hangar, the extreme close-ups during the Statue of Liberty climax—and working well with the LOCATION demands of *SHADOW OF A DOUBT*. The director was impressed enough that, when he embarked on his first independent production, *ROPE*—whose 10-minute takes would demand an unflappable technician—he brought Valentine onboard.

Nominated five times for an ACADEMY AWARD—often for Deanna Durbin musicals like *Mad about Music* and *Spring Parade*—Valentine finally won for the 1948 Technicolor epic *Joan of Arc*, starring INGRID BERGMAN. He died the next year in Cheviot Hills, CA, at 48.

References

"Joseph A. Valentine," *Cyranos*, http://www.cyranos.ch/spvale-e.htm; "Joseph Valentine," *IMDb*, http://www.imdb.com/name/nm0884252; Joseph A. Valentine, "Using an Actual Town Instead of Movie Sets," *American Cinematographer* (October 1942), http://the.hitchcock.zone/wiki/American_Cinematographer_%281942%29_-_Using_an_Actual_Town_Instead_of_Movie_Sets.

VALLI, ALIDA (1921–2006)

Italian-born actress of Austrian heritage—her hometown, Pula, is now part of Croatia—who came from an old and illustrious family. She herself was christened the Baroness Alida Maria Laura Altenburger von Marckenstein-Frauenberg. Moving to Rome at 15 to study acting, she began with roles in the Italian cinema's deliberately shallow, luxuriously posh "white telephone" films; by her early 20s, she had progressed to more serious dramas, which sometimes earned the wrath of Mussolini's political censors (although the dictator himself remained one of her most ardent fans).

DAVID O. SELZNICK "discovered" her after the war and signed her to a personal contract, hoping to repeat his success with INGRID BERGMAN and billing her,

Vertigo teamed Kim Novak and James Stewart in Alfred Hitchcock's most complex study of identity and obsession. *Paramount Pictures/Photofest © Paramount Pictures*

to foster comparisons with Garbo, as simply "Valli." The actress disliked the gimmick ("People get me mixed up with Rudy Vallee," she complained) but dutifully went to work, appearing in a radio adaptation of *SPELLBOUND*, playing the Bergman part, and making her American film debut in *THE PARADINE CASE*. Her dark hauteur apparently left Hitchcock cold, but cinematographer LEE GARMES made the most of her elegant cheekbones, lighting her with the sort of tender, worshipful devotion he'd once brought to MARLENE DIETRICH.

This film, however, was no *Morocco*, and American audiences failed to take to the raven-haired beauty or to any of her subsequent Hollywood movies. The actress soon returned to Europe and an unforgettable role in *The Third Man* as Harry Lime's unwaveringly devoted love (opposite another Selznick STAR, JOSEPH COTTEN); the movie capitalized on her chilly, unreadable gaze, and her simple, unblinking walk toward the camera and away from the friend who betrayed her lover is one of the cinema's great endings.

Roles in Luchino Visconti's *Senso*, Michelangelo Antonioni's *Il Grido*, and Georges Franju's *Eyes without a Face* followed, and for a while, other great directors continued to seek her out—CLAUDE CHABROL, Pier Paolo Pasolini, Bernardo Bertolucci. (Even if Valli was forced to do the occasional horror film, then at least those were directed by Mario Bava and Dario Argento.) But as she grew older, finding work became difficult, and although she continued to appear onstage and on Italian television, money grew tight; eventually the baroness accepted a small government pension for impoverished artists. She died in Rome at age 84.

References
"Alida Valli," *IMDb*, http://www.imdb.com/name/nm0885098/bio?ref_=nm_ov_bio_sm; Nadine Brozan, "Alida Valli, 84, Actress Memorable in 'The Third Man,' Dies," *New York Times*, April 25, 2006, http://www.nytimes.com/2006/04/25/movies/25valli.html?_r=0; John Francis Lane, "Alida Valli," *Guardian*, April 24, 2006, http://www.theguardian.com/news/2006/apr/24/guardianobituaries.film; Bob Thomas, *Selznick* (New York: Pocket Books, 1972), 244.

VALLI, VIRGINIA (1898–1968)
Chicago-born performer on the stage since her middle teens who made her movie debut in 1916. A star by the early '20s, she appeared in actor John Gilbert's only film as director, *Love's Penalty*, the King Vidor picture *Wild Oranges*, and a variety of comedies and romantic dramas. As part of SIR MICHAEL BALCON's plan to use American celebrities to broaden the appeal of British pictures, in 1925 she was imported to star in Alfred Hitchcock's first film, *THE PLEASURE GARDEN*, as Patsy, the far more worldly—but intrinsically far more moral—of the story's two chorus girls.

Her demands for expensive accommodations and travel drove Hitchcock and assistant ALMA REVILLE to distraction, and the picture failed to impress mogul C. M. WOOLF; put back on the shelf, it was only released in 1927, after *THE LODGER* had become a surprise hit (a surprise, at least, to Woolf, who had wanted to write that one off as well). By that time, however, Valli's fame was already in steep decline, having been dropped by her studio the previous year. She continued working for a while and then retired in 1931 after marrying Charles Farrell; she died in Palm Springs of a stroke at 70.

References
Patrick McGilligan, *Alfred Hitchcock: A Life in Darkness and Light* (New York: HarperCollins, 2003), 68–70; Donald Spoto, *The Dark Side of Genius: The Life of Alfred Hitchcock* (New York: Da Capo Press, 1999), 80, 81, 86; François Truffaut, *Hitchcock/Truffaut*, rev. ed. (New York: Touchstone, 1985), 31–39; "Virginia Valli," *IMDb*, http://www.imdb.com/name/nm0885128.

VENTIMIGLIA, GAETANO (1888–1973)
Catania-born filmmaker from an aristocratic family—he would occasionally use his baronial title in movie credits and sometimes "Gaetano di Ventimiglia"—in the industry since 1916, first in Italian movies and then in German and British productions. A gifted photographer and inventor, he was the cameraman on Alfred Hitchcock's first film, *THE PLEASURE GARDEN*, in 1925, where his chief contribution was disastrous—it was his suggestion that Hitchcock avoid paying duty on the film stock by hiding it when the crew traveled throughout Europe, a petty

crime that, when discovered, led to their supply being confiscated.

His next film for Hitchcock, *THE MOUNTAIN EAGLE*, remains lost, but Ventimiglia served as director of photography for the director's signature early success *THE LODGER*. It is, along with *THE RING*, Hitchcock's most visual bit of early storytelling, and the images that remain in the mind—the startling initial close-up of the screaming BLONDE, the pacing footsteps of the boarder upstairs—are ones Ventimiglia captured. His credits after that are desultory and cease altogether in 1928, save for one more film in 1938, back in his native Italy, where he was a professor at the state film school. He died at age 85.

References

"Gaetano di Ventimiglia," *IMDb*, http://www.imdb.com/name/nm0893248; Patrick McGilligan, *Alfred Hitchcock: A Life in Darkness and Light* (New York: HarperCollins, 2003), 68–69, 81, 95; H. Mario Raimondo-Souto, *Motion Picture Photography: A History, 1891–1960* (Jefferson, NC: McFarland, 2006), 149–50; Donald Spoto, *The Dark Side of Genius: The Life of Alfred Hitchcock* (New York: Da Capo Press, 1999), 77–80, 83, 86; François Truffaut, *Hitchcock/Truffaut*, rev. ed. (New York: Touchstone, 1985), 31–39.

VERNON, JOHN (1932–2005)

Saskatchewan-born actor who studied theater in Canada and at the Royal Academy of Dramatic Art. He was a regular presence on Canadian TV beginning in the '50s and made his American debut, offscreen, as the voice of Big Brother in the 1956 adaptation of *1984*.

Although Vernon was a classically trained performer who'd appeared in Shakespeare and Chekhov onstage, in the movies, his imposing baritone and pockmarked features conspired to type him as sleazy villains, from *Point Blank* in 1967 through several "women-in-chains" exploitation movies in the 1980s. His most famous heavies were the liberal mayor of San Francisco in *Dirty Harry* and the bullying Dean Wormer in *Animal House*; his one role for Hitchcock was in the ill-fated *TOPAZ*, playing the revolutionary leader Rico Parra under a not particularly convincing false beard.

A busy actor, Vernon retained a sense of humor about his career; later in life, he would often parody his bad-guy parts in comedies or provide the voices for villains in children's cartoons. He died of complications from heart surgery in Los Angeles at 72.

References

"Actor John Vernon of 'Animal House' Dies," *USA Today*, February 3, 2005, http://usatoday30.usatoday.com/life/people/2005-02-03-vernon-obit_x.htm; Adam Bernstein, "John Vernon, 72, 'Animal House' Dean," *Washington Post*, February 4, 2005; "John Vernon," *IMDb*, http://www.imdb.com/name/nm0006893/bio?ref_=nm_ov_bio_sm.

VERTIGO (US 1958)

DIRECTOR: Alfred Hitchcock.
SCREENPLAY: Alec Coppel and Samuel A. Taylor, based on the novel *D'Entre les Morts* by Boileau-Narcejac.
PRODUCERS: Herbert Coleman (Alfred Hitchcock, uncredited).
CINEMATOGRAPHY: Robert Burks.
EDITOR: George Tomasini.
ORIGINAL MUSIC: Bernard Herrmann.
CAST: James Stewart (John "Scottie" Ferguson), Kim Novak (Madeleine Elster/Judy Barton), Barbara Bel Geddes (Midge Wood), Tom Helmore (Gavin Elster), Henry Jones (Coroner).
RUNNING TIME: 128 minutes. Color.
RELEASED THROUGH: Paramount.

After seeing a police officer plunge to his death, San Francisco detective John "Scottie" Ferguson retires from the force on a disability pension, so traumatized by the event that heights now wrack him with crippling fear and dizzying nausea. He's lured back for a private case, though, when an old college friend, Gavin Elster, asks him to keep an eye on his wife, Madeleine—not because he suspects she's unfaithful but because he fears she's emotionally disturbed and may even be suicidal.

Scottie shadows the beautiful Madeleine and discovers she has a preoccupation with an ancestor—Carlotta Valdes, a 19th-century beauty who lost her mind and took her own life after her rich lover took their illegitimate child and sent Carlotta away. Madeleine grows more and more obsessed with the woman and one afternoon throws herself into San Francisco Bay. Scottie rescues her and, hiding his identity, begins to form a friendship with Madeleine, who swears she has no memory of the event.

The two spend time together and quickly fall in love. Madeleine begins to share more of her story with him, including a recurring dream about an old Spanish mission. Scottie, convinced that it's a memory of a real place she once visited, drives her down to one to confront her with the reality. But a suddenly distraught Madeleine runs inside the church, climbing the bell tower. Crippled by his acrophobia, Scottie cannot follow and watches as she leaps, screaming, to her death.

An inquest all but blames Scottie for Madeleine's suicide; a mourning Elster leaves for Europe. Scottie has a breakdown and checks into a sanitarium. Months later, he sees Judy Barton, a saleswoman who looks like Madeleine. He follows her and asks her out. Then, as a relationship begins, he starts to aggressively make her over—having her wear the same clothes, even dye her hair the same color—as Madeleine.

What he doesn't realize at first is that she *is* Madeleine—or rather had pretended to be her so that Elster could throw his dead wife from the bell tower and have a witness to her "suicide." Scottie was picked solely because they knew he could never follow her up the stairs.

Unaware of all this, Scottie begins to fall in love with the made-over Judy—until one day he sees her wearing some of Madeleine's jewelry. Telling her they're going out to dinner, he drives her to the old mission instead and pulls her up the stairs of the bell tower, confronting her with her lies. The emotional shock cures Scottie of his acrophobia. A tearful Judy confesses. But then a nun from the mission, hearing voices, enters suddenly and a startled Judy falls to her death, this time for real—while Scottie can only stand and look down.

A film that's superficially about a fear of heights but much more hauntingly about the depths of obsession—while standing as the pinnacle of its director's long career.

Alfred Hitchcock had been interested in the mystery novels of the French duo PIERRE BOILEAU and THOMAS NARCEJAC since the early '50s, when he had reportedly just missed out on the rights to *Celle Qui N'Etait Plus*—bought by HENRI-GEORGES CLOUZOT and turned into the influential thriller *LES DIABOLIQUES*. When Hitchcock signed his new deal with PARAMOUNT, one of his first requests was that they get a copy of Boileau-Narcejac's new book *D'Entre les Morts* and work up an English synopsis.

The rights were obtained in early 1955, and shortly after *THE WRONG MAN* wrapped, preproduction began. It ended up being a particularly difficult and protracted period. Always loath to have to break in a new writer, Hitchcock turned to one of the screenwriters of the previous picture, Maxwell Anderson. (ANGUS MACPHAIL, the other screenwriter and a longtime Hitchcock colleague, had a drinking problem and frankly told the director he simply wasn't up to such a major project.) But Anderson's new screenplay was even more heavily literary than the last—he titled it *Darkling, I Listen*, a line from Keats—and it was deemed unusable.

Health concerns—an abdominal hernia the director had tried to ignore for years finally necessitated surgery—brought another delay, and also some breathing room as screenwriter ALEC COPPEL tried a brand-new adaptation. But then Hitchcock needed to return to the hospital, this time for gall bladder surgery. When he emerged, he had to admit that Coppel hadn't quite gotten it either. Then came the final indignity—although JAMES STEWART was set for the hero, costar VERA MILES announced that she was pregnant with her third child and would be unable to appear in a film still called *From amongst the Dead*.

Hitchcock was furious. He had signed Miles to a personal contract, trying to mold her—choosing not just her projects but also her hair and clothes, even off set—in the way that he later would with TIPPI HEDREN. But Miles had her own ideas—unlike Hedren, she'd already made a number of other films with other directors, so she knew something about the industry, and she had no interest in being made over or turned into a major STAR. ("Hitchcock," she said years later, "had a bit of a Pygmalion Complex.") She was also newly married, for the second time, and eager to spend more time with her family. Personally affronted, Hitchcock told her that, while one child was to be expected, three was simply "vulgar." Eventually, he let her contract lapse. As for Miles, she had no regrets. "He got his picture," she reflected, decades later. "And I got a son."

Now Hitchcock was without a leading lady—and he realized, rereading the Coppel efforts, still without a suitable script. A new writer was brought on, SAMUEL A. TAYLOR, who'd had a recent success with the romantic *Sabrina*. He also knew the Bay Area well, a plus, as Hitchcock had already decided on some LOCATIONS, even sketching rough storyboards, including an old mission church and the Golden Gate Bridge. Taylor made progress quickly, and Hitchcock's agent, LEW WASSERMAN, suggested a current top star, KIM NOVAK, for the female lead; it required a loan-out from Columbia, where she was under contract. (As part of the deal, that studio got the services of Stewart for a follow-up Novak picture, *Bell, Book and Candle*.)

Her signing brought some new delays and headaches: Novak had a scheduled vacation she was determined to take, and when she was ready to start, she began by arguing with EDITH HEAD over her wardrobe, saying she never wore the COLOR gray and that the skirt-suit and dark pumps made her legs look thick. (She was right, as ALMA REVILLE pointed out later—they did make her legs look thick.) But as usual, Hitchcock had visualized the heroine's look months in advance, and he refused to compromise. Eventually Novak gave in and wore the suit and the heels. Still, "he learned very early on that I was not the ideal woman for him," said Novak, decades later. "He liked a woman to be very pliable, very flexible as far as doing everything the way he wanted."

Finally, in September 1957, shooting could begin. Novak continued to be a problem, at least in Hitchcock's eyes; "Kim's head was full of her own ideas," he complained to Hedda Hopper. As usual, he had no interest in the METHOD, motivations, or actors who didn't hit their marks or look in the appropriate screen direction, and he tried to leave Novak to her own devices (which was actually liberating in her mind). Directing BARBARA BEL GEDDES as

Stewart's ex-girlfriend was easier; when Hitchcock told her for her close-ups to simply look up or down and she did, her reactions cut together—in the scene in which Midge listens while Scottie talks obtusely about their former relationship—is one of her best moments in the picture and a small clear-cut example of the director's PURE CINEMA of MONTAGE.

There were no problems with Stewart, however—giving his darkest, most complex performance as a man full of childlike terrors and almost embarrassingly frank SEXUAL obsessions. And technical difficulties were handled with skill—a matte painting standing in for a bell tower that wasn't there, a model turned on its side substituting for a full-scale STAIRCASE, and a pioneering DOLLY zoom (later dubbed the "*Vertigo* effect") creating the sensation of a background simply dropping away before your eyes.

Postproduction, however, buried Hitchcock in an uncharacteristic avalanche of second-guessings and sudden doubts. Could he end the film as he wished, with Scottie standing alone on the tower? (No, said the prevailing rules of CENSORSHIP—you're letting the murderer get away.) Was giving away the twist—that Madeleine and Judy were the same person—something to be saved for the end or revealed earlier? Did the movie work at all? (When Alma raised a small objection—about that one shot in which Novak's calves did look fat—Hitchcock fell into a funk, reporting to colleagues that obviously his wife "hated" the film.)

But the fixes were made. The sequence with Novak was shortened. A censor-friendly ending, with Scottie and Midge listening to news reports of the police tracking down Elster, was filmed (but never shown). And after trying it both ways—with and without the early revelation of Judy's duplicity—Hitchcock finally decided with his initial instinct and gave the mystery away early. As always, suspense trumped surprise.

Finally, by 1958, a project that had begun four years earlier—and survived three different screenwriters, two leading ladies, and a pair of surgeries for Hitchcock—was at last ready. And, really, perfect.

Hitchcock's pantheon is crowded with contenders. *PSYCHO*, with its narrative experiments and pitch-black humor, *NOTORIOUS* with its curdled romanticism, *SHADOW OF A DOUBT* with its assault on small-town innocence—each film has its disciples. As does the brilliant exercise in montage and VOYEURISM that is *REAR WINDOW*; the meditation on DOUBLES and GUILT that is *STRANGERS ON A TRAIN*; and the mad, pure, almost surreally entertaining assault that is *NORTH BY NORTHWEST*. Yet *Vertigo* stands apart. Perhaps because it so clearly stands for Hitchcock and his own divided self.

As in *Strangers on a Train* and as in *Psycho*, the theme of doppelgängers is explicit in *Vertigo*—a theme underlined by the production design that, at Hitchcock's insistence, included mirrors and reflecting images whenever possible. But it is more than the idea of Judy pretending to be Madeleine. It goes to the split nature of Scottie himself, a supposedly hardened big-city detective who's reduced to a fainting panic by heights, a lanky, silver-haired adult haunted by a child's sweaty, madhouse nightmares. Judy plays two parts—the soft-spoken elegant BLONDE sophisticate, the brassy small-town redheaded shop girl—but Scottie contains two parts. And in the end he is both creator and destroyer, bringing Madeleine back to life and then literally dragging her to her death.

The film functions as its own double, too, as it portrays women as either victims or vixens, lovers or MOTHERS, objectifying them in its MALE GAZE and decrying that objectification at the same time. The credits begin with a woman broken into parts—an EYE, lips—and the early days of Scottie's relationship with Judy is the story of him trying to reassemble those parts. She must wear a suit in this color and cut; her hair, eyebrows, and nails must all be dyed, plucked, painted just so. And when she protests, he tells her it "can't matter" to her how she looks; he is the male, and helping create (or, in this case, re-create) an object that pleases him visually should be her only concern, a job for which, he promises at first, he'll pay her for.

It sounds like a relationship between a man and a kept woman, a reflection of the Carlotta Valdes story, and it is the strongest illustration of one of the film's other themes: masculine power and a man's unfettered freedom. In fact, that's a phrase that occurs three times in the movie. First, when Gavin Elster, talking about the old Barbary Coast days, rhapsodizes over an era when there was "power, freedom"; then, when Pop, the old bookstore owner who recounts Carlotta's cruel abandonment, explains, "You know, a man could do that in those days. They had the power, and the freedom." And then, finally, they are words that Scottie throws back in Judy's face, pointing out that, when Elster's wife was dead and her money his, when he finally did have "all of that freedom and that power," he deserted her, leaving her with only a few pieces of jewelry—gems that she, being a sentimental woman, couldn't help but take out and wear.

And yet, the film suggests, even as men use their own power to keep women imprisoned, they're rarely free themselves. How free is Scottie, imprisoned by his memories of a pale, mysterious blonde? How free are any of us when our relationships are ruled by memories, past hurts, unrequited loves, unrecovered losses?

Vertigo is a story of obsession, of FETISH and wish fulfillment, and it stands as perhaps the clearest exposition and exploration of Hitchcock's not-so-secret urge to control—the way that Scottie supervises every bit of Judy's transformation is precisely the way Hitchcock supervised the public image (and, if allowed, the social life) of those actresses he truly fixated on. Yet there's an unconscious, unexpected bit of doubling, too, in the casting of Novak; signed to a contract by Columbia mogul Harry Cohn, who wanted nothing more than a new Rita Hayworth, his own Marilyn Monroe, she was constantly molded and made over in real life, too (and mocked whenever she pushed to do something different or personal).

"That always was amazing to me," Novak said about the studios. "They hire you because they think you have something special. Yet they feel the need to make you over into what they want, into something else." Judy, she said later, was "just me, when I first got to Hollywood," and the things Judy went through—the hard, appraising gaze turned on her; the demands for change and attempts at control—were things Novak had gone through, too, as she struggled to hold on to her own IDENTITY. Her experiences fueled the warmth and sympathy that she brought to the role. "I really identified with the movie because it was saying, 'Please, see who I am,'" she said. "'Fall in love with *me*.'" Or as Judy asks Scottie, "Couldn't you like me, just the way I am?" or, even more heartbreakingly, "If I do what you tell me, will you love me?"

But it is too late for her and too late for Scottie (who, in another example of the film's pairings, loses her twice at that bell tower—first as Madeleine and then as Judy). He begins the film hanging from a precipice and ends standing at another, in both instances powerless, in both instances alone—and this is the way he shall remain. (Although his friend Midge remains devoted to him, he's utterly clueless—and his complaints about her being "motherly" and her soothing "You're not lost, mother's here"—suggests their relationship will remain utterly sexless, too.)

Perhaps one of the greatest, unexpected ironies of *Vertigo* was that all the difficulties that arose during its preproduction helped it, not only in the casting of Novak—a far more vibrant personality than Miles—but also with the extended rewrites, which gave Hitchcock a chance to plan and replan his imagery. There is the motif of concentric circles, of dizzying bottomless whirlpools, that begins with SAUL BASS's titles and BERNARD HERRMANN's spiraling music and then continues with the way Madeleine (copying Carlotta) wears her hair in a tight circular bun and carries a round, tightly arranged bouquet of flowers or how the camera spins around Scottie and Judy when they kiss. And there is the color green—always a signifier for Hitchcock of dreams and sometimes menace—that reoccurs throughout the film, from Madeleine's green car and dress to the neon light that bathes Judy's cheap hotel room, and the fog filter that gives scenes in the cemetery, Muir Woods, and Judy's rooms an additional hazy, dreamlike quality. But then the entire film feels somewhat like a dream, a dream from which we cannot—and do not wish to—wake.

Vertigo was released to mixed reviews and moderate box office. Publicly, Hitchcock would sometimes disparage Novak's performance; privately, he would blame Stewart for being too old for the part (a conviction that convinced the director to delay *North by Northwest*, which he had promised to Stewart, just long enough so that the actor had to begin work on *Bell, Book and Candle*, thereby "forcing" Hitchcock to cast CARY GRANT instead). That *Vertigo* was not a

bigger hit disappointed a filmmaker who always felt that the final verdict on any film came from the audience.

But slowly, the critical tide turned. And today, many see it as one of cinema's premiere achievements and Hitchcock's finest film. As well as his most nakedly revealing.

References
Richard Freedman, "'Psycho' Actress Defends Hitchcock," *Spokesman Review*, June 25, 1983, http://the.hitchcock.zone/ wiki/The%20Spokesman-Review%20 %2825%2FJun%2F1983%29%20-%20 %27Psycho%27%20actress%20defends%20 Hitchcock; Patrick McGilligan, *Alfred Hitchcock: A Life in Darkness and Light* (New York: HarperCollins, 2003), 540–49, 552–57; Kim Novak, interview with the author, October 1996; *Obsessed with Vertigo: New Life for Hitchcock's Masterpiece*, directed by Harrison Engle (1997), documentary, http://the.hitchcock.zone/wiki/ Obsessed_with_Vertigo:_New_Life_for _Hitchcock's_Masterpiece_%281997%29 _-_transcript; Donald Spoto, *The Dark Side of Genius: The Life of Alfred Hitchcock* (New York: Da Capo Press, 1999), 393–99; Donald Spoto, *Spellbound by Beauty: Alfred Hitchcock and His Leading Ladies* (New York: Harmony Books, 2008), 222–27; François Truffaut, *Hitchcock/Truffaut*, rev. ed. (New York: Touchstone, 1985), 243–48.

VIERTEL, PETER (1920–2007)
Dresden-born author raised in a literary family—his parents were writers Salka and Berthold Viertel—who grew up in Southern California after the family left Germany. The Viertel home in Santa Monica was a famous and flexible salon, always full of poets and filmmakers, and after graduation from college, Viertel began his screenwriting career by working on the screenplay for *SABOTEUR*—a lively enough film but one

whose script basically consists of ideas and situations lifted from other Hitchcock pictures, spiced up with some bon mots courtesy of DOROTHY PARKER.

After finishing *Saboteur* and *The Hard Way*, a tough proletarian drama, Viertel served with the O.S.S. during World War II; come peacetime, he resumed his writing career and a colorful life marked by his strong friendships with domineering personalities, like Ernest Hemingway and John Huston. He did some on-location rewrites for Huston on *The African Queen* and later fictionalized the experience as the excellent novel *White Hunter, Black Heart* (years later made into a film by Clint Eastwood). In 1960, Viertel married Deborah Kerr, settled in Europe, and wrote novels.

He died at 86 in Marbella, Spain.

References

Ronald Bergan, "Peter Viertel," *Guardian*, November 7, 2007, http://www .theguardian.com/news/2007/nov/07/ guardianobituaries.booksobituaries; Douglas Martin, "Peter Viertel, 86, Author and Screenwriter Is Dead," *New York Times*, November 6, 2007, http://www .nytimes.com/2007/11/06/arts/06viertel .html?ref=obituaries&_r=0; "Peter Viertel," *IMDb*, http://www.imdb.com/name/ nm0896830/bio?ref_=nm_ov_bio_sm.

VILLAGE OF STARS

One of the many projects announced in the early '60s, this was to be based on the novel by the same name by Arthur David Beaty (writing under the name "Paul Stanton") about a pilot sent on a bombing mission; the mission is aborted, but the bomb has already been armed and will explode if the plane—which is running out of fuel— dips below a specific altitude. Although the adaptation rights were purchased, it seems that this project—like *Trap for a Solitary Man*—never got much beyond a simple press release.

References

Patrick McGilligan, *Alfred Hitchcock: A Life in Darkness and Light* (New York: HarperCollins, 2003), 609, 611; "Mr. Hitchcock's Plans," *Times*, September 23, 1960, http://the.hitchcock.zone/wiki/The _Times_%2823/Sep/1960%29_-_Mr. _Hitchcock's_plans.

VISUAL EFFECTS

Hitchcock films are primarily visual ones, and the importance of specific images always trumps petty considerations about reality; what matters chiefly is that the image feels right and conveys the proper emotion. This was something he learned from his first days as a filmmaker in the '20s, observing the great German EXPRESSIONISTS, and brought to his own films; although it's most obvious in the early silents, it's an idea that he incorporated into much of his work, always pushing the "rightness" of an image over the reality. (There is, for example, no logical reason in *VERTIGO* for the made-over Judy to emerge from her hotel room bathroom in a fog; there is a very thematic one.)

The first and most important use of visual effects in Hitchcock films, then, is to create images that exist not in life but in the minds and hearts of their characters. An early clear example is in *THE LODGER*, in which it's necessary to show the nervous pacing of the tenant in the room above; Hitchcock's camera shows the ceiling, which then dissolves into a plate-glass floor to illustrate the man's nervous walking, the thudding of his footsteps, and how his worrisome presence literally hangs over the landlady's family.

Other visual effects dramatize a character's emotional or physical state. In the first *THE MAN WHO KNEW TOO MUCH* and *THE LADY VANISHES*, a swirling parade of faces or images suggest turmoil or mental confusion; in *Vertigo*, the DOLLY zoom at the top of the bell tower STAIRS helps us experience the same disorienting nausea as the hero. The overly brilliant whites of *SPELLBOUND*, the murderous red flashes of *MARNIE*, the gaily waltzing couples of *SHADOW OF A DOUBT*—these are effects that discard the camera's objectivity for SUBJECTIVITY, showing us things that only the characters might see or think and taking us inside their disturbed minds.

But Hitchcock, always the master technician, was just as skilled at using visual effects to heighten reality and always took a sort of boyish pride in describing in detail just how he and his cinematographers had tricked the audience into seeing something that they hadn't—the Schüfftan process, for example, which literally did it all with mirrors, turning still photographs into the backgrounds for *MURDER!* and the first *The Man Who Knew Too Much*. Or the brilliant crash sequence in *FOREIGN CORRESPONDENT* that had the plane hitting the ocean and water pouring in, all in a single shot—a problem finally solved, the director revealed, by making the back-projection screen out of fragile rice paper and then sending thousands of gallons bursting through it. (He relates the "secrets" of all, with great glee, in *HITCHCOCK/TRUFFAUT*.)

Working with skilled cinematographers and visual-effects wizards—from JACK E. COX in Britain to JOHN P. FULTON in Hollywood—Hitchcock would build memorable moments around carefully engineered images, whether it was the burst of bloody crimson covering the screen in *Spellbound*, Fry's spectacular fall from the Statue of Liberty in *SABOTEUR*, or the carousel catastrophe from *STRANGERS ON A TRAIN*. The director's greatest effects triumph came with *THE BIRDS*, which contained more than 400 separate optical effects and an approach that combined real birds, mechanical models, and extraordinarily difficult multiple exposures supervised by Ub Iwerks, a Disney veteran who had perfected the sodium-vapor process that made them possible.

Hitchcock's films were made, of course, decades before computer-generated images took over the world of special effects; for his 50-year career, he essentially used the same tools he always had. The miniatures, matte paintings, and multiple exposures improved with time and larger budgets, and his imagination never diminished. Yet his stubborn and somewhat old-fashioned preference for studio work sometimes hampered him; decades after other directors were filming their performers inside actual moving cars, Hitchcock still used a studio mock-up and a back-projection screen. Whether the unreality of that process added to the surreal power of *Marnie* or the antique charms of *FAMILY PLOT*—or is just a sign of a once-meticulous director distracted by personal issues or ill health—is a question for each viewer to decide.

References

Kyle B. Counts and Steve Rubin, "The Making of The Birds," *Cinemafantastique* (1980), http://the.hitchcock.zone/wiki/Cinemafantastique_%281980%29_-_The_Making_of_Alfred_Hitchcock%27s_The_Birds; Donald Spoto, *The Dark Side of Genius: The Life of Alfred Hitchcock* (New York: Da Capo Press, 1999), 67–71; François Truffaut, *Hitchcock/Truffaut*, rev. ed. (New York: Touchstone, 1985), 65, 135–36, 197.

VOYEURISM

"We've become a race of Peeping Toms. What people ought to do is get outside their own house and look in for a change."

—Stella

The nurse in *REAR WINDOW* is talking about voyeurism, or scopophilia, but SIGMUND FREUD's term for it—*schaulust*, or "pleasure in seeing"—may be the best in this context. For what is a love of movies but a pleasure in seeing—in experiencing places and things we never normally would, in watching the unguarded, unembarrassed actions of others? To go to a movie is, in itself, an act of voyeurism, a vicarious thrill garnered from peeping in at the concealed or forbidden; the act is doubled in Hitchcock's films, so many of which center around the art of looking and most often specifically on THE MALE GAZE, that cold appraising look that reduces women to sexual objects and then attaches a calculated worth.

It is actually one of the first images we get in the first completed Hitchcock film, *THE PLEASURE GARDEN*, in which a theatergoer spies on a chorine's legs through his opera glasses. It a simple, stark image of both SEXUAL pleasure and alienated removal (of anger, too—the chorus girl is aware of it and stares back, answering his gaze with her own, as decades later, Thorwald will, too, in *Rear Window*).

Observing life from a safe and chilly distance; this is an integral part of voyeurism and an integral part of watching in Hitchcock's films, as his characters routinely spy on activities they're afraid or unable to participate in. The spy who cannot bring himself to carry out his mission watches someone else do it through a telescope in *SECRET AGENT*; the bachelor who is resistant to commitment uses a telephoto lens to peer in on a variety of marriages and relationships in *Rear Window*. Safely removed, protected by the fragile barrier of a window, they watch others do what they cannot.

Yet they are not innocent; as Hitchcock's CATHOLIC lessons taught him, to observe a sin and not attempt to stop it is, in some way, to participate in that sin yourself. It is a secret sharing he extends to the audience. When Jeff picks up that phallic lens and uses it to stare at the voluptuous "Miss Torso" in *Rear Window*, we stare with him; when Norman takes the picture off the wall to peep at Marion undressing in the bathroom in *PSYCHO*, we peep eagerly, too. (As an added emphasis, the painting covering the peephole is one of the Old Testament's story of Susanna being surprised in her bath.) We watch men watching beautiful women—the loathsome Judge Horfield practically smacking his lips over Gay Keane's bare shoulder in *THE PARADINE CASE*, the obsessed Scottie Ferguson wordlessly pursuing Madeleine through the streets and alleys of San Francisco in *VERTIGO*—and we share in their pleasure. And in their GUILT.

It is a hall of mirrors—we go to the theater to see a film in which a director watches an actor watching an actress. But if we look hard enough, in that final mirror, we see ourselves.

References

"Catechism of the Catholic Church," *The Holy See*, http://www.vatican.va/archive/ccc_css/archive/catechism/p3s1c1a8.htm; Laura Mulvey, "Visual Pleasure and Narrative Cinema," *Screen* (Autumn 1975), 6–18; George Ritzer, ed., *Encyclopedia of Social Theory* (Thousand Oaks, CA: SAGE, 2004), 467–68.

WALKER, ROBERT (1918–1951)

Born in Salt Lake City, he found refuge from an unhappy childhood in acting. Later, he found a benefactor in his wealthy aunt, a Bonwit Teller executive in Manhattan who invited the teen into her home and paid for his tuition at the American Academy of Dramatic Arts. There he met aspiring actress Phylis Isley—soon to change her name to Jennifer Jones. The two married in 1939 and began looking for work, chiefly in New York. Walker eventually landed some jobs on radio, and the couple had two sons. "I was only 19 but even then I knew there could never be anyone else," he later said, remembering the day he met her. "I didn't consider myself 'good enough' for her. She made me want to be somebody. We were happy. Or at least I thought we were."

After DAVID O. SELZNICK discovered Jones in 1941, the couple relocated to Hollywood, where Walker got a deal with MGM and Jones signed a personal contract with the mogul. Physically slight and projecting the eager neediness of a puppy, Walker soon began getting wholesome juvenile parts, often as young soldiers; in *Since You Went Away*, he costarred with Jones, playing her tragic love in uniform.

But there was just as much melodrama offscreen; apparently Jones and Selznick had been having an affair for some time, and Jones and Walker separated during filming. They divorced in 1945. Walker, who had been traumatized as a child by his parents' divorce, went very quickly to pieces, drinking heavily, causing public scenes, and eventually having a breakdown. The end of his own marriage, he said, left his life "completely wrecked."

Although Walker still managed to make several interesting films during this period—including *The Clock* with the similarly fragile Judy Garland and *One Touch of Venus* with Ava Gardner—his emotional state continued to deteriorate. He cycled through a brief marriage to John Ford's daughter Barbara, had run-ins with the police, and in 1949 entered the Menninger Clinic for further psychiatric care.

One of his first films after his release was Alfred Hitchcock's *STRANGERS ON A TRAIN*. The years of alcoholism had coarsened Walker's features; the one-time boy next door looked a decade older than he was. But casting him against type appealed to Hitchcock, who—after being denied on *THE LODGER* and *SUSPICION*—was finally going to have his leading man play a psycho (and achieve perhaps another small, subterranean dig at Selznick; there was probably no actor the mogul less wanted to see onscreen).

Walker, knowing this was his best chance at a comeback, seized it. His Bruno Antony is charming, stylish, funny; he's also the brightest STAR among Hitchcock's villainous if stereotypical gays, devoted to his MOTHER and flashy clothes, full of airy

Teresa Wright brought an alert intelligence to *Shadow of a Doubt*, a film the director often named as his favorite. *Universal Pictures/Photofest © Universal Pictures*

witticisms, fixated on younger and more athletic men. (In some ways, the movie plays like a nightmarish metaphor for casual, anonymous gay sex—Bruno is the pickup who won't go away and soon threatens the closeted hero's respectable life.) Moving from strength to strength—the repartee on the train, the cold-eyed murder, the scene at the party—it's Walker's finest performance and the best thing in a great movie.

It might have been the start of a second career; soon Walker began filming a new movie, the (very bad) anti-Communist film *My Son John*, chiefly so he could work with Helen Hayes. But he couldn't stop drinking, and his nerves were always rubbed raw; at home one night in Los Angeles, a doctor-prescribed shot of a powerful sedative combined fatally with the liquor already in his system. Walker was only 32. He left *My Son John* unfinished; the studio finally pieced his worst film together using outtakes from his best one, *Strangers on a Train*.

References

"Robert Walker," *Hollywood.com*, http://www.hollywood.com/celebrities/robert-walker-57523337; "Robert Walker," *IMDb*, http://www.imdb.com/name/nm0908153/bio?ref_=nm_ov_bio_sm; "Robert Walker Biography," *Robert Walker Tribute*, http://www.robertwalkertribute.com/biobeginning.htm; David Thomson, *The New Biographical Dictionary of Film* (New York: Knopf, 2002), 910.

WALTZES FROM VIENNA (GB 1934)

> DIRECTOR: Alfred Hitchcock.
> SCREENPLAY: Guy Bolton, Alma Reville, based on the play by Heinz Reichert and Ernst Marischka.
> PRODUCER: Tom Arnold.
> CINEMATOGRAPHY: Glen McWilliams.
> EDITOR: Charles Frend.
> MUSIC: Johann Strauss Sr. and Johann Strauss, adapted by Hubert Bath.
> CAST: Jessie Matthews (Rasi), Edmund Gwenn (Johann Strauss Sr.), Fay Compton (Countess Helga), Esmond Knight (Johann Strauss).
> RUNNING TIME: 80 minutes. Black and white.
> RELEASED THROUGH: Gaumont British Distributors.

It is 19th-century Vienna, and Johann "Schani" Straus and his beloved Rasi are so immersed in performing his latest piece—and so in love—that they don't realize that there's a fire downstairs in the café. They leave the smoky building and go next door to a dressmaker's, where Schani meets the older, elegant countess, who has heard his work and wants him to set some of her poetry to music.

Schani goes off to his job—the second violinist in the orchestra of his father, the great Johann Strauss Sr. But the two men are constantly at odds, and today, it comes to a head, with the son criticizing the older man's music and the father dismissing the younger man from his position.

Schani returns to Rasi, where the sounds of the bakery inspire him, giving him the rhythms he needs to finish a new piece, setting the countess's words to music. When the noblewoman hears it, she impulsively gives him a kiss, and Schani finds himself suddenly torn between the two women. Finally, Rasi gives him an ultimatum—stay with her and take a job in the bakery or leave and go on with his music.

When the countess invites Schani to attend a famous festival, however, he can't refuse—and when she conspires to make sure his father will be late, he can't help but take his place and debut *The Blue Danube* to raves. When his father arrives, though, he is furious—and now both Rasi and the countess's husband are enraged about the affair going on beneath their noses.

Afterward, both run separately to Schani's apartment to confront him with the countess—but the countess slips away undiscovered, and Rasi, to protect him from the enraged count, takes her place, pretending to have been there all the while. The couple reconciles, and even Schani's father grudgingly admits his son's genius, now signing his autographs Johann Strauss *Senior*.

A sour note.

Having ended his relationship with BRITISH INTERNATIONAL PICTURES, and with three commercial disappointments—*THE SKIN GAME, RICH AND STRANGE*, and *NUMBER 17*—behind him, Hitchcock was both at a low point and without any pressing engagements. When an independent producer offered the job of directing the film version of *WALTZES FROM VIENNA*—a two-year hit on the stage—Hitchcock took it on.

At first, the director seemed to approach the challenge of an operetta with some new ideas and at least a flash of interest. The opening sequence, with the fire engine racing to the bake shop, has the same fast cutting and stylized sound effects as a similar opening sequence in *The Skin Game*; he makes some amusing connections between the musique còncrete of the bakery and Strauss's new composition, and the premiere of "The Blue Danube" is smartly edited to the rhythms of that familiar waltz.

But the material itself gave him nothing to hold onto. It did have, as almost all his early films did, a romantic triangle; there was also a nod to the dramas of backstage life and the struggle for IDENTITY. But he seemed uninterested in the father-son conflict, one he had rarely explored—Hitchcock's parental dramas almost always involve MOTHERS—and the book provided a "musical without much music," he observed. The whole thing had as much substance as a Viennese pastry.

More critically, the director felt somewhat at the mercy of his leading players—JESSIE MATTHEWS, who played Rasi, was a major British STAR of the time, and ESMOND KNIGHT, who played Schani, had created the role in the West End. They were clearly far more integral to the production than Hitchcock was, and left feeling superfluous—and perhaps endangered—Hitchcock responded by insulting both of them regularly and cutting down

Matthews's part as much as possible. "An imperious young man who knew nothing about musicals," is how Matthews remembered him later. "I thought the film was perfectly dreadful."

Audiences agreed, and the movie became his fourth middling release in a row. Hitchcock, at liberty again, needed to do something different and great, and he needed to do it soon. Luckily *THE MAN WHO KNEW TOO MUCH* was just around the corner.

References

Patrick McGilligan, *Alfred Hitchcock: A Life in Darkness and Light* (New York: HarperCollins, 2003), 150–52; Donald Spoto, *The Dark Side of Genius: The Life of Alfred Hitchcock* (New York: Da Capo Press, 1999), 134–37; François Truffaut, *Hitchcock/Truffaut*, rev. ed. (New York: Touchstone, 1985), 85–86.

WARNER BROS.

A studio founded by Harry, Albert, Sam, and Jack Warner, four brothers from a Polish immigrant family who got into the industry early. One of their first successes was as exhibitors showing *The Great Train Robbery* in tough mining towns throughout Pennsylvania. Within a decade, they had begun producing their own films; Warner Brothers Pictures was incorporated in 1923.

The studio became a contender with *The Jazz Singer*, an early sound film that rescued the company from debt and allowed it to expand. During the '30s, Warner Bros. became best known for its "Gold Diggers" musicals and hard-edged gangster films, as well as a pugnacious, working-class attitude; during the '40s, it concentrated on war films and glossier "women's pictures," like *Now, Voyager* and *Mildred Pierce*.

Warner Bros. first entered Hitchcock's life after the war as the American distributor for TRANSATLANTIC

PICTURES; when that company sank, a new multipicture contract was negotiated with Hitchcock alone, which allowed him to choose and produce his own directing projects.

Hitchcock would go on to make *STAGE FRIGHT, I CONFESS, STRANGERS ON A TRAIN, DIAL M FOR MURDER*, and *THE WRONG MAN* for the studio; of the five films, though, only *Strangers on a Train* and *The Wrong Man* show the director operating at the peak of his powers. Hitchcock would later complain that Jack Warner had vetoed his original casting for *I Confess*, imposed RUTH ROMAN on him as a leading lady for *Strangers on a Train*, and insisted that he shoot *Dial M for Murder* in 3-D, even though the process was already fading in popularity.

Without Warner Bros., Hitchcock went on to make his best films at PARAMOUNT and his largest profits at UNIVERSAL; without Hitchcock, Warner Bros. went on to change and transform itself through a variety of acquisitions and mergers. As a result, its back catalog is particularly deep and rich in classics; in addition to the films Hitchcock made for the studio, its home-entertainment division now also has the rights to many of the films Hitchcock made for others.

References

Donald Spoto, *The Dark Side of Genius: The Life of Alfred Hitchcock* (New York: Da Capo Press, 1999), 324, 337–38, 342; "Company Overview," *Warner Bros.*, http://www.warnerbros.com/studio/about/company-overview.

WASSERMAN, LEW (1913–2002)

Cleveland-born businessman whose first job in the entertainment industry was walking the aisles as a movie usher. At 23, he went to work for Chicago's Music Corporation of America as a booking agent, soon convincing MCA to send him to Los Angeles, where they would buy a talent agency and begin getting more involved in motion picture production.

Hitchcock moved to MCA after the death of his own agent, Myron Selznick; he was eventually represented by Wasserman, who became the agency's president in 1948. Wasserman's sober, dark-suited style won Hitchcock's approval, but more than that, the director appreciated the agent's creativity; Wasserman not only popularized the idea of selling a studio an already-assembled package of director and cast, but also he pioneered profit-participation deals in which STARS like JAMES STEWART worked for a smaller up-front fee but could reap millions in back-end percentages.

As Hitchcock's agent, Wasserman engineered a generous deal that gave the director eventual ownership of his productions; once MCA bought UNIVERSAL, Wasserman then bought back those rights, making Hitchcock a millionaire many times over (and, because he paid him in stock, the studio's third-largest shareholder).

While the two men respected each other, however, as the 1960s began, their relationship changed; Wasserman's chief concern became quarterly profits, and as a result, he found himself turning down Hitchcock projects that seemed uncommercial (the director's longed-for adaptation of *MARY ROSE*) or urging other ones purely for the sake of the box office (an adaptation of the best-selling *TOPAZ*). Although they remained friends, Hitchcock felt the relationship cooling in the 1970s; when he finally decided to close up his office on the lot, he asked someone else to tell Wasserman for him.

Wasserman remained a major force in entertainment, philanthropy, and government for years. (He was one of the driving forces behind Ronald Reagan's entry into politics and made Jack Valenti into Hollywood's premiere lobbyist at the MPAA.) He sold MCA to Matsushita Electric in 1990 (Seagram bought a controlling interest in 1995); Wasserman remained on the board until 1998. He died in Beverly Hills in 2002 of a stroke. The final days of Sam Rothstein in Martin Scorsese's *Casino*—a creative businessman pushed out by corporate interests—is in many ways an affectionate and knowing tribute, right down to the carefully tailored clothes and enormous eyeglasses.

References

Brian Lamb, "When Hollywood Had a King," *Booknotes*, http://www.booknotes.org/Watch/159444-1/Connie+Bruck.aspx; Dennis McDougal, "The Last Mogul: Lew Wasserman, MCA and the Hidden History of Hollywood," *Dennis McDougal*, http://www.dennismcdougal.com/_br_the_last_mogul__lew_wasserman__mca_and_the_hidden_history_of_hollywood_24553.htm; Donald Spoto, *The Dark Side of Genius: The Life of Alfred Hitchcock* (New York: Da Capo Press, 1999), 417–18.

WATCHTOWER OVER TOMORROW (US 1945)

DIRECTOR: John Cromwell, Harold F. Kress.
SCREENPLAY: Ben Hecht, Karl Lamb.
PRODUCER: Jerome S. Bresler.
CINEMATOGRAPHY: Uncredited (Lester White).
EDITOR: Uncredited.
ORIGINAL MUSIC: Uncredited.
CAST: John Nesbitt (Narrator), US secretary of State Edward R. Stettinius Jr. (Himself).
RUNNING TIME: 15 minutes. Black and white.
RELEASED THROUGH: War Activities Committee of the Motion Picture Industry.

A US war propaganda short heralding the United Nations as a future force for peace. Hitchcock participated in story conferences for the film and was said to have done some of the directing, as was Elia Kazan. Neither took any credit, nor did most of the crew or the actors onscreen, including George Zucco, Miles Mander, and Lionel Stander.

Reference

Patrick McGilligan, *Alfred Hitchcock: A Life in Darkness and Light* (New York: HarperCollins, 2003), 368–70.

WATSON, WYLIE (1889–1966)

Lanarkshire-born performer raised in a family of Scottish entertainers. His mother and father were with the Carl Rosa Opera Company, and Watson later joined his parents, along with his sister, in a traveling, turn-of-the-century variety act. Watson, a "boy soprano," also played the cello; later, as a teenager, he would join another company and tour the world.

It was when he was 40 and on vacation in America that he got his first movie role, a bit part in an early musical called *It's a Great Life*; it led to little in Hollywood, but after returning to England, he began a film career as a character actor. His most memorable role came in 1935 in Hitchcock's *THE 39 STEPS* as "Mr. Memory," the fatally dedicated music hall performer. Four years later, Hitchcock cast him again in *JAMAICA INN* as "Salvation" Watkins, the verse-quoting cutthroat in Sir Humphrey's gang.

Watson never rose above supporting roles; his small stature, tiny moustache, and fussy manner seemed to type him as conductors, stage managers, and butlers. He had quite a different part in *Brighton Rock*, though, as Spicer and another memorable role in *Whiskey Galore!* In 1952, he retired to Australia, returning for just one more supporting role in *The Sundowners* in 1960. He died in Australia at age 77.

References

Peter Hutchings, "Wylie Watson," *BFI Screenonline,* http://www.screenonline .org.uk/people/id/880716; "Wylie Watson," *IMDb,* http://www.imdb.com/name/ nm0914931/bio?ref_=nm_ov_bio_sm.

WAXMAN, FRANZ (1906–1967)

Silesia-born musician raised by wealthy, disapproving parents who preferred he go into finance. He got a job as a bank teller but used it to pay for music lessons and then started playing the piano in a dance band, the Weintraub Syncopaters. Although his great love remained the classics, Waxman would soon be working in the German film industry, first as an orchestrator (he wrote the charts for Frederick Hollander's score for *The Blue Angel*) and then as composer (debuting with FRITZ LANG's *Liliom,* shot in France in 1933).

By then, Waxman—who was already partially blind as the result of a childhood accident—had fled Germany with his wife after being badly beaten in Berlin by a gang of anti-Semites. Following the well-worn route of Lang, Billy Wilder, and other artists at that time, the Waxmans stayed in Paris for a while and then moved on to Los Angeles. In Hollywood, he was befriended by director James Whale, who hired him to do the score for 1935's *The Bride of Frankenstein.*

Waxman's work for that film—with its stirring marches, lush romantic interludes, and individual character motifs—drew comparisons to Wagner and steady employment. It was his swirling score for *REBECCA,* however, that made him an in-demand film composer; Waxman would go on to provide Hitchcock with scores for *SUSPICION, REAR WINDOW,* and *THE PARADINE CASE* (which recycled some of his *Rebecca* themes).

Like the similarly versatile DMITRI TIOMKIN, Waxman was the perfect collaborator for a film director. If the movie had great images and dramatic situations (*Sunset Boulevard, A Place in the Sun*), then his scores heightened that emotion; if the movie was somewhat lacking (*Elephant Walk, Taras Bulba*), then his music minimized the flaws. (He was nominated 12 times for Academy Awards and his scores for *Sunset Boulevard* and *A Place in the Sun* both won, back to back.)

Although Waxman's career began to slow in the late '50s, he had already begun to write more serious orchestral works, culminating in 1965's *The Song of Terezin,* based on the lives of children in the Thereseienstadt concentration camp. He died from cancer at 60 in Los Angeles.

References

"About Waxman," *Franz Waxman,* http:// franzwaxman.com/about-waxman; "Franz Waxman," *IMDb,* http://www.imdb.com/ name/nm0000077/bio?ref_=nm_ov_bio _sm; David Raksin, "Franz Waxman," *American Composers Orchestra,* http://www .americancomposers.org/raksin_waxman .htm; John Waxman, "Cinema's Exiles: From Hitler to Hollywood—Franz Waxman," *PBS,* http://www.pbs.org/wnet/cinemasexiles/ biographies/biography-franz-waxman/195.

WAYNE, NAUNTON (1901–1970)

Glamorgan-born performer, the son of a solicitor who made his stage debut in 1920. Effortlessly amiable, he excelled in revues, where it often fell to him to introduce the performers and tie the various sketches together. By the end of the decade, he was a popular London star, appearing regularly onstage and in nightclubs.

Wayne made his film debut in 1932, but *THE LADY VANISHES* in 1938 was the first movie to give him a major role as Caldicott, a cartoon Englishman on a trip with BASIL RADFORD's equally cricket-obsessed Charters. It is a cheekily satiric yet, in the end, quietly approving portrayal of English values, and the two actors nearly stole the film—so much so that they would regularly reteam over their careers in *Night Train to Munich* and *Crook's Tour* (which gave the characters new adventures) and such classics as *Dead of Night* and *Whiskey Galore!*, which basically repurposed them under different names.

Throughout it all, however, the dapper little Welshman persevered, no matter what difficulty he faced—fascists, murderers, even death itself. "He was," the London *Times* wrote once about his screen persona, "a man battling, with intense mental activity, against a world of almost insoluble problems; that most of them were trivial, and that conversational irrelevancies attracted him more than conversational points, was an indication not of the silliness but of the complexity of his world."

Wayne also appeared in the comic *The Titfield Thunderbolt*, the noir-ish *Circle of Danger*, and the London production of *Arsenic and Old Lace*, a four-year run; decades later, he proved his versatility by appearing in a musical version of *Vanity Fair*. He died in Surrey at age 69.

References
"Naunton Wayne," *IMDb*, http://www.imdb.com/name/nm0915614; "Obituary: Mr. Naunton Wayne," *Times*, November 18, 1970, http://the.hitchcock.zone/wiki/The_Times_%2818/Nov/1970%29_-_Obituary:_Naunton_Wayne; Matthew Sweet, "Mustard and Cress," *Guardian*, December 29, 2007, http://www.theguardian.com/film/2007/dec/29/film.

WEBB, ROY (1888–1982)
New York–born musician who studied classical composition at Columbia and then went on to work on Broadway, contributing both music and, with his brother Kenneth S. Webb, plays. When the talkies arrived, he headed for Hollywood, where he scored the early musical *Rio Rita* in 1929.

Webb would spend more than 30 years at RKO, where he eventually replaced mentor Max Steiner as head of the studio's music department. Webb's best-remembered work may have been for producer Val Lewton's stylish cycle of B-movie horror films, particularly *Cat People* and *The Body Snatcher*. For Hitchcock, he was the (uncredited) musical director on *MR. AND MRS. SMITH* and contributed the romantic score for *NOTORIOUS*.

That movie's moody mix of love and danger suited Webb's talents; he had already notched such genre credits as *Murder, My Sweet* and *The Spiral Staircase* and would go on to contribute music to such seminal noirs as *Crossfire*, *The Locket*, *The Window*, and the immortal *Out of the Past*. But his fortunes were linked, and fell, with RKO's, and when the studio disappeared, so did the constant stream of work.

Webb freelanced for a few more years and then retired, his last job coming in 1960 for an episode of TV's *Wagon Train*. He died of a heart attack in Santa Monica at age 94.

References
Uncle Dave Lewis, "Roy Webb Biography," *AllMusic*, http://www.allmusic.com/artist/roy-webb-mn0000355252/biography; "Roy Webb," *IMDb*, http://www.imdb.com/name/nm0002202/bio?ref_=nm_ov_bio_sm.

"WET SATURDAY" (US; ORIGINALLY AIRED SEPTEMBER 30, 1956)

DIRECTOR: Alfred Hitchcock.
SCREENPLAY: Marian B. Cockrell, based on the story by John Collier.
PRODUCER: Joan Harrison.
CINEMATOGRAPHY: John L. Russell.
EDITOR: Edward W. Williams.
ORIGINAL MUSIC: Stanley Wilson.
CAST: Sir Cedric Hardwicke (Mr. Princey), John Williams (Capt. Smollet).
RUNNING TIME: 30 minutes with commercials. Black and white.
ORIGINALLY BROADCAST BY: CBS.

When a disturbed young woman kills a teacher in a fit of jealousy, her very proper father sets out to frame someone else for the crime. A subpar installment of *ALFRED HITCHCOCK PRESENTS*, notable only for its pairing of two of the director's favorite English actors.

References

Tim Brooks and Earle Marsh, *The Complete Directory to Prime Time Network TV Shows*, 8th ed. (New York: Ballantine Books, 2003), 29; Jack Edmond Nolan, "Hitchcock's TV Films," *Film Fan Monthly* (June 1968), 3–6.

WHITE, ETHEL LINA (1876–1944)

Monmouthshire-born author and the daughter of an inventor who began publishing short pieces as a child but came to novel writing as an adult. After her first three books made little impression, she turned to mysteries, publishing *Put Out the Light* in 1931. Her 1936 thriller *The Wheel Spins*, about a temporary case of amnesia, became—after some thorough rewriting by the scenarists, who added comic cricket fans and a love interest—Hitchcock's *THE LADY VANISHES* and was adapted twice more over the years.

A popular writer at the time whose books tended toward the neo-Gothic with their slowly relentless killers and alternately terrified and resourceful heroines, White was often compared to Mary Roberts Rinehart; her story "An Unlocked Window" later became an episode of *ALFRED HITCHCOCK PRESENTS*, and Hollywood bought her books *Midnight House* (made in 1945 as *The Unseen*) and *Some Must Watch* (filmed in 1946 as *The Spiral Staircase*). She died in London at 68.

References

Martin Edwards, "Ethel Lina White," *Do You Write under Your Own Name*, April 13, 2010, http://doyouwriteunderyourownname.blogspot.com/2010/04/ethel-lina-white.html; "Ethel Lina White," *IMDb*, http://www.imdb.com/name/nm0924781; Christina Fowler, "Invisible Ink: Ethel Lina White," *Independent*, October 14, 2012, http://www.independent.co.uk/arts-entertainment/books/features/invisible-ink-no-145—ethel-lina-white-8210245.html; Patrick McGilligan, *Alfred Hitchcock: A Life in Darkness and Light* (New York: HarperCollins, 2003), 206–7.

THE WHITE SHADOW (GB 1923)

DIRECTOR: Graham Cutts.
SCREENPLAY: Alfred Hitchcock, based on the novel *Children of Change* by Michael Morton.
PRODUCERS: Sir Michael Balcon, Victor Saville.
CINEMATOGRAPHY: Claude L. McDonnell.
EDITOR: Alfred Hitchcock.
CAST: Betty Compson (Nancy Brent/Georgina Brent), Clive Brook (Robin Field), A. B. Imeson (Mr. Brent), Henry Victor (Louis Chadwick).
RUNNING TIME: 82 minutes. Black and white.
RELEASED THROUGH: Woolf & Freedman Film Service.

Nancy and Georgina Brent are twins—and identical only in appearance, with Nancy leading a wild and impetuous life, while Georgina lives quietly at the family's estate. After a furious quarrel with their father, Nancy leaves the house; later, her father follows to look for her. But both disappear, and Mrs. Brent dies of a broken heart.

Georgina goes to London, then Paris, in hopes of finding her missing family. But her father has lost his mind and become a homeless beggar, and Nancy has become the habitué of a decadent club, The Cat Who Laughs. Robin, an old beau of Nancy's, appears and mistakes Georgina for Nancy; Georgina allows him, first to protect Nancy's name, but later because she's fallen for him herself.

Finally, Georgina finds and confronts Nancy—but Nancy refuses to return home. Her health broken by disappointment, Georgina goes to a Swiss sanitarium. Robin finds her there, still assuming she is Nancy and wishing to marry her. Georgina arranges for Nancy to take her place—and accept Robin's proposal—then slips away to die. When she does, her soul—the "white shadow"—passes to her sister.

Returning home to England, Nancy's car strikes an old man. It is her father, and he not only survives the accident but also discovers it has restored his memory. Reconciled, father and daughter return to their country estate.

A once lost, now (almost) rediscovered film.

Hitchcock made five pictures with director GRAHAM CUTTS, serving as assistant director, screenwriter, and production designer. This was the second of the five, and while it's impossible to reliably point out Hitchcock's touches, the story—with its themes of DOUBLES and a dramatic love triangle—certainly is of a piece with the rest of his work. There are also a few visual embellishments, like the framing of certain dramatic scenes, that suggest the proscenium arch of a theater—and the role playing of the characters themselves and their toying with IDENTITY—that he would explore at length later.

But whereas the first Cutts-Hitchcock collaboration, WOMAN TO WOMAN, had been a huge success, this deliberate follow-up—which reunited some of the cast, as well as the crew—was an immediate critical and commercial failure. A significant one, too, earning the long-simmering enmity of mogul C. M. WOOLF, who seemed to blame Hitchcock's script for its failure and whose bias would bedevil the director for the next decade (fed by Cutts's apparent envy over Hitchcock's burgeoning new career).

After decades of being lost, several reels of the film, roughly comprising the first 40 minutes, were discovered in New Zealand. Seeing as Hitchcock's first film as a full director, NUMBER 13, was abandoned unfinished; his first short, ALWAYS TELL YOUR WIFE, is missing half its footage; and his first feature as an assistant director, Woman to Woman, remains completely lost, this half-movie, however imperfect and wildly melodramatic, remains as much of the very early Hitchcock as we're ever likely to see.

References

Patrick McGilligan, Alfred Hitchcock: A Life in Darkness and Light (New York: HarperCollins, 2003), 60; Donald Spoto, The Dark Side of Genius: The Life of Alfred Hitchcock (New York: Da Capo Press, 1999), 59; François Truffaut, Hitchcock/Truffaut, rev. ed. (New York: Touchstone, 1985), 30; Aylin Zafar, "Lost for 80 Years, Alfred Hitchcock's Earliest Known Film Makes Its Debut," Time, September 23, 2011, http://newsfeed.time.com/2011/09/23/lost-for-80-years-alfred-hitchcocks-earliest-known-film-makes-its-debut.

WHITLOCK, ALBERT
(1915–1999)

London-born filmmaker who began his film career at 14 working as a messenger boy for GAUMONT. He progressed from there to building sets and painting prop signs. His collaboration with Alfred Hitchcock began with *THE MAN WHO KNEW TOO MUCH*, for which he assisted in some of the miniature work, and continued through *THE 39 STEPS, SABOTAGE, YOUNG AND INNOCENT, THE LADY VANISHES*, and finally *JAMAICA INN*, with Whitlock now working as part of the art department. Whitlock remained in Britain during the war, but by the 1950s, he was in Hollywood, having developed a formidable reputation for matte paintings—careful works of art that, when combined with a separate piece of film featuring live action, added in expertly faked, completely believable backgrounds. (Some of his more fantastic work was done for television's *Star Trek*.)

For his first decade in the States, Whitlock was busy at Walt Disney; in 1961, he switched to UNIVERSAL, where he began again working with Hitchcock, helping him with the complicated effects for *THE BIRDS*, where he was credited with "pictorial designs." He would rack up additional credits—sometimes as "pictorial designer," sometimes for "special photographic effects"—on *MARNIE, TORN CURTAIN, TOPAZ, FRENZY*, and *FAMILY PLOT*, making him the only Hitchcock colleague, apart from ALMA REVILLE, who could truly say he was with the director both at the beginning and the very end.

Whitlock won Academy Awards for his fine work on two dreadful movies, *Earthquake* and *The Hindenburg*; he was also, in an inside JOKE, cast as the kidnapped industrialist in Mel Brooks's Hitchcock parody *HIGH ANXIETY* and provided the mattes for one last non-Hitch-cock Hitchcock film, *Psycho II*. He died in Santa Barbara at 84.

References

"Albert Whitlock," *IMDb*, http://www.imdb.com/name/nm0926087/bio?ref_=nm_ov_bio_sm; Jonathan Jones, "Masters of Illusion," *Guardian*, September 27, 2002, http://www.theguardian.com/film/2002/sep/27/artsfeatures2.

WHITTY, DAME MAY
(1865–1948)

Liverpool-born performer and the daughter of a journalist onstage since 1881, appearing in both London and Broadway productions. She made her film debut in 1914 in *Enoch Arden*, but movie appearances were rare until 1937, when she repeated her stage success in the Hollywood version of *Night Must Fall*; in 1938, she was the disappearing Miss Froy in Alfred Hitchcock's *THE LADY VANISHES*, a gentle governess who is, in reality, a British agent.

Whitty—who was the first actress to be made a dame commander of the British Empire, honored in 1918 for her wartime work—relocated to Hollywood, where she became a busy performer in the '40s, appearing in *Gaslight* and Hitchcock's *SUSPICION*, among others. She received Oscar nominations for both *Night Must Fall* and *Mrs. Miniver* (although she did not win) and remained a dedicated and good-humored performer even more than 60 years into her career. "I've got everything Betty Grable has," she quipped, "only I've had it longer."

She died in Beverly Hills of cancer at 82.

References

"Dame May Whitty," *IMDb*, http://www.imdb.com/name/nm0926599/bio?ref_=nm_ov_bio_sm; "Dame May Whitty Biography," *Journal of Life*, http://dame-may-whitty.journal-of-life

.com/#!biographies; Alfred E. Twomey and Arthur F. McClure, *The Versatiles: Supporting Character Players in the Cinema, 1930–1955* (New York: Castle Books, 1969), 237.

WHO KILLED COCK ROBIN? (US 1935)

DIRECTOR: Uncredited (David Hand).
SCREENPLAY: Uncredited (William Cottrell, Joe Grant, Bob Kuwahara).
PRODUCER: Walt Disney.
CINEMATOGRAPHY: Uncredited.
EDITOR: Uncredited.
ORIGINAL MUSIC: Uncredited (Frank Churchill).
CAST: Uncredited (Billy Bletcher, Clarence Nash, Purv Pullen, Martha Wentworth).
RUNNING TIME: 8 minutes. Black and white.
RELEASED THROUGH: United Artists.

A Silly Symphonies cartoon short made by Walt Disney but released through United Artists, based on the nursery rhyme. Several of the animal characters are caricatures of then-current Hollywood STARS, including Bing Crosby and Mae West, and the story revolves around a murder trial. As one of Hitchcock's PLAY WITHIN A PLAY touches, it is the movie Mrs. Verloc watches in *SABOTAGE* in between learning of her brother's death and killing her husband; the film first distracts her from her grief and then compounds it, and its mix of violence and humor matches Hitchcock's own approach to his work.

Hitchcock was an admirer of Disney, and not only for his business acumen, careful storyboarding, and visual creativity; the special matte process used in *THE BIRDS* (and the less-convincing mechanical horse in *MARNIE*) had both been originally developed at the Disney studios, where past and future Hitchcock collaborator ALBERT WHITLOCK had landed in the '50s after moving to America. A plan for a more clear-cut collaboration—Hitchcock wanted to shoot some of his proposed, early-'60s feature *THE BLIND MAN* at Disneyland—reportedly fell apart after Disney saw *PSYCHO*, however, and the film was never made.

References

Patrick McGilligan, *Alfred Hitchcock: A Life in Darkness and Light* (New York: Harper-Collins, 2003), 60, 622; "Sabotage by Alfred Hitchcock," *Disney Archives and Mysteries*, http://marciodisneyarchives.blogspot.com/2010/08/sabotage-by-alfred-hitchcock.html.

WILDER, THORNTON (1897–1975)

Madison, WI–born author whose domineering, disapproving father was a journalist and, for eight years, the US consul general in China. Education and intellectualism were stressed in the family, and four of the five Wilder children went on to become writers. Educated at private prep schools Oberlin and Princeton, Wilder published his first novel at 30; his next, *The Bridge at San Luis Rey*, was a best seller and won the Pulitzer Prize. He would win two more Pulitzers for his plays *Our Town* and *The Skin of Our Teeth*.

Hitchcock, who greatly admired *Our Town*, asked the playwright to work on the screenplay for *SHADOW OF A DOUBT*; it would be Wilder's first original feature (he had previously adapted *Our Town* for the movies) and confirm Hitchcock's preference for using novelists for initial movie treatments, which he always viewed as the real creative work. (The actual screenwriting was often done by a veteran scenarist, or as Hitchcock sometimes called them, a "stooge.") Hitchcock and Wilder looked at locations in Santa Rosa together, and Wilder delivered a prose outline for the movie, although his time on the project was cut short due to his upcoming intelligence work for the US Army. Hitchcock, though, treasured the collaboration and inserted an unusual, extra title in the opening credits acknowledging Wilder's contributions.

After the war, Wilder's busy career would resume, and he would have another unexpected commercial success with *The Matchmaker*, a rewrite of one of his earlier plays, *The Merchant of Yonkers*. (The play would later be reworked into the musical *Hello, Dolly!*) Although he remained deeply closeted and somewhat introverted, Wilder was an indefatigable and sparkling letter writer; while a number of critics carped, calling him everything from bourgeois to a plagiarist (there were a number of similarities noted between *Finnegan's Wake* and *The Skin of Our Teeth*), he remained a popular and respected American author. He died at 78 in Hamden, CT.

References

Patrick McGilligan, *Alfred Hitchcock: A Life in Darkness and Light* (New York: HarperCollins, 2003), 308–13; Donald Spoto, *The Dark Side of Genius: The Life of Alfred Hitchcock* (New York: Da Capo Press, 1999), 256–58; "Thornton Wilder (1897–1975), Playwright and Novelist," *Queers in History*, http://queerhistory.blogspot.com/2012/04/thornton-wilder-1897-1975-playwright.html; "Thornton Wilder Biography," *Thornton Wilder Society*, http://www.twildersociety.org/biography; François Truffaut, *Hitchcock/Truffaut*, rev. ed. (New York: Touchstone, 1985), 151–53.

WILDING, MICHAEL (1912–1979)

Essex-born performer who entered the industry as an artist. He soon switched to acting, making his film debut in 1933. Starting in bit parts, Wilding was a STAR by World War II, often playing valiant military men or elegant aristocrats; for six straight years, 1947 to 1952, he was voted among Britain's most popular movie actors.

Neither of his back-to-back pictures for Hitchcock, *UNDER CAPRICORN* and *STAGE FRIGHT*, were successes, however, with the usually heroic Wilding stuck playing rather vague characters; his follow-up Hollywood projects would be almost equally unmemorable, although he would have a small supporting part in the 1960 hit *The World of Suzie Wong* and guest star on an episode of *THE ALFRED HITCHCOCK HOUR* in 1963.

Married four times, once to Elizabeth Taylor, the bluntly self-deprecating Wilding ("I was the worst actor I ever came across") found roles harder to get as his epilepsy, a lifelong condition, began to worsen in middle age; he tried working as an agent for a while, representing his ex-wife's new husband Richard Burton, and then when that failed, he went back to taking on whatever small parts he could find. He died at 66 after having a seizure and falling down the stairs at his home in Chichester.

References

"Michael Wilding," *IMDb*, http://www.imdb.com/name/nm0928697/bio?ref_=nm_ov_bio_sm; "Mr. Michael Wilding," *Times*, November 16, 1979, http://the.hitchcock.zone/wiki/The_Times_%2816/Nov/1979%29_-_Obituary:_Michael_Wilding.

WILLIAMS, EMLYN (1905–1987)

Flintshire-born author and performer from a Welsh working-class family who won several scholarships, including a place at Oxford, where he was in the dramatic society. After graduation, he joined a repertory company and began writing his own comedies and dramas; the grim *Night Must Fall*, a pioneering study of a psychopathic killer, was a major success in 1935, with Williams also starring as the madman. (It was later made twice as a film.) A subsequent play and equal success, *The Corn Is Green*, told the fictionalized story of his poor childhood and the help provided by an exceptional teacher.

Williams provided some dialogue for the script to the 1934 version of *THE MAN WHO KNEW TOO MUCH* and had a good part in *JAMAICA INN* as Harry the Peddler, perhaps the most dangerous member of Sir Humphrey's gang. He would go on to appear in *The Stars Look Down*, *The Scarf*, and *Ivanhoe*, as well as in the (ultimately abandoned) Josef von Sternberg picture *I, Claudius* and the version of *THE WRECK OF THE MARY DEARE* made after Hitchcock had moved on to *NORTH BY NORTHWEST*. Later in life, Williams wrote a novelistic true-crime book, *Beyond Belief*, and successfully toured in a one-man show as Charles Dickens.

He died at 81 from cancer in his home in London.

References

"Emlyn Williams," *Encyclopaedia Britannica*, http://www.britannica.com/biography/Emlyn-Williams; "Emlyn Williams," *IMDb*, http://www.imdb.com/name/nm0930539/bio?ref_=nm_ov_bio_sm; Albin Krebs, "Emlyn Williams, Welsh Actor and Writer, Dies," *New York Times*, September 26, 1987, http://www.nytimes.com/1987/09/26/obituaries/emlyn-williams-welsh-actor-and-writer-dies.html.

WILLIAMS, JOHN (1903–1983)

Buckinghamshire-born performer who made his stage debut at 13 as one of the Darling children in *Peter Pan*. As an adult, he moved to America, where he had a steady stage career in New York and, for two decades, a less notable film one in Hollywood. (His small part in *THE PARADINE CASE* was made even smaller by the edits of producer DAVID O. SELZNICK.)

He won a Tony, however, playing the inspector in the Broadway production of *DIAL M FOR MURDER*; when Hitchcock hired him to repeat the role in the 1954 movie, his film career began in earnest. Tall, with a regimental moustache and quietly amused delivery, Williams played countless butlers and stiff-upper-lip authority figures; a favorite of Hitchcock's, he was the insurance investigator in *TO CATCH A THIEF* and guest-starred on no less than 10 episodes of *ALFRED HITCHCOCK PRESENTS*, 3 of them directed by Hitchcock.

Williams also starred in the HITCHCOCKIAN *Midnight Lace*; a TV adaptation of ROBERT BLOCH's "Yours Truly, Jack the Ripper"; *Sabrina*; *Witness for the Prosecution*; and the 1974 film of *Lost in the Stars*—although oddly he may be best remembered in America for appearing in the longest-running commercial in TV history, a record ad for "120 Music Masterpieces." He died at 80 of an aneurysm in La Jolla.

References

"John Williams," *IMDb*, http://www.imdb.com/name/nm0002369/bio?ref_=nm_ov_bio_sm; "Obituary: John Williams," *Times*, May 10, 1983, http://the.hitchcock.zone/wiki/The_Times_%2810/May/1983%29_-_Obituary:_John_Williams.

WILLIAMS, JOHN (1932–)

New York–born musician whose father played in small jazz bands. The family later moved to California, where Williams attended high school and college before continuing his musical studies at Manhattan's Juilliard. By the 1950s, he was a regular session musician and an orchestrator helping Henry Mancini, BERNARD HERRMANN, and other film composers.

Williams received his first screen credit in 1960 and became a steady collaborator of producer Irwin Allen, writing the themes for TV's *Lost in Space* and *Time Tunnel* (and, later, scores for the movies *The Poseidon Adventure* and *The Towering Inferno*). A dependable presence at UNIVERSAL, in 1976, he contributed the whimsical music for *FAMILY PLOT*. His most famous scores, however, will always be his stirring compositions for Steven Spielberg and George Lucas, including *Star Wars*; *Raiders of the Lost Ark*; *Jurassic Park*; *E.T. the Extra-Terrestrial*; *Schindler's List*; and, of course, *Jaws*.

References

"John Williams," *IMDb*, http://www.imdb.com/name/nm0002354; Patrick McGilligan, *Alfred Hitchcock: A Life in Darkness and Light* (New York: HarperCollins, 2003), 729; Patsy Morita, "John Williams: Biography," *AllMusic*, http://www.allmusic.com/artist/john-williams-mn0000232480/biography.

WOLFE, IAN (1896–1992)

Canton, IL–born performer who spent the first 15 years of his career onstage, where he mastered a clipped, vaguely English intonation. That, plus premature baldness, seemed to type him as a British butler, a part he played regularly in films for more than 50 years. He made an amazing 300 film and television appearances, many uncredited, among which the best known are the 1935 *The Raven*; *The Prince and the Pauper*; *Now, Voyager*; *Bedlam*; *Witness for the Prosecution*; and the *Star Trek* episodes "All Our Yesterdays" and "Bread and Circuses." For Hitchcock, he played Stiles in *FOREIGN CORRESPONDENT* and Robert, the butler with the blackjack, in *SABOTEUR*. His last appearance was in Warren Beatty's *Dick Tracy* in 1990. He died at 95 in Los Angeles.

References

"Ian Wolfe," *Hollywood.com*, http://www.hollywood.com/celebrities/ian-wolfe-57302946; "Ian Wolfe," *IMDb*, http://www.imdb.com/name/nm0938052; Alfred E. Twomey and Arthur F. McClure, *The Versatiles: Supporting Character Players in the Cinema, 1930–1955* (New York: Castle Books, 1969), 243.

WOMAN TO WOMAN (1922)

DIRECTOR: Graham Cutts.
SCREENPLAY: Alfred Hitchcock, Graham Cutts, based on the play by Michael Morton.
PRODUCERS: Sir Michael Balcon, Victor Saville.
CINEMATOGRAPHY: Claude L. McDonnell.
EDITOR: Alma Reville.
CAST: Clive Brook (David Compton), Betty Compson (Louise Boucher).
RUNNING TIME: 82 minutes. Black and white.
RELEASED THROUGH: Woolf & Freedman Film Service.

English officer David Compton and French dancer Louise Boucher are in love—but shortly after getting her pregnant and right before their marriage, they are accidentally separated. He goes off to war, is wounded at the front, and loses his memory; Louise changes her name and raises their son alone. Years later, David, still suffering from partial amnesia, returns to England, resumes his old life, and marries. One night, he goes to Louise's show and recognizes her; recognizing him, Louise gives David and his new wife the custody of her son and, after a final performance, dies of heartbreak.

The first of several films Hitchcock was to make with GRAHAM CUTTS, serving as the older man's assistant director, art director, scenarist, and occasional editor, the melodrama was a particular hit, encouraging the cast and crew to reteam for *THE WHITE SHADOW*. That film, unfortunately, failed; this one is now regarded as completely lost, save for a press book and a few stills. Still, *Woman to Woman* does show the earliest versions of some Hitchcock tropes—the theatrical setting, the romantic triangle (and its cast list—with young Victor McClaglen as "Nubian slave"—hints tantalizingly at some exotic touches). It's also the first picture on which Hitchcock and ALMA REVILLE, his future wife, collaborated. And there's another, prophetic connection to his later work; the film was distributed in America by Lewis J. Selznick, father of Myron and DAVID O. SELZNICK.

References

Michael Brooke, "Woman to Woman," *BFI Most Wanted: The Hunt for Britain's Missing Films*, http://old.bfi.org.uk/national archive/news/mostwanted/woman-to-woman.html; Patrick McGilligan, *Alfred Hitchcock: A Life in Darkness and Light* (New York: HarperCollins, 2003), 56–60; Donald Spoto, *The Dark Side of Genius: The Life of Alfred Hitchcock* (New York: Da Capo Press, 1999), 59; François Truffaut, *Hitchcock/Truffaut*, rev. ed. (New York: Touchstone, 1985), 29.

WOOD, ROBIN (1931–2009)

London-born author who studied at Cambridge, falling under the sway of literary critic F. R. Leavis and graduating with a commitment to academia. Over the rest of his life, he would teach in England, Sweden, France, and Canada, where he would spend the bulk of his career. His first writing on Hitchcock, an analysis of *PSYCHO*, was rejected by Britain's *Sight and Sound* magazine but later published by *CAHIERS DU CINEMA*; it would become a pivotal chapter in his book *HITCHCOCK'S FILMS* in 1965.

Although the French had formed their own Alfred Hitchcock appreciation society some time before—in fact, it was ERIC ROHMER, in his role as *Cahiers* editor, who accepted Wood's piece—*Hitchcock's Films* was not only one of the first strong defenses in English of the director's work but also a landmark in film criticism that combined a close reading of the films' imagery with an understanding of their morality. It remains essential reading.

"The book certainly got reactions," Wood later recalled. "A lot of people thought it was ridiculous, this idea of taking Hitchcock seriously. He was seen as simply an entertainer; one was merely amused by his films, had a few shocks, a few laughs, and that was it. But it was also reviewed in a way that wasn't entirely dismissive, and then it gradually caught on."

Although Wood would later write perceptively of Arthur Penn, Howard Hawks, Ingmar Bergman, and other filmmakers, his singular appreciation of Hitchcock never wavered; it did take on new dimensions, however, as its author did, too, gradually becoming more Marxist in his analyses and also finally coming out as a gay man. An expanded and revised edition of the book looking at the director's work from those new perspectives, *Hitchcock's Films Revisited*, appeared in 1989.

He died of leukemia in Toronto at 78.

References

William Grimes, "Robin Wood, Film Critic Who Wrote on Hitchcock, Dies at 78," *New York Times*, December 22, 2009, http://www.nytimes.com/2009/12/22/arts/22wood.html?_r=0; Armen Svadjian, "A Life in Criticism: Robin Wood at 75," *Your Flesh*, January 1, 2006, http://yourfleshmag.com/books/a-life-in-film-criticism-robin-wood-at-75/am.

WOOLF, C(HARLES) M(OSS)
(1879–1942)

London-born mogul who entered film-making after World War I. He would head up various companies and remain a force in film distribution for decades, succeeded finally by his sons John and James, who formed Romulus Films. From the start, Woolf père was a successful if unimaginative businessman; anything that seemed to hint at "European" influences (rather than good old-fashioned, straightforward English storytelling) drew his immediate wrath.

It's unclear when and why his antipathy to Alfred Hitchcock began; it's possible he blamed the then-screenwriter for the failure of the somewhat-metaphysical *THE WHITE SHADOW*. But once Hitchcock began directing, Woolf almost invariably disapproved of the ambitious results, successively pronouncing *THE PLEASURE GARDEN, THE MOUNTAIN EAGLE,* and *THE LODGER* all unreleasable and returning them to the shelf (until some edits in *The Lodger,* and some screenings arranged by Hitchcock's mentor, SIR MICHAEL BALCON, were met with success—then all three films rapidly received real distribution).

Woolf's stubbornly low opinion of the director never changed; he said 1934's *THE MAN WHO KNEW TOO MUCH* was rubbish and announced he was going to take it away and give it to another director to reshoot. Hitchcock, who at that point in his career desperately needed a comeback, begged the mogul to release the film as it was; Woolf finally, grudgingly agreed, as Hitchcock's name still might draw some publicity, but put the film out as a B movie. It was a hit anyway, much to Woolf's annoyance.

He died on New Year's Eve at age 63 in London.

References

Patrick McGilligan, *Alfred Hitchcock: A Life in Darkness and Light* (New York: HarperCollins, 2003), 60, 168; A. R. Phillips, "C. M. Woolf," *Hitchcock Report,* https://thehitchcockreport.wordpress.com/tag/c-m-woolf; Donald Spoto, *The Dark Side of Genius: The Life of Alfred Hitchcock* (New York: Da Capo Press, 1999), 84–85, 88–89.

WOOLRICH, CORNELL
(1903–1968)

New York–born author whose family splintered when he was young. He lived for a while with his father in Mexico and then moved back to Manhattan when he was 12, where he would share an apartment with his mother for most of the next 40 years.

Woolrich went (sporadically) to Columbia University, where he fell heavily under the influence of the works of F. Scott Fitzgerald; he published his first book, *Cover Charge,* in 1926. By the early '30s, though, with Fitzgerald's career in decline, his imitators were faring even worse; eventually Woolrich switched styles and genres, turning to popular "pulp" mysteries.

Although some of his works fit comfortably within the hard-boiled genre of tough detectives and clever professional criminals, Woolrich's most lasting books are more definitively noir, full of lies, insomnia, GUILT, and revenge; typically, in a Woolrich story, an innocent choice suddenly opens up a frightening new world, a love affair slowly leads to murder.

Woolrich's most famous works are the "Black" books—*The Bride Wore Black, The Black Curtain, Black Alibi, The Black Angel, The Black Path of Fear,* and *Rendezvous in Black*—all written between 1940 and 1948, many adapted for movies. He also wrote short stories and published under the names "William Irish" and "George Hopley." Hitchcock and his production staff were clearly close readers of Woolrich; his short story "It Had to Be Murder" was expanded into *REAR WINDOW, The Black Curtain* was condensed for an episode of

THE ALFRED HITCHCOCK HOUR, three other short stories became episodes of *ALFRED HITCHCOCK PRESENTS*, and a fourth was directed by Hitchcock himself for the television anthology *SUSPICION*.

Briefly married (the marriage was later annulled), Woolrich was gay and deeply conflicted about it, as he was about much in his life; he drank heavily and would sometimes disguise himself as a sailor and pick up men at the piers. After his mother died, he became even more reclusive, although ill health—he had lost a leg due to an infection—certainly played a part. He died in New York at 64. He left his entire estate to Columbia to endow writing scholarships in honor of his mother.

References

"Cornell Woolrich," *IMDb*, http://www.imdb.com/name/nm0941280; "Cornell Woolrich Biography," *Literal Media*, http://www.literalmedia.com/index.php?option=com_content&view=article&id=56&Itemid=76; Wallace Stroby, "Into the Night: Cornell Woolrich's Art of Darkness Revisited," *Wallace Stroby*, http://www.wallacestroby.com/writings_woolrich.html.

WORLD WAR II

Throughout the '30s, Hitchcock had been chafing at—and publicly complaining about—the state of the British film industry. He told INTERVIEWERS he yearned to work with top American STARS, like Gary Cooper and CAROLE LOMBARD. He criticized English filmmaking for being too staid and CENSORIOUS. He bristled at the budget limitations put on him by studio heads. It was clear that he wanted a bigger field to play in, and when some careful hunting finally brought a deal from DAVID O. SELZNICK, he packed up his family (and his family's cook and housekeeper) and left in 1939. He would not return to direct another feature until *UNDER CAPRICORN* a decade later.

His relocation to America wasn't an unusual one at that time. Many past and future Hitchcock colleagues—CHARLES LAUGHTON, DAME MAY WHITTY, EDMUND GWENN—had made the move to Hollywood in the late '30s, and most never returned. Yet because Hitchcock was so admired in the industry, some saw his departure from England on the eve of war as ungrateful, even unpatriotic.

His old mentor SIR MICHAEL BALCON wrote an opinion piece—that wounded Hitchcock deeply—railing against these deserters, referring slightingly to the director as a former "plump junior technician." And even decades after Hitchcock's death, a British journalist—in an otherwise affectionate piece on actors BASIL RADFORD and NAUNTON WAYNE—would sneer at the director of *THE LADY VANISHES* as a "man who suspected that war was coming, and had already decided to sit it out in Hollywood drinking orange juice." It's not a fair attack.

It is true that Hitchcock left in March 1939 (while Britain was technically still at peace). Once war did break out, though, obviously his health and weight made him ineligible for active service; he did not rush immediately back home to offer to direct propaganda films or join a documentary unit recording combat footage. He mostly stayed in America with his family and (unsuccessfully) urged his mother to leave England, too, and join them. And on that basis, he was considered by some to be a shirker. Yet throughout the '40s, Hitchcock's films are invariably pro-Allies, anti-Nazi, and forcefully in favor of the war.

True, in some of them, current events are kept successfully at bay; both *REBECCA* and *SUSPICION* might as well be period pieces set in the '30s (when, in fact, their original source novels were written). Yet their very "English-ness" is a kind of propaganda push, too—this verdant peaceful country of great manor houses and dotty neighbors was something that needed defending, and Hitchcock's faux-British films, admittedly full of tea-cozy stereotypes, nonetheless reminded audiences of what might be lost if it wasn't.

Hitchcock's other wartime films are more obvious and ardent in their patriotism. *FOREIGN CORRESPONDENT* ends with a blatant speech to the American audience, exhorting them to support Britain and prepare for war; *SABOTEUR* shows the dangers of the spies and Nazi sympathizers in our midst. And *LIFEBOAT*, his most explicit (and frustratingly misunderstood) prowar film, gathers together—as *The Lady Vanishes* did—a motley collection of travelers in peril. This time they represent classes, not countries—wealthy industrialists and artists, middle-class professionals, lower-class workers. But the message is the same: Stop your squabbling, and unite against a common and formidable enemy.

For all this patriotic tub thumping, Hitchcock was not insensitive to the horrors of war; in *SPELLBOUND*, John Ballantyne (who is admittedly disturbed and clearly suffering from posttraumatic stress disorder) talks about how much he hates fighting. But the director knew that totalitarianism was even worse, and he always had; even if his 1930s films in Britain weren't allowed to be too specific about their villains for fear of losing the German market, there was little doubt who those continental agents in *THE MAN WHO KNEW TOO MUCH, THE 39 STEPS, SABOTAGE, SECRET AGENT*, and *The Lady Vanishes* were really working for.

Nor did Hitchcock let go of that theme once the war had ended. *NOTORIOUS* warns presciently of the danger that escaped Nazis can still cause; *ROPE* (like *SHADOW OF A DOUBT* before it) points out that hateful theories of superior races and of people worthy of extermination don't have to be expounded by someone with a German accent to be bigoted and dangerous. They can come, in fact, from your well-dressed Uncle Charlie or a pair of elegant prep-school boys. (The connection between the very rich and the ultraright is one Hitchcock draws again and again; in *Lifeboat* it's the wealthy survivors who first warm up to the German sailor, the workers who remain suspicious.)

And these are merely the features Hitchcock put his name to. In Hollywood, he often lent a few ideas or several days' work to many more propaganda films; he never took credit, but they reportedly include *WATCHTOWER OVER TOMORROW* and the ambitious feature *FOREVER AND A DAY*. (He even paid personally to have a British short, *Men of the Lightship*, reworked and redubbed with American actors for the US market.) He cochaired with Whitty a fund-raising drive to evacuate children from an English orphanage and resettle them in Canada and the United States.

Hitchcock also went back to England in 1944 to direct two shorts for the British Ministry of Information, *BON VOYAGE* and *AVENTURE MALGACHE*. (There were problems later, as there had been with John Huston's *Let There Be Light* and the US Army, but there always are when you mix independent artists with official propaganda.) And he returned after the war, too, to voluntarily supervise a particularly disturbing documentary of the Holocaust (one put aside for years for fear of offending a just-pacified Germany but finally broadcast on television as *MEMORY OF THE CAMPS*).

As the postwar world turned into a Cold War one, Hitchcock's view changed, too; the villains in his films were not Nazis now but Communists (even though privately he would do what he could in real life to aid victims of the Hollywood black-list). But the old worries about authoritarian regimes didn't go away. They never had, and neither did his genuinely spirited reaction to them—even when he was sitting in his sunny Hollywood kitchen, drinking orange juice.

References
Patrick McGilligan, *Alfred Hitchcock: A Life in Darkness and Light* (New York: HarperCollins, 2003), 270–74, 280–81, 372–74; Donald Spoto, *The Dark Side of Genius: The Life of Alfred Hitchcock* (New York: Da Capo Press, 1999), 235–36; Matthew Sweet, "Mustard and Cress," *Guardian*, December 29, 2007, http://www.theguardian.com/film/2007/dec/29/film; François Truffaut, *Hitchcock/Truffaut*, rev. ed. (New York: Touchstone, 1985), 159–61; J. Danvers Williams, "What I'd Do to the Stars," *Film Weekly*, March 4, 1939, http://the.hitchcock.zone/wiki/Film_Weekly_%281939%29_-_What_I'd_Do_to_the_Stars.

THE WRECK OF THE MARY DEARE

This was to be Alfred Hitchcock's next production after *VERTIGO*. Set up at MGM, Hitchcock and screenwriter ERNEST LEHMAN worked on the script (and delayed working on the script) for some time, until Lehman finally confessed to the director that he couldn't find any way to make it interesting. Based on a novel by Hammond Innes, it was the story of sabotage aboard a Merchant Marine ship, something Lehman couldn't get a handle on, and ended with a courtroom drama, a genre Hitchcock was never comfortable with.

Instead, they decided to do an entirely new picture, a man-on-the-run epic that eventually became *NORTH BY NORTHWEST*. The Wreck of the Mary Deare, meanwhile, eventually got a script from Hitchcock friend Eric Ambler, with

Michael Anderson (of *Around the World in 80 Days*) signed to direct. The finished project proved Hitchcock and Lehman's reservations correct, although it did mark one missed opportunity—the chance to direct Gary Cooper in a movie, whom the director had wanted since *FOREIGN CORRESPONDENT* and never been able to sign.

Reference
Donald Spoto, *The Dark Side of Genius: The Life of Alfred Hitchcock* (New York: Da Capo Press, 1999), 388–89, 391–93.

WRIGHT, TERESA (1918–2005)

New York–born, New Jersey–raised performer who began in school plays and summer stock and then understudied the role of Emily in the original Broadway production of THORNTON WILDER's *Our Town*. (She eventually took over the role when Martha Scott left for Hollywood.) That stage hit was followed by another, *Life with Father*, and a movie deal with Samuel Goldwyn. Wright—who wittily but firmly had it written into her contract that she never be required to pose for corny publicity photographs "attired in firecrackers and holding skyrockets for the Fourth of July" or "looking insinuatingly at a turkey for Thanksgiving"—immediately established herself as a bright young STAR, winning Oscar nominations for her first three films: *The Little Foxes, Mrs. Miniver*, and *Pride of the Yankees*. (She won for *Mrs. Miniver*.)

Her fourth film, on loan-out from Goldwyn, would be *SHADOW OF A DOUBT* (which also reunited her with Wilder and with actress PATRICIA COLLINGE, who'd had a memorable role in *The Little Foxes*). Hitchcock called Wright in for a meeting without first sending her the screenplay. Instead, there in his office, he acted it out.

"He told the story like no one else has ever told a story," she remembered later.

"He used anything on his desk as a prop, whether it was a glass or a pencil or a book, to make a sound, do sound effects. He'd do steps. He'd do anything he could as a storyteller to lure you into his story. And he told that story so beautifully that I was just absolutely mesmerized. And when I finally saw the film, I said, 'I've seen this film. I saw it in his office.'"

Hitchcock liked Wright and was particularly patient with her on the set and open to suggestions. When she balked at a romantic scene with MACDONALD CAREY, he tried another approach (Collinge actually did the rewrite). When there was a particularly specific bit of staging, he took the time to explain why it needed to be done that way.

"The interesting thing about *Shadow of a Doubt* is the twins theme, like when she says, 'We really are twins. We think things the same,'" Wright said. "One piece of direction I absolutely do remember, I was just lying on a bed some way or other, having a rest. He said, 'No, I want you to lie there with your hands behind your head.' He told me exactly how it was, but he explained why. 'Because,' he said, 'we are going to come from a shot of Uncle Charlie lying on the bed. I want this duplicated.' Those kinds of things make it harder for young Charlie and the audience to accept him as anything except this charming uncle of hers."

Afterward, Wright went on to deliver a fine, unforced performance in *The Best Years of Our Lives*, but disagreements with Goldwyn over publicity efforts and her own independence led to her contract being dropped in 1948. Wright pronounced herself glad—"The types of contracts standardized in the motion picture industry between players and producers are archaic in form and absurd in concept," she declared—and went on to do *The Men* with newcomer Marlon Brando, but it soon became difficult to get the best roles without a studio behind her, and the pictures grew smaller.

She continued to do very good work, mostly on stage and television now, appearing in the original broadcast version of *The Miracle Worker* and several episodes of *THE ALFRED HITCHCOCK HOUR*. Her last film was *The Rainmaker* in 1997. She died of a heart attack at 86 in New Haven.

References

Beyond Doubt: The Making of Hitchcock's Favorite Film, directed by Laurent Bouzereau (2000), documentary, http://the.hitchcock.zone/wiki/Beyond_Doubt:_The_Making_of_Hitchcock's_Favorite_Film_%282000%29_-_transcript; Douglas Martin, "Teresa Wright, Stage and Film Star, Dies at 86," *New York Times*, March 8, 2005, http://www.nytimes.com/2005/03/08/theater/teresa-wright-stage-and-film-star-dies-at-86.html?_r=0; "Teresa Wright," *IMDb*, http://www.imdb.com/name/nm0942863/bio; David Thomson, *The New Biographical Dictionary of Film* (New York: Knopf, 2002), 948–49.

THE WRONG MAN (US 1956)

DIRECTOR: Alfred Hitchcock.
SCREENPLAY: Maxwell Anderson, Angus MacPhail, based on the book *The True Story of Christopher Emanuel Balestrero* by Maxwell Anderson and the *Life* article "A Case of Identity" by Herbert Brean.
PRODUCERS: Herbert Coleman (Alfred Hitchcock, uncredited).
CINEMATOGRAPHY: Robert Burks.
EDITOR: George Tomasini.
ORIGINAL MUSIC: Bernard Herrmann.
CAST: Henry Fonda (Manny Balestrero), Vera Miles (Rose Balestrero), Anthony Quayle (Frank D. O'Connor), Harold Stone (Det. Lt. Bowers), Esther Minicotti (Mama Balestrero).
RUNNING TIME: 105 minutes. Black and white.
RELEASED THROUGH: Warner Bros.

Manny Balestrero lives a quiet life of routine. He leaves his home in Queens and
takes the subway into Manhattan, where he
plays the bass in a nightclub's dance band.
He makes $85 a week—enough to support
his family but not so much that he doesn't
dream about small things he feels he can't
afford, like a car or a vacation. With a dentist's bill due, he takes his wife's insurance
policy into the agency, hoping to borrow a
little bit against it. And then his routine life
turns upside down.

Two women at the office identify him
as a man who held them up previously. The
police pick him up and bring him before
other people who were robbed in the neighborhood—owners of a deli and a liquor
store. His handwriting seems to match a
holdup note. Manny is arrested, booked,
briefly jailed (until his family can make
bail), and then put on trial—for crimes he
did not commit and yet has no alibi for.

The Balestreros hire an inexpensive lawyer, but the case against Manny
is strong. Rose Balestrero, Manny's wife,
grows more and more dejected, eventually slipping into a dangerous depression.
The trial begins, and the evidence seems
unshakeable. Dull, too—so much so that
a juror complains in open court about the
tediousness of the testimony. A mistrial is
declared and a new trial rescheduled.

Then, while Manny prays desperately,
the real stickup man—a double for the
quiet musician—is arrested and confesses.
Manny is finally free—although for now,
his wife remains institutionalized.

One of Hitchcock's most CATHOLIC
films—and in some ways an act of penance
for all the rest.

The idea of an innocent person,
imprisoned by an uncaring authority, was
planted—actually forced—into Hitchcock's psyche back in childhood, when his
father had prevailed on the local constabu-
lary to lock up little Alfred in a cell for five
minutes to teach him some sort of lesson.
Hitchcock claimed not to know the real
reason behind it—he was a meek boy, he
insisted, whose father used to call him, in
rather Biblical terms, his "little lamb without a spot"—but the experience stayed deep
within him.

It would regularly reappear, though,
in his movies. Right from *THE LODGER*,
Hitchcock's films are full of people who
are wrongfully accused (*BLACKMAIL,
MURDER!, THE 39 STEPS, SABOTEUR,
NORTH BY NORTHWEST*) or even knowingly allow themselves to be to serve a
greater good (*UNDER CAPRICORN, I
CONFESS, TORN CURTAIN*). The traumatic memory of that spotless little lamb
standing in a dark and thickly barred cell
never left Hitchcock, yet for decades he had
merely exploited it for entertainment. Now
he would dive deep into its dark center.

Although the mid-'50s had been busy
with the back-to-back successes of *TO
CATCH A THIEF* and *THE MAN WHO
KNEW TOO MUCH*, Hitchcock still hadn't
given WARNER BROS. the production he
owed them under his old contract. So he
happily seized on a *Life* magazine article
Warner Bros. already had the rights to
about the 1953 arrest of a musician at the
Stork Club and his eventual trial for crimes
he hadn't committed. The picture was an
uncomplicated one logistically, without any
elaborate sets or effects, and—apart from
some brief LOCATION FILMING in New
York—could be mostly done in the economical comfort of the studio.

Hitchcock chose lauded playwright
Maxwell Anderson to do the screenplay,
and Anderson turned his research into
the case into a stand-alone book, *The True
Story of Christopher Emmanuel Balestrero*.
But the script was more poetic than practical, and the director's old if somewhat
alcoholic colleague ANGUS MACPHAIL

was brought on to do further research and another draft. HENRY FONDA, the film's sole STAR, was cast as Balestrero; VERA MILES, a new Hitchcock "discovery" (although she already had several other important credits), would continue to be groomed for stardom by being cast as Manny's fragile wife, Rose.

Production began in March at the story's real-life locations in Queens, Manhattan, and upstate New York, before moving back to Los Angeles for studio work. Shooting went without any reported difficulties—although Hitchcock reportedly cut the location work short due to the uncomfortable cold—and BERNARD HERRMANN supplied a subdued, slightly jazzy score.

The result was an unusual picture, out of character for the director in its documentary style, grim BLACK-AND-WHITE photography, and total absence of humor. (Significantly, Hitchcock even did away with his usually whimsical, winking CAMEO—instead, he appeared at the very beginning of the film, silhouetted on a deeply shadowed soundstage, soberly announcing to the audience that this was a different sort of crime story and that everything they were about to see was true.)

The visuals would drive that home with a look that owed more to newsreel photography (and perhaps the Italian Neorealists) than to Hitchcock's most recent, high-colored entertainments. Real locations are used, and even when sets are necessary, the set decoration is precise, right down to the products from a local bakery or the rumblings of the Queens subway. Manny's police booking—the calmly cold, dehumanizing process of fingerprinting, arraignment, and final incarceration—is done with hollow precision. (It was a sequence Hitchcock had been thinking about since at least *Blackmail* and a situation he had briefly touched on in *THE PARADINE CASE*.) Only in one feverish shot at the end—after Manny has been locked in the cell and the camera, while looking at him, begins to revolve with the mad tumult of his own emotions—is there a touch of the old, EXPRESSIONIST SUBJECTIVITY.

Emphasized particularly is the KAFKAESQUE feel of the entire experience and the helplessness that Manny feels. "It's nothing for an innocent man to worry about," the lead detective says at the beginning, a sentiment he repeats several times. ("If you haven't done anything, you have nothing to fear," he offers later, along with, "An innocent man has nothing to fear, remember that"—a phrase later borrowed for the film's posters.) But in Hitchcock's films, innocence is merely a construct, a fleeting virtue borne strictly of circumstance and the judgment of others. GUILT is far more pervasive and far harder to define, let alone ever truly discard.

And as always in Hitchcock's films, the repetition of phrases, even words, is never insignificant. Does an innocent man truly have nothing to worry about, nothing to fear? In the '50s, many disagreed. Although Senator Joseph McCarthy had been formally censured by the Senate in 1954 (he would die in 1957), the era he gave his name to lived on; the story of a quiet law-abiding citizen suddenly forced to defend his own character and confront strange witnesses must have resonated not only with viewers but also with Hitchcock himself, who had seen several friends and associates banned or "gray-listed" by nervous moguls after the Washington witch trials (people who, to his credit, Hitchcock would continue to find work for, particularly on his television programs).

More than politics, though, *The Wrong Man* is about religion and faith. It's not just that, as Manny, Fonda has the face of a fasting saint; it's that Manny is a Roman Catholic who lives his faith every day. When he's first booked and told to go through his pockets, he pulls out a rosary; the police allow him to take it into his cell, and Manny continues to say his novenas, fingering the beads even as he sits in court, listening to people bearing false witness. And if his prayers seem to be going unanswered, then that hinges on a pivotal theological point: Manny, it seems, has been praying for help. Better, his old MOTHER says, he should pray for strength—left unsaid is the belief that real grace comes not from asking God to end your trials but from imploring Him to give you the faith you need to face them.

It is not a theological distinction the majority of American audiences would draw, but it meant something to Hitchcock—and indeed, once Manny meekly surrenders himself to God's plans and prays only for the resolve needed to live through them, his suffering is swiftly ended. A close-up of Manny's imploring face silently whispering prayers dissolves into a close-up of the real criminal—who is quickly apprehended and whose arrest finally brings Manny's anguish to an end.

Or does it? A strong component of *The Wrong Man* is the way that not only the innocent are punished but also the innocent spouses of the innocent; Rose Balestrero first blames herself (if her wisdom teeth hadn't bothered her, then they wouldn't have needed to borrow money; if she were a better wife, then Manny's paycheck would have gone further) and then Manny (How can she really be sure he didn't do it?) and then slips into first paranoia and then clinical depression. Finally, she is committed to a sanitarium.

It's Manny's pleasant, low-key lawyer who first notices her changing mood; Manny himself is too involved in the case. (In a pivotal scene, Hitchcock's camera watches the worried attorney watching Rose while an uncomprehending Manny talks only about the upcoming trial.) But the trouble grows and grows (Miles is very good as suggesting first the barely contained hysteria and then the bleak despair) and eventually there is nothing left but a bed in a room where the windows are as heavily screened as the ones in Manny's cell. A final title card announces that, within two years, Rose was "completely cured," but faithful audiences knew better than to accept these sort of endings from Hitchcock; like the stories on his television show, which always wrapped up with his assertion that the murderer was eventually caught, we know that true tales like these and horrors like the Balestreros' are rarely so firmly resolved.

The film was released to some confusion among mainstream audiences, who missed the usual Hitchcock verve and found it difficult to identify with such an unemotional, even passive hero. (Like Job or the early Christian martyrs, Manny's purpose is not to fight—this is no movie about an amateur detective or incensed avenger—but simply to endure.) In France, it was embraced by critics, where its themes of spirituality and injustice were picked apart, and FRANÇOIS TRUFFAUT—whose ardor for it cooled over the years—initially called it Hitchcock's "best film," comparing it favorably to Robert Bresson's *A Man Escaped*. In America, though, it was seen as a disappointing change of pace from the sort of thrillers that reviewers and fans had come to expect from the "Master of Suspense."

They were about to have a far deeper shock with *VERTIGO*.

References

Patrick McGilligan, *Alfred Hitchcock: A Life in Darkness and Light* (New York: Harper-Collins, 2003), 414, 532–38; Eric Rohmer and Claude Chabrol, *Hitchcock: The First*

Forty-Four Films, translated by Stanley Hochman (New York: Frederick Ungar, 1979), 145–52; Donald Spoto, *The Dark Side of Genius: The Life of Alfred Hitchcock* (New York: Da Capo Press, 1999), 374–80; François Truffaut, *Hitchcock/Truffaut*, rev. ed. (New York: Touchstone, 1985), 235–43; François Truffaut, "The Wrong Man," *Hitchcock Zone*, http://the.hitch cock.zone/wiki/Fran%C3%A7ois_Truf faut_%281957%29_-_The_Wrong_Man.

WYMAN, JANE (1917–2007)

St. Joseph, MO–born performer (some sources give 1914 as her birthdate). Her working-class parents were in the midst of a divorce when her father died, and Wyman eventually ended up with a foster family. Her new father was the city's chief of detectives, and home life was strict; Wyman got some singing jobs on local radio and dropped out of high school to move to Hollywood and become an actress.

Wyman's career began in the mid-'30s with bit parts, but by the '40s, she was an established performer and eventually a leading lady, bringing quiet warmth and wide-eyed sympathy to *The Lost Weekend* and *The Yearling* and winning an Oscar as the mute rape victim of *Johnny Belinda*. Hitchcock cast her as acting student Eve Gill in *STAGE FRIGHT*, but at 33, Wyman seemed too old to still be playing such a childlike character, and the director seemed to focus most of his attention on MARLENE DIETRICH and the veteran supporting cast.

Wyman had strong parts later in the decade in Douglas Sirk's *Magnificent Obsession* and *All That Heaven Allows* and later found a regular home on television; she had her own anthology show for a while and was a regular on many others, having a long run on the 1980s hit *Falcon Crest*. Married four times, her second husband was then–B actor and future

president Ronald Reagan; although there were always stories and gossip about the union and the real reason for their divorce, Wyman refused to speak against him and claimed, as a loyal Republican, to vote for him every chance she got.

She died at 90 in Palm Springs.

References

"Jane Wyman," *Biography*, http:// www.biography.com/people/jane -wyman-245894; "Jane Wyman," *IMDb*, http://www.imdb.com/name/nm0943837/ bio?ref_=nm_ov_bio_sm; Richard Severo, "Jane Wyman, 90, Star of Film and TV Is Dead," *New York Times*, September 11, 2007, http://www.nytimes .com/2007/09/11/movies/11wyman.html; David Thomson, *The New Biographical Dictionary of Film* (New York: Knopf, 2002), 950.

WYNDHAM-LEWIS, D. B. (1891–1969)

Liverpool-born author who began writing humor columns for newspapers and later turned to biographies, often of French historical figures, and screenplays. His most famous script was for the original *THE MAN WHO KNEW TOO MUCH*, on which he was one of five writers. (He received a story credit on the 1956 remake, as well.) Wyndham-Lewis returned to journalism and historical biographies in the 1940s; his most famous work, outside of the Hitchcock film, was probably editing *The Stuffed Owl*, a satirical anthology of bad verse. He died at 78 in Altea, Spain.

References

"D. B. Wyndham-Lewis," *James Boswell. info*, http://www.jamesboswell.info/ scholars/d-b-wyndham-lewis; "Lewis, D. B. Wyndham (Dominic Bevan Wyndham), 1891–1969," *SNAC*, http://socialarchive .iath.virginia.edu/ark:/99166/w67945vw.

Y

YOUNG, ROBERT (1907–1998)

Chicago-born performer from a working-class family who moved regularly during his childhood. He attended high school in Los Angeles and, after graduation, landed a job at the Pasadena Playhouse, touring with a repertory company before signing with MGM in 1931. Pleasantly amiable and unremarkably good looking, Young soon found himself safely stuck in the second tier of the studio's leading men, while Clark Gable got all the sexy roles; Spencer Tracy, the serious jobs; and Robert Taylor, the handsome leading-man parts. Young felt overlooked and underappreciated, and when the studio lent him to GAUMONT BRITISH for a pair of pictures, he took it as a further rebuke.

One of those movies turned out to be *SECRET AGENT*, however, which gave Young one of his best roles during that decade, allowing him to be both silkily romantic and coldly menacing. It also won him kudos from Hitchcock, who later lavishly praised his performance—"He is completely at ease on the set, and he always knows his lines to the dot. His is a faultless technique"—although that might also have been the director's passive-aggressive way of criticizing STAR JOHN GIELGUD, with whom he'd been disappointed.

Still, Young's career began to pick up after he returned to America—and got an unexpected boost when his MGM contract ended and he was able to seek out better

parts, including roles in *Claudia, The Canterville Ghost*, and *The Enchanted Cottage*. A particular standout was the grim noir *Crossfire*, with Young investigating an anti-Semitic attack. Like many of Hollywood's supporting actors, he later found true stardom on television, spending most of the '50s as the wise parent in *Father Knows Best* and then returning the next decade as family doctor *Marcus Welby, M.D.*

The twinkling persona was perhaps his best acting job; privately, Young drank heavily, had always battled depression, and in 1991 attempted suicide. After his recovery, he led efforts to improve mental-health treatment in his old home state of Illinois. Young died at 91 of respiratory failure in Westlake Village, CA.

References

Alfred Hitchcock, "My Screen Memories," *Film Weekly* (May 1936), http://the.hitchcock.zone/wiki/Film_Weekly_%281936%29_-_My_Screen_Memories; "Robert Young," *IMDb*, http://www.imdb.com/name/nm0001870/bio?ref_=nm_ov_bio_sm; David Thomson, *The New Biographical Dictionary of Film* (New York: Knopf, 2002), 954–55; Bernard Weinraub, "Robert Young of 'Father Knows Best' Dies at 91," *New York Times*, July 23, 1998, http://www.nytimes.com/1998/07/23/arts/robert-young-of-father-knows-best-dies-at-91.html?pagewanted=all.

Derrick de Marney, right, Edward Rigby, and Nova Pilbeam barely survive the wreck of her car in *Young and Innocent. Gaumont British Picture Corporation of America/Photofest © Gaumont British Picture Corporation of America*

YOUNG AND INNOCENT (GB 1937)

DIRECTOR: Alfred Hitchcock.
SCREENPLAY: Charles Bennett, Edwin Greenwood, Anthony Armstrong, Gerald Savory, and Alma Reville, based on the novel *A Shilling for Candles* by Josephine Tey.
PRODUCER: Uncredited (Edward Black).

CINEMATOGRAPHY: Bernard Knowles.
EDITOR: Charles Frend.
ORIGINAL MUSIC: Jack Beaver, Louis Levy.
CAST: Nova Pilbeam (Erica Burgoyne), Derrick de Marney (Robert Tisdale), Percy Marmont (Col. Burgoyne), Edward Rigby (Old Will), George Curzon (Guy).
RUNNING TIME: 83 minutes. Black and white.
RELEASED THROUGH: General Film Distributors.

A famous actress and her ex-husband argue ferociously; the next day, her protégée, Robert, finds her on the beach, strangled with the belt to his own lost raincoat. The police rapidly decide he's the murderer, and seeing the case against him—and the incompetent lawyer he's been assigned—Robert impulsively escapes in hopes of proving his innocence.

On the run, he sees Erica, the daughter of the chief constable; she had met him at the police station and knows him to be a fugitive but feels sorry for him, and Robert gradually convinces her of his plight. He also persuades her to join him on his mission: Find the man who had his raincoat, and he'll find the real murderer.

Evading the police (and Erica's nosy aunt), they eventually track the coat down to a tramp, Old Will, who says a man with a strange twitch gave it to him—although by then its belt was already missing. Finding a box of matches from the Grand Hotel in one of the pockets, the three decide to go there in hopes of finding the murderer.

The police follow them, but just as they are arresting Robert, the drummer in the hotel dance band—who has been increasingly agitated since he saw Old Will appear—collapses, his eye twitching furiously. Old Will identifies him as the man who gave him the coat, and Robert is cleared.

A gentler Hitchcock.

After the dark espionage thriller SECRET AGENT and the even grimmer SABOTAGE, the director clearly felt he and his audience needed something lighter, so CHARLES BENNETT and other writers were charged with adapting the JOSEPHINE TEY mystery *A Shilling for Candles*. Liberally adapting, too—Tey's regular hero, Inspector Alan Grant, was completely written out and two minor characters were made the young hero and heroine. The tone was determinedly breezy and teen friendly—in fact, Erica, with her widowed father, much-loved roadster, and amateur detective work, seemed modeled on Nancy Drew, the American young-adult heroine then featured in regular best sellers (and whose own popular film series would begin the next year).

In some ways, *Young and Innocent* almost feels like Hitchcock's apology to his fans for his last two films. There is little onscreen violence and no coldly calculated disappointments of an audience's expectations. (In *Sabotage*, Hitchcock had dared to kill not only a small boy but also a puppy; here, not only is the danger to the two leads minimized, but also the welfare of Erica's scruffy dog is a constant concern.) There is a momentary bit of suspense when a sinkhole begins to swallow Erica's car (until, in a sequence that foreshadows NORTH BY NORTHWEST, Robert lifts her to safety), but at no point does the murderer menace either character. It is a careful, "tasteful" film. That, of course, is not necessarily what Hitchcock had already become famous for, and today the movie can seem especially tame.

Yet even in this more family-friendly project, the familiar Hitchcock themes poke through. Erica is, for all her youth, a maternal figure—easily and naturally acting the MOTHER to her four younger brothers, worrying that Robert hasn't eaten, practically taking charge and administering first aid when people faint. After Hitchcock lost his own mother, these characters would eventually become less lauded (the clueless Midge in VERTIGO), even forbidding, but for now they are still welcome.

And, of course, the story revolves around what was already a stock situation for him, the character presumed GUILTY until proven innocent, as well as contrasting the roles played badly by his protagonists (the tramp dresses up uncomfortably as a rich man, Robert "disguises" himself by putting on a pair of thick glasses) to the world of professional pretense his antagonist moves in. (He plays the drums in a blackface dance band; his ex-wife is an actress.) All the world's a stage, but not all of us are equally proficient players.

Although Hitchcock was patient with Pilbeam on the set—he was perhaps paternally protective of a young STAR who'd been a child actress in *THE MAN WHO KNEW TOO MUCH* just three years before—and he praised her performance afterward, she doesn't shine in the part; there's something a little washed out about her close-ups, and the editing does her no favors by repeatedly using the same bad reaction shot of her in the sinkhole sequence. Derrick de Marney is equally forgettable as the hero, and George Curzon overacts dreadfully as the twitching villain. (Only the veteran character actors— Edward Rigby, as the colorful tramp; Mary Clare, as Erica's nosy aunt; and PERCY MARMONT, as Erica's disappointed father—add any real interest to the proceedings.)

Still, the story moves along briskly, and there are some flashes of signature style—as when the worst parts of the marital quarrel that begins the film are drowned out by crashing thunder or a scream turns into the screech of seagulls. And the movie features a crane shot that's both a dry run for the "key" shot in *NOTORIOUS* and famous in its own right—starting up high in the Grand Hotel, the camera soars over the crowded lobby and ballroom, passing over the heads of blissful dancers before going closer, closer, closer on the drummer in the band, until only his twitching EYES fill the screen.

Good natured and good humored, from its punning title (she's young, he's innocent) to Hitchcock's own extended CAMEO as a frustrated photographer, it's a pleasant trifle. And although badly received in the United States (where distributors cut one of its most charming scenes, set at a children's birthday party, and *Time* pronounced it "tedious"), it did point back to *THE 39 STEPS* and the director's fondness for mixing comedy and suspense— something he would soon indulge to even greater effect in *THE LADY VANISHES*.

References

Patrick McGilligan, *Alfred Hitchcock: A Life in Darkness and Light* (New York: HarperCollins, 2003), 194–97; Donald Spoto, *The Dark Side of Genius: The Life of Alfred Hitchcock* (New York: Da Capo Press, 1999), 163–67; Donald Spoto, *Spellbound by Beauty: Alfred Hitchcock and His Leading Ladies* (New York: Harmony Books, 2008), 72–75; François Truffaut, *Hitchcock/ Truffaut*, rev. ed. (New York: Touchstone, 1985), 111–16.

BIBLIOGRAPHY

Agee, James. *Agee on Film*. 2 vols. New York: Grossett Universal Library, 1969.

Barr, Charles. *English Hitchcock*. Petaluma, CA: Cameron Books, 2002.

Baxter, Anne. *Intermission: A True Story*. New York: G. P. Putnam's Sons, 1976.

Behlmer, Rudy, ed. *Memo from David O. Selznick*. New York: Viking Press, 1972.

Bergman, Ingrid, and Alan Burgess. *My Story*. New York: Delacorte Press, 1980.

Bloch, Robert. *Psycho*. New York: Award Books, 1975.

Bogdanovich, Peter. *The Cinema of Alfred Hitchcock*. New York: Museum of Modern Art Film Library, Doubleday, 1963.

———. *Pieces of Time*. New York: Arbor House, 1973.

———. *Who the Devil Made It*. New York: Alfred A. Knopf, 1997.

———. *Who the Hell's in It*. New York: Knopf, 2004.

Buchan, John. *The Thirty-Nine Steps*. New York: Popular Library, 1963.

Butler, Ivan. *Horror in the Cinema*. New York: A. S. Barnes, 1970.

Canning, Victor. *The Rainbird Pattern*. New York: Ace Books, 1980.

Cohen, Paula Marantz. *Alfred Hitchcock: The Legacy of Victorianism*. Lexington: University of Kentucky Press, 1995.

Coleman, Herbert. *The Man Who Knew Hitchcock: A Hollywood Memoir*. Lanham, MD: Scarecrow Press, 2007.

du Maurier, Daphne. *Rebecca*. New York: Avon Books, 1979.

Falk, Quentin. *Mr. Hitchcock*. London: Haus, 2007.

Fontaine, Joan. *No Bed of Roses*. New York: William Morrow, 1978.

Gardiner, Dorothy, and Kathrine Sorley, eds. *Raymond Chandler Speaking*. Boston: Houghton Mifflin, 1962.

Gardner, Gerald. *The Censorship Papers: Movie Censorship Letters from the Hays Office, 1934–1968*. New York: Dodd, Mead, 1987.

Gielgud, John. *Early Stages: An Autobiography*. San Francisco: Mercury House, 1989.

Gottlieb, Sidney, ed. *Alfred Hitchcock: Interviews*. Jackson: University Press of Mississippi, 2003.

Gram, Martin, Jr., and Patrik Wikstrom. *The Alfred Hitchcock Presents Companion*. Whiteford, MD: OTR, 2001.

Granger, Farley, with Robert Calhoun. *Include Me Out: My Life from Goldwyn to Broadway*. New York: St. Martin's Press, 2007.

Greene, Graham. *The Pleasure Dome: The Collected Film Criticism of Graham Greene*. London: Oxford University Press, 1980.

Griffith, Richard, and Arthur Mayer. *The Movies*. Rev. ed. New York: Simon and Schuster, 1971.

Highsmith, Patricia. *Strangers on a Train*. Baltimore: Penguin Books, 1974.

Hotchner, A. E. *Doris Day: Her Own Story*. New York: William Morrow, 1975.

Hunter, Evan. *Me and Hitch*. London: Faber and Faber, 1997.

Kael, Pauline. *5001 Nights at the Movies: A Guide from A to Z*. New York: Holt, Rinehart and Winston, 1982.

——. *Reeling*. New York: Warner Books, 1976.

Kracauer, Siegfried. *From Caligari to Hitler: A Psychological History of the German Film*. Princeton, NJ: Princeton University Press, 2004.

La Bern, Arthur. *Frenzy*. Previously published as *Goodbye Piccadilly, Farewell Leicester Square*. New York: Paperback Library, 1972.

Laurents, Arthur. *The Rest of the Story*. Milwaukee, WI: Applause, 2012.

LaValley, Albert, ed. *Focus on Hitchcock*. Englewood Cliffs, NJ: Prentice Hall, 1972.

Leigh, Janet, with Christopher Nickens. *Psycho: The Classic Thriller*. New York: Harmony Books, 1995.

McDevitt, Jim, and Eric San Juan. *A Year of Hitchcock: 52 Weeks with the Master of Suspense*. Lanham, MD: Scarecrow Press, 2011.

McGilligan, Patrick, ed. *Alfred Hitchcock: A Life in Darkness and Light*. New York: HarperCollins, 2003.

——. *Backstory: Interviews with Screenwriters of the 60s*. Berkeley: University of California Press, 1997.

Moorehead, Caroline. *Sidney Bernstein: A Biography*. London: Jonathan Cape, 1984.

O'Connell, Pat Hitchcock, and Laurent Bouzereau. *Alma Hitchcock: The Woman behind the Man*. New York: Berkeley Trade, 2004.

Perry, George. *The Films of Alfred Hitchcock*. London: Studio Vista, Dutton, 1970.

Rebello, Stephen. *Alfred Hitchcock and the Making of Psycho*. New York: HarperPerennial, 1991.

Rohmer, Eric, and Claude Chabrol. *Hitchcock: The First Forty-Four Films*. Translated by Stanley Hochman. New York: Frederick Ungar, 1979.

Ryall, Tom. *Alfred Hitchcock and the British Cinema*. London: Continuum International, 1996.

Sarris, Andrew. *The American Cinema: Directors and Directions, 1929–1968*. New York: Dutton, 1968.

Shipman, David, ed. *Movie Talk: Who Said What about Whom in the Movies*. New York: St. Martin's Press, 1988.

Spoto, Donald. *The Dark Side of Genius: The Life of Alfred Hitchcock*. New York: Da Capo Press, 1999.

——. *Laurence Olivier: A Biography*. New York: Harper Paperbacks, 1993.

——. *Spellbound by Beauty: Alfred Hitchcock and His Leading Ladies*. New York: Harmony Books, 2008.

Starr, Michael Seth. *Hiding in Plain Sight: The Secret Life of Raymond Burr*. Milwaukee, WI: Applause, 2008.

Taylor, John Russell. *Hitch: The Life and Times of Alfred Hitchcock*. Boston: Da Capo Press, 1996.

Thomas, Bob. *Selznick*. New York: Pocket Books, 1972.

Thomson, David. *The New Biographical Dictionary of Film*. New York: Knopf, 2002.

Truffaut, François. *Hitchcock/Truffaut*. Rev. ed. New York: Touchstone, 1985.

Twomey, Alfred E., and Arthur F. McClure. *The Versatiles: Supporting Character Players in the Cinema, 1930–1955*. New York: Castle Books, 1969.

Wiley, Mason, and Damien Bona. *Inside Oscar*. 10th anniversary ed. New York: Ballantine Books, 1996.

Williams, Tom. *A Mysterious Something in the Light: The Life of Raymond Chandler*. Chicago: University of Chicago Press, 2013.

Wood, Robin. *Hitchcock's Films*. New York: Paperback Library, 1969.

Woolrich, Cornell. *Rear Window and Other Stories*. New York: Penguin Books, 1994.

Wydra, Thilo. *Grace: A Biography*. New York: Skyhorse, 2014.

INDEX

Academy Awards, 1, *113*, 122, 358, 437
adaptations, 1–3
Agee, James, 3
Aherne, Brian, 3
Albertson, Frank, 4
alcohol, 4, 142
The Alfred Hitchcock Hour, 5–6
Alfred Hitchcock Presents, 4–5, *11*
Alfred Hitchcock: A Life in Darkness and Light,
4–5, 74, 85, 164, 171, 268, 412
Allen, Jay Presson, 6–7, 117, 163, 182, 220, 257,
262
Allgood, Sara, 7
Always Tell Your Wife, 8, 168, 172
Anderson, Dame Judith, 8, 149, 218, 357
Anderson, Lindsay, 9, 16, 335
Anderson, Maxwell, 248, 483, 611
Andrews, Julie, 9, 10, 296, 419; *Torn Curtain*,
and the making of, 460–63
anecdotes, 10–11
Angel, Heather, 11
Archibald, William, 11–12
Armstrong, Charlotte, 12
"Arthur," 12
Ashcroft, Dame Peggy, 12, 313, 448
Ashenden, 2, 146, 266, 386
Atterbury, Malcolm, 13
Auber, Brigitte, 5, 13, 85
auteur theory, the, 13, 26, 49–50, 184, 200, 300,
385
Aventure Malgache, 15–16

"Back for Christmas," 17
Bagdasarian, Ross, 17–18
Baker, Diane, 18–19, 156, 163, 213, 257, 272–74
Balcon, Sir Michael, 19–20, 36, 41, 110, 135, 237,
269–81

Balsam, Martin, 20
"Bang! You're Dead," 20–21
Bankhead, Tallulah, 21, 28, 108, 179, 189,
232, 298, 406; *Lifeboat*, and the making of,
230–33
Banks, Leslie, 21–22, 195, 252, 424
"Banquo's Chair," 22
Baring, Norah, 22
Barnes, George, 22–23
Barry, Joan, 23
Barrymore, Ethel, 23, 210
Bass, Saul, 24, 301, 486; *Psycho*, and the contro-
versy over, 227, 339
Basserman, Albert, 24–25
Bates, Florence, 25
Baxter, Anne, 25–26, 179
Bazin, Andre, 10, 26, 49, 189, 240, 370
Bel Geddes, Barbara, 27, 217, 483–84
Belloc-Lowndes, Marie, 27, 193, 237
Benchley, Robert, 28
Bendix, William, 28
Bennett, Charles, 28–29, 124, 304, 386, 417, 446
Bergman, Ingrid, 4–5, *18*, 29–31, 39, *134*, 161,
173, 228, 240, 298, 389, *473*; *Notorious*, and
the making of, 303–7; *Spellbound*, and the
making of, 408–12; *Under Capricorn*, and
the making of, 472–75
Bernstein, Sidney, 31, 74, 152, 173, 242, 391,
465; *Memory of the Camps*, and the making
of, 269–70; *Transatlantic Pictures*, and the
founding of, 319, 465
Best, Edna, 36, 39, 56, 252, 260
birds, 12, 31–32, 57, 162, 182, 188, 235, 380
The Birds, 32, 33–35, 109, 131, 159, 162–63,
182–83, 276, 302, 306
Black, Karen, 35, 154; *Family Plot*, and the making of, 112–14

ABOUT THE AUTHOR

Stephen Whitty has a BFA in film from NYU's Tisch School of the Arts and has been writing for and about films for more than thirty years. His prize-winning fiction, essays, and reviews have been published in America and Europe, and he has lectured at NYU, Rutgers, and other universities. A two-time chair of the New York Film Critics Circle, he lives in New Jersey.